CHILDREN, FAMILIES, AND STATES

Studies in Contemporary European History

Editors:
Konrad Jarausch, University of North Carolina, Chapel Hill
Henry Rousso, Institut d'histoire du temps présent, CNRS, Paris

CHILDREN, FAMILIES, AND STATES

Time Policies of Childcare, Preschool, and Primary Education in Europe

Edited by

Karen Hagemann, Konrad H. Jarausch, and Cristina Allemann-Ghionda

berghahn
NEW YORK · OXFORD
www.berghahnbooks.com

First published in 2011 by
Berghahn Books
www.berghahnbooks.com

©2011, 2014 Karen Hagemann, Konrad H. Jarausch,
and Cristina Allemann-Ghionda
First paperback edition published in 2014.

Library of Congress Cataloging-in-Publication Data

Children, families, states : time policies of childcare, preschool, and primary
education in Europe / edited by Karen Hagemann, Konrad H. Jarausch,
Cristina Allemann-Ghionda.
   p. cm. — (Studies in contemporary European history ; v. 8)
   Includes bibliographical references and index.
ISBN 978-0-85745-096-8 (hardback) -- ISBN 978-0-85745-097-5 (institutional
ebook) -- ISBN 978-1-78238-095-5 (paperback) -- ISBN 978-1-78238-096-2
(retail ebook)
   1. Child care—Government policy—Europe. 2. Early childhood
education—Government policy—Europe. 3. Family policy—Europe.
4. Child welfare—Europe. I. Hagemann, Karen. II. Jarausch, Konrad
Hugo. III. Allemann-Ghionda, Cristina, 1949–

HQ778.7.E85C57 2011
372.12'44094--dc22

                                                      2010029809

British Library Cataloguing in Publication Data

A catalogue record for this book is available from the British Library.

Printed on acid-free paper

ISBN: 978-1-78238-095-5 paperback
ISBN: 978-1-78238-096-2 retail ebook

Printed with support of the Volkswagen Foundation.

CONTENTS

III. Case Studies: Time Policies of Childcare, Preschool, and Primary Education in Europe

A. *All-Day Childcare and Education Systems in Western Europe*

B. *Part-Time Pre- and Primary School Systems with Additional Childcare in West-Central Europe*

C. All-Day Childcare and Part-Time Pre- and Primary School Systems in Eastern Europe

TABLES, FIGURES, AND ILLUSTRATIONS

TABLES

FIGURES

Figure 7.1. Structural and agency factors assumed to influence time management in compulsory education   159

ILLUSTRATIONS

Illustration 1.1. Lunch break in an all-day primary school located in southern Switzerland, run by Catholic nuns from Suore di San Giuseppe in Italy, for children of Italian workers, 1919. (Congregazione delle Suore di San Giuseppe, Cuneo. We want to thank the congregazione for allowing us to use this photo.)   17

Illustration 1.2. School education in the interwar period: First grade of a half-day primary school for boys in Dresden, Germany, 1930. (BPK, no. 30021510)   19

Illustration 1.3. Reform-pedagogic-oriented childcare in the interwar period: Coeducative age-mixed group of preschool children playing with wood material in a kindergarten of the Pestalozzi-Fröbel-House in Berlin, Germany, 1927. (BPK, no. 30030957)   23

Illustration 1.4. School education in the occupied East during World War II: Mixed-age, coeducated class in a camp of children of resettled Ethnic Germans from Volhynia in Aussig (Protectorate Bohemia), 1940. (BPK, no. 30000876, photograph by Liselotte Purper)   24

Illustration 1.5. After-school care in the postwar period: *Wärmestube* (literally "Heated Room") for primary school children that offered a warm lunch after school and a place to do the homework, West Berlin, Germany, 1949. (BPK, no. 30019349)   25

Illustration 1.6. Schooling in postwar Europe: A French coeducative all-day class in the 1950s in a small town in the Basque region. (BPK, no. 50002368)   28

Illustration 1.7. Educational reform in the 1960s and 1970s: "*Kinderkollektiv*" (Children's Collective), a group of children in a "storefront daycare center," organized by parents, Frankfurt/M., West Germany, 1970. (BPK, no. 30001862, photograph by Abisag Tüllmann)   30

Illustration 1.8. All-day education under communism: East German "day school" in Weißenfels. A teacher helps elementary school children with their homework, late 1950s. (BPK, no. 00076938)   32

PREFACE

This book analyzes the connections between the important policy fields of *education, welfare, labor, family, and gender* by focusing on two related issues of increasing relevance: the development of a *full-time childcare, preschool and primary education system for all children* as well as the drive for a *reconciliation of family and work*. For both issues the time structure of childcare and schooling is a crucial problem, because it governs the quality of formal care and education and the ability of women to pursue a career equal to men. To highlight this aspect, hitherto largely ignored by scholarship, we propose the analytical concept of *time policy,* defined as a policy of the state and other actors that determines the time structure of childcare and schooling.

Increasingly, educational experts and national policymakers agree that a state-funded, full-time childcare and pre- and primary school system is a "public good" that should be accessible to *all* children. In recent reports the Organization for Economic Co-operation and Development (OECD), UNESCO, and the European Commission emphasize the importance of investing in this "future capital." They argue that it is not enough to demand an extension of early childhood education and care and to insist that every child gets a high-quality primary education. Instead, these international organizations point out that it is also necessary to think about the time structure of these facilities and the linking of early childhood care with education programs and primary education—in the interest of *children, parents, women in particular, and society as a whole*.

For children a high-quality system of full-time childcare and schooling is important, because an education, which attempts to do more than transfer basic knowledge, needs time in which they can develop their cognitive, social, and artistic skills. As a recent comparative study by the German Institute for International Pedagogical Research shows, a full-time education enhances the "integrated holistic learning process" of children. Similarly, other surveys suggest that childcare and after-school programs as well as extracurricular activities offer children the opportunity to meet friends, participate in sports, or explore the arts or sciences, coupled with occasions for social and emotional development. A full-time education allows the growing number of only children to interact with peers and thus offers an important opportunity for social learning. Moreover, a full-time care and education system is superior to part-time provision in compensating for the unequal chances of children from different social, cultural, ethnic, and racial backgrounds and in helping children from migrant families to learn the language and culture of their new homeland. This is of particular importance because since the 1960s the percentage of the immigrant population in most Western European countries has been increasing; today an average of 10–12 percent of the population is "foreign born." A recent OECD publication, which compared the results of the 2003 survey by the Program for International Student Assessment (PISA), revealed that in the majority of the Western European countries 25–40 percent of the first-generation immigrant pupils performed below the average level of native-born students. The OECD, UNESCO, and the European Commission therefore all emphasize that a high-quality full-time system of care and education is indispensable if a society wants equal opportunities for native-born children from disadvantaged social, ethnic, and racial backgrounds as well as first- and second-generation immigrant children.

For parents an affordable high-quality full-time childcare and school system is important because more and more have and wish to combine family obligations and paid work outside their home. This is difficult if childcare facilities and schools are only open during a limited part of the workday. Because the number of single-parent families and "double-earner" households is increasing everywhere, a time policy based on the model of the "male-breadwinner" family, which assumes that the mother stays at home to take care of the children, is obsolete. More and more parents—double and single—who work full-time need additional childcare before and after pre- and primary school that extends beyond the six hours per day that the OECD defines as the minimum for a "full-time" school. Moreover, in order to meet the growing demand for employees who are available around the clock, this out-of-school care must offer flexible services. In addition, the OECD Economics Department emphasizes the importance of flexible working-time arrangements for parents. If a society aims for a reconciliation of family and work on a more equitable basis for women, double and single parents need to be enabled to reduce the number of weekly working hours in their job flexibly for some years, and fathers need to be encouraged to share the responsibility for childcare.

For the majority of mothers in single and two-parent families it is crucial to be able to support their family with full-time paid work if they want to. They are, in spite of all the rhetoric about gender equality, still more often responsible for childcare. A flexible "educare" system that takes into account their time constraints as employees is a key precondition for equal "social citizenship." The consequences of mothers being unable to earn an individual income, whether because they cannot afford childcare or after-school care for their children or because they only have access to formal part-time care and education, can be dire. According to a 2005 Labor Force Survey, 36 percent of all employed women and 60 percent of all employed mothers worked part-time in the European Community in contrast to only 8 percent of all employed men and 4 percent of all employed fathers. Limited access to the labor market and lasting part-time work (which of course also has several other causes) curtails not only women's income and career prospects, but also impairs their social security benefits and pensions, which remain dependent on their status in the labor market. For the growing numbers of single mothers and their children the consequences of a time policy of childcare and schooling that does not allow them full-time work are particularly problematic. Most of them struggle hard to survive and some are forced to live on welfare. It is no coincidence that women and children in single-parent families are the poorest group in many postindustrial countries.

The number of poor children who live in families with an income below the poverty line is generally increasing in Europe. Many of them come from immigrant families, because their parents are more often subject to unemployment. Already before the recent financial crisis, an alarming EU social report from 2008 stated that every fifth child in Europe lived in poverty. Half of these children grow up with a single parent, in a large family with more than three children, or in an immigrant family. The European Commission therefore demands that societies invest in the infrastructure of their childcare and school system and extend its daily and weekly time schedules. Equal access to high-quality full-time childcare and schooling should be a social right of every citizen, not least of all because it guarantees the future of postindustrial societies.

Finally, *for societies as a whole* the time policy of their childcare, pre- and primary school system has also become an increasingly pressing issue, as it has a profound impact on the development of the welfare system and labor market. Above all, the dramatic decline of the birth rate that endangers the future of their welfare and pension system has forced more and more European countries to rethink their childcare and schooling policy. Comparative studies show that in welfare states which offer an institutionalized, high-quality, full-time "educare" system and support dual-earner families and single parents, more children are born than in welfare states that cling to the outdated "male-breadwinner/female-homemaker" model or its "modernized" variant that allows mothers to earn a "supplementary income" with part-time work. In addition, postindustrial economies with a declining population cannot forego the increasingly qualified workforce of women. It is simply too expensive for a society to have women who receive a higher education to stop working outside the home after they have their first or second child. The difficulties that women face when they try to combine family with a career are thus not only their "personal problem," but belong to society as a whole, which is deprived of potential children and future workers to sustain the economy.

In order to explore these complex issues, the book presents a comparative analysis of the evolution of different time systems of childcare, preschool and primary education in Eastern and Western Europe since 1945. By focusing on the time policy of childcare and schooling, the various chapters seek to establish which economic, political, social, and cultural factors have determined the specific time structure in different countries in the past and present. The aim of this comparative stocktaking is to understand the conditions necessary for a reform of the time policy of a system of childcare and schooling so that it will respond more successfully to the competing interests of children, parents, women in particular, and societies.

The first section of the book introduces the concept of "time policy" as a new approach to a comparative analysis of childcare and schooling by describing the theoretical and methodological framework of the volume and summarizing the results of its comparative analysis. Its first chapter traces the historical development of childcare, pre- and primary schooling since the early nineteenth century, while its second chapter surveys the changes since the 1990s from the perspective of social and political sciences. The three chapters in the second section analyze major trends of family policies in Eastern and Western Europe after 1945, reflect on their impact on the time structure of childcare and schooling, and in turn analyze the consequences of different time policies on the employment of parents, in particular women, and the development of the birth rate. They provide the historical background for the third and main section of twelve national cases studies from Western and Eastern Europe, which present distinctive developments but also show some similarities, even across the former Iron Curtain. In our analysis we differentiate between three groups of time policy systems, which also structure the order of the national case studies in the book: (1) all-day childcare and education systems in Western Europe (Britain, France, Italy, Norway, Spain, and Sweden); (2) part-time preschool and primary school systems with additional childcare in

West-Central Europe (the Federal Republic of Germany and Switzerland); and (3) all-day childcare and part-time pre- and primary school systems in Eastern Europe (the German Democratic Republic, the Czech Republic, Hungary, and Russia).

The volume is the product of an interdisciplinary and international co-operation. Karen Hagemann, then at the Center for Interdisciplinary Studies on Women and Gender at the Technical University in Berlin, started the research for a comparative study of the subject in 2000. She was joined by Cristina Allemann-Ghionda, a specialist in comparative education at the University of Cologne, and Konrad Jarausch, the former director of the Center for Research on Contemporary History in Potsdam in initiating a Volkswagen Foundation project in 2003, titled *The German Half-Day Model: A European Sonderweg? The 'Time Policy' of Public Education in Post-War Europe: An East-West Comparison.* In order to obtain a comprehensive picture of the time structures and policies of European childcare and school systems, this team brought together scholars from education, history, political science, and sociology, hailing from thirteen countries. During a first workshop in Potsdam in 2006 this group discussed the state of research and the theoretical and methodological approaches of various disciplines in order to develop a shared analytical framework for comparative research. One year later in Cologne, the same scholars met with additional experts to present the results of their research on national developments and put them into a comparative perspective.

This book contains the fruits of this truly collaborative enterprise. Since thirty scholars generously contributed by presenting papers and participating in the discussion, we would like to thank everyone who was actively involved in the project. By selecting the most significant papers we tried to produce a coherent volume, which turned out to be quite a challenge, since the texts hailed from many different national and disciplinary backgrounds. Reaching this aim required intensive cooperation with the authors and extensive rewriting of the papers. But this was a rewarding process, because it helped us to understand the peculiarities of each national case and forced us also to question many of our initial assumptions.

Though we edited the texts together, the main responsibility for the final version of all chapters lay in the hands of Karen Hagemann. We are very grateful to our editorial assistant Brandon Hunziker, who not only struggled hard to produce a coherent and readable text out of the different disciplinary and national drafts, but also provided helpful critical feedback. We also would like to thank the two readers of the book manuscript, who helped us with their comments, Thomas Goldstein, who did the final proofreading, and Friederike Brühöfener, who worked as a research assistant and helped with the index. Finally, we want to express our special gratitude for the project's support by the German Federal Ministry of Education and Research as well as for the generous funding by the Volkswagen Foundation for making this book possible. We are very pleased that the book is now being published in a paperback edition, because the subject of time policies of childcare and school education is gaining increasing importance for states, children, and families due to the global trend to flexible working hours and patchwork careers.

Chapel Hill and Cologne, July 2013
Karen Hagemann, Konrad H. Jarausch, and Cristina Allemann-Ghionda

Part I

INTRODUCTION

*Time Policy—A New Approach for
the Comparative Analysis of
Childcare and Education*

Chapter 1

CHILDREN, FAMILIES, AND STATES

Time Policies of Childcare and Schooling
in a Comparative Historical Perspective

Karen Hagemann, Konrad H. Jarausch,
and Cristina Allemann-Ghionda

One searches international handbooks and encyclopedias on childcare and schooling in vain for the term *time policy*. The time structure of childcare and education systems and the policies of the state as well as the social and political actors that shape them are rarely topics of interest for politicians, journalists, or scholars. At first glance, the reason for this neglect seems obvious: Since full-day childcare and all-day schools are today either the norm or at least a widely used option in most countries, it has appeared to be unnecessary to study their time structure and the policies that generated it.[1] Not surprisingly, research on this subject began in countries with a "half-day" or "part-time" system where the majority of childcare facilities *and* schools are open only half of the day or slightly longer.[2] This is still the case in Austria, the Federal Republic of Germany, Italy, and the German parts of Switzerland. This time structure makes it difficult for parents to combine family and paid work, because it presupposes a "stay-at-home mom" and is predicated on the "male-breadwinner/female-homemaker" family model. It also discriminates against children from low-income and immigrant families, because it hinders educational opportunities and reinforces social differences.[3]

The time policy of care and education is, however, also a crucial problem for most other countries, because it is at the center of two closely related issues of increasing political relevance: the need for a state-funded, high-quality, flexible, full-time childcare and school system educating all children and for the reconciliation of family and work responsibilities on a basis more equitable for women. Recent research by sociologists Janet

Notes for this chapter begin on page 42.

C. Gornick and Marcia K. Meyers and others emphasizes that it is not enough to demand the extension of early childhood care and education and to ensure that every child gets a high-quality pre- and primary school education; it is also necessary to consider the time structure of these facilities—in the interest of children, families, the society, and the state.[4]

It is for these reasons that this book focuses on the time policy of childcare and pre- and primary schools, which we define as a policy implemented by the state as well as different social and political actors that determines the time structure of the care and education system. We place this time policy squarely at the center of five connected policy fields—education, labor, welfare, family, and gender—and ask which economic, political, social, and cultural factors have shaped the specific time structures and related time policies in Western and Eastern European countries since the end of the Second World War.[5] Our aim is to determine the conditions necessary for reforming the time policy of childcare and schooling so as to make it respond more adequately to the interests of children, parents, particularly women, and society.

After outlining the book's theoretical and methodological framework, this introduction will summarize the results of our historical comparison of the time structure of the care and education systems in the twelve European countries that we have selected for this study. These cases include for Western Europe: Britain, the Federal Republic of Germany, France, Italy, Norway, Spain, Sweden, and Switzerland; and for Eastern Europe: the German Democratic Republic, the Czech Republic, Hungary, and Russia. Although each case exhibits its own distinctive development, our comparison seeks to uncover not only the differences but also the similarities that transcend the borders of the nation-states and their specific economic and political systems. The focus of the book is the post-1945 period until the present. Our comparative survey in the introduction, however, begins in the early nineteenth century and ends with the transformation of communist Eastern Europe in 1989–1990. An additional chapter by Kimberly Morgan analyzes the developments since 1990.

"Time Policy"—Some Theoretical and Methodological Reflections

Time policies of childcare and schooling are difficult to analyze because they are the result of complex interactions among education, labor, welfare, family, and gender policies. Thus, taken alone, none of the common discipline-specific theoretical and methodological approaches used by educationists, sociologists, political scientists, and historians is sufficient to investigate the time structure of a care and education system and compare it with others. Only an interdisciplinary approach that draws from each of these fields is equal to this task. Educational research can help to define and understand the dimension of time in childcare and schooling and explore its implications for children. The social sciences, particularly gender studies, provide theoretical and methodological tools for analyzing the connections between labor and the family as well as welfare and childcare, and emphasize the importance of gender as a crucial category of analysis. Historical scholarship provides a framework for comparison of long-term development and emphasizes the usefulness of a multiperspective approach that focuses on the interplay of different economic, political, social, and cultural factors. Finally, political science offers the concept of path dependency, which allows us to understand how policies—and the institutions that implement them—evolve over a long period of time.

Analyzing the Time Structure of Childcare and Schooling

Any analysis of the time structure of childcare and schooling must first begin by reflecting on what we actually mean when we speak of the time spent in childcare or school, as this includes more than just the hours spent in these facilities. It also comprises early-morning care, lunchtime, after-school programs, and extracurricular activities, all of which have an enormous influence on children's education and socialization. A cursory glance at different childcare and school systems immediately reveals a wide variety of daily and weekly time structures, ranging from boarding care services and schools, various kinds of full- and part-time childcare and schooling, and special schools that integrate formal and informal education, to half-day schools with after-school care and extracurricular activities. In order to make this variety of forms of childcare and schooling and their different time structures transparent, whenever possible we use the national terms or their literal translations and explain its specific meaning. Following the Organisation for Economic Co-operation and Development (OECD), we define as *all-* or *full-day* a timetable of at least 30 weekly hours. *Half-day* or *part-time* is attendance from 12.5 to 25 hours per week; that is, a child should be in a childcare facility or school at least 2.5 hours daily.[6]

To study the variety and complexity of school-related time structures in Europe, the German Institute for International Pedagogical Research organized a comparative research project entitled "Time for Schooling" in the early 1990s.[7] Directed by comparative educationalist Wolfgang Mitter, the project proposed a new concept of "school time" that sought to account for the various physical and psychological factors that influence educational outcomes. It differentiated between the following three dimensions: first, *teaching time* calculated on the basis of official schedules and including practical work, project work, examination time, and field trips in addition to classroom hours; second, the *time spent in school,* including instructional time as well as breaks and extracurricular activities on school premises; and third, *school-related time,* for example, traveling to and from school, completing homework, or tutoring.[8] Although useful, Mitter's approach ignores how closely the time structure of schooling is often connected to "out-of-school" care services before and after regular school hours and extracurricular activities off the school premises.[9] To remedy this, we therefore propose a fourth dimension, namely, the *time spent in care services and other formal activities that complement time in school.* This approach can also aid the analysis of the *time structure and related time policies of childcare services* by differentiating between the time used for teaching and learning, the total time spent in the childcare facility, and time related to the childcare service, especially the time spent traveling to and from home. Such an understanding of time is helpful because it emphasizes that the time spent in formal care and education constitutes an important part of children's lives and shapes their daily routines.

Due to the diversity of time structures of all-day education and the different connections between childcare and schooling, the German UNESCO Institute for Education distinguishes four school types: the traditional divided all-day school, the modern conjunct all-day school (*verbundene Ganztagsschule*) and its variant the day school (*Tagesheimschule* or *Tagesschule*), and finally the open all-day school (*offene Ganztagsschule*). The traditional *divided all-day school* has lessons in the morning and afternoon, which are divided by a long lunch break that students usually spend at home. The *conjunct all-day school* has lessons, including art and sports, throughout the entire school day, provides children with a school lunch (mandatory or optional), and also offers additional extracurricular activities. Both school types start between 8:00 and 9:00 A.M. and end between 3:00 and 5:00 P.M. The *day school* is a variant of the conjunct all-day school and offers parents additional childcare services before and after official school hours. The *open all-day school* is a half-day or part-time school combined with elements of full-time childcare services and/or extracurricular activities, which parents and children can use voluntarily. This last school type, which in many cases does not really deserve the label "all-day school," is extremely diverse. Such institutions range from half-day schools that offer lunch and childcare before and after school hours every weekday between 7:00 A.M. and 5:00 or 6:00 P.M. to schools that offer such services only for a few hours on certain days of the week. In addition, the UNESCO Institute for Education differentiates between two types of *half-day* or *part-time school:* schools with a regular and reliable schedule that is the same for each day of the week (usually from 8:00 A.M. to 1:00 or 2:00 P.M.) and schools with an un-regulated weekly schedule that is different every day.[10]

With respect to childcare, preschool, and out-of-school services, we follow, whenever possible, the terminology of the OECD. *Crèches* are professional center-based services for infants and toddlers. *Kindergartens* are today professional center-based programs, usually for children from 3–6 years with predominantly educational aims; however, in the past in most countries, they belonged like crèches to the health or welfare system and often were understood as facilities that provided simply childcare. Parallel to kindergartens, there exist several other forms of childcare facilities for children in this age group, which are considered mainly as a form of social service. *Preschools,* on the other hand, are usually understood as schools, i.e., a form of publicly controlled preprimary education, and were also in the past part of the education system. In some countries, they offer programs for children from 3–6 years; in others they are limited to the last one or two years before the start of primary school. In addition we define professionally organized programs usually offered for children in the primary school age, which can take place inside or outside the school, as *out-of-school* or *after-school services.* The phrase *early childhood care and education* is used by the OECD and in current research as a global term encompassing all arrangements providing care and education for children under compulsory school age. The similar term *early childhood education* emphasizes more strongly that all childcare service is also education and promotes universal programs before primary education, which starts with compulsory school education and is followed by secondary education.[11]

Because the forms of childcare, preschools, and primary schools vary so much and their time structure is often so closely interrelated, we analyze them together and differentiate only very broadly between three clusters of time systems:

1. All-day (or full-day) systems of childcare, preschools, and primary schooling (often also called full-day);

2. Part-time preschool and primary school systems with additional childcare;

3. All-day childcare and part-time pre- and primary school systems.

The main criterion for this distinction is the dominant time structure of the compulsory preschool and primary school system, because the time policy for childcare usually depends on the time structure of the school system, complements it, and in most countries is far less coherent. In our study, the first cluster includes Britain, France, Italy, Norway, Spain, and Sweden in Western Europe; the second cluster includes the Federal Republic of Germany and Switzerland in West-Central Europe; and the third cluster includes the Czech Republic, the German Democratic Republic,

Hungary, and Russia in Eastern Europe. We would like to stress, however, that the distinction between these three clusters of time systems suggests a more clear-cut difference than what we found in reality, since most countries offer a mix of part- and full-time care and education. Two examples of "mixed systems" are Italy and Switzerland. In both states, the dissimilarities between regions are more pronounced than in most other countries. We placed them in different groups, because we focus on the dominant time structure.

The Implications of the Time Structure of Formal Care and Education for Children

Educational and sociological research on the implications of the time structure of childcare and schooling for children is still underdeveloped but is urgently needed. This research should explore the hypothesis that an obligatory and conjunct all-day childcare and education system would offer children from disadvantaged backgrounds more equal social chances. In particular, in countries with a half-day and part-time childcare and school system like Austria and the FRG, the supporters of a reform have argued since the early 1960s that the introduction of obligatory and conjunct all-day schools would enhance the chances of children from disadvantaged backgrounds, together with other structural reforms like the introduction of obligatory early childhood education and the abolition of a tracked school system. References for this argument were and are other countries with a comprehensive all-day-school system.[12] After the implementation of the Program for International Student Assessment (PISA) by the OECD and the publication of its first comparative study in 2001, it became undeniable that the Austrian, and in particular the German school system, performed poorly in educating children from lower social backgrounds in general, and first- and second-generation immigrant children in particular. Countries like Canada and Sweden that had performed much better were discussed as examples for a necessary reform.[13]

The question of how far school education supports social mobility in a society or is the most effective cause of social distinction is indeed increasingly urgent in industrialized countries. Sociologist Pierre Bourdieu has criticized since the 1970s that in most societies the education system itself privileges children from middle and upper classes in a variety of ways: its immanent structures, insufficient and unequal funding, inadequate training of educational personnel, and informal mechanisms of sociocultural exclusion. He thus demands reforms that are driven by a commitment to create more social and ethnical equality.[14]

How to improve the school performance of immigrant students is one of the most urgent problems for many European states with an increasing immigrant population. Already since the 1970s, the Council of the European Union has addressed this issue, but in the last two decades it has become more and more pressing.[15] Europe today matches North America in its significance as a region of immigration. Net immigration in Europe in 2003 stood at 3.7 per 1,000 inhabitants, compared to 3.1 in the United States. The region now hosts a population of 56.1 million "migrants,"[16] compared to 40.8 million in North America.[17] There is every indication that Europe's importance as a target region will further increase. However, the forms of migration are very different in European countries; some like Belgium, Britain, and France are former colonial powers, which mostly integrated citizens of their ex-colonies. Others like Austria and the FRG became immigration countries only after World War II; they recruited foreign "guest workers" originally for a short-term stay. But many of these laborers stayed and later brought their families to their new home countries.[18] Today 6 percent of the population in Europe (EU 25)[19] are so-called foreigners; many more people have a "migrant background" — which includes "citizens" as well as "foreigners" — from first-, second-, and sometimes even third-generation migrant families.[20]

Whether compulsory all-day education can help children with a migrant background to perform better in school is a question that needs to be studied further. The 2006 OECD survey *Where Immigrant Students Succeed — A Comparative Review of Performance and Engagement in PISA 2003* does not discuss the implications of different time structures. It only refers to the tracked system as one plausible cause for the extreme differences in the performance of immigrant children in the seventeen countries included in the study.[21] Its authors emphasize other factors as preconditions for higher success rates, like compulsory early childhood education with language programs, systematic language education with qualified teachers in schools, extracurricular programs for homework and other activities, and the high-quality training of educational personnel.[22] We argue, however, that all pedagogical measures listed above are much easier to implement in all-day care and education facilities, because they provide more time. In addition, they can help to diminish the influence of the family and thus compensate for social origin.[23]

To study the implications of different forms of all-day schooling for children, the German Federal Ministry of Education and Research currently funds a research project called StEG (*Studie zur Entwicklung von Ganztagsschulen*).[24] One aspect of this study addresses the consequences of all-day schooling for children from lower social and migrant backgrounds. The first results of this project indicate that all-day schools can, indeed, contribute to a better performance of children from lower social classes and immigrant families, but only if they are sufficiently funded, free and compulsory, offer enough opportunities for language learning

and extracurricular activities, and possess well-trained and highly motivated educational personnel.[25] Due to insufficient research, we will not be
able to address the implication of all-day childcare and education for children, especially those from disadvantaged backgrounds, systematically
in this volume. Nevertheless, we believe it is important to emphasize this
point to foster more research.

Gendering Labor, Welfare, and Childcare

Of central importance for understanding different national time policies
of childcare and schooling are cultural traditions. Comparison shows how
despite similar economic situations and demographic problems, different
concepts of childrearing and education produce highly divergent time
policies. It also demonstrates the influence of gender concepts, in particular the dominant notions of the gender-specific division of labor in the
economy, society, and politics, and the related family model.[26] Following
historian Joan W. Scott, we understand "gender" in our analysis as both an
important subject of investigation and a method of doing research that can
illuminate a whole range of social cleavages and cultural practices.[27] As
Scott recently emphasized, gender as a methodology mainly involves asking historical questions and thinking critically about how the meanings of
sexual differences are produced, deployed, and changed.[28] In order to integrate the gender dimensions systematically in our comparative analysis
of the time policies of childcare and schooling, we will apply this dynamic
and relational concept of gender and draw on the extensive literature on
gender, labor, childcare, and welfare states.[29]

Since the late 1980s, feminist scholars have sought to overcome the
limits of "mainstream" research that was mainly studying the emergence
and development of welfare states. One key objective of much sociological scholarship was to arrive at a typology of welfare state development.
Thus, the analysis concentrated on the relationship between the state and
the economy in general and work and welfare state benefits in particular.
"Work" was defined as paid employment, and "welfare state legislation"
as eligibility for access to benefits that permit, promote, or prevent "decommodification," defined as the possibility, created by the welfare state,
of acquiring a measure of financial security without paid employment.[30]

The concept of decommodification came to particular prominence
through the pathbreaking work of sociologist Gøsta Esping-Andersen.
In his 1990 study *The Three Worlds of Welfare Capitalism,* he introduced a
typology of welfare regimes that has had an enormous influence over
subsequent research. He divided capitalist welfare states into three categories—*social democratic, liberal,* and *conservative-corporatist regimes*—based

largely on the quality of social rights; the manner in which the state, market, and family are interconnected; and the effects on the structures of social inequality. Esping-Andersen describes the three welfare regimes in ideal-typical fashion as follows: In the *social democratic welfare regime,* which is typical of the Scandinavian countries, social rights are universal. There is a wide range of public services adapted to the expectations of the middle classes. A large proportion of women are integrated into the labor market. In the *liberal welfare regime,* for example in the United States and Britain, social rights are comparatively modest and based on need. These systems emphasize individual responsibility and market solutions. State intervention in the market and the family is limited. The consequence is a polarization of the social structure. Women's labor market participation is quite high because they receive little state support to stay at home. Finally, in *conservative-corporatist regimes* such as the Federal Republic of Germany, France, Italy, Austria, Switzerland, and Spain, social rights are based on class and status. The existing social hierarchies are bolstered by a strong state. The church and the family are central pillars of this welfare system, and the state intervenes only when the family is no longer able to provide for its members. Because the "male-breadwinner/female-homemaker" family plays an important role in the reproduction of these societies, the state does not actively support female employment. Only France since the 1960s represents an exception in this regard.[31]

While welcoming this typology as an improvement over older approaches, feminist scholars have criticized its insufficient attention to the important dimensions of society and family, owing to the focus on the transfer payments between state and market. Sociologist Jane Lewis, like others, chided Esping-Andersen for neglecting two areas that are central to structuring welfare regimes and determining equal social and political opportunities for women. First, his model does not offer a way to place a value on unpaid social care in the family, which is largely done by women, and the associated problem of inadequate social protection for these women. Second, it ignores the importance of a "mixed economy" in providing social services. As a result, this typology does not adequately account for the fact that all participating institutions—the state, market, and family—provided social care services to different degrees at different times.[32]

This critique, which was shared by many feminist scholars, led to calls for the systematic integration of gender into analyses of welfare regimes. They argued that any research on the welfare state that seeks to engage in a "gender neutral" analysis while defining work exclusively as paid employment proceeds implicitly from the norm of the "male breadwinner," elevating it to a "universal" yardstick. Only by integrating the gender dimension can one understand the gender-hierarchical division of labor in society and the family and thus adequately account for unpaid social care work in a theory of welfare regimes. Only then does it become possible to conceptualize childcare as both unpaid work by women in the family and as a social care service provided by the market or state.[33]

Proceeding from these assumptions, feminist scholars have endeavored to integrate gender more systematically into the analysis of welfare states.[34] Two alternative approaches became most influential. The first was developed by sociologists Ann Shola Orloff and Julia O'Connor and focuses on the question of equal social citizenship for women, i.e., their equal access to all economic and social rights as a precondition for equal political participation.[35] In order to include this dimension in the analysis of welfare states, they introduced the concept of "commodification" as an antonym to decommodification. They use the concept of commodification to measure the degree of state social benefits that not only afford women equal access to the labor market but also allow them to maintain their own households, with or without children, independent of a husband. Childcare is one important factor in their analysis.[36]

The second approach has been proposed by political scientist Diane Sainsbury. Like Jane Lewis, she suggests focusing the analysis of welfare systems on the different positioning of women and men along the spectrum of the "male-breadwinner/female-homemaker" family model and its variants that determine different levels of part-time employment for wives and mothers. After all, she argues, this model significantly affects economic and social systems, and prevents the equal, autonomous participation of both sexes in economic, social, and, consequently, political life. Sainsbury has thus recommended distinguishing between two types of welfare states and corresponding mixed forms, namely, those that follow the "breadwinner model" and those that follow the "individual model." The latter model essentially assumes that "each spouse is individually responsible for his or her own maintenance, and that the husband and his wife share the tasks of financial support and care of their children."[37]

Esping-Andersen himself also took up the feminist critique and integrated it into his model in his later publications. He acknowledged that the distribution of tasks and levels of equality between the sexes are important preconditions for successful family policy. For him, a "women-friendly policy" and equality between the sexes are now the "main challenges for welfare state reform."[38]

Though helpful for our gendered analysis of labor, welfare, and childcare, these approaches still share four conceptual weaknesses. First, they usually focus only on the care and education of infants, toddlers, and preschool children; second, they offer no room for a systematic analysis of school systems and their important role in the development of welfare states, because schools are usually conceptualized as part of education, not welfare policy; third, following this logic they don't connect the analysis of childcare, preschool, and primary school education; and fourth, their concepts apply only to an analysis of capitalist welfare regimes. Our comparative study therefore required an expansion in three directions. We had to include not just childcare but also pre- and primary schools as well as out-of-school care in our analysis of the time structure of care and education systems; as a consequence we had to link our analysis of welfare systems to a discussion of educational systems and conceptualize both childcare and schooling as important issues of social policy;[39] and finally, we needed to find a way of integrating communist welfare systems into our typology.

This last point was particularly important, because many concepts of the welfare state have great difficulty in dealing with social policy in the communist countries and thus also the transformation processes after their demise in 1989–1990. This transformation from centralist to pluralist welfare systems produced a "welfare mix" that depended mainly on three factors: the specific economic, social, and political situation of these countries; the different national traditions of their welfare state policies before 1945; and the specific version of the authoritarian-paternalistic welfare state that prevailed under the communist regime, whose gender-specific social policy sought to intervene in reproduction within the family.[40]

Two models proved particularly helpful in the debate on the appropriate conceptualization of welfare-state policy in communist Eastern Europe. The first was sociologist Toni Makkai's proposal to integrate a fourth type of a "state-socialist welfare regime" into Esping-Andersen's model. She uses this term to refer to a regime "that stressed collectivization so that production and consumption could be centrally planned and controlled. This also included the provision of welfare services by the state on egalitarian principles."[41] The second was the suggestion by social policy scholar Bob Deacon that we understand communist welfare regimes as "bureaucratic state collectivist systems of welfare."[42] Both authors emphasize the necessity of paying close attention to the specific national "welfare state mix" and the changes it underwent as well as the considerable discrepancy between socialist aspirations and practices.

Comparison and Path Dependency

The history of different national care and education systems in Eastern and Western Europe reveals that the wide variety of daily and weekly time structures was shaped by a complicated interplay of economic, social, demographic, and cultural factors. Our theoretical and methodological approach to the comparative analysis of this interplay of multiple factors is based on the elaborate German debate on the possibilities and limits of comparison in historical scholarship. One conclusion of this discussion, in which historians such as Jürgen Kocka and Hartmut Kaelble played a leading role, concerned the importance of exploring both the origins of differences between the national discourses, policies, and practices, *and* the similarities that crossed the boundaries of nations and political systems.[43]

For our comparative, long-term analysis of the development of the time policies of childcare, preschools, and primary schooling, the concept of *path dependency* introduced by Paul Pierson and other political scientists has proved particularly useful. This concept stresses the processual character of policies and the institutions that implement them, and seeks to explain the "hardening" of solutions once they have been found. It assumes that with the establishment of a pattern, the passage of time, and repeated use, the material and cultural costs of change rise. As a result, major economic, social, and political pressures are necessary in order to institute far-reaching reforms. Education systems, like welfare state regimes, therefore tend to evidence a high degree of path dependency.[44]

Because we wanted to understand which circumstances promoted or hindered the reform of the time policy of childcare and schooling and shaped different paths of development, our long-term analysis focused on the interplay among the following six factors:

1. The *legal and institutional foundations of childcare* and the *education system,* which developed over time, particularly the role of the state, the responsibility within the state of different governmental departments and levels of state administration, and the status of nonprofit providers (such as churches and charitable associations);

2. The *economic and labor market situation,* the *financial strength of the state,* and the *system of funding of childcare services and schools,* which varies greatly from predominantly public financing through mixed forms of funding to largely private financing;

3. The *demographic development of society* and the *population policy of the state;*

4. The *dominant cultural concepts (and competing ideas) of childcare and schooling,* in particular notions about the role of the family and the state in the upbringing of children and their education;

5. The *hegemonic concept of the gender order,* especially the family model and related ideas of an "appropriate" gender-specific division of labor in family and society, as well as variants and alternative concepts;

6. And finally, the *structure of the overall political system,* the *specific political constellation,* and the *ability of different interest groups,* such as churches, political

parties, the women's movement, or teachers' and parents' organizations, *to assert their position in the normative debate over questions of childcare and schooling* and the *political decision-making process.*

We have found that the relevance of these six factors changes over time and varies significantly from country to country, as does their specific interplay.

The time horizon of our comparative analysis tries to explore long-term trends and developmental paths as well as shorter conjunctures in which reforms became possible. The foundations of most national patterns were already being laid in the nineteenth century with the introduction of compulsory schooling, but many systems experienced significant periods of educational reform thereafter, preceded or followed by longer periods of stagnation. We thus needed to begin our analysis before the end of the Second World War, often already in the nineteenth century, but given the enormity of the social, political, and economic changes after 1945, we had to pay particular attention to the postwar period. Moreover, in both Eastern and Western Europe, the 1960s and 1970s proved to be critical periods for the reform of childcare and education policies. Finally, the initial years of transformation after the collapse of the Soviet system were especially important in the former communist countries of East-Central Europe. The concept of path dependency proved particularly useful for understanding the remarkable continuity of national systems across such historical caesuras.

Patterns of Time Policy for Childcare and Schooling in Europe

The many differences in the time policies of the national systems of childcare und schooling have a long history going back to the late eighteenth century. At the same time, historical analysis also reveals striking parallels in the emergence and development of national childcare and school systems as well as in the pedagogical debates associated with them, which can be explained by the similar social problems and intensive transfer of ideas in Europe.[45]

The Emergence of Different Time Structures of Childcare and Schooling

Beginning in the late eighteenth century, childcare and preschool facilities were established throughout Europe on the initiative of individual notables, charitable associations, municipal administrations, and church parishes. Their founders shared similar ideas and increasingly exchanged them on an international level, which explains why new, pioneering concepts and model institutions influenced subsequent projects all across Europe.[46] Five sometimes competing, but more often complementary motives seem to have come together across the continent:

1. The concern of churches for the moral and religious development of children, whom they hoped to guide with early moral and religious education;

2. The increased interest of enlightened pedagogues in the education of a child with the objective of enhancing its abilities and strengthening its individual character;

3. The political desire of "patriots" for a national education, which they regarded as a central element in promoting their "national culture";

4. The economic interest of entrepreneurs and businessmen in securing the cheaper labor of women and mothers for work in the factories;

5. The hope of bourgeois social reformers to protect the unsupervised children of employed working-class mothers from feared "neglect," which "destroys morals" and thus society.[47]

These motives led to the development of three main types of institutions of early childhood care and education during the nineteenth century in Europe that dominated until the middle of the twentieth century. The first were the *Kinderbewahranstalten,* all-day nurseries for the unsupervised children of the working class, which arose after 1800. They were usually established by confessional organizations out of charitable and moral motives and represented the majority of childcare institutions up to World War II. Second, beginning around 1840, pedagogically engaged individuals and nonconfessional associations, inspired by the example of the German pedagogue Friedrich Fröbel, founded kindergartens that were usually open half-day and were conceived as educational institutions dedicated to fostering child development. They were supposed to complement upbringing in the family and were mainly attended by middle-class children. From the beginning, middle- and upper-class women throughout Europe became active in the "kindergarten movement." In keeping with the maternalist concept favored by the majority of the bourgeois women's movement, they regarded their engagement as a form of "social work" appropriate to their sex and as an important step towards their own emancipation.[48] Third, confessional schools for young children that took a Christian missionary approach also became important from mid-century on. They were run by all of the churches and usually open half-days as well. Like the kindergarten, they were intended only to supplement childrearing within the family.[49] In particular, the Catholic Church was active in this area because it sought to influence the moral and religious upbringing of children. Otherwise Catholicism opposed any form of public, collective care and education for children, clinging until well into the second half of the twentieth century to the principle that childcare and childrearing were primarily the task of the family and of mothers, whose paid employment it perceived as "destructive to the family."[50]

Since the late nineteenth century, formal out-of-school care for primary school children was established mainly out of charitable motives, at first only in those countries in which the half-day school system had taken root. These encompassed all regions of the German Empire, including the Prussian-controlled areas of partitioned Poland and the Austro-Hungarian Empire, with the regions of Bohemia and Moravia, as well as the United Kingdom of Italy founded in 1861. Various factors conspired to establish the half-day school system, which became a long-lived developmental path in these regions.[51]

Until the end of the nineteenth century, instruction in the private schools and secondary public schools lasted usually all day but was divided into two parts. The school day was interrupted by a long lunch break, which

ILLUSTRATION 1.1: Lunch break in an all-day primary school located in southern Switzerland, run by Catholic nuns from Suore di San Giuseppe in Italy, for children of Italian workers, 1919.

was to be spent at home with the family. With the introduction of compulsory schooling in Prussia in 1763 and the rest of the German-speaking
region during the following decades, all-day instruction with a long lunch
break was also launched in public primary schools. But it proved difficult
to enforce, since it meant a radical intervention in the working and living conditions of broad segments of the population, and it could not be
reconciled with the common practice of child labor. Accordingly, nearly
all school regulations provided for numerous exceptions. The most common were the so-called summer school, which offered shorter school days
during the summer months so that children could work in agriculture; the
factory school, which combined regulated child factory work with significantly reduced school attendance in the early morning and late evening;
and the rural half-day school. Instruction in morning or afternoon "shifts"
also offered a pragmatic solution to the widespread problems of school
financing, which led to shortages of classroom space and teachers. In 1872,
half-day instruction gained, under specific conditions, official recognition,
first in Prussia and later in the other states of the German Empire.[52]

In the mid-nineteenth century, half-day instruction also began to become common in the secondary schools. The main reason for this shift was
concern about "the overburdening of pupils," advanced by physicians
and educators since the 1830s. They argued that the lengthy school day,
in conjunction with hours of homework and ever-longer travel to school,
was making students nervous and sickly. Boys got too little exercise and
might ultimately even become unfit for military service. The solution they
recommended was the introduction of instruction in the mornings only,
which was permitted for the secondary schools in Prussia in 1890 and
soon spread throughout Germany.[53] The municipal primary schools followed suit, introducing morning instruction in larger numbers after 1900.
The development in the other states of the German Empire as well as in
other regions of Central Europe was similar and here too codified in legislation and institutions.[54]

The reform pedagogical initiatives of the late nineteenth century, which
promoted new forms of all-day schooling combining instruction and leisure activities, failed to halt this trend towards half-day education.[55] With
its critique of the so-called *Lernschule* focused on rote learning, and its call
for schoolwork that emerged from the needs and interests of children and
youth, reform pedagogy gained adherents only among the culturally critical circles of the educated middle class, particularly the youth movement,
the labor movement, and segments of organized primary school teachers.
Until the 1960s, the dominant view in the German-speaking region was
that the purpose of school was to convey knowledge.[56] Social and cultural

education was regarded as the task of the family, and only when the family failed should the public welfare system intervene.

In contrast, England and France, and the states in their sphere of influence, retained the traditional divided all-day school system with lessons in the morning and the afternoon and a long lunch break. From 1900 on, England gradually transformed its institutions into a modern conjunct all-day school system, with classes in the mornings and afternoons and a school lunch. French schools followed decades later; moreover, lunch here usually remained optional. After-school care was not established before the 1960s, if at all.[57] The main reason for this different development was that in both countries a universal compulsory primary school system was only established in the second half of the nineteenth century, much later than in Prussia and the other Central European states. In England, the enforcement of compulsory all-day schooling and the gradual extension of the hours of instruction in primary schools were weapons in the struggle against widespread child factory labor. In France, the chief motivation for all-day instruction was the republican aspiration to create a radically "laicist" state-controlled school that would break the dominance of the Catholic Church in education and thus in the state.

In England, the expansion of the primary school system was largely the work of nonprofit private institutions, among them the National So-

ILLUSTRATION 1.2: School education in the interwar period: First grade of a half-day primary school for boys in Dresden, Germany, 1930.

ciety, which was affiliated with the Church of England. From 1833 on, the central government supported their work with growing subsidies. The Forster Act of 1870 stipulated that public schools must be established in regions where the private schools were insufficient to meet local needs and it enacted the first guidelines, although these still left a good deal of scope to school providers, whether private or public. It was not until 1876 that schooling was made compulsory for all, more than a century later than in Prussia. At the same time, factory work during school hours was prohibited for children up to the age of ten. Children between the ages of ten and fourteen were only allowed to work as so-called half-timers, having to attend school for the other half of the day. Only in 1920 was the half-time system finally abolished and all-day schooling made compulsory.[58]

Part of the enforcement of the modern conjunct all-day school in England was the introduction of school lunch, which a growing number of schools offered from the late nineteenth century on. At first they did so primarily for welfare reasons and later increasingly for the sake of social education, since shared meals were believed to promote community. The first law on school meals was enacted in 1906. The Education Act of 1944 finally required the Local Education Authorities to provide every child with a school meal.[59] In Austria and Germany, private charity organizations had also launched school meal initiatives since the end of the nineteenth century, but only as temporary social assistance for sick and needy children. These offerings were significantly expanded during the hardship years of the First and Second World Wars, but quickly dismantled in the postwar period. Although in most working-class households, a hot lunch at home was probably the exception, the middle-class myth of the significance of the shared family meal in creating community persisted well into the post–World War II period and prevented the introduction of universal school lunches on the English model.[60]

In France, the all-day school day was introduced by the Third Republic together with compulsory primary instruction in 1882. Republican politicians sought to place the school system, which had been controlled largely by the Catholic Church, under exclusive state oversight, freeing it from the tutelage of an often antirepublican clergy. The declared objective was the "laicist" school with no religious instruction whatsoever, which was finally mandated in 1905 by a law separating churches and state. This laicist policy had two consequences for school organization that are still felt today. First was the organization of schools as conjunct all-day institutions. Republican school reformers regarded primary school teachers as the *prêtres laïcs* (secular priests) of republican national education and wanted to exert as comprehensive an influence as possible on the malleable "souls of children." Second, as a concession to the Catholic Church, however, primary school students were given one free day and secondary school students one free morning in the middle of the week. This was supposed to allow those parents who insisted on it to send their children to religion classes provided by the church. In order to maintain the stipulated weekly classroom hours, the school administration had no choice but to introduce all-day instruction on the remaining days. Another circumstance also promoted all-day schools: In agrarian-dominated France, the Ministry of Education tried to mollify farmers opposed to compulsory schooling by introducing a long (nearly ten-week) summer holiday so that children could help with the farm work and harvest. Thus, from the beginning, the childrens' school day in France was oriented toward the adult working day.[61]

By the first decades of the twentieth century, the basic patterns of the time structure of childcare and schooling had already been set in most European countries. In later decades, the time policy of care and education followed the path taken earlier by each country with only minor modifications. Both the English and the French models of a full-day school, time structure exerted a strong influence on the countries that belonged to their empires or were influenced by their culture. The German half-day model, on the other hand, influenced not only all of the regions that belonged to the German and Austro-Hungarian Empires but also the Nordic countries and parts of Eastern and Southern Europe well into the twentieth century.[62]

For the evolution of the all-day time policy of the Scandinavian education system, Sweden is the best example, because its development set standards for the other Nordic countries. Until the 1940s the main aim of the education policy of the Swedish state was the improvement of primary school education. Compulsory schooling was formally launched in Sweden already in 1842, but until the introduction of the first national "standard syllabus" in 1900, the quality of the six-year primary school, which was directed mainly towards the children of farmers and workers, differed vastly between town and countryside. Decisions on the curriculum and temporal organization of education were made locally. School attendance was not strictly compulsory, because home instruction was permitted and a variety of different school types existed, like "mobile schools," "part-time schools" with shift-classes, and "minimum courses," but primarily in rural areas. Here the school year usually lasted only for four to five months and the half-day school with at most five hours was the norm, because parents needed their children for farm work or other labor.[63] With the introduction of the first national "standard syllabus" in 1900, part-time schools with shift-classes were abolished. In 1912 all forms of child labor were prohibited. After World War I the Social Democratic Workers' Party of Sweden (*Sveriges socialdemokratiska arbetareparti,* SAP) entered the government for the first time and increasingly pushed for a school reform, most importantly an extension of compulsory education. One result was the national "standard syllabus" of 1919 with six full years of compulsory education and an average of 28–30 hours per week for primary school children. During the 1920s, the recommendations of this syllabus slowly became the norm against the fierce resistance of the conservatives.[64]

After the SAP took over the government again in 1932, the party intensively propagated a new concept of social welfare that included free school meals and extracurricular activities, free kindergartens, and free after-school centers. These ideas gained increasing influence and formed the social democratic welfare and education policy from the 1940s on, which systematically sought to expand the social functions of education and aimed for more gender equality. The reforms, however, did not change the weekly teaching time in compulsory education, which stayed remarkably stable after 1919. Only the years of compulsory primary education were increased to seven in 1937. What changed were the teaching conditions and the time schedule. With the introduction of school lunches, extracurricular activities, and after-school programs, the publicly funded primary school slowly developed from a half-day or divided all-day school to a conjunct all-day school.[65]

The reform of education policy in Sweden was fostered by the increasing influence of reform pedagogical ideas in interwar Europe. After the First World War, socialist or social democratic variants developed alongside bourgeois reform pedagogy. Their proponents sought not only to reform the state school system by introducing "polytechnical" schools (*Arbeitsschulen*) and/or comprehensive schools (*Einheitsschulen*), but also to reform childcare and out-of-school care. The countries where progressive pedagogical ideas became especially influential after the World War I were Austria, Germany, and Sweden. A strong social democratic labor movement influenced education and welfare policies in all three states. Thus all-day kindergartens and schools with a reform-pedagogical orientation were mainly founded in major European cities like Berlin, Hamburg, Stockholm, or Vienna, which were governed by a social democratic city council.[66]

The interwar period was a decisive phase in the development of education systems and welfare states throughout Europe. The emergence of a broad publicly funded school system, which was increasingly subject to legislation and thus standardization, served to entrench existing national differences. Childcare was in most European countries still understood as

ILLUSTRATION 1.3: Reform-pedagogic-oriented childcare in the interwar period:
Coeducative age-mixed group of preschool children playing with wood material in
a kindergarten of the Pestalozzi-Fröbel-House in Berlin, Germany, 1927.

a part of the welfare—not the education—system. It was usually funded by the state only if no private institutions were willing and able to do so. Thus, until World War II, the churches and charitable associations continued to be in most countries the largest providers of childcare.

The Second World War played an important, albeit ambivalent role in the development of childcare and schooling in Europe. Since the wartime economy required a greater deployment of female labor, most governments of the leading war powers dramatically increased the number of places in daycare services. This was even the case in neutral states like Sweden with a booming war industry that supplied the armies of the fighting states. After 1945, this childcare service was only partially dismantled in most countries that were involved in World War II, because many widowed and divorced women now had to support their families. One exception here was Britain, where as part of its demobilization, the government closed most of the publicly funded childcare facilities after the war. Thus World War II was in many European countries a key period in the expansion of all-day childcare.[67] At the same time, however, the National Socialist annexation and occupation of large parts of the European continent as well as saturation bombing destroyed the material infrastructure of schools and childcare facilities in many regions (especially the cities of Central and Eastern Europe).[68]

ILLUSTRATION 1.4: School education in the occupied East during World War II: Mixed-age, coeducated class in a camp of children of resettled Ethnic Germans from Volhynia in Aussig (Protectorate Bohemia), 1940.

The Development of Childcare and Schooling in Western Europe after 1945

After the Second World War, nearly all Western European countries picked up where their prewar childcare and school systems had left off in order to reestablish both as quickly as possible. The late 1940s and the 1950s therefore appear to have been a period of restoration and stagnation in educational policy. Until the late 1950s, far-reaching structural reforms of the childcare and education system were limited everywhere. For most countries in the West, the most important changes in this period were an increase in the years of compulsory schooling and the extension of the secondary school system.[69]

A crucial contributing factor to this stagnation was the importance accorded to the family in the social and political reorganization of postwar societies. Everywhere in Western Europe, policies aimed to stabilize the

ILLUSTRATION 1.5: After-school care in the postwar period: *Wärmestube* (literally "Heated Room") for primary school children that offered a warm lunch after school and a place to do homework, West Berlin, Germany, 1949.

family and further entrench the "male-breadwinner/female-homemaker" model first formulated in the Enlightenment. In the 1950s this was even the case in Norway and Sweden. Here, their social democratic governments worked to modernize societies through policies that aimed at social integration and equality, which rhetorically included the goal of "women's emancipation," although a broad public debate that questioned the traditional gender roles and demanded real gender equality did not emerge before the early 1960s.[70]

The restoration of the model of the male-breadwinner/female-homemaker in postwar societies was made possible because of the "economic miracle" that many Western European countries experienced from the 1950s on. For the first time even wives and mothers from working-class families were able to avoid paid employment or to work only very limited hours. But it was also the product of constant public promotion of the family ideal and massive legal and institutional safeguards. These included, among other things, welfare and educational policies that blocked the expansion of public all-day childcare services. As a result, the male-breadwinner/female-homemaker family model shaped most postwar societies in Western Europe more than ever before.[71]

A change in education and childcare policies slowly started in the late 1950s. The economic boom led to a growing need for labor, to which most Western European states responded with two labor market policies: they recruited "foreign" laborers and tried to raise female employment. One of the countries with the highest increase of "guest workers" was the FRG.[72] After the GDR had closed its borders in 1961, the flourishing West German economy needed labor even more urgently than before. One way to solve this problem was the active recruitment of "guest workers," a government program that already had started in 1955 and continued until 1973.[73] Another way was the expansion of female part-time work.[74] From the early 1960s on, industry in the FRG promoted, increasingly supported by the government, part-time work for wives and mothers because it could be "reconciled" with their domestic and familial "duties." A similar development started in other European countries such as Austria, Italy, Switzerland, and England. The model of the male-breadwinner/female-homemaker family was partly adapted to the needs of the labor market by allowing housewives to earn some "surplus income." Full-time employment was still common mainly for single, divorced, or widowed women, while part-time employment became increasingly widespread among wives and mothers. Their opportunities on the job market, however, remained quite limited. One consequence was a relatively low level of female employment—56 percent in Austria, 53 percent in West Germany, and 42 percent in Italy—even in the late 1980s. In Great Britain, where the Conservative government in the 1970s and 1980s began to move towards a family model that also expected married women to earn an individual income, the rate of employment among women in the late 1980s was 63 percent, although the proportion working part-time was quite high. (See table 1.1)

After 1945, the Catholic Church also played a key role in enforcing the model of the male-breadwinner/female-homemaker family in many Western European countries. In Catholic doctrine, the aim of all welfare measures still was to stabilize this family form, which the church considered the bedrock of society and the state. Social policies thus had to ensure that a married woman stayed in the home taking care of her family. Childcare and conjunct all-day schools were regarded as means to thwart this agenda, because they allowed women to work for a living outside the home. Nevertheless, the influence of the Catholic Church varied greatly, even in heavily Catholic countries, as a comparison between France, Austria, the FRG, Spain, and Italy shows.

Based on a strong laicist tradition and motivated by labor market and population policy concerns, the Gaullist government in France began systematically expanding the full-time *école maternelle* to supplement the all-day primary school in the 1960s, encountering little resistance from the Catholic Church, while at the same time in Austria and the FRG, the conservative Christian-democratic parties in power and the Catholic Church firmly rejected any such programs.[75] In Spain, the influence of the Catholic Church remained so strong under the authoritarian Franco regime that it largely determined school policy. Here the church unequivocally supported the traditional divided all-day structure for schools, which was also implemented in preschools. The number of preschool places only expanded after the change of political regime in 1975. The new democratic government in Spain, while allowing the Catholic Church to maintain an extensive private childcare and school system, curtailed its influence over public pre- and primary schools. Because both retained a divided all-day time structure after 1975, parents could not use them as substitutes for childcare, since their opening hours were not only shorter than the typical working day but were still interrupted by a long lunch break spent at home. The number of places in childcare and out-of-school care was very limited.[76] As a result, the rate of female employment in the late 1980s was extraordinarily low in Spain at only 38 percent. (See table 1.1)

A similar compromise between the Catholic Church and the state was reached in Italy, where a mix of various time policies emerged beginning in the 1960s. The Italian proponents of all-day schools used mainly reform pedagogical and only rarely labor market arguments for expanding all-day childcare and education. The differences between urban and rural regions were especially pronounced in this country. All-day childcare services and schools gained increasing influence from the 1970s on, above all in the large cities of the industrialized North. But even there different types of all-day schools coexisted. Depending on local labor market demand and the time structure of childcare and schooling, the percentage of working women varied greatly from region to region.[77]

Since the 1960s, significant differences between the Western welfare states did appear in the areas of women's, family, and educational policy. At the same time, the varying paths of development in time policies for childcare and schooling became more entrenched. One effect of this development was that specific mixtures of welfare systems, family models, and time policies of childcare and schooling began to take shape, which cannot be captured alone by an extended welfare state model based on Esping-Andersen.

In France, which according to his model was a conservative-corporatist welfare state, the ideal of the "dual-earner" family was gradually accepted after the late 1960s, mainly because of the demands of the labor market and

ILLUSTRATION 1.6: Schooling in postwar Europe: A French coeducative all-day class in the 1950s in a small town in the Basque region.

the reluctance of politicians to recruit foreign laborers as extensively as in the FRG. Also based on its natalist tradition, the French state pursued an "explicit" family policy that was overseen by government institutions and which supported female employment. Indeed, since the interwar period, the "family" itself was legally recognized as an institution that played an important role in the maintenance of social cohesion and order. In the 1970s and 1980s, full-time employment for women rose continuously and became quite normal for mothers. The result was a relatively high female employment rate of 57 percent in the late 1980s.[78] (See table 1.1)

A similar development occurred since the late 1950s in Sweden, where the booming economy needed more female labor and the government was also reluctant to recruit as many "guest workers" as the FRG. Norway followed the Swedish model a decade later. In the late 1980s, both countries had higher female employment rates, at 84 and 71 percent, respectively, than almost any other West European state. Only Denmark, which pursued a similar policy, had a comparable proportion of women in the workforce, at 75 percent. (See table 1.1) The great majority of mothers in these Scandinavian countries worked part-time, however, mostly in the greatly increasing public service sector. This development was promoted by the systematic expansion of full-time childcare services and all-day pre- and primary schools. Pursuing a social democratic welfare policy, the governments of the three Nordic states supported this development by fostering a family policy that aimed for gender equality and allowed both parents the combination of family and paid work. Earlier than most other Western European states (with the exception of France) they made their political goal the "dual-earner family."[79]

Britain, in contrast, a liberal welfare state according to Esping-Andersen's model, had a modern, comprehensive all-day school system, despite its relatively underdeveloped and mainly privately run care services for kindergarten and preschool children persisting into the 1980s. The proportion of women in the workforce was nevertheless comparatively high. In the British welfare system, women increasingly had to work, regardless of their marital status and number of children, in order to secure their own place in the social insurance system. Here, under an aggressively neoliberal Conservative government, the trend was from "welfare" for families to "workfare" for individuals.[80]

The 1960s and 1970s were a period of reform and expansion of public childcare and schooling all over Western Europe. Education was now generally defined as a means to promote "equal opportunities" and economic growth. In this context, kindergarten and preschools were increasingly regarded as part of the education and no longer of the welfare system. Some countries, such as France, Sweden, and later also Britain, that were expanding their full-time offerings, oriented time policies explicitly on both educational and labor market policy goals, therefore gradually embracing the new model of the "double-earner" family. This change was fueled in France and Sweden by a strong women's movement, which, in cooperation with trade unions and social democratic, socialist, or communist parties, increasingly pushed through the provision of full-time childcare, thus allowing women to combine family and career.[81]

For several reasons, this change did not occur to the same degree in Austria and the Federal Republic of Germany. Counted among the conservative-corporatist welfare states, they in fact adhered longest to the male-breadwinner/female-homemaker family model, albeit in a "modernized" version that accepted part-time employment for women. Because of Germany's National Socialist past, both the student movement and the autonomous women's movement were wary of the state's influence over children and thus primarily supported the independent, antiauthoritarian *Kinderladen* (literally "children's stores") movement. Many autonomous feminists also rejected cooperation with the trade unions and the established political parties such as the Social Democrats.[82]

ILLUSTRATION 1.7: Educational reform in the 1960s and 1970s: "*Kinderkollektiv*" (Children's Collective), a group of children in a "storefront daycare center," organized by parents, Frankfurt/M., West Germany, 1970.

The Development of Childcare and Schooling in Eastern Europe after 1945

After the Second World War, providing education proved extremely difficult for most Eastern European countries. With the towns and economy in ruins, the basic material conditions, including classrooms, teachers, and schoolbooks, were all in short supply. The first aim was thus the enforcement and extension of compulsory education for all children. In addition, communist Eastern European societies, in particular the Soviet Union, had to take care of the numerous orphaned and homeless children after the war. Debates about a "socialist school reform," which should enhance the "socialist education" of children as the "future of the society," could only come later and thus started in most communist countries some years after the war. All Eastern European states continued to follow the Germanic tradition and kept the half-day school.[83]

The development in the Eastern bloc, however, took a quite a different path after World War II, not only economically and politically, but also socially and culturally. Most important in the first decade was economic reconstruction. This aim formed the demands of the planned economy, primarily determined social and labor market policy, and thus defined the approach to female employment and childcare until the late 1950s. An accelerated policy of industrialization to compensate for war damage led to a massive mobilization of female labor in industry since the 1950s, which further intensified in the 1960s. In practice, the extraordinary need for labor led to a *duty* for men and women alike to work full-time, as the majority of state social benefits were tied to this.[84] At the same time, all communist states propagated women's employment outside the home as a path to equality between the sexes in keeping with the traditional socialist theory of "women's emancipation." The expansion of public childcare was also intended to allow mothers to work full-time.

The old revolutionary demand to relieve the burdens of "working women" by collectivizing housework, which had already failed in the Soviet Union in the 1930s, was not seriously pursued after 1945.[85] In the East, the introduction of technologies that were facilitating housework in the West foundered on economic priorities, since consumer goods industries were less developed than heavy industry. The one exception was the "goulash communism" of Hungary after the revolution of 1956. In the other countries, this one-sided orientation of economic policy only began to change after the Soviet crushing of the Prague Spring in 1968, when governments offered more consumer goods to compensate for political repression. The communist welfare states were thus quite authoritarian and paternalistic.

In spite of the rhetoric of equality, the Eastern states never seriously called into question the gender-specific division of labor in the family and society. In practice, the model remained the dual-earner/female-homemaker family similar to France and Sweden. The extent to which the public all-day childcare and school systems were expanded depended largely on the demands of the industrial labor market, which varied widely according to the degree of industrialization and the different needs for labor. Therefore there were also marked differences in the rate of female employment, which in 1988 ranged from 48 percent in the CSSR to 88 percent in the GDR (see table 1.1).[86] Because the CSSR had an oversupply of labor during the 1970s and 1980s, the government did everything in its power to keep the mothers of small children out of the labor market as long as possible. In the GDR, in contrast, full-time childcare services were especially well developed because labor was extremely scarce. From the 1970s on, the GDR had more children between the ages of three and twelve in childcare or out-of-school care facilities than any other European country, East or West.

Apart from economic concerns, population policy motives increasingly came to exert influence over family and time policy throughout the

Eastern bloc. The accelerating fall in the birth rate was to be halted by all means. This trend became evident in the late 1960s, particularly in the CSSR and Hungary, but also in the GDR, where an all-day time policy was an important measure of population policy.[87] In addition to these economic and demographic reasons for expanding full-time childcare systems for children of kindergarten, preschool, and primary school age, the communist states also pursued political and cultural goals. Of particular importance was the desire to educate "future socialist citizens." The official model here was the Soviet Union, which the GDR sought to follow in particular.[88] But all of the extensive reforms attempted from the late 1950s on, such as the introduction of "boarding schools" and later "day schools" (*Tagesschulen*) in the GDR and "extended-day schools" (*shkola prodlennogo dnya*) in the SU, were limited in both countries. In Russia no more than

ILLUSTRATION 1.8: All-day education under communism: East German "day school" in Weißenfels. A teacher helps elementary school children with their homework, late 1950s.

37 percent of all students (compulsory grades 1–8) were enrolled in an "extended-day school" in 1985. The number of "day schools" in the GDR was even more limited; no more than 133 existed in the whole republic. Mainly economic reasons stifled these reform attempts, as they were simply too expensive. Both governments also restrained these experiments, because of the resistance of teachers and parents who rejected an excessive control of the state over education.[89] In contrast to a widespread misperception, all communist states kept the half-day time structure for the majority of their schools, which they complemented with extensive full-time childcare and out-of-school care services.

Finally, the national variants of childcare and school systems and the associated time policies in the communist states were also influenced by differing political circumstances and cultural traditions. Because of the direct confrontation with the West, the education system of the GDR was strongly oriented towards the Soviet model and from the outset suppressed as "bourgeois" any reform pedagogical tradition that did not conform to the declared aims of socialist education.[90] In contrast, the reform pedagogical tradition continued to be cultivated in the CSSR.[91] Yet in the primarily agrarian Poland of the 1960s, a clearly national-political, Catholic tradition emphasized the role of the family as the site of national education. Therefore, all-day childcare services were only well developed in industrial urban regions.[92]

In addition, in the GDR and the FRG, which more than any other countries represented the competition between political-economic systems during the Cold War, time policies were influenced to a great extent by attempts to disassociate themselves from "the other" ideological camp. While the West polemically embraced half-day school and childrearing within the family as sign of democratic choice, the East supported collective all-day education and employment for mothers as symbol of socialist progress.[93] In the postwar era, both states represented two closely connected extremes in the time policy of childcare and schooling as well as female employment.

Divergence and Convergence of Time Policies in Western and Eastern Europe during the late 1980s

Towards the end of the 1980s, the result of these diverse developments in Western and Eastern Europe was a heterogeneous mix of welfare state regimes, family models, and time policies of the various childcare, preschool, and primary school systems. Due to the specific tensions between national historical developmental paths and labor market, population, family, and education policies, the level of female and maternal employment was quite different in each country. (See table 1.1)[94] As one major outcome of our comparative research, we are able to distinguish between six groups of welfare states, their dominant family models, and their usual time policy for the late 1980s.

First, the *social democratic welfare states in Northern Europe with an egalitarian version of the "dual-earner" family model* (but nevertheless no equal division of labor in the family and society), a very high percentage of employed women and part-time working mothers, and in most countries an *extended all-day time policy for childcare and schooling.* Here the differences between Denmark, Norway, and Sweden are interesting, since Denmark and Sweden had modern conjunct all-day schools, the latter with an extensive out-of-school service program, while Norway only had a reliable full-time school of six hours per day, but no additional out-of-school services. The childcare and school system in all three centralized states was publicly funded and controlled.

Second, the *conservative-corporatist Western European welfare states with a dominant "dual-earner/female-homemaker" family model* (Belgium and France) or the *"male breadwinner/female-homemaker-supplementary-earner" family model* (Netherlands) and different forms of *all-day time policy for childcare and schooling.* In Belgium and France the pre- and primary schools were modern conjunct all-day schools, although France offered additional out-of-school care and Belgium did not. At least in France, the percentage of employed women was above the European average, but not as high as in Scandinavia and some of the socialist countries; the rate of part-time working mothers was relatively low compared to the Scandinavian states. The Netherlands retained the traditional divided all-day school schedule in pre- and primary schools with a long lunch break at home and no provision for additional out-of-school care. The rate of female employment was here close to the European average, and the percentage of mothers working part-time was higher than in any other European country. The Dutch state systematically supported part-time work for women. The childcare and school system was in all three countries publicly funded and controlled; private schools and childcare facilities were allowed, but they had to be licensed and were supervised by the state. In particular in the Netherlands, the percentage of private schools that were subsidized by the state was high.

Third, the *conservative-corporatist welfare states in Southern Europe with a diminishing influence of the "male-breadwinner/female-homemaker" family model* and a gradually increasing acceptance of part-time and even full-time work for mothers. The percentage of employed women was, however, relatively low compared to other European countries and the opportunities for women to work part-time were limited. The *care and education sys-*

tems were rather mixed, with the dominance either of the traditional divided all-day-pre- and primary school schedule, as in Portugal and Spain, or a hybrid system as in Italy. The school system was publicly funded and controlled; private schools were allowed, but they had to be licensed and were supervised by the state. Childcare was mostly privately organized and funded; here too the churches played an important role as providers. The regional differences were also extremely developed.

Fourth, the *liberal Western European welfare states with a diminishing influence of the "male-breadwinner/female-homemaker–supplementary-earner" family model, an increasing importance of the "individual-earner" model, and a mix of time policies,* private part-time care for children under five, and a modern conjunct all-day schedule for pre- and primary school children. In Britain, in particular, the percentage of employed women was high, although the majority of mothers there worked part-time. The school system was publicly funded and controlled, while the percentage of privately funded schools was relatively high compared to other countries. Childcare was mostly provided by private institutions.

Fifth, the *conservative-corporatist West-Central European welfare states, following the model of the "male-breadwinner/female-homemaker–supplementary-earner" family* and consequently *a half-day or part-time policy in childcare and schooling* in Austria, Germany, and German-speaking Switzerland. The school system was publicly funded and controlled while the small percentage of private schools had to be licensed and were supervised by the state. Childcare was funded on the principle of subsidiarity; the result was a very high percentage of private, mostly church-related providers of childcare who were subsidized by public funding and controlled by the state. In all three countries, the rate of female employment was below or close to the European average and the percentage of mothers working part-time was high.

Sixth, the *authoritarian-paternalistic communist welfare states in Eastern Europe with their ideal of the "dual-earner" family* (which in practice was a "dual-earner/female-homemaker" family), a high percentage of employed women in most countries, and only limited opportunities for mothers to work part-time as well as *varying availability of all-day care and education.* In the former CSSR, the GDR, Hungary, and Russia, the dominant type of school was a "reliable" half-day school with integrated full-time out-of-school care. The childcare and school system was publicly funded and controlled. The only exceptions were childcare facilities in state-run factories and farms and in some countries a small percentage of church-funded kindergartens.

Table 1.1 presents an overview of these six groups organized in the three clusters of time systems of childcare and education we proposed earlier.

TABLE 1.1: Children in childcare, preschool, and "out-of-school" services, daily opening hours of primary schools, and female employment rates in Europe, 1987–1989 [95]

Country	Reporting year	Children under the age of 3	Children between the age of 3 and compulsory school age (including preschool)	Children of primary school age		Female employment in 1988 (women 15–64 years)	Percentage of employed mothers who work part-time
				Length and form of school day (and form of lunch for students)	Out-of-school services		
1. All-day childcare and education systems in Western Europe							
Social democratic welfare states in Northern Europe *"Dual-earner" family model (in practice with female responsibility for family and household)* All-day care and education, publicly funded and controlled							
Denmark	1989–1990	48%	85%	MADS (6 hrs.) [b]	36%	76%	
Norway	1988	8%	51%	RHDS (5–6 hrs.) [b]	none	71%	65%
Sweden	1988	31%	64%	MADS (6–7 hrs.) [b]	the norm	84%	68%
Conservative-corporatist welfare states in Western Europe *"Dual-earner" family model* (Belgium and France) *(in practice with female responsibility for family and household)* or *"male breadwinner/female-part-time-earner" family model* (Netherlands) Different forms and levels of all-day care and education, publicly funded and controlled							
Belgium	1989	25%	95% [c]	MADS (8 hrs.) [b]	Rare	45%	
France	1988	20%	98% [c]	MADS (8 hrs.) [b]	the norm	57%	28%
Netherlands	1989	2%	50–55%	TADS (6–7 hrs.) [a]	1%	49%	84%
Conservative-corporatist welfare states in Southern Europe *"Male-breadwinner/female-homemaker-supplementary-earner" family model,* increasingly accepting part-time and even full-time work for mothers Mixed system (Italy) or traditional divided all-day-education (Portugal and Spain), pre- and primary school education publicly funded and controlled, childcare mostly provided by private institutions							
Italy	1990	5–6%	75–92% [c]	max. 6.5 hrs. mixed system	None	42%	33%
Portugal	1990	6%	40%	TADS (6 hrs.) [a]	6%%	56%	32%
Spain	1987–1988	2–3%	68%	TADS (8 hrs.) [a]	None	38%	34%
Liberal welfare states in Western Europe *"Male-breadwinner/female-homemaker-supplementary-earner" family model,* increasingly accepting the "individual-earner" model *(in practice with female responsibility for family and household)* and thereby full-time work for mothers All-day school education and private formal part-time childcare, primary school education publicly funded and controlled (starts with the age of 5), childcare mostly provided by private institutions							
Great Britain	1988	2%	40%	MADS (6.5 hrs.) [b]	none	63%	68%
Ireland	1989	3%	50–60%	MADS (6.5 hrs.) [b]	none	39%	—

2. Part-time pre- and primary school systems with additional childcare in West-Central Europe						
Conservative-corporatist welfare states in West-Central Europe *"Male-breadwinner/female-homemaker–supplementary-earner" family model* Half-day care and education, pre- and primary school education publicly funded and controlled, childcare funding based on the principle of subsidiarity						
Austria	1988	1%	75%	UHDS (4–5 hrs.)	1%	56%	44%
FRG	1989–1990	3%	79%	UHDS (4–5 hrs)	4%	53%	59%
Switzerland (German-speaking parts)	No data only for the German speaking part available						
3. All-day childcare and part-time pre- and primary school systems in Eastern Europe						
Communist authoritarian-paternalist welfare states in Eastern and East-Central Europe *"Dual-earner" family model (in practice with female responsibility for family and household)* All-day care and education, publicly funded and controlled						
CSSR	1988	17%	82%	RHDS (5–6 hrs.) [b]	50%	18%	20%
GDR	1988	80%	94%	RHDS (5–6 hrs.) [b]	82%	88 %	27 %
Hungary	1988	25%	85%	RHDS (5–6 hrs.) [b]	66%	62%	8%
Poland	1988	11%	60%	RHDS (5–6 hrs.) [b]	none	68%	5%

Notes:

MADS: Modern all-day school system

TADS: Traditional all-day school system with lessons in the morning and in the afternoon

RHDS: "Reliable" half-day school system (= school begins and ends at the same time every day)

UHDS: "Unreliable" half-day school system (= varying school hours)

a) Long lunch break at home.

b) Lunch at school (mandatory or optional for students).

c) State-funded preschool since the age of three.

Even a cursory glance at the table reveals significant differences not only among the three clusters and six groups of countries described above, but also within each individual cluster and even each group. Apart from the time structure, the level of female employment, and the extent of part-time work among mothers, the political system (centralized or federative) that controlled childcare and schooling, and the forms of funding and the quantitative level of provision of care and education facilities for children under twelve were also important indicators. According to the latter standard, in the late 1980s, Denmark and Sweden had the best developed publicly funded care and education systems in Northern Europe, and France and Belgium the best systems in Western Europe.[96]

In Denmark and Sweden, public childcare was available for 85 and 64 percent of children aged three to six, respectively. In both countries, these facilities, which were usually open all day, were overwhelmingly run and funded by municipal authorities. In the centralized political systems of both states, their work was regulated by general guidelines. In Sweden, these regulations stipulated that all six-year-olds had to attend preschool at least three hours a day. School attendance in both countries was compulsory for children over the age of seven. Denmark and Sweden, along with France, were also the only countries in Europe to provide not just a well-developed all-day school system for primary school children, but also out-of-school care for a large proportion of them. Denmark provided after-school facilities for 36 percent of primary school children, while in Sweden this service was the norm.[97]

The centralized and state-funded educational and childcare systems in France and Belgium also offered a well-developed range of facilities, providing places for nearly 100 and 95 percent of preschool children, respectively. While in France the overwhelming majority of educational and childcare institutions was in state hands, 20 percent were maintained by nongovernmental providers, particularly the Catholic Church. Also important is the fact that in France, additional childcare was available outside regular school hours. The situation was different in Belgium, where before- or after-school facilities for children were rare.[98]

In the federal republics of Germany and Austria, where 79 and 75 percent of preschool children aged three to six were covered by childcare services, respectively, the rate of provision was average, although a closer analysis of both states reveals significant regional differences due to their federal systems. According to the principle of subsidiarity, providers in the FRG were mainly private welfare organizations, which maintained nearly 70 percent of all facilities, while approximately 30 percent were run by municipalities and only a very small number by companies and associations. The situation in Austria was similar. The opening hours of childcare services varied greatly in the two countries. The most common form of childcare operated half a day in the mornings. Preschool was not yet mandatory, while school attendance was only compulsory from the age of six. The provision of care for primary-school-age children was far less favorable; in the FRG, facilities were only available for 4 percent of all children, and in Austria merely for 1 percent.[99] At the same time, the half-day system still applied in the state-funded and controlled schools. In 1988–1989, only 1 percent of primary school children and 5 percent of all school children in the FRG attended an all-day school.[100] Moreover, in both states the federative political system that delegated the responsibility for childcare and schooling to the states and communities did not allow for energetic and consistent reforms on the national level.

In the late 1980s, Britain and Portugal were among the countries in Western Europe with the least developed system of public preschool care and education. In both countries, only 40 percent of three- to five-year-olds attended a childcare facility or preschool. These were largely private nursery schools, which usually provided all-day services, but more than half of the children attended only in the mornings or afternoons, since they were very expensive. In Britain, compulsory education began at the age of five, however. Moreover, by the 1970s, the all-day comprehensive school where children ate lunch at school had become the rule. Additional care facilities outside school hours existed only rarely. These average figures conceal significant regional differences, since England, Northern Ireland, Scotland, and Wales have their own, separate educational legislation and administration.[101]

Most of the centralized communist states of Eastern Europe were far better at providing care facilities for pre- and primary school children in the late 1980s. In the GDR, 94 percent of three- to-six-year-olds attended an all-day kindergarten in 1988, and 82 percent attended an out-of-school center before and after their half-day primary school. In Hungary in that same year, 85 percent and in the CSSR 82 percent went to a childcare center before preschool, but in Poland only 60 percent did so. Here, too, the average figures conceal large regional differences. Thus in rural Poland, the corresponding figure was only 33 percent, while a similar rural/urban gap was also evident in the CSSR and Hungary. Though these two countries had extensive all-day childcare offerings, in Poland the half-day system dominated: only 38 percent of all children between the ages of three and five who attended kindergarten also had a place in a childcare center, and in the countryside, the figure reached only 21 percent. The preschool sections of the primary schools in Poland, which all six-year-old children had to attend, were open between three and five hours a day. In all three countries, the primary schools were organized as reliable half-day schools, but while 66 percent of children in Hungary and 50 percent in the CSSR also had a place in an out-of-school care center in 1988, such facilities were completely absent in Poland.[102]

This overview shows how difficult it is to give precise information about even the quantitative degree of provision, because most of the available figures represent national averages. They cannot be adequately interpreted without additional information on the specific structure of each national and regional care and education system and its political, economic, and social context. They conceal significant regional differences and also say nothing about chances of access or differences in quality. A particularly important aspect of *access* to childcare and schooling is children's legal entitlement, i.e., the question of the age at which children may be enrolled in childcare and preschools and when compulsory schooling begins. It is rather important whether access is defined as a right of all children or perceived as only a "compensatory measure" for children from disadvantaged social and ethnic backgrounds as well as from immigrant families. Finally, the fees that parents have to pay are key determinants of access to childcare, out-of-school-care, and private primary schools. High fees exclude children from lower social and ethnic backgrounds and children from migrant families.

The quality of childcare and schooling depends in large part on the average amount of money invested per child, which directly influences such aspects as average class size, school facilities and equipment, and the quality of food provided. Similarly important are the qualifications of the staff in childcare facilities and schools, i.e., the content and level of professional training and salaries, which reflect the state and society's appreciation of the work done by childcare staff and teachers. Finally, the pedagogical goals a state pursues and their implementation also influence the quality of childcare, preschooling, and primary schooling.[103] The OECD distinguishes here between two traditions of early childhood care and education: the "readiness for school tradition," which is more oriented towards early cognitive development, and the "social pedagogy tradition," which emphasizes children's right to play and focuses more on children's emotional and social development.[104] The former dominates in Western and Southern Europe, particularly in the English-speaking and Latin countries, as well as in Eastern Europe, while the latter is characteristic of Northern and West-Central Europe.[105] In practice, both traditions coexist in most countries and influence each other. They also have a considerable impact on the style of teaching in pre- and primary schools.[106]

Taken together, these factors shape access to and quality of childcare, preschools, and primary schooling. Unfortunately, we were not able to explore these important dimensions of childcare and education in our comparative study of time structures and time politics in similar detail. Nevertheless, we wish to emphasize that it is not enough just to offer full-time childcare and schooling. Children and parents need a state-funded, *high-quality*, and full-time system of childcare, preschools, and primary schools, flexible enough to meet the needs of children from different ethnic and social backgrounds including immigrant children as well as working parents. Only then can we achieve the aim of a future-oriented care and education that offers equal opportunities to all children regardless of their origin.

Conclusion

A comparison of the development of time policies in Eastern and Western Europe up to 1990 reveals a strong path dependency of the time structure of childcare and schooling extending back to the nineteenth century.

Through the establishment of compulsory primary schooling, different time structures gradually emerged, which were permanently codified in laws and institutional structures. These consisted chiefly of three types of schools: the traditional divided all-day school, the modern conjunct all-day school, and the half-day or part-time school. Modern all-day schools and day schools had existed since the end of the nineteenth century, but were at first organized mainly as private reform pedagogical schools and so-called public laboratory schools. Both school types only gained greater influence in most Western European countries in the post-1945 period, in particular in the reform era of the 1960 and 1970s.

The basic structures of the childcare and out-of-school care systems had already taken shape by the interwar period. Once again a strong path dependency is in evidence. All-day care served primarily as a "social welfare" measure for "needy children" from families that did not function "properly" or had a mother working outside the home, while half-day or part-time care was considered the norm for "education" of "normal" children from better-off families. We can observe this distinction everywhere. Until the 1950s, the first approach was dominant all over Europe.

Only with the reform era of the 1960s and 1970s did the "educational" approach to childcare and all-day schools gain significant influence in most European countries. During this period, the systematic extension of childcare began everywhere—albeit for different reasons. In most Western European countries, a major argument was the desire to improve the possibilities for early learning. Care for children between three and six was now perceived more as "education" than "care," while the reforms of the school system were defined as an investment in "human capital" and thus indispensable for economic development. In addition, the needs of the labor market and the increasing influence of the new women's movement played an important role in the West, because feminists everywhere demanded equal social citizenship rights for women. However, only when these economic, social, and political factors worked together and gained a strong influence did an increasing number of kindergartens and preschools become all-day facilities. Otherwise the half-day or part-time services in childcare and preschools continued to dominate. In the communist countries of the East, it was mainly the labor shortage that required a full-time care policy in order to allow women's integration into the labor market. Later, demographic motives also drove this time policy. But for economic and financial reasons, the majority of schools in the communist states remained half-day schools, which were combined in most countries with extensive childcare and out-of-school care.

In spite of these general trends, the interplay of the six factors that shaped time policies discussed at the beginning of this essay produced specific policy mixes in each of the countries that have become ever more pronounced. Today, in most European countries, postcommunist Eastern and Western welfare states alike, a pragmatic blend has come to dominate the time policies of childcare and schooling, as the following chapter by Kimberly Morgan demonstrates. This mixture is supported by an increasing combination of public and private structures of welfare and childcare and by a discourse of shared responsibility. It is no longer the state *or* the family, but rather the state *and* the family—as well as the market—that are responsible for the provision of childcare. In all countries, schooling is still largely the responsibility of the state, but the influence of the private sector is increasing even in countries, such as Austria or Germany, with no strong tradition of private schools.

Traditional dichotomies such as the tension between the interests of children and parents, in particular mothers, are thus becoming obsolete. Both interests can and should be combined in the right policy mix. All states, not just in Europe, need to respond with a more pragmatic blend of time policies in childcare and schooling to changing family patterns such as lower birth rates, higher divorce rates, single-parent families, and a wide variety of other family models that differ from the so-called normal family of father, mother, and children. Since the old time structures of education no longer work in the twenty-first century, the challenge is to develop new time policies that help children, parents, women, and society as a whole to cope with postindustrial realities.

Notes

The article is mostly based on the comparative research that Karen Hagemann has done since 2000 for the project "The German Half-Day Model: A European Sonderweg? The 'Time Politics' of Child Care, Pre-School and Elementary School Education in Post-War Europe (1945–2000)," funded by the Volkswagen Foundation. She is the primary author of this introductory chapter.

We would like to thank Ann Taylor Allen and Sonya Michel for their critical comments, Pamela Selwyn for her support with the translation, and Brandon Hunziker for his careful editing.

1. Compendia that compare education systems only sometimes mention how their time schedules are generally organized; see, for example, Oskar Anweiler et al., eds., *Bildungssysteme in Europa: Entwicklung und Struktur des Bildungswesens in zehn Ländern* (Weinheim, 1996); Hans Döbert et al., eds., *The Education Systems of Europe* (Dordrecht, 2007). The OECD and the Information Network on Education in Europe (EURYDICE) provide useful data collections on the childcare and school systems in Europe. In the

descriptions of the national school systems, the database EURYDICE includes the keyword "organization of school time" with subthemes such as "organization of the school year" and "weekly and daily timetable." See EURYDICE, *Organisation of School Time in Europe: Primary and General Secondary Education, 2007–08 School Year* (Brussels, 2009). Retrieved 18 February 2008: http://eacea.ec.europa.eu/education/eurydice/documents/calendars/102EN.pdf. The OECD provides information on the time structures of early childhood education and care systems and uses the terms *length of day, full-day,* and *half-day.* See OECD, *Starting Strong I: Early Childhood Education and Care* (Paris, 2001); OECD, *Starting Strong II: Early Childhood Education and Care* (Paris, 2006).

2. See, for example, Joachim Lohmann, *Das Problem der Ganztagsschule. Eine historisch-vergleichende und systematische Untersuchung* (Ratingen, 1965); Joachim Lohmann, "Die Entwicklung des Halb- und Ganztagsschulwesens. Eine vergleichende Darstellung in verschiedenen Ländern," *Paedagogica Historica* 7, no. 1 (1967): 132–81; Harald Ludwig, *Entstehung und Entwicklung der modernen Ganztagsschule in Deutschland,* 2 vols. (Cologne, 1993); Gerlind Schmidt, "Die Ganztagsschule in einigen Ländern Europas. Vergleichende Analyse im Rahmen des Projekts 'Zeit für Schule,'" in *Die Zeitdimension in der Schule als Gegenstand des Bildungsvergleichs,* ed. Wolfgang Mitter and Botho von Kopp (Cologne, 1994), 45–112; Marie-Madeleine Compère, ed., *Histoire du temps scolaire en Europe* (Paris, 1997); Jürgen Rekus, ed., *Ganztagsschule in pädagogischer Verantwortung* (Münster, 2003); Jürgen Rekus and Volker Ladenthin, eds., *Die Ganztagsschule. Alltag, Reform, Geschichte, Theorie* (Weinheim, 2005); Hans-Uwe Otto and Thomas Coelen, eds., *Ganztägige Bildungssysteme. Innovation durch Vergleich* (Münster, 2005); Cristina Allemann-Ghionda, "Ganztagssysteme in Europa—Zeitstrukturierung im internationalen Vergleich," in *Grundbegriffe der Ganztagsbildung: Das Handbuch,* ed. Hans-Uwe Otto and Thomas Coelen (Wiesbaden, 2008), 674–83; Cristina Allemann-Ghionda, "Ganztagschule im europäischen Vergleich: Zeitpolitiken modernisieren—durch Vergleich Standards setzen?" *Zeitschrift für Pädagogik,* supplement no. 54 (2009): 190–208.

3. On the FRG, see the chapter by Karen Hagemann; on Italy (in comparison to France), the chapter by Cristina Allemann-Ghionda; on Switzerland, the chapter by Claudia Crotti in this volume. Only the most recent research on this subjects emphasizes the importance of the gender dimension: see Sandra Bonfiglioli, "Le politiche di riorganizzazione dei tempi della città: sviluppo della qualità della vita e del territorio," in *Cosa vogliono le donne. Cosa fanno le donne per conciliare lavoro e famiglia* (Milan, 2001), 54–59; Karen Hagemann and Karin Gottschall, "Die Halbtagsschule in Deutschland—ein Sonderfall in Europa?" *Aus Politik und Zeitgeschichte,* B 41 (2002): 12–22; Karen Hagemann, "Between Ideology and Economy: The 'Time Politics' of Child Care and Public Education in the Two Germanys," *Social Politics* 13, no. 1 (2006): 217–60.

4. See Janet C. Gornick and Marcia K. Meyers, *Families That Work: Policies for Reconciling Parenthood and Employment* (New York, 2003), 185–235. See also the chapters by Kimberly Morgan and Livia Sz. Oláh in this volume.

5. In this volume we only differentiate between Eastern and Western European countries; in the former, we include all (post-)communist East-Central European countries. We don't use the phrase "Central and Western European Countries," because the West-Central European countries have become part of Western Europe.

6. See Tine Rostgård and Torben Fridberg, *Caring for Children and Older People: A Comparison of European Policies and Practices* (Copenhagen, 1998); OECD, *Starting Strong II,* 229.

7. Wolfgang Mitter, "Einführung des Projektleiters," in *Zeit für Schule. Polen, Sowjetunion,* ed. Heliodor Muszynski and Leonid Novikov (Cologne, 1990), vii–xii.

8. Ibid., xi.

9. Following the OECD, we use the term *out-of-school care* for all types of institutionalized care services before and after school; the term *after-school care* includes only the time after school. See OECD, *Starting Strong II*, 228.
10. See Tino Bargel and Manfred Kuthe, *Ganztagsschule. Untersuchungen zu Angebot und Nachfrage, Versorgung und Bedarf* (Bad Honnef, 1991), 9ff.
11. For more on the terminiogy see, OECD, *Starting Strong II*, 227–31.
12. See Carl-Ludwig Furck, "Schule für das Jahr 2000. Ein utopischer Plan," *Neue Sammlung* 3 (1963): 501–8.
13. See OECD, *PISA: Schülerleistungen im internationalen Vergleich. Im Auftrag der Kultusminister der Länder und in Zusammenarbeit mit dem Bundesministerium für Bildung und Forschung* (Bonn, 2001); OECD, *PISA: Measuring Student Knowledge and Skills. The PISA 2000 Assessment of Reading, Mathematical and Scientific Literacy* (Paris, 2000); Jürgen Baumert et al., eds, *Herkunftsbedingte Disparitäten im Bildungswesen: Differenzielle Bildungsprozesse und Probleme der Verteilungsgerechtigkeit: Vertiefende Analysen im Rahmen von PISA 2000* (Wiesbaden, 2006).
14. See Pierre Bourdieu and Jean-Claude Passeron, *Die Illusion der Chancengleicheit. Untersuchungen zur Soziologie des Bildungswesens in Frankreich* (Stuttgart, 1971); Pierre Bourdieu and Jean-Claude Passeron, *Reproduction in Education, Society, and Culture* (London, 1990).
15. See for example, The Commission of European Communities, *Education of Migrant Workers' Children in the European Community* (Luxembourg, 1975); The European Parliament, *The Teaching of Immigrants in the European Union* (Luxembourg, 1997).
16. One major problem of all statistics is what they count as "migrants." Recent statistics differentiate between "foreigners" (*Ausländer*), i.e., people who have no citizenship in their host country (this category covers usually only a very limited percentage of "people with a migrant background"); "migrants" (*Immigranten*), who themselves moved for a variety of reasons (economic, political, social, or cultural) from one country to another; and "people with a migration background" (*Personen mit Migrationshintergrund*), which include all people from first-, second-, and sometimes even third-generation migrant families.
17. European Commission, "Migration and Asylum in Numbers." Retrieved 20 December 2009: http://ec.europa.eu/justice_home/doc_centre/immigration/statistics/doc_immigration_statistics_en.htm; see also International Organization on Migration, *World Migration Report 2003: Managing Migration—Challenges and Responses for People on the Move* (Geneva, 2003); OECD, *Trends in International Migration 2003* (Paris, 2004).
18. For the postwar period, see Klaus J. Bade, *Migration in European History* (Malden, MA, 2003), esp. 217–75.
19. The "EU 25" includes the twenty-five East and West European states that had joined the EU until 31 December 2006.
20. Sandra Lavenex, "Focus Migration Europäische Union," *Länderprofil Europäische Union*, ed. Hamburg Institute of International Economics (HWWI), no. 17 (March 2009): 1.
21. OECD, *Where Immigrant Students Succeed—A Comparative Review of Performance and Engagement in PISA 2003* (Paris, 2006), 12, 32, 71, and 73.
22. Ibid., 7–11 and 153–55.
23. This is particularly important, because recent studies emphazise the importance of differences in the family background and its unequal perception by teachers as one reason for the extreme differences in school performance beween "native" and "migrant" children. See, for example, Cornelia Kristen, "Ethnische Unterschiede im deutschen Schulsystem," *Aus Politik und Zeitgeschichte*, B 21-22 (2003): 26–32; Ludger Wößmann, "Familiärer Hintergrund, Schulsystem und Schülerleistungen im internationalen Vergleich," *Aus Politik und Zeitgeschichte*, B 21-22 (2003): 33–38. On the extremely different

performance between "native" and "migrant" children in the FRG, see Beauftragte für Migration, Flüchtlinge und Integration (ed.), *Daten – Fakten – Trends: Bildung und Ausbildung* (Berlin, 2004).

24. For the first results, see Ludwig Stecher et al., eds., *Ganztägige Bildung und Betreuung, Zeitschrift für Pädagogik*. 54th supplement (Weinheim and Basel, 2009); and http://www.projekt-steg.de/.

25. See Christine Steiner, "Mehr Chancengleichheit durch die Ganztagsschule?" in Stecher, *Ganztägige Bildung,* 81–105; Natalie Fischer, Hans-Peter Kuhn and Eckhard Klieme, "Was kann die Ganztagsschule leisten?" in Stecher, *Ganztägige Bildung* 131–67.

26. Exceptions are Hagemann and Gottschall, "Die Halbtagsschule"; Hagemann, "Between Ideology."

27. As a classical text, see Joan Wallach Scott, "Gender: A Useful Category of Historical Analysis," reprinted in *Gender and the Politics of History,* ed. Joan Wallach Scott (New York, 1988), 28–50. For a more recent debate see "AHR Forum: Revisiting 'Gender: A Useful Category of Historical Analysis,'" *American Historical Review* 113, no. 5 (2008): 1344–430; "Gender and Change: Agency, Chronology and Periodization," special issue, *Gender & History* 20, no. 3 (2008). 453–678.

28. Joan W. Scott, "Unanswered Questions," in "AHR Forum," 1423.

29. See the following important studies: Seth Koven and Sonya Michel, eds., *Mothers of a New World: Maternalist Politics and the Origins of Welfare State* (New York, 1993); Mary E. Daly, *The Gender Division of Welfare: The Impact of the British and German Welfare States* (Cambridge, UK, 2000); Rianne Mahon and Sonya Michel, eds., *Child Care Policy at the Crossroads: Gender and Welfare State Restructuring* (London, 2003); Mary E. Daly and Katherine Rake, eds., *Gender and the Welfare State: Care, Work and Welfare in Europe and the USA* (Cambridge, UK, 2003); Gornick and Meyer, *Families That Work;* Ute Gerhard and Trudie Knijn, eds., *Working Mothers in Europe: A Comparison of Policies and Practices* (Cheltenham, 2005); Kimberly Morgan, *Working Mothers and the Welfare State: Religion and the Politics of Work-Family Policies in Western Europe and the United States* (Berkeley, CA, 2006); Daniela Del Boca and Cecile Wetzels, eds., *Social Policies, Labour Markets and Motherhood: A Comparative Analysis of European Countries* (Cambridge, UK, 2007).

30. See, for example, Normann Furniss and Timothy Tilton, *The Case for the Welfare State* (Bloomington, IN, 1977); Gerhard A. Ritter, *Der Sozialstaat. Entstehung und Entwicklung im internationalen Vergleich* (Munich, 1991).

31. Gøsta Esping-Andersen, *Three Worlds of Welfare Capitalism* (Princeton, NJ, 1990), 26f.

32. Jane Lewis, "Bezahlte Arbeit, unbezahlte Arbeit und wohlfahrtsstaatliche Leistungen," in *Das Private ist ökonomisch. Widersprüche der Ökonomisierung privater Familien- und Haushalts-Dienstleistungen,* ed. Ute Behning (Berlin, 1997), 67–86. See also Jane Lewis, ed., *Women and Social Policies in Europe: Work, Family and the State* (Aldershot, 1993); Jane Lewis et al., eds., *Gender, Social Care and Welfare State Restructuring in Europe* (Aldershot, 1998); Diane Sainsbury, ed., *Gendering Welfare States* (London, 1994), 2ff., 8–26, and 26–44.

33. See, for example, Linda Gordon, ed., *Women, the State and Welfare* (Madison, WI, 1990); Gisela Bock and Pat Thane, eds., *Maternity and Gender Politics: Women and the Rise of the European Welfare States, 1880s–1950s* (London, 1991); Arnlaug Leira, *Welfare States and Working Mothers: The Scandinavian Experience* (Cambridge, UK, 1994); Sainsbury, *Gendering;* Diane Sainsbury, *Gender, Equality and Welfare States* (Cambridge, UK, 1996); Christina Bergqvist et al., eds., *Equal Democracies? Gender and Politics in the Nordic Countries* (Oslo, 1999).

34. See, for example, Siv Gustafson, "Childcare Types of Welfare States," in Sainsbury, *Gendering,* 45–61; Sonya Michel, *Children's Interests / Mothers' Rights: The Shaping of America's Child Care Policy* (New Haven, CT, 1999), 282–85.

35. Ann Shola Orloff, "Gender and the Social Rights of Citizenship: State Policies and Gender Relations in Comparative Research," *American Sociological Review* 58, no. 3 (1993): 303–28; O'Connor, *Gender*; Julia O'Connor et al., eds., *States, Markets, Families: Gender, Liberalism and Social Policy in Australia, Canada, Great Britain and the United States* (Cambridge, UK, 1999). See also Jet Bussemaker, *Citizenship and Welfare State Reform in Europe* (London, 1999).
36. See Orloff, "Gender"; O'Connor, *Gender*; O'Connor et al., *States*, 109ff.
37. Diane Sainsbury, "Women's and Men's Social Rights: Gendering Dimensions of Welfare States," in *Gendering*, ed. Sainsbury, 150–69, 153; Sainsbury, *Gender*. See also Lewis, *Gender, Social Care*.
38. See Gøsta Esping Andersen, "Towards the Good Society, Once Again?" in *Why We Need a New Welfare State*, ed. Gøsta Esping Andersen et al. (Oxford, 2002), 20; Gøsta Esping Andersen, "A Child-Centered Social Investment Strategy," and "A New Gender Contract," in *Why We Need*, 26–67 and 68–95.
39. See Jutta Allmendinger, "Bildungsarmut. Zur Verschränkung von Bildungs- und Sozialpolitik," *Soziale Welt* 50 (1999): 35–50; Jutta Allmendinger and Stephan Leibfried, "Bildungsarmut," *Aus Politik und Zeitgeschichte*, B 21-22 (2003): 12–18.
40. See Gøsta Esping-Andersen, ed., *Welfare States in Transition: National Adaptions in Global Economies* (London, 1996); Zsuzsa Ferge and Jon Eivind Kolberg, eds., *Social Policy in a Changing Europe* (Boulder, CO, 1992), 201–22; Ferge, "Freedom and Security," *International Review of Comparative Public Policy* 7 (1996): 19. For the debate on the conceptualization of communist welfare states, see also the chapter by Dorottya Szikra in this volume.
41. Toni Makkai, "Social Policy and Gender in Eastern Europe," in Sainsbury, *Gendering*, 189.
42. Bob Deacon, *The New Eastern Europe: Social Policy Past, Present and Future* (London, 1992), 167–69.
43. Hartmut Kaelble, *Der historische Vergleich. Eine Einführung zum 19. und 20. Jahrhundert* (Frankfurt/M., 1999); Heinz-Gerhard Haupt and Jürgen Kocka, eds., *Geschichte und Vergleich* (Frankfurt/M., 1996); Hartmut Kaelble and Jürgen Schriewer, eds., *Diskurse und Entwicklungspfade. Der Gesellschaftsvergleich in den Geschichts- und Sozialwissenschaften* (Frankfurt/M., 1999); the volume by Deborah Cohen and Maura O'Connor, eds., *Comparison and History: Europe in Cross-National Perspective* (New York, 2004), presents this mostly German and European debate to an American audience.
44. Paul Pierson, "Increasing Returns, Path Dependency, and the Study of Politics," *American Political Science Review* 94, no. 2 (2000): 251–67. See also the chapter by Kimberly Morgan in this volume.
45. Jean-Noël Luc, "Pour une histoire européenne, nationale et locale de la préscolarisation," in "L'école maternelle en Europe XIXe-XXe siècles," ed. Jean-Noël Luc, special issue, *Revue Histoire de l'Éducation*, Service d'Histoire de l'Éducation (1999): 5–22, 8ff. On the historical development of kindergartens and preschools in Europe, see Luc, *L'école maternelle*.
46. See Luc, "La Diffusion des modèles de préscolarisation en Europe dans la première moitié du XIXe siècle," in Luc, *L'école maternelle*, 189–206.
47. See Luc, "Pour une histoire," 8f.
48. On the concept of maternalism, see Koven and Michel, *Mothers of a New World*; Ann Taylor Allen, "Öffentliche und private Mutterschaft. Die internationale Kindergartenbewegung 1840–1914," in *Frauen zwischen Familie und Schule. Professionalisierungsstrategien bürgerlicher Frauen im internationalen Vergleich*, ed. Juliane Jacobi (Cologne, 1994), 7–27; Ann Taylor Allen, *Feminism and Motherhood in Western Europe, 1890–1970: The Maternal Dilemma* (New York, 2005).

49. See Luc, "Pour une histoire," 12ff.
50. See Luc, "La Diffusion," 202ff.
51. On the development of the time structure of school systems, see Compère, *Histoire du temps*; Lohmann, *Das Problem*; Lohmann, "Die Entwicklung."
52. See Lohmann, *Das Problem*, 13–24.
53. Ibid., 25–45. See also the chapter by Hagemann in this volume.
54. Lohmann, *Das Problem*, 45ff. See also Karen Hagemann, "Die Ganztagsschule als Politikum: Die westdeutsche Entwicklung in gesellschafts- und geschlechtergeschichtlicher Perspektive," *Zeitschrift für Pädagogik*, supplement no. 54 (2009): 209–29.
55. The term *reform pedagogic* is not common in American English, since the phrase *progressive education* is used more often. But because both terms do not have the same meaning, we use the European term *reform pedagogic*. Common also are the phrases "*éducation nouvelle*," "new education," or "*Reformpädagogik*." For more, see Ehrenhard Skiera, *Reformpädagogik in Geschichte und Gegenwart. Eine kritische Einführung* (Munich, 2003); Jürgen Oelkers, *Reformpädagogik—eine kritische Dogmengeschichte* (Weinheim, 2005); Dianne Ravitch, *Left Back: A Century of Battles over School Reform* (New York, 2000); Kevin J. Brehony, "From the particular to the general, the continuous to the discontinuous: progressive education revisited," *History of Education* 30, no. 5 (2001): 413–32.
56. Harald Ludwig, "Moderne Ganztagsschule als Leitmodell von Schulreform im 20. Jahrhundert. Historische Entwicklung und reformpädagogische Ursprünge der heutigen Ganztagsschule," *Die Ganztagsschule* 35, no. 2/3 (1995): 68–89.
57. Lohmann, "Die Entwicklung." See also Jürgen Rolle and Edith Kesberg, *Materialienband zur Hortgeschichte* (Cologne, 1989).
58. R. E. Williams, "England und Wales," in *Schulen in Europa*, ed. Walter Schultze (Weinheim, 1969), vol. 2, pt. A, 12ff.; Lohmann, *Problem*, 48ff.
59. Lohmann, *Problem*, 60ff.; Williams, "England und Wales," 71ff.
60. Lohmann, *Problem*, 77ff.
61. See Antoine Prost, *Histoire de l'enseignement en France (1800–1967)* (Paris, 1968); Raymond Grew and Patrick J Harrigan, eds., *School, State and Society: The Growth of Elementary Schooling in Nineteeth-Century France* (Ann Arbor, MI, 1991). See also the chapter by Allemann-Ghionda in this volume.
62. See the chapters by Allemann-Ghionda, Hana Hašková, Anatoli Rakhkochkine, and Szikra in this volume.
63. Wilhelm Sjöstrand, *Pedagogikens historia. III: 2. Utvecklingen i Sverige under tiden 1805–1920* (Lund, 1965).
64. Lisbeth Lundahl, "I moralens, produktionens och det sunda förnuftets namn: Det svenska högerpartiets skolpolitik 1904–1962" (PhD diss., Lund University, 1989), 82f.
65. Alfred Oftedal Telhaug et al., "From Collectivism to Individualism? Education as Nation Building in a Scandinavian Perspective," *Scandinavian Journal of Educational Research* 48, no. 2 (2004): 141–58; Gustav E. Karlsen, *Utdanning, styring og marked: Norsk utdanningspolitikk i et internnasjonalt perspektiv* (Oslo, 2002). See also the chapters by Lisbeth Lundahl and Tora Korsvold in this volume.
66. Luc, *L'école maternelle*; Michael Seyfarth-Stubenrauch and Ehrenhardt Skiera, eds., *Reformpädagogik und Schulreform in Europa. Grundlagen, Geschichte, Aktualität*, vol. 1 (Baltmannsweiler, 1996). See also the chapters by Lundahl, Korsvold, and Hagemann in this volume.
67. See Luc, *L'école maternelle*; Compère, *Histoire du temps*. One exception in this respect was Britain, were the Conservative government after 1951 reduced the number of daycare sites dramatically. See the chapter by Sally Tomlinson in this volume.
68. See the chapters by Hagemann, Hašková, Rakhkochkine, and Szikra in this volume.

69. On the development of school systems, see also Anweiler et al., *Bildungssysteme*; John Boli and Francisco O. Ramírez, "Compulsory Schooling in the Western Cultural Context," in *Emergent Issues in Education. Comparative Perspectives*, ed. Robert F. Arnove et al. (Albany, 1992), 25–38; Compère, *Histoire du temps*; Otto and Coelen, *Ganztägige Bildungssysteme*; Schmidt, "Die Ganztagsschule"; Rekus and Ladenthin, *Die Ganztagsschule*. On childcare and preschools see Michel, *Children's Interests*, 281–97; Rolf Torstendahl, ed., *Social Policy and Gender System in the Two German States and Sweden, 1945–1989* (Uppsala, 1999); Luc, *L'école maternelle*; Eric Plaisance, *L'école maternelle en France depuis la fin de la Seconde Guerre mondiale* (Paris, 1984); Wolfgang Tietze, "Vorschulische Erziehung in den Ländern der EG," in *Zukunft der Bildung in Europa: Nationale Vielfalt und europäische Einheit*, ed. Klaus Schleicher (Darmstadt, 1993), 217–41.

70. See the chapter by Korsvold in this volume.

71. See also Allen, *Feminism*, 209–26; Nadine Lefaucheur, "Maternity, Family and State," in *History of Women in the West: Toward a Cultural Identity in the Twentieth Century*, ed. Francoise Thébaud et al. (Cambridge, MA, 1994), 432–52; Franz Höllinger, "Frauenerwerbsarbeit und Wandel der Geschlechtsrollen im internationalen Vergleich," *Kölner Zeitschrift für Soziologie und Sozialpsychologie* 43, no. 4, (1991): 753–71; Manfred Garhammer, "Familiale und gesellschaftliche Arbeitsteilung—ein europäischer Vergleich," *Zeitschrift für Familienforschung* 9, no. 1 (1997): 28–70; Gerhard and Knijn, *Working Mothers*. See also Alva Myrdal and Viola Klein, *Women's Two Roles. Home and Work* (London, 1956); the chapters by Allemann-Ghionda, Jeanne Fagnani, Hagemann, and Tomlinson in this volume.

72. European Parliament, *The Teaching*, 12–14; Veysel Özcan and Stefan Grimbacher, "Focus Migration Deutschland," *Länderprofil Europäische Union*, ed. Hamburg Institute of International Economics (HWWI), no. 1 (May 2007): 1–9.

73. See Rita Chin, *The Guest Worker Question in Postwar Germany* (Cambridge, UK, 2007); and the chapter by Hageman in this volume.

74. See Christine von Oertzen, *The Pleasure of a Surplus Income: Part-Time Work, Gender Politics, and Social Change in West Germany, 1955–1969* (New York, 2007).

75. See Birgit Fix, *Church-State Relations and the Development of Child Care in Austria, Belgium, Germany, and the Netherlands, Families and Family Policies in Europe: Comparative Perspectives* (Frankfurt/M., 2000), 304–21. On Germany see Lukas Rolli-Alkemper, *Familie im Wiederaufbau. Katholizismus und bürgerliches Familienideal in der Bundesrepublik Deutschland, 1945–1965* (Paderborn, 2000).

76. See the chapter by Celia Valiente in this volume.

77. See the chapter by Allemann-Ghionda in this volume.

78. For the early development, see Kristen Stromberg, *Childers, Fathers, Families, and the State in France, 1914–1945* (Ithaca, NY, 2003); Sandra Ehrmann, *Familenpolitk in Frankreich und Deutschland im Vergleich* (Frankfurt/M., 1999); and also the chapter by Fagnani in this volume.

79. See Bergqvist, *Equal Democracies*, 137–160; Leira, *Working Parents*, 15–44; the chapters by Korsvold and Lundahl in this volume.

80. See the chapters by Kevin J. Brehony and Kristen D. Nawrotzki as well as Tomlinson in this volume.

81. On Austria, see Josef Scheipl and Helmut Seel, *Die Entwicklung des österreichischen Schulwesens in der Zweiten Republik 1945–1987* (Graz, 1988); Josef Scheipl and Otto Vág, *Über die Geschichte der Vorschulerziehung in Österreich und in Ungarn* (Graz, 1993).

82. See Hagemann, "Between Ideology"; Ingela K. Naumann, "Childcare and Feminism in West Germany and Sweden in the 1960s and 1970s," *Journal of European Social Policy* 15, no. 1 (2005): 47–63, as well as the chapters by Korsvold and Fagnani in this volume.

83. See Anweiler, *Bildungssysteme*, 143–92; see also the chapters by Hašková, Rakhkochkine, and Szikra in this volume.

84. See the chapters by Hašková, Rakhkochkine, and Szikra in this volume; on Poland, see Jacqueline Heinen and Monika Wator, "Child Care in Poland before, during, and after the Transition: Still a Women's Business," *Social Politics* 13, no. 2 (2006): 189–216; Renata Siemienska, "Gendered Perceptions: Women in the Labour Market in Poland," *Women's History Review* 5, no. 4 (1996): 553–66; on Hungary, see Lynne Haney, "Familial Welfare: Building the Hungarian Welfare Society, 1948–1968," *Social Politics* 7, no. 1 (2000): 101–22.

85. See Britta Schmitt, *Zivilgesellschaft, Frauenpolitik und Frauenbewegung in Rußland. Von 1917 bis zur Gegenwart* (Königstein/T., 1997), 154–208.

86. See Pavla Horska, "Historical Models of Central European Families: Czechs and Slovaks," *Journal of Family History* 19, no. 2 (1994): 99–106; Sharon L. Wolchik, "The Status of Women in a Socialist Order: Czechoslovakia, 1948–1978," *Slavic Review* 38, no. 3. (1978): 123–42; Sharon L. Wolchik, "Women and the Politics of Gender in Communist and Post-Communist Central and Eastern Europe," in *Eastern Europe: Politics, Culture and Society since 1939*, ed. Sabina R. Ramet (Bloomington, IN, 1998), 285–304.

87. See the chapters by Hašková, Monika Mattes, and Szrika in this volume.

88. See Botho von Kopp, *Die sozialistische Schule zwischen Lernen und Erziehen: Eine vergleichende Studie über den Erziehungsauftrag der Schule in der "entwickelten sozialistischen Gesellschaft"* (Cologne, 1983).

89. See the chapters by Mattes and Rakhkochkine in this volume.

90. Christa Uhlig, "Reformpädagogik contra Sozialistische Pädagogik: Aspekte der reformpädagogischen Diskussion in den vierziger und fünfziger Jahren," in *Erziehung und Erziehungswissenschaft in der BRD und der DDR*, ed. Dietrich Hoffmann and Karl Neumann, 2 vols. (Weinheim, 1994), vol. 1, 251–73; Dietrich Benner and Herwart Kemper, *Theorie und Geschichte der Reformpädagogik: Staatliche Schulreform und Schulversuche in SBZ und DDR* (Weinheim, 2004).

91. See Karel Rydl, "Länderstudie Tschechische Republik," in Seyfarth-Stubenrauch and Skiera, *Reformpädagogik*, vol. 2, 487–95.

92. See Klemens Trzebiatowski, "Vorschulerziehung in der Volksrepublik Polen," *Sozialpädagogische Blätter* 34, no. 2 (1983): 58–61; Jacek Bednarski and Zbigniew Jasiewicz, "The Family as a Cultural Unit. Tradition and Modernity in Cultural Activity within the Family in Poland," in *The Family and its Culture: An Investigation in Seven East and West European Countries*, ed. Manfred Biskup et al. (Budapest, 1984), 281–344; Jacqueline Heinen, "Ideology, Economics, and the Politics of Child Care in Poland before and after the Transition," in Michel and Mahon, *Child Care Policy*, 71–94.

93. Hagemann, "Between Economy."

94. Daly and Ranke's volume *Gender and the Welfare State* provides an excellent comparative framework for the European welfare states and the United States from a gender perspective, focused, however, on current developments. For cross-national similarities and differences, see 152–63.

95. See Hagemann, "Between Ideology," 226f. For the additional data, see Marlene Lohkamp-Himmighofen, "Ansätze zur Förderung der Vereinbarkeit von Familie und Beruf," in *Zwölf Wege der Familienpolitik in der Europäischen Gemeinschaft. Eigenständige Systeme und vergleichbare Qualitäten? — Länderberichte*, ed. Erika Neubauer et al. (Stuttgart, 1993), 322 and 342; Susanne Schunter-Kleemann, ed., *Herrenhaus Europa. Geschlechterverhältnisse im Wohlfahrtsstaat* (Berlin, 1992), 341, 372ff., 378, 382, and 384; Steven Saxonberg and Tomáš Sirovátka, "Failing Family Policy in Post/communist Central Europe," *Journal of Comparative Policy Analysis* 8, no. 2 (2006): 185–202.

96. On the situation in different European countries in the 1980s, see Anweiler et al., *Bildungssysteme;* Peter Moss, *Childcare and Equality of Opportunity: Consolidated Report to the European Commission. Final Version* (Brussels, 1988); Schmidt, *Die Ganztagsschule;* Monika Renz, "Ganztagsschule in anderen EG-Ländern—Wie sieht die Realität aus?" *Die Ganztagsschule* 34, no. 1–2 (1994): 3–18.

97. On Sweden and Norway, see the chapters by Korvold and Lundahl in this volume; on Denmark, see Josef Rubin, "Schule in Dänemark und Schweden," *Die Ganztagsschule* 21, no. 3–4, (1981): 68–73; Christina Bergqvist and Anita Nyberg, "Welfare State Restructuring and Child Care in Sweden," in Michel and Mahon, *Child Care Policy,* 287–308; Anette Borchorst, "Danish Child Care Policy: Continuity Rather than Radical Change," in Michel and Mahon, *Child Care Policy,* 267–86; Monique Kremer, "The Politics of Ideals of Care: Danish and Flemish Child Care Policy Compared," *Social Politics* 13, no. 2 (2006): 261–87.

98. On France, see the chapters by Allemann-Ghionda and Fagnani in this volume; on Belgium, see Marc Depaepe and Ferre Laevers, "Preschool Education in Belgium," in *International Handbook of Early Childhood Education,* ed. Gary A. Woodwill et al. (New York, 1992), 93–103; Kimberly Morgan, "Does Anyone Have a 'Libre Choix'? Subversive Liberalism and the Politics of French Child Care Policy," in Michel and Mahon, *Child Care Policy,* 143–70; Kremer, "The Politics of Ideals"; Kremer, "The Illusion of Free Choice: Ideals of Care and Child Care Policy in the Flemish and Dutch Welfare States," in Michel and Mahon, *Child Care Policy,* 113–43.

99. On the FRG, see the chapter by Hagemann in this volume; on Austria, see Österreichisches Statistisches Zentralamt, ed., *Krippen, Kindergärten und Horte (Kindertagesheime). Berichtsjahr 1998/99,* Beiträge zur österreichischen Statistik (Vienna, 1999); Ulrike Popp, "The All-Day School In Public Discourses and Policies: The Case of Post-1945 Austria" (paper presented at the International and Interdisciplinary Conference "The German Half-Day Model: A European Sonderweg? The 'Time Politics' of Child Care, Pre-School and Elementary School Education in Post-War Europe," Cologne, 1–3 March 2007). For more see http://www.time-politics.com.

100. See Heinz Günter Holtappels, ed., *Ganztagserziehung in der Schule. Modelle, Forschungsbefunde und Perspektiven* (Opladen, 1995), 35ff.; Bargel and Kuthe, *Ganztagsschule,* 137ff.

101. See the chapters on Britain in this volume by Brehony and Nawrotzki as well as Tomlinson; Daniel Wincott, "Paradoxes of New Labour Social Policy: Towards Universal Childcare in Europe's 'Most Liberal' Welfare Regime," *Social Politics* 12, no. 2 (2006): 286–312; Vicky Randall, "Childcare in Britain, or How Do You Restructure Nothing?" in Michel and Mahon, *Child Care Policy,* 219–38.

102. See the papers by Hašková, Mattes, Szikra, and Rakhkochkine in this volume; Heinen and Wator, "Child Care"; Haney, "Familial Welfare."

103. OECD, *Bildungspolitische Analyse 1999: Erziehung und Betreuung im Vorschulalter,* ed. Zentrum für Forschung und Innovation im Bildungswesen (Paris, 1999).

104. OECD, *Starting Strong II,* 136–41. See also Borchorst, "Danish Child Care."

105. Hans-Günther Rossbach and Wolfgang Tietze, "Vorschulische Erziehung in den Ländern der Europäischen Union—Eine vergleichende Studie," *Zeitschrift für Pädagogik* (Beiheft) no. 32 (1994): 336–48.

106. See Jürgen Oelkers and Fritz Osterwalder, eds., *Die neue Erziehung. Beiträge zur Internationalität der Reformpädagogik* (Bern, 1999).

Chapter 2

THE POLITICS OF TIME

Comparing and Explaining Current Work-Family Policies— Theoretical and Methodological Reflections

Kimberly J. Morgan

In recent years, the discourse surrounding work and family policy in Europe has undergone a substantial change. It is clear that the male-breadwinner model—in which men are full-time breadwinners and women are full-time caregivers—is largely a relic of the past. As a result, academics, activists, and policymakers are increasingly calling for policies that will help mothers work for pay and provide high-quality care for children. International organizations have embraced these goals as well, with the European Union setting targets for mothers' employment and childcare provision, and the Organisation for Economic Co-operation and Development (OECD) chiding states who lack adequate early childhood care and education programs. Despite this apparent paradigm shift in thinking about mothers' employment and child development, the nexus of work-family policies still varies considerably from country to country.

Explaining these variations exceeds the capacity of one book chapter. Instead, this chapter discusses some of the methodological issues that arise when studying work-family policy in comparative perspective. Moreover, it examines some of the theoretical tools that may help us explain contemporary "time politics." Comparing work-family policies across countries is fraught with complexity. Parents' decisions on work and care are shaped by the nexus of at least four different policy sectors, each one with its own distinctive features that render cross-national comparison difficult. Thus, the first step in any comparative account is careful specification of the policies to be compared and analysis of the ways in which different benefits, services, and labor market arrangements intersect to shape an overall model of work-family policy.

Notes for this chapter begin on page 68.

The comparative welfare state literature offers some useful theoretical insights for explaining the origins of different policy systems, particularly if one modifies these tools to take into consideration the gendered nature of the policies being studied. The research agenda informing this scholarship has its limits, however, most notably in its neglect of the educational and social services sectors. These areas of public policy have political dynamics that diverge from conventional accounts of welfare state politics. In addition, the contemporary politics of work and family continue to be shaped by the legacies of the past. For that reason, analysis of contemporary politics should consider the effects of path dependency—the notion that, once in place, public policies and other institutions tend to reproduce themselves, making it difficult for a country to move away from a well-trodden pathway. By employing a sophisticated variant of path dependency that explores the precise mechanisms of institutional reproduction, we can examine how policies have become seemingly locked in place but also the potential openings for change in the years to come.

The chapter is organized as follows. First, I sketch out the range of policies that affect the care of children and women's employment, including childcare, parental leave, working time policies, and school systems. This section discusses how the multifaceted nature of these programs and policies creates challenges for those seeking to do cross-national comparisons. The following section lays out some of the theoretical tools that can be employed to help make sense of this complexity, including gendered approaches to the welfare state, ways to think about the origins of social service and educational systems, and theories about both institutional continuity and change.

Challenges in Comparing Childcare and School Systems

Parents' decisions on work and care are affected by four interlocking but often distinct sectors of public policy: early childhood education and care services, school systems, paid leave time, and part-time or flexible work arrangements. Cross-national comparison of these policies is a complex enterprise, as the actual meaning of these policies differs from country to country. In addition, these components of public policy fit together in distinct ways in each country. This section will discuss some of the most important dimensions of these policy areas and how these policies structure time for parents and children differently from place to place.

One complexity of childcare systems is how the boundary is drawn between early education and care programs. In most countries, early childhood education and daycare are conceptualized as separate services, with the former providing pedagogical stimulation to children over the age of three, and the latter often seen as caretaking programs for children whose parents are at work. Along with this conceptual distinction is a bureaucratic one: daycare programs usually fall within the jurisdiction of social services or welfare departments, whereas preschools are overseen by education ministries. Daycare also usually requires financial contributions from parents, whereas preschools may be free of charge like the school system. Nonetheless, the line between daycare and preschool can be ambiguous.[1] Increasingly, scholars, parents, and government policymakers recognize that the "caretaking" side of preschools and daycare programs in many countries also seek to provide developmental stimulation. The growing scholarly use of the term *early childhood education and care* to describe early childhood services signifies an intellectual shift, albeit one that has not yet begun to inform domestic policymaking in most countries.[2]

The Nordic states are exceptional in that they lack any differentiation between care and education programs for young children. With the expansion of public childcare that began in the late 1960s and 1970s, all services for children from infancy to age seven (the mandatory school age) were initially developed under the auspices of one bureaucratic agency—social affairs departments of each country—rather than being divided between education and social affairs ministries. While structured to meet the needs of working parents, most of these programs have a strong pedagogic component. In fact, the educational dimension was highlighted in Sweden in the 1990s when responsibility for all early childhood education and care programs was shifted from the Ministry of Social Affairs to the Ministry of Education and a national curriculum was adopted for these programs.[3]

A second important dimension of childcare and schools systems concerns the length of time that programs are available. To some degree, this overlaps with the division between education and care services: "Daycare" tends to be available for 8–10 hours per day and is more amenable to parents' working schedules, whereas early education programs are open only to fulfill educational goals. As a result, kindergartens, which are usually open for children of three and older, and preschools often are open for half a day or a few days a week and usually are closed during part or all of the summer. For example, in Austria and Germany (particularly in its western part, in the "old" federal states), preschools like primary schools usually close by lunchtime, and after-school care is minimal. There are important exceptions that complicate the picture, however. In France, Belgium, and Italy, for example, preschools, as are most other schools, are open for a lengthy school day (often 8:30 A.M.–4:30 P.M. in France and Italy; 8:30 A.M.–3:30 P.M. in Belgium). And in Eastern Europe, one legacy of communism is that kindergarten programs are available on a full-time basis.

Since the collapse of these regimes, childcare for children under three has declined dramatically in many of these states, but the full-day preschools remain in most countries.[4]

Although childcare services usually are open for a full working day, parents do not necessarily use them full-time. In the Netherlands, for example, very few children are placed in childcare five days a week. One reason for this is that government subsidies to childcare have been inadequate, thus making it prohibitively expensive for low-income parents to purchase full-time care.[5] In addition, the very high prevalence of part-time work among Dutch women helps explain why parents use only part-day services, although the decision to work part-time is likely also related to the high cost of care. Thus, although official statistics report that about 24 percent of children under three are in daycare, there are places in full-time care for only about half of those children.

Further complicating early childhood education and care systems is the mix of public and private programs. In many Nordic countries, government policy has sought to contain or squeeze out the private market of care. Even family-style daycare—care for smaller groups of children that is provided in private homes—is so heavily subsidized that it is considered part of the public system. In other countries, however, the range of cash and tax subsidies offered to parents for childcare can make it difficult to draw clean boundaries between the public and private sectors. In Britain, Ireland, and the Netherlands, demand subsidies are the predominant form of public spending on daycare, as government policy has sought to foster private provision of services rather than create broadly available public childcare programs. Thus, in some countries, private provision appears to fill some of the gaps left by lack of public provision, although full information on the extent of the private sector is often lacking.

All of these caveats make it difficult to construct a simple indicator of early childhood care and education provision. Table 2.1 shows enrollment rates in formal childcare and preschool education in a large number of European countries, but should be approached with caution. For one thing, these data do not distinguish between part-time and full-time programs. They also do not reveal anything about the cost of these programs—in some countries, access to some early childhood program is free of charge, but in others the cost of the program limits parents' access or imposes a heavy financial burden on them.

School systems are another critical piece of the childcare puzzle for parents. Here, there are differences in both the age at which children enter the school system and the length of the school day. In Sweden, Denmark, and Finland, the mandatory age of entry into schools is relatively late—age

TABLE 2.1: Enrollment in licensed childcare and preschool programs, Europe 2004–2005[6]

	0–2-year-old children	3–6-year-old children (or until school age)
Austria	9%	80%
Belgium	Crèches, family daycare: ▶ 34% (Flanders) ▶ 18% (Wallonia) Preschool: ▶ 90% of 2 1/2-year-olds	100%
Czech Republic	Minimal	88%
Denmark	15% of under 1-year-olds 85% of 1–2-year-olds	95% of 3–5-year-olds 88% of 6-year-olds
Finland	1% of under 1-year-olds 37% of 1–2-year-olds	69% of 3–5-year-olds 67% of 6-year-olds
France	18% in family daycare 8% in crèches 6% other licensed arrangements 35% of 2-year-olds in preschool	100%
Germany	9% ▶ 3% (Western federal states) ▶ 37% (Eastern federal states)	90% ▶ 90% (Western federal states) (24% full-time) ▶ 99% (Eastern federal states) (98% full-time)
Great Britain (England only)	26% in private nurseries, childminders, playgroups	95% of 3–4-year-olds in playgroups, nurseries 100% of 4–5-year-olds in reception class, nursery school
Hungary	9%	87%
Italy	19%	70–90% (depending on region)
Netherlands	23% (Most services used part-time)	89% of 2 1/2–4-year-olds 100% of 4–6-year-olds (Most services used part-time)
Norway	3% of children under 1 54% of 1–2-year-olds	91% of 3–5-year-olds
Poland	2%	36%
Portugal	13%	76%
Spain	21%	99%
Sweden	0% of children under 1 67% of 1–2-year-olds	95% of 3–5-year-olds 84% of 6-year-olds

Note:
Different sources (e.g., OECD, European Union, national figures) often show different figures on childcare and preschool enrollment. This table reports data mostly from the OECD's *Starting Strong* report and Nordic Social-Statistical Committee volumes because they provided more detailed breakdowns (e.g., by age group, region) than that which is normally available.

seven—although children can now enter a pre-primary class at the age of six that is free but voluntary.[7] Compulsory schooling begins at age five or six in most other European countries. The hours spent in primary school then vary considerably, with fewer annual hours in the Nordic countries, the Central-Western (Austria and the FRG) and some of the East European ones (e.g., Poland, Hungary), and fairly long hours of schooling in Italy, the Netherlands, Belgium, Ireland, and France (see figure 2.1).

These figures on total hours do not take into account schedules, however, or the existence of lunch facilities at schools. In Austria, Germany, and Dutch primary schools, for instance, lunch facilities are often lacking. Daily school hours are short in Austria and West Germany and with their "half-day-system," i.e., schools are open only half of the day and usually do not offer an after-school program. The East German federal states (*Länder*) are different in this regard, as here most schools tend to have an after-school program—a tradition that reaches back to the former GDR. (See Table 2.2.) By contrast, lunch is usually available at schools in France and the Nordic countries. It also is essential to take into account after-school programs for children in primary education. Although the official hours at school are shorter in the Nordic countries, they generally have well-developed after-school services. Such services are less prevalent in much of the rest of Europe.

Parental leave is another key component of work-family policy systems. All European countries provide a mandatory, paid maternity leave

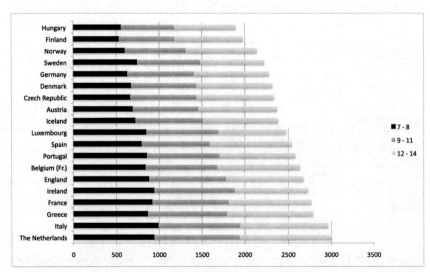

FIGURE 2.1: Average number hours per year of compulsory instruction time, Europe 2005[8]

Note:
Belgian data available for French-speaking region only; ages 12–14 refers only to children aged 12–13.

TABLE 2.2: Normal opening hours of primary schools in the European Union, 2004[9]

Country	Opening hours	Meals, supervision during lunch?
Austria	8:00–12:00 A.M. or 1:00 P.M.	Few schools
Belgium	8:30–12:00 A.M. 1:30–3:30 or 4:00 P.M. (except Wednesday afternoon)	Many schools
Denmark	8:00 A.M.–3:00 P.M.	Yes
Finland	19–30 hours per week, by age	Yes
France	8:30 A.M.–3:30 or 4:30 P.M.	Usually
Germany	8:00–12:30 A.M. hours increase with age	Very few schools
Great Britain	9:00–12:00 P.M. and 1:00–3:30 P.M. Hours increase with age	Yes
Ireland	9:00 A.M.–2:00 P.M.	Supervision
Italy	8:00–12:30 A.M. or 8:00 A.M.–4:30 P.M. (min 27 hours a week, max of 30)	Yes for the latter
Netherlands	8:30–12:00 A.M. and 1:15–3:30 P.M.	Yes if organized by parents
Portugal	9:00–12:00 A.M. and 2:00–4:00 P.M. or 1:00–3:00 P.M. 8:00 A.M.–1:00 P.M. or 1:00–6:00 P.M. (two shift scheme)	Yes
Spain	9:00–12:00 A.M. and 3:00–5:00 P.M.	Increasing
Sweden	Flex-time patterns (20–25 hours)	Yes for those in school 5 hours

lasting around three or four months and paid at a relatively high replacement rate. For countries in the European Union, a 1992 directive mandates that women have the right to fourteen weeks of maternity leave paid at the level workers normally receive for absences due to illness, and that member states offer at least an unpaid parental leave of three months that parents can take until their child's eighth birthday. Parental leave, if it exists, generally follows the period of maternity leave and is open to both parents, but these leaves vary considerably both in the length of leave and their remuneration.[10] Some countries offer paid parental leave whereas others only guarantee rights to unpaid leave. There is yet another form of leave, "care leave," that can be distinguished from parental leave in that it usually is longer but paid at a low rate, if at all.[11] In France and Finland, for example, there are flat-rate payments for parents who leave work for up to three years to care for a child.[12] Many of the East and Central-Western European countries also have paid care leaves for two to four years. (See Table 2.3.)

A final set of work-family policies are measures that enable part-time or flexible work schedules. Such work is widespread among women, es-

TABLE 2.3: Compensation for statutory parental leave in the European Community, 2003[13]

Compensation		Country
None		Greece, Ireland, Netherlands, Portugal, Spain, UK
Flat-rate	Means-tested	Poland
	Lower for higher-income claimants	Germany pre-2007
	Not means-tested	Austria, Belgium, France, Finland, Luxembourg, Slovakia
Proportional to pay	Below 80% of pay	Finland, Hungary, Italy, Germany since 2007
	80%—90% of pay	Denmark, Sweden
	100% of salary	Norway, Slovenia

Note:
In Finland, the first 26 weeks are not means-tested but paid at a flat-rate, and the second 26 weeks are proportional to pay.

pecially for mothers of young children, although this is more prevalent in some countries than in others. In some countries, parents have the right to work a reduced day while their children are below a certain age. However, one should clarify the meaning of "part-time," as this differs between countries. In Sweden, parents of children under eight are entitled to work six hours a day and many of them do, which results in their being classified as part-time workers. The situation in the Netherlands is quite different, as many women who work part-time work less than twenty hours a week. (See Figure 2.2.)

How do these pieces of public policy fit together to shape the lives of parents and children? In the Nordic countries, France, and Belgium, public policy covers most of parents' childcare needs through a mix of services, subsidies, and paid parental care. In Sweden, for example, all mothers take advantage of a generous and lengthy parental leave that also includes two months of "daddy-only" time. These are nontransferable months that must be taken by fathers or else are lost to the parents. In 2004, men took almost 19 percent of parental leave benefit time. All children then go to full-day preschool, although parents who work only six hours a day will usually pick up their children early from these programs. Once children start primary school, there are after-school programs that round out the day. Thus, Swedish policy generally meets most parental needs through a mix of public services and subsidized parental care.

French and Belgian policies also cover many parents' needs but do so through a more heterogeneous set of arrangements than in Sweden. Paid

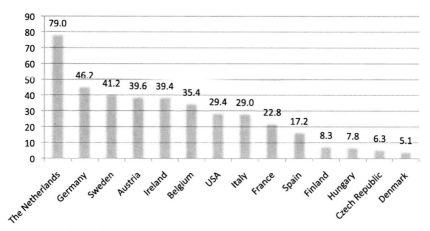

FIGURE 2.2: Share of part-time work for mothers, youngest child under six, Europe 2002[14]

Note:
These data are for women aged 15 to 64. Part-time work is employment for less than 30 hours per week.
In Sweden, however, this is measured as employment under 35 hours per week.

maternity leave is relatively short and is followed either by subsidized maternal caring time in France (at a low rate)[15] or subsidized childcare in both countries that is mostly publicly provided or funded. Then, by the age of two and a half or three, nearly all children are in preschool, with either parents (or relatives) taking over care at the end of the school day or public subsidies helping to pay for the remaining hours of childcare. Some municipalities fund after-school services at these schools as well. Once children start primary school, they are at school for a fairly long day, after which parents provide care, use public subsidies to pay a childminder, or in some places depend on after-school services.

Other countries rely considerably more on parental care. In Hungary, there is a long care leave that is paid at a reasonable rate for those who have previously been employed and is available until a child reaches the age of three.[16] Because there are few care services available, nearly all mothers take this leave. Many children then attend preschools that are open for a full day and begin primary school at the age of six. The Dutch model lacks a lengthy parental leave but instead relies on a combination of part-time work and care. Following a short maternity leave, many women work part-time and make part-time use of subsidized childcare services. This pattern continues into a child's primary school years, owing to the lack of lunch or after-school care in Dutch schools—both of which make it difficult for both parents (or a single parent) to work full-time.[17]

In Germany—and especially the western federal states—the pattern was for many years one of a short maternity leave, parental care that was either unsubsidized or paid at a low rate, and a limited supply of child-care. Preschools and primary schools have covered only half of the day, leaving parents to provide care for the rest of the day. There has been some change in the policy model, however, as the government in 2006 adopted a longer, better-paid parental leave and is committed to a expansion in daycare services and all-day schools by 2013.[18] The situation has been different in the eastern federal states, where there are more full-day preschools, more childcare for children below the age of three, and longer school schedules.

The comparative picture sketched above raises many questions about why public policies structure the time of parents and children so differently. While some systems rely heavily on parental (usually maternal) care, others have developed public education and care services or subsidize privately provided care. There also are clear differences in the conceptualization of education and care services for children below the mandatory school age, with three models: first, the Nordic countries' "educare" model, in which education and care for all children below the age of seven are provided by the same services; second, the long-day educational model of France, Belgium, Italy, and Eastern Europe, in which there is a division between services based on age and in which although they are seen as educational in purpose, preschools are open for a long school day; and third, the short-day pedagogic model of Britain, Germany, Austria, and the Netherlands, in which there also is a division between education and care, and preschools are open for only part of the day.

The remaining sections of this chapter reflect upon some of the theoretical dimensions of these public policies, examining some conceptual tools that may help to explain these patterns.

Policies for Work and Family: Theoretical Dimensions

Some of the theoretical challenges of explaining differences in work-family policies across nations stem from the very complexities of the policies described above. While it is the nexus of different policy sectors that shapes the overall environment for working parents, each sector may be marked by its own distinctive politics. One cannot assume that the same forces and ideas guide daycare, preschool, parental leave, and working time policy. In fact, the lack of coordination between these areas can produce an incoherent array of policies that fail to address parents' needs. In addition, welfare and educational systems often have deep historical roots, with current policy arrangements reflecting previous debates and beliefs that have become institutionalized in contemporary programs and services. For that reason, one should adopt a temporal perspective on these policies, looking not only at how path dependency has shaped contemporary policy arrangements and political debates but also at potential openings for change.

Gendering Welfare State Politics

There is a vast literature on the welfare state that should help explain the mix of public and private caring arrangements in different countries. One prominent approach links the size and shape of welfare states to the power resources of the left, arguing that strong social democratic parties produce large, universalistic welfare states. Several scholars have applied this approach to explain why the social democratic welfare states in Northern Europe also have extensive public childcare services and high rates of women's workforce participation.[19] One variant of this approach focuses on corporatist bargaining systems: in countries with well-institutionalized corporatist bargaining and strong unions, we could expect greater attentiveness to labor market policy, and thus to the needs of women workers. Finally, the Soviet-bloc countries represented an extreme version of left ideology, one that held all adults as workers and thus created childcare and preschool services so that women would work outside the home.

While often persuasive, these accounts can only take us so far in explaining patterns of public policy. One problem is that, outside of the Nordic countries, left parties and trade unions have not always been faithful, or very committed, champions of gender equality and mothers' workforce participation. Initially, social democratic parties and unions were heavily oriented towards the needs of male workers, and many long favored the male-breadwinner/female-caregiver model. Left parties and unions have moved towards supporting mothers' employment and gender equality policies, but these shifts have occurred in different countries, at different times, and with varying degrees of enthusiasm. In addition, work-family policies are not only about questions of economic redistribution and labor market policy, but also reflect beliefs about gender roles and children's socialization. These values, as expressed by both mass opinion and political organizations, are likely to shape the political dynamics around these policies.

One way we could supplement these accounts is to focus on women's power resources—the mobilization of women's movements and/or women within political parties and trade unions. Political scientists Rianne Mahon and Christina Bergqvist emphasize that women's mobilization within trade unions and political parties played a critical role in highlighting questions of gender equality within these male-dominated organizations in Scandinavia.[20] Similarly, political sociologist Ingela A. Naumann argues that differences in both the influence and identities of feminist movements in West Germany and Sweden help explain different childcare policies. In West Germany, the women's movement was divided between antifamilial and new maternalist strands, neither of which lobbied much for improved childcare services. By contrast, Swedish feminists did not reject the family and viewed employment as the path to women's autonomy, which made childcare an important objective.[21] Looking back further in history, maternalist movements played a critical role in debates about mothers' employment and childcare policy in the late nineteenth and early twentieth centuries, shaping the development of kindergartens, family allowances, and other services for families.[22]

We could also examine the role of religion in shaping values about gender roles and the family. Christian democrats have long championed the male-breadwinner family model and, in most countries, continue to favor policies that maximize parental caring time at home. Where these parties compete with left parties, the latter may moderate their stance on work-family policies so as not to alienate more traditionally minded voters. This could explain why social democratic parties in Germany, Austria, and the Netherlands were long reticent with regard to the nonmaternal care of children. The near absence of religiously based parties in the Nordic countries, and their weakness in France, helps explain why the issue of mothers' employment has been less controversial in those societies than in some other parts of Europe.[23]

There may also be culturally and historically specific dimensions to debates over mothers' employment. In the Federal Republic of Germany, for example, aversion to childcare spanned the political spectrum for decades and was influenced by both the Third Reich and the Cold War. Childcare was denounced as "collective education" and became associated with totalitarian regimes, creating aversion to all forms of all-day childcare and school education.[24] In some parts of Eastern Europe, the collapse of communism either generated a backlash against the previous system or revealed long-suppressed preferences about the maternal care of young children. In Poland and Hungary, for example, there appears to be little public support for the idea of mothers working while their children are below the age of three. Thus, no government in Hungary since the collapse of state socialism has advocated the two-earner model, as to do so would go against the dominant currents of public opinion.[25]

The Politics of Social and Educational Services

Another dimension of contemporary work and family politics concerns the creation of social and educational services, and the relationships between these two sectors. Here, the existing literature on the welfare state may be less useful. Thus far, much welfare state research has focused on benefit programs in which the maximum role for the state is to determine eligibility criteria for programs and send out checks. Social and educational services require policymakers to decide not only who is entitled to these programs, but who will actually provide them, raising questions about intergovernmental relations, the role of private actors in social provision, and the personnel who will staff these programs. More generally, it is unclear that education fits well in the reigning welfare state typologies and frameworks.

In reflecting upon the historic forces that have shaped social services politics, sociologist Jens Alber suggests we should focus less on class politics than on another set of political divisions—conflicts over religion and center-periphery relations.[26] In many countries, contemporary civil society has its historic roots in social and political conflicts over religion in the nineteenth century. The clashes between religious and secular forces as well as among competing religious groups produced a mobilization of civil society actors to preserve their influence over a traditional area of responsibility—welfare and educational services for children and families.[27] In some countries, religious parties would ultimately gain political power and their welfare policies would reflect their belief in the principle of subsidiarity—the idea that human needs should be met at the lowest level of society. If families could not assure these needs, then voluntary organizations should do so, including those religious organizations that, often with considerable public funding, provide primary education, kindergarten, childcare, and other welfare services.

While Alber's focus is on social services, his framework may also help us understand the historical construction of education systems, which often emerged out of religiously based conflicts over who would have responsibility for socializing the nation's children. Similarly, education systems reflect historic settlements over the organization of territorial power, with some states devolving responsibility for primary and secondary schools to lower levels of government (Switzerland and West Germany), and others creating highly centralized education systems (France and Sweden).

We can see the legacy of these historic arrangements in the structure of welfare states and educational systems today. Although the religious basis of the voluntary sector faded over time, the principle of subsidiarity has endured in countries such as West Germany and the Netherlands.[28] As a result, the central state is not directly involved in providing these services; instead, publicly funded yet privately provided programs are the norm. This may make it more difficult to develop a coherent set of programs that address the needs of working parents. In France, Sweden, and the other

Nordic countries, by contrast, a principle of reverse-subsidiarity would develop whereby the state assumed responsibility for educational and social service programs. In recent decades, there have been efforts in France and Sweden, however, to promote a greater role for voluntary organizations in the provision of social services, which appears to have worked more in France than in Sweden.[29] The same was true in the communist regimes of Eastern Europe, where the state held a monopoly over education and social services.[30] Since the collapse of communism, civil society has reemerged in many of these countries, and voluntary organizations have gained an increased role in social provision. Still, the nonprofit sector continues to play a relatively small role in providing educational and social programs there.[31]

Alber's center-periphery divide concerns the division of responsibility between national, regional, and municipal levels of government. Historically, the presence or absence of these divisions shaped the construction of a unitary or federal state, and this would have consequences for the provision of social welfare and educational services. In unitary countries, the central state often finances these programs if not actually providing them. In federal systems, by contrast, lower levels of government usually have responsibility for many social and educational programs, and they will fight to protect their prerogatives in these areas. In recent years, there has been a trend towards devolution in many countries of both Western and Eastern Europe, but it is unclear whether this trend is beneficial or harmful to service provision.

The development of welfare and educational services also raises questions of personnel: who will staff these programs and what will be the training, working conditions, and pay of these workers? The split between educational and social services reflects, to some degree, divisions between the different types of workers who staff these programs. In many countries, these workers are trained separately and conceptualize their roles in quite distinct ways. In preschools, these workers often are called "teachers" and see themselves as primarily providing education, not care. Asking them to take care of less "educable" children, such as those below the age of three, or to oversee lunch facilities or after-school time is asking them to do care work, and not education, and this may be fiercely resented. By contrast, daycare workers often receive less professional training, have lower salaries, and may not see themselves as engaged in pedagogic work. In general, different systems of training instill a particular identity in these workers, which in turn affects the likelihood of collective mobilization to defend their interests. In France, for example, preschool teachers have the same degree of qualification (tertiary level) and are in the same unions as primary school teachers, and these unions have been a powerful force in education politics. Daycare workers are less organized, lack the connection to the primary school teachers, and have been less influential in social policy debates.

As the above discussion has revealed, work-family policies often have deep historical roots. Why do these historical structures endure? Is there no likelihood of change in the years to come? Recent debates in the social sciences about path dependency can shed light on these questions.

Path Dependency and the Potential for Change

Today's welfare states and educational systems are the accretion of more than a century of public policymaking. While motivations driving policy in one era might be quite different from those of later years, the legacies of earlier policy choices are often quite enduring. This is particularly evident in the case of modern childcare systems, which in recent decades have not only included policies to address the rise of mothers' participation in the labor force but also reflect the ways in which modern mass education systems were founded at earlier points in history. For example, France and Belgium first incorporated preschools into the national education system over one hundred years ago, embedding these programs in powerful national bureaucracies that would later propel their expansion. But because these programs are entrenched as part of the education system, there remains a sharp divide between daycare and early education programs.[32] In many Eastern European countries, the post–World War II period was a critical juncture, as this was the time when full-day primary and preschool programs were implemented, as well as childcare programs for children under three. Although the latter system of care has unraveled after 1989, the long-day school programs have endured.

These kinds of policies reflect the well-known effects of institutionalization, or path dependency.[33] Path dependence, simply put, is the notion that once one starts down a particular path, one is likely to stay on that road. Researchers often assess path dependency in the context of a critical juncture or moment. These events become institutionalized through mechanisms such as increasing returns, whereby the costs of switching from a particular path rise over time and the benefits of remaining on the existing path increase.[34] Increasing returns reflect institutional "stickiness," as policies and institutions put binding constraints on behavior while also offering "mental maps" that guide people through the complexity of political life.[35] Political scientist Paul Pierson also finds "lock-in" effects of policies that induce changes in individual behavior, which in turn generate expectations about public policy. As a result, decisions made at a particular moment in history may be difficult to alter later on.[36]

While attention to the path dependency of social programs is essential, it should not blind us to the possibilities for policy change. One of the significant criticisms leveled at historical institutionalism is that it is unduly static. In response, political scientist Kathleen Thelen suggests paying more attention to the fact that political and social life is characterized by both stability and change, with change that is at times, but not always, bounded by preexisting institutions.[37] Thelen thus argues that scholars need to identify the precise mechanisms that reproduce institutions, so as to better evaluate the forces that could alter those mechanisms. Adopting a temporal perspective on the welfare state can help us to identify the mechanisms that produce stability in political or social arrangements and observe whether change in those mechanisms can give rise to policy reform.

What are the mechanisms that make work-family policies stable and enduring? Social and educational services create constituencies of providers and the staff that work in these programs. Not surprisingly, these constituencies develop a strong interest in the status quo. Teachers unions, for example, have been a powerful force in the politics of many countries, and social services providers of either the nonprofit or for-profit variety will often lobby to protect the subsidies they receive. In addition, social programs become embedded in the fabric of social relations, affecting the behavior of citizens and their expectations about their own lives and the state's responsibilities in ways that prove resistant to change.[38] For example, policies that support the male-breadwinner model influence the way people organize work and care, as well as their beliefs about what the state should and should not do in this area. By contrast, policies that increase women's workforce participation create new expectations about state responsibilities, generating pressure on politicians to fund programs such as childcare or parental leave. In Denmark and Sweden, for example, policy shifts that augmented women's employment in the 1970s put tremendous political pressures on governments to increase their investment in childcare and expand the generosity of parental leave. Even as these states faced economic downturns and budgetary shortfalls in subsequent years, the commitment to gender egalitarian work-family policies has not wavered.[39]

At the same time, however, the social embeddedness of the welfare state can also be a source of dynamism and change. People inhabit a world that is bounded not only by the institutions of the welfare state, but by a larger set of economic, social, and cultural forces. Thus, despite policies that perpetuate the male-breadwinner model across the Western world, rapid economic growth in the decades after the Second World War and rising levels of women's education generated new, gender egalitarian values. Throughout Europe, women's workforce participation rates have increased in recent years, generating tensions in existing social policy arrangements and new demands by parents for more assistance. The response to these demands is in no way guaranteed, but rising levels of women's employment have put new issues on the agenda and spurred political competition over who could best meet the needs of working parents. The irrepressible dynamism of complex societies often unsettles existing social and political arrangements, opening up space for new beliefs, demands, and policies.

Outside actors also can create openings for policy reform. The European Union is increasingly setting the agenda on work-family issues by pressuring the member-states to develop childcare and parental leave policies. The international transmission of ideas has long been an important source of new policy ideas, and the EU now is a vital source of this kind of policy learning. Yet another international actor that has influenced domestic debates about work and family has been the OECD.[40] In recent years, for example, its Program for International Student Assessment (PISA) has provided internationally comparative data on the performance of students. This data has shown that some countries are doing comparatively poorly in the area of academic achievement, generating pressures for policy reform. In West Germany, for example, the revelation that students from minority and low-income families were doing particularly badly in the education system produced a "PISA-shock" that then made preschool and all-day education a higher priority than in the past.[41]

How governments respond to these demands will be shaped by existing policy arrangements. Faced with new problems, policymakers often reach for established repertoires of action, for example by modernizing existing programs or services to fit new needs.[42] In addition, previous policies can affect contemporary politics because they tend to generate both mass and bureaucratic constituencies with a stake in the status quo. In fact, sometimes the absence of past policies can create space for more innovation than in countries where long-standing programs are embedded in the fabric of societal and political expectations.[43] Where the terrain is littered with the institutional detritus of past policies, we are less likely to see bold reform than an incremental reform of the status quo. For that reason, uncovering the historical construction of contemporary policies is essential. Even if changes occur, the degree and nature of this change is likely to be bounded by existing institutional arrangements.

Conclusion

This chapter highlighted some of the methodological and theoretical issues raised by comparisons of work-family policies across European countries. As the above sections showed, one useful tool for interpreting contemporary policy is the notion of path dependency—the idea that events and decisions of the past shape political debates today. Childcare and education systems, in particular, appear to bear the effects of path dependency. One could argue, however, that path-dependent accounts are excessively static and, for reform advocates, depressingly pessimistic. How can change be achieved if we are all locked in structures inherited from the distant past?

One approach is to study periods of dramatic change in an effort to understand why significant reform has been possible in some countries during specific periods in time. We could focus, for example, on the abrupt shift in public policies towards working mothers in the Nordic countries in the 1970s, honing in on the political conditions that made this shift possible. There may also be ways to build on the institutional inheritances of the past. In France, for example, the gap between educational and care programs is wide, yet policymakers have added services and subsidies to the existing educational infrastructure that meet the needs of parents. Thus, while preschools themselves are not entirely structured around the working schedules of parents, municipal governments fund their own after-school care programs that make use of existing school facilities but do not require teachers to provide this care. Subsidies for family daycare also help parents cover the hours after school. While the French education system is a behemoth that is difficult to reform, modifications around this edifice can significantly improve the lives of families.

It is interesting to see that in at least some of the East European states, education systems have maintained the schedules developed under communism. While apparently valued mostly for their pedagogic values, full-day preschools in Hungary and the Czech Republic resemble the programs found in the Nordic states that attempt to fuse educational and caregiving goals. Thus, although women's employment rates have dropped significantly since 1989, this inheritance from the communist past may again become an important support to mothers' employment. In short, analysis of the historical construction of childcare, education systems, and other work-family policies will not only enlighten us about the politics of the past, but also can point the way to future openings for change.

Notes

1. Soo-Hyang Choi, "Early Childhood Care? Development? Education?" *UNESCO Policy Brief on Early Childhood* 1 (March 2002).

2. Lenira Haddad, *An Integrated Approach to Early Childhood Education and Care*, UNESCO Early Childhood and Family Policy Series, no. 3 (Paris, 2002).

3. Hillevi Lenz Tagushi and Ingmarie Munkammar, *Consolidating Governmental Early Childhood Education and Care Services under the Ministry of Education and Science: A Swedish Case Study*, UNESCO Early Childhood and Family Policy Series, no. 6 (Paris, 2003).

4. Eva Fodor, *Parental Insurance and Childcare: Statements and Comments*. Retrieved 25 October 2007: http://www.almp.org/pdf/sweden04/hunSWE04.pdf; Organization for Economic Co-operation and Development, *An Overview of ECEC Systems in the Participating Countries* (Paris, 2001), 158.

5. Willem Adema, *Babies and Bosses: Reconciling Work and Family Life* (Paris, 2002), vol. 1, 89–90.

6. OECD, *Starting Strong II: Early Childhood Education and Care* (Paris, 2006), 76–77; Nordic country data from the Nordic Social-Statistical Committee, *Social Protection in the Nordic Countries in 2005* (Copenhagen, 2007), 228; Data for Spain and Poland from the OECD Family Database. Retrieved 8 August 2008: http://www.oecd.org/els/social/family/database; and OECD Education Database. Retrieved 8 August 2008: http://www.oecd.org/education/database.

7. Michelle J. Neuman, "Hand in Hand: Improving the Links between ECEC and Schools in OECD Countries" (paper prepared for the consultative meeting on international developments in ECEC, Columbia University, 11–12 May 2002).

8. OECD, *Education at a Glance* (Paris, 2007), 369.

9. Eurostat, *Development of a Methodology for the Collection of Harmonized Statistics on Childcare* (Luxembourg, 2004), 99.

10. Not all countries have done this. Sweden, for example, had only a parental leave, offering no specific entitlement to a maternity leave. This was changed in 1995 to comply with the EU's pregnancy directive.

11. Kimberly J. Morgan and Kathrin Zippel, "Paid to Care: The Origins and Effect of Care Leave Policies in Western Europe," *Social Politics* 10, no. 1 (2003): 49–85.

12. Jacqueline Heinen and Heini Martiskainene de Koenigswarter, "Framing Citizenship in France and Finland in the 1990s: Restructuring Motherhood, Work, and Care," *Social Politics* 8, no. 2 (2001): 170–81.

13. European Foundation for the Improvement of Living and Working Conditions, *Family-Related Leave and Industrial Relations*. Retrieved 8 August 2008: http://www.eurofound.europa.eu/eiro/2004/03/study/tn0403101s.htm.

14. OECD, *Society at a Glance: OECD Social Indicators* (Paris, 2005), 41.

15. The benefit is over €500 per month, roughly one-half of the French minimum wage. See Hélène Périvier, "Emploi des mères et garde des jeunes enfants: l'impossible réforme?" *Droit Social* 9/10 (2003): 797–800. Parents with one child can receive it for six months after the end of maternity leave, and those with two or more can receive the benefit until the child turns three.

16. The payment for leave is a two-tier system. All parents caring for a child until the age of three can receive a flat-rate benefit (equal to the minimum old-age pension). Those who have been in paid work for at least 180 days in the two years before the child is born have the right to receive 70 percent of previous income, up to a ceiling. See Fodor, *Parental Insurance*, 2.

17. For the Dutch policy see Monique Kremer, "The Illusion of Free Choice: Ideals of Care and Child Care Policy in the Flemish and Dutch Welfare State," in *Child Care Policy at the Crossroads: Gender and Welfare Restructuring*, ed. Sonya Michel and Rianne Mahon (London, 2002), 113–42.

18. The parental leave pays two-thirds of one's previous wages up to a ceiling for twelve months, with two additional months of paid leave available if the other parent takes them. See Karen Hagemann, "Between Ideology and Economy: The 'Time Politics' of Childcare and Public Education in the Two Germanys," *Social Politics* 13, no. 1 (2006): 217–60, and her chapter in this book.

19. Gøsta Esping-Andersen, *The Social Foundations of Postindustrial Economies* (Oxford, 1999); Evelyne Huber and John D. Stephens, "Partisan Governance, Women's Employment, and the Social Democratic Service State," *American Sociological Review* 65 (2000): 323–42.

20. Rianne Mahon, "Childcare in Canada and Sweden: Policy and Politics," *Social Politics* 4, no. 3 (1997): 382–418; Christina Bergqvist et al., "The Debate on Childcare Policies," in *Equal Democracies? Gender and Politics in the Nordic Countries,"* ed. Christina Bergqvist et al. (Oslo, 1999), 137–56.

21. Ingela K. Naumann, "Childcare and Feminism in West Germany and Sweden in the 1960s and 1970s," *Journal of European Social Policy* 15, no. 1 (2005): 47–63; see also Hagemann, "Between Ideology."

22. Seth Koven and Sonya Michel, eds., *Mothers of a New World: Maternalist Politics and the Origins of Welfare States* (New York, 1993).

23. Kimberly J. Morgan, *Working Mothers and the Welfare State: Religion and the Politics of Work-Family Policies in Western Europe and the United States* (Palo Alto, CA, 2006).

24. See Wiebke Kolbe, "Gender and Parenthood in West German Family Policies from the 1960s to the 1980s," in *State Policy and Gender System in the Two German States and Sweden, 1945–1989,* ed. Rolf Torstendahl (Uppsala, 1999), 133–68; Hagemann, "Between Ideology."

25. Fodor, *Parental Insurance,* 4.

26. Jens Alber, "A Framework for the Comparative Study of Social Services," *Journal of European Social Policy* 5, no. 2 (1995): 131–49.

27. Josef Schmid, "Verbändewohlfahrt im modernen Wohlfahrtsstaat: Strukturbildende Effekte des Staat-Kirche-Konflikts," *Historical Social Research* 20, no. 2 (1995): 88–118.

28. Morgan, *Working Mothers,* 82–88.

29. Edith Archambault, *Le secteur sans but lucratif: Associations et fondations en France* (Paris, 1996), 15–17; Johan Vamstad, "The Third Sector in the Swedish Welfare State: A Curiosity or a Relevant Factor?" (paper presented at the ISTR-EMES Conference, Paris, 26–29 April 2005).

30. We can see the contrast within Germany in the decades after 1945, as confessional welfare associations provided much of the available childcare and kindergartens in the western regions, but hardly any of the programs available in the East under the communist regime. See Adalbert Evers and Birgit Riedel, *Changing Family Structures and Social Policy: Childcare Services in Europe and Social Cohesion,* TSFEPS Report, August 2002. Retrieved 25 October 2007: http://www.emes.net/fileadmin/emes/PDF_files/Child_care/National_Reports/Child_care_NR_D.pdf.

31. Marta Korintus et al., *National Report, Hungary: Mapping of Care Services and the Care Workforce* (London, 2001), 13; Haddad, *An Integrated Approach,* 8.

32. Kimberly J. Morgan, "Forging the Frontiers between State, Church, and Family: Religious Cleavages and the Origins of Early Childhood Care and Education Policies in France, Sweden, and Germany," *Politics and Society,* 30, no. 1 (2002): 113–48.

33. Kathleen Thelen, "Historical Institutionalism in Comparative Politics," *Annual Reviews in Political Science* 2 (1999): 369–404.

34. Douglass C. North, *Institutions, Institutional Change and Economic Performance* (Cambridge, UK, 1990), 95–98.

35. Paul Pierson, "Increasing Returns, Path Dependence, and the Study of Politics," *American Political Science Review* 94, no. 2 (2000): 251–67.

36. Paul Pierson, *Dismantling the Welfare State? Reagan, Thatcher and the Politics of Retrenchment* (Cambridge, UK, 1994).

37. Kathleen Thelen, "How Institutions Evolve: Insights from Comparative-Historical Analysis," in *Comparative Historical Analysis in the Social Sciences*, ed. James Mahoney and Dietrich Rueschemeyer (New York, 2002), 208–40.

38. Gøsta Esping-Andersen, *Three Worlds of Welfare Capitalism* (Princeton, NJ, 1990), 141.

39. See Anette Borchorst, "Still Friendly: Danish Women and Welfare State Restructuring," and Anita Nyberg, "How Are Swedish Women Faring? Childcare as a Gauge," in *Social Politics* 8, no. 2 (2001): 203–5 and 206–9.

40. Rianne Mahon, "The OECD and the Reconciliation Agenda: Competing Frames," in *Children in Context: Changing Families and Welfare States*, ed. Jane Lewis (London, 2007), 173–97.

41. Evers and Riedel, *Changing Family Structures*, 5–6; Hagemann, "Between Economy."

42. Heidi Gottfried and Jacqueline O'Reilly, "Reregulating Breadwinner Models in Socially Conservative Welfare Systems: Comparing Germany and Japan," *Social Politics* 9, no. 1 (2002): 29–59.

43. Daniel Wincott, "Paradoxes of New Labour Social Policy: Toward Universal Childcare in Europe's 'Most Liberal' Welfare Regime?" *Social Politics* 13, no. 2 (2006): 286–312.

Part II

BACKGROUND AND CONTEXT

Family Policies in Comparison

Chapter 3

FAMILY LAW AND GENDER EQUALITY
Comparing Family Policies in Postwar Western Europe

Ute Gerhard

Comparing national politics and policies towards the family in Western Europe is an inherently complex endeavor. Above all, the form that state intervention takes ultimately depends on important variations in the national structures of family life, cultural traditions, and existing institutional arrangements. Moreover, widely differing policies aimed at the family are often subsumed under the broad heading "family policy," although implicit measures influence, if often unintentionally, an individual's lifestyle within the family. At the same time, explicit family policy, such as measures designed to provide material support to families with children or raise the birth rate, whose effects and success rates are questionable, cannot be measured with any confidence. It is thus impossible to give an overall comparative survey.[1] Nonetheless, a number of approaches exist that can help us not only describe influences on family policy, changes in family structure, or compare statistical data between nations but also identify typologies or so-called policy regimes, and thus place nations into specific groups. Over the past two decades, the most prominent such approach has been sociologist Gøsta Esping-Andersen's typology of welfare regimes, each of which is characterized by a particular relationship between the state, the market, and the family. This typology enables us to group countries according to dominant institutional and cultural patterns as well as the logic that inform their social policies.[2]

In addition, Esping-Andersen's concept of a "welfare regime" facilitates comparative analyses of welfare states that focus not only on the relationship between the state and the economy but also take into account a whole set of legal, institutional, and cultural factors that also characterize different family forms. Esping-Andersen's distinction among three types of welfare regimes, however, has been criticized from many quarters, especially feminist scholars who note its failure to appreciate the role of gender, as is discussed in the introduction of this book.[3] To his credit, Esping-Andersen has responded positively to feminist criticism of his conceptual model by acknowledging that the distribution of tasks and levels of equality between the sexes are important preconditions for successful family policy. In other words, he understands that "women-friendly policy" and equality between the sexes are the "main challenges for welfare state reform."[4]

For our purposes, family policy refers to "a particular kind of social policy, i.e., a set of political interventions explicitly aiming at or implicitly operating to improve the life situations of individuals in the context of their family rights and obligations."[5] As a result of the feminist insistence on the meaning of the family in the analysis of the welfare state, important new criteria have emerged for comparing various European family policies. A regime-centered approach that takes into account the multiple developmental paths, social contexts, and cultural traditions can still prove useful for defining criteria that will enable us to distinguish more effectively and interpret the findings from various nations. Moreover, such an approach can help reveal the connections between typologies of family regimes and each nation's specific principles with regard to welfare, even though an examination of several additional factors is still necessary to complete an analysis of family policy.

In her important study *The State and the Family*, sociologist Anne Gauthier distinguishes four family policy models that provide further justification for this gendered approach to welfare state analysis:[6] first, a *French pronatalist model*; second, an *English noninterventionist model* that views the family as a private matter; third, a *Nordic proegalitarian model* that is based largely on a concept of gender equality and aims to support two working parents; fourth, a *German protraditional model* that supports the man as the breadwinner but that invests a fairly large sum in social transfers and subsidies for families. She also mentions a fifth, a *hybrid form* represented by the Southern European model, which is characterized by a traditional reliance on extended networks for family support.[7]

In the following, I analyze only a few specific national examples that, while not covering all of Western Europe, nonetheless represent distinct types of family policy. My selection of these countries is determined by the impact and role of family law or, better, "families of law" (*Rechtskreise*) in each of them. As previous research on the history of the family, the contemporary family, and social policies have shown, law has and continues to exercise significant influence on the reality of family structure and in particular on the status of women and children within it.[8] Indeed, legal norms and their application are not only a product of political, social, and cultural transformation, but also the driving force behind it. Since it is an instrument of both control and liberation, law exhibits a double character. The legal framework thus not only constrains but also empowers individuals by defining rights and obligations that function as a precondition for autonomous social relations and agency. In his recent study *The Trajectories of European Societies 1945–2000*, sociologist Göran Therborn also attributes significant influence to "European jurisprudence and the different styles of law," concluding, "In the case of Europe, this is above all a question of the difference between the English common law and the civil law of the continent."[9] Therborn places particular emphasis on the legacies of family law of the 1900s that have "largely shaped the development of family and gender relations in the twentieth century."[10]

In this chapter, I first offer an overview of European trends in the transformation of the family since 1945. They represent both a template and a challenge to modern, sustainable family policy. From there, I examine several different "families of law" that provide the organizing principle for my selection of four exemplary countries: France, Great Britain, Germany, and Sweden.[11] My thesis is that national styles in family policy reveal their roots in the historical context of developments in family law. In the conclusion, I highlight some of the main challenges that confront family policy today, namely, the redistribution of responsibilities for childcare between state and family as part of a necessary "update of the gender contract" in Western Europe.[12]

Change in the Family in Western Europe

A major characteristic of the European family today is the growing plurality of "family forms" or "forms of private living."[13] In addition to the nuclear family, modern societies in Europe and elsewhere are increasingly characterized by one-parent households, cohabiting couples with or without children, and homosexual couples. Moreover, recent decades have seen a growth in the number of singles as well as so-called patchwork families composed of stepfamilies or elderly people living together. This plurality of lifestyles, however, is by no means a historically new phenomenon, but has appeared in the history of the family during various phases of social transformation. Indeed, it represents a sign and even engine of social change.[14] In fact, research on the history of the family in Europe has described the numerous forms of family that have evolved during modern times as a distinctively European phenomenon when measured against the development of the family elsewhere.[15]

Despite these historical precedents, it is still valid to speak of a pluralization of private forms of life over the past forty years, especially when we compare current circumstances to the early postwar period. This phase, which lasted from 1945 to the mid-1960s, is generally characterized as the "Golden Age of Marriage" in the industrialized West, "because never before in the history of our cultural area … [had] there been so many married people, so few divorces and such a relatively high number of children per family, [with] non-married couples … nearly unknown."[16] Taking the 1950s as a starting point of our comparison, we must therefore remember that these years represent the heyday of the nuclear family in nearly all Western countries. Indeed, this family form was so ubiquitous that sociologist Talcott Parsons suggested that it possessed universal validity, a thesis that he expanded in his structural-functional theory with a traditional gender role model (his pattern variables).[17] But as sociologist René König had already critically noted, Parson's ideal family type was informed by a number of theoretical prejudices that obscured the reality of family structure and life in the industrialized world.[18]

Thus, in the aftermath of World War II, family sociology as well as child psychology played a significant role in restoring the normative family model of devoted motherliness to compensate for the loss of paternal authority as well as reestablishing security and normalcy in the postwar family.[19] This new familialism of the early postwar period was part of a so-called normalization process that served to defend the traditional hierarchical gender order and has been linked by historians to a broader remasculinization of the state and politics not only in West Germany but also in other parts of Western Europe and the United States.[20] As late as 1962, a UNESCO study of several countries uncovered the following norms: "Single women *must* work; married women without [any children] or [with] grown-up children *may* work; married women with small children *must not* work."[21]

Beginning in the mid-1960s, however, one can begin to discern a sustainable change in family structure that was driven by major transitions in the economy, social relations, and, by extension, values. Important forces for the transformation of values were in the 1960s and 1970s the New Left, protest movements, and the new women's movement. These trends led to the emergence of new lifestyles as well as changes in gender relations and relations between parents and children. The most visible sign of this development was the decline in the birth rate in many countries beginning in the 1970s. That decade also witnessed a rise in the divorce rate, a drop in the number of marriages and a devaluation of marriage in general, an increase in children born out of wedlock, and an increased acceptance of alternative forms of partnership and parenting. Despite differences among nations in the levels as well as in the timing and tempo of change, research has shown that a common feature in the evolution of family life patterns in Europe since the 1970s has been "a convergence towards diversity." Demographer Anton Kuijsten has condensed the major trends into four main periods: the 1960s are marked by limiting family size due to decreased births; the 1970s by an increased number of premarital cohabitations, divorces, and postponements of births; the 1980s by postponement of marriage until a child announces its arrival; and the late 1980s and 1990s by renouncing marriage even after children have been born.[22] However, these major trends mask the specific variations and developments within different nations.

The growing number of private lifestyles is due in large measure to marriage's relative loss of significance. In light of this "ever increasing individualism," in her book *The End of Marriage*, sociologist Jane Lewis has questioned whether or not marriage as an institution was reaching its end.[23] After all, marriage is no longer a prerequisite for either a lifetime partnership or a sexual relationship, nor must it serve as a prelude to parenthood. This change in values can be deduced from the falling number of marriages in Europe, which has also been accompanied by an increase in age of men and women at their first marriage and a rise in divorce rates.[24] In addition, this development corresponded to a dramatic increase in the number of children born out of wedlock,[25] with Sweden and Denmark already leading this trend in the 1970s, France and Britain catching up by the 1990s, and Austria, Greece, Spain, and Italy occupying the other end of the spectrum.[26] Scandinavian countries, and in particular Sweden, lead in all three indicators: decline of marriages, increase of divorce rates, and children born out of wedlock. In terms of divorce, Sweden along with Denmark, Britain, and the former East Germany stand out. With regard to "illegitimate" births, France matches Scandinavia's rate. It is also interesting that the number of divorces in almost all countries began to increase in the 1970s (albeit at different rates), independent of the reforms in divorce legislation that were implemented later in some of them.[27] Finally, this general decline in the significance of marriage can also be seen in the growing variety of household configurations in Europe. So, while a couple with children still represents the most common form of family, it has become increasingly acceptable for couples to live without children.

A declining birth rate, which is generally seen as a symptom of a broader social crisis, has almost always been the primary reason for government intervention in family issues. A case in point is France, which in the 1830s led the way in passing the first population measures in response to a drop in the birth rate.[28] Still, it was not until the early twentieth century that Europe experienced its first significant demographic change due to declining birth rates, which dropped steadily until the 1930s. Moreover, by the turn of the twentieth century, West European households, which averaged four people, were already smaller than their Eastern European counterparts. This development was due above all to the higher age at first marriage for men and women as well as an increase in the number of unmarried adults.[29]

The second demographic transition, which was caused above all by the widespread availability of reliable birth control and has been far more dramatic than previous changes, began in all Western European countries in second half of the 1960s.[30] As a contemporary observer has put it, this "period of free fall in fertility" came "like a bolt from the blue."[31] In comparison to today's birth rates in the EU, Germany, with 1.3 children per woman, has one of the lowest fertility rates in Western Europe, followed only by Greece and Spain. Due to its Catholic heritage and later industrialization, Ireland, on the other hand, exhibits a peculiar dynamic: since the 1960s the birth rate there has been cut nearly in half, sinking from 4.0 in 1960 to just barely 2.0 per woman in 1996.[32]

A rough summary of the data and research on the transformation of the family over the past half century shows that despite clear differences in levels, timing, and tempo of change among nations, there exists a common trend towards individualization, deinstitutionalization, and pluralization. In addition, one can discern a fundamental split in all countries between a family and a nonfamily sector, with a growing polarization between one-income and two-income forms of private life. Thus, as Kuijsten has concluded, "pluralization is everywhere, but everywhere it has another face."[33] This development not only moves family poverty or that of single parents to the center of the family policy debate but also raises the issue of gender equality, or, more specifically, assuring equal access for women and mothers to gainful employment while at the same time equalizing the division of labor in everyday care for both women and men. The most important insight that comparative research has yielded thus far is that the countries with the highest rates of female employment (Denmark, France, Norway, and Sweden) also have the highest birth rates. Those countries that were among the last to change their family policy to pursue more gender equality (Greece, Spain, Italy, and Germany) and have the lowest female employment rates also have the lowest birth rates in Western Europe. This indicates that it is not the legal equality of partners, which often is interpreted as an indicator of "modernity," that is responsible for lower birth rates today, but instead the persistence of traditional gender arrangements and family models, in particular the dominance of the male-breadwinner model.[34]

Family Regimes and Families of Law

Although my analysis focuses on developments of family policies in Western Europe and stresses the role of path dependency in family law, I am aware that these factors are just a few of the many responsible for the social changes since the end of World War II. In addition to the trend towards ongoing deinstitutionalization and individualization, we must also recognize the role played by political and social movements as well as specific cultural, economic, and political influences. Nevertheless, the modern history of law reveals that national peculiarities and cultural traditions—for example, basic assumptions about the role of the family, the social order, and particularly the gender order—are preserved in family law much longer than in other areas of civil rights, and thus often contradict basic principles of liberal democracies such as the freedom and equality of all human beings. In most European countries, therefore, we can observe a cultural lag between civil law, mostly marriage and family law, or, in some cases, even "an enclave of unequal law" until the middle of the twentieth century.[35] This lag is the result of the explicit and systematic inequality of women within nineteenth-century concepts of family law that informed forms of state and jurisprudence throughout Western Europe. Despite the various contexts and circumstances within different countries, republican as well as liberal discourses share "overlapping vocabularies" that produce the same basic differentiation between public and private spheres and relegate women to the private sphere.[36] Moreover, the concept of marriage as an institution provided common ground in marriage and family law in civil society.

In the political theory of civil society, marriage and the family were considered a basic institution and a fundamental component of stable social relations. Indeed, they were viewed as the "germ cell" and main pillar of the state. As an institution, marriage was characterized by its hierarchical ordering of the sexes, which helped regulate and legitimate the gender order. It defined the man as the "head of household" and furnished him with the authority to make economic decisions necessary for its maintenance. The woman, on the other hand, was required to fulfill her "marital duties" and subordinate herself to her husband while providing a wide variety of personal services for family members as well as in her husband's business. This bourgeois family model, in which the woman sacrificed her individual rights to the "higher good of morality," served as cornerstone of the nineteenth-century state and thus as a political end in and of itself. Reactions to demands for women's emancipation that emerged from the Enlightenment, in classical liberal theory, or during the Restoration era all shared this same basic position on marriage. For, as an institution, marriage was not simply a "legal" but, above all, a "moral relationship" that differed from other contracts that were based on the "free will" of the consenting parties. For this reason, divorce was not permitted. In practice, the relationship was built on the supposed inequality of the sexes. As the German writer Wilhelm Heinrich Riehl so poignantly put it in 1855, "If it were not for husband and wife, one could think people destined to an earthly existence of freedom and equality. But because God created woman and men, he made inequality and dependence basic elements of human development."[37] With this basic gendered assumption of all legal theories of the family since the nineteenth century in mind, we must now examine how family policy developed in mid-twentieth-century societies and whether the "paths" in family law briefly sketched in the following pages continue to shape differing national policy regimes today.[38]

Due to its demographic concerns about low birth rates as well as deeply rooted familial-institutional motives, France has the longest history of state intervention in family life. Indeed, the republican concept of the state, *L'Etat paternaliste*, was itself closely connected to the rigid patriarchalism in the French Civil Code. As a result, interventionist family policy in France, and in particular the strong sociopolitical commitment to childcare, derives from cultural traditions stemming from Napoleon's 1804 Code Civil, whose articles on family law, in contrast to other law codes inspired by the Enlightenment such as the Prussian General Code of 1794, gave fathers unrestricted, even despotic power over their children. Neither offspring born out of wedlock nor their mothers enjoyed any rights or protection whatsoever. Indeed, as Article 340 makes clear, even *inquiring* into paternity was forbidden.[39] In addition, there is a clear connection between the rigid paternal power over children that is rooted in the republican concept of the state and its view of motherhood as encompassing specific civic duties and virtues exercised by women, such as maternal caregiving and love for children, with both serving the interest of the state. In general, state education, which sought to socialize children into a shared culture and language and shape them into an egalitarian, active citizenry, played a central role in the process of nation building, secularization, and separation of church and state.[40] The introduction of full-time schooling in 1881 was thus not just a pedagogical project but part of the Third Republic's broader political project to instill in children the republican principles of freedom, equality, and active citizenship. So, while schooling was free, it was also placed under strict government control.[41]

Given its explicit aim of promoting the equality of opportunity for children as future citizens, mothers, including those who worked, were to be encouraged and protected. Since the end of the nineteenth century, a broad social consensus supported this linkage between citizenship and education, which was also advocated by a social movement organized around family issues and an Alliance Nationale contre la Dépopulation (a pronatalist society). Passed in 1939, the "Code de la Famille" served as the basis for the subsequent growth of family policy as "a central structural feature of social policy development" after World War II.[42] The specific "paternalistic" direction of the French welfare state, with its generous provisions for families with more than two children, was based on two "logics of public action," one of them "natalist" supporting a rising birth rate and the other "familialist" that sought the redistribution of wealth between families with children and families with none.[43] This horizontal redistribution is consistent with a conception of the family as the fundamental social institution of the French nation whose protection is the obligation of the state. At the same time, increasing family allowances and support for the most needy children, mothers, and families also aims to achieve a vertical increase in social equality.[44]

For our purposes, it is particularly noteworthy that the specifically misogynist laws in Napoleon's Civil Code of 1804 that accorded unrestricted authority to husbands remained on the books until 1938. Moreover, despite having been the first to claim human rights for women during the French Revolution, French women only won the right to vote in 1944. In fact, it was not until the 1970s, a period of changing social and cultural norms, that the notion that the state should remain neutral in regard to private lifestyles gained currency.[45] At the same time, however, France does appear to have achieved a broad consensus on the need for women to be both mothers and workers much earlier than most other countries. The major reason for this was that in France—similar to Sweden—the complementary agrarian division of labor between the sexes had been dominant longer than in other earlier industrialized countries. It was therefore culturally more commonplace and accepted that women work outside the house, even in the cities, because many of the female and male workers came from the countryside.[46] As is the case in most other European countries, increasingly few French couples take the vows of marriage. Likewise, divorce rates in France are also rising, and nearly as many children are born out of wedlock as in Scandinavia. In 1989, a decision of the French Supreme Court effectively recognized this trend when it awarded the same legal status to unmarried couples in consensual unions that married couples had long since enjoyed.[47] Not surprisingly, countries whose laws derive from the French Civil Code such as Belgium and Luxembourg exhibit similarities and variations that explicitly follow the French legal model. In contrast, the Netherlands, which up until 1956 had kept the principle of wives' legal inequality, finally followed the liberal British welfare model in the 1980s by designating marriage and family a private matter.[48]

Family policy in Britain, in contrast, was for a long time characterized by a form of nonintervention derived from common law as well as the residual influences of its former liberal welfare regime. According to this view, it is not the state's place to regulate citizens' private affairs unless need arises as a result of poverty or a particular vulnerability. In contrast to the unmarried woman, who already in medieval jurisprudence was viewed as an independent legal agent, the wife lost her status as legal subject until the twentieth century. As the eighteenth-century jurist William Blackstone, whose famous commentary on English common law became the standard work on the subject, notes, "In law husband and wife are one person, and the husband is that person."[49] The legal situation of wives contradicted earlier constitutional achievements in England, including its parliamentary traditions, separation of powers, and constitutional guarantee of property. Thus during the nineteenth century, civil law came under increasing pressure.

Beginning in the 1870s, the first suffrage campaigns of the English Women's Movement along with John Stuart Mill's important intervention on behalf of women's rights led to the passage of the Married Women's Property Acts. Although at first the property of married women was protected only on behalf of their inherited family property and did not offer women equal status, this legislation concerning women's right to hold property still helped pave the way for the idea of individual freedom that was consistent with the liberal ideology of "possessive individualism."[50] However, the invocation of marriage as an indissoluble institution rather than as a private contract survived until the 1960s. A number of legislative acts, including the so-called Marriage Bill of 1937 that expanded the grounds for divorce with equal rights for women, were taken before a radical reform of the divorce law in the 1960s finally introduced no-fault divorce in Britain. This transformation of marriage from institution to "an unnecessary legal concept" and a private relationship, along with the change from husbands and wives to men and women as parents, however, "tended to run ahead of social reality," as in practice, women remained economically dependent doing unpaid care work at home.[51] Several regulations of parenting have accepted private control over marriage and divorce, although parents are expected to negotiate their respective parental roles before applying to end the union.[52]

By permitting divorce through mutual consent and abandoning the principle of guilt, the state basically abdicated all responsibility for regulating marriage and the family. For, in contrast to continental marriage laws, the marriage contract in common law is a purely private affair. Indeed, it more closely resembles a labor contract as it presupposes the autonomy and equality of the contracting partners, thereby essentially excluding the

possibility of state intervention.[53] Obviously, the relationship between social change and law on the one hand, and behavior and legal reform on the
other, is both more vague and liberal in countries with common law — including the United States — than in countries where explicit family policy
regulates marital relations through legal provisions concerning marriage
contract contents. Thus the British welfare state links benefits not to families but rather to individuals, single parents, and children in need.[54]

In Germany, the ideal of the male-breadwinner family has had a strong
influence on its welfare regime, which is built upon a corporatist-conservative policy model. Transfer payments are largely based on employment
and its accompanying benefits. As a result, family policy is determined by
a broader social policy agenda that is designed above all to benefit wage
earners and to uphold a specific gender-hierarchical division of labor. This
anchoring and significance of the family as an institution can be observed
in all German-speaking countries and serves as "the basis for German Social Policy."[55] Indeed, concepts of marriage and the family that were developed in the mid-nineteenth century found their way into the Civil Code
(*Bürgerliches Gesetzbuch*) of 1900, including some particularly backward-
looking paragraphs that complicated divorce, limited married women's
property rights, and denied claims from "illegitimate" children.[56] In addition, Article 6 of the West German Basic Law (*Grundgesetz*) of 1949, which
guarantees special protection to marriage and the family, also derives from
these nineteenth-century concepts. As a result, until the passage of legislation guaranteeing equality in 1953, married women were legally subject to
their husband's right to make decisions for the family. Indeed, it was not
until the broad reforms of marriage and family law in 1977 that women
were no longer legally required to perform household duties, which often
meant they were found guilty in divorce proceedings. Since the end of the
1970s, West Germany has increasingly recognized the need for various
reforms, especially in regard to questions of alimony and the custody of
children after divorce. Moreover, to compensate for the lost income that
resulted from women leaving the labor market to have and raise children,
in 1986 the state introduced a parental leave with modest cash benefits, re-
newing it in 1992. Other reforms included the right, established in 1996, to
at least a half-day place in kindergarten for each child starting at age four,
the improvement in child rights in 1998, and, most recently, the introduction of payments to parents (*Elterngeld*) in 2006 based on their previous
income. For the first time in West German history, legislation (supported
by a coalition of Christian and Social Democrats) has sought to stabilize a
link between paid work and family for women and men.

Finally, the German education system has also served to reproduce
nineteenth-century middle-class gender relations. Above all, until now in

the former West Germany only a half-day of instruction is offered in most kindergartens and schools.[57] As a result, the academic success of children depends largely on their parents, and especially their mother's presence at home to help with homework.[58] Moreover, the tripartite structure of the school system serves as a gatekeeper to various careers and professions[59] and, as confirmed by the studies of the OECD Program for International Student Assessment (PISA), strengthens the social inequalities of a class society.[60] Thus a number of institutional and cultural factors have led to delays and persistent deficits in German family policies. To this day, German family policy has not only discouraged women from participating fully in the labor market but has also enshrined the male-breadwinner model in its welfare regime in such a way as to produce a "double standard of social security."[61] And despite decades of criticism, the West German system is perpetuated by tax policies such as the so-called marriage partner splitting provision that privileges unequal marriage relationships and thus favors stay-at-home wives. Finally, the often-cited culture of German family life has also helped to cement the patriarchal middle-class family model. Indeed, from its inception, German family sociology has viewed this model as "the foundation of German social policy,"[62] which has been invoked time and again as a part of German national identity ever since.[63]

It should be emphasized, however, that all changes and delays in German family policies after 1945 concern West Germany only. In fact, compared to the GDR, West Germany made a conscious attempt to appear conservative in order to highlight the supposedly negative aspects of women's emancipation under socialism and particularly in the raising of children on the collective model. After all, a crucial aspect of the East German system was its intention to ease women's participation in the labor market.[64] By 1970, the rate of employment of East German women was already 20 percent higher than that of their West German counterparts, and in 1989 the ratio of East German women in the workforce reached almost 90 percent (including students and apprentices), in contrast to 55 percent in the West.[65]

The divided history of the two German states with regard to family policies[66] thus forces us think about the effects of various social policies and legislation, especially on the different attitudes and everyday practices of working mothers in Western and Eastern Germany.[67] This comparison is particularly telling because here—as in a sociological experiment—the social policies of two very different political systems and their effects on behavior after forty years of separate history can be observed against the background of a once shared cultural tradition and political history. As a result of these different trajectories, there are still significant differences in the forms of private life, for example, the number of children born out of wedlock. In 2003, more than half of all children in Eastern Germany were born to unmarried mothers, making the proportion of such nonconjugal births 36 percent higher than in Western Germany.[68] This life pattern also suggests that children of unmarried mothers today do not grow up outside of marriage-like partnership relations, but instead that for a majority of couples in Germany, living together without being married may be a transitional state on the road to parenthood—a trend that can also be observed in other Western European countries like Britain.[69]

In order to complete this consideration of law, legal cultures, and their influence on state family policies, we must consider the case of Sweden.[70] Often considered the model of a successful policy for balancing family and work, Sweden also demonstrates the importance of law under the principle of equality, not in terms of protection for the family, but rather through individualization and institutionalization of individuals' civil rights. Comparative legal studies and the history of law treat the Scandinavian countries as a possessing a separate legal tradition.[71] Though closer to continental legal traditions than Great Britain or North America, Scandinavian jurisprudence is characterized by rather pragmatic interpretations that often lead to practical reforms. Moreover, the rapid transformation from an agrarian to a modern industrial society at the beginning of the twentieth century undoubtedly benefited women, as they were spared the detour through the bourgeois patriarchal gender ordering that occurred in much of Western Europe during the nineteenth century. Although a sex-based guardianship of all women, both married and unmarried, was only formally abolished in Scandinavia during the second half of the twentieth century, married women's ability to act independently was closely linked to the rather early granting of property rights to all women that occurred there. Already in 1874, women in Sweden were granted the right to dispose of their separate property and own earnings.[72] Even before they won the right to vote in 1919, Scandinavian women were involved in initiatives for legal reform through membership in women's organizations and political parties. As a result, they were able to participate in public debates, in family law committees, and even in the Swedish parliament. In fact, the marriage reform of 1920 in Sweden emerged from a close cooperation among the Nordic legislators and feminist activists. The new family law provided for equal property rights, divorce liberalization, and the complete abolition of male authority as well as equal custody of children. This rather early gender equality in marriage, which was based on the individual rights of both spouses and at the same time on a progressive understanding of gender roles and gender difference, is characterized as the "Nordic model of marriage."[73] One of the greatest symbols of gender justice, moreover, is the claim for maintenance payments from the fathers of illegitimate children, which was rooted in the "Danske Lov" of 1763 and extended in all Scandinavian countries at the beginning of twentieth century.

In addition to these legal innovations, the particular Swedish development was the result of political circumstances. Above all, the Swedish women's movement succeeded in forming alliances with movements and organizations dominated by men, such as the peasant movement and the Social Democratic Party.[74] Since the late 1960s, moreover, the Swedish as well as the Scandinavian way of social and family policy has been characterized by a distinct and radical policy of equality that was accompanied by a change of the ideas about motherhood and the collectivization of childcare.[75] In addition to the increased availability of public childcare and separate taxation for individuals even if they are married, a policy introduced in the 1970s, the Swedish welfare state has consistently individualized social and family law and gradually abandoned women-specific protective legislation. Following the elimination of health insurance for spouses and widows' pensions in the late 1980s, marriage as a maintenance institution was abolished. And yet here, too, it remains to be seen whether or not the 1995 reform of parental leave, which introduced a "daddy quota" and more attention to fathers' rights, will enable the family to overcome the remaining gendered divisions of work within the family and in the labor market.

Conclusion

As we have seen, given the numerous variations in national patterns and structures of family life as well as different forms of private living, comparing national politics and policies towards the family in Western Europe is a complex undertaking. Taking the 1950s, the heyday of the nuclear family, as a starting point, there is, however, a common underlying feature in the development of family life patterns in Western Europe, namely, the "convergence to diversity." All countries exhibit a declining significance of marriage accompanied by an increasing social acceptance of alternative forms of partnership and parenthood outside of wedlock. Against the background of these family changes with nation-specific variants and developments, my goal in this chapter has been to explain various national styles of family policies by referring particularly to cultural legacies and legal traditions. The organizing principle at the base of each of these exemplary cases of family policy regimes derives from one of four different "families of law"—the French Civil Code, English common law, the Central European or Germanic tradition, and the Nordic model of marriage. A comparison of these policy regimes reveals that those countries that have failed to apply fully the principle of equality as the primary motor of civil rights within gender relations, and especially within the family, are now facing major problems, above all lower birth rates.

In addition to gender justice, the organization of childcare emerges as a key issue that will serve as a benchmark for progress in women- and particularly child-friendly family policy. Since the 1990s, Western Europe has experienced a remarkable shift in political thinking about childcare and the boundaries between public and private responsibilities, particularly with regard to children under the age of three.[76] Moreover, within the European Union there is a political consensus that childcare policies are essential in reducing gender inequalities. Likewise, there is an increasing awareness that early childhood education should be included among children's democratic rights.[77] However, because childcare has become a central political issue in the process of social change as well as the changed definition of motherhood, childhood, parenthood, and gender roles, the different national contexts, path dependencies, ideologies, and legal cultures become all the more obvious or, at least seem to be at different stages. France and the Nordic countries have a long history of state intervention and state responsibility in this regard. In countries such as Germany and the Netherlands, on the other hand, the right to give care for younger children is, although in a different degree, still understood as the responsibility first and foremost of parents, which in practice usually means mothers. The British Labor government is on its way to change this and offers parents with children in a preschool age more public funded all-day childcare.[78]

Given the dramatic changes in the family and demography in general, a balanced and just distribution of care and work in the family and on the labor market will be a key challenge for future welfare and family policy. Because they fail to consider, recognize, and compensate adequately those who raise children or care for the elderly, social and family policies in a few West European countries appear undemocratic and indeed quite irresponsible in terms of achieving solidarity. As a result, they render any generational contract nearly impossible. This deficit in family policy, moreover, should be considered part of a broader deficit in democracy within the European Union, whose achievements remain focused on paid work and thus follow the logic of a common market, not the prerequisites of welfare for all. Although the Amsterdam Treaty of 1997 set new standards for gender equality, as far as the reconciliation of family and professional life or caring needs and responsibilities are concerned, progress in achieving them remains slow. With respect to unpaid care work, it is not governments, but also men and fathers who must act. The right and indeed duty to provide care and not only receive it might also prove to be a gain for men, and not just a loss of convenience. The task of the future, therefore, is to remedy this deficit in care by updating the gender contract and introducing new institutional solutions that make men and women equally responsible for care and other work within the family.

Notes

1. Franz-Xaver Kaufmann, "Politics and Policies towards the Family in Europe: A Framework and an Inquiry into their Differences and Convergences," in *Family Life and Family Policies in Europe*, vol. 2, *Problems and Issues in Comparative Perspective*, ed. Kaufmann et al. (Oxford, 2002), 453.
2. Gøsta Esping-Andersen, *The Three Worlds of Welfare Capitalism* (Cambridge, UK, 1990); and Gøsta Esping-Andersen, "After the Golden Age? Welfare State Dilemmas in a Global Economy," in *Welfare States in Transition: National Adaptations in Global Economies*, ed. Gøsta Esping-Andersen (London, 1996), 1–31.
3. See Jane Lewis, "Gender and the Development of Welfare Regimes," *Journal of Social Policy* 2 (1992): 159–73; Ann Shola Orloff, "Gender and the Social Rights of Citizenship: The Comparative Analysis of Gender Relations and Welfare States," *American Sociological Review* 58, no. 3 (1993): 303–28; Mary Daly, "Comparing Welfare States: Towards a Gender Friendly Approach," in *Gendering Welfare States*, ed. Diane Sainsbury (London, 1994), 101–17; Ruth Lister, "Citizenship: Towards a Feminist Synthesis," *Feminist Review* 57 (1997): 28–48; Anneli Anttonen and Jorma Sipilä, "European Social Care Services. Is it Possible to Identify Models?" *Journal of European Social Policy* 6, no. 2 (1996): 87–100; Arnlaug Leira, *Working Parents and the Welfare State: Family Change and Policy Reform in Scandinavia* (Cambridge, UK, 2002); Ruth Lister et al., *Gendering Citizenship in Western Europe: New Challenges for Citizenship Research in a Cross-National Context* (Bristol, 2007). See for more the introduction by Karen Hagemann, Konrad H. Jarausch, and Cristina Allemann-Ghionda in this volume.
4. See Gøsta Esping Andersen, "Towards the Good Society, Once Again?" in *Why We Need a New Welfare State*, ed. Esping-Andersen et al. (Oxford, 2002), 1–26; Helga Hernes, *Welfare State and Women Power: Essays in State Feminism* (Oslo, 1987); and the introduction by Hagemann et al. in this volume.
5. Kaufmann, "Politics and Policies," 434.
6. See Anne H. Gauthier, *The State and the Family: A Comparative Analysis of Family Policies in Industrialized Countries* (Oxford, 1996), 203–5.
7. Ibid.; see also Beat Fux, "Which Models of the Family are Encouraged or Discouraged by Different Family Policies," in *Family Life*, ed. Kaufmann et al., 363–418; Linda Hantrais and Marie T. Letablier, *Families and Family Policies in Europe* (London, 1996); as to the problems of comparison, see Bundesministerium für Familie, Senioren, Frauen und Jugend, *Siebter Familienbericht: Familien zwischen Flexibilität und Verlässlichkeit. Perspektiven für eine lebenslaufbezogene Familienpolitik*, Deutscher Bundestag Drucks. 16/1360 (Berlin, 2006): 36.
8. See Ute Gerhard, *Verhältnisse und Verhinderungen: Frauenarbeit, Familie und Rechte der Frauen im 19. Jahrhundert* (Frankfurt/M., 1978); Ute Gerhard, "Die Rechtsstellung der

Frau in der bürgerlichen Gesellschaft des 19. Jahrhunderts," in *Bürgertum im 19. Jahrhundert*, ed. Jürgen Kocka (Munich, 1988), 439–68; Ute Gerhard, *Gleichheit ohne Angleichung: Frauen im Recht* (Munich, 1990); Ute Gerhard, *Debating Women's Equality: Toward a Feminist Theory of Law from a European Perspective* (New Brunswick, NJ, 2001).

9. Göran Therborn, *European Modernity and Beyond: The Trajectory of European Societies, 1945–2000* (London, 1995), 103.

10. Ibid., 105.

11. See also Ute Gerhard, "Mothers between Individualization and Institutions: Cultural Images of Welfare Policy," in *Working and Mothering in Europe: A Comparison of Policies and Practices*, ed. Ute Gerhard et al. (Cheltenham, 2005), 18–40; Kaufmann, "Politics and Policies," 458.

12. Anne Lise Ellingsaeter and Arnlaug Leira, *Politicising Parenthood in Scandinavia: Gender Relations in Welfare State* (Bristol, 2006).

13. For the distinction between these two terms "family forms" or "forms of private living," see Franz-Xaver Kaufmann and Hans-Joachim Schulze, "Comparing Family Life in the Frame of National Policies: An Introduction," in *Family Life*, ed. Kaufmann et al., 4.

14. See Heidi Rosenbaum, *Formen der Familie* (Frankfurt/M., 1978).

15. See William J. Goode, *Soziologie der Familie* (Munich, 1967); Richard Laslett, "Introduction: The History of the Family," in *Household and Family in Past Time*, ed. Peter Wall and Richard Laslett (Cambridge, UK, 1972), 1–89; Michael Mitterauer and Reinhard Sieder, *Historische Familienforschung* (Frankfurt/M., 1982).

16. See Rosemarie Nave-Herz, "Die These über den 'Zerfall der Familie,'" in *Die Diagnosefähigkeit der Soziologie*, ed. Jürgen Friedrichs et al. (Opladen, 1998), 294.

17. Talcott Parsons, *The Social System* (Glencoe, IL, 1951).

18. René König, "Soziologie der Familie," in *Handbuch der empirischen Sozialforschung*, ed. René König (Stuttgart, 1969), 253.

19. Gerhard Baumert, *Deutsche Familien nach dem Kriege* (Darmstadt, 1954); see also René König, "Familie und Autorität: Der deutsche Vater im Jahre 1955," in *Materialien zur Soziologie der Familie*, ed. René König (Cologne, 1974), 214–30.

20. Robert G. Moeller, "Forum: The 'Remasculinization' of Germany in the 1950s," *Signs: Journal of Women in Culture and Society* 24, no. 1 (1998): 104–27; for Norway, see Arnlaug Leira, *Welfare States and Working Mothers: The Scandinavian Experience* (Cambridge, UK, 1992).

21. Quoted in Ingrid N. Sommerkorn, "Die erwerbstätige Mutter in der Bundesrepublik: Einstellungs- und Problemveränderungen," in *Wandel und Kontinuität der Familie in der Bundesrepublik Deutschland*, ed. Rosemarie Nave-Herz (Stuttgart, 1988), 132.

22. Anton Kuijsten, "Variation and Change in the Forms of Private Life in the 1980s," in *Family Life*, Kaufmann et al., 21.

23. See Jane Lewis, *The End of Marriage? Individualism and Intimate Relation* (Cheltenham, 2001).

24. For more detail, see Henrika Strohmeier et al., *Familienpolitik und Familie in Europa: Literaturbericht* (Düsseldorf, 2006).

25. See Kuijsten, "Variation," 36.

26. Isabel M. Torremocha, "Lone-Parenthood and Social Policies for Lone-parent Families in Europe," in *Family Life*, ed. Kaufmann et al., 182.

27. Ibid., 30.

28. Karen Offen, "Depopulation, Nationalism, and Feminism in Fin-de-Siècle France," *American Historical Review* 89, no. 3 (1984): 648–76.

29. Bundesministerium für Familie, *Siebter Familienbericht*, 14.

30. Ibid., 68ff.

31. Cited in Kuijsten, "Variation," 32.
32. Ibid., 33.
33. Ibid., 50.
34. Steffen Kröhnert and Reiner Klingholz, "Geschlechterrollen und Kinderwunsch," *Dokumente: Zeitschrift für den deutsch-französischen Dialog* 61, no. 5 (2005): 21–32.
35. Dieter Grimm, "Bürgerlichkeit im Recht," in *Bürger und Bürgerlichkeit im 19. Jahrhundert*, ed. Jürgen Kocka (Göttingen, 1987), 340–71.
36. Joan B. Landes, "The Performance of Citizenship: Democracy, Gender, and Difference in the French Revolution," in *Democracy and Difference: Contesting the Boundaries of the Political*, ed. Seyla Benhabib (Princeton, NJ, 1996), 295.
37. Wilhelm H. Riehl, *Die Naturgeschichte des Volkes als Grundlage einer deutschen Social-Politik: Die Familie* (Stuttgart, 1855), 3.
38. See for the following also Gerhard, "Mothers."
39. See Ute Gerhard, "Legal Particularism and the Complexity of Women's Rights in Nineteenth-Century Germany," in *Private Law and Social Inequality in the Industrial Age: Comparing Legal Cultures in Britain, France, Germany and the United States*, ed. Willibald Steinmetz (Oxford, 2000), 137–55; Ute Gerhard, *Debating*, 136–40; Marianne Weber, *Ehefrau und Mutter in der Rechtsentwicklung* (Tübingen, 1907), 318.
40. Cécile Laborde, "Republican Citizenship and the Crisis of Integration in France," in *Lineages of European Citizenship: Rights, Belonging and Participation in Eleven Nation States*, ed. Richard Bellamy et al. (New York, 2004), 46–72.
41. Mechthild Veil, "Ganztagsschule mit Tradition: Frankreich," *Aus Politik und Zeitgeschichte* B41 (2002): 29–37.
42. Kaufmann, "Politics and Policies," 460–62.
43. Marie T. Letablier and Ingrid Jönsson, "Childcare Policies in Europe: Comparing the Logics behind Public Action," in Gerhard, *Working and Mothering*, 41–57.
44. In detail see Franz Schultheis, *Familien und Politik—Formen wohlfahrtsstaatlicher Regulierung von Familie im deutsch-französischen Gesellschaftsvergleich* (Konstanz, 1999).
45. On France, see also the chapter by Jeanne Fagnani in this volume.
46. Letablier and Jönsson, *Childcare Policies*, 45.
47. Kaufmann, "Politics and Policies," 462.
48. Arnlaug Leira et al., "Kinship and Informal Support: Care Resources for the First Generation of Working Mothers in Norway, Italy and Spain," in *Working and Mothering*, ed. Gerhard et al., 131–61; Jan Künzler, "Paths Towards a Modernization of Gender Relations, Policies, and Family Building," in *Family Life*, ed. Kaufmann et al., 252–98.
49. Quoted in Ursula Vogel, "Zwischen Privileg und Gewalt: Die Geschlechterdifferenz im englischen Common Law," in *Differenz und Gleichheit: Menschenrechte haben (k)ein Geschlecht*, ed. Ute Gerhard et al. (Frankfurt/M., 1990), 217–23.
50. See Crawford B. Macpherson, *The Political Theory of Possessive Individualism: Hobbes to Locke* (Oxford, 1962).
51. Lewis, *The End of Marriage*, 113; see also Kathleen Kiernan et al., *Lone Motherhood in Twentieth-Century Britain: From Footnote to Front Page* (Oxford, 1998).
52. On Britain see the chapters by Kevin J. Brehony and Kristen D. Nawrotzki as well as Sally Tomlinson in this volume.
53. Willibald Steinmetz, "Introduction: Towards a Comparative History of Legal Cultures, 1750–1950," in *Private Law and Social Inequality in the Industrial Age: Comparing Legal Cultures in Britain, France, Germany and the United States*, ed. Willibald Steinmetz (Oxford, 2000), 1–43; see also Spiros Simitis, "The Case of the Employment Relationship: Elements of a Comparison," in Steinmetz, *Private Law*, 181–202.
54. Kaufmann, "Politics and Policies," 472.

55. Thus the subtitle of Riehl's book *The Family*.

56. Gerhard, *Verhältnisse und Verhinderungen*, 154–79; Gerhard, *Debating*, 122–48.

57. See the chapter by Karen Hagemann in this volume.

58. Karin Gottschall and Karen Hagemann, "Die Halbtagsschule in Deutschland: Ein Sonderfall in Europa?" *Aus Politik und Zeitgeschichte* B 41 (2002): 12–22; Karen Hagemann, "Between Ideology and Economy: The 'Time Politics' of Child Care and Public Education in the Two Germanys," *Social Politics* 13, no. 1 (2006): 217–60.

59. Ludwig von Friedeburg, *Bildungsreform in Deutschland. Geschichte und gesellschaftlicher Widerspruch* (Frankfurt/M., 1989).

60. See for more the introduction in this volume by Karen Hagemann, Konrad H. Jarausch, and Cristina Allemann-Ghionda.

61. See Linda Gordon, ed. *Women, the State and Welfare* (Madison, WI, 1990); Barbara Riedmüller, "Armutspolitik und Familienpolitik: Die Armut der Familie ist die Armut der Frauen," in *Politik der Armut und die Spaltung des Sozialstaates*, ed. Stephan Leibfried and Florian Tennstedt (Frankfurt/M., 1985), 311–35; Ute Gerhard et al., *Auf Kosten der Frauen: Frauenrechte im Sozialstaat* (Weinheim, 1988).

62. See Riehl, *Die Familie*.

63. Carl von Rotteck, "Art: Familie," in *Das Staatslexikon. Encyklopädie der sämmtlichen Staatswissenschaften für alle Stände*, ed. Carl v. Rotteck and Carl Welcker (Altona, 1846), 592.

64. For more see the chapter by Monika Mattes in this volume.

65. Hagemann, "Between Ideology," 256f.; also, Gunnar Winkler, ed., *Frauenreport '90* (Berlin, 1990).

66. In detail Ute Gerhard, "Die staatlich institutionalisierte 'Lösung' der Frauenfrage: Zur Geschichte der Geschlechterverhältnisse in der DDR," in *Sozialgeschichte der DDR*, ed. Hartmut Kaelble et al. (Stuttgart, 1994), 383–403.

67. Isolde Ludwig et al., *Managerinnen des Alltags: Strategien erwerbstätiger Mütter in Ost- und Westdeutschland* (Berlin, 2002).

68. Silke Bothfeld et al., *WSI FrauenDatenReport* (Berlin, 2005), 49.

69. See Lewis, *The End of Marriage*.

70. For more on the Nordic countries, see the chapters by Tora Korsvold and Lisbeth Lundahl in this volume.

71. Ditlev Tamm, "Einführung: Skandinavien als selbständiger Rechtskreis," in *Handbuch der Quellen und Literatur der neueren europäischen Privatrechtsgeschichte. Das 19. Jahrhundert. Die Nordischen Länder*, ed. Helmut Coing (Munich, 1987), 3–18.

72. See Ute Gerhard "Historical Perspectives," in *Gendering Citizenship in Western Europe*, ed. Ruth Lister et al., 34.

73. Kari Melby et al., "The Nordic Model of Marriage," *Women's History Review* 15, no. 4 (2006): 651–61.

74. Barbara Hobson, "Frauenbewegung für Staatsbürgerrechte—Das Beispiel Schweden," *Feministische Studien* 14, no. 2 (1996): 18–34; Teresa Kulawik, *Wohlfahrtsstaat und Mutterschaft—Schweden und Deutschland 1870–1912* (Frankfurt/M., 1999).

75. Arnlaug Leira, *Working Parents*, 32; see also Ellingsaeter and Leira, *Politicising Parenthood*.

76. Lister et al., *Gendering Citizenship*, 109–36.

77. See the Parental Leave Directive of 1996, the Recommendation of Childcare 1992 and the targets set for the provision of childcare services at the European Council meeting in Barcelona 2002.

78. See the chapters by Kevin J. Brehony and Kristen D. Nawrotzki as well as Sally Tomlinson in this volume.

Chapter 4

FROM EQUALITY TO DIFFERENCE?

Comparing Gendered Family Policies
in Post-1945 Eastern Europe

Jacqueline Heinen

The debates surrounding the process of postcommunist integration of Eastern European countries in Europe have paid scant attention to the social and even less to the gender dimensions of the issue. This neglect could be seen clearly in the European Commission's millennium program "Agenda 2000" and the criticism that it sparked within the European Parliament.[1] As it stands, European institutions interfere relatively little, at least not in a substantial way, in the social and family policies of the Eastern European countries that joined the European Union in May 2004—the Czech Republic, Estonia, Latvia, Lithuania, Poland, Slovakia, Hungary, and Slovenia—and even less so in issues concerning the condition of women.[2] This lack of involvement, however, comes as little surprise. On the one hand, the EU Treaty of Nice from February 2001, which reformed the institutional structure of the European Union to withstand eastward expansion, leaves little room for such intervention. On the other hand, such issues were also not a priority for most governments in the region. Although they felt compelled to change a number of laws in order to comply with the *acquis communautaire* (the total body of European law), they failed to develop new policy instruments that would enable them to enforce the new regulations.[3] And even when they did begin to tackle family policies, they did so primarily for demographic reasons, as evidenced by the 2005 *Green Paper—Confronting Demographic Change: A New Solidarity between the Generations* published by the European Commission.[4]

Notes for this chapter begin on page 109.

Drawing on the work of social scientist Richard Titmuss, sociologist Linda Hantrais has argued that family policies are best "characterized as policies that identify families as the deliberate target of specific actions, and where the measures initiated are designed to have an impact on family resources and ultimately, on family structure."[5] While useful, this definition does not apply to all member states of the "EU-25" (the twenty-five states that since May 2004 belong to the extended European Community), and even less in all new member states, as not all governments use the term *family policy*, identify the family as a target, or have specific departments responsible for it. Moreover, the definition still leaves open the question of the gender dimension of family policies as well as their impact on women's status and the gendered division of labor in society. In fact, the analysis of social and family policies can help uncover the various factors that shape social relations between the sexes, especially in periods of economic, social, and political upheaval. The transformation of Eastern Europe over the past fifteen years has been carried out in an almost exclusively masculine setting. Indeed, few women participated actively in the formulation of state policy at the very moment when parliaments across the region were beginning to shape new and durable social relations for the future. It is thus all the more important to scrutinize how these policies have affected the divide between the public and private spheres.

Of course, any discussion of (post)communist Eastern Europe as a single region runs the risk of eliding important economic, cultural, and other differences among the several countries that constitute it. This holds particularly true during a period of rapid transformation that witnessed them all moving away from the economic and political models of communism. In addition, each country exhibits significant differences in the circumstances of their individual, and especially female, citizens. This was the case before the collapse of communism, in particular in the areas of training and employment, and remains the case today in terms of educational level, age, place of residence, and above all standard of living.

Nevertheless, it is important to emphasize the similarities that have and continue to exist in social policies, especially those that have important implications for women's place in the labor market and the family. The analysis of these countries' family policies since 1945 can help us better understand the gendered dimensions of state actions and how they have shaped lives of women as well as their strategies for meeting the responsibilities of having a family. And despite the differences in each country's transformation since 1989, the available data, together with comparisons to Western European countries, make it possible to discern underlying tendencies that illustrate common features, especially in terms of gender relations and their influence on social policy. As economists Janneke Plantenga and Chantal Remery have shown, strong similarities can be found in areas such as women's employment rate, fertility rates, levels of childcare coverage for children aged three and under, and parental leave, which, to the detriment of mothers, was generally framed as a family, and not as an individual right.[6] Moreover, opinions on marriage and the family in Eastern European countries also converged in important respects.[7] Indeed, the experience of the transition seems to have encouraged a return to more traditional attitudes, while patterns of family formation have become increasingly deinstitutionalized.[8]

Material difficulties encountered by Eastern European citizens over the past fifteen years have generally enhanced the idealization of the family's role in society and raising children. This occurred despite the fact that the market economy exalted the individual and most of these countries experienced rising rates of divorce and extramarital births as well as decreasing marriage rates and a growing percentage of single women.[9] The idealization of the traditional middle-class breadwinner family model, which was strengthened by nationalist rhetoric encouraging women to prioritize their role as mothers, has helped to mask sexual inequality and pave the way for sexist attitudes, whether in politics or the economy.[10] Indeed, it has been harder in these countries than in the West to tackle the issue of inequality between the sexes head-on, especially since the concept of gender equality itself remains locked within the context of past debates. In fact, this concept has suffered enormously from the legacy of communist ideology, which proclaimed the emancipation of women as a great accomplishment of "genuine socialism." More than anything else, this legacy explains the rejection of all ideas linked to feminism among the majority of citizens in the postcommunist Eastern European countries. As sociologist Alena Heitlinger observed, "To call yourself a feminist is to invite abuse and ridicule,"[11] because the term *feminism* is linked to the "egalitarian" discourse of a now bankrupt political ideology and system. "Claiming distinct rights for women," social scientist Julia Szalai thus points out, "is generally seen as an expression of hostility towards the family in Hungary."[12]

Although equal civil and political rights of men and women existed largely in name only under communism, universal social rights ensured a minimum guarantee against the risks of personal misfortune. Drawing on the classic and still useful typology of sociologist Thomas H. Marshall, who differentiates between civil, political, and social citizenship, these rights constituted a kind of "social citizenship" and were particularly important for women's status.[13] The abolition of private property and the severe limitations of freedom of expression, organization, travel, and other liberties under communism, however, largely emptied civil rights of their content in the former communist regimes. Political rights proclaimed in constitutions were mainly formal, given the passive role of the "elected" state organs. After the transition of 1989, democratic freedoms, along with the civil and political rights normally guaranteed in a liberal state based on law, have been restored in all Eastern European countries, but many of the previous social structures and legal provisions have been rejected, above all because of budgetary constraints. Thus the notion of public care, which had existed under the previous regime, has essentially disappeared from the political agenda altogether. The state's concern with reducing spending led to a fundamental reconsideration of universal welfare provisions. The support and services that families had once received from the state or state-owned enterprises are increasingly rendered by the families themselves. This shift of burdens, moreover, came at a time when high unemployment made shouldering them all the more difficult for these families.[14]

In most Eastern European countries, many forms of social protection have been limited to the poorest members of society. As a result, only families whose per capita income falls below a certain percentage of the average wage are entitled to social welfare benefits. At the same time, the deterioration, both quantitatively and qualitatively, of public benefits and services, particularly in the area of childcare and early childhood education, has contributed to a marked increase in social polarization. In contrast to the successful minority embodied by the new affluent classes, the majority of the population faces economic hardship. Large or one-parent families are the most vulnerable, with women, as was also the case before 1989, affected most because they continue to shoulder the heaviest domestic duties, especially childcare.

In this chapter I concentrate on measures directly related to family and childcare policies in the areas of allowances, employment, services, and work leaves under communism and since its collapse.[15] Due to limitations of space, I focus on the Eastern European states that joined the European Union in May 2004 and analyze their similarities more than their differences. For the same reason, I will not enter into the ongoing debates concerning welfare state typologies or where Eastern European countries stand in relation to the other European countries in the West.[16] There have been several attempts to place communist and postcommunist countries into mainstream welfare regime typologies, in particular in an extended model of sociologist Gøsta Esping-Andersen's differentiation between "liberal," "conservative-corporatist," and "social democratic" welfare regimes.[17] Recent scholarship, however, agrees that most of the former communist states were in the past a specific type of a "paternalist and authoritarian socialist welfare regime" and are at present "mixed welfare regimes."[18]

Main Features of Family Policies under Communism

The universal social rights that guaranteed on a moderate level certain equality also represented one of the key means through which the "paternalist and authoritarian socialist welfare regime" ensured the submission of individual citizens during the communist era. Social welfare was used for the political and cultural integration of citizens in the socialist society. Family policy, childcare, and education were part of this "grand compromise" in which the state offered social security in exchange for the suppression of political and civil rights. As social scientist Tine Rostgaard has noted recently, "Under the command economies, family allowances tended to be generous." In the last years before the transition, "resources devoted to this policy area far exceeded those in the Organisation of Economic Co-operation and Development countries."[19]

Job protection, with its related benefits (mostly free services and state-controlled subsidies in domains like housing, health, transportation, and basic food supplies) conferred certain welfare-like traits to the "socialist state," even if many of these services reflected the general dysfunction and economic waste that was endemic in communist countries. The subsidy system ensured that certain basic needs were met and offered a minimum of protection to the individual. At the same time, state subsidies secured the free use of various services and maintained prices at an artificially low level for a number of basic necessities.[20]

Women were encouraged to work full-time, and laws provided special entitlements for mothers of young children. In many respects, childcare coverage for three- to six-year-olds in Eastern European countries appeared similar to that of Nordic ones. Paid maternity leaves ranged from two to six months after birth. During the 1970s, paid childcare leaves were introduced as well as leaves to care for a sick child. Single mothers had priority access to childcare and preschool for toddlers and enjoyed twice the standard family or childcare benefits. Thus on the surface, this system appeared very positive and progressive and compared quite favorably to Western welfare states. Measured as a proportion of real wages, family allowances were higher than in the West. In fact, public expenditures for family allowances were two or three times higher in Eastern European countries than in Sweden, often considered the most generous welfare state in the West.[21]

In ideological and political terms, however, a closer examination of family policy in practice reveals serious contradictions and incoherencies in respect of women's social status and the importance attributed to the family. Communists claimed to minimize the function of the family by reducing it to an entity defined mainly by its duties towards society, especially reproduction. In fact, constitutions and family laws were founded on an explicitly egalitarian gender model.[22] But these laws coexisted with specific regulations and practices that worked to reinforce a more traditional model of gender relationships in which women were—next to their paid work—responsible for family and household. Although the official policy claimed to emancipate women through work and through the socialization of education and childcare, it proved incapable of reaching these lofty goals.[23]

Most of the protective measures mentioned above aimed at encouraging women to reconcile occupational and domestic tasks. In contrast to the initial project of female emancipation, in practice this policy goal entailed stressing women's roles as mothers and asking them explicitly to take care of children and other dependent persons. Traditional views concerning younger children, who were to be cared for at home, also prevailed, and the number of crèches remained limited. The coverage rate for children under age three within formalized childcare ranged from 5 to 15 percent in most Eastern European countries despite the fact that an extended break from active participation in the labor force often had a deleterious impact on careers, including delays in or even barriers to training, promotion, and access to supervisory positions.[24] Thus, social and family policies—next to cultural and religious factors—contributed to the maintenance and even the reinforcement of the sexual division of labor in terms of horizontal and vertical job segregation, the wage gap, and the low level of division of labor within the family.[25] Indeed, they actually added to the dual burden that women had to shoulder. The amount of unpaid work done at home in the 1970s and 1980s differed among various countries in Eastern and Western Europe. But while house and family work was on average more or less similar in both parts of the continent, the paid weekly workload was nearly twice as high for women in Eastern Europe.[26]

The Family as a Refuge

The attempts of authoritarian communist regimes to transform the family into an instrument of social control encountered the resistance of populations who were victims of their incompetence in the economic field. In direct opposition to the discourse and goals of the state, citizens across Eastern Europe often valorized the family as a refuge that marked the border between "us" and "them" (the "other," the state). For many, the family became the only space that permitted the development of personal initiative and autonomy. As time went on, the positive value assigned to the private sphere increased in inverse proportion to the rejection of continued state intervention into personal life.[27] This trend strengthened as communist state authorities proved themselves to be incapable of satisfying people's most immediate consumer needs, which in turn helped stimulate the development of a black market. The first consequence of official policy in the economic and political field was thus to enhance the prestige of the private sphere. Second, but no less importantly, official policy worked to conceal and even reinforce gender differences. As a result, most citizens of these countries deeply internalized the double burden as something normal and linked to a seemingly natural difference of status between both sexes.[28]

Therefore, while we should avoid any excessive generalizations, it is important to remember how certain measures adopted in the past (e.g., parental leave, which initially was a maternity leave) were able, if only partially, to respond to the more or less explicit interests of women. And by claiming such policies as their own, women actually helped to strengthen the traditional division of labor in the family and conventional family norms. By focusing their energy on the family and accepting the practiced gendered division of labor in the family and in society, they supported these norms and at the same time willingly or unwillingly the regime. Factors that contributed to differences in the reaction of women's attitude to work and, by extension, the degree of importance they assigned to their family duties were the level of education and the type of job they had. Their perception of the role of the "mother-wife" also varied according to their practice of taking or not taking (and for how long) parental leave. In addition, history, religion, the influence of nationalism, and the type of social politics enforced since World War II have contributed to the differences in various Eastern European countries concerning the divide between the private and public spheres.[29]

The Outcome of Social Transformations in the Field of Family

The collapse of communism brought long-denied democratic liberties and the construction of a new state, based on law, that guaranteed civil and political as well as certain social rights that had not been necessary under the planned socialist economy of full employment (for example, unemployment benefits). At first, during this so-called phase of transition, hopes, which often bordered on illusions, about the expected benefits of the market economy were so great that most people took it for granted that social rights would be extended and state services improved. The rejection of the very notion of egalitarianism that had been tainted by communism contributed in the discourse to a minimization of the risk of increased inequality as a result of the neoliberal transition of which many social researchers and experts had warned.[30]

Events, however, quickly confirmed the fears of these experts. The spectacular rise of unemployment, accompanied by a general neglect of social questions in the face of the production crisis, led to the erosion or outright elimination of the social benefits that had been enjoyed under the former regimes. The euphoria and confidence in the neoliberal economy soon gave way to nostalgic feelings about the "security" and "egalitarian" nature of the former system. As sociologist Barbara Einhorn pointed out at an early stage of the transformation, "T.H. Marshall's earlier prioritizing of the 'social rights of citizenship' has renewed relevance in the face of the growing social inequalities and poverty in Central and East Europe."[31]

In terms of marriage, new laws have upheld the principle of equality of women and men that existed under communism. But with regard to social security, the first years of transition focused more on the destruction of the old system than the construction of a new one. Indeed, no former communist country has managed to establish a coherent and supportive family policy in place of the old one. Whatever the stated intentions with respect to family policies, housing, health, or social assistance might have been, economic constraints almost always ended up prevailing over the promises contained in the official rhetoric. Above all, these changes have weakened or eliminated altogether the old protective laws that conferred privileges on mothers or parents of young children (such as parental leave and leave for care of sick children) and on single mothers or fathers (such as priority of access to childcare centers and nursery schools, doubling of family or care allowances, privileged tax status, etc.).[32]

Various factors have contributed to the deterioration of social conditions and the policies pursued by the various governments of the region to reform their economies have differed in numerous ways. Still, one can observe a common dynamic in the majority of the measures undertaken in family policy and their consequences for women both as workers and mothers.

Changes in the Structure of Social Protection

After 1990, drastic reductions in state budgets drove legislators to reform a whole series of legal clauses and structures in an attempt to protect against new risks linked to the logic of the market economy. Their main priorities, not surprisingly, were unemployment and poverty. Most Eastern European countries made a series of choices of principle, not least of all to satisfy the neoliberal demands of the International Monetary Fund (IMF), which made financial assistance contingent upon the adoption of new measures designed to curtail the budget deficit. Thus, across the region postcommunist governments reduced state subsidies for consumption, disengaged the state from the administration of social security on behalf of independent firms, devolved administrative responsibilities to the local or regional level, and created a new system of funding based on dues from employers and employees.[33]

Policy paradigms for expenditures on family benefits and family support programs have diverged in many ways depending on a country's fiscal condition. But the general tendency was to restrain spending by reducing the overall costs of social welfare. Throughout the 1990s, the value of family allowance benefits, for example, declined by about one-half in most of Eastern European countries.[34] These reductions were obtained either through direct cuts, by failing to adjust benefits to the cost of living, or through the continued link of benefits to wage-based social security contributions. And yet at the same time, the number of self-employed, informally employed, and unemployed grew massively.[35] In many cases, this led to a narrowing of eligibility requirements; previously universal provisions became means tested and targeted to specific groups. This is the case in Bulgaria, Slovenia, Slovakia, the Czech Republic, and in Poland. In the latter country, only families with per capita incomes below one-fourth of the average wage are entitled to benefits. Moreover, the number of these "target people" in several countries has been progressively reduced to include only the most impoverished individuals.

Taken together, these restrictions have had a highly negative impact on families. In the Eastern European countries, the very high percentage of children who are in institutional care because they are orphans or have been abandoned is seen as an indication of the financial and practical problems that parents face in raising their children in the postcommunist era.[36] As Hantrais has pointed out, "raising a large family is more often than not equated with poverty."[37]

Impact of Gender-Targeted Policies

These changes have proved particularly consequential for women. According to Ewa Ruminska-Zimny, the UN's regional advisor on "gender and the economy," "Policies in many transition countries of the 1990s were run against the worldwide trends, which increasingly acknowledged women's contribution to economic growth as a result of empirical studies."[38] Although employment patterns do not indicate that unemployment is consistently higher today for women as compared to men, the proportion of women among the long-term unemployed has grown everywhere in the region. In 2001, women's unemployment rate, which ranged from 5 to 15 percent (reaching 7 to 33 percent among younger women), was only higher than men's in the Czech Republic, Estonia, Poland, Slovakia, and Slovenia.[39] These official rates of unemployment, however, only indirectly reflect women's withdrawal from the labor market when those on maternity and parental leave are counted, as is the case in the Czech Republic and Hungary, as economically inactive and thus excluded from the employment count. In addition, all those women are not counted as unemployed who have no access to unemployment benefits or have exhausted their entitlements.[40]

Due to traditional patterns of sharing (or as is often the case *not* sharing) the responsibility for raising a family and of full-time work for both women and men, it comes as little surprise that women have been affected more by the changes described above.[41] In contrast to most Western European countries, part-time work remains lower than 10 percent in most of the Eastern European countries, and even lower than 5 percent in many of them. Moreover, they face discrimination on the job market, as employers tend to prefer to hire male workers to offset the costs of maternity,[42] but government policies often encouraged them to leave the labor market, either through attractive parental leave schemes (as in Hungary) or through early retirement policies (as in the Czech Republic and in Poland).[43]

This trend, moreover, has been exacerbated by a number of pronatalist incentives for childbearing—backed by religious groups and conservative parties—that aim to reverse the decline of fertility in the region. From a relatively high level in the 1980s, fertility rates have fallen dramatically over the past two decades. In 1980, in the Czech Republic and Hungary, for example, they reached 2.3 and 2.2, respectively, as a result of pronatalist policies and other factors. In Britain and Sweden, it was in the same year 1.7 and in France, 1.9. Today the Eastern European countries have the lowest fertility rates on record, with an average of 1.2 to 1.3 percent in 2002.[44] Thus, their governments encourage women to take advantage of the opportunity to stay at home with their children. In Slovenia, the family allowance increases by 20 percent if the child does not attend kindergarten. Likewise, a new child benefit has been created for Hungarian families with three or more children and progressively larger tax credits have been provided for the second, third, and all subsequent children.[45] The result is that the employment rate for mothers with children under three now stands at 30 percent. But at the same time, new rules have been introduced in the pension system that, along with time off for caring, will substantially reduce the level of the pension for women. A similar scheme has been developed in Poland.[46] Although these incentives have had relatively little effect on fertility rates, they have had a strong impact on the course of women's lives.

Not surprisingly, the press never fails to highlight so-called success stories of women entrepreneurs that implicitly testify that women are men's equals. But such stories hide the trends towards the feminization of poverty that have been documented in various studies.[47] Single mothers constitute a disproportionate percentage of those who live on the threshold of poverty, especially since the laws that had once assured them a certain level of protection from the state were abolished in many Eastern European countries during the first wave of reforms in the early 1990s. Among the younger generation, the most worrying symptoms of the deterioration of women's financial situation are the increase in domestic violence as well as the growing extent of prostitution and sex trade.[48] In the older generation, retired women receive pensions that are on average substantially lower than those of men because they are calculated according to past income and women's mandatory retirement age is still lower than men's in most of Eastern European countries.[49] The wage gap, moreover, has remained stable, and in some cases increased, over the last fifteen years. The wages of women range from 70 to 90 percent of their male counterparts in the workforce. Though significant in size, this difference is nonetheless comparably less or smaller than the difference prevailing in Western European countries.[50] Finally, as a consequence of various pension reforms, the level of benefits that women receive is rather low, and across the region women's pensions are nearly 40 percent lower than men's.[51] Thus on the whole, women do suffer from several forms of highly consequential discrimination in the area of social protection that are reinforced by other trends in family policies since 1989.

The Inverted Effects of Parental Leave

In a number of countries, the protective laws of the old regime, which had provided special entitlements for mothers of young children, were among the first to be questioned by postcommunist governments. This applied especially to childcare leave. Under the pressure of requirements for entry into the European Union, efforts were made to modify the law in an egalitarian direction. Parental leave and leave to care for sick children, for example, have been made available to fathers without restriction, which was not the case before 1989. But a close examination of the legislation shows that this concession remains quite formal. The language of the law continues to emphasize the role of women, while the father only appears incidentally at the very end of the text. One should not be surprised, then, if parental leave continues to be taken almost exclusively by women and not by men.[52]

As for other social protection entitlements, the changes introduced in the law concerning the length of the leave and the level of payment, both crucial questions, differed greatly from one country to another.[53] In Poland, for example, childcare leave, which had been one of most attractive social policies under communism, has lost much of its appeal as the right to return to a job after a leave has been abolished in cases of mass layoffs or company closings. In addition, financial compensation for childcare, as limited as it was (about one-quarter of the average salary), has declined dramatically. Whereas in Hungary, childcare fees for a parent with two young children constitute about half of her or his wages, in Poland they are means-tested, and if the person is entitled to receive them, they constitute barely 75 percent of the net minimum wage.[54] This measure, therefore, has been largely robbed of its initial content, even more so when the rate of unemployment is taken into account. As a result, the proportion of Polish women, for example, availing themselves of childcare leave has decreased by two-thirds between 1990 and 1996 and continues to decline to this day.[55] The same is true for leave for care of sick children (sixty days per year), which since 1995 has also been available for men. As it is, very few women (to say nothing of men) use it today for fear of losing their jobs.

In contrast, the vast majority of Czech women do take parental leave. As is the case in Poland, this benefit is also means-tested. At the same time, however, it is much higher than in Poland, and women's right to return to their jobs has been maintained. Likewise, Hungary has established a universal benefit that increases with the number of children, and most low- or mid-qualified women take advantage of it.[56] But recent studies have highlighted that long-term benefits may be creating traps for women or work disincentives, especially for those with low skills or who occupy an otherwise weak position in the labor market.[57]

These various examples illustrate the ambiguity of protective measures such as parental leave when they are conceived as a family right, which in effect means that they target women specifically. But they also show that women often do not exercise this right for fear of losing their job or because it might limit their autonomy in terms of their bearing children; when crèches are closing one after the other, as is the case in most Eastern countries, having a young child becomes an obstacle to getting a job.

The Deterioration in Childcare Services

Public services, especially in the areas of health and education, have similarly suffered the inevitable consequences of budgetary constraints, which have led to a marked deterioration of eligibility criteria. Consequently, many local structures and legal provisions were considered to be too onerous and were called into question throughout Eastern Europe. This occurred just at the moment when social services previously linked to companies (health centers, facilities for children, canteens, convalescent homes, etc.) were also disappearing. Indeed, the transition has had a major impact on company involvement in the provision of social services. Because of financial constraints, enterprise restructuring, and liquidation, childcare institutions run by companies before the reform were closed during the first years after 1989. The disappearance of these services was, moreover, accompanied by a process of decentralization that served to broaden internal disparities within countries. As services for families are generally delivered at the local level, the inequalities are especially palpable in the field of childcare. In most countries, the state has been gradually delegating the responsibility to local governments, the voluntary sector, and private initiatives. Thus with the exception of the Baltic countries and Slovenia, childcare coverage for children three and under has fallen to less than 10 percent, and sometimes less than 5 or even 2 percent across the region. In fact, statistics show that even the proportion of children three to six years old are now well below most Western countries.[58]

However, the decrease in the number of children cared for in collective facilities was not caused solely by the limitation of potential capacity alone. On the one hand, the decline in the birth rate helped curb the demand. On the other hand, the rise in the cost of services in public institutions has played the decisive role in reducing attendance. For many families, the prohibitive cost discourages any desire of turning to outside childcare, all the more so when they must allow for various supplementary expenses such as food and special activities. The price of a meal, which before had been practically free, has now become an insurmountable obstacle for low-income households and especially the minority families among them.[59] In this way the current system very clearly favors the middle levels of society at the expense of the most impoverished ones. And as for unemployed women, the impact of closing care institutions that are considered to be too costly (like crèches, kindergartens, and hospitals) means more work within the family.

At the same time, the process of privatization has had some positive consequences. For example, there has been a diversification and improvement in the quality of certain services such as caring and educational work. This progress, however, almost always rests on a commercial basis consisting of private companies whose primary objective is to make profits. The ultimate result is thus a reinforcement of class divisions since income determines who has access to quality services. The decentralization of services, above all the transfer of responsibility for subsidizing childcare facilities from the central to local governments, has also had contradictory results. Ideally, it allows for a better response to those in need and provides a more rational management of services. But it also generates inequalities between rich and poor regions even though basic needs are far greater in the most impoverished places. This phenomenon is particularly acute in Poland where the network of childcare centers has suffered a near total collapse. In Poland, three-quarters of childcare centers have been closed between 1989 and 2002. In this country of 38 million inhabitants, only four hundred centers remain today. But the phenomenon can also be observed in other countries of the region, such as Romania, Slovakia, or the Czech Republic. In the latter, the childcare network, which before 1989 had covered 20 percent of children three and under, also collapsed. By 2004, only sixty crèches from the previous regime survived.[60]

Unemployed mothers of small children thus find themselves in a no-win situation. While the lack of an income forces them to take care of their children themselves, they lose the freedom of movement that would allow them to seek a job actively or undergo training that might improve their chances of finding one. Taken together, these conditions lead one to conclude that for the greater part of Eastern European countries' citizens, the consequences of the postcommunist transformation in terms of social policy have been, on balance, negative.

Conclusion

The picture that emerges from the preceding analysis illustrates clearly that the transition to a market economy and liberal state was accompanied by neither introduction of more choice for families nor greater autonomy for women. The state's overriding concern to reduce spending brought strong tensions between civil and social rights. The reconsideration of universal welfare provisions could thus be considered part of a broader "deciviliz-ing" trend identified by sociologist Zsuzsa Ferge.[61] This confirms the continued utility of Marshall's typology of citizenship, which distinguishes between different kinds of rights of citizenship and suggests how each is affected by the relationship between the public and private sphere as well as the degree to which they affect the social and political condition of individuals. As political theorist Anne Phillips argues, "Democratization remains an empty promise unless it pushes on to address power relations between rich and poor, white and black, women and men."[62] Analyzing family policies and dissociating the various levels and nature of rights is necessary to determine the social status of men and women facing the outcomes of the ongoing changes in Eastern Europe. In other words, are they in a position to exercise their (old and new) rights? In this sense, the notion of "entitlement failures" is quite useful "for judging the effectiveness of procedures for resource allocation."[63]

In practice, the protective measures that were afforded to women under communism did not expand their autonomy as individuals. Nevertheless, these measures were positively appreciated by employed women, who made extensive use of them despite their ambiguous character. The mere reduction or wholesale elimination of such rights hinders the exercise of women's individual liberties. The drastic fall in the birth rate can be interpreted as a sign of resistance by young women faced with financial difficulties as well as a response to employers who treat them as "unreliable labor" because they are liable to have children.

The existence of the discriminatory practices described in these pages reflects the fact that women continue to be perceived (and perceive themselves) as potential mothers. Their supposed availability to their families—and, more generally, to all dependents—restricts their freedom of movement, while the crumbling of childcare provisions increases their marginalization on the economic and political plane. As Linda Hantrais asserts, "Traditional family values resurfaced as women were forced back into family care work, while child poverty became a major concern for governments. Family policy can be said to have been refamilialized."[64] It is therefore not surprising that the older generation is pessimistic and that women workers, in particular low-qualified ones, express both criticism towards the outcome of the transition and nostalgia for the past.

Nevertheless, contrary to numerous forecasts dating from the beginning of the 1990s, the rate of women's labor activity, though weakened, has not declined nearly as rapidly or significantly as men's. On the one hand, the need to work is a question of survival for the family, which is completely dependent on their wages. But on the other hand, it also reflects changes in attitudes among young women in particular, who express career aspirations and display a much more assertive attitude towards work than their elders did just a decade ago. While certain protective laws (for single mothers, for example) are appreciated as achievements that should have been maintained, other laws, which privilege the role of the mother at the expense of the father, have begun to be seen as a kind of discrimination that strengthens sexual inequalities.[65]

One should not exclude the possibility of future changes in policies and in behaviors. Financial difficulties (per capita income, funds available) do represent a major obstacle for changing family policies. Indeed, many Eastern European countries today find themselves in a similar situation as Southern European states did when they joined the European Community after a long period of authoritarian rule (Greece joined the EC in 1981, followed by Portugal and Spain in 1986). This leaves the road open for possible changes in the future. Moreover, the generational factor must also be taken into account. Reactions of different groups are informed by past experiences, and the younger generation is more inclined to oppose policies that limit their choices. The coming years will thus determine whether the postcommunist countries of Eastern Europe will be able to foster a comprehensive approach encouraging gender equality, not only in social protection and family policies, but in the realms of labor, the law, and politics as well.

Notes

1. European Commission, "Agenda 2000: For a Stronger and Wider Europe," *Bulletin of the European Union*, Supplement 5/97, no. 5 (1997). Retrieved 5 October 2008: http://europa .eu.int/comm/dg1a/agenda2000/en/agenda.htm; European Parliament, *Report on the Communication from the Commission "Agenda 2000—For a Stronger and Wider Union,"* reporters Arie Oostlander and Enrique Baron Crespo, 1997, COM(97)2000—C4–0371/97.

2. United Nations, Economic and Social Council, *Gender Aspect of the Social Security and Pensions in the UNECE Region*, 2004, ECE/AC.28/2004/8.

3. Julien Damon, "Les politiques familiales en Europe," *Cahiers français* 322 (2004): 401–8; Yann Favier, "L'impact du droit européen sur le droit des prestations familiales," *Informations sociales* 129 (2006): 120–29; Jacqueline Heinen and Stéphane Portet, "Social and Political Citizenship in Eastern Europe: The Polish Case," in *Gender Justice, Development and Rights*, ed. Maxine Molyneux and Shahra Razavi (Oxford, 2002), 141–69; Jacqueline Heinen and Stéphane Portet, eds., "Egalité des sexes en Europe centrale et orientale: Entre espoir et déconvenues," *Transitions* 44, no. 1 (2004).

4. European Commission, *Green Paper—Confronting Demographic Change: A New Solidarity between the Generations*, 16 March 2005, COM (Brussels, 2005), 94.

5. Linda Hantrais, *Family Policy Matters Responding to Family Change in Europe* (Bristol, 2004), 132.

6. Janneke Plantenga and Chantal Remery, *Reconciliation of Work and Private Life: A Comparative Review of Thirty European Countries* (Luxembourg, 2005), 28–34.

7. Jean-François Tchernia, "Les valeurs familiales des Européens: Des conceptions diverses à l'oeuvre," *Informations sociales* 124 (June, 2005): 86; European Values Study, *European Values Study—3rd. Wave*, Central Archive for Empirical Social Research, University of Cologne. Retrieved 2 May 2006: http://zacat.gesis.org/webview/index.jsp.

8. Hantrais, *Family Policy*, 67.

9. UNICEF, *Women in Transition: The Monee Project* (Regional Monitoring Report, 6) (Florence, 1999), 43 and 47.

10. Katherine Verdery, "From Parent-State to Family Patriarchs: Gender and Nation in Contemporary Eastern Europe," *East European Politics and Societies* 8, no. 2 (1994): 225–55; Jacqueline Heinen, "Clashes and Ordeals of Women's Citizenship in Central and Eastern Europe," in *Women and Citizenship in Central and East Europe*, ed. Jasmina Lukic et al. (Aldershot, 2006), 81–100.

11. Alena Heitlinger, "Framing Feminism in Post-Communist Czech Republic," *Communist and Post-Communist Studies* 29, no. 1 (1996): 78.

12. Julia Szalai, "Women and Democratization: Some Notes on Recent Changes, in Hungary," in *Women and Democracy: Latin American and Central and Eastern Europe*, ed. Jane

S. Jaquette and Sharon L. Wolchik (Baltimore, 1989), 197. On the rejection of feminism by Russian women, see Larissa Lissyutkina, "Emancipation Without Feminism: The Historical and Socio-cultural Context of Women's Movement in Russia," in *Women and Political Change: Perspectives from East-Central Europe*, ed. Sue Bridger (London, 1999), 168–87.

13. Thomas H. Marshall, *Citizenship and Social Class* (London, 1992). For a feminist criticism of Marshall's typology, see Barbara Hobson and Ruth Lister, "Citizenship," in *Contested Concepts in Gender and Social Politics*, ed. Barbara Hobson et al. (Cheltenham, 2002).

14. See, for example, Olivier J. Blanchard et al., eds., *The Transition in Eastern Europe* (Chicago, 1994).

15. This chapter does not discuss other topics such as family configurations, the aging of the population, other types of care services (for elderly, etc.), perceptions of family policy, the effects on individuals' behavior, or the role of the voluntary sector in shaping family policies today.

16. See Rianne Mahon, "Introduction," in *Childcare Policy at the Crossroads: Gender and Welfare State Restructuring*, ed. Sonya Michel and Rianne Mahon (New York, 2002), 1–27; Damon, "Les politiques familiales"; Hantrais, *Family Policy*. For more on this debate, see also the chapter by Dorottya Szikra in this volume.

17. See Gøsta Esping-Andersen, *The Three Worlds of Welfare Capitalism* (London, 1990). See for more the introduction by Karen Hagemann, Konrad H. Jarausch, and Cristina Allemann-Ghionda in this volume.

18. See for example, Julia Szalai, "Poverty and the Traps of Post-communist Welfare Reforms in Hungary: The New Challenges of EU-accession," *Revija za Socijalnu Politiku* 13, no. 3 (2005): 309–33. See for more the discussion in the introduction by Hagemann et al. in this volume.

19. Tine Rostgaard, *Family Support Policy in Central and Eastern Europe: A Decade and a Half of Transition*, ed. The Council of Europe and UNESCO (Paris, 2004), 15.

20. Blanchard, *The Transition*.

21. UNICEF, *Women in Transition*, 44; Rostgaard, *Family Support*, 17.

22. Olivier Büttner, "Les anciens textes fondateurs dans les pays de l'Est," *Informations sociales* 124 (2005): 42–52.

23. See the chapter by Hana Hašková in this volume.

24. UNICEF, *Women in Transition*, 55.

25. See the chapters by Hana Hašková, Dorottya Szikra, and Monika Mattes in this volume.

26. See UNICEF, *Women in Transition*, 25.

27. Heinen, "Clashes."

28. Antonina Kloskowska, "Les attitudes à l'égard de la condition de la femme dans les familles ouvrières polonaises," in *Images de la femme dans la société*, ed. Paul-Henry Chombart de Lauwe (Paris, 1964); see also Alena Heitlinger, *Women and State Socialism — Sex Inequality in the Soviet Union and Czechoslovakia* (London, 1979).

29. Renata Siemienska, "Women, Work, and Gender Equality in Poland: Reality and its Social Perception," in *Women, State and Party in Eastern Europe*, ed. Sharon L. Wolchik and Alfred G. Meyer (Durham, NC, 1985); Alena Kohler-Wagnerowa, *Die Frau im Sozialismus — Beispiel CSRR* (Hamburg, 1974); Jacqueline Heinen, *Chômage et devenir de la main-d'oeuvre féminine en Pologne — Le coût de la transition* (Paris, 1995).

30. OECD, *Unemployment in Transition Countries: Transient or Persistent?* (Paris, 1994); UNICEF, *Women in Transition*.

31. Barbara Einhorn, *Cinderella Goes to Market: Citizenship, Gender and Women's Movements in East Central Europe* (London, 1993), 258.

32. See Rostgaard, *Family Support*; UNICEF, *Women in Transition*.

33. See Salvatore Zecchini, ed., *Lessons from the Economic Transition: Central and Eastern Europe in the 1990s* (Boston, 1997).

34. UN, *Gender Aspect*, 13; UNICEF, *Women in Transition*, 50; Rostgaard, *Family Support*, 17.

35. UN, *Gender Aspect*, 4.

36. Every Child, *Family Matters: A Study of Institutional Childcare in Central and Eastern Europe and the Former Soviet Union* (London, 2005), 10. Retrieved 20 October 2008: http://www.everychild.org.uk/media/documents; UNICEF, *Women in Transition*, 15.

37. Hantrais, *Family Policy*, 177.

38. Ewa Ruminska-Zimny, *Gender Aspects of Changes in the Labour Markets in Transition Economies*, ed. United Nations Economic Commission for Europe (UNECE) (New York, 2002). Retrieved 1 October 2008: http://www.unece.org/commission/2002/Ruminska-Zimny.pdf.

39. UNICEF, *Women in Transition*, 29.

40. UNICEF, *Women in Transition*, 6f.

41. Plantenga and Remery, *Reconciliation*, 89; Rostgaard, *Family Support*, 12.

42. There are numerous examples, in Poland, in the Czech Republic and elsewhere, of young women taking on contracts in which they promise not to get pregnant during a given period for fear of dismissal. See Hantrais, *Family Policy*, 87; Jacqueline Heinen and Monika Wator, "Childcare in Poland before, during and after the Transition—Still a Women's Business," *Social Politics* 13, no. 2 (2006): 197; Alena Krizkova, "Entre transition et stéréotypes de genre: Les femmes tchèques sur le marché du travail," in *Egalité des sexes en Europe centrale et orientale: Entre espoir et déconvenues. Transitions*, ed. Jacqueline Heinen and Stéphane Portet, 44, no. 1 (2004): 114; Ruminska-Zimny, *Gender Aspects*, 8.

43. Jill M. Bystydzienski, "The Effects of the Economic and Political Transition on Women and Families in Poland," in *Women and Political Change: Perspectives from East-Central Europe*, ed. Sue Bridger (London, 1999), 90–109; Jacqueline Heinen, "East European Transition, Labor Markets and Gender: In the Light of Three Cases: Poland, Hungary and Bulgaria," *Polish Population Review* 15 (1999): 106–27.

44. Plantenga and Remery, *Reconciliation*, 31; Globalis, *The Development of Fertility Rates*. Retrieved 10 October 2008: http://globalis.gvu.unu.edu/indicator.cfm?IndicatorID=138.

45. UN, *Gender Aspect*, 4; Rostgaard, *Family Support*, 26.

46. UN, *Gender Aspect*, 6.

47. UNICEF, *Women in Transition*.

48. Ruminska-Zimny, *Gender Aspects*, 6.

49. This is to say nothing of the fact that years of military service are figured into the pension, while those spent on parental leave are in most cases not.

50. UNICEF, *Women in Transition*, 33.

51. Elaine Fultz and Silke Steinhilber, "The Gender Dimensions of Social Security Reform in the Czech Republic, Hungary and Poland," in *The Gender Dimensions of Social Security Reform in Central and Eastern Europe: Case Studies of the Czech Republic, Hungary and Poland*, ed. Elaine Fultz et al. (Budapest, 2003), 13–41; European Commission, *Social Protection in the 13 Candidate Countries: A Comparative Analysis* (Brussels, 2003); United Nations Research Institute for Social Development (UNRISD), *Gender Equality: Striving for Justice in an Unequal World* (Geneva, 2005).

52. Rostgaard, *Family Support*, 14–30.

53. For more about the various configurations enforced during the transition period in Central-East-Europe, see Plantenga and Remery, *Reconciliation*, 2005.

54. Heinen and Wator, "Childcare in Poland." The same trend occurred in other countries in the region, which have either reduced the range of those eligible for an allowance (as

in Bulgaria and Russia) or completely done away with the right to parental leave, as has occurred in several ex-Soviet republics. See Kornelia Merdjanska and Panova Rossica, "The Family Enclosure in the Bulgarian Context: From Herodotus to the End of the Twentieth Century," *The European Journal of Women's Studies* 2 (1995): 21–32; UNICEF, *Women in Transition*, 55.

55. Bozena Balcerzak-Paradowska, "Publiczne instytucje spolecznych a rodzina," in *Partnerstwo w rodzinie i na rzecz rodiziny* (Warsaw, 1997), 58.

56. Lynne Haney, "'But We are Still Mothers': Gender and the Construction of Need in Post-Socialist Hungary," *Social Politics* 4, no. 2 (1997): 208–24.

57. See Linda Hantrais, ed., *Gendered Policies in Europe: Reconciling Employment and Family Life* (London, 2000), 108–23; Fultz and Steinhilber, "The Gender Dimensions."

58. Plantenga and Remery, *Reconciliation*, 34–35 and 84; see also Rostgaard, *Family Support*, 20–25.

59. See also the chapter by Dorottya Szikra in this volume.

60. See Heinen and Wator, "Childcare in Poland"; OECD, *Starting Strong II: Early Childhood Education and Care* (Paris, 2006), 85; UNICEF, *Women in Transition*, 54–55; see also the chapters by Hana Hašková and Dorottya Szrika in this volume.

61. Zsuzsa Ferge, "L'évolution des politiques sociales en Hongrie depuis la transformation du système," *Revue d'études comparatives Est-Ouest* 29, no. 3 (1998): 35–59.

62. Anne Phillips, "Identity Politics: Have We Now Had Enough?" (communication at the GEP International Conference, "New Challenges to Gender, Democracy, Welfare States," Vilvorde, Denmark, 18–20 August 2000).

63. Diane Elson, "Gender Justice, Human Rights and Neo-liberal Economic Policies," in *Gender Justice, Development and Rights*, ed. Maxine Molyneux and Shahra Razavi (Oxford, 2002), 102.

64. Hantrais, *Family Policy Matters*, 204.

65. Heinen and Portet, *Egalité des sexes*.

Chapter 5

FAMILY POLICIES AND BIRTH RATES
Childbearing, Female Work, and the Time Policy of Early Childhood Education in Postwar Europe

Livia Sz. Oláh

During the second half of the twentieth century, family patterns across Europe underwent extensive changes. New family forms emerged alongside of the traditional nuclear family (i.e., a married couple with children), which, based on the male-breadwinner family model, prescribed a strict separation of gender roles and, by extension, the tasks and opportunities of both sexes. The dominant pattern of the 1950s, which were characterized by early marriage and childbearing and thus worked to restrict women's role to the home, weakened over time. As marriage and childbearing have increasingly been postponed to the age of the late twenties and early thirties, it has become possible for women to gain experience in the public sphere through, among other things, higher education and paid work. In addition, both fertility rates and marriage rates have decreased as the connection between marriage and childbearing weakened, especially given the availability of effective, modern contraceptives. The decline in birth rates preceded the decline of marriage rates, which produced a new diversity of couple relationships such as nonmarital cohabitation, in which childbearing has become increasingly common, and living-apart-together relationships.[1] Moreover, due to the increasing prevalence of these more fragile relationships, the stability of partnerships decreased while the rates of divorce and separation rose. As a result, the share of single-parent, and especially single-mother, families has grown. The prospect of having to raise one's children alone has become a reality for many parents, a fact that may also have reinforced the decline in fertility as well as strengthened women's role beyond the private sphere.[2] Indeed, changing family patterns have been accompanied by rising female employment rates, and the

Notes for this chapter begin on page 128.

dual-earner-family model has become more common as educational systems and labor markets across the continent increasingly displayed a relatively high level of gender equality.[3] At the beginning of the twenty-first century, the traditional male-breadwinner/female-homemaker model applies to an ever shrinking proportion of couple relationships in Europe.

The changes in partnership patterns along with the postponement of parenthood and substantial female participation in the work force have led to fertility rates lower than 2.1 children per woman on average, which is below the replacement level. Such low fertility rates had already appeared in the 1970s in Northern and Western Europe, in the 1980s in the Mediterranean countries, and in the 1990s in Eastern Europe. By the end of the twentieth century, virtually all European states posted fertility rates below the replacement level, although significant differences remained from country to country. While Nordic countries and French-, Dutch-, and English-speaking countries displayed moderate fertility rates, birth rates in German-speaking societies, Southern Europe, and the former communist countries of Eastern Europe fell below 1.5 children per woman.[4] (See Figure 5.1.)

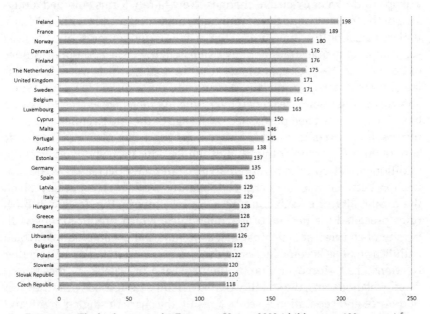

FIGURE 5.1: The birth rates in the European Union, 2003 (children per 100 women) [5]

As demonstrated by demographer Peter McDonald, a "safety zone" for low fertility exists somewhere around 1.5 births per woman.[6] Above that level, the reduction in the size of subsequent generations occurs slowly and relatively smoothly, thus allowing the effect of low fertility on future labor supply to be mitigated by immigration. When fertility remains below 1.5 children per woman for an extended period of time, however, the rapidly increasing proportion of elderly in the population exerts an upward pressure on public expenditures, particularly on pensions but also on the costs for health and elderly care, and thus jeopardizes the future of the welfare state. As a result, low fertility has become an issue that policymakers in Europe can ill afford to ignore.[7]

In addressing this issue, policymakers can draw on a considerable body of research. Numerous recent studies have carefully examined the link between childbearing trends and institutional settings.[8] And yet, the time structure of childcare, preschool, and primary schooling, which constitute an important dimension of institutional settings, has received relatively little attention from scholars and policymakers alike. For a number of reasons, however, the interplay between the time policies of early childhood education and fertility is an important and complex issue that demands further study. First, the diversity of family constellations and women's presence in the labor market require a set of childcare arrangements that allow motherhood and nonfamily roles to be combined beyond the immediate months following a childbirth, which are usually addressed through maternity- or parental-leave programs.[9] Second, (pre)school schedules determine the compatibility of these roles, as short school days and/or long midday breaks without provision of lunch at school for the children make it inherently difficult for mothers to fulfill multiple roles. Third, women's sense of entitlement to time of their own—that is, time in addition to that spent doing paid work—appears to have strengthened over the past several decades, thus limiting family sizes even further. Only effective time policies for childcare, preschool, and primary education have succeeded in accommodating this demand.[10]

A better understanding of fertility trends in relation to a certain policy context is thus necessary for policymaking that aims to achieve sustainable development. In this chapter, I explore the various factors linking the time policies of early childhood education and birth rates in Europe. I begin by discussing the theoretical and methodological approach that informs my analysis before turning to the empirical findings and results of my research. In the empirical analysis, I first address the changes that have occurred in the relationship between female participation in the labor force and fertility rates from the late 1960s to the early 2000s. In a second step, I integrate the dimension of time policies of early childhood education. I conclude with a discussion of why and how specific time policies are more or less supportive of childbearing, which is a key issue for the future of the welfare state and one that must be addressed by any future reforms.

Analyzing Fertility Rates: Theoretical Reflections

As mentioned above, with the exception of most of the former communist countries of the Eastern bloc, below-replacement-level fertility rates are not a recent phenomenon in Europe. As fertility declined to and remained at extremely low levels during the 1990s, the debate over the causes of low birth rates intensified in the demographic and economic literature.[11] For it was clear to scholars and policymakers alike that this decline would very likely have severe implications for the population age structure as well as the sustainability of the welfare state, not just in several Mediterranean and Eastern European countries where it is most profound, but in some countries of Western Europe as well. And yet despite its undeniable importance for fertility decisions and behavior, the influence of the time dimension of childcare, preschool, and primary school education policies on childbearing trends has remained largely unexamined.

In order to understand better this important aspect of childcare and education policies, my analysis draws on a combination of gender equity theory[12] and risk aversion theory.[13] Both theories suggest that women and men living in modern societies enjoy, for the most part, equal access to education at all levels and work for their living as individuals, irrespective of gender. The male-breadwinner/female-homemaker family model is perceived of as obsolete. With the exception of the former communist countries of Eastern Europe, however, this is a relatively recent development. The ideal of the male-breadwinner family, with its socially prescribed gender roles, persisted as the dominant form of family organization in the industrialized world up until the late 1960s and in some places well into the 1970s and 1980s. The relatively high level of gender equity attained in individual-oriented social and economic institutions such as the school system and labor market has not been matched, however, in family-oriented institutions, especially not families with children, in which women continue to perform the lion's share of household and childcare work.[14] The low level of gender equity in the family constrains women's opportunities in other spheres as well, including the labor market. Having only one or two children, or often none at all, has thus become a strategy followed by many women who wish to keep their options open or pursue a professional career. For the first time in history, women in industrialized countries have nearly total control over their own fertility, because they can rely on modern, efficient contraceptives.[15] Thus in societies where a large proportion of women see no other way to improve their opportunities other than severely limiting their family sizes, fertility has fallen to unprecedented low levels.[16] In East Germany, for example, total fertility rates fell below one birth per woman for a period of six years following unification in 1990, and have remained below 1.5 children per woman ever since. These rates, which resulted from the replacement of the former regime's family policies with those of the West German state, stand in stark contrast to the moderate fertility level displayed in the country in the decades before 1990.[17] This case also illustrates the role that policy models play in reducing or rather sustaining the gap between gender equity levels in individual-oriented social institutions and in the family, which in turn influences childbearing behavior. While a number of policy measures promoted the dual-earner model in the former GDR, West German policies support the male-breadwinner family ideal instead, as seen, for instance, in both the scarcity of public childcare provision for young children and the half-day system of early childhood education such as the primary school.[18] Such a radical change basically pushed East German women into a de facto birth strike, which has been unmatched in scale, if not as a phenomenon per se, in Europe.[19]

Another important question confronting policymakers is why participating in the labor force, which is a key component in gender equity theory, remains, in contrast to the 1940s and 1950s, important for women even after they enter a partnership. The answer to this question can be found in the concepts of uncertainty and risk.[20] A high level of youth unemployment over an extended period of time in a number of European countries,[21] combined with high economic aspirations and a reluctance to accept, if only temporarily, a lower living standard than in one's parental home,[22] have strengthened the sense of being able to support oneself, irrespective of gender, among many young people. In addition, because of the growing instability of couple relationships, young women have become increasingly risk averse. This trend can be observed, for example, in the rather high divorce rates and growing prevalence of nonmarital cohabiting relationships that have proved even more fragile than marriages. Moreover, women are increasingly aware of the gender-unequal outcomes that result from the dissolution of partnerships, which often leave women, much more so than men, to cope with economic hardship, especially if they have children.[23] As a result, young people, especially young women in modern societies, seek to minimize the risk of economic insecurity by postponing having families and reducing the number of children they have or plan to have. Instead, they seek to advance their position in the labor market by investing in their human capital, both in terms of educational attainment and employment experience.[24] Irreversible decisions such as childbearing are thus greatly affected by family policies that either support or constrain the combination of parenthood and gainful employment. From this perspective, the time policies of early childhood education are especially important. For if paid work and childrearing are rendered incompatible due to short opening hours in daycare, a lack of school-lunch provision and of after-school activity centers for children, women may feel compelled to choose between the "high-risk project" of motherhood and the rather secure path of continuous participation in the labor market, which inevitably reduces birth rates, sometimes to a dangerously low level for society.

Whereas the vast majority of young people eventually become parents, the timing of this transition has enormous consequences for a country's overall fertility rate. While it only takes one child to become a parent, a country's population cannot replace itself when the majority of couples have just one child. Given certain biological and social constraints, delayed parenthood often results in small family sizes. In addition, the postponement of the first birth strengthens women's sense of entitlement to time for themselves. This sense is particularly developed if they went through much of early adulthood without the responsibility of caring for children. If the public time policies of early childhood education cannot meet such demands from mothers and easily accessible, market-based solutions are also absent, many women may refrain from further childbearing after their first child.[25] This is due not least of all to the fact that fathers in most societies have shown themselves to be, on the whole, unwilling to increase substantially their involvement in the care of children.[26] Other women who have yet to become mothers but have learned of the experiences of new mothers from relatives, friends, neighbors, or colleagues may decide to abstain from motherhood altogether. In conjunction, these factors can firmly establish a low fertility rate that can be difficult to change.

My analytical model for exploring the relationship between time policies, female work, and birth rates is thus based on the following three premises: First, the gap between the levels of gender equity in individual-oriented social institutions versus family-oriented institutions emerged as substantial proportions of women engaged in paid work even after marriage and the birth of their first child. Second, women's participation in the labor force beyond the first years of young adulthood and early phases of their own families has been reinforced as the male-breadwinner model has increasingly become unviable economically due to the growing uncertainties in the labor market and substantial business-cycle fluctuations.[27] And third, plans for birth and employment as well as fertility and work behaviors have become connected through a process of "circular cumulative causality" (i.e., all three components affecting each other) in modern societies.[28] Women are increasingly aware of the time constraints that particular family policies impose on them in their choices about childbearing and employment. Drawing on aggregate-level data from several relevant measures for European countries of the Organisation for Economic Co-operation and Development (OECD), my analysis will explore the mechanisms around the time policies of early childhood education and the reconciliation of employment and motherhood.

Time Policies and the Reconciliation of Paid Work and Motherhood

Economists have argued that there is a link between increasing rates of female employment and the simultaneous decline of birth rates from the late 1960s onwards. These trends have contributed to a substantial increase in women's economic independence, seen as the main cause of low fertility. Particularly influential here was the approach of the "New Home Economics," which expanded the field of family and consumption economics in the early 1960s that had begun forty years earlier as household economics.[29] According to their analysis, as women's earning power rose, the time they spent caring for children became more "expensive," which increased the opportunity cost of having children. As a result, couples' desire to have more than one or two children has been reduced.[30] However, the cost of the time that mothers, who were not engaged in paid work, spent raising children was negligible. They thus had little impact on birth rates in countries that were still dominated by the male-breadwinner family model, since women customarily left the workforce upon entering motherhood. As this pattern has changed, however, the opportunity cost of childbearing has greatly increased, as has the gap between gender equity levels in the labor market and in the family.[31] Together, these factors have worked to push fertility levels down even further. Having prepared themselves for a long career, more and more young women have also carefully planned out childbearing (both number and timing). Among other things, they have considered how best to combine the dual responsibilities of work and family under given structures of social support, and constantly revise further plans based on employment opportunities and number of children they may already have.[32]

Indeed, studies have shown a rather strong negative correlation between birth rates and women's participation in the labor market in the 1960s and 1970s when family policy support for dual-earner families remained quite limited, even in countries with relatively high levels of female employment, such as the Nordic states.[33] Consequently, the high level of participation of women in paid work suppressed fertility rates in these countries. The Scandinavian countries were "forerunners" in this respect. In other countries of the developed world, the problem of reconciling employment and family life had not yet arisen in the 1960s and 1970s, and thus birth rates remained comparably high. The same general conclusion can be drawn from the data on European countries alone. In this period, the time policies of early childhood education had not yet emerged as an important issue, largely because mothers usually withdrew from the labor market after the birth of their first child. Unfortunately, there are no comparable data on female participation in the labor market for this period from former communist countries, whose regimes' commitment to full employment for both women and men was accompanied by policies that made family life and childrearing manageable.[34] These countries have thus not been included in the studies on this period.

In the 1980s, the rate of female employment continued to rise all over Europe. At the same time, birth rates continued to fall. However, the relationship between female employment and fertility began to change by the end of the decade in all OECD countries.[35] While retaining the focus on Western Europe but also including, unlike other studies, OECD countries from the former Eastern bloc, the same basic picture emerges, with the highest fertility *and* employment rates found in the Nordic countries. Communist Eastern European societies including the GDR show moderate levels of fertility and female employment, whereas the Western German-speaking and the Mediterranean countries, with the exception of Portugal, score low in both areas. In those two groups, the limited availability of public childcare for young children,[36] the specific time schedule of public daycare centers, and the particular organization of the school day in primary schools[37] are likely to have contributed to the relatively modest increase of female employment levels since the late 1960s. At the same time, however, they appear to have driven fertility rates below the critical level of 1.5 children per woman.

Data from the twenty-seven countries of the EU and Norway show that the positive correlation between the levels of female employment and fertility remains evident at the beginning of the twenty-first century. Unlike in the late 1980s and early 1990s, we now find a large number of states, particularly the German-speaking countries and all the Southern and Eastern European states, demonstrating very low birth rates that in many cases also correspond to relatively low levels of female employment. The decrease in both areas for the former communist countries can be explained by the severe cutbacks of policy provisions that previously facilitated the combination of paid work and family life.[38] Countries of Northern and Western Europe with a female employment rate of at least 60 percent also exhibit relatively high fertility rates,[39] while societies in which female employment rates are around 50 percent or less tend to belong to the low fertility group. Because countries with high levels of female employment do not display extremely low birth rates and those with low female employment rates do, traditional economic reasoning fails to explain current European trends in childbearing. In fact, the data demonstrate that the dual-earner family has become well established in all European countries. Thus, fertility levels have become sensitive to the gender equity gap, which made the reconciliation of parenthood and employment, including the organization of early childhood education, an important policy priority.

Although the dual-earner-family model does not imply that both earners — husband and wife — work full-time, it still constrains their time use, since both devote a certain amount of their time to paid work, thereby reducing the number of hours available for other activities such as caring for children. Shorter working hours for at least one of the parents, usually the mother, may thus prove to be an effective strategy for reconciling employment and childrearing responsibilities while also providing women with some free time of their own, which, in turn, will further influence their childbearing decisions.

Following this reasoning, very low fertility would be expected only in countries with rather limited opportunities for part-time work.[40] However, Figure 5.2 shows this is not really the case.

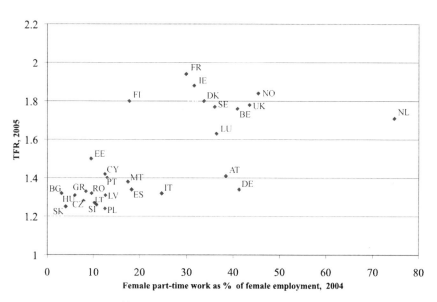

FIGURE 5.2: Correlation[a] between the percentage of women working part-time and total fertility rate in the European Union and Norway in 2004–2005[b][41]

Notes:
(a) Pearson's coefficient of correlation = 0.66174; TFR = Total Fertility Rates.
(b) Percentage of women working part-time among all employed women (ages 15–64 years) in the European Union and Norway in 2004 and total fertility rates in 2005.

Most states with extremely low birth rates, such as those of Eastern and Southern Europe, also exhibit low rates (under 20 percent) of female part-time employment. However, in Austria and Germany, with comparably low fertility rates, about one-third of women are employed in part-time jobs. This share exceeds that seen in France and equals that of the Nordic countries, which all are societies with the highest fertility rates in Europe.[42] This suggests that in addition to the availability of part-time work, other factors, very likely including the time policies for early childhood education that allow for a certain flexibility in family life arrangements, also have an important influence on childbearing behavior.

As mentioned above, the dual-earner-family model is today in the everyday lives of many couples well established in most European countries. Nevertheless, mothers of very young children may prefer to stay home to care for the children themselves by taking advantage, where available, of generous maternity- or parental-leave programs.[43] Thus, we would expect at best a weak correlation between the enrollment of children under the age of three in some kind of childcare facility and a country's fertility rate.[44] But, as Figure 5.3 shows, we in fact find a strong positive correlation between the two.

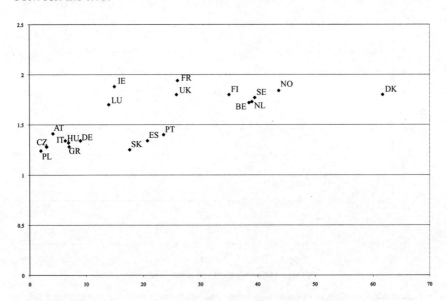

FIGURE 5.3: Correlation[a] between the percentage of under-three-year-old children in childcare and total fertility rate in the European Union and Norway in the early 2000s[b][45]

Notes:
(a) Pearson's coefficient of correlation = 0.71401;TRT = Total Fertility Rates.
(b) Correlation between the percentage of under-three-year-old children enrolled in public childcare facilities in the European Union and Norway in the early 2000s and total fertility rates in 2005.

Indeed, the majority of countries with the smallest proportion of young children enrolled in childcare, in particular Austria, Germany, the Czech Republic, and Hungary, also provide a rather long leave of absence for parents who wish to take care of their children at home.[46] At the same time, they also display fertility rates below the critical level. This suggests that limited provision of public daycare for very young children has done very little to increase birth rates for the following years. Such a conclusion is supported further when we look at the difference between the desired and the realized average number of children as shown in the data from the most recent results of the Population Policy Acceptance Study and from Eurostat in relation to the proportion of children below the age of three who are enrolled in public childcare.[47] Here we find a rather strong negative correlation reflected by a substantial gap between desired and observed fertility in countries with small proportions of very young children in public daycare. This stands in stark contrast to countries with a high level of childcare enrollment. Yet, the gap between desired and actually realized fertility is quite small and of similar extent for German-speaking countries as for Finland or the Netherlands. This suggests that we should turn our attention to the varying degrees of desire for having children, because in contrast to Germany and Austria, whose fertility rates have drifted below the critical level, fertility rates in Finland and the Netherlands have been above 1.5 births per woman for nearly the entire period under consideration.

Time Policies and Childbearing Desires

Research has shown that the ideal family size, like other goals and aspirations in life, is affected by the social context in which young women are socialized.[48] During the formative years of childhood and young adulthood, individuals internalize social norms and learn about the possibilities and constraints under which plans for their professional and family lives are to be realized. Work and childbearing behaviors are part of this process of realizing previous plans while at the same time generating new ones based on past experiences and outcomes from previous behavior. Living in a very low fertility context for longer periods, perhaps growing up as an only child, having many friends and schoolmates who are only children, or knowing other couples who remained childless in order to pursue other life goals is likely to affect one's own plans for having—or not having—children in the future.

As we have seen, nearly all European countries have exhibited below-replacement fertility rates for quite some time. And yet at the same time, birth rates have varied substantially from one country to another. To better understand the interplay between fertility desires and the surrounding society, we must first consider the occurrence of childlessness across various cohorts that may affect the fertility plans and behavior of subsequent generations.[49] It has been shown that in contrast to women born before 1950, the proportion of women who have never become mothers increased among the younger cohorts in most European societies.[50] Nevertheless, only a few states—Austria, Britain, Germany, Italy, and the Netherlands—have reached very high rates of childlessness (around 20 percent), and mainly among women born in the mid-1960s, the youngest cohort for which we have data on childlessness in nearly all countries. For Germany, such a high incidence of childlessness can already be seen for women born in the mid-1950s. And while we do not have data for later cohorts in that country, there is no indication that the level of childlessness would have decreased since. In fact, just the opposite appears true. Germany and Austria are projected to have the highest rate of childlessness in Europe even among women born in the mid-1970s, with about every fourth woman ending her reproductive years without even a single child.[51] Interestingly, Belgian women and the 1965 cohort in Poland also display levels of childlessness of around 15 percent, which may signal future changes in the level and/or timing of fertility in those countries.

On the basis of data from the Eurobarometer Survey 2002, we can also examine the relationship between actual childlessness and the desired level of childlessness.[52] Among women born in 1955 who reached the end of their reproductive period by the early 2000s, we find a rather strong positive correlation between their level of childlessness and that desired by women between the ages of eighteen and thirty-four in twenty EU-OECD countries (see Figure 5.4).

This seems to support the socialization argument put forth by sociologists and demographers Joshua Goldstein, Wolfgang Lutz, and Maria Rita Testa, according to which desired family size eventually adjusts to a country's fertility rate.[54] Does this mean, then, that experiencing a very low fertility rate for a long time is a precondition that generates a relatively high level of desired childlessness in a society? Figure 5.5 shows that this is not really the case.

Among the twenty-seven countries of the European Union, there are only four states where the proportion of women aged eighteen to thirty-four years who wanted "no child" is at or above 10 percent. In most countries, the proportion is between 0 and 5 (or at most 6) percent. The four states that exhibit rather high levels of desired childlessness are Germany, Austria, the Netherlands, and Belgium. The two latter countries are among the few in Europe with nearly no experience of birth rates at or below the critical level of 1.5 births per woman. Why, then, would a significant share

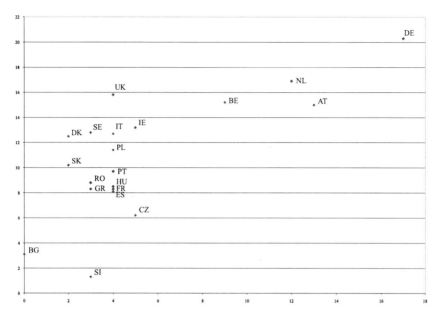

Figure 5.4: Correlation between the percentage of childless women born in 1955 and the percentage of eighteen- to thirty-four-year-old women with "0 child" as ideal family size in the European Union in the early 2000s[53]

Note: Pearson's coefficient of correlation = 0.72167.

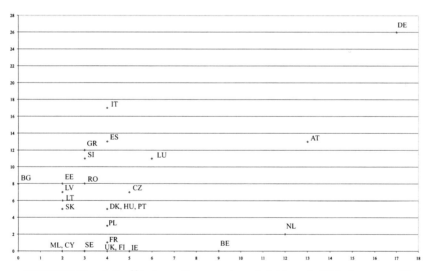

FIGURE 5.5: Correlation[a] between the percentage of eighteen- to thirty-four-year-old women with "0 child" as ideal family size and length of experience[b] of fertility below the critical level[c] in the European Community[d] in the early 2000s[55]

Notes:
(a) Pearson's coefficient of correlation = 0.42598.
(b) Number of years in the period 1970–2000.
(c) Fertility below the critical level, i.e.: TFR=1.5.
(d) EU-27.

of young women desire in such a society never to become a mother? In the case of the Netherlands, time policies are likely to have contributed to this sentiment, as the opening hours in preschool institutions are often limited, school days end around 3 P.M., and the lack of school lunch provision further constrains parents', and usually mothers', time, thus making it difficult to engage in other activities including paid work.[56] This, in turn, can eventually lead to a growing share of risk-averse women who are not willing to give up other opportunities for the sake of motherhood. Given the circular cumulative causality between work- and childbearing plans and behaviors, such a development may have rather serious consequences for fertility in the long term.

As a further "test" of the socialization argument, we must also consider the relationship between the frequency of small family size ideals (i.e., zero or one child) among women in the main childbearing ages and the length of the period below the critical level of fertility. We find that nearly 40 percent of German women and almost 30 percent of Austrian women have such limited family size aspirations. Likewise, in Romania and Belgium, every fifth woman desires a very small family, although neither of these countries have a long experience of very low birth rates. In fact, Germany is the only country where both the proportion of women with small family size desires is exceptionally large and the length of the period when fertility has remained below 1.5 births per woman is exceptionally long, about three decades. Austria also has relatively long experience of very low fertility, but not longer than either Spain or Italy, where about 15 percent of women prefer a small family, most likely because of their strong familistic tradition.[57] This again suggests the need to delve more deeply into the particular social contexts of different countries. The reason that the German-speaking countries have the largest proportion of young women who desire to have no children or at most a single child is very likely to be found in the great difficulties of combining motherhood and work or other aspirations in the public sphere in these societies, as the example of West Germany demonstrates. Moreover, the time policies of early childhood education seem to reinforce these difficulties, thereby reducing not only the actual fertility rate, but the desire to have children as well.

Conclusion

The time policies of early childhood education are thus clearly an important issue for the development of fertility in modern societies in which the dual-earner family model is well established. In this chapter, I have presented both the theoretical and empirical underpinnings for this argument. As the gap of gender equity in the educational system and the labor market versus that in the family has widened, increasing numbers of women have become aware of the risks of having more than a very limited number of children. Unless family policy measures are perceived as effective in reducing the insecurity linked to motherhood, fertility can and in many cases has fallen to dangerously low levels for society, thereby jeopardizing economic growth and the future of the welfare state. Indeed, easy access to efficient contraceptives empowered women to control, and if they find it necessary, greatly limit their childbearing. At the same time, self-realization has become an accepted goal for all individuals, irrespective of gender, due to changes in societal norms all over Europe in the past decades.[58] However, despite similarities in individual life goals as well as in the availability of modern contraceptives, fertility rates have remained well above the critical level of 1.5 births per woman in a number of countries, but not in others. This again suggests the importance of the particular social context and policy measures.

We have seen that the relationship between female employment rates and fertility had changed by the late twentieth century. Countries with low rates of female employment exhibit rather low birth rates whereas societies with high levels of women's labor-force participation display fertility well above the critical level of 1.5 births per woman. This new pattern, however, has not been linked to the availability of part-time work, because countries with limited opportunities for women to work less than full-time (such as in Southern Europe) and with a substantial proportion of employed women in part-time positions (e.g., German-speaking countries) both exhibit very low fertility rates. Furthermore, the findings indicate that generous parental leave programs have fallen short of their goal of preventing the further decline of fertility, whereas public childcare provision, even for children below the age of three, seems to promote further childbearing. Access to high-quality daycare services also appears to produce a greater desire to have children as well as to facilitate the realization of that desire. But this only occurs when such services are combined with time policies of early childhood education that allow women to engage in both paid work and in other activities beyond childrearing.

Countries that neglect the necessity of effective time policies for early childhood education will, therefore, only heighten the risk of increasing the proportion of childless or one-child families. Given that a high frequency of small families in a society may reinforce similar desires in the next generations, this may suppress birth rates below the critical level in the long run. The importance of time policies in the organization of childcare, primary school schedules, and other aspects of early childhood education for childbearing plans and behavior is particularly evident in countries with comparatively brief experiences of very low fertility levels. Because these countries have not yet established a durable low-fertility path, they may still have time to act decisively by implementing new and more effective time policies. It is therefore likely that the role of policymaking in the development of childbearing trends will become increasingly prominent in the years to come.

Notes

I would like to thank the Swedish Council for Working Life and Social Research (FAS), whose grant of a postdoctoral research fellowship enabled me to complete the research and writing of this chapter.

1. John C. Caldwell and Thomas Schindlmayr, "Explanations of the Fertility Crisis in Modern Societies: A Search for Commonalities," *Population Studies* 57, no. 3 (2003): 244.
2. Barbara Hobson and Livia Sz. Oláh, "Tournant positif ou 'grève des ventres'? Formes de résistance au modèle de l'homme gagne-pain et à la restructuration de l'État-providence," *Recherches et Prévisions* 83 (2006): 48.
3. Peter McDonald, "Gender Equity, Social Institutions and the Future of Fertility," *Journal of Population Research* 17, no. 1 (2000): 4.
4. Council of Europe, *Recent Demographic Developments in Europe* (Strasbourg, different years); Eurostat, *Total Fertility Rate*. Retrieved 12 February 2007: http://epp.eurostat .ec.europa.eu/portal/page?_pageid=1090,30070682,1090_33076576&_dad=portal&_ schema=PORTAL.
5. Council of Europe, *Recent Demographic Developments in Europe* (Paris, 2003). Retrieved 3 November 2008: http://www.coe.int/t/e/social_cohesion/population/demographic_ year_book.
6. Peter McDonald, "Low Fertility and the State: The Efficacy of Policy," *Population and Development Review* 32, no. 3 (2006): 485.
7. See also "Documents. The IMF on Policies Responding to Demographic Change," *Population and Development Review* 30, no. 4 (2004): 783–89.
8. For some of the latest studies on this topics see, Thomas A. Di Prete et al., "Do Cross-national Differences in the Costs of Children Generate Cross-national Differences in Fertility Rates?" *Population Research and Policy Review* 22, no. 4 (2003): 439–77; Janet C. Gornick and Marcia Meyers, *Families that Work: Policies for Reconciling Parenthood and Employment* (New York, 2003); Ronald R. Rindfuss et al., "The Changing Institutional Context of Low Fertility," *Population Research and Policy Review* 22, no. 5–6 (2003): 411–38; Barbara Hobson and Livia Sz. Oláh, "Birthstrikes? Agency and Capabilities in the Reconciliation of Employment and Family," *Marriage and Family Review* 39, no. 3/4 (2006): 197–227.
9. Harriet B. Presser, "Can We Make Time for Children? The Economy, Work Schedules and Childcare," *Demography* 26, no. 4 (1989): 523.
10. Harriet B. Presser, "Comment: A Gender Perspective for Understanding Low Fertility in Post-Transitional Societies," *Population and Development Review* 27, Supplement: Global Fertility Transition (2001): 179–80.
11. For an overview, see Hobson and Oláh, "Tournant positif," 49–51.

12. For a thorough presentation of the gender equity theory, see McDonald, "Gender Equity," 1–11.
13. See Ulrich Beck, *World Risk Society* (Cambridge, UK, 1999); Hobson and Oláh, "Tournant positif," 50; and Peter McDonald, "Low Fertility in Australia: Evidence, Causes and Policy Responses," *People and Place* 8, no. 1 (2000): 14–16.
14. Richard Breen and Lynn Prince Cook, "The Persistence of the Gendered Division of Domestic Labor," *European Sociological Review* 21, no. 1 (2005): 43f.
15. Presser, "Comment," 178.
16. McDonald, "Low Fertility and the State," 492–93.
17. Institut national d'études démographiques (INED), *Population in Figures. Database: Total Period Rate.* Retrieved 6 February 2007: http://www.ined.fr/en/pop_figures/developed _countries/situation/one_indicator.
18. See Karen Hagemann, "Between Ideology and Economy: The 'Time Politics' of Childcare and Public Education in the Two Germanys," *Social Politics* 13, no. 2 (2006): 217–22 and 225; Michaela Kreyenfeld, "Fertility Decisions in the FRG and GDR: An Analysis with Data from the German Fertility and Family Survey," *Demographic Research*, Special Collection 3, art. 11 (2004): 278–84 and 307; and also the chapter by Karen Hagemann in this volume.
19. Hobson and Oláh, "Birthstrikes?" 200–202, 217–18.
20. Hobson and Oláh, "Tournant positif," 50.
21. John Micklewright and Kitty Stewart, "Is the Well-Being of Children Converging in the European Union?" *Economic Journal* 109, no. 459 (1999): F701; OECD, "Labour Market Performance since 1994 and Future Challenges," in *Employment Outlook 2006*, OECD (Paris, 2006), 34 and 37.
22. Dirk J. van de Kaa, "Anchored Narratives: The Story and Findings of Half a Century of Research into the Determinants of Fertility," *Population Studies* 50, no. 3 (1996): 413–14; Gianpiero Dalla Zuanna, "The Banquet of Aeolus: A Familistic Interpretation of Italy's Lowest Low Fertility," *Demographic Research* 4, art. 5 (2001): 150–51.
23. Hans-Jürgen Andress et al., "The Economic Consequences of Partnership Dissolution—A Comparative Analysis of Panel Studies from Belgium, Germany, Great Britain, Italy, and Sweden," *European Sociological Review* 22, no. 5 (2006): 551. For an overview of studies on the economic consequences of divorce, see also Michael Gähler, "Life After Divorce: Economic, Social and Psychological Well-being among Swedish Adults and Children Following Family Dissolution" (PhD diss., Stockholm University, 1998), chapter 2.
24. McDonald, "Low Fertility in Australia," 15.
25. Paola di Giulio and Antonella Pinnelli, "The Gender System in Developed Countries: Macro and Micro Evidence," in *Genders in the Life Course: Demographic Issues*, ed. Antonella Pinnelli et al. (Dordrecht, 2007), 35.
26. Presser, "Comment," 179–80.
27. Valerie Kincade Oppenheimer, "Women's Rising Employment and the Future of the Family in Industrial Societies," *Population and Development Review* 20, no. 2 (1994): 315–18 and 331–34; Hobson and Oláh, "Tournant positif," 46.
28. Eva M. Bernhardt, "Fertility and Employment," *European Sociological Review* 9, no. 1 (1993): 34–35.
29. Shoshana Grossbard-Shechtman, "The New Home Economics at Columbia and Chicago," *Feminist Economics* 7, no. 3 (2001): 103–4.
30. Gary S. Becker, *A Treatise on the Family* (Cambridge, MA, 1991), 140.
31. Heather Joshi, "The Opportunity Costs of Childbearing: More than Mothers' Business," *Journal of Population Economics* 11, no. 2 (1998): 161–63.

32. Karin L. Brewster and Ronald R. Rindfuss, "Fertility and Women's Employment in Industrialized Nations," *Annual Review of Sociology* 26, (2000): 289–90.

33. See for example Brewster and Rindfuss, "Fertility and Women's Employment," 278; Namkee Ahn and Pedro Mira, "A Note on the Changing Relationship between Fertility and Female Employment Rates in Developed Countries," *Journal of Population Economics* 15, no. 4 (2002): 668; Rindfuss et al., "The Changing Institutional Context," 424.

34. Livia Sz. Oláh, "'Sweden, the Middle Way': A Feminist Approach," *European Journal of Women's Studies* 5, no. 1 (1998): 48 and 52.

35. Brewster and Rindfuss, "Fertility and Women's Employment," 283; Ahn and Mira, "A Note," 669; Rindfuss et al., "The Changing Institutional Context," 424–25.

36. OECD, "Balancing Work and Family Life: Helping Parents into Paid Employment," in *Employment Outlook 2001*, OECD (Paris, 2001), 143–45.

37. Hagemann, "Between Ideology," 217–18; Celia Valiente, "Central State Childcare Policies in Postauthoritarian Spain: Implications for Gender and Carework Arrangements," *Gender and Society* 17, no. 2 (2003): 289–90.

38. Gillian Pascall and Nick Manning, "Gender and Social Policy: Comparing Welfare States in Central and Eastern Europe and the Former Soviet Union," *Journal of European Social Policy* 10, no. 3 (2000): 248–50 and 252–56; Jirina Kocourková, "Leave Arrangements and Childcare Services in Central Europe: Policies and Practices before and after the Transition," *Community, Work & Family* 5, no. 3 (2002): 311–12 and 314–15.

39. I refer here to a broad age range between 15 and 64 years, but the same picture is seen also when focusing on women aged 15–39 years. See Livia Sz. Oláh, "Höga födelsetal i länder med utbyggd barnomsorg" *Välfärd*, no. 3 (Statistics Sweden, 2007): 6–7, 6.

40. It was indeed shown for Italy that limited availability of public childcare and part-time employment suppresses fertility. See Daniela Del Boca, "The Effect of Childcare and Part-Time Opportunities on Participation and Fertility Decisions in Italy," *Journal of Population Economics* 15, no. 3 (2002): 568.

41. Eurostat, *Total Fertility Rate*; LFS Series – Part-time employment; Retrieved: February 17, 2010 from http://epp.eurostat.ec.europa.eu/portal/page/portal/employment_unemployment_lfs/data/database.

42. Ibid.

43. For thorough overviews of such programs, see for example Kocourková, "Leave Arrangements," 306–13; Tommy Ferrarini, "Parental Leave Institutions in Eighteen Postwar Welfare States" (PhD diss., Stockholm University, 2003); Anne H. Gauthier, "Family Policies in Industrialized Countries: Is There Convergence?" *Population (English Edition)* 57, no. 3 (2002): 460–64.

44. OECD, *OECD Family Database*, PF11: Enrollment in Day-care and Pre-schools. Retrieved 5 February 2007: http://www.oecd.org/els/social/family/database.

45. Eurostat, *Total Fertility Rate*; OECD, *OECD Family Database*.

46. Gauthier, "Family Policies," 470; Kocourková, "Leave arrangements," 308–9.

47. Data on the desired average number of children in the first years of the twenty-first century are extracted from Bundesinstitut für Bevölkerungsforschung [BiB] and the Robert Bosch Foundation, eds., *The Demographic Future of Europe—Facts, Figures, Policies: Results of the Population Policy Acceptance Study (PPAS). Dialog*, 10. Retrieved 2 February 2007: http://www.bib-demographie.de/dialog_ppas_e.pdf. Eurostat-data on total fertility rates in 2004 are used for realized fertility.

48. Joshua Goldstein et al., "The Emergence of Sub-replacement Family Size Ideals in Europe," *Population Research and Policy Review* 22, no. 5–6 (2003): 490–91; Wolfgang Lutz and Vegard Skirbekk, "Policies Addressing the Tempo Effect in Low-Fertility Countries," *Population and Development Review* 31, no. 4 (2005): 703.

49. A cohort is constituted by people born in the same year.

50. Jean-Paul Sardon and Glenn D. Robertson, "Recent Demographic Trends in the Developed Countries," *Population (English Edition)* 59, no. 2 (2004): 300f.

51. Tomás Sobotka, "Postponement of Childbearing and Low Fertility in Europe" (PhD diss., University of Groningen, 2004), 143–45.

52. Francesco C. Billari, "The Transition to Parenthood in European Societies," in *Policy Implications of Changing Family Formation: Study Prepared for the European Population Conference 2005, Population Studies,* no. 49, ed. Linda Hantrais et al. (Strasbourg, 2006), 78.

53. Ibid.; Sardon and Robertsson, "Recent Demographic Trends," 300–301.

54. Goldstein et al., "The Emergence," 490–91.

55. Billari, "The Transition to Parenthood," 78; INED, *Population in Figures.*

56. European Commission, "Childcare Services," in *Reconciliation of Work and Private Life: A Comparative Review of Thirty European Countries* (Luxembourg, 2005), 42.

57. David Sven Reher, "Family Ties in Western Europe: Persistent Contrasts," *Population and Development Review* 24, no. 2 (1998): 234 and 215.

58. Dirk J. van de Kaa, "Postmodern Fertility Preferences: From Changing Value Orientation to New Behavior," *Population and Development Review* 27 Supplement: Global Fertility Transition (2001): 301f., 314, and 324.

Part III

CASE STUDIES

Time Policies of Childcare, Preschool, and Primary Education In Europe

Section A

All-Day Childcare and Education Systems
in Western Europe

Chapter 6

THE BEST INTEREST OF THE CHILD
Early Childhood Education in Norway and Sweden since 1945

Tora Korsvold

The labor and family policies of the Norwegian and Swedish states offer a remarkably wide selection of publicly funded social welfare programs and services. In keeping with the strong egalitarian traditions of these countries, their welfare policies are "universal" in orientation—that is, they are available for everybody—and aim for a decommodification of social rights. Like the other Scandinavian welfare states, they are maintained by a high level of direct taxation on both the working population and businesses, as well as a variety of special taxes.[1] Indeed, given their scope, in order to function effectively they require a large number of employees and a high income tax to pay for them. Social democracy was the driving force behind social reform in Scandinavia. It "pursued a welfare state that would promote a quality of the highest standards, not an equality of minimal needs."[2]

In the comparative scholarship on welfare states, Norway and Sweden are often regarded as representing the most highly developed type of welfare state, models for gender equality, and the best system of "public measures for children."[3] Current data confirm this judgment. Norway and Sweden are among the countries with the highest rate of female employment. In 2004, 73 percent of all Norwegian and 71 percent of all Swedish women were employed, compared to an average in the European Union of 55 percent. Forty-six percent of all employed Norwegian and 37 percent of all employed Swedish women worked part-time; the EU average was 31 percent. This is the highest female participation rate in the workforce in the European Union. Even France, with its high rate of female employment (67 percent full-time, 30 percent part-time), ranks below Norway and Sweden. The high level of female employment in Norway and Sweden is the result of a welfare policy that has been based on the dual-earner family model for more than three decades, and a labor policy that has offered women many (part-time) jobs in a greatly expanding public service sector. Public all-day childcare for children up to the age of six and after-school care are key components of this welfare and labor policy. In 2003, 44 percent of all children between the ages of one and three in Norway and 65 percent in Sweden were enrolled in a publicly funded childcare facility. The percentage of three- to five-year-old children was even higher, at 86 and 94 percent, respectively.[4] The quality of these public childcare programs is by all measures higher than in most other European countries. As is the case in France, the statistics indicate that the idea of mothers working outside the home and even small children being cared for during the day in a childcare center enjoys widespread cultural acceptance in Scandinavia, which is supported by the fact that childcare is considered in Norway and in Sweden a public responsibility, and is financed by the state, local municipalities, and modest parental fees. With its women- and children-friendly orientation, this publicly funded and institutionalized welfare state policy has contributed crucially to a relatively high fertility rate of 1.9 in both countries, a level that far exceeds the EU average of 1.5 in 2007.[5] All attempts by conservative parties to change this policy when they controlled the government proved unsuccessful in the long run, which can be seen as yet another sign of the policy's effectiveness and popularity.[6]

The unique combination of high-tech capitalism and a women- and children-friendly welfare policy in Norway and Sweden owes its success above all to the modern and highly industrialized economy in these countries, both of which possess a large public-service sector and a well-educated workforce. Unlike most of Europe, Sweden enjoyed peace and neutrality throughout the twentieth century, a condition that enabled it to develop a prosperous modern economy. Indeed, even during World War II, Sweden, while officially neutral, was able to sustain its economy by supplying Nazi Germany with iron ore, steel, machine parts, and other products.[7] Emerging from the war with its economy more or less intact, Sweden experienced a postwar boom that enabled the Swedish Social Democratic Workers Party (Sveriges socialdemokratiska arbetareparti, SAP) the dominant force in Swedish politics since 1945, to create its unique welfare state.

Norway, on the other hand, was occupied in April 1940 by the German *Wehrmacht*, and thus experienced exploitation and humiliation at the hands of the Third Reich until the end of the war. Nevertheless, after

1945 the Norwegian Social Democrats, like their counterparts in Sweden, initiated a similarly ambitious program of social reform that aimed at reducing income inequality, eliminating poverty, expanding social services for all citizens, and increasing public holdings in the economy. While Norway's industrial economy continued to lag behind Sweden's until the 1960s, in 1963 it asserted sovereign rights over natural resources in its sector of the North Sea. The exploitation of its maritime oil and gas reserves over the past four decades has made Norway one of the richest countries in Europe, second only to Luxembourg, and indeed the entire world.[8] The citizens of both states enjoy a high and relatively equal standard of living, and although inequalities and income disparity are increasing, compared with children in most other European countries, Norwegian and Swedish children are privileged, at least in material terms.[9]

By using a comparative historical approach that takes into account economy, politics, and culture, in this chapter I explore the key factors that influenced the development of the early childhood education policy in Norway and Sweden and outline the context-specific patterns and characteristics of each childcare system and its time structure.[10] With my analysis I attempt to answer two main questions: First, which factors supported the establishment of a public childcare and preschool system in both states? And second, which factors stimulated the creation of an all-day time policy for early childhood education?

A comparison of Norway and Sweden can prove highly revealing, because both countries exhibit several similarities in the growth of their childcare sectors, which have become largely a public responsibility. At the same time, both welfare states have been shaped by different priorities in solving the issue of reconciling family and work and organizing childcare. A close comparison can shed light on several often-overlooked differences between Scandinavian welfare states in the long-term origins and development of public childcare.[11] These differences are especially evident in the specific way both systems responded to the new demands of the postwar labor market to integrate women as well as how they dealt with the need to reconcile family and work. If we want to understand these differences, we cannot simply analyze the economic and political conditions and the important role of the state. We also need to study cultural conceptions of the "role of the state" in education and childcare, the "duties of families and mothers," and the "appropriate gender order."[12] My analysis thus draws on historical scholarship that has demonstrated the impact of culture and gender on early childhood education.[13]

In order to shed light on the origins and development of the childcare system and its time policy in Norway and Sweden, I first describe developments in the 1930s and 1940s, when a vision of the modern Scandinavian welfare state began to emerge, and then turn to the 1950s, when the practical implementation of this vision started. From there, I examine the 1960s and 1970s, when the structural changes in the labor markets, above all the large-scale entry of women into the workforce, stimulated a new approach to the "women's question" and childcare. Finally, I reflect on the new challenges facing the labor market today and their possible impact on time policies.

The State, Population, and Childcare in the 1930s and 1940s

The public interest in childcare in Norway and Sweden can be traced back to the first half of the nineteenth century.[14] Until the second half of the twentieth century, however, provisions for children in both states were divided along class lines. Starting in the 1830s, crèches (*asyl*) offered all-day care for children of poor, working-class mothers. The main function of these crèches, which were often free of charge, was to supervise their small children and prevent "social damage." Somewhat later, kindergartens (*barnehager* or *barnträdgårder*) were established with parents having to pay for their half-day service. They followed the ideas of German educator Friedrich Fröbel and aimed for a better cognitive and social education of middle-class children. Both types of institutions were local and mostly private initiatives. As was the case elsewhere in Europe, the main providers of both forms of childcare were churches (in Sweden mainly the Protestant Church) and philanthropic associations.[15]

It was not until the early 1930s that social reformers began discussing new ideas about the relationship between the state, the family, work, and childcare and questioning the class-based approach to childcare and childhood. Already in 1928, Social Democrats in Sweden put forward the program of the *folkhemmet* (people's home), an essentially new vision for society based on notions of equality, well-being, and social solidarity that has guided the creation of the country's welfare state ever since. Indeed, realizing the goals of the people's home was the core political aim of the Social Democrats who, in alliance with the Agrarian Party, enjoyed broad popular support and dominated Sweden's politics from 1932 to 1976.[16] The Social Democratic Labor Party of Norway took over the government for the first time in 1935 and remained in power until 1981 (except for the exile period between 1940 and 1945 and the years of opposition between 1965 and 1971).[17] In both countries, early childhood education became an important field of social democratic policy. But unlike in Sweden where the discourse about this policy field had already begun to take shape in the 1930s, the family did not figure much at all in public policy discourse in Norway until the 1950s, when a specific family policy began to emerge there as well.[18] Sweden, therefore, had a head start of more than two decades.

One of the leading intellectuals in Sweden pushing for a fundamental rethinking of the state's role in childcare was the Social Democrat Alva Myrdal, who had campaigned for equal rights for women since the 1920s. Above all, Myrdal demanded a social policy that would allow married mothers to combine motherhood and paid work outside the home. Together with her husband Gunnar Myrdal, she helped to set a new tone in the ongoing public discussion about the "threatening decline" of the Swedish population. They coauthored the book *Crisis in the Population Question,* which was published in Swedish in 1934. The basic premise of this book was that new social reforms were needed to promote individual liberty and equality, in particular for women. Above all, the Myrdals advocated a double-earner family model and public all-day childcare. Only such a modernization of family policy, they argued, could halt the decline of the birth rate.[19]

In 1935, growing fears of the declining birth rate, which were common throughout Europe, led the social democratic government to establish a parliamentary Commission on Population, of which Gunnar Myrdal was a member. Following his suggestions, the commission declared that if the government wanted to increase the birth rate, social reforms would be necessary. One of the first new measures designed to meet the demographic crisis was a governmental subsidy for private childcare institutions. The commission argued that even if this might not raise the birth rate, it would still help to produce higher-quality children.[20]

Like her husband, Alva Myrdal became a leader of Swedish social democracy. In 1943, she was appointed to the party's program committee that was tasked with drafting a postwar party program. In that same year, she joined the Government Commission on International Postwar Aid and Reconstruction. Early childhood education was one of the fields in which her ideas became most influential. She demanded that all children, regardless of their social background, should have the opportunity to attend an "expanded nursery school" (*storbarnkammar*) that should integrate children from all classes and eliminate all differences that existed between the traditional day nurseries and kindergartens.[21] This more pedagogically oriented form of childcare should help children to become "better citizens." At the same time it would offer a more effective way of providing supervision of "endangered children."[22] This proposal was part of her larger agenda to attain greater social equality by reducing differences in the standard of living and by providing equal access to education to all children. State subsidies should provide certain services for the public, such as "expanded nurseries" and "good schools" that provided children with meals, both of which would help to reach this goal. But according to Myrdal, these reforms would only prove efficacious if the state showed people how they could make the best possible use of these services. In fact, Myrdal's approach to childcare and education was informed by the strong belief that raising children in a modern industrial society was simply too difficult and complex a task for parents to cope with on their own.[23]

Equally important to the discourse on social reform in Swedish social democracy were Alva Myrdal's ideas regarding the "women's questions." She insisted on the double role of women as mothers and workers. In her view, every citizen who is capable of working should have a paid job, including married mothers with small children, because she saw economic independence as a precondition for equal citizenship of men and women alike.[24] Like her ideas on early childhood education, this position, which is widely accepted today in the Nordic countries, was very radical in the 1930s. But during the 1940s and 1950s, her reform agenda gained increasing influence and acceptance in the Swedish Social Democratic Party.[25]

Equality, the Labor Market, and Family Policy in the 1950s and 1960s

Following World War II, interest in the welfare of young children grew in both countries considerably. Politicians of all parties now regarded public investment in children not just as a social and moral good and a necessary condition for peace and democracy, but also as a premise for continued economic development. One of the first examples of this policy change was the introduction of child allowances in Norway (1946) and Sweden (1947). A flat-rate, tax-free child allowance, which was granted to the mother regardless of the employment status of both parents, replaced the old child tax deduction. In Sweden, this child allowance was given to all mothers, with very few exceptions. In Norway, the allowance was only paid to mothers with two or more children.[26]

The introduction of a child allowance was in both countries the first family policy reform after the war. Many more reforms followed in the next decades, first in Sweden and usually ten years later in Norway. The major reason for this time gap was the different economic situation of both countries. In Norway, the postwar demobilization had led to a more conservative social and family policy. As was the case in other countries involved in the war, the family became the core institution for the reconstruction of the social and political order. Norway's first political priority after the war was to put men back to work. Women were encouraged to concentrate on domestic life. The care of young children remained their exclusive responsibility. The government stimulated new industries and invested in the infrastructure of the still more agrarian country by building roads and expanding the electrical power supply. Female work in industry and the service sector was not needed until the 1960s. The low female employment rate in postwar Norway is an indicator of this development, with mostly single mothers engaged in paid work outside the household. In 1950, only 26 percent of all Norwegian women fifteen years or older were employed. By 1960, this percentage had declined to 24 percent where it hardly budged for the next decade, reaching 25 percent in 1970.[27]

Sweden, which had suffered less during the war years, began to prosper soon after World War II. Stimulated by aid from the Marshall Plan, it experienced an "economic miracle" during the 1950s and was able to build a modern, export-oriented market economy while at the same time quickly expanding the size of its public service sector, both of which required a skilled work force. Because of this economic postwar boom, the Swedish government found itself in a unique position to construct, earlier and more effectively than its Nordic neighbors, a welfare state that included public services for young children. Part of the economic growth was a dramatic increase in the percentage of women who worked outside the home. In 1950, 35 percent of all Swedish women between the ages of 15 and 64 were employed. By 1960, this rate had risen to 50 percent, climbing to 59 percent by 1970. Not only single women, but increasingly married women and mothers as well began working in industry and the service sector. In 1945, the percentage of employed married women was less than 11 percent. In 1950, it had risen to 15 percent, 25 percent in 1960, and 33 percent in 1966. Yet, the difference between the average rate of female employment (54 percent) and the employment rate of mothers with children under sixteen (47 percent) was still considerable in 1965. A decade later, however, these rates had converged at 68 and 66 percent, respectively. This high degree of integration of female labor in general and married women in particular in Sweden was unique in postwar Europe. This development was largely the result of an increase in the public service sector, in which already by 1960 more than 57 percent of the employees were women.[28]

In the 1950s and 1960s, social democratic governments in both Norway and Sweden worked to modernize their societies through policies that aimed at social integration and equality. Indeed, both considered it the state's duty to provide equality of opportunity for all members of society.[29] Education, which they perceived as a microcosm of society, became one of the most important policy arenas in which to achieve this ambitious goal. In order to contribute to democratic socialization, they advocated the "comprehensive school" as a site of interaction among children from different social backgrounds.[30] The focus of education reform in the early postwar years was thus compulsory school education, not childcare, which was still defined as a form of welfare.

Throughout the 1950s and 1960s, the Swedish debate on childcare was driven largely by the increase of women's, including mother's, participation in the workforce.[31] Already in 1951 the Swedish Committee for Childcare, which had been established five years earlier, presented a report entitled *Day Nurseries and Preschools* (*Daghem och förskolor*). Its authors argued that if women chose paid work outside of the home over their previously prescribed role as housewives, society, represented by the state, should support them by providing childcare services.[32] The government was aware of this challenge, but it did not develop an effective response until the 1960s.[33] Although small public grants for private childcare facilities had been available since the 1940s and were dramatically raised in the 1950s, until the 1970s the demand for public childcare was far greater than the supply. In 1965, only 3 percent of all preschool children under six were in public childcare, mostly day nurseries, while another 4 percent attended private institutions, many of which were kindergartens and preschools (mostly open only half days). The majority of the children of working mothers were still supervised in private care arrangements, including childminders, relatives, or neighbors. In 1975, the percentage of preschool children under six in public childcare was considerably higher at 17 percent, but the number of publicly funded places remained insufficient.[34] As a result, in the 1960s the goal of governmental policy increasingly became to provide all groups of children, especially those from less privileged backgrounds, equal access to publicly funded, all-day childcare and education.[35]

One important factor that supported this change in Sweden was the emerging debate over gender roles (*kjönsrolledebatten*) since the early 1960s. As was the case in Norway, until then the political discourse on equality in the postwar era had focused above all on promoting equal opportunity (social, economic, and geographic) for all groups in society.[36] But this began to change as an increasing number of women inside and outside the Social Democratic Party, together with trade unions, demanded that men and women should have equal roles in society. They questioned the ideal of the male-breadwinner family, which was still widely accepted in the 1950s. The idea that men and women should enjoy equal opportunities in employment and that married women should be able to achieve economic independence through paid work outside the home gained widespread acceptance. Promoting this idea was above all the Swedish women's movement, which closely cooperated with the government, the Social Democratic Party, and the trade unions.[37] As women's rights achieved greater acceptance in Sweden, a new time policy that sought to balance paid work and childcare began to emerge.

A similar process occurred in Norway a decade later. One reason for this time lag was that female employment there began to rise later than in Sweden.[38] But more importantly, until the late 1960s the Norwegian labor government pursued a more conservative family policy that aimed for the universalization of the male-breadwinner family.[39] The 1950s are therefore described in the literature on Norway as the "golden era of the family" or the "era of a happy childhood."[40] Even the majority of Norwegian women supported this policy and did not demand more all-day childcare facilities. One example is the National Union of Housewives, which in the 1960s established "housewives' preschools" (*Husmødrenes barnehager*). These were not conceived of as a way to help working mothers, but rather as a way of making life easier and more comfortable for "stay-at-home-moms" and their children. While the latter had the opportunity to socialize with their peers, mothers were able to complete their household chores without distractions.[41] As a result of this policy, the percentage of children between the ages of three and six who attended childcare centers in 1965 was quite low at 3 percent, and indeed considerably lower than in Sweden where the percentage stood at 7 percent. The employment rate of mothers with younger children of 15 percent in 1960 also reflected the Norwegian family policy. In that same year, Sweden posted a rate of 37 percent.[42] It was not until the late 1960s, when the percentage of women and mothers who worked outside the home began to increase steadily in Norway as well, that the discourse there also started to change and all-day childcare became a demand.

This demand for all-day childcare, however, faced serious challenges in both countries. Above all, it ran counter to the dominant cultural ideal of children and "a good childhood." This longstanding Nordic ideal held that children belonged to their families and the best place for them to enjoy "free" or unstructured play with their peers would be an outdoor environment close to their own homes. Given the continued resonance of agrarian values in the postwar period, it is not surprising that a childhood in the countryside was perceived in both countries as the best possible option.[43] Indeed, this ideal was shared even by social democratic politicians until the 1950s. Its persistence is illustrated by a debate in the parliamentary Commission on Day Nurseries and Preschools. The majority of the committee members believed that longer stays in day nurseries would have a deleterious impact on early childhood development. Citing the opinions of psychologists and other experts, their report noted that day nurseries posed a potential risk for young children's, and especially infants' physical and mental health.[44]

In both countries, the idea that the family was the "best possible" environment for raising children informed—in Sweden until the 1950s and in Norway until the 1960s—a specific gender model for childcare. Most experts, including child psychologists, doctors, and educational scientists, argued that nursery schools (*lekskolan*) and kindergartens should be supported for "the sake of the children," but should not be open longer than four hours each day. They advocated half-day childcare and preschool as the best solution for children aged three to six, because all-day nurseries would keep young children away from home for too long. In their opinion, children under the age of three should not attend such institutions at all, but instead should stay at home with their mothers, who were considered the best qualified to care for them. Children under three, so they argued, remained in a "presocial phase" and thus were unable to benefit from being together with other children in their peer group.[45] The only accepted exceptions to this rule were children of single and working mothers who needed to earn a living for the family because of their unfortunate circumstances. For these children, day nurseries were perceived of as a necessary welfare measure.[46]

This discourse on childcare, children, and childhood created a "regime of truth" that was shaped above all by child psychology. Its arguments were part of a powerful strategy to prevent the extension of all-day childcare. In Norway, this discourse was so influential that until the 1960s, the Norwegian government hesitated to support childcare, especially day nurseries (*daghjem*). When in 1963 the Norwegian state finally started to subsidize day nurseries and kindergartens (or *barnehager*), child experts still continued to regard public day nurseries as harmful to children. They went on to argue that three to four hours was the maximum amount of time that would still be in the best interest of the child.[47] Their argumentation, moreover, was highly gendered, because it demanded that the mother stay at home and take care of her children.[48]

A New Time Policy of Childcare since the Late 1960s

By the end of the 1960s, the main goal of early childhood education in Sweden became, despite all resistance, to provide all-day places in public childcare to all those who needed them, especially the rapidly increasing number of mothers who worked outside the home. A consensus emerged within both the discourse on welfare and the discourse on gender equality that public resources should concentrate primarily on day nurseries. This was a paradigmatic change, because until then the priority for public funding had been given to half-day nursery schools.[49] In 1963, the Swedish parliament raised the yearly subsidy of childcare by 25 percent. Two years later, it passed a bill excluding half-day nursery schools from further subsidies. Henceforth all resources were to be concentrated on day nurseries. To meet the needs of both women and industry, the government thus undertook a fundamental reform of its childcare policy. The number of places rose from 18,000 in 1965 to 125,000 in 1975 after the National Preschool Act was introduced in 1974. This law obligated local authorities to expand public early childhood education. The municipalities were now required to provide all six-year-olds with at least 525 hours of free preschooling (i.e., part-time education). For younger children, however, eligibility for a place in a public childcare was linked to their parents' employment status. Exceptions were made primarily for children in need of special support. Until 1985, when the social democratic government increased its efforts, the demand for public childcare was always greater than the supply.[50]

At the same time that the Swedish government was expanding the number of places in publicly funded all-day nursery schools, it also started to reform the older system of private day nurseries, which were primarily childcare institutions, and half-day-kindergartens that focused on education. Both institutions were merged to form the modern, publicly funded all-day centers (*dagis*), which closely integrate education and childcare as inseparable activities for all children between the ages of one and six. The main goal of this reform was the improvement of early childhood education, which was now perceived as part of the education system. As was the case in other European countries, a new understanding of education as an economic resource that could stimulate labor supply and thereby economic growth influenced this reform. Industrial growth in turn meant increased welfare for all.[51] This new thinking directly affected the time structure of childcare: the former reservations against all-day childcare and education were no longer tenable in a modern economy that needed female labor. A new understanding of childhood, in which young children would spend some time at home and some at all-day centers, along with a new gender contract, which recognized a woman's right to pursue her own career and achieve economic independence, were better suited to the needs of Sweden's expanding labor market.

From the beginning, a basic assumption of the Scandinavian welfare state was the importance of striving for inclusion and integration in society. To achieve this goal and overcome social divisions in society, beginning in the 1960s policymakers increasingly focused on early childhood education. Among other things, they aimed for a combination of education and care in full-time daycare centers for all children between the ages of one and six. This new development corresponded in many ways to the vision of childcare and gender equality that Alva Myrdal had first articulated in the 1930s. Indeed, her ideas provided a rhetorical framework for the social democratic discourse in Sweden and Norway in the 1960s and 1970s. The driving force behind the changes in childcare and education policy, however, was not Myrdal's vision of improving the "quality" of children or advancing "mothers' right to paid work." Instead, it was above all the new realities of the labor market and the economy that laid bare the need for a more effective system of childcare and education.[52] Different than West Germany, both countries preferred to integrate more married women and mothers into the labor market, instead of recruiting a large numbers of foreign "guest workers."[53]

However, the resistance against all-day childcare persisted much longer in Norway than in Sweden. Public provision of childcare in Norway did not begin until the Kindergarten Act came into force in 1975. This was due not just to the conservative family policy and the weaker demand for female labor in the 1950s and 1960s, but also to the more enduring persistence of the cultural ideal of "a good childhood." This concept went hand in hand with a deeply rooted ambiguity regarding the institutionalization of childcare. The 1975 decision of the Norwegian parliament to adopt in the first childcare law "kindergarten" (*barnehage*) instead of "preschool" (*førskole*) as the official term for all childcare institutions reflected the desire to "protect the golden age of childhood."[54] The Kindergarten Act explicitly defined daycare centers as a municipal domain. However, municipalities were not obliged to provide daycare, but only to plan such services. In order to pursue a national daycare policy, the government thus developed a financial incentive system. For each child they enrolled, approved centers received a government grant calculated according to the child's age and attendance. This grant, however, covered only one-third of the operating costs; the remaining sum had to be shared by the parents and the owner (public or private). It was not until 1997 that the Norwegian government made six the age for starting school. Of course, daycare centers existed in Norway before the Kindergarten Act, but as a result of this law, twenty years later all municipalities offered daycare services, even though the levels of coverage varied considerably (between 25 and 91 percent of all eligible children) from place to place.[55]

Thus, the 1960s in Sweden and the 1970s in Norway marked the beginning of a new policy that aimed to increase and accelerate the building of full-time childcare centers. This new policy sought to accommodate the growing demand for a time policy that would seek to balance care and work. Public institutions for childcare shifted from the domain of social policy to that of labor policy. Indeed, childcare became increasingly subordinated to the demands of industrial growth, women's right to work, and the household's purchasing power. According to this new logic, the best way to improve conditions for children was to give both parents the opportunity to enter paid employment. As a result, the double-earner family model became the norm.

Consequently, governments in both countries developed a generous work-oriented family policy that ultimately resulted in transforming mothers and fathers alike into breadwinners and caregivers. Two of the most important instruments were a reform of the tax system and the parental leave policy. Here Norway's government acted first by reforming its tax codes in 1969 in order to encourage greater gender equality. Sweden followed in 1971. Since there were no longer tax or other benefits for families with only male breadwinners, they came to depend more and more on both incomes for their livelihoods, even if income disparities between husbands and wives continued to persist.[56] In 1973, the Swedish government introduced paid parental leave. Norway passed a similar law in 1977. The expectation in both countries, but most clearly in Sweden, was for parents to return to their jobs after a period of paid leave, and entrust their child(ren) to public care, which was now described as equally good and necessary as private care in the family.[57]

This development clearly fostered the equality of women, but at the same time raised important questions concerning the position of children. Now that all children could benefit from institutional pedagogical care, policymakers, educators, and other experts increasingly argued—as Alva Myrdal had in the 1930s—that raising children was too difficult for parents to do on their own. They would need public support; in their eyes, parental care in the home remained important, but was not enough. Instead, children needed to develop cultural and social skills for their future life. The best possible place to do this was, these experts argued, all-day childcare. They now considered the time spent in a day nursery as an important aspect of childhood, because modern society would demand that competent and well-socialized citizens cooperate with each other in an ever-changing environment. In short, by the end of the 1970s, a new concept of childhood based on the idea of the "modern public childcare child" had emerged that would have enormous consequences for public policy and found broad support in society.[58]

The Time Policy of Childcare Today

As was the case in the 1960s and 1970s, there remains today a clear relationship between special care arrangements for small children and the continuing evolution of the labor market. Unlike many advanced industrial societies, childcare provisions in the two Scandinavian countries have not fallen victim to the trend towards state retrenchment that has occurred in the wake of globalization and neoliberalism. On the contrary, public childcare provision has steadily increased. In fact, during the 1990s in Norway, which had always lagged behind Sweden in this area, childcare emerged as one of the most extensive areas of the welfare state. One of the main goals of the Norwegian government since the end of 1980s has been to fund childcare centers fully for all children. As a result, most childcare centers in Norway today provide all-day care for children as young as one or two years of age.[59]

Today all childcare centers in Norway and Sweden are funded and, for the most part, owned and operated by municipalities. Parents only pay a portion of the costs. Early childhood education is seen as a public responsibility, not the task of employers or private institutions like the churches. Indeed, access to early childhood education is considered a child's right. Unsurprisingly, childcare arrangements, their coverage and alternatives to them, and how they are to be paid for are, therefore, among the most important issues that shape the discourse on childcare in Scandinavia. But while this discourse does reflect budgetary concerns, it is equally informed by ideological preferences.

Since the mid-1990s, childcare debates in Sweden and Norway have been increasingly influenced by growing demand for a so-called freedom of choice. Conservatives have argued that parents should have a greater degree of choice between public childcare and a more family-based welfare. As a consequence of this debate, in the 1990s Norway introduced provisions including the cash benefit for parents with small children (*kontantstøtte*), while both states have instituted various new allowances for maternity and paternity leaves (i.e., a leave quota for fathers, the "daddy quota").

In 1998, after several years of highly contested debate, Norway introduced the *kontantstøtte* for one-year-olds. A year later, this benefit was extended for two- and three-year-olds. Despite the existence of numerous public services aimed at reconciling work and family, many parents with small children continued to complain about the lack of time that they could spend with their families. They thus demanded a new time policy that would achieve a better balance between paid work and care. Indeed, the *kontantstøtte*, which was proposed by the more conservative Norwegian Christian Democratic Party, was designed to enable parents to spend less time at work and more time at home with their families. Social Democrats, however, argued that the *kontantstøtte* would have a long-term negative impact on gender equality. Moreover, they believed that this new benefit would only help to reproduce a traditional gender order and potentially increase women's dependency on their husband's wages, thereby making it harder to reenter the labor market. Finally, critics of this policy thought that the *kontantstøtte* ran the risk of isolating underprivileged children and mothers at home, hardly the outcome welfare policy should bring about. Instead, Social Democrats argued that children could continue to attend childcare centers part-time at the same time that their parent received the cash benefit.[60] In contrast to this cash-for-care reform plan, the extension of parental leave, including for fathers, in Norway in 1993 and Sweden in 1994 was not controversial. In 1994, fathers' share of total maternity, paternity, and parental leave benefit days per year was 12 percent in Sweden and 3.9 percent in Norway; ten years later, their portion had increased to 19.7 percent in Sweden and 9.0 percent in Norway.[61]

These two reforms represent distinctly different approaches to time policy and achieving gender balance in paid work and childcare.[62] Although the so-called "daddy quota" challenges traditional gender roles, the cash-for-care reform strengthens them. The "daddy quota" is still the pattern of the social democratic welfare regime, which prevailed throughout the 1970s. The new, more conservative regime, therefore, has retained some aspects of the social democratic agenda, but at the same time, with its emphasis on free choice, also reflects the concerns of neo-liberalism, at least rhetorically.

In the labor market, the trend has been towards achieving greater flexibility in working hours, also a reflection of neoliberal priorities. Here again, the idea of freedom of choice confirms a growing concern with the individualization of childcare. The new and ever-changing demands of a labor market that aims for unlimited access to its human resources and more flexibility have and continue to shape the time policy of work and childcare.[63] This development of the modern labor market is increasingly rendering old work schedules irrelevant and with them the standards according to which the time policy of childcare is formulated. It presents one of the most challenging problems to future welfare state reform in Norway and Sweden and many other highly industrialized countries, namely, how to combine in a humane way the necessities of the labor market with the needs of parents and children.[64]

Conclusion

Exploring the roots of early childhood education can help us understand some of the differences regarding gender, work, and the family in the Scandinavian welfare states, which are usually perceived as one similar group of "social democratic" welfare regimes. The analysis here has demonstrated that we need to pay more attention to the cultural factors that have shaped welfare states and welfare policies if we want to understand the differences between Scandinavian welfare states—in our case, Norway and Sweden. At first glance, both states appear to exhibit remarkably similar patterns in terms of their time policy of childcare. But an historical approach that integrates the cultural dimension, including the prevailing ideas about the gender order and education, has revealed key differences. These differences were shaped not least of all by the divergent history during World War II, which put both states at different starting points in 1945. As a result, Sweden experienced an economic boom in the 1950s while the process of industrial modernization in Norway was delayed for nearly a decade. Cultural traditions and prevailing concepts of the role of the family and the state, the gender order, education, and childhood also influenced the distinct development in both countries. In addition, the role of the Social Democratic Party and the intellectual influence of individual leaders like Alva and Gunnar Myrdal in Sweden had a profound effect.

And yet, despite all the differences in the paths these states took, both achieved universal and public early childhood education and emerged as societies that fully embrace the double-earner family model. In addition, we see in both countries an active, interventionist state that sought to regulate mothers' and fathers' time for work and childcare, even if they took different approaches to doing so. Moreover, the outcome in each country has been essentially the same: a new care contract between the state and families. Of course, the construction of this new care contract, which rested not least of all upon the expansion of childcare centers, was driven most notably by economic demands and realities. At the same time, notions of greater equality and democratic rights also contributed to its development. Thus, the time policy that they constructed encouraged gender equality in parenting and work as well as the right of children of all social backgrounds to enjoy a happy childhood with their peers in publicly funded childcare centers. In short, the two Scandinavian countries have proven remarkably successful in balancing work and care, and thus are usually cited as models for effective welfare policy in Europe.

Notes

1. "Scandinavia" normally refers to the Scandinavian peninsula (Norway and Sweden), to the area of Scandinavian languages (Denmark, Iceland, Norway, and Sweden), and to a variation of welfare regimes: the Scandinavian social democratic welfare regime (Denmark, Norway, and Sweden). See Gøsta Esping-Andersen, *The Three Worlds of Welfare*

Capitalism (Cambridge, UK, 1990), 9–34. In this chapter, I mostly use the term in the first and third meaning.

2. Esping-Andersen, *The Three Worlds*, 27; Gøsta Esping-Andersen, "Towards the Good-Society, Once Again?" and "A Child-Centred Social Investment-Strategy," in *Why We Need a New Welfare State*, ed. Gøsta Esping-Andersen et al. (Oxford, 2002), 1–15 and 16–67. See also the introduction by Karen Hagemann, Konrad H. Jarausch, and Cristina Allemann-Ghionda in this volume.

3. Arnlaug Leira, *Welfare States and Working Mothers: The Scandinavian Experience* (Cambridge, UK, 1992); Arnlaug Leira, *Working Parents and the Welfare State: Family Change and Policy Reform in Scandinavia* (Cambridge, UK, 2002); Anne Lise Ellingsæter and Arnlaug Leira, eds., *Politicising Parenthood in Scandinavia: Gender Relations in Welfare State* (Bristol, 2006).

4. OECD, *Starting Strong II: Early Childhood Education and Care* (Paris, 2006), 78; Dietmar Rauch, "Is There Really a Scandinavian Social Service Model? A Comparison of Childcare and Elderlycare in Six European Countries," *Acta Sociologica* 50, no. 3 (2007): 249–69.

5. Populations Reference Bureau, *2007 World Population Data Sheet* (Washington, DC, 2007), 9; Gerda Neyer et al., *Fertilität, Familiengründung und Familienerweiterung in den nordischen Ländern*, Max Planck Institute für demographische Forschung, Working Paper (Rostock, 2006), 45.

6. See Wiebke Kolbe, *Elternschaft im Wohlfahrtsstaat. Schweden und die Bundesrepublik im Vergleich 1945–1995* (Frankfurt/M., 2002); Christina Bergquist and Anita Nyberg, "Welfare State Restructuring and Child Care in Sweden," in *Child Care Policy at the Crossroads: Gender and Welfare State Restructuring*, ed. Sonya Michel and Rianne Mahon (New York, 2002), 287–308.

7. Byron J. Nordstrom, *Scandinavia since 1500* (Minneapolis, 2000), 315–19.

8. For more, see Fritz Hodne, *The Norwegian Economy 1920–1980* (New York, 1983).

9. An-Magritt Jensen et al., "Childhood and Generation in Norway: Money, Time and Space," in *Children's Welfare in Ageing Europe*, ed. An-Magritt Jensen et al. (Trondheim, 2004), vol. 1: 335–402.

10. I am drawing on sociologist Arnlaug Leira's definition and use the term *childcare* for all forms of childcare and preschool facilities for which public approval is required and public subsidies are provided. See Leira, *Welfare States*, 65 and 95.

11. Jane Lewis, *Gender, Social Care, and Welfare State Restructuring in Europe* (Aldershot, 1998).

12. See Ann Taylor Allen, *Feminism and Motherhood in Western Europe 1890–1970: The Maternal Dilemma* (New York, 2005), 8–15.

13. On the history of the concept of public childcare, see Gunnhild Kyle, *Gästarbeterska i manssamhället: Studier om industriarbetande kvinnors villkor i Sverige* (Stockholm, 1979); Anne Lise Seip, *Veiene til velferdsstaten: Norsk sosialpolitikk 1920–1970* (Oslo, 1994); Tora Korsvold, "Profesjonalisert barndom: statlige intensjoner og kvinnelig praksis på barnehagens arena 1945–1990" (PhD diss., University of Trondheim, 1997); Christina Bergqvist, ed., *Equal Democracies? Gender and Politics in the Nordic Countries* (Oslo, 1999); Ann Katrin Hatje, *Fraan treklang till triangeldrama: Barnträdgaarden som ett kvinnligt samhällsprojekt under 1880–1940-talen* (Lund, 1999).

14. Because of this long tradition, scholarship on these two countries as pioneers of the advocacy of children's interests and rights as well as child provision is quite extensive. See, for example, Göran Therborn, "The Politics of Childhood: The Rights of Children since the Constitution of Modern Childhood: A Comparative Study of Western Nations," in *Families of Nations*, ed. F. G. Castles (Aldershot, 1993), 241–91; Mirja Satka and Gudny

Bjoerk Eydal, "The History of Nordic Welfare Policies for Children," in *Beyond the Competent Child. Exploring Contemporary Childhoods in the Nordic Welfare Societies*, ed. Helene Brembeck et al. (Roskilde, 2005), 33–60; Baldur Kristjansson, "The Making of Nordic Childhoods," in *Nordic Childhoods and Early Education: Philosophy Research, Policy, and Practice in Denmark, Finland, Iceland, Norway, and Sweden*, ed. Johanna Einarsdottir and Judith Wagner (Greenwich, CT, 2006), 13–42.

15. Tora Korsvold, *For alle barn. Barnehagens framvekst i velferdsstaten* (Oslo, 1998), 51–74; Hatje, *Fraan treklang*, 31–125.

16. See Francis Sejersted, *Sosialdemokratiets tidsalder: Norge og Sverige i det 20. århundre* (Oslo, 2005), 163–75.

17. Berge Furre, *Vaart hundreaar. Norsk historie 1905–1990* (Oslo, 1991), 138, 187, and 331–35.

18. Korsvold, "Profesjonalisert barndom," 397–411; Inger Elisabeth Haavet, "Framveksten av velferdsstatens familiepolitikk i Norge og Sverige," *Tidsskrift for velferdsforskning* 2 (1999): 46–62.

19. Alva Myrdal and Gunnar Myrdal, *Kris i befolkningsfrågan* (Stockholm, 1934).

20. Karl Gustav Hammarlund, *Barnet och barnomsorgen. Bilden av barnet i ett socialpolitiskt project* (Göteborg, 1998), 41–60.

21. Alva Myrdal, *Stadsbarn. En bok om deras fostran* (Stockholm, 1935), 158.

22. For more, see Ann-Katrin Hatje, "Private and Public Welfare: Sweden's Childcare in Comparative Perspective," in *Civil Society in the Baltic Sea Region*, ed. Norbert Götz and Jörg Hackmann (Aldershot, 2003), 119–32.

23. Alva Myrdal, *Morgonbris* no. 1 (1935): 7; Alva Myrdal, *Stadsbarn*, 179; Hatje, *Fraan treklang*, 224–28.

24. Alva Myrdal, *Folk och familj* (Stockholm, 1944); Hatje, *Fraan treklang*, 224–26.

25. Christina Florin and Bengt Nilsson, "'Something in the Nature of a Bloodless Revolution': How New Gender Relations Became Gender Equality Policy in Sweden in the Nineteen-Sixties and Seventies," in *State Policy and Gender System in two German States and Sweden, 1945–1989*, ed. Rolf Thorstendahl (Lund, 1999), 11–79.

26. Tora Korsvold, *Barn og barndom i velferdsstatens smaabarnspolitikk. En sammenlignende studie av Sverige, Norge og Tyskland 1945–2000* (Oslo, 2008), 51 and 115.

27. Ida Blom and Soelvi Sogner, *Med kjoennsperspektiv på norsk historie* (Oslo, 1999), 345.

28. Kolbe, *Elternschaft*, 448f.

29. Sejersted, *Sosialdemokratiets tidsalder*, 231–357.

30. See Alfred Telhaug et al., "The Nordic Model in Education: Education as Part of the Political System in the last 50 Years," *Scandinavian Journal of Educational Research* 50 (2006): 245–83.

31. Florin and Nilsson, "Something in the Nature," 31–48.

32. Swedish Committee for Childcare, *Daghem och förskolor*, Official Report SOU 1951: 15 (Stockholm, 1951), 138.

33. Bergquist and Nyberg, "Welfare State," 288.

34. Ibid.

35. Jonas Hinnfors, "Swedish Parties and Family Policy, 1960–1980: Stability through Change," in Thorstendahl, *State Policy*, 105ff.

36. See Bengt Henningsen, *Der Wohlfahrtsstaat Schweden: Nordeuropäischen Studien* (Baden Baden, 1986).

37. Florin and Nilson, "Something in the Nature;" Ingela K. Naumann, "Childcare and Feminism in West Germany and Sweden in the 1960s and 1970s," *Journal of European Social Policy* 15, no. 1 (2005): 47–63.

38. Korsvold, *Barn og barndom*, 113–33.

39. Gro Hagemann, "Housewife and citizen?" in *Twentieth-Century Housewives: Meanings and Implications of Unpaid Work*, ed. Gro Hagemann and H. Roll Hansen (Oslo, 2005), 28–36.
40. Monica Rudberg, *Dydige, sterke, lykkelige barn. Ideer om oppdragelse i borgerlig tradisjon* (Oslo, 1983), 217.
41. Korsvold, *For alle barn*, 70f.
42. Korsvold, *Barn og barndom*, 59–70 and 125–32.
43. Hammarlund, *Barnet och barnomsorgen*, 167; Tora Korsvold and Mette Nygaard, "Barndomsforståelser i offentlige dokumenter om barnehagen," *Prisme* 1 (2006): 7–8.
44. Swedish Committee for Childcare, *Daghem och förskolor*, 523.
45. Ibid., 183; *Komitéen til å urede visse spørsmål om daginstitusjoner m.v. for barn*, oppnevnt ved kgl. res. av 6. Mars 1959. Vedlegg 1. Barnets psykologiske utvikling i førskolealder (Oslo, 1959), 63f.
46. On the history of motherhood and childhood, see Sonya Michel, *Children's Interests/ Mothers' Rights: The Shaping of America's Childcare Policy* (New Haven, CT, 1999); Allen, *Feminism and Motherhood*.
47. St. meld. nr. 1 (1962–63) *Om retningslinjer for utbygging og drift av daginstitusjoner for barn* (Oslo, 1963), 63.
48. At the same time we find a similar debate in other countries like West Germany or the United States; see the chapter by Karen Hagemann in this volume and Michel, *Children's Interests*, chapters 2 and 3.
49. Hammarlund, *Barnet och barnomsorgen*, 182–83.
50. Hinnfors, "Stability," 105; Bergquist and Nyberg, "Welfare State," 288.
51. Telhaug et al., "The Nordic Model," 246–56.
52. See also Celia Winkler, *Single Mothers and the State: The Politics of Care in Sweden and the United States* (Lanham, MD, 2002), 122.
53. For more, see the introduction by Karen Hagemann, Konrad H. Jarausch, and Cristina Allemann-Ghionda in this volume.
54. Stortingstidende, Inst. O. nr. 69 (1974–75) *Innstilling fra den forsterkede sosialkomité om lov om barnehager m.v.; 11* (Oslo, 1975); Korsvold, *Profesjonalisert barndom*, 123–25.
55. T. C. Reitan, "Getting a Head Start: Early Provision of Daycare Among Municipalities in Norway," *International Journal of Social Welfare* 6, no. 4 (1997): 268–78.
56. Florin and Nilsson, "Something in the Nature," 72.
57. Hammarlund, *Barnet och barnomsorgen*, 141–65.
58. Korsvold, *Barn og barndom*, 78–84, 137–48.
59. Ibid., 170.
60. Ibid., 163–170.
61. Anita Haataja, *Fathers' Use of Paternity and Parental Leave in the Nordic Countries* (Helsinki, 2009), 8ff.
62. Berit Brandt and Elin Kvande, "Father Presence in Childcare," in *Children and the Changing Family: Between Transformation and Negotiation*, ed. An-Magritt Jensen and Lorna McKee (London, 2003), 61–75.
63. Tora Korsvold and Nina Volckmar, "Velferdspolitikken i skole og barnehage: En Reorientering?" in *Pedagogikk og politikk*, ed. Petter Aasen et al. (Oslo, 2004), 233–46; Sejersted, *Sosialdemokratiets tidsalder*, 506.
64. An-Magritt Jensen and Jens Qvortrup, "Summary — A Childhood Mosaic: What Did We Learn?" in *Children's Welfare in Ageing Europe*, ed. An-Magritt Jensen et al. (Trondheim, 2004), vol. 1, 820–25.

Chapter 7

THE SCANDINAVIAN MODEL
The Time Policy of Primary School Education in Twentieth-Century Sweden

Lisbeth Lundahl

The Scandinavian countries are often described as prominent examples of social democratic welfare regimes characterized by universalism.[1] According to sociologist Gøsta Esping-Andersen, who has identified three major types of welfare states (social democratic, liberal, and conservative), the social democratic regime is defined by a welfare policy that not only targets those most in need but also seeks to cover the entire population. It accomplishes this through a high level of wealth redistribution and social insurance. This welfare state model assumes full employment and a high degree of social solidarity.[2] However, Esping-Andersen's welfare-state typology is analytical rather than empirical. As recent research has shown, in practice all welfare regimes are a mix of different policies, which change over time, depending on the specific economic, political, and social development.[3]

In this chapter, I adopt a welfare-regime perspective for describing and analyzing time allocation politics in Scandinavian and Swedish school education. This perspective can help us to understand better the interconnectedness of welfare and education systems. In contrast to most scholarship in both the educational and social sciences, my analysis assumes that resources allocated to education, including time, as well as the way that education, childcare, and other aspects of the welfare system are organized, reflect the dominant outlook on the relationships between the economy, social welfare, the state, and the family. This perspective has not been emphasized in most of the scholarly literature, which instead has tended to examine education policy and welfare research separately.[4]

Notes for this chapter begin on page 171.

I begin with a brief theoretical discussion of education and time policy in a welfare state perspective, in which I identify five sets of factors that frame and influence the allocation of time for school children's comprehensive education and care. From there, I analyze the Swedish example in a long-term perspective by focusing on three time periods during which questions concerning the time policy of compulsory education have been high on the political agenda: First, the period 1900–1945, during which the quality of primary education steadily improved. The 1920s, when conservative groups fought strongly against full-time education for all children, were especially important during this time. Second, the period 1945–1975, which saw the development and consolidation of a nine-year comprehensive education. Here the 1970s, when the social democratic government investigated the possibilities of combining school children's education and leisure time into an "integrated school day," were critical. This initiative proved highly controversial, since nonsocialist politicians regarded it as an effort to diminish parents' responsibility to care for their children. And third, the period 1975–2005, an era of decentralization, deregulation, and market initiatives in welfare politics. In this period, the early 2000s were particular important, as it was then that the government launched an experiment among nine hundred Swedish compulsory schools that allowed them to abandon the regulation of the national timetable and gave them considerable autonomy to allocate time as they deemed necessary in order to attain national and local educational goals. At the same time, however, regulations regarding the minimum number of teaching hours and the length of school days remained in place. In the conclusion, I discuss structural and actor-related factors that frame and influence time allocation politics of school education in Sweden and elsewhere in Scandinavia.

Education and Time Policy in a Welfare State Perspective

The relationships between the state, civil society, and the economy frame and influence the ways in which educational reforms are carried out in various national and local contexts. In addition, they determine the response to global trends. More generally, the welfare state context affects how education is structured and influences its content. In this framework, I propose to differentiate between four analytical aspects of education policy: value base, instrumentality, governance, and key actors.[5]

The *value base* aspect refers to the degree to which equality, integration, social differentiation, and elitism are present in education. In the ideal-typical social democratic welfare state, equal opportunity for education is considered a major vehicle for social progress and justice. As a result, a system of public, comprehensive education with little stratification is preferred over private or even mixed approaches. In contrast, ideas of competition and achievement are prominent in the liberal paradigm of the welfare state, and links to the market economy are stronger. Competitiveness is regarded as natural and beneficial, with individual enterprise and self-empowerment promoted at all levels of community life. Public and private services with considerable freedom of choice are offered. Early educational stratification is prominent in both liberal and conservative welfare states, but they are underpinned by different ideologies. Individuality and choice are important in liberal welfare states, while patriarchy and hierarchy are the foundations of the conservative welfare state.

The *instrumentality* aspect refers to the dual function of education, which provides individuals with social security and a connection to their community while at the same time contributing to economic growth by producing and reproducing human capital. In conservative and social democratic paradigms, the sociocultural functions of schools and education are stressed more than in liberal welfare states, even if their economic role remains crucial.

Finally, the aspects of *governance* and *key actors* refer to the source and agency of educational change and control as well as the degree of centralization and standardization. The lowest level of standardization is expected in liberal welfare states, where educational governance is divided among several key actors. More standardized education is expected in both social democratic and conservative-corporatist welfare regimes, where the state and the organizations of social partners, like trade unions and employer associations, continue to be significant.

Similarly, it can be assumed that the timeframes of school education are affected by a number of structural and agency factors related to the welfare state context (see Figure 7.1). In the following discussion, I will define the five most important and analyze each on the basis of examples from the social democratic welfare context. The first factor is the function assigned by the state to education. In a social democratic welfare regime, the state is relatively strong, social democratic parties are influential, and education is assigned great importance and multiple functions, implying a preference to invest considerable time and other resources in education at all levels. The second factor is the demand of the economy and labor market. Other decisive factors include the need for children and women in the workforce and the ability of various labor market organizations representing both employers and workers to enforce their policies in relation to each other and to the state. In Scandinavian countries, these actors ("Big State, Big Union, Big Business") became increasingly well organized from the 1930s onwards. Their views on issues such as women entering the labor

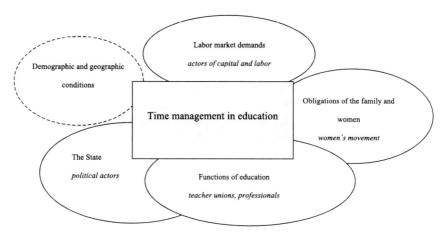

FIGURE 7.1: Structural and agency factors assumed to influence time management in compulsory education

market must therefore also be taken into account.[6] The historically defined obligations of the family and the division of responsibilities between men and women comprise a third factor that could affect time management in the education of younger children. The power of the women's movement to change conditions and achieve greater gender equality—for example, by demanding high-quality education, childcare, and after-school care of school children—is yet another important factor. Finally, although not a function of the welfare state, demographic and geographic factors can also influence time management in education. For example, in sparsely populated parts of Nordic countries, so-called mobile schools and part-time schools were common during the first part of the twentieth century. I will return to these factors in the following analysis and the conclusion.

Common Features of Scandinavian Education Policy in Retrospect

Although the welfare and educational systems of Scandinavian countries are hardly identical, they do share important characteristics. Throughout the twentieth century, education policies in Scandinavia have sought to provide equal educational opportunities regardless of gender, social class, and geographical background. Other common features include the formation of a strong interventionist state and the widely held view that economic growth and welfare, both individual and collective, are highly interdependent.[7] As historian Pauli Kettunen notes, the fact that "all five

Nordic countries shared a particularly strong trust in the harmony between the objectives of social equality, political democracy and economic
prosperity was expressed in manifestations of the Nordic cooperation as
early as in the late 1930s."[8] This view was clearly reflected in Scandinavian education politics, which were shaped by the widespread belief that
bringing together children from different social classes would promote
social integration and citizenship. Equal educational opportunities would
also guarantee efficient recruitment to different positions in society and
optimal use of human resources.

After World War II, the ruling social democratic parties in Scandinavia
sought to expand the social functions of education. From the 1960s on,
education was increasingly regarded as a crucial factor for both economic
growth and development, even though social motives remained strong.[9]
Both sets of motives underpinned the comprehensive school reforms that
occurred in the Nordic countries in the 1960s. Moreover, efforts were
made to introduce a common Nordic comprehensive school system, but
they were largely unsuccessful.[10] State governance of compulsory education became stronger and more comprehensive, but to a lesser extent in
Denmark than in the other Nordic countries.[11]

Beginning in the 1970s, and above all in the 1990s, the education systems in all Scandinavian countries were radically transformed, if to varying degrees, by a long-term process of decentralization, deregulation, and
marketization.[12] In 1976, the Swedish Social Democrats were voted out
of power after an exceptionally long period in office. They had run the
government since 1932, in average obtaining 41–54 percent of the popular vote. Between 1976 and 1982 as well as between 1991 and 1994, a conservative government was in power. In general, since the 1970s politics in
the Scandinavian countries have become increasingly unstable, as a new,
well-educated middle class rose to prominence and the traditional working class declined. While the educational reforms during this period were
of a similar nature and occurred at the same time, they were implemented
somewhat differently in each country. At the same time, the extensive
changes in the education and welfare state system met little resistance.
Indeed, they were perceived as an "inevitable" or "necessary" reaction
to the rapid social and technological developments that were occurring
at the time.[13] The effects of these changes were often quite dramatic. A
European comparison shows that the transfer of responsibilities to municipalities and schools has been most extensive in the Nordic countries,
leading to growing differences between schools and students.[14] Equality
and uniformity are gradually being replaced by diversity and fragmentation. At the same time, however, the Nordic countries continue to deviate
from other countries of the Organisation for Economic Co-operation and

Development in several important respects, as they continue to adhere to many aspects of traditional social democratic education policy. They too are an example of long-lasting path dependency. Education and welfare state systems seem to be influenced everywhere in a very strong way by institutional, legal, and cultural traditions.[15] For example, the comprehensive education system has survived largely unchallenged and there remains limited tracking and separation of students at the secondary level. With the exception of Denmark, the percentage of students in private institutions is well below the OECD average.[16] Moreover, in comparison to other countries in Europe and elsewhere in the world, variations between schools are still small and social segregation is low.[17] In general, all Scandinavian education systems do well in the comparative surveys of fifteen-year-old school children's scholastic performance by the Program for International Student Assessment (PISA), which has been implemented and organized by the OECD since 2000.[18]

Education Policies and Time Allocation in Sweden, 1900–2007

The development of the time policy of the Swedish education system can, as described earlier, be separated into three main periods: 1900–1945, when the quality of primary education was significantly improved, albeit not without resistance; 1945–1975, when nine-year comprehensive education was developed and consolidated, but also showed its first signs of crisis; and 1975–2005, when welfare and education was subject to decentralization, deregulation, and market initiatives. As Table 7.1 shows, despite all

TABLE 7.1: Teaching time allocation in Swedish compulsory education (hours per week), 1919–2007[19]

Policy document	Maximum number of teaching hours			
	Grades 1–2 (ages 7–8)	Grade 3 (age 9)	Grades 4–6 (ages 10–12)	Grades 1–6 (ages 7–12)
1919 standard syllabus	28	28 plus craft lessons	30 plus craft or domestic science	—
1955 standard syllabus	28	30	34 (grade 4) 36 (grades 5–6)	—
1962 and 1969 national curricula	20 (grade 1) 24 (grade 2)	30	34 (grade 4) 35 (grade 5–6)	—
1980 national curriculum	Regulated the total number of hours of each subject in grades 1–3 and 4–6.			
1994 national curriculum	Regulates the minimum total number of hours of each subject for all 9 years.			

changes in these three periods, the teaching hours per week in compulsory education (grades one through six) have proven remarkably stable. A student in grade six, for example, has had an average of 34–35 weekly hours of instruction for the larger part of the last century. What changed was not the amount of teaching hours per week, but the teaching conditions, the usage of the teaching time, and the context (including lunch, the offering of childcare, and extracurricular activities).

The Early Years (1900–1945)

At the beginning of the twentieth century, Sweden was still a relatively poor, agrarian country that had not yet industrialized. The quality of the six-year primary school, which was directed mainly towards the children of farmers and workers, differed vastly between rural areas and cities. Decisions on the curriculum and temporal organization of education were made locally. Until 1955, moreover, the national standard syllabus served only as a recommendation and example.[20] School attendance was not compulsory, home instruction was permitted, and a variety of different school types existed. "Mobile schools," "part-time schools" with shift-classes, so-called minimum courses, and teaching groups of children of various ages, however, were to be found primarily in sparsely populated rural areas. The school year normally lasted for four to five months, as many children were needed for farm work or other labor, and the school day lasted at most five hours long.[21]

With the introduction of the first standard syllabus in 1900, the poorest forms of school education, "part-time schools" with shift-classes, were abolished. Poverty was no longer an acceptable reason for exceptions from the required schedule of teaching hours. Above all, the excessive time children needed to get to and from school was now used as an argument in favor of half-time education and other schools with an "exceptional" time schedule. In 1914, more than 30 percent of all students in primary education attended schools with half-time instruction (e.g., with lessons every other day).[22]

In 1917, the Social Democratic Workers' Party of Sweden (Sveriges socialdemokratiska arbetareparti, SAP) entered the government for the first time as part of a coalition with the Liberal Party. This coalition was intermittently in power until 1926. Both parties pushed for school reform. In 1919, the Ministry of Education introduced a new national standard syllabus, which recommended 28 to 30 teaching hours per week or five hours per day. The ministry also demanded that local municipalities work to improve the conditions of their primary schools. It enforced the appointment of full-time school inspectors whose task it was to monitor the quality of the instruction, textbooks, premises, hygienic conditions, and other aspects of the educational setting. These school inspectors played an important role in the implementation of the desired school reform. In 1920, already less than 25 percent of students were in half-day education.[23]

Conservative groups in certain parts of Sweden, however, particularly in rural areas, responded to this development with considerable resistance. Their campaign against the so-called full-time instruction of five hours demanded by the new standard syllabus and an improvement of the school buildings and other material conditions of schooling has been characterized by historian Viktor Fredriksson as "one of the most heated that primary school has ever had to endure" in Sweden.[24] In a series of articles entitled "Luxury Education of Citizens" that appeared in 1921 in one of Sweden's largest daily newspapers, a spokesman for the so-called popular movement, which fought against an extension of the school time and the construction of new schools, argued that the school reform would destroy the economy of poor municipalities and force the majority of children to receive an education that was unnecessary for their future economic and social roles as farmers and workers. It was not until after the economy recovered from the postwar recession of the early 1920s that the popular movement lost momentum. From the mid-1920s on, the national standard syllabus of 1919 and the demands and recommendations that it made for a school reform became increasingly the norm.[25]

In 1932, the SAP again took over the government. During the 1930s, Sweden's economy and politics were characterized by well-organized relationships between industry and the union movement. In 1938, these social partners reached an important agreement (*Saltsjöbadsavtalet*) that ended a period of countless strikes and lockouts. This historic compromise rested on the agreement by the Swedish Confederation of Trade Unions to work towards industrial peace and limit wage demands and the Swedish Employers' Confederation's acceptance of the welfare policies of the social democratic government. By that time, the country's demographic and socioeconomic situation had changed considerably. Increasing numbers of Swedes lived in cities. World War II boosted Sweden's industry, creating an economic boom. As a result, the number of salaried employees exceeded that of farmers in the 1940s.[26]

This economic upswing increased the demand for female labor, and not just single women. Wives and mothers were also needed to fill jobs in Sweden's industrial sector. Together with a decreasing birth rate, this stimulated a public debate about how the state should best respond. Two of the most important voices in this debate belonged to Alva and Gunnar Myrdal, both social scientists and leading Social Democrats. Already in 1934 they had published their highly controversial book *Crisis in the Popu-*

lation Issue, which, among other things, promoted the idea of public child-care and other kinds of support for families and mothers. The Myrdals argued that the costs and responsibilities of childrearing must be shared by society and the state and should not be shouldered by individual families alone. They argued, "If we want to stop the decreasing fertility rates, there is no other alternative than very radical distribution and social policies. ... In the future society, families and children must be protected in ways much different than is currently the case."[27] Beginning in the 1930s, the Myrdals and other advocates of a new concept of social welfare thus recommended free healthcare for children, free school meals, free kindergartens, and after-school centers as well as education stipends for talented young people.

These ideas gained increasing currency and formed not only the welfare state and family policy of the Swedish Social Democratic Workers' Party, but also its education policy. Since then, social democratic welfare and family policy measures have included improved housing for poor, large families, the provision of maternity leave, and an increase of childcare facilities. The SAP introduced this policy in the late 1930s in response to the declining birth rates and the obvious fact that an increasing number of mothers were forced to support the family income and do paid work outside their homes. In the booming economy of the 1940s, the extension of childcare became imperative for the Swedish government.

An important part of the introduction of a more family-friendly and social policy became the reform of the education system. During the 1930s and 1940s, the major aim here was the extension of the compulsory education of all children from six to seven years, which was introduced in 1937. However, the law stated that this policy should be implemented over a twelve-year transition period. At the same time, a far-reaching "program of a rationalization" of the education system was launched. Its aim was the closing of small rural schools and the elimination of all remaining forms of part-time instruction.[28]

Development and Consolidation (1945–1975)

The "Swedish model" of welfare state development, which reached its peak in the late 1950s and the 1960s, had three main components: industrial rationalization and restructuring, an active labor-market policy, and a cohesive wage policy.[29] Together these three components formed a strong corporatist state. As sociologist James Fulcher concludes, "If any non-fascist society can be considered corporatist, Sweden in the 1950s and 1960s fits the bill."[30] The concept of a "strong society," which was coined in the 1960s by the former social democratic prime minister Tage Erlander, illustrates a view of state and society that gradually came to dominate Swedish welfare policy.

An important part of this concept of a "strong society" was a family-friendly policy, which the social democratic government began to introduce in the 1930s and expanded in the postwar era.[31] In 1946, for example, the government decided to supply free school meals to all children in primary education, not just to those who were poor or had a long commute to school. This reform not only promoted children's health, but it also facilitated the gainful employment of women as well as full-time instruction. The introduction of free school meals, however, was consistently met with opposition from the right. Ever since the idea was first proposed by the public commission on population matters (*Befolkningskommissionen*) in the 1930s, the conservative parties, in particular the Right Party, had argued against it. They feared that free school meals would cause women to neglect their work as housewives. In the 1950s, they also contended that parents, not the state, should pay for school meals.[32] This resistance proved, however, unsuccessful. Since the 1960s, family policy reform began to include the expansion of daycare centers and other forms of all-day public childcare that aimed to facilitate the combination of family and work by mothers.[33] These reforms were seen as especially necessary because the booming Swedish economy of the 1960s urgently required more female labor.[34]

The Swedish labor movement, which constituted another important component of the "strong society," also sought a fundamental reform of the education system. After World War II, many people came to believe that reforms that aimed to modernize and expand common education were necessary to promote the development of the national economy and become internationally competitive. As was the case in the 1920s, the educational reform agenda was set to a large extent by the SAP and the trade unions, and hence reflected their aim to combine initiatives for equality and efficiency. Their primary concern was to ensure equal access to education and thereby equal opportunities in society, regardless of class, gender, and geographical origin. In this respect, the introduction of the nine-year comprehensive school together with a more modern new national "standard curriculum" in 1962, after a ten-year trial period, can be seen as a symbol of social democratic dominance.[35]

However, despite the fact that the Social Democrats governed Sweden until 1976, major educational reforms were generally based on a broad political consensus. This was an important precondition for their success, which differentiates the Swedish development from, for example, West Germany's. There similar educational reforms proposed in the 1960s and early 1970s were much less successful, not least of all because of the sharp and irreconcilable ideological differences between the two leading parties, which produced educational agendas that were wholly incompatible with each other.[36] During the 1950s and 1960s, debates over comprehensive school reforms revolved around specific questions such as whether and when pupils should be separated into specific tracks within the school, but did not question the reforms per se. Moreover, educational politics in Sweden during this period were completely centralized: schooling was, on the whole, a "state business." Indeed, as educationist Guy Neave has noted, in Sweden "non-state schools are so few as to be scarcely visible." The strong centralization of the education system in Sweden was another precondition for a successful reform in this period, which we do not find in other countries like Austria or West Germany with its federative political system and enduring time policy.[37]

From 1955 on, Sweden had a national time schedule that for the first time established an obligatory number of school hours in every subject for each grade. The 1962 national curriculum of the nine-year compulsory comprehensive education program stated the number of weekly teaching hours (see Table 7.1).[38] Examples of time schedules were appended to the curriculum plan, according to which a typical school week for children in grades three through six (nine to twelve years old) should have six to seven hours of lessons per day, Monday to Friday, and three on Saturdays. The 1969 national curriculum did not change this basic arrangement.[39]

Time management in primary and secondary education was essentially a nonissue for the political agenda in the postwar period, and thus caused no political debates or controversy. In the late 1960s, however, psychologists and educationalists, but also the broader public, began to regard the internal function and working environment of comprehensive compulsory schools as increasingly problematic—as is evident in professional journals and daily newspapers. Descriptions of absenteeism, bullying, and a lack of discipline in schools prompted considerable public concern and debate. In 1970, a parliamentary committee called "Schools' Inner Work" (*Skolans Inre Arbete*), was appointed to investigate the situation and propose solutions, both "general or individual, that include the whole life environment of the pupils."[40] Based on the committee's proposals, in 1975 parliament introduced the "integrated school day" (*samlad skoldag*). This reform aimed to give school children equal access to culture and leisure activities, as well as more opportunities for educational support and social training. The integrated school day meant that schools were expected to organize free activities with an educational purpose between and after scheduled lessons. The contents and extent of such extracurricular activities were to be decided by the local school board.[41] However, the deterioration of financial circumstances made full implementation of the integrated school day reforms difficult. Furthermore, the reforms met with conceptual resistance from non–social democratic politicians, who argued that they would diminish parents' motivation and opportunities to care for their children.[42] As a result of the financial restrictions and political resistance, a decade later, slightly more than a third of all children aged seven to twelve attended schools with integrated school days.[43] Increases in the number of so-called leisure time centers and family daycare homes for school children aged seven to twelve were also promoted, a development that overlapped with the implementation of integrated school days.[44]

Decentralization, Deregulation, and Market Initiatives (1975–2005)

In the 1970s, after twenty-five years of continuous growth under social democratic rule, Sweden entered a period of economic and political instability. Challenged by structural changes and economic recessions, the welfare system came under criticism from both the right and left. In the 1970s and early 1980s, a "social investment strategy" that included a more activist labor market policy and more education reforms prevailed, whereas the strategies of the late 1980s and 1990s were characterized by state cutbacks, deregulation, and the introduction of market solutions.[45] In 1976 the Center Party, Moderate Party, and Liberal Party formed a center-right government, which ruled until 1982. From 1982 until 1991, and again from 1994 until 2006 the Social Democratic Workers' Party was in office. During the 1970s, the new government took the first steps towards implementing greater local responsibility and autonomy. The 1980 national curriculum guide of compulsory education manifested a trend towards governance by objectives. In 1989, under social democratic rule, the government implemented a more clear-cut division of labor between the state and local levels, with responsibilities for education being further devolved to municipalities and schools.[46] While in office from 1991–1994, the liberal-conservative government took even more far-reaching steps toward local autonomy and attempted to break "the state school monopoly" by introducing a quasi-market for education. In particular, generous state subsidies fueled the establishment of independent schools. At the same time, they promoted parental choice between public or independent schools. The 1993 decision to deliver all state subsidies to the municipalities as a lump sum meant that a powerful central steering mechanism was abandoned. Both socialist and nonsocialist governments contributed to this development, although they had different motives for doing so. The Social Democrats regarded decentralization as a necessary means to attain educational goals where older strategies had failed. They believed that local political authorities should become more engaged than they previously had been and that parents and pupils be granted greater influence over educational decisions. The conservative parties aimed to reduce the power of politicians and bureaucrats in favor of schools, parents, and private interests. The transfer of responsibilities to the municipalities along with increased opportunities for choosing a school, housing segregation, and budget cuts all contributed to growing differences between them. In his recent study, educationalist Jan-Eric Gustafsson concludes that "the results [of this new policy] point to a strong and mainly linear increase in school segregation in terms of foreign status, grades, and educational background from 1992 to 2000."[47]

In 1975, the government and the Swedish Association of Local Authorities agreed on a rapid expansion of school childcare.[48] However, it took considerable time to achieve this goal, and ten years later, such care covered only 37 percent of all seven- to nine-year-old children (22 percent in "leisure time centers"). By 1995, that number had climbed to 52 percent (48 percent in "leisure time centers") and would reach 75 percent in 2005 (74 percent in "leisure time centers"). However, the proportion of ten- to twelve-year-olds in school childcare has always been low, and currently stands at 11 percent. Since the 1990s, moreover, there has also been a continuous and problematic trend towards larger groups and fewer staff in the "leisure time centers," with large differences among different municipalities.[49]

One result of decentralization and deregulation has been an increase in local communities' ability to allocate school hours. An international comparison by the European Commission, *Key Data on Education in Europe*, has described the Swedish education system as uniquely decentralized in this respect in 2005.[50] In 1999, the Swedish Parliament decided on a five-year experiment in which compulsory schools in approximately 80 of Sweden's 290 municipalities were excluded from national time-schedule regulations. Using the national curriculum and course syllabi as guides, schools in these municipalities were permitted to create their own timetables and freely distribute teaching hours between different subjects and activities within a minimum timeframe of 6,665 total annual teaching hours.[51] The main goal was to remove a governing mechanism that, at best, had become redundant and, at worst, impeded governance by objectives. In addition, it sought to adapt instruction to individual pupils and permit essential modernization of education.[52] For a long time, the idea of abandoning the national timetable had solid support from both politicians and school leaders, whereas opinions among teachers varied. However, a decision on this reform has been delayed and different parties have increasingly expressed reservations about it.

Interestingly, the experiment of time allocation did not include increased local autonomy in determining the length of school days. The participating schools were to follow the general guidelines of the Education Act, with pupils' work scheduled from Mondays to Fridays and distributed as evenly as possible across these days. The Education Act also stipulates that it would be up to the local school board to decide the length of the school day, including when it begins and ends, something that the experiment did not intend to change.[53]

Conclusion

A striking element in Sweden's history of time policy is the stability with which the school day or week has been conceived and materialized over time. Since the beginning of the twentieth century, i.e., well before the creation of the modern Swedish welfare state, a "normal" school day in the fifth or sixth grade of primary education has consisted on average of six hours (Saturdays excluded). Since the normal syllabus was introduced in 1900, part-time teaching or mobile schools have been considered inferior or special alternatives, acceptable only in cases where students had to travel long distances to school. It is important to note, however, that the so-called special forms of time management were actively defended by conservative groups in the 1910s and 1920s and remained common well into the 1930s. Since the mid-1920s, however, full-time instruction in compulsory schools has not been seriously questioned. In contrast, school childcare and the extent to which schools should be responsible for extracurricular activities have proved to be somewhat more controversial issues. This observation leads one to ask, what are the possible explanations for the prevalence of full-time schooling in Sweden, and more generally, what factors are important for our understanding of the time policy education? To answer these questions, Esping-Andersen's welfare regime model is helpful, as it focuses on the different relationships and division of responsibility between the state, family, and economy. At the same time, the interplay of the other factors discussed here as well as the long-term influence of path dependency that his model neglects are also important.[54]

State power and the legitimacy of the public welfare system are characteristics of social democratic welfare states like Sweden. Much more than is the case in liberal and corporatist-conservative welfare states, such states are expected to care for their citizens and compensate for children's disparate needs. This implies, of course, a redistribution of resources and high levels of taxation. In the case of younger preschool children, debates on whether daycare centers are always beneficial have occasionally flared up in Sweden, with some nonsocialist parties advocating the introduction of a childcare allowance for parents who choose to stay home with their small children. However, on the whole, regardless of considerable class-based variations, public institutions for childcare, education, and, more generally, the public welfare system still enjoy strong popular support.[55] Swedish citizens trust these institutions sufficiently to send their children to them for many hours each day. The fact that these welfare services are universal and of high quality and do not simply target children with special needs has been important in achieving this popular support.[56]

Unlike other education systems such as West Germany's, childcare and teaching professionals in Sweden have not had a major effect on the time policy of education. Teachers have struggled to limit more detailed time regulations beyond regular teaching hours, particularly in the 1980s and 1990s, but have not engaged in questions regarding the length of students' school days. However, the school inspectors that have been appointed since 1919 were very important in reducing the number of schools with substandard management, thereby helping to implement the political agenda laid down in the national standard syllabi.

Family, economy, and labor market needs have also affected how education and childcare are organized. In contrast to some other countries, Sweden was poor well into the twentieth century and most families could not afford to follow the male-breadwinner model. As a result, the proposals put forward by the Myrdals appeared at a time when most women had to work outside the home for economic reasons. Poverty strongly contributed to decreasing fertility rates, and the social policies of the 1930s and 1940s, including free school meals, were largely responses to these conditions. Child labor was prohibited in 1912. The rapid rationalization of agriculture and growing numbers of people moving into the cities during the first half of the twentieth century meant that the labor of children was no longer required in farming. Up until that time, this had been an important reason for demanding shorter school terms and school weeks.

Swedish industry developed an urgent need for manpower during the boom of the 1950s and 1960s. Faced with the choice between recruiting immigrants or women, industry and government preferred the latter as the primary labor reserve. In discussions held between social partners, mainly trade unions and employer organizations, the trade union confederation was reluctant to increase immigration due to concerns that employers would use it as an opportunity to lower wages. The rapid expansion of public childcare in the 1960s and 1970s was directly aimed at facilitating women's gainful employment.[57] Needless to say, the idea of half-day schools was hardly the first thought in the minds of reformers at the time. Furthermore, the Swedish women's liberation movement, which gained strength in the late 1960s and the 1970s, wholeheartedly supported the expansion of high-quality preschool and in-school childcare, since it would enable women to combine work and family responsibilities. However, the

Social Democratic Women's Association strongly advocated the introduction of a six-hour workday in order to help families make ends meet.

Demographic and geographic factors may have also contributed to the establishment of full-day teaching as the "normal" principle for organizing time. Before the introduction of public transportation for schools after 1945, children in sparsely populated areas often had to walk very long distances between their homes and school. Attending just a couple of lessons would have been a waste of time. Similarly, on cold winter days it would have been wasteful not to make full use of the classrooms once their wood stoves had been heated.

In isolation, none of the above factors can explain the emergence of a time policy of compulsory education. The Swedish example illustrates that a combination of factors must be considered. The welfare regime model, which denotes specific relationships between the state, civil society, and economy, may serve as a wide frame of reference. However, the Swedish case also illustrates the multitude of factors at work, many of which are probably unique to each country. Finally, one cannot disregard the importance of path dependency in the evolution of time policies. The bitter struggle over half-time instruction had already ended in the interwar period, and the groups defending it have come to be seen as reactionary. Since the 1960s, the vast majority of Swedish society has come to support all-day education, thus making it nearly impossible to change it now. Once a system of full-time comprehensive system of instruction has been established, profound political, social, and economic changes would be required before radical changes to the education system could be seriously considered. Now that the majority of Swedish women are gainfully employed, it will be nearly impossible to mobilize support to reduce resources allocated to schools and childcare.

Notes

1. Anne-Lise Arnesen and Lisbeth Lundahl, "Still Social and Democratic? Inclusive Education Policies in the Nordic Welfare States," *Scandinavian Journal of Educational Research* 50, no. 3 (2006): 285–300.

2. Gøsta Esping-Andersen, *The Three Worlds of Welfare Capitalism* (Cambridge, UK, 1996), 26–32. For more, see the introduction by Karen Hagemann, Konrad H. Jarausch, and Cristina Allemann-Ghionda in this volume.

3. See for example, Julia O'Connor et al., eds., *States, Markets, Families: Gender, Liberalism and Social Policy in Australia, Canada, Great Britain and the United States* (Cambridge, UK, 1999).

4. Arnesen and Lundahl, "Still Social"; Thomas S. Popkewitz et al., "Review of Research on Education Governance and Social Integration and Exclusion," *Uppsala Reports on Education* 35 (Uppsala, 1999).

5. Arnesen and Lundahl, "Still Social."

6. Lisbeth Lundahl, *Efter svensk modell: SAF, LO och utbildningspolitiken 1944–1990* (Umeå, 1997).

7. Niels F. Christiansen and Klaus Petersen, "The Dynamics of Social Solidarity: The Danish Welfare State, 1900–2000," *Scandinavian Journal of History* 26, no. 3 (2001): 177–96; Gudmundur Jonsson, "The Icelandic Welfare State in the Twentieth Century," *Scandinavian Journal of History* 26 (2001): 249–67; Pauli Kettunen, "The Nordic Welfare State in Finland," *Scandinavian Journal of History* 26, no. 3 (2001): 225–47; Urban Lundberg and Klas Åmark, "Social Rights and Social Security: The Swedish Welfare State, 1900–2000," *Scandinavian Journal of History* 26, no. 3 (2001): 157–76; Stein Kuhnle, *The Nordic Approach to General Welfare.* Retrieved 15 October 2005: http://www.nnn.se/intro/approach.htm.

8. Kettunen, "The Nordic Welfare State," 26.

9. Alfred Oftedal Telhaug et al., "From Collectivism to Individualism? Education as Nation Building in a Scandinavian Perspective," *Scandinavian Journal of Educational Research* 48, no. 2 (2004): 141–58; Gustav E. Karlsen, *Utdanning, styring og marked: Norsk utdanningspolitikk i et internasjonalt perspektiv* (Oslo, 2002).

10. Oftedal Telhaug,"From Collectivism," 142.

11. Ibid.

12. Ingolfur A. Johannesson et al., "Modern Educational Sagas: Legitimation of Ideas and Practices in Icelandic Education," *Scandinavian Journal of Educational Research* 46, no. 3 (2002): 265–82; Karlsen, *Utdanning, styring og marked*; Lisbeth Lundahl, "A Matter of Self-Governance and Control: The Reconstruction of Swedish Education Policy 1980–2003," *European Education* 37, no. 1 (2005): 10–25.

13. Ingolfur A. Johannesson, "An Inevitable Progress? Educational Restructuring in Finland, Iceland and Sweden at the Turn of the Millennium," *Scandinavian Journal of Educational Research* 46, no. 3 (2002): 325–39; Sverker Lindblad et al., "Educating for the New Sweden?" *Scandinavian Journal of Educational Research* 46, no. 3 (2002): 283–303; Risto Rinne et al., "Shoots of Revisionist Education Policy or Just Slow Adjustment? The Finnish Case of Educational Reconstruction," *Journal of Education Policy* 17, no. 6 (2002): 643–48.

14. European Commission, *Key Data on Education in Europe 2005* (Brussels, 2005).

15. For this concept see the introduction of this volume.

16. OECD, *Education at a Glance. OECD Indicators 2005.* Retrieved 3 December 2006: http://www.oecd.org/edu/eag2005.

17. Stephen P. Jenkins et al., *Social Segregation in Secondary Schools: How Does England Compare with Other Countries?* Retrieved 10 October 2005: http://www.iser.essex.ac.uk/pubs/workpaps/pdf/2006-02.pdf.

18. OECD, "English Summary and Comment," in *PISA 2000: Svenska femtonåringars läsförmåga och kunnande i matematik och naturvetenskap i ett internationellt perspektiv* (Stockholm, 2001), 4–7.

19. *National Curriculum for Compulsory Schools of 1962* [Läroplan för grundskolan] (Stockholm, 1962); *Curriculum for Compulsory Schools of 1969* (Stockholm, 1969); *Curriculum for Compulsory Schools of 1980* (Stockholm 1980); *Curricula for the Compulsory Comprehensive School System* [Läroplaner för det obligatoriska skolväsandet] (Stockholm, 1994).

20. Sixten Marklund, *Skolsverige 1950–1975. 3. Från Visby-kompromissen till SIA* (Stockholm, 1983), 32.

21. Wilhelm Sjöstrand, *Pedagogikens historia. III: 2. Utvecklingen i Sverige under tiden 1805–1920* (Lund, 1965).

22. Viktor Fredriksson, ed., *Svenska folkskolans historia. V. Det svenska folkundervisningsväsendet 1920–1942* (Stockholm, 1950); for the historical development, see also Leon Boucher, *Tradition and Change in Swedish Education* (Oxford, 1982), 7–20; Rolland G. Paulston, *Educational Change in Sweden: Planning and Accepting the Comprehensive School Reforms* (New York, 1968), 13–34.

23. Fredriksson, *Svenska folkskolans historia*, 53.

24. Ibid.

25. Lisbeth Lundahl, "I moralens, produktionens och det sunda förnuftets namn: Det svenska högerpartiets skolpolitik 1904–1962" (PhD diss., Lund University, 1989), 82f.

26. Lisbeth Lundahl, "A Common Denominator? Swedish Employers, Trade Unions and Vocational Education," *International Journal of Training and Development* 1, no. 2 (1997): 91–103. For the development of industry and the economic growth in Sweden in the 1940s and 1950s, see also Lars Magnusson, *An Economic History of Sweden* (London, 2000), 200–231.

27. Alva Myrdal and Gunnar Myrdal, *Kris i befolkningsfrågan* (Stockholm, 1935), 139f

28. Lundahl, "I moralens."

29. James Fulcher, *Labour Movements, Employers and the State: Conflict and Cooperation in Britain and Sweden* (Oxford, 1991).

30. Ibid., 285.

31. See the chapter by Tora Korsvold on childcare in Sweden in this volume.

32. Lundahl, "I moralens."

33. Christer Thörnqvist, "Family-friendly Labor Market Policies and Careers in Sweden—and the Lack of Them," *British Journal of Guidance and Counselling* 34, no. 3 (2006): 309–26. See also the chapter by Korsvold in this volume.

34. Lundahl, *Efter svensk modell*. See also the chapter by Korsvold in this volume.

35. For social democracy and the school system, see, for example, Bo Lindensjö, "From Liberal Common School to State Primary School: A Main Line in Social Democratic Educational Policy," in *Creating Social Democracy: A Century of the Social Democratic Labor Party in Sweden*, ed. Klaus Misgeld et al. (University Park, PA, 1992), 307–37.

36. See the chapter by Karen Hagemann on West Germany in this volume.

37. Guy Neave, "Editorial," *European Journal of Education* 20, no. 4 (1985): 319. See the chapter by Hagemann in this volume.

38. See *Curriculum for Compulsory Schools of 1962*.

39. See *Curriculum for Compulsory Schools of 1969*.

40. Swedish Government Official Report (SOU) 1974: 53. *Skolans arbetsmiljö: Betänkande avgivet av Utredningen om skolans inre arbete—SIA* (Stockholm, 1974), 68.

41. Marklund, *Skolsverige*, 393.

42. Bo Lindensjö and Ulf P. Lundgren, *Utbildningsreformer och politisk styrning* (Stockholm, 2000), 79.

43. SOU 1985:12. *Skolbarnsomsorgen. Betänkande av fritidshemskommittén*, Socialdepartementet (Stockholm, 1985).

44. See the chapter by Korsvold in this volume.

45. For the economic and political problems, see Magnusson, *An Economic History of Sweden*, 269–80.

46. Lisbeth Lundahl, "Sweden: Decentralization, Deregulation, Quasi-Markets—and Then What?" *Journal of Education Policy* 17, no. 6 (2002): 687–97; Lundahl, "A Matter of Self-Governance."

47. Jan-Eric Gustafsson, *Barns utbildningssituation. Bidrag till ett kommunalt barnindex* (Stockholm, 2006), 93 (translated by LL).
48. SOU 1985:12, *Skolbarnsomsorgen.*
49. Swedish National Agency for Education, Report no. 283: *Descriptive Data on Pre-school Activities, School-age Childcare, Schools and Adult Education in Sweden 2006.* Retrieved 25 January 2009: http://www.skolverket.se/sb/d/193/url.
50. European Commission, *Key Data on Education in Europe 2005* (Brussels, 2005), 99.
51. Mikaela Nyroos et al., "A Matter of Timing: Time Use, Freedom and Influence in School from a Pupil Perspective," *European Educational Research Journal* 3 no. 4 (2004): 743–58.
52. Linda Rönnberg, "A Recent Swedish Attempt to Weaken State Control and Strengthen School Autonomy: The Experiment with Local Time Schedules," *European Educational Research Journal* 6, no. 3 (2007): 214–31.
53. Swedish Code of Statutes (SFS) 1985: 1100: *Skollag.*
54. For the concept of path dependency, see the introductions to this volume.
55. See Stefan Svallfors, "Class, Attitudes and the Welfare State: Sweden in Comparative Perspective," *Social Policy and Administration* 38, no. 2 (2004): 119–38.
56. Thörnqvist, "Family-Friendly Labor Market Policies."
57. Lisbeth Lundahl, "A Common Denominator?"

Chapter 8

CONTINUITIES AND CHANGES— TENSIONS AND AMBIGUITIES
Childcare and Preschool Policies in France

Jeanne Fagnani

Together with the countries of Scandinavia, France leads the European Union in public childcare provision and benefits aimed at reducing childcare costs for families.[1] Since the late 1960s, female participation in the French labor force, as is the case in nearly all states of the Organisation of Economic Co-operation and Development (OECD), has increased steadily. What distinguishes France, however, from many other economically similar European states—with the exception of the Nordic countries—is its high rate of maternal employment. In 2007, 75.4 percent of mothers with two children under sixteen years of age were employed outside of the home compared to only 67.7 percent in Germany, 60.0 percent in Spain, and 53.6 percent in Italy.[2] A primary reason for this is that working mothers in France have access to more generous public assistance and services than most of their counterparts in other European welfare states. It is also a long-standing tradition for women in France to participate in the labor force, dating back to the beginning of the twentieth century.[3] Equally important is the prevailing attitude of French policymakers and the public towards the significance of education of small children. The large-scale arrival of women into the labor market since the 1970s has prompted policymakers to introduce a wide range of services for working parents. In turn, these services enabled still more mothers to work outside of the home. In 2007, the French state subsidized family daycare for 18 percent and crèche service for 27 percent of children under the age of three living with full-time working parents. A further 35 percent of two- to three-year-olds were enrolled in the free full-day preschools (*écoles maternelles*). In addition, nearly 100 percent of children aged three to six attended *écoles mater-*

Notes for this chapter begin on page 193.

nelles, which follow the primary school schedule of 8:30 A.M. to 4:30 P.M., and around 12 percent of children under six participated in an after-school program of some kind.[4] These family and labor policies have contributed at the same time to maintain one of the highest fertility rates in Europe. Indeed, France's fertility rate of 2.0 in 2008 stands high above the European Union average of 1.5, and much higher than countries with a similar economy such as Austria (1.4), Germany, and Italy (both 1.3).[5]

Since the 1990s, however, significant organizational changes in the workplace have accompanied the development of atypical, irregular, and often unforeseeable working time schedules. This global development has rendered the reconciliation of family and work more difficult for parents and has far-reaching consequences for the daily schedule of all family members. Moreover, it poses serious challenges to France's common family policy because policymakers have difficulties in coping with conflicting interests within the family. Therefore, given these changes, how do those involved in the development and implementation of family policy tackle the issue of the "best interests" and welfare of children with two working parents?

By focusing on children under seven, I argue in this chapter that childcare policies in France are currently being driven more by labor market pressure and mothers' rights to paid work than the "best interests" of the child. After some methodological reflections, I give a historical overview of childcare and preschool education policies. I emphasize the continuities and changes in childcare policies and highlight the ways in which the boundaries between the state, families, and the market have been redrawn. In addition, I explore the rationales underpinning the policy changes in the area of childcare as well as the stakes involved at each stage of their development. Afterward, I analyze the reforms introduced since the 1990s in an attempt to shed light on what is at stake from perspective of "the best interests of the child" and public support to mothers' employment. Finally, I point out some of the tensions and dilemmas policymakers are currently facing in regard to childcare policies in France.

Some Methodological Reflections

During a given workweek, around 36 percent of French children under the age of three are cared for only by their parents, in most cases their mother.[6] Indeed, a significant proportion of mothers of young children are on parental leave and therefore do not work until the child is old enough to attend nursery school. And when they do work, it is usually on a part-time basis. Difficult working conditions, in particular work schedules that do not match the operating hours of public childcare facilities, as well as long commuting times and difficulties coping with the responsibilities of work and family, encourage these mothers to devote all of their time to raising their children.

Most mothers, however, resume their jobs after maternity leave and, as a result, have to rely on publicly subsidized childcare arrangements. During the sixteen weeks of maternity leave, they receive an earnings-related allowance (paid by the health insurance scheme) to cover living expenses. Many mothers, especially career-oriented professionals, resume their full-time jobs and thus devote a great deal of time to paid work. In particular, mothers with only one child under the age of three are economically active (80 percent in 2008). And among them, 54 percent were working full-time.[7]

While one might think that the implementation of the thirty-five-hour workweek for all employees in 1998 would have helped working parents combine family and work, upon closer examination it becomes clear that for many just the opposite occurred. Above all, many French firms responded to this new law by implementing more flexible and irregular working hours as a way of coping with the demands of an intensely competitive global economy, which shapes their internal working patterns and practices.[8] The development of flexible, irregular, and often not family-friendly work schedules, along with an increase in workload, has created new difficulties for families in which both parents are employed in managing their everyday life.[9] As a result, they are increasingly forced to rely on multiple—formal and informal—childcare arrangements with the result being that their children are likely to spend considerable time outside the home with different caregivers and educators.[10]

In light of these circumstances, it is important to investigate the effects of these new working conditions and parental rhythms of life and work on children's welfare. Is the right of children to spend enough time with their parents guaranteed? Where and how are young children cared for when both parents work full-time? Have policymakers been addressing these issues in a way that accounts for the long-standing French traditions of "quality of care" for children? My aim here is to offer some preliminary answers to these questions.

Drawing on the work of political scientist Peter Hall, who developed a tripartite model of the politics of social change, my analysis of changes in childcare policies since the 1970s will distinguish at each stage in the development:[11]

- *a process of first order change,* whereby instrument settings are changed (for example, the level at which childcare benefits and related tax deductions were set), while the overall goals and instruments of policy remain the same.

- *a process of second order change,* during which the instruments of policy as well as their settings are altered even though the overall goals of policy remain the same. For example, in the 1980s and 1990s, successive French governments with political majorities both on the right and left created new childcare allowances that would increase regularly in order to support mothers' employment and create new jobs in the care sector.

- *a process of third order change or paradigm shift,* which occurs when a radical policy shift produces simultaneous changes in all three components of policy: the instrument settings, the instruments themselves, and the hierarchy of goals behind policy. One example here is the move of French family policy from the "male-breadwinner model" to the "dual-earner model."

Peter Hall has used this tripartite model of the politics of social change to characterize this new pattern of behavior that has increasingly replaced older ones in politics, society, and the economy and to understand the processes whereby such patterns shift. His goal is to disaggregate the concept of "social learning," which he defines "as a deliberate attempt to adjust the goals or techniques of policy in response to past experience and new information. Learning is indicated when policy changes are the result of such a process."[12] The development of family policy in France illustrates well the usefulness of this model. During the 1980s, policymakers at the governmental level, citing research showing that fertility rates in West Germany were much lower than in France while the extent of female participation in the labor force was higher in France, extended public provision of childcare services as a means of further supporting mothers' employment.[13] Despite resistance from some organized social interests such as the more conservative family associations, boundaries between the state, families, and the market have been redrawn, providing clear evidence that the increasing entry of women into the labor force has been a key force for change in the French welfare system. Hall's model is thus appropriate for analyzing the evolution of French childcare policy since the paradigmatic shift that began in the 1970s.

Likewise, the theory of path dependency, according to which reforms are framed by past commitments and specific institutional arrangements, can also prove useful for investigating how the policies and the logic behind them have evolved in this arena, because public childcare services provided to working parents are embedded in a set of broader institutional arrangements.[14] As is the case in Scandinavia, the French government pursues an explicit family policy that is overseen by government institutions and is the subject of official reports produced annually. Indeed, the "family" itself is legally recognized as an institution that plays an important role in the maintenance of social cohesion and order. The appointment of a minister or of a secretary of state responsible for family issues by the French government since the 1970s further demonstrates the importance accorded to family policy. The principal institution responsible for it is the Caisse Nationale d'Allocations Familiales (CNAF), the National Family Allowance Fund, which oversees a large network of 123 Caisses d'Allocations Familiales (CAF), Local Allowance Funds. Theoretically, the social partners (including family organizations) represented on the executive board of the CNAF periodically determine the modes of intervention in family policy. In practice, however, decisions are made by the central government, whether previously approved by the executive board or not. It is only at the local level that the executive boards of the Family Allowance Funds have any real decision-making power and some room for maneuver in the provision and development of childcare services. Focusing on childcare policies in isolation would therefore not prove fruitful, because the goal of this chapter is to examine the overall organization of these policies and then place them in their institutional, historical, and cultural context.[15]

The Development of Public Daycare and Preschool Education

In order to understand the foundations of current childcare policy, one must first remember that children in France have historically been considered to be both a private and a public resource. They represent a "common good" and the "wealth of the nation," which, in return, bears certain obligations towards them. This long-standing tradition stretching back to the nineteenth century also helps to explain why crèches and *écoles maternelles* enjoy such widespread popular support.[16]

Indeed, the history of public childcare in France is inextricably linked to the notion that the state has an obligation to protect maternity, childhood, and the capacity of women to work outside the home. This conception, which is deeply embedded in republican ideals and prevailing ideas about citizenship, developed towards the end of the nineteenth century when it was generally agreed that the state, above all for demographic reasons (concern about the decline in fertility), needed to pay greater attention to motherhood and childrearing.[17] Therefore, in a context of conflicts between clericalists and anticlerical republicans over the control over education, the former *salles d'asile* were incorporated into the national, secular education system and renamed *écoles maternelles* in 1881. The republican government did not trust the education in the *salles d'asile*, which were opened since the 1820s as childcare and preschool institutions by charitable organizations, most of them controlled by the Catholic Church.

Subsequent legislation replaced nuns with state-employed teachers and established a national ministry responsible for the education of children aged three and older. Because many working-class mothers already participated in the labor force, *écoles maternelles* were open full-time to match their working schedule. As far as children under three years are concerned, the crèches had a separate development: this childcare system has been developed from a welfare model in which health improvement and protection from infant mortality and risk were paramount. Crèches first appeared in the 1840s, run by charities and catering to under-three-year-old children whose mothers worked. However their expansion took place only in the twentieth century in a context of growing concern about the demographic issue.

During the three decades that followed the end of World War II, legislators were, in fact, particularly concerned not only about the decreasing fertility rate but also about the high infant mortality rate. Protecting the physical health of children and pregnant women was thus placed at the forefront of the policy agenda. In this postwar context of demographic anxiety, the Protection Maternelle et Infantile (PMI) services were developed and reinforced. These services were a national public system of preventive healthcare and health promotion for all mothers and children from birth through age six. They have played an important role by assuming responsibility for the quality of public childcare provision. In addition to training and licensing childminders, they also license and monitor care services outside the school system so as to ensure compliance with health (including preventive health exams and vaccinations), safety, nutrition, and staffing standards.

Until the 1960s, the French government, as was the case elsewhere in Europe, promoted the "male-breadwinner/female-homemaker" family model by offering generous assistance to families in which only the man worked outside of the home.[18] In order to encourage mothers to stay home, couples with at least two children were offered financial incentives in the form of the Allocation de Salaire Unique (Single Salary Allowance). But beginning in the 1970s, the hierarchy of goals and the set of instruments employed to guide childcare policy shifted radically. Female work was increasingly needed in the labor market. Therefore, the government started a childcare policy that supported employment of married women and mothers. This policy shift was accompanied by substantial changes in the discourse exerted by policymakers who now supported the idea of the "double role" of women as mothers and employees. In addition, since the early 1970s, the new women's movement played a significant role in the public discourse on family and work as women's organizations demanded public childcare service. Against this background, political actors—in particular after the Socialists came to power in 1981 with the presidential election of François Mitterrand—were inclined to win women's votes on the basis of their support for childcare provision.[19]

At the same time, the level of the Single Salary Allowance was progressively reduced and restricted to low-income families, and in 1978 abolished altogether. Due to an acute labor shortage and a growing demand for qualified women to fill jobs in the tertiary sector (education, health, social services, administration, banking, etc.), the French government began to establish community-funded daycare centers (crèches) in an attempt to attract women into the workforce. As a result, not only did the labor force participation of women in general increase, but so too did that of mothers. Between 1962 and 1990 the participation rate of mothers between the ages of twenty-five and forty-nine and living with two children under the age of sixteen rose from 26 to 75 percent.[20] (See Table 8.1.)

TABLE 8.1: The development of the female labor force participation in France, 1975–2006[21]

Women aged	Percentage of employed women of the age group in the year			
	1975	1985	1995	2006
15–24	50%	44%	31%	31%
25–49	60%	72%	80%	82%
50 and more	43%	40%	44%	55%

This, in turn, stimulated demand for the expansion of public daycare facilities and other social services. This demand stemmed directly from the urban middle classes and was actively supported by the women's movement, which was strongly advocating greater gender equality in the labor market. Together, these factors provided a powerful impetus for a radical change in childcare policy and moved French policymakers to incorporate the model of the "working mother" into their plans for reform. As a result, a growing proportion of unpaid private childcare was assumed by paid public provision.

As more mothers entered the work force, politicians increasingly sought to win women's votes on the basis of their support for childcare provision. Likewise, policymakers became increasingly receptive to the arguments of early childhood specialists in favor of crèches. They soon moved to increase funding for local CAFs so that they could assume partial responsibility for the operating expenses of public childcare services, including crèches, and improve the quality of care for infants and young children. At the same time, legislators took yet another decisive step by creating a new childcare allowance for families in which the mother worked outside of the home. This decision was particularly symbolic because it also decreed that the Single Salary Allowance would henceforth be granted only to low-income families. Accompanying these reforms of public childcare policies, moreover, were new initiatives in the private sector. At the instigation of the respective Works' Committees, for example, several French companies established recreational centers and holiday camps for their employees' children.

The growing number of crèche slots and the increasing attendance of young children in *écoles maternelles* in the 1970s proved to be the decisive impetus to new childcare policies that placed greater emphasis on the "quality" of childcare provision. This is evidenced by a 1977 labor law that accorded "registered childminders" with the same rights and status as employees in other industries. Until then, their rights as workers had been restricted by the vagueness and ambiguity of their positions. In addition, this law marked the first steps towards the social recognition of the importance of the quality of childcare. The militant action and information campaigns organized by the National Association of Nursery Nurses, doctors in the Protection Maternelle et Infantile services, and psychologists to achieve such recognition were thus beginning to bear fruit. Finally, this legislation promoted the early socialization of young children by stressing that crèches offered an "ideal" preparation for nursery school.

When the French Socialist Party under François Mitterand came to power in 1981, trade unionists and policymakers spoke increasingly of the need to develop a childcare policy "to assist mothers" in balancing the dual responsibilities of work and family. As a result, funding allocated by both local authorities and the National Family Allowance Fund for the construction of crèches was substantially increased. As a corollary, the number of places available in childcare centers has been regularly augmented. By 2006, a total of 265,000 places were available: *crèches collectives* (147,467 slots) are publicly subsidized daycare centers in which 11 percent of children of all children under three are cared for by trained staff, either on a full-time or a part-time basis; *crèches familiales* (62,630 slots), which care for 17 percent of children under three, are organized by registered childminders who look after no more than three children in their own home and are paid by the local authority and monitored by qualified state infant care personnel; and *halte-garderies* (56,000 slots), which provide supplementary childcare, occasionally or for few hours a day and no more than twenty hours per week.[22] In combination with a change in women's attitudes vis-à-vis paid work, the development of these new public policies oriented toward working mothers interacted with the change in women's attitudes to produce a snowball effect that resulted in a rise in women's employment rates. (See Table 8.2.)

TABLE 8.2: The labor force participation[a] of mothers living with a partner—according to the number of children (aged less than eighteen) in France, 1990–2005[23]

Women	Percentage of employed mothers	
	1990	2005
Without any children under 18	60%	76%
1 child	77%	84%
2 children	74%	78%
3 children and more	44%	57%

(a) Including part-time work

The existence of *écoles maternelles* added to the growing movement in favor of shared public responsibility for young children.[24] Here too the number of available places has increased dramatically since the 1970s. In 2007, 18 percent of the children between the ages of two and three and 99 percent of those aged three to six attended, either on a full- or part-time basis, these free nursery schools.[25] On-site cafeterias and out-of-school-hours care centers have enabled more mothers to work full-time. Furthermore, with financial assistance from local CAFs, local authorities have gone a long way towards developing recreational infrastructure designed to occupy children on Wednesday (when all schools including nursery schools are closed; childcare facilities, however, are open) and after school.[26] Therefore, mothers are able to work on a full-time basis if they want or need to.

As a result of these reforms of the late 1970s and 1980s, it has become socially acceptable for a child under the age of three to be taken care of in public daycare facilities for the whole day while his or her parents are at work. Moreover, the early socialization that this care provides is often held in high esteem, particularly by educated professionals. Indeed, the probability that a child will attend a crèche increases significantly if his or her mother possesses a high level of education. In 2004, 12 percent of those children whose parents were in senior or middle management or worked as supervisors were enrolled in daycare, compared with only 7 percent of children from working-class families.[27] Among children aged three and under whose mothers work full-time, 30 percent of those living in well-off families (top fifth quintile of income) were cared for in a crèche. This, again, compares to only 22 percent of those living in the poorest families (first and second quintiles).[28] The development of the public infrastructure for childcare and the benefits linked to such care have thus corresponded directly to changes in child-rearing norms. France's historical legacy in the area of childcare therefore created a favorable context for the described development.

Promoting "Freedom of Choice"?
Individualized Formal Childcare Arrangements

Since the beginning of the 1990s, socioeconomic constraints and public concern about the dramatic rise in the unemployment rate have been the main drivers of second order change in childcare policies. Against the background of rising unemployment, in 1994 the right-oriented neo-Gaullist government decided to exploit the job-creating potential of the childcare sector by dramatically increasing childcare allowances and introducing special tax breaks designed to help families better meet the costs of "individualized" care arrangements (registered childminders and home helpers such as "nannies"). The government hoped to encourage families with young children to create employment while at the same time bringing more domestic workers into the formal economy. Adopting the rhetoric of "free choice for parents," and "diversification of childcare arrangements" to draw popular support, successive governments on both the left and right have begun to use family policy as a tool to fight unemployment without challenging the overall terms of the "working mother" model. At the same time, increasing internal flexibility (often employer driven and not always family friendly) in the workplace—in particular the development of irregular or nontraditional working hours—has led to rising demand for more "flexible" forms of childcare arrangements.

It is in this context that the issue of the children's interest, in terms of both the amount of time they spend with both parents and of the protection of their biological rhythms, seems to have been relegated to the backburner of the policy agenda. In order to increase the number of crèches, policymakers, including those in the ministry responsible for family policies, local authorities, and the CNAF, have established new ways to fund childcare facilities while at the same time developing more flexible regulations in regard to the skills of crèche workers (as shortage of qualified staff make it difficult to open new crèches).

Outsourcing of Care Work and the Promotion of Individualized Formal Childcare Arrangements

Regardless of their political leanings, in the 1990s French governments started to give priority to the development of "individual" childcare arrangements. Their underlying aim was to reduce the cost of hiring workers in the childcare sector. Both the CNAF and the state agreed to pay a portion of the social security contributions and salaries of registered but privately hired childminders and "nannies." To be eligible for such care, both parents with at least one child under the age of six must be either employed, registered as unemployed, or attending a training course.

The reduction in the cost of this type of childcare, however, was accompanied by an increase in the professionalism of childminders, who are now required to undergo training in the five years following their initial registration (since July 2005, 120 hours in total). These measures achieved considerable success, with the number of families receiving the childcare allowance associated with a registered childminder rising from 110,000 in 1991 to 686,000 in 2008. This childcare allowance covers the social security contributions to be paid by the employer of the registered childminder. An additional and income-related financial contribution is also given to the family.[29] As a result, with the exception of care provided by one of the parents on parental leave, the most common type of care arrangement for one- to three-year-old children of working parents is now the registered childminder. A second childcare allowance covers part of the social security contributions that must be paid by families who employ a nanny in their home to care for their child(ren). In addition, these families may deduct 50 percent, up to €6,000 per year, of the real costs from their income tax.

Despite vociferous criticism from women's associations, in 1994 the government also decided to encourage working parents who have a second child to opt to stay at home after the maternity (or paternity) leave. To do so, it provided these parents with a flat-rate child rearing benefit, the Allocation Parentale d'Education (APE), on the condition that they stop working or work only on a part-time basis until the child reaches the age of three. To be eligible for this benefit, parents were required to have worked or have been registered as unemployed before the birth. Despite a gender-neutral rhetoric, 98 percent of beneficiaries are currently women, thus reinforcing the widely held view that caring remains the primary responsibility of the mother.[30]

Given this disparity, the Socialist government that resumed power in 1995 made a serious attempt to encourage a more equal division of unpaid work between mothers and fathers. Official rhetoric on family issues began emphasizing the right of *both parents* to be present with a newborn baby. This ultimately resulted in the decision to extend paternity leave (paid at a full rate under a certain ceiling) from three to eleven days from January 2002. Today, approximately seven out of ten children under the age of three from dual-income families attend either a crèche or nursery school or are the subject of subsidized childcare, whether in the form of a registered childminder, help in their own home, or one of the two parents receiving the APE. In fact, this figure already exceeds the 2010 target that was set at the European Summit of Barcelona in 2002.[31]

Changes in the Instrumental Setting: The Reform of 2004

In 2004, a process of first order change took place when the conservative government headed by Prime Minister Dominique de Villepin introduced a reform of the system of childcare allowances. Above all, this reform replaced the two former childcare allowances with a single one, the Complément de libre choix du mode de garde (Supplement for the Freedom of Choice of Childcare Arrangements). This allowance is income related, and its amount also varies according to the type of childcare arrangement and the age of the child. Thanks to the significant increase in the amount of the allowance, it has become easier for low-income families to afford registered childminders than had previously been the case under the two-allowance system. But in reality, the only significant change in this reform was the provision of an allowance to parents with a single child under the age of three with the Complément de libre choix d'activité (Supplement for the Freedom of Choice to Work). This allowance is basically the equivalent of the former child-rearing benefit, but can only be received if the mother (or the father) has been continuously employed for at least two years before the child's birth. As a result of this new condition, mothers or fathers holding insecure or undeclared jobs are ineligible for this allowance. But the amount of the allowance is low at €552 per month in 2010 (if the parent does not work), and even decreases if the parent works part time. In 2006, the government introduced additional measures to benefit large families with at least three children. Following the birth of a third child or more, one of the two parents can take advantage of an allowance of €790 per month (in 2010) for a total of twelve months on condition that one parent stops working completely. This measure aims to encourage fathers who earn modest salaries to consider taking parental leave.

The Predicament of Childcare Policy: What Is at Stake?

In spite of its many successes—in particular a spectacular decline in the infant mortality rate since the end of World War II—French family policy is facing new challenges linked to dramatic changes in both the labor market and in the family sphere.[32] Policymakers and their social partners (executive boards of the CAFs, local authorities, employers, the trade unions, etc.) are confronted with increasing tensions resulting from contradictory demands of these social partners and must cope with conflicting interests within the family.

Dilemmas for Policymakers: Coping with Conflicting Interests Within the Family

The thirty-five-hour legislation passed in 1998 and modified in 2000 has reduced the average working time in France considerably. As a result, significant organizational changes in the workplace and intensification of work have gone hand-in-hand with a development of irregular and/or unforeseeable working-time schedules. The results of a survey conducted in 2003 among a representative sample of recipients of child benefits who have one child under the age of three indicate, for example, that 19 percent of the parents (father or mother) have irregular and unforeseeable work schedules. The combined impact of these developments has led many parents, especially mothers and fathers in senior or middle management positions or who work as supervisors and are thus often confronted with long working hours, to declare that their professional constraints make it difficult to organize childcare. Thirty-three percent of parents with at least one child under the age of three answered in the survey that their working schedules can "sometimes" or "often" make it difficult to organize child-care. This percentage is even higher in the group of parents who rely on a home helper to look after their child(ren) while they are at work—most of them being upper-middle-income families. Some 67 percent of parents face difficulties in this regard.[33]

Although the data in this area are scarce, it is likely that the time these parents are able to devote to their children during the work week has decreased and indeed sometimes during the weekend as well. This may well be the case despite the fact that the institutions responsible for childcare policies provide parents with various opportunities to cope with these professional constraints. For instance, according to the regulation of public childcare facilities, children can attend a crèche as well as an *école maternelle* for up to ten hours per working day.[34] In order to accommodate these changes in the workplace and enable working parents to meet the demands of their employers, the number of privately run but publicly funded childcare services and crèches that operate twenty-four hours a day, seven days a week, has increased over the past decade.

Due to these changes in work schedules and childcare policies, a significant proportion of children under three now spend large amounts of their time in outside childcare. For example, a survey carried out in 2005 on a representative sample of families with at least one child aged under seven has shown that among children aged three and under, 25 percent of those attending crèches spend more than 42.5 hours each week in crèches, 25 percent of those cared for by childminders spend more than 44 hours with them in the childminder's home, and 25 percent of those cared for by nannies spend more than 46 hours at home with nannies.[35] At the same time, nearly 60 percent of full-time registered childminders stated that they worked more than 45 hours a week.[36] Moreover, parents are often obliged to rely on multiple childcare arrangements during the same day and/or over the week, especially when their work schedules overlap. Consequently, staff in the childcare sector often mention and even denounce the fact that parents frequently match their child's daily and biological rhythms with their work schedules without taking their child's needs sufficiently into consideration.[37]

Given these circumstances, staff in childcare facilities and childminders are under increasing pressure to accept and adapt their own working hours to the needs of the growing numbers of parents confronted with flexible or irregular working hours. Taking into account their own family obligations, individuals employed in the childcare sector are also striving to protect their own interests. Not surprisingly, they are very reluctant to accept more flexible working hours. Registered childminders—if they can afford to—will often refuse to look after a child beyond standard working hours.[38] As a result, young children are often cared for by different persons and institutions within the same day, a situation that can prove to have a negative impact on their welfare and development.[39] This is especially the case for only children, children from single-parent households, or children whose parents both have irregular work schedules.[40]

In 2003, a report commissioned by the Haut Conseil de la Population et de la Famille emphasized the advantages and drawbacks of existing childcare arrangements from the point of view of children.[41] Underlining the importance of language learning on the cognitive and psychomotor development of children as well as the risks of infectious diseases in crèches, the report recommended both an increase in places in crèches and the further development of training programs to improve the skills of childminders and nannies at home. According to the report's authors, the current situation was far from satisfactory. Research on childminders has provided evidence that 49 percent have no qualification whatsoever, while another 35 percent are only poorly qualified.[42] The problem becomes all the more glaring if we take into account the lack of professional training for caregivers engaged in the home. These workers are exempt from all training and education requirements and are not supervised by PMI services despite the fact that parents who hire these workers receive public funding through childcare allowances. However revealing its findings are, this report neglected other aspects of children's welfare, not least of all the impact of the new working conditions of a growing proportion of parents on the daily rhythms of their children and the amount of time they spent with them.

Putting these issues on the policy agenda and getting them the media coverage they deserve, however, has proved difficult. The reasons for this lack of interest in both the government and general public are numerous, but three main explanations present themselves. First and most obviously, these issues are relatively new and insufficiently researched. Surveys on the amount of parental time invested in children are scarce and do not include adequate data to investigate the impact of working conditions on the time spent with children and on their daily rhythms. The most recent study, which is based on data from the "Time Use" survey conducted in 1998–1999 by the Institut national de la statistique et des études économiques (National Institute for Economic Studies, INSEE), did assess the time invested in family life, but did not take into consideration the childcare arrangements.[43] Moreover, this study was completed prior to the implementation of the thirty-five-hour laws.

Second, fighting unemployment and promoting gender equality on the labor market have been given priority over childcare on the policy agenda. Successive governments and advisory boards of family allowance funds have strongly advocated opening hours that are more in tune with the needs of working parents. In addition, they have promoted the development of more "flexible" childcare arrangements. In fact, enhancing women's employment, especially since the European Council of Lisbon in March 2000 and the creation of the European Employment Strategy, has stood so high on the policy agenda that in 2004 the Ministère du travail, des relations sociales, de la famille et de la solidarité, which is in charge of family affairs, introduced a measure promoting the creation of crèches in private companies by providing them with tax deductions. The ministry also required that CAFs partially fund these new crèches. But according to the Education Law passed in July 1989 on the regulation of children's attendance of nursery school, "Every child who reaches the age of three has the right to attend a nursery school as close as possible to his or her residence" in order to spare the child any fatigue related to long commuting time that could be potentially detrimental to his or her welfare.[44] Therefore, when policymakers adopted this measure, they turned a blind eye to the fact that the average commuting time in France has increased dramatically over the last two decades.[45] In addition, in November 2006 the responsible ministry presented a new *Plan petite enfance* (Childcare Program).[46] Citing the development of nontraditional work schedules, it stated that public childcare workers should work and be present "at various moments of the day, for instance very early in the morning and late in the evening." It did not, however, mention the possible impact that these new schedules would have on children's wellbeing.

Third, since the end of the nineteenth century, childcare policies have been at the forefront of social policy agenda. Indeed, it seems that in French collective memory, "quality of care" and concerns about children's interests are often taken for granted. In this context, the position of the child ombudsmen (*défenseur des enfants*), charged with the protection of the "interests of the child," was created in 2000. But its mission and its financial means are relatively limited.[47] And while the child ombudsmen have given annual reports on children's issues since 2000, they have concentrated on such issues as child abuse, violence within the family and at school, prevention of delinquency, the impact of poverty and parents' unemployment, the influence of divorce, and the adoption of children by gay couples. The only exception was the 2003 report, which mentioned the everyday life of young children. Following controversies among early childhood specialists, this report criticized the growing number of children between the ages two and three years old who were attending nursery school. Emphasizing research results by experts, it argued that because the *école maternelle* was not adapted to the special needs of children in this age group in terms of their biological rhythms, language learning and cognitive development might be impaired. Children of that age should, the report concluded, instead receive care in crèches or by registered childminders.[48] The *école maternelle* is indeed a school, not a kindergarten. Staffing consists primarily of teachers (*professeurs des écoles*). In addition, classes usually include (at least for a half day) an assistant (*agent spécialisé des écoles maternelles*). In 2003, there was on average one teacher to every twenty-seven children. In crèches, staffing standards are also set at the national level: there is to be one adult for every five babies, and one adult for every eight toddlers under three years. According to the Education Law, only children from an underprivileged social background, upon reaching the age of two, are given first priority at an *école maternelle*. However, the shortage of places in crèches, particularly in rural areas and the fact that the *école maternelle* is free to parents remain strong incentives to place two- to three-year-olds in them.

Given the new circumstances resulting from structural changes in the labor market and at the workplace, family policy in France is forced to cope with conflicting interests within the family. Above all, it seeks to promote children's welfare and allow them to spend time with their parents while at the same time providing women with the employment opportunities on an equal footing with men. As a result, policymakers are confronted with the following dilemma: Either they must make it a priority (for the sake of gender equality on the labor market) to help parents, in particular mothers, to adapt to the realities of the world of work and the demands of the employers so that they can keep their job or advance in their careers. In doing so, they will need to acknowledge that the effects of the organizational changes in the workplace on family life and children's wellbeing could prove to be contrary to the principles on which French family policy is founded. Or, if they attempt to focus more on the protection of children's welfare (for example, keeping in tune with their biological rhythms), policymakers must refuse to support the implementation of irregular and flexible work schedules that are contributing to the growing disruption of the traditional rhythms of the family. Taking into account the enduring gender division of unpaid work in France, this option might undermine gains in gender equality at the workplace by penalizing certain categories of mothers in occupational terms, particularly the most poorly skilled. In some cases, policymakers would be helping to exclude them from the labor market altogether. The effect of the thirty-five-hour work week has only further exacerbated the difficulties of coping with these tensions and divergent interests.

Conclusion

Since the 1970s, successive governments in France, whether on the right or left of the political spectrum, have radically changed childcare policies in response to societal pressure and—according to the model introduced by Peter Hall—a process of third order change took place, which only occurs when radical policy shift produces simultaneous changes in all three components of policy: the instrument settings, the instruments themselves, and the hierarchy of goals behind policy. The expansion of publicly provided childcare corresponded to a rise in female participation in the labor force, which in turn fueled political demands for still more public social services. These policy shifts gained widespread public support. As a result, the family policy branch of the social security system has proved to be immune to cutbacks in provision for children. And despite the general attempt to rein in public expenditures, childcare policies continue to be a growth area in the French welfare state. This mirrors the relative importance of the issue of how best to balance work and family life in the social and political agenda. But after the turn of the millennium in France, changes have been incremental and represent a process of first order change, in which instrument settings are changed, while the overall goals and instruments of policy remain the same. Issues related to the work/life balance have rarely strayed from their stable trajectory and have largely developed in accordance with the path dependency theory.[49]

Unlike Britain, Germany, or the Netherlands, it is still socially acceptable in France for children under the age of three to be cared for outside of the home in formal childcare provisions for the whole day while their parents are at work.[50] Early socialization is even considered to be of great value, particularly by the educated middle classes. The result is that among the member states of the European Union, France has one of the highest employment rates for mothers with young children. In addition, France tops, alongside of Ireland, the list of EU fertility rates. Over the last few decades, the progressive introduction of measures and schemes to support "working mothers" and the modernization of childrearing norms have coalesced to justify in the eyes of couples, and above all women, both having children and being present in the labor market. At the same time, the right of fathers to make a commitment to family life has made its mark on the social and political debate, as evidenced by the introduction of two weeks' statutory paternity leave, a measure that has had a strong symbolic impact. The French parental leave scheme could also be viewed as a welfare measure that yields more leisure time and reduces pressure on families with young children, above all in low-income families. Through this scheme, parents' social right to provide care for their young children has been validated and recognized.[51] Moreover, policies encouraging paid care outside the family have had some positive results in terms of the inclusion of women in the work force. This has especially been the case for unqualified or low-skilled immigrant women, whose employment rate has been increasing rapidly and who, thanks to childcare allowances, receive guarantees of social rights and a minimum wage.

Nevertheless, the reforms that have been introduced since the mid-1980s in the realm of childcare illustrate the growing influence that employment policies have had on French family policy. Despite the rhetoric promoting "freedom of choice," due to the unbalanced power relationships between employers and employees, the fight against unemployment and the development of "workfare" policies have been given first priority. This confirms that welfare state regimes are closely interrelated with different labor market institutions and policies.[52] By providing working parents with more flexible childcare arrangements to meet the demands of their employers, policymakers have been inclined to give second place to children's interests on the policy agenda. It is noteworthy, however, that recent research has once again demonstrated that nontraditional work schedules and long working hours may have detrimental effects on children's wellbeing and on the quality of interactions within the family.[53] Other research has shown that a more equal division of responsibility between parents in early childhood can have numerous positive effects on that child's future wellbeing and success.[54]

Given the rapid organizational changes in the workplace, should not policymakers be paying more attention to the wellbeing of children? Is it socially equitable to maximize female labor market participation in order to underpin economic growth and to comply with the European Union gender equality policy without at the same time taking into consideration the best interests of the child? Could a new policy design simultaneously provide both men and women with a genuine choice to provide both paid and unpaid care while spending enough time with their children? These are some of the questions that policymakers need to address as they consider new approaches to childcare in France.

Notes

1. All working parents are provided with childcare allowances. These childcare allowances are, however, income-related, which means that poor working families are given more generous allowances than well-off families.

2. OECD, *Family database* (Paris, 2009). Retrieved 27 December 2009: http://www.oecd.org/dataoecd/1/37/43199008.xls. See also *Babies and Bosses: Reconciling Work and Family Life,* vol. 5, *A Synthesis of Findings for OECD Countries* (Paris, 2007).

3. For more, see Susan Pedersen, *Family, Dependence, and the Origins of the Welfare State. Britain and France, 1914–1945* (Cambridge, UK, 1993).

4. OECD, *Starting Strong II: Early Childhood Education and Care* (Paris, 2006), 325–26; Kimberly Morgan, "Does Anyone Have a 'Libre Choix'? Subversive Liberalism and the Politics of French Childcare Policy," in *Childcare Policy at the Crossroads: Gender and Welfare State Restructuring,* ed. Sonya Michel and Rianne Mahon (New York, 2002), 146.

5. Eurostat, *Demographic and Socio-economics Factors Indicators: Fertility Rate, 2008.* Retrieved 24 January 2009: http://ec.europa.eu/health/ph_information/dissemination/echi/echi_1_en.htm#5; see also Jeanne Fagnani, "Family Policies in France and Germany: Sisters or Distant Cousins?" *Community, Work and Family* 10, no. 1 (2007): 39–56.

6. Marie Ruault and Audrey Daniel, "Les modes d'accueil des enfants de moins de six ans," *Études et résultats,* Direction de la recherche, des études, de l'évaluation et des statistiques, (DREES), no. 235 (2003): 1–11. Retrieved 24 January 2009: http://www.sante.gouv.fr/drees/etude-resultat.

7. Institut national de la statistique et des études économiques (INSEE), *Enquête Emploi* (Paris, 2006). Retrieved 24 January 2009: http://www.insee.fr/fr/ffc/chifcle.

8. Jeanne Fagnani and Marie Thérèse Letablier, "Work and Family Life Balance: The Impact of the 35 Hour Laws in France," *Work, Employment and Society* 18, no. 3 (2004): 551–72. See also Diane Perrons et al., eds., *Gender Divisions and Working Time in the New Economy* (Northampton, MA, 2006).

9. Sophie Bressé et al., "La garde des enfants en dehors des plages horaires standard," *Études et Résultats,* Direction de la recherche, des études, de l'évaluation et des statistiques (DREES): no. 551 (2007): 2–8.

10. Jeanne Fagnani and Marie Thérèse Letablier, "Caring Rights and Responsibilities of Families in the French Welfare State," in *Care Arrangements and Social Integration in European Societies,* ed. Birgit Pfau-Effinger and Barbara Geissler (Berlin, 2005), 153–72.

11. Peter Hall, "Policy Paradigms, Social Learning and the State: The Case of Economic Policymaking in Britain," *Comparative Politics* 25, no. 3 (1993): 275–96.

12. Ibid., 278.
13. Fagnani, "Family Policies," 39–56.
14. For more on path dependency, see the introduction in this volume.
15. Jeanne Fagnani, "Family Policy in France," in *International Encyclopedia of Social Policy,* ed. Tony Fitzpatrick et al. (Oxford, 2006), vol. 3, 501–6.
16. Kimberly Morgan, "Forging the Frontiers between State, Church and Family: Religious Cleavages and the Origins of Early Childhood Education and Care Policies in France, Sweden and Germany," *Politics and Society* 30, no. 1 (2002): 113–48.
17. Jean-Noël Luc, *L'invention du jeune enfant au 19ème siècle. De la salle d'asile à l'école maternelle* (Paris, 1993).
18. Fagnani, "Family Policy," 501–6.
19. See Kristina Schulz, *Der lange Atem der Provokation. Die Frauenbewegung in der Bundesrepublik und in Frankreich 1968–1976* (Frankfurt/M., 2002).
20. INSEE, *Census 1962 and 1990.*
21. INSEE, *Enquêtes Emploi* (Paris, 2008). Retrieved 24 January 2009: http://www.insee.fr/fr/themes/tableau.asp?reg_id=0&ref_id=NATCCF03103.
22. Guillaume Bailleau, "L'accueil collectif et en crèches familiales des enfants de moins de six ans en 2006," *Études et Résultats,* DREES, no 608 (2007): 1–8.
23. INSEE, *Enquêtes Emploi* (Paris, 1990 and 2005). Retrieved 25 January 2009: http://www.insee.fr/fr/methodes/default.asp?page=definitions/enquete-emploi.htm.
24. Morgan, "Forging the Frontiers," 30.
25. Information provided by the Caisse Nationale d'Allocations Familiales (National Family Allowance Fund, CNAF) (Paris, 2009).
26. The lesson-free Wednesday afternoon was created in the nineteenth century for religious education outside school. Its introduction was a compromise between a secular state and the Catholic Church, which in return accepted state control of the whole education system and secular compulsory schools. See Luc, *L'invention du jeune enfant.*
27. Ruault and Daniel, "Les modes d'accueil," 235.
28. Sophie Bressé and Bénédicte Galtier, "La conciliation entre vie familiale et vie professionnelle selon le niveau de vie des familles," *Études et Résultats,* DREES, no. 465 (2006): 1–10.
29. CNAF. Retrieved 24 January 2009: http://www.caf.fr/wps/portal.
30. Bressé and Galtier, "La conciliation."
31. See Barcelona European Council, *Presidency Conclusions,* 15 and 16 March 2002, SN 100/1/02 rev 1.
32. The infant mortality rate declined from 52 per thousand in 1950 to 7.3 in 1990 and 4.1 in 2002. L'Institut national d'études démographiques (INED) (Paris, 2008).
33. Centre de recherche pour l'étude et l'observation des conditions de vie (CREDOC), *Les allocataires de la Prestation d'accueil du jeune enfant,* Report for CNAF (Paris, 2006), 113.
34. Included in the "*Code de l'action sociale*" (Social policy regulation). Retrieved 24 January 2009: http://daniel.calin.free.fr/textoff/code_action_sociale.html.
35. Ruault and Daniel, "Les modes d'accueil," 235.
36. Nathalie Blanpain and Milan Momic, "Les assistantes maternelles en 2005," *Études et Résultats,* DREES, no. 581 (2007): 2–8.
37. Evelyne Renaudat, "Les dernières réformes des modes de financement aux crèches," *Recherches et prévisions,* no. 85 (2006): 76–82.
38. For instance, if it is difficult for parents to find another childcare arrangement or if she is highly valued by the family.
39. Rachel Schumacher and Elizabeth Hoffmann, *Continuity of Care: Charting Progress for Babies in Childcare Research-Based Rationale,* Center for Law and Social Policy (CLASP),

Washington DC, 1–7 August 2008. Retrieved 24 January 2009: http://www.clasp.org/publications/cp_rationale3.pdf.

40. Bressé, "La garde," 551.
41. The Haut Conseil (established in 1985) has only advisory powers. It provides advice to the government on family issues and demography.
42. Blanpain and Momic, "Les assistantes maternelles," no. 581, 6.
43. See more generally Louis Lesnard and Alain Chenu, *Disponibilité parentale et activités familiales. Les emplois du temps familiaux dans la France des années 1980 et 1990*. Report for the Haut Conseil de la Famille et de la Population (Paris, 2003).
44. Education Law of 10 July1989, art. 2. Retrieved 24 January 2009: http://www.ac-nancy-metz.fr/VieScolaire/Textes_circ/LoiOrient.htm.
45. George Crague, "Des lieux de travail de plus en plus variables et temporaires," *Economie et Statistique*, no. 369–370 (2003): 25–37.
46. Ministère du travail, des relations sociales, de la famille et de la solidarité, *Plan petite enfance*, 10 November 2006. Retrieved 24 January 2009: http://www.social.gouv.fr/htm/dossiers/dpm/index.htm.
47. La Défenseure des enfants. Retrieved 24 January 2009: http://www.defenseurdesenfants.fr.
48. Ibid.
49. See Jeanne Fagnani, "Les réformes de la politique familiale en Allemagne: l'enjeu démographique," *Institut Français des relations Internationales* (IFRI) no 71 (2009), Coll. Notes du CERFA. Retrieved 27 December 2009: http://www.ifri.org/frontDispatcher/ifri/publications/note_du_cerfa_1046782795256.
50. Fagnani and Letablier, "Caring Rights," 156.
51. See more generally Sheila Kamerman and Alfred Kahn, eds., *Beyond Child Poverty: The Social Exclusion of Children* (New York, 2002).
52. For a more general discussion, see Gøsta Esping-Andersen, *Social Foundations of Postindustrial Economies* (Oxford, 1999).
53. Lyndal Strazdins et al., "Unsociable Work? Nonstandard Work Schedules, Family Relationships and Children's Well-being," *Journal of Marriage and the Family* 68, no. 2 (2006): 394–410.
54. For a more general discussion, see Paul Gregg and Elizabeth Washbrook, *The Effects of Early Maternal Employment on Child Development in the UK*, CMPO Working Paper Series 03/070 (Bristol, 2003).

Chapter 9

CONTRASTING POLICIES OF ALL-DAY EDUCATION

Preschools and Primary Schools
in France and Italy since 1945

Cristina Allemann-Ghionda

The education systems of France and Italy both feature an all-day time policy for their pre- and primary schools. But while in France all-day education has long since been the norm, in Italy it is only one option in a hybrid system that continues to be dominated by part-time schooling. One result of this difference is that the term *time policy* is only known in Italy. Here the phrase *politiche temporali* (literally, "time policies") was introduced some years ago by educationalists and social scientists who studied social and family policies.[1] According to a study produced by the Italian National Institute of Statistics, it is necessary to coordinate the daily and weekly schedule of schools, workplaces, and public services more effectively in order to help parents reconcile family obligations and paid work on a more equitable basis for women.[2] While the reconciliation of family life and work time has also been a subject of debate in France, in Italy experts and policymakers have focused more on offering parents greater choice and flexibility in childcare, including in terms of time schedules.[3]

At first glance, the fact that all-day schools exist in France and in Italy might suggest that the two countries share a similar educational philosophy that accords a strong role for the state in education. Upon closer examination, however, major differences can be discerned. Above all, all-day education has a much longer tradition in France, where it was introduced along with compulsory schooling in 1881. In France, until 1945 the most common form of all-day education for primary schools was the divided all-day school, with lessons in the morning and afternoon and a long

Notes for this chapter begin on page 215.

lunch break at home. The basic structures of French school time policy underwent remarkably little change until the 1960s. In Italy, the traditional form of all-day schooling with lessons in the morning and the afternoon often, but not in all cases, separated by a long lunch break at home was, as in other parts of Europe, common in private schools, most of which were run by the Catholic Church, long before the introduction of compulsory education between 1859 and 1861. It was not until the early 1970s, however, that all-day education was funded as a result of a new school law. According to the educationalist Giuseppe Cerini, all-day schooling in Italy developed in four phases: first, a preliminary stage in the 1950s and 1960s; second, the institutional and legal establishment of all-day schools in the 1970s; third, a phase of consolidation in the 1980s and 1990s; and fourth, a period beginning in 2000 characterized by new developments.[4] In contrast to France, the history of all-day schooling in Italy has thus been characterized by discontinuity.

In addition, the political, social, and pedagogical arguments that led to the implementation of all-day schools in France and Italy also exhibit important differences. In France, the state and Catholic Church have been strictly separated since the early twentieth century. In fact, successive governments confirmed compulsory public all-day education to reinforce this separation.[5] In Italy, no such separation between the state and the Catholic Church exists. Instead, there is a long tradition of political and institutional cooperation between the two. Unlike in Austria and Germany, in Italy beginning in the 1960s, Catholic educationalists actively supported the establishment of all-day schools. At the same time, however, all-day schooling was never made compulsory as it was in France, and, as a result, is not nearly as available. Not surprisingly, the pedagogical goals of all-day schooling as well as their implementation in the two countries also feature important differences.

In the following, I compare the development of the all-day time policy in the French and Italian primary school systems. My comparison centers on the question of why and how the patterns of the all-day time structure were introduced in the public primary school systems of these two countries.[6] In the first part, I examine the chronological development of the all-day policy in both countries. Because it is less well known, I pay more attention to the Italian case. In the second part, I analyze the similarities and differences in the two systems by addressing the following four factors that proved to be the most significant in both countries:

1. The political and pedagogical arguments used to legitimate all-day schooling;

2. The relationship between school time policies, gainful employment of mothers, and the development of the birth rate;

3. The prevailing notions of the role of the state and families in education; and

4. The structural inclusiveness of the school systems.

In the conclusion, I place the results of this comparison in a broader context in order to identify patterns of path dependency in the development of school time policy in both countries.[7]

The Time Structure of the Public Primary School System to 1945

The French all-day model, which is characterized by the strong authority of a highly centralized state, is the result of an education policy that was first discussed and designed during the French Revolution. In his 1792 *Report and Draft of a Decree of the General Organization of the Public School System,* the Marquis de Condorcet called for the implementation of compulsory schooling.[8] When the Third Republic finally implemented compulsory public education in 1882, both political interests and economic needs informed all-day time policy. Three political principles, each of which was formed by the idea that public education had to foster the social, cultural, and political unity of the French nation, proved crucial: *gratuité* (school had to be free for everybody), *loyauté* (school had to shape students into citizens loyal to the Republic), and *laïcité* (the separation between the state and the churches). This third and especially enduring principle was set down in law in 1905. In addition, the republican government took into account the needs of the large agricultural sector. Peasants in particular needed their children to help with farm work during the summer months. These factors—both ideological and practical—helped establish the all-day time structure in France.[9]

In Italy, compulsory education was first established in the Kingdom of Piedmont-Sardinia and Lombardy by the Casati Law of 1859, which was extended to the entire Kingdom of Italy after unification in 1861. According to this law, all children over six were required to attend the *scuola elementare* for at least two years. Although the Italian state remained a constitutional monarchy until the founding of the republic in 1946, its educational philosophy had much in common with that of France.[10] Most importantly, Italian politicians generally agreed that the state needed to exercise control over the nation's education system. While the Catholic Church, which had dominated the Italian education system for centuries, was not to be marginalized altogether, the government, guided by the principle of a free church within a free state, did seek to curtail its traditional influence somewhat and gradually replace most of its schools with state-run institutions. Still, the state explicitly recognized private schools and paternal authority as important pillars of Italian education. The Casati Law underwent several amendments, but remained in force until 1923. Soon after taking power in 1922, the Fascist government under Benito Mussolini began work on an extensive school reform, and in 1923 implemented the so-called Gentile Reform, named after Mussolini's first minister of education, philosopher Giovanni Gentile. This reform extended compulsory school education until the age of fourteen and created a highly selective two-track secondary school system that was designed to preserve social distinctions and prevent social mobility, while striving to educate an elite. In addition, the Lateran Pacts of 1929 defined the relationship between the Italian state and the Catholic Church and its role in the education system for decades to come. This concordat, which remains in force today, stipulated on the one hand that Catholic religious teaching was to be part of the curriculum of public schools, and on the other confirmed that private Catholic schools could continue to exist, but only when approved and supervised by the state.[11]

The Italian education system was not initially conceived as an all-day system. Indeed, the state lacked the resources to finance traditional all-day education, which was common for private primary and secondary schools, for all public primary and secondary schools. Shift classes in agrarian regions and half-day schooling in urban areas thus became the norm. This time policy was in harmony with the ideal of the "male-breadwinner/female-homemaker" family, which stood at the foundation of social, family, and education policy in Italy well into the 1960s. During the Fascist era, this family model and the idealization of women as mothers and housewives had played a particularly prominent role in the regime's political propaganda.[12] However, the Fascist government complemented half-day schooling with a program of collective after-school education that included leisure activities and paramilitary training aimed at molding children and youth into loyal Fascist citizens.[13]

Reconstruction and Stagnation:
From the Postwar Years to the Late 1950s

The lack of political stability in France in the wake of World War II caused all far-reaching plans for educational reform, for example the Langevin-Wallon plan of 1947, to fail. It was thus not until the end of the 1950s that the French government was able to initiate a fundamental reform of the education system.[14] As was the case in several other European countries, the need for an ever better-educated workforce to fuel the postwar boom led education to be seen as an "economic resource." Above all, policy-makers agreed that the percentage of students with a secondary education had to be increased significantly. There was also a growing recognition that teaching methods needed to be modernized.[15] Pedagogic innovations proposed by Célestin Freinet and other reform-minded educationalists of the *éducation nouvelle* movement began to transform teaching styles in primary school classrooms. In fact, the French all-day schedule offered a conducive time framework for realizing the reformers' vision of a multi-faceted, active education that would equip students with the knowledge and skills necessary for their later entrance into the labor market.[16]

In Italy, World War II was followed by a period of transition and con-tradictory tendencies in education policy. From the liberation in 1943 until 1946, when the First Republic of Italy was founded, the Western Allies pursued a broad policy of the "reeducation" of the Italian population that included not least of all rebuilding and reforming the Italian school sys-tem. First and foremost, they sought to "cleanse" school education of the legacy of the Mussolini regime, which in practice meant replacing Fascist principals and teachers and fundamentally revising the structures of the educational system and its curriculum. Inspired by the ideas of the Ameri-can philosopher and educationalist John Dewey and other educational re-formers, the Allies saw the establishment of a comprehensive, integrated all-day school system as a pillar of their plan to create a more democratic education system that would, they hoped, foster greater equality and so-cial mobility in postfascist Italy.[17] With the end of the Allied occupation in January 1947, however, Italy entered into a period of political restoration. In the free and universal election in April 1948 the Democrazia Cristiana (DC), under the undisputed leadership of Alcide De Gasperi, defeated the Popular Front of the Communist and Socialist Party with 48 percent of the vote. Despite strong opposition from the Partito Comunista Italiano (PCI), the DC, which enjoyed the support of the Vatican, would dominate Italian educational policy for the next four decades. As a consequence, the Italian school system continued to be shaped by the Gentile Reform of 1923, especially in secondary education. Under the DC government, school structures returned to the patterns established by the Fascist re-gime and remained unchanged until 1962. While compulsory schooling was officially set at eight years, the majority of Italian students did not attend more than five, and only an elite of about 5 percent completed sec-ondary education.[18]

Family policy, which continued to be based on the conservative ideal of the male-breadwinner/female-homemaker family, became an important tool in the project to "restore" Italian society after World War II. Women were to stay home and dedicate themselves to raising their children. Not surprisingly, in 1951 only 21 percent of the Italian women were employed. Many more, however, worked unofficially as "supporting family members" in agriculture or small businesses without ever being counted in the labor market statistics or being paid for their work.[19] The "Economic Miracle" that began in the 1950s with the support of the Marshall Plan increased Italian businesses' demand for labor, especially in the more industrialized north. Thus began a massive migration from the impoverished south to the booming industrial cities in the north. More and more women began to enter the labor market and as they did, their expectations concerning education and gainful occupation started to change.[20] Married women, however, still required the permission of their husbands to work outside the home. Furthermore, it was not until 1975, when the Italian Parliament approved equal rights for women and men, that their official legal status experienced a substantial improvement.[21]

In the 1950s, the extended nature of the Italian family meant that the children of working mothers, whether in industry, on the farm, or in small business, could be taken care of by other family members when they were not in school. This task usually fell to grandmothers or other elderly relatives, but older children, especially in rural areas, were also expected to help out on the farm or look after their younger siblings. All-day care and education were thus seen largely as measures of "social help" for very poor, disadvantaged, and neglected children and were provided primarily by charity organizations. At the time, there was no widespread demand for such care. By the late 1950s, however, a new debate about all-day schooling began to emerge as part of the broader discussion concerning the need for a new, reformed pedagogy in Italy. This and other public and political debates helped pave the way for the structural reforms that would eventually transform the Italian education system in the 1960s and 1970s.[22]

The Era of Structural and Curricular Reforms: 1960s to 1980s

As was the case in many other European countries, radical social and economic change in the decades following the end of World War II engendered new ways of thinking about education and educational policy in the 1960s and 1970s in both France and Italy.[23] From 1958 to 1969, France was led by a conservative government headed by Charles de Gaulle. Despite de Gaulle's firm grip on power for most of this decade, beginning in the mid-1960s the communist and socialist opposition gained increasing influence in debates over social issues, not least of all education. Above all, they argued that the much-touted social equality of the French education system was nothing more than a rhetorical fig leaf that masked deep inequalities. Their position was supported by social scientists whose empirical research demonstrated that educational institutions were not "just" and equally accessible to everyone, but rather played a central role in reproducing social differences and inequalities. In their path-breaking 1970 book *La reproduction: Eléments pour une théorie du système d'enseignement*, sociologists Pierre Bourdieu and Jean-Claude Passeron offered convincing evidence of the many failures of the French education system. This important work influenced educational debates not just in France, but in many Western European countries, including Italy.[24]

As a result of this debate, it became clear that the selective and elitist structures of the education system stood in the way of increasing the number of the more qualified, better-educated workers required to sustain the growing French economy. Since the late 1950s, critics had been demanding that all levels of education be opened to people from all social backgrounds, and first passed reforms in 1959. The mass demonstrations and strikes that roiled France in May 1968 severely challenged de Gaulle's legitimacy and forced the government to embark on a policy of reform. The structural reforms of the education system that his government initiated—generally available preschool education for ages three to six since 1968, integrated special education of handicapped students—had no effect on the existing all-day time structure of schools, which remained the norm. Beginning in the 1960s, however, the traditional divided-time structure was increasingly replaced by a more modern version that included a school lunch as well as extracurricular activities.[25] Comprehensive lower secondary school was introduced later, in 1975, again without altering the weekly time pattern.

An intense debate over the need for an educational reform also began in Italy in the 1960s. There the structural reforms of the education system that occurred in the 1960s and 1970s were closely linked to the goal of establishing a modern form of all-day education. The agenda for educational reform was driven primarily by the politically and pedagogically motivated critique of the class structure of the two-track Italian school system, which was, critics maintained, inherently socially exclusive. In 1962, a new center-left government led by the DC initiated a series of structural reforms that radically changed the elitist and segregated Italian school system. Most importantly, it merged the two tracks in lower secondary schools into a comprehensive school (*scuola media unica*), which included grades six to eight.[26] The "historic compromise" between the DC and PCI under Prime Minister Aldo Moro, who held office from 1963 to 1968 and then again from 1974 to 1976, created a political climate more conducive to educational reform. In 1968, the government introduced public provision of all-day preschool for three- to six-year-old children. A decade later, in 1977, the "special education" for physically or mentally handicapped children in separated classes that had been established with the Gentile Reform of 1923 was abolished, and such children were integrated into regular education with targeted assistance from specialized teachers. Finally, in 1985, under Bettino Craxi, the first socialist prime minister (1983 to 1987) and head of the Partito Socialista Italiano (PSI), the primary school curriculum was adapted to contemporary pedagogical theories and teaching methods.[27]

The Italian debate on all-day schooling (literally "full-time schooling" or *scuola a tempo pieno*) focused primarily on primary schools. Unlike other European countries such as Austria and West Germany, proponents from across the political spectrum supported all-day school education, which was generally considered to be the best possible pedagogical approach to—at least partially—counteract and compensate for the class differences between students as well as to integrate students with special educational needs into the regular classroom.[28] The international movement for education based on the idea of a new reformed pedagogy, in particular the American concept of a "progressive education" and French *éducation nouvelle,* influenced the social and pedagogical arguments in favor of all-day education. The political culture in Italy during the 1960s and 1970s offered fertile ground for such an approach, as did the Italian tradition of Montessori education, which also required an all-day schedule.[29]

Two of the most important voices in the emerging Italian debate on full-time schooling belonged to the Catholic educationalists Cesare Scurati and Franco Lombardi. In their 1982 book *Pedagogia: termini e problemi* they referred to the pedagogical approach of "personalism," which promotes the "full human development" (physical and mental as well as social and cultural) of all students. If school education was to accomplish this ambitious goal, they argued, it needed to adapt to the unique characteristics of each individual student. Moreover, it should no longer be limited to knowledge accumulation and cognitive "learning" alone, but instead be designed to promote student creativity, for example by integrating arts and music into the curriculum. According to Scurati and Lombardi, a more "well-rounded" education would contribute positively to the integration of the individual in the community. To reach these goals, they called for a new set of individualized and cooperative methods of instruction as well as an all-day curriculum, because such pedagogical innovation required more time spent in school in order to be effective. At the same time, these reformers emphasized that school was just one, albeit the most important, "agency" of education in society.[30]

Scurati and Lombardi also cited the changing conditions of family life as a key argument for the necessity of all-day schooling. They emphasized that in Italy the family had ceased to be a "patriarchal" institution, but instead was increasingly reduced to a core of two parents and one or two children, or a household headed by a single mother. These new family types, they argued, could no longer guarantee the necessary socialization of children that extended families had provided in the past. In addition, they referred to the rising percentage of gainfully employed mothers and the consequences of urban life, which limited children's opportunities for outdoor play. Only all-day schooling, they concluded, could compensate for these changing living conditions.[31]

In 1971, a center-left coalition government led by the DC passed a new School Law that established the legal foundations for all-day primary schooling.[32] It was not until 1979, however, that the option of a "longer school time" for lower secondary education was introduced. Still, by the late 1970s, the legal framework for all-day education for the entire Italian school system from preschool to lower secondary education was in place, even if it was not, as was the case in France, compulsory. Importantly, the impetus for this reform came not from government itself, but from the trade unions, the parliamentary opposition, and a strong extraparliamentary movement that emerged during the so-called years of lead (*anni di piombo*), the period between 1969 and the late 1970s during which Italy was deeply affected by widespread social conflict, opposing political extremisms, and violence.[33] The School Law of 1971 was itself a direct response to a general strike that, among other things, demanded equal access to education.

The new Italian School Law provided for a variety of forms of all-day primary education. For example, additional afternoon classes were introduced to help less-privileged students with their homework. Similarly, some schools offered extracurricular activities on a voluntary basis for those students whose parents were both employed, or extended the regular twenty-four-hour weekly schedule by adding art and sports. Other schools opted for a compulsory forty-hour weekly schedule.[34] Despite these innovations, the implementation of all-day schooling proved to be a slow and very uneven process that differed widely from region to region. While in 1980 around 50 percent of students attended all-day schools in highly industrialized northern cities like Milan, Bologna, and Modena, only 3 to 4 percent did in the larger cities of the south like Naples, Bari, and Palermo.[35] This uneven distribution of all-day education reflected the economic divide separating the north and the south of Italy, urban and rural areas, and the peninsula and the numerous larger and smaller islands. This divide was further reinforced by the different stages of development of the education system in different regions, because the realization of all-day schooling depended in large measure on the political priorities, cooperation, and financial situation of regional school administrations.

Despite this uneven start, the 1980s did see the consolidation of all-day schooling in Italy. In 1990, a structural reform of the primary school system introduced important changes that favored all-day schools. Most importantly, the curriculum now had to be taught in modules, which required more school time. In addition, three teachers were made responsible for two classrooms, which encouraged team-teaching and more active, individualized teaching methods in small groups.[36] Thus, while all-day schooling had still not been implemented in all regions of Italy, by the mid-1990s it had gained widespread acceptance in Italian politics and society.

The Emergence of Neoliberal Thinking: 1990s to 2008

The all-day time structure of the French pre- and primary school system has undergone very little change since the 1960s. French children first enter the *école maternelle,* which, without being compulsory, is attended by 100 percent of three- to six-year-olds.[37] They are then enrolled in the *école primaire,* which lasts another five years and includes twenty-four lessons per week. Wednesdays (alternatively, in some places, Thursdays) are entirely free and can be used for religious education. Lunchtime is usually between 12:00 and 2:00 P.M. and a warm, complete meal is available in every school canteen, the quality of which is controlled by the state. School meals are inexpensive, with prices adapted to parents' income and their number of children. Parents with six or more children pay nothing at all. On average, about half of French students eat lunch at school.[38] Moreover, pre- and primary schools offer some kind of out-of-school supervision after regular school hours. This care, called *études surveillées* (supervised individual work), can be used for homework. But while it is available to all students, it is mostly weaker students seeking extra help with their homework who take advantage of it. The state guarantees supervision in and outside the school buildings while also cooperating with local communities to provide transportation to and from school.[39]

In France, the discussion of the time policy of primary schooling has largely focused on the free Wednesday and school holidays, in particular the very long summer break. Since a high percentage of French women are employed, parents need to find informal or formal care arrangements for the free Wednesday and school holidays. To facilitate the reconciliation of family and work, an increasing number of schools use their partial administrative autonomy to replace the free Wednesday with a free Saturday, a policy that the government supports so long as a majority of the parents concur. Other schools cooperate with out-of-school institutions that offer regularly scheduled extracurricular activities on Wednesdays and organize summer camps. In particular, physical education classes organized by schools in cooperation with the Union Nationale des Sports Scolaires et Universitaires are often held on Wednesdays.[40]

The arrangement of school schedules is, however, not simply a question of time management. It also affects the *rythme scolaire*, i.e., a distribution and sequence of lessons and other activities during the school day and week that reflect students' changing level of energy and attention. Here as well, the traditionally very demanding, cognitively oriented curriculum of the French primary school system has undergone important changes over the last few decades. Particularly important has been the attempt to organize a more active and stimulating learning process for students by introducing variations in teaching methods. Since the 1990s, French primary schools have offered more and more optional extracurricular activities during lunchtime and after school as a way of diversifying the students' learning experience. The so-called *foyer socio-éducatif* (socio-educational center), for example, organizes a variety of activities such as theater, editing the school newspaper, the UNESCO Club, and sports.[41]

This multifaceted offering is only possible because of French teachers' high level of training. Since 1991, the standardized education of preschool and primary school teachers in teacher colleges at the tertiary level, the Instituts Universitaires pour la Formation des Maîtres (IUFM), has guaranteed that teachers are highly qualified.[42] At school their work is supported by the Centre de Documentation et d'Information, which helps teachers and students develop projects for independent learning by providing books, new media, and other resources. In addition, qualified support staff and nonteaching personnel assist teachers in schools. On average, 28 percent of school employees are non-teachers.[43] The nonteaching personnel are responsible for, among other things, supervising the lunch break and all types of independent student work, including homework after school. The most important members of this support staff are the "main educational advisors" (*conseiller principal d'éducation*), usually undergraduate or graduate students who receive the minimum wage for work.[44] In short, since the 1990s an important goal of the increasingly neoliberal politics of the French government, which had alternated between a left-wing coalition and a right-wing coalition, was to give schools more autonomy and offer parents and students greater choice.

In Italy, the instability that has marked politics since early 1990s has also influenced the formulation of education policy. Between 1992 and 1994, the DC experienced a severe crisis that ultimately caused it to split into several smaller parties. At the same time, the Socialist Party and other minor co-governing parties were dissolved altogether. Benefiting from this situation was the media mogul Silvio Berlusconi, who became prime minister in 1994. After only two years in office, however, he was forced to step down in 1996, paving the way for a new center-left coalition that governed until 2001. The national elections of 2001 returned Berlusconi and his center-right coalition to power. The 2006 elections brought victory for another center-left coalition, but its tenure was brief, and Berlusconi resumed power yet again in 2008. The result of this tumultuous period was the increasing polarization of Italian political culture. The kind of political consensus between the left and the right that had characterized the 1960s and 1970s at least in some fields was no longer possible, a circumstance that had an enormous impact on education policy.

Throughout the 1990s, all-day education remained widely accepted in Italy. In fact, as was the case in the 1960s and 1970s, competing political groups presented surprisingly similar arguments for the need to expand all-day education further. In light of the increasing instability and polarization of Italian politics, this represents a remarkable continuity. This general consensus, however, did not lead to the final implementation of all-day education in Italy. Indeed, by the 2000–2001 school year, only 22 percent of children were enrolled in an all-day primary school. Likewise, the uneven regional distribution of all-day schools persisted: while up to 85 percent of the primary school students (like in the province of Milan) in the large cities of the north attended an all-day school, fewer than 5 percent in most small cities, rural areas, the south, and the Italian islands did. Thus, more than three decades after it was first introduced, all-day schooling in Italy remained largely confined to the economically prosperous, more urbanized regions of the country.[45] Nevertheless, the idea of all-day schools continued to enjoy widespread acceptance in Italy, above all because such schools were often of a higher quality. One precondition for the increasing quality of primary school education is the training of its staff. All-day schools only employ trained, qualified staff as supervisors for the lunch break and other nonacademic, optional activities. In addition, in 2004 a reform act mandated university education for all primary school teachers.[46]

The political consensus on the organization of all-day schooling gradually began to be questioned. The first sign of weakening support came with the so-called Berlinguer Reform (named after the minister of education Luigi Berlinguer) passed by the center-left government led by Massimo D'Alema in 2000. In addition to a fundamental reorganization of the curriculum of primary and secondary schools, this law called for the revision of time structures by implementing the so-called longer school time, which until then had been common mostly in lower secondary education, for primary schools. The change in terminology from "all-day school" to "longer school time" signaled an important shift in the time policy and, more generally, in education policy, even if the center-left government did not yet question the general importance or potential efficacy of all-day schooling.

Such questioning, however, began when a new center-right coalition under Berlusconi was elected and Letizia Moratti, a businesswoman whose main experience prior to entering government was in the insurance and telecommunications industry, became the new minister of education. She was responsible for the so-called Moratti reform in 2003, which limited the number of hours students could spend each day at school to eight (including a two-hour lunch break). The law stipulated that the time for compulsory "educational and teaching activities" in primary school for all students should not exceed 891 hours per year, i.e., 27 hours per week in a school year of 33 weeks. In order to personalize the curriculum, primary school students could also participate in optional activities that would be offered for 99 hours per year, i.e., three hours per week.[47] In that same year, the government passed a new law requiring that all-day schooling only be offered for children whose parents specifically requested it. In arguing for this new law, the government emphasized the role of families and social groups as "cultural and educational resources for students" and called for more "individualized instruction." The second law therefore demanded that schools, in cooperation with other public and private educational institutions, offer up to 300 hours per year of additional optional courses outside of school, for example in museums and sport clubs.[48]

Upon retaking power in 2008, Berlusconi's new cabinet resumed the education policy of his earlier government. One of its first acts was to reduce the hours dedicated to the compulsory curriculum for lower secondary schools from 32 to 29 weekly lessons.[49] Another program from the same year, which was designed to promote economic development and to stabilize public expenditure, mandated a modification of the student/teacher ratio by one point "for the sake of better qualification of school services" and a "full enhancement of teachers' professional skills" until the school year 2011–12. In addition, the law demanded a huge 17-percent reduction in the size of the administrative and support staff.[50] Promoted with neoliberal slogans, this program, itself part of a larger policy of austerity in public administration, envisaged the cancellation of team-teaching, the reduction of teaching hours, and the drastic marginalization of all the activities that had transformed the traditional half-day school into, at the very least, a "longer time school."

Parents and teachers responded to this policy with street demonstrations that drew support from trade unions and the political opposition. They feared that this new program would reduce school education once again to the teaching of essential skills like reading, writing, and arithmetic, while more elaborate cognitive, artistic, and social skills would disappear from the pedagogical agenda altogether. In response to the protest, the law was amended to give parents of primary school children the choice between a weekly schedule of 24, 27, 30, or 40 hours. In addition, classes with an all-day schedule were again required to have two teachers, which had been a distinctive feature of primary school since the reform of 1990.[51]

This neoliberal education policy signaled the transition in Italy from a widely accepted all-day time policy, which since the 1960s has found widespread support across the political spectrum, to an optional hybrid model in which all-day education is available to only a minority of children depending on their region. Indeed, this new policy is incrementally undermining the structural and material foundations upon which all-day education rests. According to the neoliberal logic that guides the current Berlusconi government, a leaner school is a better school.

Differences and Convergences: France and Italy in Comparison

Arguments for All-day Primary Schooling

In the late nineteenth century, political and economic factors moved the French state to establish a compulsory public school system based on an all-day time structure. Until the late 1950s, arguments coming from the movement for reformed pedagogy played hardly any role at all in the French debate on all-day schooling. This changed, however, during the period of reform in the 1960s and 1970s, when such arguments began to gain currency and shape debates on both the curriculum and teaching methods in the French all-day school. But unlike in Italy, they never proved pivotal. Nor did the arguments of feminists, as there already existed a widespread social and political consensus in support of all-day schools. Growing pressure from the feminist movement, which was very active and influential in France from the 1960s on, did, however, contribute to the systematic extension of the all-day preschool education as well as the gradual implementation of out-of-school care, public programs for the school-free-Wednesday, and the introduction of the undivided school day with a school lunch and supervision during the lunch break. All of these measures helped French women reconcile family and work outside the home.[52]

In contrast, social and pedagogical arguments in Italy proved instrumental in producing the educational reforms of the 1960s and 1970s that led to the implementation of all-day schooling. During this period, the entire cultural and political spectrum in Italy gradually came to accept all-day education as a means of promoting social equality and a more individualized approach to the education of all children. Unlike in France in the late nineteenth century, political arguments such as the need to strengthen national identity or to limit the influence of the Catholic Church played no role in the movement towards all-day education in Italy. On the contrary, the relationship between the Italian state and the Catholic Church had been effectively settled with the concordat of 1929, which produced a lasting compromise that persisted long after 1945. A side effect of this compromise was that the state and church as well as a broad political coalition all focused on *education*, not childcare. Preschools were defined as educational, and *not* childcare, institutions. As in France, they were and are part of the public education system.[53] Finally, feminist arguments did, much more so than in France, contribute to the implementation and expansion of all-day education in Italy. The strong Italian women's movement of the 1970s demanded a system of state-supported all-day childcare and schools that would allow women to reconcile motherhood and employment.

School Time Policies, Employment of Mothers, and Birth Rates

Comparative research has convincingly shown that an all-day care and education policy, especially when combined with a family policy based on the "double-earner" family and a labor market policy that supports part-time work, contributes to higher birth rates. Such a policy mix allows mothers to reconcile family obligations with paid work outside the home.[54] The case of France confirms this finding. There, all-day care and education is considered normal, and preschool education for children is available all over the French territory for all children from the age of two. All children in the age group from three to six are enrolled in preschool education. In addition, 35 percent of all two- to three-year-old children are enrolled in an *école maternelle*, 18 percent of all under-three-year-olds are placed in the care of accredited daycare providers, and 8 percent are in crèche services.[55] Not surprisingly, the percentage of employed women and mothers is, in comparison with most other European countries, high, and part-time work is common. In 2004, 64 percent of all women aged fifteen to sixty-five and 65 percent of all mothers with a child under six were employed, while another 24 percent of all female employees worked part-time. The evidence suggests that these factors have played a decisive role in elevating France's birth rate, which reached 1.98 in 2006, the second highest in Europe after Iceland.[56]

The situation is much more ambivalent in Italy, which in 2006 posted a birth rate of just 1.35, one of the lowest in Europe.[57] Here too the correlation between female employment and birth rate is striking: only 51 percent of all women aged fifteen to sixty-five and 45 percent of all mothers with a child under six were employed in 2005, one of the lowest rates in the European Union. A major reason for this is the lack of childcare for children under three: one-third of all childcare requests remain unfulfilled, with the percentage much higher in the south than in the north. While 29 percent of all female employees worked part-time in 2005, there are stark regional differences in the rate of female employment. Not surprisingly, women are much more likely to be employed in the north, where the unemployment rate is much lower, job opportunities for women more abundant, and, not least of all, a much better system of all-day care and education exists.[58]

As noted above, the implementation of all-day education in Italy proved regionally uneven, reflecting the vast economic and social differences in the country. On average, less than one-quarter of all Italian children of primary school age currently attend an all-day school. While 80 percent of all three- to six-year-old children are enrolled in preschool, a childcare place is available for 6 percent of children under two.[59] As a result, most mothers with small children must, if they want to work outside the home, seek private childcare of some kind. Still, it must be said that during the last three decades, Italian governments have pursued a family policy that aims to promote gender equality and help reconcile the responsibilities of family and paid work.[60] But as is the case in many other policy areas, the extreme disparities between the north and south have hampered the practical implementation of this potentially beneficial policy.[61]

Despite numerous obstacles, women's participation in the labor market has increased steadily over the past four decades.[62] In response to urging from the EU, today Italian politicians have made increasing female employment an important part of their political agenda, not least of all because they believe it will stimulate economic growth.[63] Indeed, they have finally recognized that the relatively low rate of female employment neither reflects a certain preference for family life and the upbringing of children nor does it encourage a higher birth rate. Recent research has shown that this apparent contradiction (low female employment/low birth rate) is due above all to the shortage of part-time jobs, the shrinking family network that previously supported working mothers, and the lack, especially in southern regions and in rural areas, of all-day childcare and school schedules that are compatible with the working hours of parents, and especially mothers.[64] In addition, the rapid increase in the percentage of women with a higher education has also put downward pressure on the birth rate. In 2006, 71 percent of all women aged twenty-five to thirty-four had at least a high-school diploma.[65] An increasing percentage of such women dedicate themselves to pursuing their careers and, as a result, forgo having children. Here, too, the insufficient care system for children under two and the unreliable or nonexistent offering of all-day primary schools inform these women's choices. Still, an all-day education for every child remains a widely accepted idea in Italian society, if not necessarily among the leaders of the current center-right government.[66] The outdated opinion that mothers should stay at home to care for their children, moreover, finds little support in both France and Italy, at least as far as public debate is concerned.

States, Schools, and Families

In France, the supremacy of the state in determining education policy is unquestioned. Traditionally, the French public school system assumes educational responsibilities that in other countries, especially those with a half-day school system, are considered the exclusive domain of families.[67] Over the past few decades, however, French education policy has allowed for a greater degree of decentralization and school autonomy, thereby encouraging more participation on the part of parents as well as increased cooperation with institutions outside the schools. With this policy the government has facilitated a much-needed modernization of education and enabled schools to develop in ways that meet the needs of their students and communities. And yet despite these changes, it is still widely accepted that the all-day time policy determined by the state shapes the daily life of families.[68] This preeminent role of the French state does not, however, mean that the rights and responsibilities of parents are restricted or they are excluded from participation in public education. In fact, the desire for cooperation between schools and parents is explicitly mentioned on the official website of the Ministry of Education: "Parents are full members of the educational community. ... They are involved in the decision-making process, most notably by electing representatives to the various decision-making bodies."[69]

In Italy as well, the central state is responsible for school education, even though schools were given greater autonomy over their affairs in 1997. However, the strong Italian tradition of half-day schooling, which prevails to this day (78 percent of all primary schools are half-day or part-time schools), accords a much larger role for the family in children's education. In accordance with Catholic social theory, the family is considered the most important institution in society for the raising and education of children. The issue of shared responsibilities—if not dialogue—between the state and the family was therefore a constant topic of debate since the implementation of compulsory schooling.

Since the 1960s, the role of the family in education occupied an important place in debates about education policy. Citing the "erosion of the traditional extended family," educationalists, sociologists, and politicians alike all argued that all-day education in pre- and primary schools was necessary to compensate for the social and cultural deficits in children's socialization in the family. Their arguments were further influenced by the ideas of the international reform pedagogic movement.[70] The institution of all-day education in Italian schools went hand in hand with the introduction of a new legal framework that allowed for the more democratic participation of parents in schools.[71] Indeed, the involvement of parents became an important goal of all schools, as the state declared its intention to strengthen, not question, parental responsibility for the education of their children. While education policy has continued along this path since the early 2000s, it has sought to encourage families to become more involved in and responsible for all aspects of school education.

The cooperation between schools and families has thus become an important topic in the current debate on education in both countries. As is the case elsewhere in Europe, parents in France and Italy expect more choice and flexibility from the public care and education system. Increasing public discontent with the upbringing and education of children at home, in particular in low-income and migrant families, has also contributed to the growing importance of family education in the broader political debate on education in general. Unlike in the past, the response to the putative "failure of family socialization" is no longer to call for more education by the state, but instead for greater responsibility on the part of families.

The Inclusive Structure of the French and Italian School

Despite important differences, the all-day school policies in France and Italy share several common features, which are based on the goals of social compensation and inclusiveness:

- In both countries, all-day education is combined with a comprehensive school structure; primary school lasts five years, and lower secondary education keeps all students together for three, in France for four more years. The selection and tracking of students in France and Italy thus begins relatively late.

- The all-day pattern covers the entire range from pre- and primary school to lower secondary education (in France also upper secondary education); in Italy, however, the focus is mainly on pre- and primary schools.

- Neither country provides any form of separated "special education" for students with disabilities and special needs. Instead, such students are integrated in regular classes whenever possible, and the aim is an inclusive pedagogy.

- Both teachers and support staff have university training; this applies to all sectors of formal education.

Both countries face difficult social, ethnic, and regional disparities in the education system. While 100 percent of the French students are enrolled in an all-day school, the quality of the education they receive depends to a large degree on the social and ethnic composition of their school district. Social marginalization and truancy of students with socially deprived backgrounds, for example, has proved to be a persistent problem in French primary schools.[72] In Italy, less than a quarter of all primary school students have access to an all-day school. Moreover, the quality of education in the poorer agrarian regions of the south as well as the Italian islands often does not reach the levels of the wealthier urban centers in the north. As data derived from the comparative survey of the Program for International Student Assessment (PISA) suggest, the French school system has addressed the issue of social inequality more effectively than its Italian counterpart (and most other immigration countries).[73] To what extent the long tradition of universal, all-day schooling for all students contributed to France's better achievement in terms of compensating social inequality remains an open question that demands further exploration.

Conclusion

The historical comparison of the French model of universal all-day schooling and the Italian model of an optional all-day education reveals different patterns of path dependence. In France, the predominant pattern is stability and continuity. There the all-day model survived numerous social changes as well as the shifting political coalitions of the government after 1945. In Italy, the implementation and expansion of all-day schooling from the 1960s to the late 1990s found support from across the political spectrum, a remarkable fact given the enormous ideological differences between left-wing, center, and right-wing political parties. Still, the all-day schools that this policy produced took root in a school system that was (and still is) dominated by half-day or part-time school schedules. Since 2003, a center-right government that consistently pursued a neoliberal policy and preferred the model of a "lean school" has been undermining the foundations of all-day schooling in Italy.

The French and the Italian models of all-day schooling are situated in a continuum of all-day school policies that is flanked on one side by universal, state-provided, all-day education (France, United Kingdom, Denmark, Sweden), and on the other by half-day education (Austria and Germany).

Despite their numerous similarities, France and Italy find themselves on different spots on this continuum.[74] According to the typology developed by sociologist Gøsta Esping-Andersen, France represents a conservative-corporatist welfare state that offers universal all-day education for all children, while paying particular attention to the problems of children from less-privileged social strata and ethnic groups. In this respect, it is not much different than the social-democratic welfare state model exemplified by Sweden.[75] The Italian state, in contrast, offers all-day education only as an option in a broader mix of time policies in which, for a variety of reasons, the half-day structure remains the most prominent. While it does attempt to take into account the needs of the less-privileged students, it does so with much less political and financial support than in France. The quickly changing political coalitions that have governed Italy since the foundation of the republic in 1946, but even more so since the 1980s, have prevented the creation of strong continuities in education reform policy, thus further contributing to the hybrid character of the Italian time policy. Italy's welfare state thus combines elements of the Christian-conservative and the liberal welfare states identified by Esping-Andersen.

We must, however, be careful in drawing any definite conclusions. There are many indications that the French model of a republican school is not as stable as it is often portrayed in the literature. Sociologist François Dubet, for example, titled one of his studies of the French education system *The Decline of the Institution*. In it, he warns against any attempt to idealize the myth of the republican school.[76] For sociologist Yves Careil, the supremacy of the state has been eroded by liberal ideas.[77] Philosopher and educationalist Louis Porcher describes ordinary dysfunctions, for example, the frequent absences of teachers.[78] The Italian education system is, as far as all-day school is concerned, open, optional, and, in comparison to France, deregulated. Yet even if it has increasingly incorporated neoliberal elements such as greater local autonomy, a flexible time-table, and parental choice, it still remains the product of an educational policy designed and supervised by a centralized state.

Notes

I would like to thank Ireneusz Białecki, Carla Collicelli, and my coeditors for their helpful suggestions and critical comments on earlier versions of the chapter.

1. Sandra Bonfiglioli, "Le politiche di riorganizzazione dei tempi della città: sviluppo della qualità della vita e del territorio," in *Cosa vogliono le donne. Cosa fanno le donne per conciliare lavoro e famiglia* (Milan, 2001), 54–59.

2. Rita Ranaldi and Maria Clelia Romano, *Conciliare lavoro e famiglia. Una sfida quotidiana* (Rome, 2008), 39.
3. See the chapter by Jeanne Fagnani in this volume.
4. Giuseppe Cerini, "Il contributo del tempo pieno alla scuola italiana," *Insegnare* 3, no. 11–12 (2003): 10–15.
5. See the introduction by Karen Hagemann, Konrad H. Jarausch, and Cristina Allemann-Ghionda in this volume.
6. Cristina Allemann-Ghionda, *Einführung in die vergleichende Erziehungswissenschaft* (Weinheim, 2004), 158ff.
7. For more on path dependency, see the introduction in this volume. The state of research on all-day schooling in France and Italy is not equally developed. For Italy, see Annali della Pubblica Istruzione, "La scuola elementare a tempo pieno," *Studi e documenti degli annali della Pubblica Istruzione* 1, no. 13–14 (1980): 125–46. For France, see Wolfgang Hörner, "Das französische Ganztagsmodell," *Aus Politik und Zeitgeschichte* B 23 (2008): 15–21; Wolfgang Hörner, "Ganztagsschule in Italien," in *Ganztägige Bildungssysteme: Innovation durch Vergleich*, ed. Hans-Uwe Otto and Thomas Coelen (Munich, 2005), 63–72. On the French preschool system, see the chapter by Fagnani in this volume. General comparisons on the time structure of European school systems can be found in Gerlind Schmidt, "Die Ganztagsschule in einigen Ländern Europas. Vergleichende Analyse im Rahmen des Projekts 'Zeit für Schule,'" in *Die Zeitdimension der Schule als Gegenstand des Bildungsvergleichs*, ed. Wolfgang Mitter and Botho von Kopp (Cologne, 1994), 46–112; Hermann-Günter Hesse and Christoph Kodron, eds., *Zeit für Schule*, 7 vols. (Cologne, 1990–1991); Otto and Coelen, *Ganztägige Bildungssysteme*; Cristina Allemann-Ghionda, "Zeitstrukturen (vor-)schulischer Bildung in Europa," in *Grundbegriffe der Ganztagsbildung: Das Handbuch*, ed. Hans-Uwe Otto and Thomas Coelen (Wiesbaden, 2008), 674–83; Cristina Allemann-Ghionda, "Ganztagsschule im europäischen Vergleich. Zeitpolitiken modernisieren—durch Vergleich Standards setzen?" *Zeitschrift für Pädagogik* (Supplement) no. 54 (2009): 190–208.
8. Marie Jean Antoine Nicolas de Caritat, Marquis de Condorcet, *Rapport et projet de décret sur l'organisation générale de l'instruction publique* (Paris, 1792).
9. For more see the introduction by Hagemann, Jarausch, and Allemann-Ghionda in this volume.
10. Günter Brinkmann and Wolfgang Hörner, "Italy," in *The Education Systems of Europe*, ed. Wolfgang Hörner et al. (Dordrecht, 2007), 394. During Napoleonic domination, some elements of the French educational system were incorporated; see Franco Cambi, *Storia della pedagogia* (Rome, 1997), 412.
11. Michael Riccards, *Vicars of Christ: Popes, Power, and Politics in the Modern World* (New York, 1998).
12. Victoria de Grazia, *How Fascism Ruled Women: Italy, 1922–1945* (Berkeley, CA, 1993), 77–115.
13. Cambi, *Storia della pedagogia*, 483.
14. Wolfgang Hörner, "France," in Hörner et al., *The Education Systems*, 263–83.
15. Antoine Prost, *Histoire de l'enseignement en France, 1800–1967* (Paris, 1968). See also Hörner, "France."
16. Ehrenhardt Skierka, "Länderstudie Frankreich," in *Reformpädagogk und Schulreform in Europa*, ed. Michael Seyfart-Stubenrauch and Ehrenhardt Kierka (Baltmannsweiler, 1996), 419–36.
17. Cristina Allemann-Ghionda, "Dewey in Postwar-Italy: The Case of Re-Education," *Studies in Philosophy and Education* 19 (2000): 53–67.
18. Brinkmann and Hörner, "Italy."

19. See Penelope Morris, ed., *Women in Italy, 1945–1960: An Interdisciplinary Study* (Basingstoke, 2006).

20. Centro Studi Investimenti Sociali (CENSIS), *42° rapporto annuale sulla situazione sociale del Paese* (Rome, 2008), Retrieved 5 March 2008: http://www.censis.it.

21. On the evolution of women's rights and feminism in Italy, see Lucia Chiavola Birnbaum, *Liberazione della donna: Feminism in Italy* (Middletown, CT, 1986).

22. Siegfried Baur, "Verlängerte Unterrichtszeit in Italien," in Otto and Coelen, *Ganztägige Bildungssysteme*, 73–80.

23. John Boli and Francisco O. Ramírez, "Compulsory Schooling in the Western Cultural Context," in *Emergent Issues in Education: Comparative Perspectives*, ed. Robert F. Arnove et al. (Albany, NY, 1992), 25–38.

24. Pierre Bourdieu and Jean-Claude Passeron, *La reproduction. Eléments pour une théorie du système d'enseignement* (Paris, 1970).

25. Hörner, "Ganztagsschule in Frankreich," in Otto and Coelen, *Ganztägige Bildungssysteme*; see also Mechthild Veil, "Ganztagsschule mit Tradition: Frankreich," *Aus Politik und Zeitgeschichte*, B 41 (2002): 29–37.

26. Brinkmann and Hörner, "Italy," 397.

27. Ibid., 394–407; see also Cristina Allemann-Ghionda, *Schule, Bildung und Pluralität. Sechs Fallstudien im europäischen Vergleich* (Bern, 2002), 210–15.

28. For example, the Catholic priest Don Lorenzo Milani, *La scuola di Barbiana* (Firenze, 1967); and the left-wing educationalist Aldo Visalberghi, "Aspetti sociologici della scolarizzazione: importanza della scuola integrata," *Riforma della scuola*, no. 10 (1966): 14–19.

29. See Jürgen Oelkers and Tobias Rülcker, eds., *Die neue Erziehung. Beiträge zur Internationalität der Reformpädagogik* (Bern, 1999); Harald Ludwig, "Die Montessori-Schule," in Seyfarth-Stubenrauch and Skiera, *Reformpädagogik*, 237–52.

30. Cesare Scurati and Franco V. Lombardi, *Pedagogia: termini e problemi* (Milan, 1982), 425ff.

31. Ibid.

32. Parlamento italiano, Legge 24 settembre 1971, no. 820 (Attività integrative, insegnamenti speciali, avvio del tempo pieno nella scuola elementare) (Rome, 1971).

33. Baur, "Verlängerte Unterrichtszeit," 75.

34. Sergio Neri, "Il tempo scolastico," in *Scuola elementare e nuovi programmi*, ed. Benedetto Vertecchi (Firenze, 1982), 219.

35. CENSIS, *Tempo-scuola: quanto e come?* (Milan, 1984), 96.

36. Baur, "Verlängerte Unterrichtszeit," 76. For a critical view of the reform of primary school, see Franco Frabboni, "Programmi e riforma della scuola elementare dieci anni dopo. Molti sì, altrettanti 'ni,'" *Scuola e Città*, 46 (1995): 522–27.

37. See the chapter by Fagnani in this volume.

38. Official website of the French Ministry of Education, retrieved 9 February 2009: http://www.education.gouv.fr/pid218/vie-au-college.html, translated by CAG.

39. Hörner, "France," 263–83.

40. Ibid., 266f.

41. Ibid.

42. A reform of teacher education is integrating it into universities from 2010 on. "Réforme des enseignants: du nouveau." Retrieved 16 May 2009: http://info.france2.fr/education/52426500-fr.php.

43. Christian Alix, "'Schule und Ganztagsschule sind identisch.' Frankreichs Schulsystem in der Praxis—ein Blick nach Marseille," in *Bildung und Innovation*, 14 August 2003. Retrieved 9 February 2009: http://www.bildungsserver.de/innovationsportal/bildungplus.html?artid=217.

44. Hörner, "Das französische Ganztagsmodell," 20.
45. Baur, "Verlängerte Unterrichtszeit," 79; see also Ranaldi and Romano, *Conciliare lavoro*, 38.
46. Ministero dell'Istruzione, dell'Università e della Ricerca (MIUR), "Decreto legislativo no. 59 del 19/2/2004" (Rome, 2004).
47. EURYDICE, *Descriptions of National Educational Systems, Italy 2007/08*, Retrieved 9 February 2009: http://eacea.ec.europa.eu/portal/page/portal/Eurydice/EuryPage?country=IT&lang=EN&fragment=25.
48. Osservatorio sulla scuola dell'autonomia, *Rapporto sulla scuola dell'autonomia* (Rome, 2003). Retrieved 9 February 2009: http://www.pubblica.istruzione.it.
49. "Riforme: Il tempo prolungato nella scuola secondaria di I° grado," *Orizzonte Scuola* (22 January 2009).
50. MIUR, "Decreto legislativo no. 59"; Parlamento Italiano, Legge 6 agosto 2008, n. 133, "Conversione in legge, con modificazioni, del decreto-legge 25 giugno 2008, no. 112, recante disposizioni urgenti per lo sviluppo economico, la semplificazione, la competitività, la stabilizzazione della finanza pubblica e la sperequazione tributaria" in *Gazzetta Ufficiale* n. 195 (21 August 2008), Suppl. Ordinario n. 196. Retrieved 5 February 2008: http://www.camera.it/parlam/leggi/08133L.htm.
51. "Scuola, maestro unico 'facoltativo,'" *Corriere della Sera*, 12 December 2008, 2–3.
52. See the chapter by Fagnani in this volume; see also Kimberly Morgan, "Does Anyone Have a 'Libre Choix'? Subversive Liberalism and the Politics of French Child Care Policy," in *Child Care Policy at the Crossroads: Gender and Welfare State Restructuring*, ed. Sonya Michel and Rianne Mahon (London, 2003), 143–70.
53. For Spain, see the chapter by Celia Valiente in this volume. For Italy, see Vincent Della Salla, "'Modernization' and Welfare-State Restructuring in Italy: The Impact on Child Care," in Michel and Mahon, *Child Care Policy*, 171–90.
54. Hans Bertram, "Nachhaltige Familienpolitik und demografische Entwicklung. Zeit, Geld und Infrastruktur als Elemente einer demografiebewussten Familienpolitik." *Zeitschrift für Pädagogik* 55, no. 1 (2009): 37–55. See also the chapter by Livia Sz. Oláh in this volume.
55. OECD, *Starting Strong II: Early Childhood Education and Care* (Paris, 2006), 326.
56. Ibid., 325; Population Reference Bureau (PRB), *Fertility Rates for Low Birth-Rate Countries, 1995 to Most Recent Year*. Retrieved 1 July 2008: http://www.prb.org/pdf07/TFRTable .pdf.
57. Ibid.
58. OECD, *Starting Strong II*, 359; PRB, *Fertility Rates*.
59. Ranaldi and Romano, *Conciliare lavoro*, 37.
60. One of the measures is the law on parental leave. See Istituto Nazionale Previdenza Sociale, "La Maternità." Retrieved 9 February 2009: http://www.inps.it/home/default .asp?ItemDir=4797. On the policies aiming at the reconciliation of family and work, see Chiara Saraceno, "La conciliazione di responsabilità familiari e attività lavorative in Italia: paradossi ed equilibri imperfetti," *Polis*, no. 2 (2003): 199–218; Della Salla, "Modernization."
61. Ranaldi and Romano, *Conciliare lavoro*, 12 and 37.
62. CENSIS, *42° Rapporto annuale*.
63. Della Salla, "Modernization," 182ff.
64. Daniela Del Boca et al., "Why are Fertility and Women's Employment Rates So Low in Italy? Lessons from France and the UK," *IZA Discussion Paper*, no. 1274 (Bonn, 2004).
65. CENSIS, *42° Rapporto annuale*.
66. Enzo Catarsi, ed., *La scuola a tempo pieno in Italia: una grande utopia?* (Pisa, 2004).

67. Hörner, "Das französische Ganztagsmodell."

68. François Dubet and Danilo Martuccelli, *A l'école: Sociologie de l'expérience scolaire* (Paris, 1996), 45.

69. Le Ministère d'Education Nationale, *Les parents d'élèves.* Retrieved on 9 February 2009: http://www.education.gouv.fr/cid2659/les-parents-d-eleves.html.

70. Allemann-Ghionda, "Dewey."

71. In Italy, the democratic participation of parents in school affairs is regulated by a law from 1973. See the official website of the Ministry of Education. Retrieved on 9 February, 2009: http://www.pubblica.istruzione.it/index_famiglie.shtml.

72. François Dubet, *Faits d'école* (Paris, 2008).

73. See Petra Stanat and Gayle Christensen, *Where Immigrant Students Succeed: A Comparative Review of Performance and Engagement in PISA* (Paris, 2006). On the integration of migrants, see Jean-Paul Payet, "The Paradox of Ethnicity in French Secondary Schools," in *Youth and Work in the Post-Industrial City of North America and Europe*, ed. Laurence Roulleau-Berger (Leiden, 2003), 59–71, and Louis Porcher, *L'éducation comparée: Pour aujourd'hui et pour demain* (Paris, 2009), 196f; for Italy, see Roberta Ricucci, "Educating Immigrant Children in a 'Newcomer' Immigration Country A Case Study," *Intercultural Education* 19, no. 5 (2008): 449–60.

74. See Konrad H. Jarausch and Cristina Allemann-Ghionda, "Zeitpolitik der Kinderbetreuung und Grundschulerziehung," *Aus Politik und Zeitgeschichte* B 23 (2008): 3–7.

75. For the welfare state typology, see this volume's introduction and Gøsta Esping-Andersen, *Three Worlds of Welfare Capitalism* (Princeton, NJ, 1990), 26f.

76. François Dubet, *Le déclin de l'institution* (Paris, 2002); see also Dubet and Martuccelli, *A l'école*, 25.

77. Yves Careil, *De l'école publique à l'école libérale. Sociologie d'un changement* (Rennes, 1998).

78. Porcher, *L'éducation comparée*, 42.

Chapter 10

(Pre)School Is Not Childcare

Preschool and Primary School Education Policies in Spain since the 1930s

Celia Valiente

After its bitterly fought civil war of 1936–1939, Spain was governed for the next three and a half decades by a right-wing authoritarian regime headed by General Francisco Franco. The only legal party under Franco's regime was the Falange Española Tradicionalista y de las JONS, known as Falange, an authoritarian party, which emphasized anticommunism, Catholicism, and nationalism. But in the 1960s, Spain began a period of unprecedented economic growth—the so-called Spanish miracle—and thus resumed the long-interrupted transition into a modern industrial economy. Still, it was only after the death of General Franco in November 1975, when Spain became a constitutional monarchy with liberal democratic institutions, that the country could begin a process of real democratization. In addition to establishing democratic rights and principles, the new Spanish constitution of 1978 devolved autonomy to the regions. In 1986 the country joined the European Economic Community, a step that gave added impetus to the rapidly progressing modernization of Spain's economy and society.

Both before and after Franco's long rule, policymakers in Spain generally conceived of childcare as an all-day welfare service. Preschool education, on the other hand, was regulated by legislation on both primary and general education and administered by the education authorities. Consequently, most preschool classes were located in primary schools. As is still the case today, compulsory education started at the age of six. Under Franco, however, the provision of preschool education was never a major goal of education policy. One major reason for this was that until the 1960s, Spain was primarily an agricultural country. Politicians thus did not perceive the need to develop early childhood education as a means of fostering economic development. It was only in the 1960s and 1970s, in the context of a European-wide debate about education reform, that this policy began to change. During this period, other goals in education policy took precedence over preschool education. Above all, policymakers focused on the extension of compulsory education from six to eight school years as well as the de facto universalization of compulsory education. As a result, the number of preschool facilities and the rates of enrollment in them remained low into the 1970s. In 1971–1972, for example, only 12 percent of three-year-olds, 42 percent of four-year-olds, and 60 percent of five-year-olds were enrolled in a preschool program of some kind. Most of the existing preschools were private and required parents to pay to enroll their children.[1]

In contrast, at 97 to 100 percent current preschool enrollment for children aged three to five ranks among the highest in the world (data for 2006–2007).[2] As a result of the dramatic increase in the number of preschool places in public centers since the 1970s, today most preschool institutions are public. In 1975–1976, only 38 percent of all preschool students were enrolled in a public center.[3] By 2007–2008, this proportion had nearly doubled to 64 percent.[4] The majority of the private schools were and continue to be administered by the Catholic Church, which since 1975 has sought to expand and secure its role in preschool education with the expectation that its work is subsidized by the state.

But (pre)school is not childcare. By 2006–2007, the proportion of Spanish children aged two or under in childcare remains one of the lowest in the EU: 5 percent for children younger than one year, 17 percent of children aged one year, and 33 percent of two-year-olds.[5] Parents cannot use preschools and primary schools as substitutions for childcare, since pre- and primary schools' hours are shorter than the typical workday and are interrupted by a long lunch break. In addition, the three-month summer holidays for pre- and primary school students are much longer than the usual one-month paid holidays of employees. This situation creates severe problems for working parents, in particular mothers, who still bear the primary responsibility for domestic and family work.

The problem of inadequate childcare became more pressing since the 1970s, when the rate of female employment in Spain began to increase rapidly. In comparative terms, at the end of the Franco's regime, the presence of women in the labor market was modest. In 1974, the percentage of employed women (from fifteen to sixty-four years) was 33 percent, far below the European Economic Community (EEC) average of 45 percent.[6] Indeed, since the majority of Spanish women did not work for wages in the 1970s, childcare was not such a pressing issue. If mothers with small children needed help, female relatives or neighbors offered informal and often unpaid childcare.

In contrast, the majority of women of working age in Spain today are employed. In the last few decades, the female employment rate has increased steadily, standing at 55 percent in 2007. The former pattern that saw most women leaving the labor market (if they were ever present there) when they married or had their first child has been reversed. By 2000, the employment rates of women aged twenty-five to thirty-four and thirty-five to forty-four reached 57 percent and 53 percent, respectively.[7] The probability of having children of preschool age is the highest in these age groups. Most Spanish women with and without children work full-time. Part-time work is still less widespread, with 12 percent of all employees and 23 percent of all women working part-time in 2007 compared to 18 and 31 percent, respectively, in the European Union. This means that even though Spain's female employment rate of 55 percent is still below the EU average of 59 percent, most Spanish women who work for wages have full-time jobs and thus enjoy a higher degree of economic independence.[8] At the same time, this fact makes it all the more urgent for them to have a sufficient system of formal childcare. The increase of preschool education in the last three decades, however, offered no real alternative in this regard.

Since the political transition in Spain in the mid-1970s, policymakers have pursued a steady extension of the number of publicly and privately provided preschool services. Political parties across the ideological spectrum supported this goal, as they had all come to see the beneficial role of early childhood education in their strategies for long-term economic development. Once the de facto universalization of compulsory schooling had been achieved in the early 1980s, more resources were channeled to noncompulsory education, including preschool. In addition, the declining birth rate helped to increase the number of children in preschool. With less money needed for compulsory education, more could be invested in the preschool sector. Finally, the growing presence of women in the labor market as well as civil society motivated politicians, now eagerly seeking to win the female vote, to lend their support to policies such as early childhood education that could be perceived as beneficial to women.

Although the time structure of the existing preschools and primary schools—an all-day school with a long lunch break and a three-month-long summer vacation—created and continues to create problems for working parents, especially working mothers, and pre- and primary school is no supplement for childcare, the question of the time structure of the education system did not play a major role in shaping debates about (pre-) school policies in pre- and post-Franco Spain. Instead, for a long time policymakers and the public remained focused on other issues, above all the role of the private sector and the influence of the Catholic Church on education.[9]

In this chapter, I focus on two key questions: first, which factors influenced the policy regarding childcare as well as pre- and primary school education before and after 1975, and second, what caused the rapid increase of public preschooling in the post-Franco era. I begin with a brief discussion of my analytical framework, and then describe the main development of the preschool policy that prevailed both during Franco's rule and the postauthoritarian period and its close relation to primary school policy. Finally, I will explain the steady expansion of preschool services since 1975.

Path Dependency and Catholicism in Social Policy

Before any new public policy can be established, political elites must perceive a situation as a "problem" that requires governmental intervention. The way in which that problem is defined in the political discourse, moreover, determines to a large extent how it is solved.[10] Problem definition is particularly important in the case of childcare because rationales for childcare policy can fall into one of several categories: economic or labor market, poverty reduction, gender equality, or education. Public policies in a given period are not only responses to problems of that time, but also reactions of policymakers to past policies. In other words, new policies are almost always shaped, at least in part, by former attempts by governments to cope with the same or similar problems. Indeed, when facing problem situations, policymakers are generally more inclined to introduce only minor changes in existing programs rather than depart radically from past policies. Policy legacies therefore tend to favor continuities in the policymaking process. This is one of the most important insights of the analytical concept of path dependency, which is employed in several social science disciplines.[11]

Both before and after 1975, childcare in Spain was firmly entrenched in the policy domain of education. Throughout the modern period, states and churches in the West have fought to control education policy and institutions. Thus in order to understand education policy in Spain, which is no exception in this regard, we must take into account the important role of the Catholic Church, which to this day remains a key actor in the Spanish education system. Spain remains a largely homogeneous Catholic country. After the expulsion of Jews in 1492 and of Muslims soon afterwards, Catholicism was the only openly active religion in Spain. Even today, 76 percent of adult Spaniards consider themselves Catholic, although the number of practicing Catholics is much lower.[12] But the high percentage of Catholics explains the continuing power of the Catholic Church in Spanish culture, society, and politics.

The literature on welfare states in the Western world has underlined the complexity of Catholicism's influence—direct and indirect—on social policymaking. Catholic social doctrine emphasizes three basic principles regarding the nature of social provision. First, social provision should be implemented by organizations of civil society, especially those operated by or affiliated with the Catholic Church. Second, social provision should preserve status differences in society, because, in Catholic thinking, each social class occupies a special place in the "divinely mandated" social order. And third, social provision should help families in taking care of their members by providing them with income when the male breadwinner, usually the father, is unable to earn a sufficient wage, rather than replacing families in their caring functions by providing them with caring services. In Catholic doctrine, the aim of all welfare measures should be to stabilize the "male-breadwinner/female-homemaker" family, which is considered the bedrock of society and the state. Social policies thus had to ensure that a married woman stayed in the home taking care of her family. Childcare was regarded as a means to thwart this agenda because it allowed women to work for a living outside the home. If we want to understand the development of preprimary school policy in Spain and other countries in which the Catholic Church was historically very influential, we therefore need to consider its role in both welfare and education.[13]

(Pre)School Policies in Franco's Spain

Childcare programs in Spain have historically been part of broader education policy. The basic structure of Spain's public education system was established by the Education Act of September 1857. This legislation, also known as the "Moyano Act" after its principal author, the minister of education Claudio Moyano, created a remarkably durable, three-tiered system of education consisting of a primary (*primera enseñanza*), secondary (*segunda enseñanza*), and university (*enseñanza superior*) level. Under the provisions of the Moyano Act, primary education was to be compulsory for children between the ages of six and nine. Thereafter, some students would advance to a noncompulsory secondary education comprising of a six-year course of study. Although they were not conceived of as an integral part of the new system, Article 105 of the Moyano Act declared that infants schools (*escuelas de párvulos*) should be established in provincial capitals and all towns and villages with populations of ten thousand or more.[14]

The Moyano Act also provided for a high degree of centralization as it gave the Ministry of Development (Ministerio de Fomento) control over "the establishment and functioning of schools and universities, the content of teaching, [and] the training and appointment of teachers."[15] At the same time, while universities were to be administered solely by the state, the act allowed both public and private institutions, including the Catholic Church, to provide primary and secondary education. This was an important political compromise with the Catholic Church, which tried to secure its long-term influence on the education system. Indeed, this basic arrangement of Spain's education system put in place by the Moyano Act remained largely unchanged for over a century, when it was finally modified by the General Education Act of August 1970.

During Franco's dictatorship, preschool policy underwent three major legislative reforms. In July 1945, the government issued a new act on pre- and primary schooling that differentiated two types of preschools: maternal schools (*escuelas maternales*) for children up to four years of age and infants schools (*escuelas de párvulos*) for children aged four and five. Only in cases where the number of children was too small could boys and girls attend the same classes. The gendered nature of this act was further underscored by the requirement that only female teachers provide preschool education. Finally, this reform reinforced the previously established norm that school should last the entire day, with five hours of instruction, which were usually interrupted by a longer lunch break and after-school activities. In contrast to the reform of 1945, the Education Act of December 1965 contained only one important innovation on preschool. In Article 18, it declared that "the state would establish (and promote that others establish) preschool centers according to its ability."[16] With this article, the government recognized for the first time the need to extend its preschool offerings. But it was only with the General Education Act of 1970 that preschool policy underwent a more fundamental revision. This act not only mandated that preschooling was henceforth to be free of charge in public preschools, but also changed the name of preschools for children up to four years of age from maternal schools (*escuelas maternales*) to kindergartens (*jardines de infancia*). Although this reform allowed for preschool children above and below the age of four to receive instruction in preschools, the act demanded that children of different ages be taught separately, with exceptions warranted only under special circumstances.

Despite the attention that these three reforms paid, at least on paper, to preschool, the number of preschool services remained very limited throughout the Franco era. In 1963–1964, preschool enrollment rates of children aged two, three, four, and five were still as low as 2 percent, 3 percent, 32 percent, and 46 percent, respectively.[17] Most preschool students lived in towns and cities and came from well-off families that were able to pay for what was at the time a mostly private service. The majority of all children under six did not attend preschool of any kind.

(Pre)School Policies in Postauthoritarian Spain

Since the end of the Franco regime, the main goal of Spanish childcare policy has been to increase the number of public preschool programs for children aged five and under to prepare them for the compulsory primary school. Because these programs offer full-day education free of charge, the absolute number of places and the proportion of children in preschools has increased dramatically ever since. In 1975–1976, 347,026 children under the age of six were enrolled in some kind of public preschool program. By 2007–2008, this figure had tripled to 1,041,426 children. Today two-thirds of all places in preschools are provided by public centers. Although the relative importance of the private sector has declined in the last three decades, it remains a crucial provider of preschool services. Unlike in other European countries, the Catholic Church in Spain has since the 1970s been highly successful in defending its territory in the Spanish educational system despite the massive expansion of public education during the same period. In 1975–1976, the number of children enrolled in preschool education who attended private centers was 573,310, while in the academic year 2007–2008, the figure stood largely unchanged at 579,089 (provisional data for 2007–2008).[18]

The policy changes initiated after 1975 have elevated Spanish preschool enrollment rates, which now stand at 97 to 100 percent for children between four and six, to among the highest in the EU (data for 2006–2007).[19] In 2002–2003, only four EU countries (Belgium, France, Italy, and Spain) could claim full enrollment (100 percent) even for four-year-old children, with an average enrollment rate in the EU of 86 percent. For three-year-old children in preschool education, only Belgium, France, and Italy (all 100 percent) exceeded the Spanish participation rate of 95 percent, which was far above the EU average of 72 percent.[20]

The Limitations of Preschool Policies in Franco's Spain

In Franco's Spain, there were no attempts to achieve gender equality through the provision of childcare. Given that the regime actively worked to undermine women's rights and status in the family, society, and politics, this should come as little surprise. Divorce was abolished and the sale and advertising of contraceptives was criminalized. Abortion was defined as a crime subject to a prison sentence. According to the official doctrine of the dictatorship, the ideal family was a hierarchical unit in which authority rested with the father, who was supposed to be its sole (or at least its primary) breadwinner. Motherhood was described not only as a woman's duty to the family, but also as her primary obligation towards the state and society. Women's crucial role as mothers was thus perceived as incompatible with other activities, above all paid work outside the home. This family policy was, moreover, strongly informed and legitimated by the doctrine of the Catholic Church.[21]

Most scholarship differentiates two periods during the Franco regime.[22] During the first period, which lasted from the mid-1930s to the end of the 1950s, the state took numerous measures to prevent women from working outside the home. Labor regulations mandated that companies fire women upon being married, while some professions, for example law and medicine, barred women altogether. In addition, married women needed their husbands' permission before signing a labor contract or engaging in a trade.[23] The Franco regime also used its childcare and preschool policy to restrict the possibilities of married women and mothers for paid work outside the home by keeping the number of programs it offered to a minimum. During this period, few politicians saw education, let alone early childhood education, as a way to improve the quality of the labor force and thereby promote economic development. Through the 1940s and 1950s, the government sought to achieve economic self-sufficiency by isolating the Spanish economy from the international market.[24] Despite the onset of industrialization, Spain remained until the 1950s a predominantly rural country, with some 50 percent of its labor force employed in agriculture.[25] Compared to other Western European countries, Spanish agricultural productivity was low, while unemployment and underemployment were high.

During the first phase of the Franco regime, the Catholic Church and the state found in each other useful allies. Catholicism was made the official religion of the country, and freedom of worship was abolished. In return for the political support of the church, the state accorded it the right to adjudicate all matters regarding marriage and the separation of married couples. With very few exceptions, a Catholic marriage was mandatory and a divorce not possible. In addition, the state conceded to the Catholic Church far-reaching influence in the education system. On the one hand, it required compulsory religious education and religious practices in all pre-, primary, and secondary schools and demanded that the school curricula conform to the teachings of the Catholic Church, which was also given the right to inspect private and public schools, including preschools. On the other, it allowed the church to administer a significant number of pre-, primary, and secondary schools on its own.[26] The church was able to fund these and many other projects because it received generous financial support from the state. Moreover, it was exempted from taxation. In turn, the Catholic Church provided the authoritarian Franco regime with much-needed political legitimacy, above all by proclaiming the civil war a crusade between the supporters of Christianity and the godless Republicans. Indeed, some officials in the Francoist state, including the government, hailed from Catholic lay organizations such as the Asociación Católica Nacional de Propagandistas.[27] This close entanglement of the Franco regime and the Catholic Church allowed the government to pursue a very conservative family policy that focused on the stabilization of the male-breadwinner family.

The second phase of the Franco regime, which most historians date from the end of the 1950s to the mid-1970s, at first brought little change. While policymakers did approve a few more liberal measures related to women's rights, including the abolition of certain obstacles to paid employment in previously barred professions, other barriers to female employment, above all the authority of the husbands to approve the labor contracts of his wife, remained in place. Official doctrine and actual policymaking continued to insist on the notion that a married woman's place was at home.[28] During the 1960s, however, the growing economy brought inevitable social changes. In 1959, the government had charted a new economic course by partially liberalizing the economy and opening it to international trade and competition. The result was a period of remarkable growth that ended two-and-a-half decades of stagnation.

The slow but steady industrialization of the country and its economic growth inspired a new debate about the necessity of educational reform. An increasing number of policymakers began to recognize the potential benefits of education for economic development. The three "Plans for Economic and Social Development" implemented in 1964–1967, 1968–1971, and 1972–1975 thus contained long sections on education.[29] The proposed reforms, however, focused on primary and secondary education. Most important was the extension of compulsory education to the age of fourteen in 1964, which proved difficult to realize. In 1963–1964, school enrollment rates for children were 74 percent for those aged twelve and 52 percent for those aged thirteen.[30] In the mid-1960s, independent sources calculated that at least one million children between the ages of six and fourteen were either not enrolled in school at all or were enrolled but did not attend it regularly.[31] Many parents either needed the income of their children or their helping hands on their farm or small business. Other parents were not able to pay for the schooling. One important precondition for a de facto universalization of compulsory schooling was therefore free education. The Education Act of December 1965 thus required that compulsory schooling should be free in the near future.

The enforcement of this major policy objective—free compulsory schooling for children aged six to thirteen—was an ambitious and highly contested project. It demanded most of the attention, energies, and financial resources of those responsible for education policy. As a result, very limited efforts were dedicated to preschooling, which reinforced the neglect of this sector of the education system.[32] The first "Plan for Economic and Social Development" in 1964 went so far as to ban the building of schools for children under the age of six.[33] Similarly, in 1972 the third plan defined compulsory education as an "absolute priority."[34] The realization of this major objective was considerably complicated by the heated debates over the best strategy. For some, the primary objective was to ensure that all children of compulsory school age were enrolled in and attended school regularly. In their opinion, the state needed to dedicate most of its resources towards increasing the number of available places in public schools for all children of compulsory school age whose parents opted for public education. Only then could the state subsidize more places in private schools for the same purpose.[35] Others favored greater state subsidies for private schools to meet the goal of free compulsory education for every child. This was, not surprisingly, the position of the providers of private schools, above all the Catholic Church. They argued that because the state extracts wealth from society in the form of taxes, public expenditures should respond to the wishes and interests of private citizens and institutions. In addition, in accordance with Catholic doctrine, they insisted that the right and duty to educate children belongs above all to parents who only delegate this right and duty to schools when children reach a certain age. It should be up to the parents, and not the state, to determine the kind of education their children should receive. If parents opt for private schools, the state should not interfere with their choice but instead facilitate it. And since in the past this choice had been available primarily to well-off families, the state should guarantee that parents of all social classes would be able to choose their preferred education by subsidizing private school.[36]

The relations between the Catholic Church and the Franco regime changed during this second phase. Increasingly, active members of the church and parts of the clergy distanced themselves from the regime, criticized the church's position and actions in the Civil War, and even gave protection and support to political dissidents. Catholics joined groups and parties across the ideological spectrum that opposed the dictatorship. Because an increasing number of Catholics and members of the church hierarchy had distanced themselves from the regime in the 1960s and 1970s, after Franco's death in 1975 the church as an institution was able to align itself with other political and social forces in the building of a new democratic regime.[37] This was an important precondition for the church's support of the new democratic state after 1975.

Because of the dominant family policy and the focus of education policy on the universalization of compulsory schooling, childcare and preschool education were not important subjects in public debate in Franco's Spain. Nevertheless, public demand for the expansion of childcare services and preschool education was increasing since the 1960s. Even official sources had to recognize the existence of families who needed childcare or preschool, especially in urban regions with a high level of female employment. Here more often than elsewhere mothers with small children worked outside the home. In such areas, the lack or scarcity of childcare and preschool services often meant that children, and above all girls, of compulsory school age had to stay home taking care of their younger siblings while their mothers were at work.[38] The extension of preschool services would thus also support the universalization of compulsory schooling.

The Expansion of Preschool Services in Postauthoritarian Spain

When Franco died in 1975, he bequeathed to the new Spanish state a preschool policy that, however limited, was part of the broader policy on education. The Ministry of Education remained in power and continued to be responsible for formulating and executing preschool policy. The ability of the ministry to meet its policy goals, however, remained severely limited. Structural and financial problems prevented a quick change in education policy. Above all, the ministry lacked sufficient facilities, staff, and teachers to offer enough preschool classes. Because of these severe problems, after 1975 politicians at the central and later the regional level found it easier to expand existing education policies than to invent a completely new policy from scratch.[39] In respect to preschools, this meant that they increasingly recognized the importance of the extension of preschool programs, but pursued this extension as an educational reform, not a reform of the childcare system or the family policy. The Ministry of Education and later regional authorities on education increased the number of preschool places in the structures of the pre-1975 system. In the late 1970s and 1980s, public preschool places were provided above all for children aged four and five, while in the 1990s and the first decade of the twenty-first century, these places were also increasingly furnished for children aged three.

This expansion policy was supported by a broad spectrum of political parties (although for different reasons): governments formed by the center-right coalition of parties of the Unión de Centro Democrático (1977–1982), the social democratic Partido Socialista Obrero Español (PSOE) (1982–1996), the conservative Partido Popular (1996–2004), and since 2004 again the PSOE, have all recognized that the expansion of preschool services was necessary if Spain were to catch up to the more developed members of the EU. All parties agreed that the relative economic and social backwardness of Spain was due not least of all to its education deficit. They now saw early childhood education as an important tool to help ensure a high-quality education for children from broader social strata, which would be increasingly necessary if the country wanted to compete economically. In particular, the PSOE promoted public preschool as a means to reduce social inequality because access to noncompulsory education was determined in the past largely by class.[40] And yet when it was in government, the conservative Partido Popular also maintained and even increased the number of publicly supported preschools. In the context of strong electoral competition from the PSOE, the conservatives sought to avoid being labeled as a party of the rich, a constituency that is more likely to use private childcare and preschool programs.[41] For the same reasons, regional governments from across the political spectrum continued to expand public preschool programs as educational policy was steadily transferred to them from the central state.

The implementation of universal, compulsory education between the ages of six and twelve was achieved in the late 1970s. Government statistics reported an enrollment rate of 100 percent for children aged thirteen years for the first time in 1981–1982.[42] This allowed the government to invest more money in the expansion of preschool services. Its growth was facilitated further by the declining number of children of compulsory school age, which meant that some of the material and human resources that had previously been dedicated to compulsory schooling could be shifted to preschool. As a result, the number of public preschool centers, and with it the rate of enrollment, climbed significantly during the 1980s.

This development was made possible by the political transition after 1975, which fundamentally changed the relationship between the Catholic Church and the state. With Article 16 of the new constitution from 1978, Spain became a nondenominational state based on freedom of religion. This very same article, however, also states that "public authorities will remain cognizant of the religious beliefs of Spanish society" and emphasized the "desirability" of the cooperation between the state, the Catholic Church, and other confessions. Thus the Spanish state continues, despite the official separation between state and church, to accord special treatment to the Catholic Church. This is also reflected in the continuation of the tax exemptions and the generous financial support the Spanish state still grants to Catholic schools, hospitals, social agencies, and cultural institutions.[43]

This political compromise allowed the Catholic Church to support the continued expansion of school education in the 1980s and 1990s because it ensured that much of it remained private and subsidized by the state. Today, most private, non-university education in Spain is supported by state funds, and most non-university educational institutions that receive state subsidies are either controlled by or directly affiliated with the Catholic Church. In 2004–2005, 84 percent of non-university students in private education attended subsidized educational institutions (*centros privados concertados*). In that same year, 72 percent of non-university students in subsidized private education attended religious schools. In exchange for state funding, subsidized private schools must not only use the same criteria as public schools in selecting students if the number of applicants exceeds the number of available places, but are also required to provide education free of charge and allow parents, students, and school staff to participate in school affairs.[44] State subsidies are a very important source of income for providers of private education. On average, in 2004–2005 the state covered 75 percent of the current expenses of private schools that received public funds.[45] Until the 1990s, the state had mainly subsidized private compulsory education, but since then it has increasingly supported private preschool education as well.[46]

The expansion of preschool services in post-Franco Spain occurred as women became increasingly active in political parties, trade unions, civil society organizations, and the growing women's movement. Today, women outnumber men in mixed associations dedicated to the promotion of social causes.[47] As a result, women have become a visible political constituency that politicians must take into consideration when determining their positions on public policy. But unlike in other Western European countries, the issue of childcare was never the first priority of the most politically active women in Spain. Even the women's movement, which was and remains divided into an explicitly feminist and a more traditional branch, did not make childcare a major priority. The feminist branch of the women's movement was established in the 1960s and early 1970s as the Franco regime underwent a gradual process of liberalization. Since the end of the regime, it has influenced policies through its involvement with left-wing political parties. When these parties began to take power in the 1980s, some of their feminist activists and leaders assumed prominent positions in the state and bureaucracy from which they could advance an agenda of gender equality.[48] But even then, they made the issue of childcare only a secondary priority. The memory of the right-wing authoritarian regime in Spain limited Spanish feminists' interest in issues concerning motherhood and childcare. After forty years of being told that mothering and caring were the most important tasks in a woman's life, the last thing Spanish feminists wanted to do after the dictatorship was focus on motherhood and childrearing. Instead, they sought to increase the range of concerns that define women's lives, such as paid employment outside the home, political participation, and control of their own bodies. This redefinition of women's roles and possibilities carefully skirts the place of motherhood and childcare in the life of the newly liberated Spanish women.[49]

Conclusion

The primary goal of this chapter was to determine which factors influenced the policy regarding all-day preschool education before and after 1975 and to explore the causes for the rapid increase of public preschooling in the post-Franco era. It argues that one of the most important factors in this area of education was the persistent role of the Catholic Church in Spanish society and politics, in particular the changed relation between the state and the church, which also defined the influence of the church on education and welfare. In addition, the unanimous perception of all-day early childhood education as *education* and not as *childcare* was and remains an important factor in determining policy. Even the Catholic Church, which has long since fought in other European countries such as Austria and West Germany against the extension of all-day schools and childcare, shared this approach. Finally, the politics of the women's movement played a major role. Unlike in other countries such as Sweden, Spanish feminists did not vehemently demand all-day childcare, which allows women to work full-time and gain financial independence from men, as a key means of achieving female emancipation.

The interplay of these factors also supported the remarkable increase of public preschooling in the post-Franco era. First and foremost, the perception of preschool education as education and not as childcare helped engender the necessary political support for the dramatic increase of preschool facilities since the late 1970s. The free preschool education has and continues to receive broad support because it includes children from all social classes and enhances their cognitive and social development. However, the time structure of Spanish preschools prevented women who needed or wanted to work full-time from using it for childcare purposes.

In addition, the compromise between the state and the Catholic Church after 1975 proved particularly important in the evolution of preschool education, as it secured for the church major influence on all sectors of non-university education. Catholicism is no longer the "state religion," but the Catholic Church still has a privileged position in the Spanish democracy and receives considerable financial support for its work in education and welfare. And despite the dramatic increase of public education, the church today administers a similar number of preschool places as it did in the

1970s, thus demonstrating its success in defending its position as a major provider of early childhood education. Together, these factors paved the way for greater acceptance of preschool education by the Catholic Church in Spain, which, like the church in Germany and elsewhere in Europe, has fought a longstanding battle against the extension of public all-day schools and childcare. Furthermore, the women's movement did not, as it did in other countries like France and Sweden, push strongly for childcare as a means to allow women to work full-time. Nevertheless, the increasing presence of women in civil society and the strength of the women's movement has compelled politicians across the ideological spectrum to pursue policies, including the expansion of preschool, that could be perceived as beneficial for women.

Notes

This chapter contains research undertaken by the project "Gender and Citizenship in Multicultural Europe: The Impact of the Contemporary Women's Movements (FEMCIT)" financed by the European Commission's Sixth Framework Program (EC contract number 028746–2).

1. Álfonso Pérez Peñasco, "Educación," in *Estudios Sociológicos sobre la Situación Social en España 1975*, ed. Fundación Foessa (Madrid, 1976), 224.
2. Ministerio de Educación, Política Social y Deporte, *Estadística de las Enseñanzas no Universitarias: Resultados Detallados del Curso 2006–2007*. Retrieved 12 August 2007: http://www.mepsyd.es/mecd/jsp/plantilla.jsp?id=310&area=estadisticas&contenido=/estadisticas/educativas/eenu/result_det/2006/resultados.html.
3. Instituto Nacional de Estadística, *Estadística de la Enseñanza en España: Curso 1975–76* (Madrid, 1977), 101–3.
4. Ministerio de Educación y Ciencia, *Datos y Cifras: Curso Escolar 2007/2008*, 3. Retrieved 12 August 2008: http://www.mepsyd.es/dctm/mepsyd/horizontales/prensa/documentos/2008/datosycifras.pdf?documentId=0901e72b80027850.
5. Ministerio de Educación, Política Social y Deporte, *Estadística de las Enseñanzas.*
6. OECD, *Historical Statistics* (Paris, 1992), 39.
7. Instituto Nacional de Estadística, *Encuesta de la Fuerza de Trabajo de la UE (UE LFS): Datos Europeos*. Retrieved 27 August 2007: http://www.ine.es/jaxi/tabla.do?path=/t22/e308/e01/l0/&file=03005.px&type=pcaxis&L=0.
8. Fabrice Romans, "Labor Market Trends 4th Quarter 2007 Data," *Eurostat DATA in Focus: Population and Social Conditions* 16 (2008): 3–4.
9. Xavier Bonal, "Interest Groups and the State in Contemporary Spanish Education Policy," *Journal of Educational Policy* 15, no. 2 (2000): 206; Pérez Peñasco, "Educación," 315.
10. Peter Bachrach and Morton S. Baratz, "Two Faces of Power," *American Political Science Review* 56, no. 4 (1962): 948–49; John W. Kingdom, *Agendas, Alternatives, and Public Policies* (Glenview, IL, 1995), 1–21.
11. Paul Pierson, *Politics in Time: History, Institutions, and Social Analysis* (Princeton, NJ, 2004), 10f.

12. Two percent of the interviewed identified themselves as belonging to other religions, 13 percent as nonbelievers, 7 percent as atheist, and 2 percent did not answer. Fifteen percent of those self-declared Catholics or believers of other religions affirmed that they attended religious services (not including social events such as weddings, first communions, or funerals) almost every Sunday or religious holiday, and 2 percent attended on various days during the week. Centro de Investigaciones Sociológicas, *Study Number 2,769* (July 2008). Retrieved 12 August 2008: http://www.cis.es/cis/opencm/ES/1_encuestas/estudios/ver.jsp?estudio=8480.

13. Francis G. Castles, "On Religion and Public Policy: Does Catholicism Make a Difference?" *European Journal of Political Research* 25, no. 1 (1994): 19–40; Mary Daly, "The Functioning Family: Catholicism and Social Policy in Germany and Ireland," *Comparative Social Research* 18 (1999): 105–33; Kimberly J. Morgan, *Working Mothers and the Welfare State: Religion and the Politics of Work-Family Policies in Western Europe and the United States* (Stanford, CA, 2006), 64, 83–86; Kees van Kersbergen, *Social Capitalism: A Study of Christian Democracy and the Welfare State* (London, 1995), 2–5, 175, and 181–91.

14. Manuel de Puelles Benítez, *Educación e Ideología en la España Contemporánea* (Barcelona, 1999), 133.

15. John M. McNair, *Education for a Changing Spain* (Manchester, 1984), 18f.

16. Translated by Celia Valiente.

17. Fundación Foessa, ed., *Informe Sociológico sobre la Situación Social de España* (Madrid, 1966), 158.

18. Instituto Nacional de Estadística, *Curso 1975–76*, 101–03; Ministerio de Educación y Ciencia, *Datos y Cifras*, 3.

19. Ministerio de Educación, Política Social y Deporte, *Estadística de las Enseñanzas.*

20. Ministerio de Educación y Ciencia, *Datos y Cifras*, 15.

21. Aurora G. Morcillo, *True Catholic Womanhood: Gender Ideology in Franco's Spain* (Dekalb, IL, 2000), 26–45; Mary Nash, "Pronatalism and Motherhood in Franco's Spain," in *Maternity and Gender Policies: Women and the Rise of the European Welfare States, 1880s-1950s*, ed. Gisela Bock and Pat Thane (London, 1991), 160; Rosario Ruiz Franco, *Eternas Menores? Las Mujeres en el Franquismo* (Madrid, 2007), 25–30.

22. Charles W. Anderson, *The Political Economy of Modern Spain: Policy-Making in an Authoritarian System* (Madison, WI, 1970), 27, 32, 206, and 221; Raymond Carr, *España 1808–1975* (Barcelona, 2002), 682–702.

23. Ruiz Franco, *Eternas Menores?* 35–47.

24. My description of economic policy in Franco's Spain is drawn largely from Anderson, *Political Economy*, 1–34, 129–31, 147–56, and 203–31; and Carr, *España*, 703–17.

25. Carr, *España*, 704.

26. McNair, *Education*, 28f.

27. Carr, *España*, 669; José Casanova, "Church, State, Nation, and Civil Society in Spain and Poland," in *The Political Dimensions of Religion*, ed. Said Amir Arjomand (Albany, NY, 1993), 107–8; Amando de Miguel, *Sociología del Franquismo: Análisis Ideológico de los Ministros del Régimen* (Barcelona, 1975), 205–09, 223; de Puelles Benítez, *Educación*, 310; Juan J. Linz, "Religión y Política en España," in *Religión y Sociedad en España*, ed. Rafael Díaz-Salazar and Salvador Giner (Madrid, 1993), 9–25.

28. Morcillo, *Catholic Womanhood*, 4; Ruiz Franco, *Eternas Menores?* 229–32.

29. Comisaría del Plan de Desarrollo Económico y Social, *Enseñanza y Formación Profesional, Investigación Científica y Técnica: Anexo al Plan de Desarrollo Económico y Social* (Madrid, 1964); Comisaría del Plan de Desarrollo Económico y Social, *Enseñanza y Formación Profesional: II Plan de Desarrollo Económico y Social* (Madrid, 1967); Comisaría del Plan

de Desarrollo Económico y Social, *III Plan de Desarrollo Económico y Social: Educación, 1972–1975* (Madrid, 1972); Pérez Peñasco, "Educación," 315.

30. Fundación Foessa, *Informe Sociológico* (1966), 158.
31. Fundación Foessa, ed., *Informe Sociológico sobre la Situación Social de España 1970* (Madrid, 1970), 85; Juan M. Lumbreras Meabe, *Momento Actual de la Enseñanza no Estatal: ¿La Gratuidad, Empresa Posible?* (Barcelona, 1973), 12.
32. McNair, *Education*, 42.
33. Comisaría del Plan de Desarrollo Económico y Social, *Plan de Desarrollo*, 20.
34. Comisaría del Plan de Desarrollo Económico y Social, *II Plan de Desarrollo*, 13.
35. De Puelles, *Educación*, 332; Fundación Foessa, *España 1970*, 845–51; McNair, *Education*, 46–47; Pérez Peñasco, "Educación," 220.
36. Juan M. Lumbreras Meabe, *Los Colegios de la Iglesia en España, ¿Son un Negocio?* (Madrid, 1960), 8–13; Lumbreras Meabe, *Enseñanza No Estatal*, 7–9; McNair, *Education*, 46f.
37. Carr, *España*, 670, 694–95; Casanova, "Church," 114–17; Linz, "Religión," 25–32.
38. Act of 17 July 1945 on primary schooling, art. 19; 1970 Education Act, art. 98; Comisaría del Plan de Desarrollo Económico y Social, *Plan de Desarrollo*, 20.
39. Celia Valiente, "The Value of an Educational Emphasis: Childcare and Restructuring in Spain since 1975," in *Childcare Policy at the Crossroads: Gender and Welfare Restructuring*, ed. Sonya Michel and Rianne Mahon (New York, 2002), 57 and 65.
40. De Puelles Benítez, *Educación*, 368–69; McNair, *Education*, 47; Pérez Peñasco, "Educación," 219–20, 226–27.
41. Valiente, "Educational Emphasis," 63; Celia Valiente, "Central State Childcare Policies in Postauthoritarian Spain: Implications for Gender and Carework Arrangements," *Gender & Society* 17, no. 2 (2003): 289.
42. Instituto Nacional de Estadística, *Estadística de la Enseñanza en España 1981–82* (Madrid, 1985), 54. In 1990, the period of compulsory education was extended to the age of sixteen.
43. Juan G. Bedoya, "Las Cuentas del Catolicismo Español," *El País*, 30 September 2006: 43; Casanova, "Church," 117; Linz, "Religión," 35.
44. The free of charge requirement does not include extracurricular activities, school meals, or school textbooks.
45. Instituto Nacional de Estadística, *Notas de Prensa—19 de Julio de 2007: Encuesta de Financiación y Gastos de la Enseñanza Privada, Curso 2004–2005*. Retrieved 27 August 2007: http://www.ine.es/prensa/np465.pdf.
46. In postauthoritarian Spain, the Catholic Church has also consistently demanded that the state grant religion academic status in the school curriculum. See Bonal, "Interest Groups," 205–6; McNair, *Education*, 144.
47. Víctor Pérez Díaz and Joaquín P. López Novo, *El Tercer Sector Social en España* (Madrid, 2003), 214–17, 231–33, and 241–42.
48. Monica Threlfall et al., eds., *Gendering Spanish Democracy* (London, 2005), 40–44.
49. Valiente, "Educational Emphasis," 65; Valiente, "Childcare Policies," 288.

Chapter 11

FROM WEAK SOCIAL DEMOCRACY TO HYBRIDIZED NEOLIBERALISM

Early Childhood Education in Britain since 1945

Kevin J. Brehony and Kristen D. Nawrotzki

In January 2006, Beverley Hughes, British Minister of State for Children, Young People, and Families, gave the keynote address at a conference in New York about economics and early childhood provision. Hughes's speech was described as "a victory lap," celebrating what she called a "revolution in early years policy" in England.[1] June 2006 government figures show the results of this revolution: near universal part-time educational provision for three- and four-year-olds in nursery classes and nursery schools as well as more than 1.5 million childcare places spread across a wide range of schedules and settings. In addition to increasing the number of places, New Labor has focused on the integration of services to provide wrap-around "educare," dawn-to-dusk care and education. This coordination of services is meant to help parents navigate "the gentle anarchy of British preschool provision," which until recently has not been concerned with a universal time policy.[2]

The results of this policy are at the first glance impressive. The Organisation for Economic Co-operation and Development (OECD) reported in 2006 that on average about 20 percent of all children under three, 96 percent of all three- to four-year-old children and 100 percent of all four- to five-year-old children in Britain have access to a regulated childcare service. All three- to five-year-old children currently have fifteen hours per week of free early education provision for the school year. Compulsory school starts after the fifth birthday and is usually an all-day school with a lunch break and a provided meal.[3]

These average numbers hide the major differences between the existing five categories of care: crèches, childminders, full-day care, out-of-school

Notes for this chapter begin on page 253.

care, and seasonal care. Crèches offer occasional care more than two hours a day/five days a week. Registered childminders provide care on domestic premises for more than two hours per day but not after 6:00 P.M. Full-day care is found in institutional settings including nurseries and children's centers open more than four continuous hours per day. Out-of-school care is for children ages three and over, before and after school and during school holidays, and seasonal care is care offered less than four hours a day, five days a week.[4] The costs to the parents vary greatly according to their income and the service. Compared to those in other developed industrial countries, parents in Britain have to pay considerable childcare fees. The OECD estimates that British parents cover in average 45 percent of the costs.[5]

Over much of the last sixty years, time spent in early childhood care and education in Britain has been related to social class and conceptions of the role of mothers within the family, society, and labor market. The children who spend the most time in formally provided care have almost always been poor and working class. Outside the ideologically and financially constrained nursery school sector, time spent in care or education by the children of middle-class families has been more limited and thus closer to the half-day system in Germany. There is little evidence for the view that time in childcare or education has been a major issue in England as distinct from its general availability and quality. However, a lack of provision of childcare or education time has, as in other countries, widely been seen as a constraint on women's labor force participation.[6]

The recent and quite massive expansion in English early years care and education provision is especially impressive when set against the background of sixty years of virtual inactivity in the state sector (except in a few localities where the political will existed). The New Labor policy revolution Hughes described in 2006 has actually been in the making for more than half a century, belatedly fulfilling British government promises of 1918 and 1944. Since the end of World War II, the British welfare state has been shaped by international and nation-specific economic and social conditions as well as by a male-breadwinner ideology. The latter delineated the sexual division of labor and the distribution of time and other resources within the family unit.[7] Its persistence and the continuation of relatively stable economic and social conditions made radical change in early years policy and provision difficult until the 1970s. In the 1980s, Thatcherite neoliberalism radically altered the English welfare state. Although it arguably did more harm than good for the economic and social welfare of England's children, its effects provided the critical juncture for a redefinition of the English welfare state. We shall argue that the response of the New Labor government—including Hughes's "revolution"—marked neither a return to the postwar social democratic welfare settlement, nor a move towards an unalloyed market-based approach. Seen through the lens of childcare and early years policy and provision, the revolution that New Labor effected in the state-family relationship appears to have been a hybrid welfare settlement with neoliberal inflections.

In this chapter, we analyze the main developments in the postwar policy debates as well as the provision of childcare and early year education in Britain since the end of World War II, with a focus on the English case.[8] We explain why, after diverging from many other European nations, English policy towards childcare and early childhood education is now showing signs of convergence with them. We contextualize these developments within the transition from social democratic to neoliberal approaches to policy. In the final section, we discuss the consequences of the childcare and preschool time policies for the theorization of welfare states and welfare regimes in order to understand more adequately the paradox of the expansion of time provided in childcare and preschool in a neoliberal era.

The Longstanding English Liberal Tradition

In political terms, the English family has long been seen as requiring privacy and independence from intervention by the state in order to fulfill its duties as the moral center of society. Where families could not perform this duty, such as in cases of extreme deprivation or at times of national crisis, the state has intervened—but only reluctantly, with the result that England has had little explicit childcare policy to speak of. English social welfare and educational provision have traditionally neglected children under age five—that is, children under compulsory school age—who were seen primarily by policymakers as the responsibility of the family and of the mother in particular. When young children have been the focus of state-sector institutions, the goal has been first to ensure services such as infant healthcare or nursery schooling and then increasingly to fill gaps in the patchwork of provision to make services universally available. Programs have normally been defined at the national level, with the Ministries of Health and Labor in charge of childcare and day nurseries and Ministry of Education overseeing infant schools (from 1839) and nursery schools (from 1918). However, responsibility for day-to-day provision has rested with local authorities, which were often circumscribed by central government spending strictures.

World War II brought significant but short-lived changes to English early years provision. Women made up slightly more than one-third of the British labor force in the first half of the twentieth century, but the war drew more married women, especially mothers, into paid employment.[9] Severe shortages in many sectors of the wartime labor market, combined with pressure from organized labor, spurred the Ministry of Health to support local authorities in opening day nurseries for children ages one to five. These accommodated up to seventy thousand children on a variety of schedules. After World War II, however, the Labor government began "positively to discourage mothers of children under two from going out to work" and in 1946 it abruptly ended its support for day nurseries.[10] Nevertheless, before, during, and after the war, relatives and individual home-based childminders provided the majority of care for children under age five. Under a 1948 act, the Ministry of Health assumed responsibility for the registration and regulation of the latter and for that of private nurseries, but the number of unregistered childminders remained in the hundreds of thousands.[11]

The Weak Social Democratic Welfare State

The liberal ideal of families fending for themselves in a free market was pushed aside in the design of the postwar welfare state, which was based upon a social democratic consensus and Keynesian economics. Following decades of economic crisis and social upheaval, coalition and Labor governments sought to ensure the family's protection from poverty and unemployment. Among other things, the Education Act of 1944 required local authorities to provide nursery schools and nursery classes for under-five-year-olds. In the face of budgetary constraints and teacher shortages, however, the government soon embargoed nursery school expansion. As a result, state-sector nursery schooling expanded very little in the decades to follow, rising from 370 nursery schools in 1946 to 648 in 1977 and declining to 516 by the year 2000.[12] The new welfare state included key measures to combat social inequality, most notably the National Insurance Act of 1946. While this act marked a massive extension of state responsibility for citizens' welfare and laid the foundations of the welfare state, the commitment to social equality was weaker than in other social democratic welfare states, such as Sweden. It also continued the earlier trend of paying little attention to the education and care of under-five-year-old children.

The care of young children was not significantly altered by mothers' wartime labor market participation, and it made readily available childminders appealing even as the number of postwar day-nursery places dwindled. With a few exceptions, during the immediate postwar years, employed mothers were forced out of full-time jobs and, if they remained in paid work, it was only part-time.[13] By 1955, despite protests from women, labor organizations, and other women's and children's advocacy organizations, 50 percent of war-time day nurseries had been closed. Moreover, the stigmatization of day nurseries as "welfare" institutions run under the Ministry of Health remained an obstacle to making them universally available.[14]

In addition, the psychoanalytic maternal separation theories of child development expert John Bowlby came to encapsulate the pronatalist ideology upon which the reduction of day nursery provision was based.[15] The fact that increasing proportions of mothers were employed part-time outside the home did not impel governments to become more responsible for providing childcare, nor did long waiting lists for day nursery and nursery school places. In fact, the Ministries of Health and Education refused working mothers priority in the allocation of postwar daycare or nursery school places.[16]

In the immediate postwar years, the "bulge" in birth rates led local education authorities to discourage "rising-fives" from enrollment in infants' classes, whose rolls reached fifty pupils on average.[17] In 1960, the government issued a circular admitting that nothing had been done to implement the part of the 1944 Education Act relevant for under-five-year-olds. In addition, it strengthened earlier restrictions on nursery expansion, citing a shortage of teachers and a lack of classroom space. The result of pre- and postwar policy was that for several decades, provision for under-five-year-old children stagnated. Whereas in 1932, 5 percent of them received some kind of state provision, 7 percent did in 1965.[18] A general shift from full-time (roughly 9:00 A.M. to 3:30 P.M.) to increasingly part-time, double-session attendance at nursery schools and classes meant that nursery education became less attractive as a form of childcare. Nursery schools in working-class areas had empty places while those in middle-class areas had extensive waiting lists.[19] Only 4 percent of three- and four-year-olds in England and Wales were in part-time private nursery schools, nursery classes, or in part- or full-time day nurseries in 1965, but these numbers were increasing.[20]

Responding to state inaction, voluntary organizations such as the Save the Children Fund began to open preschool playgroups for some of the thousands of three- and four-year-olds who lacked access to state-sector nursery education. A coordinated movement for preschool playgroups was begun in 1962 with the establishment of the Preschool Playgroups Association (later Preschool Learning Alliance).[21] Its instigator, the working-mother-turned-activist Belle Tutaev, and others were initially keen for mother-supervised, professionally guided playgroups to serve as a means of pushing for growth in state provision. However, within a decade they had changed from a nursery education pressure group to "a parent-run educational movement" emphasizing wholly play-based parent-and-child socialization.[22]

By 1976, the Preschool Playgroups Association had over ten thousand members and supported thousands of registered playgroups.[23] Its central organization received a small government grant and some local authorities eventually subsidized playgroups, which increasingly relied on unqualified low-paid and volunteer staff, especially the middle-class mothers of playgroup children. Later, they came to include toddler groups for even younger children, but most participants attended the two- to three-hour playgroup sessions no more than twice or three times each week. Although playgroups did not serve as effective childcare for working mothers, the government recognized them as childcare and not as educational institutions. Ironically, the rapid expansion of playgroups (serving around half of all three- and four-year-olds in England by 1987) took pressure off local authorities and the central government, which continued to resist state-sector nursery school expansion.[24]

In the late 1960s, after two decades of focusing on secondary schooling and its structural implications for social inequality, the British government turned its attention to compulsory primary education and, to a lesser extent, to precompulsory nursery education. The Plowden Committee's 1967 report on primary education, including infant schools for five-year-olds, did not dispense with the attachment theories and male-breadwinner ideologies that had long defined government policy, and its claims accorded with general liberal distaste for government interventions into families. While the committee found it "generally undesirable, except to prevent a greater evil, to separate mother and child for a whole day in the nursery," it did advocate half-day, nondaily nursery education for threes and fours as a means of enhancing normal child development and, potentially, reducing socioeconomic inequality.[25] To this end, the committee recommended special government funding to support nursery and primary schooling in Educational Priority Areas characterized by high levels of social and material deprivation.

The recommendations of the Plowden Committee seemed very near realization in 1972, when Margaret Thatcher, as secretary of state for education in a self-described "profamily" Conservative government, presented a White Paper on education. Thatcher promised to extend state-sector provision to include free places in nursery schools and nursery classes for 90 percent of four-year-olds and 50 percent of three-year-olds. The new scheme accorded with Plowden views about full-day care being suitable only under exceptional circumstances, and proposed that 15 percent of places in each category cover full school days. Following on Plowden Educational Priority Areas, Thatcher promised that socially deprived areas would receive funding priority in the first two years. The White Paper also recognized the work of Preschool Playgroups Association groups by increasing their funding.[26]

What made this policy consensus attractive in the 1970s? Public demand for early childhood education and for full-time care for under-five-year-olds was high and rising. Causes included declining birth rates allowing more space in schools, married women's increased participation in the paid labor market and related changes in gender roles, significant increases in the number of single-parent households, and the exceedingly high opportunity costs of childbearing for English women.[27] The government's increasing awareness of the fragmented nature of nursery education and childcare as well as unfavorable comparisons of English early years provision with those of other members of the European Economic Community and with the United States also played a role.[28]

The Preschool Playgroups Association campaigns for nursery education and for playgroups had changed public opinion regarding programs for young children, especially as playgroups brought mothers into preschool settings and broke down home/institution barriers. The Plowden Report provided social-scientific evidence in support of preschool experiences for all children, claiming that good nursery schools go beyond what good mothers or childminders could offer, giving children "what modern family life often cannot."[29] Thatcher's 1972 White Paper can also be seen as a half-hearted attempt to legitimate the crumbling postwar social democratic order in the face of increasing evidence of its failure to reduce inequality and to increase the nation's economic competitiveness.[30]

The Rise of Neoliberalism: The Thatcher Government

The White Paper, which was initially celebrated as a watershed in state-sector preschool provision, ended up a victim of economic recession, concomitant social and educational crises, and aggressive cutbacks in state-sector funding as the long postwar boom came to an end. Upon coming to power in 1979, Thatcherite Tories broke sharply with the social democratic settlement and pursued a radical neoliberal policy agenda based upon a repudiation of Keynesian economics, the advocacy of unregulated markets to increase economic growth and national well-being, deregulation of industry, and privatization of services as a means of reducing state intervention into public and private life. Representing itself as "profamily," the Thatcher government nevertheless rejected the idea of the so-called nanny state and shelved Thatcher's own 1972 White Paper recommendations in the 1980 Education Act.

The years of the Thatcher government, 1979–1990, were marked by high unemployment rates as the state was "rolled back" and deindustrialization proceeded apace. Controls on capital flows were lifted, trade unions in traditional industries were confronted and defeated by the state, and this facilitated the subsequent growth of the mainly low-wage service sector. Coupled with demographic changes, this created an increased demand for women's labor, chiefly on a part-time basis. Although women's wages were an increasing proportion of family income, leading to the decline of the male-breadwinner paradigm on which policies were based, there was no concomitant move towards redistributing care responsibilities among male and female breadwinners. Family and community cohesion were corroded in the areas most affected by deindustrialization. The number of single parents, almost all of them women, grew to record levels, a trend that would continue through the century's end.[31]

Thatcherite libertarian, neoliberal policies were linked somewhat uneasily to a traditionalist "authoritarian populist" view of the family and the state that precluded collectivist action on childcare and resisted expansion in young children education.[32] In this period, few politicians campaigned on childcare issues or nursery education, and certainly no one took up the cause of young children. A notable exception was Renee Short, a Labor Member of Parliament (MP) who was president of the Nursery Schools Association for many years. Her admiration of the USSR and the GDR was related to a belief in the collective provision of childcare in the Soviet Bloc.[33] Arguments for high-quality preschool education were also contained in the Rumbold Report of 1990 as well as reports by the Royal Society of Arts in 1994 and the Audit Commission in 1996.[34] While these interventions ensured that childcare was moved up on the policy agenda, other determinants of its rise to political significance were possibly of greater importance.

Borrowing workfare policies from the United States, the Conservative John Major government from 1990 to 1997 focused on the supposed deficits of single mothers and their dependency on welfare.[35] It identified childcare as a prime condition for helping move single parents into the workforce.[36] After a long period of political quiescence, the education and care of children moved up the political agenda so rapidly that in 1994 the Conservative government promised nursery schooling for all four-year-olds by 1997. In order to finance this objective, it introduced a nursery voucher scheme in 1996, which involved top-slicing some local authority budgets to provide the money.[37] Under the scheme, "parents who exchanged vouchers in the private or voluntary sectors were able to 'top up' the voucher with their own resources if higher fees were charged, for the part-time place or for a full-time, year-round place."[38] One unintended consequence was that preschool playgroup closures rose steeply as a result of the competition between providers vouchers were intended to stimulate.

The voucher scheme's introduction of a market mechanism into the childcare and early education sector under the banner of "choice" was not, however, a purely neoliberal policy move, as it was accompanied by state regulation of program content. This took the form of "desirable learning outcomes" that *all* voucher-receiving providers of prestatutory education and childcare, including childminders in home settings, had to work towards. Like those in the National Curriculum for school-aged children, these outcomes were mainly concerned with literacy, numeracy, and the development of personal and social skills.[39]

When Major's Conservative government ended in 1997, it was clear that neoliberal policies had failed to improve the lives of English children and their families. By then, English employment rates for single parents — which had reached 48 percent in 1979 — were now among the lowest of the advanced economies.[40] Child poverty increased significantly over the period, too: more than 1 in 3 children were in poverty in 1996–1997 compared with 1 in 10 in 1979[41] — one of the largest increases in the advanced economies.[42] By the mid-1990s, Britain had the highest proportion of children in unemployed and low-income households. Overall income inequality was expanding at a rate virtually unknown in the other advanced economies of OECD.[43]

The Conservatives in the election of 1997 pledged to give "the parent of every four-year-old child a voucher for nursery education" so they could form "a play-group, a reception class, or a nursery school in the private or state sector."[44] Labor, now reinvented as "New Labor," declared in its manifesto that "nursery vouchers … are costly and do not generate more quality nursery places." It promised to "use the money saved by scrapping nursery vouchers to guarantee places for four-year-olds … [and] set targets for universal provision for three-year-olds whose parents want it."[45] Upon being elected to power in 1997, the New Labor government abolished the nursery vouchers scheme.[46]

The formulation of New Labor's childcare and early years' education policy has not been the subject of much academic discussion. There is some evidence that it might have been partly driven by European considerations. In a debate on a nursery voucher scheme, Paul Boateng, later a New Labor minister, said,

> Childcare … strikes to the heart of our competitiveness with our European partners. As a nation, we have the worst childcare record in Europe. … That is bound to impact on our success in obtaining a skilled work force in terms of the educational advantages to children in receipt of preschool education, and, more importantly, drawing on the pool of skills that women are able to offer in the economy.[47]

This particular argument for childcare appears to have played a prominent part in New Labor's policy formation.

The European Council Recommendation "92/241/EEC" of 31 March 1992 on childcare recommended the provision of care for children whose parents were employed or seeking or training for employment.[48] Subsequently, in Britain and some other EU states that followed the model of the male-breadwinner family in their policy, arguments prioritizing economic efficiency and equal opportunities gained ground at the expense of arguments prioritizing the well-being of children.[49] How much this was due to European Union policy is debatable. As social scientist Jane Lewis has argued, "The message coming out of the EU was similar to that propounded by New Labor—that social provision had to 'modernize' in order to assist, rather than to detract from, economic growth and competitiveness."[50]

In 1998, New Labor launched its National Childcare Strategy, the first of a series of programs to massively extend and integrate childcare and early education.[51] Building on Early Excellence Center pilot programs begun in 1997, the strategy sought to integrate local childcare and education across private, voluntary, and state sectors. Its aim was to ensure access to good, affordable, informal, and institutional childcare, which was to be integrated with educational provision for children aged zero to fourteen nationwide.

The strategy was intended to meet a number of sometimes contradictory needs, including the reduction of child poverty, alleviation of labor shortages, and the need to raise educational attainment in order to adapt to globalization and to make Britain competitive in the "knowledge economy." As the policy developed, sometimes one was highlighted and at other times another. Reminiscent of Educational Priority Areas in the late 1960s, the strategy allocated special funding for disadvantaged areas, this time through the 1998 Sure Start initiative. Directed by the interdepartmental Sure Start Unit, accountable to both the Department for Education and Skills and the Department of Work and Pensions, Sure Start Children's Centers serve more than 400,000 children from birth to age four in the most disadvantaged neighborhoods in England. The centers provide nursery, childcare, and playgroup provision and postnatal and other health and employment services to families and are open on a dawn-to-dusk basis, ten hours a day, five days a week, forty-eight weeks a year.

The Childcare Strategy rhetoric relied heavily on the terms "support" and "choice" rather than on claims for state intervention within families themselves. Strategy documents declared that while "parents will always have the primary responsibility for the care and well-being of their children ... it is the Government's responsibility to ensure that parents have access to services to enable them to make genuine choices."[52] Increasing parents' ability to choose services was also at the heart of New Labor's

1999 Working Families Tax Credit, which targeted parents, including single parents, working a minimum of sixteen hours per week.

The increasing desirability of government intervention into family life was underscored by New Labor's Every Child Matters (ECM) program, founded in 2003. The program was intended as an overhaul of the child protection system and the ways in which police, health, and social services oversee the care of children at risk of abuse, neglect, or other "negative outcomes" at home or elsewhere.[53] Designed to coordinate social, health, and educational services for children and youth from birth to age nineteen, Every Child Matters embodied New Labor efforts to prevent young people from "falling through the gaps between different services" — including scheduling gaps — as well as to "improve children's lives as a whole" and "maximize their potential."[54]

Among other goals, the Every Child Matters program sought increased professionalization of those who work with children and instituted a new umbrella Minister for Children, Young People, and Families in the Department for Education and Skills. It also expanded the Sure Start program. By October 2007 there would be 1,500 Children's Centers (well ahead of the initial target of 1,000 by 2008) and the new Brown government promised another £351 million to achieve the goal of one in every community by 2010.[55] Although Children's Centers targeted families in high-poverty areas, Every Child Matters went beyond categorical state provision and promoted a Blairite discourse about "universal services," which included education, social services, health, and, for the first time, childcare.

In 2004, a Ten-Year Strategy for Childcare was added that paid specific attention to the timing and scheduling of services in addition to choice, flexibility, availability, quality, and affordability. It promised the expansion of full-service extended schools, schools open well beyond standard hours that offered breakfast, after-school activities, childcare, on-site healthcare, and other social services. The strategy was closely associated with the then-chancellor Gordon Brown. Speaking to his 2004 spending review in what has widely been quoted as support for universal childcare, Brown said that "the early part of the twenty-first century should be marked by the introduction of preschool provision for the under-5-year-olds and childcare available to all."[56]

The Ten-Year Strategy was quite explicit about its 2010 childcare scheduling "milestones," which cast aside earlier views that young children should spend only very little time away from their mothers. The 2010 milestones included:

> all parents of three- and four-year-olds offered access to wrap around childcare linked to the early education offer and available all year round from 8 A.M. to 6 P.M. weekdays; all parents of children aged 5–11 to have access to childcare from

8 A.M. to 6 P.M. weekdays all year round, based in their school or early education provider, or nearby with supervised transfer arrangements; all secondary
schools open from 8 A.M. to 6 P.M. weekdays providing extended services.[57]

At the end of 2007, the entitlement to free early education and childcare
for three- and four-year-olds having been raised from 12.5 to 15 hours a
week, the Children's Plan, another ten-year strategy, promised to extend
the entitlement to free early education and childcare to up to "15 hours
of free early education and childcare to 20,000 two-year-olds in the most
disadvantaged communities."[58]

Building upon the Ten-Year Strategy, the Childcare Act of 2006 completed a gradual long-term shift away from the traditional division of
childcare (under Ministry of Health) and nursery schooling (Department
for Education and Skills) and placed duties on local authorities and bodies
responsible for regulating and inspecting childcare. In short, all forms of
provision were to become part of a Children's Center or Extended School.
Local authorities are responsible for quality improvement and ensuring
seamless coverage of early years care and education provision for all who
want it. True to English models of educational provision more broadly,
however, a subsidiarity principle is at work whereby local authorities provide services only if no private, voluntary, or community-sector provision
is available, and in some cases parents have had to pay fees for services
that should be part of their free entitlement.[59] It places statutory duties
on local authorities not only to ensure sufficient childcare, but also to improve the well-being of young children in their area. *Well-being* is defined
in terms of the outcomes presented in the Every Child Matters program:
being healthy, staying safe, enjoying and achieving, making a positive
contribution, and attaining economic well-being.

A Regulated Market: The Early Years Foundation Stage

The state under New Labor has, like many other European states, appeared
to retreat from direction in favor of governance, the sharing of the power
to direct with private agents. In the year 2000, Curriculum Guidance for
the Foundation Stage (three to five years) was published to help practition-
ers plan how their work would contribute to early learning goals. This,
together with *Birth to Three Matters*, the nonstatutory guidance for all registered childminders and parents, and the national standards for childcare, was integrated into the Early Years Foundation Stage (EYFS), which
was statutory from 2008 as the phase of learning and development for
children from birth to the end of the academic year in which they turn five.
It was implemented in all registered early years settings and maintained

and independent schools. These settings have been required to meet the learning, development, and welfare requirements in the supporting EYFS package, and to follow the guidance associated with those requirements as appropriate. This is intended to ensure that all young children have access to an integrated learning and care experience and to secure for parents childcare of a consistent quality regardless of setting. As implemented, the curriculum for children from birth to five is no longer part of the National Curriculum.

In order to regulate the emerging mixed economy of childcare, a separate section of the Office for Standards in Education was established in 1999. This brought together the registration, investigation, enforcement, and inspection of both early education and daycare. The Office for Standards in Education uses the aims of the Every Child Matters program as part of its inspection framework and has required a small percentage of settings to close and judged a slightly larger percentage as inadequate. Critics claim this approach is "inspecting out" poor quality, rather than investing in a highly-trained and better-paid workforce.[60]

Childcare and the Welfare State

In 2003, Margaret Hodge became the first Children's Minister. At a Sure Start Conference, she declared, "Our ten year strategy is nothing less than a childcare revolution. It brings us from an era when children and families were barely at the fringes of people's concerns, to a time when childcare is at the absolute heart of the modern welfare state."[61] Hodge's perception that childcare and the contemporary welfare state were inextricably linked is one that is widely shared, but it begs the question of what kind of welfare state it is. Thus far we have used categories drawn from the sociologist Gøsta Esping-Andersen's typology of social democratic, conservative, and liberal.[62] At a certain level of abstraction, this is a useful way to think about the English state during the period we are concerned with. At the beginning of the postwar period, policies followed a somewhat diluted social democratic trajectory and focused on the reduction of social class inequality, though not as much as in Scandinavia. Later, during the Thatcher years, England embraced neoliberalism, and the role of the state was massively redefined in favor of "freedom of choice" and the market.[63]

However it is conceptualized, the welfare state constructed in the 1940s was very different in character to that of the early 2000s.[64] Large rises in women's labor market participation have undermined the assumption of the male-breadwinner family model that underlay the postwar welfare state in Britain and elsewhere. This led to the charge that Esping-Andersen's typology was gender blind as it did not register the male-breadwinner assumption.[65] As historian Sonya Michel has observed, attempts to build gender into his model have not been any more successful.[66] Recognizing this, political scientist Daniel Wincott suggests that rather than categorizing welfare regimes, we should consider them as particular welfare settlements.[67] Despite their limitations, typologies of welfare states still have a heuristic value. In this respect political scientist Rianne Mahon's mapping of the transition from maternalist policies designed to support the mother in the home to reconciliation policies to support mothers who are in paid labor assists our understanding of the history presented here. However, her triadic categorization of "neo-familialist, third way, and egalitarian" needs modification in the English context.[68] The ground has been cut from beneath the feet of the neofamilialists, who contend that mothers should have the choice to participate in the labor market or stay at home, by New Labor's highly interventionist policies that aim to get more women into the labor market.[69]

Political scientists Jonathan Hopkin and Daniel Wincott make the point that state policy configurations are typically "hybrids," containing specific social policies conforming to different "regime-types."[70] Thus, we might consider the space denoted by the "third way" as being made up of contradictory elements so that the totality is neither social democratic nor neoliberal even though neoliberal strands, such as the reliance on the market to provide much of the desired childcare, predominate in New Labor's policy repertoire. Though short of full privatization, Blair's childcare policies had much in common with Major's voucher idea and Thatcher's neoliberal approach in other areas of government in that they were focused on increasing citizens' employability. Thatcher's antistate, neoliberal policies made families or mothers alone responsible for childcare and measurably increased child poverty whereas Blair's hybrid neoliberal workfare policies sought to help women out of poverty by increasing their employability, something that could be done by nourishing and regulating the provision of flexible childcare/educare, especially in the private sector.[71]

Regarding reliance on the market, educational scientist Anne West explains that "there has been a very explicit policy drive to increase the range of providers from the private and voluntary sectors," a drive that has resulted in more four-year-olds attending academically oriented reception classes in primary schools and fewer enrolled in more play-focused state-funded nursery classes and nursery schools.[72] Private provision also enables better-off parents to combine paid work and family but disadvantages poorer ones. As social policy analysts Gillian Pascall and Jane Lewis have observed, "Relying on markets means that gender equality is likely to be a privilege (nearly) attained by better-off women" since more highly educated women who pay for childcare develop continuous careers while less highly educated women who return to low-paid part-time jobs after childbirth suffer a huge loss of income.[73]

The commodification of childcare through the introduction of the market has also had other effects, not least being the increasing cost of childcare. The Daycare Trust's 2007 survey of childcare costs noted considerable regional variation, with London and the southeast being the most expensive. Typical childcare costs are over a third of average earnings, while at the highest end of the scale, parents pay as much as £21,000 per year.[74]

Recognizing the hybrid nature of the emerging welfare regime, authors from the Institute for Public Policy Research, the New Labor-supporting think tank, coined the term the "Anglo-Social" model.[75] From Gordon Brown and his adviser, Ed Balls (later Secretary of State for Children, Schools and Families), came the label "progressive universalism," which Brown describes as a modernization of welfare that rejected old-style means testing and redistribution in favor of a regime "where all get help, but those in greatest need get the greatest support."[76] Balls explained that the cost of providing universal and high-quality care to all families free of charge was unrealistic, so tax credits would be targeted at the poorest families.[77]

In their attempts to specify the character of the emergent welfare settlement, some have had recourse to sociologist Anthony Giddens's notion of a social investment state.[78] Such a state is future oriented, and it is this that makes it necessary to invest in children. That current EU policy favors a social investment strategy has been noted by Esping-Andersen among others.[79] The formulation of social policy by the EU through the open method of coordination presents another layer of complexity that renders much of the debate about characterizing welfare states decidedly one-sided. Specifically, much of it suffers from "methodological nationalism" and, in the case of England, does not account sufficiently for Europeanization.[80] We have already implied a certain homology between New Labor's approach to childcare policy and that of the EU. Regarding women in paid labor, for example, the Barcelona European Council agreed in 2002 that "member States should remove disincentives … and strive, taking into account the demand for childcare facilities and in line with national patterns of provision, to provide childcare by 2010 to at least 90 percent of children between 3 years old and the mandatory school age and at least 33 percent of children under-3-years of age."[81] Speaking at a conference in 2004, economist Janneke Plantenga summed up the role of the EU in formulating childcare policies by saying that there is "no doubt the European Employment Strategy and the Open Method of Co-ordination have increased the political relevance of the childcare issue. The targets set and the process of peer review keep responsible ministers and civil servants alert and raises the awareness of policy makers."[82] There is much evidence that this has been the case recently in the United Kingdom.

Conclusion

Our account has highlighted an enormous lacuna at the heart of the post-war social democratic welfare settlement in England. In Marxist-feminist terms, the costs of the reproduction of labor power were to be borne by women in the family. Once the family was exposed to the cold winds of the market, deindustrialization, and the retreat of the state, the family, particularly the fractured single-parent and poor family, began to be seen as inadequate to the task. On this point, nascent EU social policy and New Labor were in the 1990s in agreement. Of course, as we have pointed out, childcare policy is not determined solely by economic requirements, even though in New Labor rhetoric it sometimes seemed to be. Capital's need for labor equipped with the right dispositions is always set against, and often contradict, the need for societies and polities to pursue social justice to preserve order. Collective and individual agents make choices that often disrupt functionalist analyses of needs and requirements, although collective agents have been noticeably absent, especially at the party-political level, in the formation of policies for childcare. However, the decisions of individuals that lead to changes in the family—such as divorce, single parenthood, and the division of labor within the home—have produced, when aggregated, considerable changes that have impacted the social, political, and economic requirements of the state and the emergent transnational formation that is the EU. In all of this, the requirements of children qua children as opposed to future citizens, workers, or family formers have rarely been considered.

New Labor's approach, a combination of its perceptions of the need of capital for women's paid labor in conditions of globalization and a strong belief in the ability of education to reduce social inequality, has, as we have shown, produced a significant expansion in the provision of childcare and early years education and the time allocated to it. The one flaw in this hybrid strategy is its reliance on private providers to implement much of it. In order to make a profit, private providers have to keep wage costs low in what is an inescapably labor-intensive service. Wages and conditions are already lower in the private sector, which tends to be more involved in care than the education-oriented public sector.[83] Moreover, market consolidation has occurred through acquisition and mergers in recent years.

Predictions of further consolidation may lead to a reduction in the flexibility of the time provision. Social differentiation is inevitable in childcare as it is in other sectors of education systems, but private provision raises the possibility of even sharper divisions in quality.[84] In this scenario, it is likely that neither the less well-off mothers nor their children will gain much benefit from the early years "policy revolution."

Notes

1. Beverley Hughes, *Building the Economic Case for Investments in Preschool* (New York, 2006). Retrieved 12 December 2006: http://www.ced.org/docs/trans_2006earlyedconf_hughes.pdf.
2. James Swift, *Kleinkindererziehung in England* (Würzburg, 1984), 89–104.
3. OECD, *Starting Strong II: Early Childhood Education and Care* (Paris, 2006), 415f.; OECD, *Babies and Bosses: Reconciling Work and Family Life,* vol. 4, *Canada, Finland, Sweden and the United Kingdom* (Paris, 2005), 113. For the development of education policy for British schools see the chapter by Sally Tomlinson in this volume.
4. Great Britain, Office for Standards in Education [OFSTED], *Annual Report of Her Majesty's Chief Inspector of Schools 2005/2006* (London, 2006), 14–16.
5. OECD, *Starting Strong II,* 415f.
6. Florence Jaumotte, "Labor Force Participation of Women: Empirical Evidence on the Role of Policy and Other Determinants in OECD Countries," *OECD Economic Studies,* no. 37 2003/2 (June 2004): 86. For more on Britain, see the chapter by Tomlinson in this volume.
7. Colin Creighton, "The Rise and Decline of the 'Male Breadwinner Family' in Britain," *Cambridge Journal of Economics* 23, no. 5 (1999): 519–41.
8. We shall focus on England as there has been significant divergence in early years policy since devolution granted powers to Wales, Scotland, and Northern Ireland in 1999.
9. Heather Joshi and P. R. Andrew Hinde, "Employment after Childbearing in Postwar Britain: Cohort Study Evidence on Contrasts within and across Generations," *European Sociological Review* 9 (1993): 204.
10. Great Britain, Ministry of Health and Ministry of Education, *Nursery Provision for Children Under Five. Circular 221/45* (London, 1945).
11. Willem Van Der Eyken, *The Preschool Years* (Harmondsworth, 1967), 1–144.
12. Nanette Whitbread, *The Evolution of the Nursery-Infant School: A History of Infant and Nursery Education in Britain, 1800–1970* (London, 1972), 104–30; Great Britain, Department for Children, Schools and Families (DfCSaF), "1a: Schools, Pupils and Teachers. Primary, Secondary and Nursery Schools: Time Series 1980 to 2000," *Statistical Bulletin: Statistics of Education, Schools in England 2000.* Retrieved 21 January 2007: http://www.dfes.gov.uk/rsgateway/DB/VOL/v000192/956-t1a.htm.
13. Catherine Hakim, *Key Issues in Women's Work: Female Heterogeneity and the Polarisation of Women's Employment, Conflict and Change in Britain—New Audit* (London, 1996), 61.
14. Denise Riley, *War in the Nursery: Theories of the Child and Mother* (London, 1983), 120f.
15. John Bowlby and Margery Fry, *Child Care and the Growth of Love* (London, 1953), 1–190.
16. Riley, *War in the Nursery,* 120–22.

17. Alasdair F. B. Roberts, "The Development of Professionalism in the Early Stages of Education," *British Journal of Educational Studies* 24, no. 3 (1976): 254–64.
18. Van Der Eyken, *The Preschool Years*, 81–90.
19. Jack Tizard, "The Objectives and Organisation of Educational and Day Care Services for Young Children," *Oxford Review of Education* 1, no. 3 (1975): 211–21.
20. Tessa Blackstone, "Some Aspects of the Structure and Extent of Nursery Education in Five European Countries," *Comparative Education* 7, no. 3 (1971): 91–105.
21. June Statham et al., *Playgroups in Three Countries: A Comparison of the Playgroup Movements in England, Ireland and the Netherlands*, Working and Occasional Paper No. 8, University of London (London, 1989), 14–15; Sue Mastel and Marjorie Dykins, "The Role of the Preschool Playgroups Association in England and Wales after Twenty-Five Years," *Early Child Development and Care* 27, no. 3 (1987): 393–417.
22. Statham et al., *Playgroups*, 10.
23. Marjorie E. Dykins, "Profile: The Preschool Playgroups Association—Playgroups in the Community," *Child: Care, Health and Development* 2, no. 3 (1976): 125–28.
24. Mastel and Dykins, "The Role."
25. England, Central Advisory Council for Education (Plowden Committee), *Children and Their Primary Schools*, 2 vols. (London, 1967), par. 330.
26. Margaret Thatcher, *Written Statement Launching Education White Paper: A 10-year Plan for Education* (6 December 1972). Retrieved 2 February 2007: http://www.margaretthatcher.org/speeches/displaydocument.asp?docid=102233; Great Britain, Department for Education and Skills (DfES), *Education: A Framework for Expansion* (London, 1972).
27. Heather E. Joshi and Hugh B. Davies, "Day Care in Europe and Mothers' Forgone Earnings," *International Labour Review* 131, no. 6 (1992): 561–79; Hugh B. Davies and Heather E. Joshi, "Gender and Income Inequality in the UK 1968–1990: Feminization of Earning or of Poverty?" *Journal of the Royal Statistical Society*, Series A, 61, no. 1 (1998): 33–61.
28. Plowden Committee, *Children*, par. 304; Tessa Blackstone, "Some Issues Concerning the Development of Nursery Education in Britain," *Paedagogica Europaea* 9, no. 1 (1974): 172–83.
29. Plowden Committee, *Children*, par. 299.
30. Xavier Bonal, "The Neoliberal Educational Agenda and the Legitimation Crisis: Old and New State Strategies," *British Journal of Sociology of Education* 24, no. 2 (2003): 159–75.
31. Jane Lewis et al., *Lone Motherhood in Twentieth-Century Britain: From Footnote to Front Page* (Oxford, 1998), 22.
32. Stuart Hall and Martin Jacques, *The Politics of Thatcherism* (London, 1983), 19–39.
33. "Renee Short Dies," *Daily Telegraph*, 19 January 2003.
34. Great Britain, Committee of Inquiry, Angela Rumbold, *Starting with Quality: The Report of the Committee of Inquiry* (London, 1990); Christopher Ball, *Start Right: The Importance of Early Learning* (London, 1994); Audit Commission for Local Authorities in England, Angela Rumbold, *Counting to Five: Education of Children Under Five* (London, 1996).
35. Jamie Peck, *Workfare States* (New York, 2001), 274ff.
36. Vicky Randall, *The Politics of Child Daycare in Britain* (Oxford, 2000), 93–95.
37. Naima Browne, "English Early Years Education: Some Sociological Dimensions," *British Journal of Sociology of Education* 17, no. 3 (1996): 365–79.
38. Anne West, "The Preschool Education Market in England from 1997: Quality, Availability, Affordability and Equity," *Oxford Review of Education* 32 (2006): 284.
39. Great Britain, Department for Education and Employment (DfEE) and School Curriculum and Assessment Authority, *Nursery Education: Desirable Outcomes for Children's Learning on Entering Compulsory Education* (London, 1996).

40. Great Britain, Treasury, *The Modernisation of Britain's Tax and Benefit System: Number One. Employment Opportunity in a Changing Labour Market* (London, 1997).
41. Gill Scott and Sue Innes, "Gender, Care, Poverty and Transitions," in *Families in Society: Boundaries and Relationships*, ed. Linda McKie et al. (Bristol, 2005), 42; Paul Gregg et al., "Poor Kids: Trends in Child Poverty in Britain, 1968–96," *Fiscal Studies* 20, no. 2 (1999): 163–87.
42. Bruce Bradbury and Markus Jäntti, *Child Poverty Across Industrialized Nations* (Florence, 1999), 18–22.
43. Great Britain, Treasury, *The Modernisation of Britain's Tax and Benefit System: Number Four. Tackling Poverty and Extending Opportunity* (London, 1999).
44. Conservative Party, *Conservative Party General Election Manifesto* (London, 1997).
45. Labour Party, *New Labour: New Life for Britain* (London, 1997).
46. Labour Party, *New Labour: Because Britain Deserves Better* (London, 1997).
47. *Hansard Parliamentary Debates, House of Commons*, vol. 176 (16 July 1990), col. 759.
48. Council of the European Communities, "Council Recommendation 92/241/EEC of 31 March 1992 on Childcare," *Official Journal of the European Communities*, L 123 (8 May 1992).
49. Inge Bleijenbergh et al., "Trading Well-Being for Economic Efficiency: The 1990 Shift in EU Childcare Policies," *Marriage and Family Review* 39, no. 3/4 (2006): 315–36.
50. Jane Lewis, *The Pursuit of Welfare Ends and Market Means and the Case of Work/Family Reconciliation Policies*. Retrieved 15 October 2006: http://www.cerium.ca/IMG/doc/JaneLewis.doc.
51. DfES and Department for Social Security (DfSS), *Meeting the Childcare Challenge: A Framework and Consultation Document* (London, 1998).
52. DfEE and DfSS, *Meeting the Childcare Challenge*.
53. DfES, *Every Child Matters. Summary* (London, 2003), 5.
54. Ibid., 5–6.
55. DfCSaF, *Press Notice: Government backs commitment for Sure Start Children's Centre in Every Community* (15 October 2007). Retrieved 25 October 2007: http://www.dfes.gov.uk/pns/DisplayPN.cgi?pn_id=2007_0190.
56. *Hansard Parliamentary Debates, House of Commons*, vol. 423 (12 July 2004), col. 1139.
57. Great Britain, Treasury, *Choice for Parents, the Best Start for Children: A Ten Year Strategy for Childcare* (London, 2004), 63.
58. DfCSaF, *The Children's Plan: Building Brighter Futures* (December 2007). Retrieved 19 December 2007: http://www.dfes.gov.uk/publications/childrensplan/downloads/The_Childrens_Plan.pdf.
59. Daycare Trust and National Centre for Social Research, *Childcare Nation? Progress on the Childcare Strategy and Priorities for the Future* (London, 2007).
60. Stephen J. Ball and Carol Vincent, "The 'Childcare Champion'? New Labour, Social Justice and the Childcare Market," *British Educational Research Journal* 31, no. 5 (2005): 557–70.
61. Margaret Hodge, "Speech to the Sure Start National Conference on 8 December 2004." Retrieved 6 February2007: http://www.dfes.gov.uk/speeches/media/documents/surestartfinal.doc.
62. Gøsta Esping-Andersen, *The Three Worlds of Welfare Capitalism* (Princeton, NJ, 1990), 26–28. For more, see the introduction by Karen Hagemann, Konrad H. Jarausch, and Cristina Allemann-Ghionda in this volume.
63. Bob Jessop, "Towards a Schumpeterian Workfare State? Preliminary Remarks on Post-Fordist Political Economy," *Studies in Political Economy* 40 (1993): 7–40.
64. Ibid.

65. Clare Bambra, "The Worlds of Welfare: Illusory and Gender Blind?" *Social Policy and Society* 3, no. 3 (2004): 201–12.
66. Sonya Michel, "Introduction: Perspectives on Childcare, East and West," *Social Politics* 13, no. 2 (2006): 145–50.
67. Daniel Wincott, "Paradoxes of New Labour Social Policy: Toward Universal Childcare in Europe's 'Most Liberal' Welfare Regime?" *Social Politics* 13, no. 2 (2006): 286–312.
68. Rianne Mahon, "The OECD and the Reconciliation Agenda: Competing Blueprints." (paper presented at the University of Oxford Conference "Challenges and Opportunities Faced by European Welfare States: The Changing Context for Child Welfare," Oxford, 7–8 January 2005), 3. Retrieved 13 January 2007: http://www.childcarecanada.org/pubs/op20/index.html.
69. Jill Kirby, Centre for Policy Studies, *The Nationalisation of Childhood* (London, 2006), 1–11.
70. Jonathan Hopkin and Daniel Wincott, "New Labour, Economic Reform and the European Social Model," *British Journal of Politics and International Relations* 8, no. 1 (2006): 52.
71. Mick Carpenter and Barbara Merrill, *Smoothing Out the Rough Edges of Welfare to Work? The Role of Community Based Organisations in Coventry* (Warwick, 2004). Retrieved 14 September 2007: http://www.britsoc.co.uk/user_doc/Carpenter.pdf.
72. West, "The Preschool Education," 293.
73. Gillian Pascall and Jane Lewis, "Emerging Gender Regimes and Policies for Gender Equality in a Wider Europe," *Journal of Social Policy* 33, no. 3 (2004): 384.
74. Daycare Trust, "News Release: 27 Percent Increase in Childcare Costs in Five Years" (8 February 2006). Retrieved 1 February 2007: http:///www.daycaretrust.org.uk/mod/fileman/files/Childcare_Costs_Survey_2006.pdf.
75. Nick Pearce and Mike Dixon, "New Model Welfare," *Prospect* 110 (May 2005).
76. Great Britain, Treasury, "Speech by the Chancellor of the Exchequer, Gordon Brown MP, at the launch of the new tax credits advertising campaign" (16 September 2002). Retrieved 21 January 2007: http://www.hm-treasury.gov.uk/speech_chex_160902.htm.
77. Ed Balls, "The Second Daycare Trust Annual Lecture" (12 January 2005), 9. Retrieved 7 February 2007: http://www.edballs.com/assets/files/f/fullspeechinprintablepdfformat_187.pdf.
78. Anthony Giddens, *The Third Way: The Renewal of Social Democracy* (Cambridge, UK, 1998).
79. Jane Lewis and Susanna Giullari, "The Adult Worker Model Family, Gender Equality and Care: The Search for New Policy Principles and the Possibilities and Problems of a Capabilities Approach," *Economy and Society* 34, no. 1 (2005): 76–104.
80. Ulrich Beck, *What is Globalization?* (Cambridge, UK, 2000), 20ff.
81. "Barcelona European Council: Summary of Presidency Conclusions," *Infobase Europe Factsheet*, 2002. Retrieved 4 February 2007: http://www.ibeurope.com/Fact/34barcelona.htm.
82. Ibid.; Janneke Plantenga, "Investing in Childcare: The Barcelona Childcare Targets and the European Social Model," in *Childcare in a Changing World*, ed. Janneke Plantenga and Melissa Siegel (Groningen, 2004), 8.
83. Claire Cameron, *Building an Integrated Workforce for a Long-term Vision of Universal Early Education and Care* (London, 2004), 9.
84. Helen Penn, "Childcare Market Management: How the United Kingdom Government Has Reshaped Its Role in Developing Early Childhood Education and Care," *Contemporary Issues in Early Childhood* 8, no. 3 (2007): 192–207.

Chapter 12

GENDER, CLASS, AND SCHOOLING

Education Policy, School Time, and the Labor Market in Post-1945 Britain

Sally Tomlinson

In March 2007, the last report of the English Equal Opportunities Commission, before it was merged with a new Commission for Equality and Human Rights, concluded that women with young children suffered more discrimination at work than any other group. This came as little surprise for most working mothers, who are accustomed to searching for a part-time job that can accommodate their children's needs or being shunted onto what is now known as the "mummy track" in business or the professions. The Organisation for Economic Co-operation and Development reported in 2005 that 70 percent of all British women aged fifteen to sixty-four participated in the labor market while 40 percent worked part-time. In 1980, the percentage was 62 and the rate of part-time work 41 percent. The largest increase occurred in the 1990s. Today, the female employment rate in Britain is nearly 10 percent above the EU and OECD average. However, the labor force participation rate of mothers with three- to six-year-old children is 60 percent, of whom 60 percent work part-time. Only 49 percent of all mothers with children under three are employed, of whom 62 percent work part-time. Compared to Sweden, which has one of the highest female employment rates in the EU (73 percent), the percentage of employed mothers with young children in Britain remains low. In Sweden this percentage is 81 percent for mothers with three- to six-year-old children and 72 percent for mother with children under three.[1]

The most common family form in Britain today is the "one-and-a-half earner family."[2] One reason for this is the childcare policy. Compared to most other European countries, the percentage of three- to five-year-old

Notes for this chapter begin on page 271.

children in childcare facilities was very high at 96 percent (three- to four-year-olds) and 100 percent (four- to five-year-olds). The majority of the children in this age group, however, only spend part of the day in child-care because until 2007 the state only paid for a maximum of 12.5 hours per week. Today, the government covers the cost of 15 hours of weekly childcare. Compared to their counterparts in other EU countries, British parents thus have relatively high expenses for childcare if they want or need full-time care. Mothers with school children, moreover, find it very difficult to work full-time. And although Britain has a comprehensive all-day school system that starts with all five-year-old children, schools are usually only open until 3:30 or 4:00 P.M., and after-school programs are rare. The missing formal "out-of-school-time provision" therefore remains a major problem for working mothers with school children, although recent government policy is to encourage "extended" schools, opening from 8 A.M. to 6 P.M., to help working parents.[3]

Compared to other countries with a half-day school system like Austria and Germany, however, the situation for working mothers with children in school is much better in Britain. The older their children, the more likely it is for mothers to be employed. The OECD reported in 2005 that the percentage of employed mothers with children between the ages of six and sixteen stood at 74 percent, higher than the average female employment rate. Fifty-five percent of these mothers, however, worked part-time.[4] More British women seem to feel that they can combine family and employment. One indicator is that compared to most Eastern and Central European as well as Mediterranean countries, the birth rate in Britain has not experienced as steep a decline since the 1980s, even if it did drop from 1.81 in 1990 to 1.60 in 2005.[5]

Nevertheless, it is important to question why women, and in particular mothers, still do not have the same opportunities on the labor market, especially considering the fact that since the 1970s there has been an increase in girls' educational achievements, the labor force has been restructured in ways that bring some benefits to women, and government has pursued policies to encourage mothers to work. This chapter argues that one major reason for these changes was the British childcare and education policy, which was largely driven by economic motives. As a result of the radical restructuring of the post-1945 welfare state into a "postwelfare state" all individuals, male and female alike, were to be drawn into the world of work. By the 1980s, the British welfare state had become a "workfare state," in which social benefits were to be progressively removed for those reluctant to work and individuals were to be regarded as "human capital" that should be prepared, encouraged, and, if necessary, even compelled to work.[6] Nevertheless, the state did not provide until the late 1990s adequate daycare and out-of-school care for mothers, who are still primarily responsible for childcare.

The aim of this chapter is to provide an overview of the changing policy of school education in Great Britain from 1945 to 2007 and illustrate its links to changes in the labor market and the employment of women. One important aspect here is the time policy that regulates the complex dimension of daily, weekly, and annual time in schooling and childcare. The chapter refers mainly to the education system in England, as the systems in Scotland, Wales, and Northern Ireland are controlled by regional governments and thus exhibit a different development.

I structure the following analysis in three time periods, which reflect the development of the British education policy: First is the period of welfare state reconstruction between 1944 and 1979, which was mainly formed by the Labor Party. In this period the normative model of the "male-breadwinner/female-homemaker" family dominated welfare and education policy.[7] It was not until the 1970s that this changed. A resurgent women's movement, improved educational achievements of girls, and changes in family and occupational structures all led to improved employment opportunities for women and changed thinking about gender roles in the family. Second is the Conservative Thatcher era in welfare and education policy between 1979 and 1997. This period saw a restructuring of the economy away from manufacturing to the service sector, which demanded more part-time, flexible workers willing to work for lower pay. While women largely filled this new role, little attention was still paid to childcare and out-of school care.[8] Third is the period of New Labor, led by Tony Blair, between 1997 and 2007, which was characterized by a transformation of the childcare and education system as well as female work. The Labor government recognized that the realities of women's employment had generated a need for a "National Child Care Strategy," i.e., a dramatic extension of childcare services. The main slogan of this new Labor policy was "Every Child Matters."[9] Much of the political interest in children, childcare, and education by New Labor, however, can be linked to its economic agenda, both in terms of getting women into the workforce and commercializing childcare and education for a profit.[10]

School Education, Labor Market, and Welfare State Reconstruction, 1944–1979

By the early twentieth century, all-day primary schools for the working classes had been established for children between the ages of five and twelve, with some senior primary schooling going up to fourteen. Old and newer grammar schools catered to the middle and lower-middle classes while "public" fee-paying schools, where students boarded or stayed for a long school day, were primarily the preserve of the upper classes. The system was openly intended to educate children from different social classes and genders for their different roles in life, with working-class girls being prepared for domestic service or factory work and middle-class girls for "white-collar" work and marriage. In 1939, 88 percent of young people left school by the age of fourteen. Only 10 percent achieved public examination passes, while a scant 5 percent went into higher education.[11]

From the early twentieth century on, state-maintained schools had been involved in offering some social care in addition to traditional teaching. After 1907, a school medical service developed, and the Education Act of 1944 required all Local Education Authorities (LEAs) to provide "milk, meals and other refreshments" during the day. School dinners, cooked and served by women who became known as "dinner ladies," became a feature of both primary and secondary schools. In addition, welfare services were expanded in schools, with free school meals and school transport as well as clothing grants being introduced.[12]

The Education Act of 1944 was the first major step in the reform of the British school system and had a lasting impact in the postwar period. This act, named after Conservative politician Richard Austen Butler, enforced the division between primary (five- to eleven-year-olds) and secondary (eleven- to fifteen-year-olds) education and made secondary education free for all students, including all children from the working class. It also proposed raising compulsory school to the age of sixteen, a measure that was not realized until 1972. In addition, this reform introduced a tripartite system of secondary education based on grammar schools, secondary technical schools, and secondary "modern" schools. While the Butler Act also allowed for the creation of comprehensive schools, which would combine the functions of these three schools, only a few were initially founded.[13]

The 1944 Education Act was part of a whole package of welfare reforms that were introduced during World War II as recognition of the broad war support by the population, in particular the working class. The new Labor government under Prime Minister Clement Attlee, elected in 1945, established the framework of the modern British welfare state, which created a national health and education system and augmented all public services.[14] During the war, the increasing demand for female labor in the expanding war industries had led to the expansion of childcare facilities, but most of them were withdrawn after 1945 as women had to surrender their jobs to the demobilized men with whom the ideology of the male-breadwinner family returned. The aim was to "rebuild families" and thereby "restabilize" postwar society. As part of this policy, the number of daycare places was cut dramatically, in particular after a Conservative government took over in 1951. The number of places fell from 62,000 in the 1940s to 22,000 in the 1960s.[15] Despite this conservative policy, however, the percentage of married women who worked rose sharply in the 1950s, from 26 percent in 1951 to 35 percent in 1961.[16] The increase in the employment of married women outside the home was even sharper in the 1960s and 1970s, and the percentage reached 62 percent in 1981. (See Table 12.1.)

Most of the married women who joined the labor market chose part-time work. The percentage of women employed part-time rose from 12 percent in 1951 to 42 percent in 1981. As in other European countries, primarily mothers worked part-time. A 1980 study revealed that the age of the youngest child in a family was a better predictor of women's economic activity than the number of dependent children. Because of the lack of childcare facilities for small children, their mothers more often stayed at home or worked part-time than any other group.[18] Each preschool child lowered women's participation rate in the early 1980s by 35 percent, each primary school child by 14 percent, and each secondary school child by 7 percent. One reason was that only 19 percent of British preschoolers had a place in a daycare center. Relatives provided the care of most children of working mothers.[19]

Despite the many social changes that occurred in the postwar era, well into the 1960s it was assumed in all social classes and political parties that men were the "breadwinners" and women's jobs were of secondary importance. This changed very slowly. In a 1980 survey, 60 percent of women felt that mothers with preschool children should stay at home while only 11 percent felt that mothers with school children should do this. For them it was easier to work, at least part-time, because of the all-day time schedule of British schools, which finished usually by 3:30 or 4:00 P.M. Full-time

TABLE 12.1: Women in the labor force, Great Britain, 1951–2000[17]

Women in labor force	1951	1961	1971	1981	1990	2000
Percentage of women of the total labor force [(a)]	31%	33%	37%	40%	—	—
Percentage of women aged 20–64	36%	42%	52%	61%	68% [(a)]	69% [(a)]
Percentage of women employed part-time [(b)] (of total labor force)	12%	26%	35%	42%	40%	41%
Percentage of married women in labor force (of all married women aged 15–59)	26%	35%	49%	62%	—	—

Notes:
(a) Women aged 15–64.
(b) Under 30 hours.

work, however, was still difficult for mothers of school children, because out-of-school-care was lacking.[20]

Until the early 1960s, the British school system also remained highly segregated according to social class. Selective examinations administered at the age of eleven sent predominantly middle-class children to grammar schools while children from working-class backgrounds attended so-called modern schools. Technical education remained underdeveloped. As it was, the postwar need for economic reconstruction resulted in a policy that sent working-class children into jobs by the age of fifteen. The Ministry of Education, controlled by Labor, justified this policy in a programmatic paper in 1945 with the argument that their employment did not require any measure of technical skill or knowledge.[21]

A period of educational reform started in Britain, as in many other European countries, in the 1960s. Now politicians of all parties recognized the economic need for expanded education for more young people, especially in science and technology, and a broad comprehensive school movement developed that aimed for equal access to education. The Labor Party won the elections in 1964 under Prime Minister Harold Wilson and shaped education policy until 1970. One year after Labor came to power, a circular of the Department of Education and Science asked all Local Education Authorities to abandon selection at eleven years and educate all children in comprehensive schools. Around two-thirds of the LEAs did this, but thirty-six districts retained full or partial selection into the 2000s. Higher education expanded with the creation of more universities after 1963, and teaching, the major career choice for middle-class girls, became a degree-level profession.[22]

In the 1970s, global economic pressures put the education system under stress as a rise in oil prices affected industry and the prospects of employment for all young people. From 1970 to 1974, when the Conservatives governed Britain, they introduced low-level vocational courses to reduce unemployment and set back the development of comprehensive education. This policy followed their belief in selection by "ability." The social democratic consensus of the education reform era of the 1960s that government should regulate resources to achieve social justice and more equal opportunities was breaking down, and welfare costs were increasingly regarded in the public as too expensive.[23]

During this same period, however, the women's movement drew attention to inequalities in education, employment opportunities and pay and pushed the government into action. As a result, in 1970 the Conservative government passed an Equal Pay Act. In 1975, the new Labor government that had come to power again the year before passed a Sex Discrimination Act, which set up an Equal Opportunities Commission to report on gender issues. Over the years, this commission regularly reported on the growth in women's employment and the various kinds of discrimination in pay, conditions, and employment they were subject to. Over ten million women, 36 percent of whom were mothers with dependent children, were engaged in full or part-time work in 1976. An increasing percentage of these working women came from migrant communities. In particular, African-Caribbean women joined the workforce, who always have been more likely to work than women form other migrant groups. Women of Indian origin, but above all Muslim women of Pakistani origin, were the least likely to work outside the home.[24]

By the end of the 1970s, politicians of all parties were criticizing schools for failing to prepare the workforce adequately, although this had more to do with changes brought by the difficult transition from an industrial to a postindustrial economy than what went on in schools. An education system that was regarded as adequate for an industrialized society with many unskilled jobs was now perceived as obsolete. Employers and business managers also criticized schools and demanded that education become more closely linked to industrial regeneration and the need to prepare for an economy under a new neoliberal regime of managerialism.[25]

Thatcherism in Education Policy, 1979–1997

The 1980s were a decade of contradictions. Although Margaret Thatcher became the first female prime minister in Britain in 1979, her Conservative government, which consequently pursued a neoliberal policy, was critical of feminist egalitarianism and ongoing changes in the family (declining birth rates, smaller families, single parenting, more divorces, etc.). Nevertheless, these changes continued, and more and more women joined the workforce. The shift from manufacturing and heavy industries to the service sector as the well as the emergence of a "knowledge economy" gave women more employment opportunities than ever before, but those opportunities were often in part-time, low-paying jobs. Working-class men also lost jobs and status, but not to the same extent. When the latter were employed, they usually had full-time jobs and higher salaries.

The Conservative government was dedicated to a free economy, deregulated markets, and choice, and thus fostered competition between schools. But while the Conservative rhetoric stressed "parental choice" of schools, in reality parents could only express a preference, and the central government continued to control the curriculum as well as assessment and teacher training. In addition, the 1980s witnessed private and business interests increasingly becoming involved in education as well as greater levels of accountability from all institutions. Over the course of seventeen years, the Conservatives passed some twenty Education Acts concerning school structures and governance, funding, resources, curriculum, pedagogy, modes of inspection, teacher professionalism and training, further and higher education, and vocational education.[26] Strategies to ration educational opportunities, "help the middle classes" escape from lower-performing, comprehensive schools, and provide vocational courses for working-class children emerged. After a long pay dispute in the mid-1980s with the teacher unions, which were dominated by women, the secretary of state for education specified the number of hours teachers should work, after which many withdrew their supervision of dinner-hour and after-school activities.[27]

But despite much right-wing opposition, comprehensive education continued to develop during the 1980s, and by 1989 some 85 percent of students were in comprehensive schools without having taken selective tests at age eleven. After 1986, all students were able to enter for a common public examination, the General Certificate of Secondary Education (GCSE), at sixteen with an Advanced Level at eighteen. As a result, educational standards as measured by public examinations began to rise, particularly for girls. From the outset, the comprehensive movement had assumed gender equality as a goal, and during the 1980s teacher attention became more focused on educating girls for a wider range of employment opportunities. Research to this point had demonstrated that girls were directed towards the humanities, languages, and domestic sciences, rather than math, technical areas, and the physical sciences. But with the introduction of the GCSE, more girls were encouraged to study these subjects. With the exception of the physical sciences, girls gradually came to outperform boys in the GCSE examinations.[28]

And yet once they entered the labor market, girls were still directed into the "caring" professions, service positions, or office work. Only a very few made it into the higher professional or managerial levels. In 1984, only 5 percent of all university professors were women, and only 3 percent of these had children. Nevertheless, sociologist Madeline Arnot has identified two positive aspects of the Thatcher era for women: the promotion of individualism and the growing need for flexible, better-qualified workers in a restructured economy. Although the ideologies of marketization and managerialism that emerged during the later 1980s were distinctly male oriented, Arnot concluded, "Cultural, demographic (lower birth rates) and labor market changes have influenced the way teachers think about the schooling of girls. Few now consider girls' education to be less important than boys."[29] Of course, there continued to be differences in the educational opportunities offered to girls from different social classes and ethnic groups.[30]

The introduction of comprehensive all-day schools made some employment possible for mothers with dependent children. Nevertheless, after-school care facilities remained inadequate during the 1980s, as did childcare for mothers with preschool-aged children.[31] In addition, while mothers were being encouraged in the Thatcher era to enter the labor force, the ideology of "good parenting" (which usually meant "mothering") was still strong. The Conservatives and the media used this ideology and increasingly blamed families for their children's poor behavior, delinquency, and wider social problems. Women in all social classes were affected by the dual message for them to "go to work" but at the same time provide "good parenting."[32]

The implementation of the 1988 Education Reform Act created even more problems for parents. This Reform Act introduced far-reaching changes in the English, Welsh, and Northern Irish Education System.[33] The four main provisions were: First, the introduction of Grant-Maintained (GM) Schools. Primary and secondary schools could remove themselves fully from their respective Local Education Authorities and would be completely funded by the central government. This reform was slow to take off, and GM schools were abolished in 1997 by the new Labor government, although the move was reinstated in 1998 in other forms. Second, local management of schools was introduced. The act allowed all schools to be taken out of the direct financial control of LEAs. Financial control would be handed to the principals and governors of a school. Third, a National Curriculum was introduced, which defined so-called key stages for schools. At each key stage, a number of educational objectives were to be achieved. "League tables," which would publish the examination results of schools, were created by the media by 1992. And fourth, an element of choice was introduced, where parents could specify which school they preferred.[34]

This newly introduced "choice" policy increased social disparities in school education. Rather than have them attend local schools, parents were now encouraged to "choose" their children's schools at the primary and secondary level. As educationalist Diane Reay has shown, mothers were more engaged in choosing schools and initiating contact with teachers than their male partners.[35] It also became more necessary for them to drive children to schools outside their locality. This proved to be above all a class issue. Middle-class mothers were quick to "play the education market game." Working-class mothers, however, had less time, resources, or knowledge to seek out the "best" schools. They were less likely to have access to a car and more likely to be working shifts or hours that prevented them from driving their children to school. They also lacked the time to contribute to their children's school or after-school activities.[36]

Now funding, more than before, tended to follow students, and schools competed for the "best" ones. Students were tested at "key stages" of seven, eleven, fourteen, and sixteen years of age. Schools that took in children from the working classes or ethnic minorities as well as students with special educational needs were more likely to be designated as "failing" and in need of special measures by the newly privatized inspectorate (Office for Standards in Education). The publication of the examination results in league tables encouraged competition, and choice quickly led to more middle-class and white flight from disadvantaged urban schools with high numbers of minority students. Social class and ethnic divisions in schooling thus became increasingly apparent even in primary schools.[37]

After-school care for the children of working mothers remained a problem too. A number of voluntary organizations encouraged schools to set up after-school activities and eventually some received government funding. As the founder of one organization, Education Extra, noted in 1996

> The issues raised by after-school provision are large and complex. They include childcare as well as education ... the relationship between schools, families and communities ... [and] the nature and future of learning and employment in a post-industrial society. ... After-school provision also has something to say about the way work is organized and how family life and working patterns are organized.[38]

Childcare and nursery provision for what was now termed the "early years" was beginning to be recognized as a serious issue. To address this problem, Conservatives introduced a short-lived voucher scheme whereby parents could "spend" their voucher in state or private nurseries. This scheme, however, was abolished in 1997 by the New Labor government, which introduced a new agenda called *Meeting the Childcare Challenge*.[39]

New Labor, the Transformation of Education, and Female Work, 1997–2007

The New Labor government under Tony Blair declared that raising standards in education would be a priority, and with the exception of 2003, one or more Education Acts were passed each year through 2007. However, the new government accepted many of the basic assumptions of conservative policy, such as "choice" of school, competition between schools, and more privatization.[40] Likewise, education continued to develop as a market commodity that was supposedly driven by consumer demand, while parents competed with each other to send their children to the "best" primary and secondary schools as measured by test results in the league tables and inspectors' reports.

The development of a "diversity of schools" also continued, with a White Paper in 2001 welcoming more "faith schools."[41] Religious primary and secondary schools affiliated with the Anglican, Roman Catholic, Methodist, and other Christian Churches all had received state funding in England since 1833. The paper demanded that this now needed to be extended to other faiths as well. By 2006, Jewish schools and a small number of Muslim, Seventh Day Adventist, Hindu, Sikh, and Greek Orthodox schools had also received state funding. Around 24 percent of the entire school population was being educated in these voluntary faith schools. Above all, middle-class white parents were seeking places at Christian schools to avoid sending their children to schools with minority children.[42]

From 2002, Blair and his closest advisors began encouraging a new kind of school called "Academies." These were to be semiprivatized, "independent" schools set up as limited companies that would be sponsored by business, religious, or other voluntary groups, but would still be funded primarily by taxpayers. By 2006, forty-four of these schools had opened with sponsors including bankers, shipping owners, football clubs, sports agencies, and religious groups. Sponsors could appoint governing bodies and control the admission of students, the hiring of staff, and the curriculum. Although some Local Education Authorities were pleased to be rid of poor schools, and parents were attracted by the idea of a completely new school, the Academy program, with four hundred eventually planned, constituted nothing less than a direct effort to hand over state schools to private interests.[43]

In the summer of 2004, all major government departments were required to produce a Five Year Strategic Plan, and the Department for Education and Skills responded by presenting their five-year plan for children and learners.[44] This plan claimed that the five principles underlying education would be greater personalization and choice in education, services opened up to new and different providers, more freedom and independence for head teachers and managers, a commitment to staff development at all levels, and partnerships with parents, Local Education Authorities, employers, and voluntary organizations. The strategy covered all areas of education from early years to further and higher education. It included plans for Children's Centers, which were to be located on or off school grounds, an extended school day running from 8 A.M. to 6 P.M., and employed such terms as "educare" and "wrap around childcare," both of which were to take place on school grounds. This strategy was clearly intended to help working mothers.[45]

Three more education acts followed, with the 2006 act declaring that LEAs were to become "champions of children" while further reducing the powers of the authorities. Successful schools were to be allowed to expand

and federate with neighboring schools, even if they remained in competition for students with them. "Choice" of school continued to be notional for many parents as schools were largely able to choose their students. Moreover, schools could remove themselves completely from the control of LEAs and become self-governing charitable trusts backed by business, charity and faith groups, or parents. While a few small groups of middle-class parents, usually with a religious orientation, had sought government backing to open their own schools, the notion that parents would have the time or knowledge to open a new school while being encouraged to work was unrealistic.[46]

In contrast to the production of contradictory policies that increased competition between schools while at the same time urging cooperation and partnership, New Labor's policies for children and childcare were less competitive. The creation of a Sure Start program from 1999, designed to bring together services for disadvantaged children aged zero to three, was eventually regarded as highly successful and did not require competitive bidding from local authorities. Maternity leave with pay after childbirth was extended, and paternity leave eventually passed as well, although few men took up the option. Children were to be "lifted out of poverty" by tax credits and working family credits for low-paid workers. While recognizing that women with children could not work unless childcare facilities were expanded, there was also a declared intention to improve services for families with young children and coordinate services more effectively. A National Childcare Strategy was announced in 1998, which promised free nursery education for all four-year-olds, then three-year-olds, as well as Early Excellence Centers that would provide models for integrating childcare with early education. Local Education Authorities were directed to set up Early Years and Childcare Partnerships between service providers, and a 2002 Education Act established an Early Years Foundation Stage of the national curriculum.[47]

In 2003, a green paper entitled *Every Child Matters* set out a new framework for services for children and young people under the age of twenty.[48] This was followed by the Children Act in 2004, which established a Minister for Children, Young People and Families, with a director of Children's Services in each Local Education Authority to combine responsibility for education, social, and children's services, including responsibility for Children's Centers and Extended Schools. But there was still much confusion between the duties of LEAs, schools, childcare services, and other social and health services, especially since many schools were now removed from local authority control. Undeterred, the Department for Education and Skills continued to provide guidance on what Extended Schools and Children's Centers were expected to offer.[49] A 2005 paper entitled *Extended*

Schools: Access to Opportunities and Services for All asserted that by 2010 all schools should offer extended services, including homework clubs, sports, music tuition, arts and crafts, visits to museums, business and enterprise activities, parenting support and family learning, and referral to specialist services as well as access to information, communication technology, and adult learning opportunities.[50] Teachers greeted much of this reform rhetoric with skepticism, as they felt they were now suffering from a surfeit of innovation. However, the clearest attempt to date made by the New Labor government to oversee coordination of all children's services came in July 2007 when, under the new prime minister, Gordon Brown, the Department for Education and Skills was split into two departments—a Department for Schools, Children and Families and a Department for Universities, Innovation and Skills. All LEAs were then required to produce yet another Children's Plan.[51]

Alongside childcare and extended schools, the new government pursued policies aimed specifically at encouraging women, especially single parents, to work. By the early 2000s, 78 percent of women in the main working ages were "economically active" in the labor market. However, the Office for National Statistics noted that "the presence of a dependent child in the family still has a major effect on the economic activity of women. [Only] 65 percent of women whose youngest child was under five were economically active. ... Among women with preschool children, 36 percent were working part-time."[52] Single mothers were less likely to be employed than other mothers, although they returned to work sooner after the birth of children than partnered mothers. Single mothers needed to earn an income, but had in general more problems reconciling their family obligations with their paid work. At the same time, hostility to those who did not provide good parenting continued. Especially single mothers bore the brunt of the stigma for failing to provide "good parenting."[53]

Under New Labor, political efforts to link parenting issues with what had come to be known as the work-life balance gained weight. Both the government and the markets recognized that women, especially in an economy that demands longer and unregulated working hours, can spend less time in the home engaging in childcare. Much of the expanded state intervention has been an attempt to mediate between work and family life. Thus, from the early 2000s, parents with children under six could request flexible working hours—a request dependent, of course, on the goodwill of the employer. From November 2007, this right was extended to parents with a child under seventeen.[54]

For all of the rhetoric that a "knowledge economy" dominates the world of work, the reality is that despite significant changes as manufacturing industries disappeared and finance and business dominated, "the new economy still leaves the vast majority of us doing jobs that have been around for years."[55] This is particularly true for women. The glass ceilings women meet in their work are pay and status, with the jobs they take being still predominantly lower paid and of lower status. Despite equal pay legislation, full-time and part-time male and female employees are still paid differentially. A Commission on Women and Work set up by the Labor government in 2004 reported that the gender pay gap in 2006 was 18 percent for full-time workers and 38 percent for part-time workers. Part-time work is not an effective strategy for an equal integration of women in the labor market. The major reason why so many British women still do part-time work are their family obligations: for mothers with school children, the extension of the public "out-of-school time provisions," which the Labor government initiated, is still insufficient. The number of places increased from 137,000 in 1997 to 490,000 in 2004, but that was not enough. The *Five Year Strategy* from 2004 set 2010 as a target for making an affordable "out-of-school" childcare place, linked to schools, for all children aged three to fourteen, but by 2010 it was clear that this had not been achieved.[56]

Conclusion

This chapter has described some of the changes in the school systems in Britain over the past fifty years to 2007, linking these with gender issues and the labor market. While the "all-day" time structure of schooling always allowed women some possibility of working, it was not until the 1970s that ideologies that defined women's place as "in the home" lost their dominant influence. Encouragement of women to enter the labor force was bound up with human capital theories that all individuals should contribute to making the national economy competitive in a globally competitive world. However, the increase in women's employment at all levels outside the home, now encouraged by all political parties in Britain, has gone some way towards achieving wider European Union aims of providing more equal social and economic opportunities for women. But in Britain, women do not yet have an equal position in the labor market with real choices, equal pay, status, and promotion prospects. The major issue is still the maternity ward. Children and childcare continue to affect the careers of women in ways that do not apply to men. Women now engage in productive labor, take a major share in the reproduction of family life and a future workforce, and contribute spending power, all of which may be good for globalizing capitalist economies, but perhaps not so good for women.

Notes

1. OECD, *Starting Strong II: Early Childhood Education and Care* (Paris, 2006), 415; OECD, *Babies and Bosses: Reconciling Work and Family Life*, vol. 4, *Canada, Finland, Sweden and the United Kingdom* (Paris, 2005), 59, 70.
2. OECD, *Babies and Bosses*, 74.
3. OECD, *Starting Strong II*, 415–18.
4. OECD, *Babies and Bosses*, 70.
5. Globalis, *United Kingdom*. Retrieved 16 October 2008: http://globalis.gvu.unu.edu/indicator_detail.cfm?IndicatorID=138&Country=GB.
6. Anthony Giddens, *The Third Way: The Renewal of Social Democracy* (Cambridge, UK, 1998), 99.
7. Sheila Rowbotham, *A Century of Women: The History of Women in Britain and the United States in the Twentieth Century* (London, 1999), 398–433.
8. For an overview of the British development of the welfare state with a gender perspective, see Mary Daly, *The Gender Division of Welfare: The Impact of the British and German Welfare State* (Cambridge, UK, 2000); for a comparative perspective, see Mary Daly and Katherine Rake, *Gender and the Welfare State: Care, Work and Welfare in Europe and the USA* (Oxford, 2003).
9. Department for Education and Skills (DfES), *Every Child Matters*, Report No. CM 5680 (London, 2003).
10. Barbara Pocock, *The Work/Life Collision* (Annandale, Australia, 2003).
11. See also Brian Simon, *Education and the Social Order 1940–1990* (London, 1991); Sally Tomlinson, *Education in a Post-Welfare Society* (Berkshire, 2005).
12. See Bernard Harris, *The Health of the Schoolchild: A History of the School Medical Service in England and Wales* (Buckingham, 1995), 26–175.
13. Simon, *Education*, 26–28.
14. June Purvis, ed., *Women's History: Britain, 1860–1945* (London, 2000), 324f.
15. Jane Lewis, *Women in Britain since 1945* (Cambridge, UK, 1992), 75.
16. Ibid., 65, 73.
17. Ibid., 65; OECD, *Babies and Bosses*, 59.
18. Lewis, *Women*, 74.
19. Ibid.
20. Ibid., 76.
21. Ministry of Education, *The Nation's Schools* (London, 1945), 13.
22. For more, see Gerald Grace, *Teachers, Ideology and Control: A Study in Urban Education* (London, 1978).
23. Tomlinson, *Education*, 13–27.
24. Sally Tomlinson, *Race and Education in Britain: Policy and Politics* (Berkshire, 2008), 48.
25. For more, see Sally Power et al., *Education and the Middle Classes* (London, 2003).
26. Tomlinson, *Education*, 30.
27. Ibid., 41.
28. Madeleine Arnot et al., *Closing the Gender Gap: Post War Education and Social Change* (Cambridge, UK, 1999), 12–31 and 125–48; see also, Robert W. Connell, "Cool Guys, Swots and Wimps: The Inter-play of Masculinity and Schooling," *Oxford Review of Education* 15, no. 3 (1989): 291–303.
29. Madeleine Arnot et al., *Educational Reform and Gender Equality in Schools* (Manchester, 1996), 162.
30. Sally Tomlinson, *Education 14–19: Critical Perspectives* (London, 1997).

31. See the chapter by Kevin J. Brehony and Kristen D. Nawrotzki on childcare and early years education in Britain in this volume.
32. Carol Vincent, *Parents and Teachers: Power and Participation* (London, 1996).
33. Scottish education legislation is separate from that of the rest of the UK.
34. Office of Public Sector Information, Education Reform Act, 1988, c. 40. Retrieved 17 October 2008: http://www.opsi.gov.uk/acts/acts1988/ukpga_19880040_en_1#Legislation-Preamble; Michael Flude and Merril Hammer, *The Education Reform Act, 1988: Its Origins and Implications* (London, 1990).
35. Diane Reay, *Class Work: Mothers' Involvement with Their Children's Primary Schooling* (London, 1998), 35–46.
36. Ibid., 136–37.
37. Ibid.
38. Kay Andrews et al., *Good Policy and Practice for After School Hours* (London, 1996), xii.
39. DfEE, *Meeting the Childcare Challenge* (London, 1998). See also the chapter by Brehony and Nawrotzki in this volume.
40. See Stephen J. Ball, *Education plc: Understanding Private Sector Participation in Public Sector Education* (London, 2007).
41. DfES, *White Paper—Schools: Achieving Success* (London, September 2001).
42. See Jo Cairns et al., eds., *Faith Schools: Consensus or Conflict?* (London, 2005), 7–13 and 49–145.
43. Francis Beckett, *The Great City Academy Fraud* (London, 2007).
44. DfES, *Five Year Strategy for Children and Learners* (London, 2004).
45. See Carol Vincent and Stephen J. Ball, *Childcare, Choice and Class Practices* (London, 2006).
46. See Ball, *Education plc*.
47. For more, see the chapter by Brehony and Nawrotzki in this volume.
48. DfES, *Every Child Matters*.
49. DfES, *Extended Schools: Access to Opportunities and Services for All—A Prospectus* (London, 2005).
50. Ibid.
51. Department for Children, Schools and Families, *The Children's Plan: Building for Brighter Futures* (London 2007).
52. Office for National Statistics, *Social Trends No. 30* (London, 2003), 75.
53. Carol Vincent et al., "Between the Estate and the State: Struggling To Be a 'Good' Mother" (paper presented at the British Educational Research Association Conference, London, 5–8 September 2007).
54. Department for Work and Pensions, *Government Action Plan: Implementing the Women and Work Commission Recommendations* (London, 2006).
55. Chris Denny, "Job Description," *Guardian*, 6 June 2000.
56. DfES, *Five Year Strategy*; OECD, *Starting Strong II*, 418.

Part-Time Pre- and Primary School Systems with Additional Childcare in West-Central Europe

Chapter 13

A West German "*Sonderweg*"?

Family, Work, and the Half-Day Time Policy of Childcare and Schooling

Karen Hagemann

In its statement on the *Seventh Family Report*, the government of the Federal Republic of Germany announced in April 2006 that it had "initiated a paradigmatic shift and was orienting its family policy more towards expanding an effective infrastructure which supports families and children for education and care as well as towards measures to integrate women into the world of work and allow for a better balance between family and work."[1] With this major policy shift, the federal government was following the recommendations of the report, which a group of experts had prepared for the Ministry for Family Affairs. They had defined as the main objective of German family policy "to catch up with the most family-friendly countries in Europe by 2010" and described the half-day system of childcare and schooling as one particularly important area of reform.[2] The authors of the *Seventh Family Report* had criticized that the Federal Republic is one of the few remaining countries in Europe where the vast majority of childcare facilities and schools are only open for half of the day. This time policy, they scathed, discriminates against children from lower socioeconomic and immigrant backgrounds by reinforcing social differences and makes it extremely difficult for parents to reconcile family life and paid work.[3]

Over the past decade, the problematic consequences of the half-day time policy have become increasingly apparent in the Federal Republic of Germany. As a result, the extension of all-day care and education for children between the ages of two and twelve has recently become an important topic of political debate. With support from the media, politicians from across the political spectrum are now calling for the expansion of all-day childcare and schooling. This represents a significant change in public discourse, which until the end of the 1990s had regarded all-day childcare and schooling as suitable only for "problem" and "latchkey" children from lower social backgrounds.[4] However, thus far the reforms that have been implemented have had limited practical impact, and the half-day system remains dominant. Moreover, the new coalition of the Christian Democratic Party (CDU), the Christian Social Party (CSU), and the Free Democratic Party (FDP), which in October 2009 replaced the former federal government formed by the CDU/CSU and the Social Democratic Party (SPD), supports the continuing demand of parents for more all-day childcare facilities and schools more rhetorically than practically.[5]

In the following chapter, I explore the complex and deeply rooted historical causes of the persistence of the West German half-day system. Because the time policies of childcare and schooling have been and continue to be so closely connected, my study focuses on both. In order to illustrate the high degree of path dependency that has characterized the evolution of the West German childcare and education system, I begin my analysis with a brief discussion of its earlier history.[6]

Continuities and Ruptures: Development Before 1945

As was the case elsewhere in Europe, institutionalized childcare for preschool children emerged in Germany in the first half of the nineteenth century. Two distinct institutional traditions developed: Since the early nineteenth century, private charitable associations, especially those run by churches, established all-day nurseries called *Warteschulen* (waiting schools) to care for the unsupervised children of working mothers. This often free childcare service was understood primarily as an "emergency social relief measure" that would protect working-class children from "moral decay" and the "dangers of the streets." Since the 1840s, individuals committed to child pedagogy and liberal reform associations founded half-day Fröbel *Kindergärten* for middle-class children. From their inception, these kindergartens, which required considerable fees from parents, were conceived of as "educational institutions" that augmented the family and promoted child development. In addition, charitable organizations launched in the second half of the nineteenth century an increasing number of so-called *Volkskindergärten* for children from lower classes, which were open all day and primarily thought of as a welfare measure.[7]

Since the end of the nineteenth century, institutionalized out-of-school care for primary school children from the working classes emerged in the form of the *Hort,* an after-school care center, and the *Tagesheim,* an all-day care facility for preschool and school-age children. They pursued goals similar to those of the *Warteschulen* and were also organized by private charitable associations.[8] This additional service became necessary, because unlike in England and France, the traditional all-day time structure of schooling, with morning and afternoon classes (from 8:00 A.M. to 12:00 P.M. and 2:00 to 4:00 P.M.) divided by a long lunch break at home, was gradually being replaced by a half-day time structure.

This process was closely related to the introduction of compulsory schooling for *all* children. In 1763, Prussia became the first German state to establish compulsory schooling, serving as a model for the other states. All Prussian children were required to enter primary school at age six and attend until grade four (if they were not sent to a private school). Upon completion, they began one of three secondary school tracks: The vast majority of the children went to the *Volksschule* (people's school), with compulsory education ending for them after the eighth grade. They usually learned only basic skills in reading, writing, and arithmetic. *Mittelschulen* (also called *Bürgerschulen* or *Realschulen*), which enrolled above all middle-class children, offered a longer and better education. However, only the *Gymnasium* led to the *Abitur*, an examination that qualified a student to study at a university. Not surprisingly, the *Gymnasium* was accessible only to a very small minority of children (and until the late nineteenth century, only boys) from the better-off, educated classes of society.[9]

Two main factors led to the introduction of the half-day time structure in *Volksschulen*. First, Prussia, like all other German states, faced enormous difficulties financing compulsory education for all children. From the beginning, the Prussian state allowed schools exemptions from the all-day time structure demanded by the School Law when they lacked classrooms and teachers. The most common form to deal with these problems was teaching in shifts (*Schichtunterricht*), with one-half of the children attending school in the morning and the other half in the afternoon. "Shift schooling" was especially widespread in rural areas, where teachers and classrooms were in short supply. Starting in 1872, Prussia officially permitted a half-day schedule for *Volksschulen* in cases where the number of children in a single class exceeded eighty, the classroom was too small, or because a community's finances prevented it from hiring a second teacher. Other German states followed this example.

Second, the states encountered enormous difficulties in enforcing compulsory, all-day schooling for working-class children who often had to work or help out at home by looking after their smaller siblings and doing other domestic chores. To deal with this problem, the state turned to "factory schools," "summer schools," and "rural half-day schools." Factory schools, which offered lessons in the early morning and evening hours, were first introduced by Saxony in 1835 for students eleven and older who worked in factories. These schools existed until 1891, when they were finally abolished. Summer schools were common in all agrarian regions of Germany. During the summer months, compulsory school hours were usually reduced to a minimum of nine hours over the course of three days. During the second half of the nineteenth century, summer schools were gradually replaced by rural half-day schools because they allowed children who had to work or help out at home to attend school more regularly.[10]

In most cities, the *Volksschulen,* whenever possible, offered a traditional form of all-day schooling with morning and afternoon classes. However, after the Prussian state officially allowed *Gymnasien* to implement a half-day schedule in 1890, they also gradually replaced their all-day schedule with a new half-day schedule. In *Gymnasien,* this shift came about largely as a result of a debate on putative "overburdening" of their male students that began in the 1830s. Teachers and doctors in particular worried that increasing numbers of students spent too much time getting to and from school, had no opportunity to eat lunch at home, and did not have enough time for their intensive homework (Prussia's guidelines required five hours per day). Since the mid-nineteenth century, more and more *Gymnasien,* especially in the larger cities, implemented a half-day schedule. After 1890, this schedule became increasingly common in Prussian *Gymnasien,* and by 1911, when the state introduced the "forty-five-minute short lesson" for all schools, it had prevailed in higher schools. Teachers at *Volksschulen* and their professional associations responded to this development by calling for the same privilege of an afternoon free to prepare their lessons. However, in the end it was the severe teacher shortage during World War I that forced school administrations to establish half-day schooling also in all *Volks-* and *Mittelschulen.* In 1920, the Prussian Ministry of Education effectively recognized half-day schooling as the norm for its tripartite school system. The other states in the Weimar Republic, which maintained the federal organization of school system, eventually followed the Prussian example. Thus began the policy path of half-day schooling that has persisted to this day.[11]

In response to this development and as an alternative to the common school education, educational reformers advocated all-day schools as a way of providing a more "holistic" approach to education that combined intellectual, social, and cultural learning. From the late nineteenth century on, they founded various forms of all-day schools like "rural boarding schools," "homebound day schools," and "nature and open air schools." Most of these school were private "laboratory schools" (*Versuchsschulen*) with high tuition rates, thus making them accessible only to middle- and upper-class children.[12] In addition, socialist educational reformers called for an end to the tripartite school system and its replacement with a new "comprehensive school" (*Einheitsschule*) for all children. These and other ideas of this movement for a reformed pedagogy finally came to fruition within the public school system during the Weimar Republic, especially in social democratic strongholds such as Berlin, Frankfurt am Main, or Hamburg where the city councils endeavored to make a quality education more accessible to children from the working classes.[13] The 1920s also saw the implementation of childcare centers in urban hubs that were similarly guided by the principles of reform pedagogy and run mostly by the social democratic welfare organization Workers' Welfare (*Arbeiterwohlfahrt*).[14]

From the outset, all-day childcare centers and schools informed by this new pedagogy were accused of nothing less than "destroying the family." By allowing mothers to work outside their home, they would, their Christian-conservative opponents argued, undermine the family as the main site of childrearing. The Catholic Church was a particularly ardent supporter of this position, which was rooted in the Catholic doctrine that the family was created by God as an end in itself, and, because of its divine provenance, stood above the state and society. It thus demanded a policy that defined childrearing as a parental duty, made schooling the obligation of the state, and tolerated institutionalized childcare only in the form of privately organized "social welfare" that supported "imperiled and indigent" families.[15]

This division of labor was enshrined in the constitution of the newly founded Weimar Republic as part of the political compromise between the Social Democrats and the Catholic Center Party and legally and institutionally cemented by the National School Conference of 1920 and the National Youth Welfare Law of 1922. Henceforth, formal childcare was considered as social welfare and was made the responsibility of the Youth Welfare Offices. However, the principle of subsidiarity (*Subsidiaritätsprinzip*) implemented by the Youth Welfare Law did allow municipalities to offer childcare services only in cases where no nonprofit provider was available, while at the same time obligating them to finance the private childcare facilities. With this legal and institutional framework now firmly in place, the Weimar Republic established a policy path that would continue for decades to come.[16]

While the Third Reich retained the basic structures of the Weimar childcare and school system, it also sought to transform, in conjunction with Nazi youth organizations, schools, childcare, and after-school care centers into institutions for the "total education of the German human being" that would shape children and youth collectively in the spirit of National Socialism. Collective NS education was thus now competing on a broad scale with family education.[17] In the field of child welfare, the NS state enforced this policy by bringing the vast majority of providers into line with Nazi institutions and ideology. All childcare facilities were henceforth placed under the umbrella of National Socialist People's Welfare (NSV). Despite this takeover, 32 percent of all childcare facilities remained in the hands of the Protestant and Catholic Church. As in other European countries, a massive expansion of childcare became urgent during World War II because female labor was needed in wartime industry. As a result, the proportion of three- to six-year-olds in all-day childcare facilities rose from 13 percent in 1930 to 31 percent in 1940 (see Table 13.1).[18]

TABLE 13.1: Childcare places for three- to six-year-old children in the German Empire and West Germany, 1910–1989[19]

Year	Number of facilities	Number of places	Degree of coverage [b]
1910	7,300 [a]	559,000	13%
1930	7,300	422,000	13%
1940	20,000	1,123,000	31%
1950	8,648	604,698	34%
1955	11,122	749,195	34%
1960	12,290	817,200	33%
1965	14,113	952,900	33%
1970	17,493	1,160,700	38%
1975	23,130	1,478,900	66%
1980	23,938 [c]	1,392,500	79%
1985	24,476 [d]	1,438,400	79%
1989	–	1,440,000	79%

Notes:
(a) The first exact nationwide survey, undertaken by the Ministry of Labor.
(b) Places in relation to children between the ages of three and six. This measurement commonly used in the FRG overestimates the actual degree of coverage, since a significant proportion of six-year-old children attended preschool facilities.
(c) After 1980 this includes the nursery schools attached to the public schools in Bavaria.
(d) Number of facilities in 1986.

In addition to these political and structural changes in the childcare and school system, the Third Reich put an end to the movement for reform pedagogy that had flourished in the Weimar Republic. After 1933, many of its supporters were forced to emigrate, were persecuted, and in some cases even murdered by the regime. Their institutions were closed or reorganized. As a result, the movement reemerged from the Nazi period greatly weakened.[20]

Reconstruction and Restoration: The Early Postwar Years

After World War II, the most basic material requirements for both child-care and schooling were sorely lacking. The first concern, therefore, was to make them available again as quickly as possible.[21] The easiest way to do this was to revive the basic structures of childcare and schooling that had prevailed in the Weimar Republic, which meant returning to what many policymakers assumed was a proven path of development. The dire material conditions also contributed to the failure of the reform initiatives introduced by the Western Allies, especially the Americans, as part of their broader Re-Education Program. In addition to the denazification of teaching and childcare personnel, this program also envisioned the introduction of all-day comprehensive schools and a more "democratic" education in general.[22]

Material circumstances, however, were not the only factor responsible for the failure of the reform initiative of the Western Allies. Just as important was the fierce resistance from middle-class liberal and Christian conservative groups, which advocated their more traditional educational policy as an alternative to the thoroughly discredited Nazi educational system, with its tendency towards totalitarian collective childrearing; the policies of the Soviet zone of occupation, which embraced the Weimar traditions of a socialist-reform pedagogy;[23] and the Re-Education Program of the Western Allies.[24] Instead, they sought to restore a shattered German national identity by reverting to the neohumanist tradition that had shaped German education since the nineteenth century. This tradition declared Christian culture to be the core of the German nation and placed special emphasis on the distinction drawn between *Bildung* and *Erziehung,* with the state assuming responsibility for *Bildung,* the intellectual and cultural education of children in schools, while the family provided *Erziehung,* the upbringing of children at home.[25]

Both liberals and Christian conservatives shared a deep skepticism towards any form of collective education of children, and regarded the family as the primary childrearing institution. Supposedly unsullied by National Socialism, the family was glorified as the foundation for the social reconstruction of the nation and a haven of stability in a country devastated by war. The Catholic Church in particular pursued a policy of restabilizing the family and re-Christianizing society. The provisions on the family and schools in the FRG's constitution—the *Grundgesetz* (Basic Law)—of May 1949 reflect this policy, effectively picking up where the corresponding articles of the Weimar constitution had left off.[26]

In short, the newly founded FRG basically continued the traditions of the Weimar Republic: Childrearing was still understood as the duty of parents, not the state, and institutional childcare was accepted only as a "social relief" measure for which the municipal youth welfare offices were accountable but had to follow the principle of subsidiarity. In the federal political system of the FRG, the responsibility for school education was once again given to the *Länder* (federal states), which already in 1948 had formed the Standing Conference of the Ministers of Education of the Federal States (Kultusministerkonferenz, KMK) to coordinate their policies.

Economic Growth and "Refamilization": The 1950s and 1960s

In this specific social and political constellation of postwar West Germany, major structural reforms of the childcare and school system had little if any chance for success. Indeed, any hope of such reform was dashed in 1955 by the Düsseldorf Agreement of the KMK, which wrote the tripartite, half-day school system into law for the next ten years and allowed all-day schools only if they were designated as "laboratory schools."[27] By 1966, only thirty-six such schools were founded in West Germany, fifteen of which were private (see Table 13.2).[28]

TABLE 13.2: Number of all-day schools in West Germany, 1954–1987[29]

Year	Total		Only primary schools	
		Of these private		Of these private
1954	1			
1957	7			
1958	8			
1966	36	15		
1977	311	98	24	4
1987	562	246	44	2

The development of the childcare system also stagnated in the first two decades after the war. Until the 1960s, the proportion of three- to six-year-olds in nursery schools or other facilities was at 34 percent not much higher than it had been during the war. However, after the war, the large number of single mothers, most of them widows, who had to earn a living prevented the reduction of the number of childcare places. (See Table 13.1.) As was the case before 1933, the vast majority of childcare facilities, 78 percent by the 1960s, were in the hands of nonprofit organizations, most of them controlled by the two main churches. Although other providers and municipalities did slowly gain more influence over the provision of childcare, by the 1980s, the churches still controlled 70 percent of all childcare facilities, albeit with large regional differences. It is therefore not surprising that more than 80 percent of all childcare facilities provided only half-day services.[30]

During the first postwar decade, all-day education was not an important subject of public discussion. Only individual reformers spoke up in favor of all-day childcare and schools as a "measure of social aid."[31] One of the most well-known supporters was Lina Meyer-Kuhlenkampf, a teacher at the Pestalozzi-Fröbel House in Berlin. She saw all-day childcare and schools as a means of helping the hundreds of thousands of women who were forced to work full-time after the war because they were either widowed or divorced or were still waiting for the return of their POW husbands.[32] Similar arguments shaped the discourse for all-day schools until the early 1960s. From 1955 on, the Gemeinnützige Gesellschaft Tagesheimschule (GGT), a newly founded interest group for all-day education made up of school teachers and educationalists dedicated to reform pedagogy, became the most influential advocate for all-day education.[33]

The debate on all-day schools first intensified during the conflict over the five-day work week, which the German Trade Union Federation (DGB) had begun calling for in 1956 with the slogan "On Saturday, Daddy belongs to me." All-day schools were now discussed as a way to harmonize work and school schedules. Pointing to the positive examples of all-day comprehensive schools in Britain, Sweden, and the United States, supporters of the five-day work week argued that family life stood to benefit enormously if school and work schedules corresponded to each other.[34]

Despite these initial efforts, resistance to all-day childcare and schooling remained strong well into the 1960s, with the Catholic Church, the Christian Democratic Party, the Christian Social Party, and the Free Democratic Party all taking strong positions against it. Siding with them were conservative Christian interest groups, certain elements within the teaching profession (primarily the conservative high school teachers' association, the Philologenverband), and many physicians. As was the case during the interwar period, opponents continued to argue that all-day education would alienate children from the family.[35] Pointing to the GDR, they also claimed that more all-day programs for children would only lead to a further increase in the employment of mothers, which in their eyes could only further damage the already threatened family. Some critics, in fact, went so far as to advocate the refusal to expand the offering of all-day education and childcare as a strategy for "combating" mothers' employment.[36]

But it was not just conservatives who opposed all-day childcare and schooling. Many Social Democrats were also reluctant to support such a fundamental reform. To be sure, the women's programs of the DGB and the Social Democratic Party repeatedly called for the "establishment and improvement of social facilities that offer relief to working women and mothers," but even their female functionaries largely agreed that all-day education was desirable only as a supplementary "social assistance measure."[37] They did not support employment either. In fact, a report of the DGB's Department of Women's Affairs for the period 1962–1964 lamented the increase in the number of working mothers: "A particularly noteworthy and unfortunate aspect of this rise in the rate of female employment is the strong increase among working mothers with children under the age of fourteen years."[38] The position of the DGB and SPD was bolstered by social scientists, who until the 1960s regarded mothers' employment as a "social problem" and repeatedly made the unsupported assertion that children could develop properly only if they received unlimited attention from their mothers.[39]

Until the late 1960s, the "male-breadwinner/female-homemaker" family remained the accepted ideal for the vast majority of West German society. Indeed, its acceptance became stronger than ever in the 1950s and 1960s as it became for the first time attainable even for working-class families. As a result of West Germany's "economic miracle" in the 1950s, more and more married working-class women could stay at home.[40] This provided the economic and social basis for the cultural hegemony of this family ideal, which, despite all of the social and cultural changes of the postwar period, remained largely unquestioned until the 1970s. Indeed, its pervasiveness was one of the most important reasons for the persistence of the half-day system in West Germany.[41]

The Cold War context also contributed greatly to the widespread acceptance of this family model and the related half-day time policy. From the outset, it was presented as a counter-image to the East German "double-earner family," which in the FRG was associated with the much-maligned system of "collective all-day childcare" that supposedly aimed at the "socialist indoctrination of children."[42] The images of the "West German housewife" and the "East German working mother," like the related images of "free and individual West German family education" and "totalitarian East German education in collective institutions," were constructed in opposition to, and strictly demarcated from, one another.[43] They served as important cultural markers of the fundamental difference between East and West. Any discourse and social change that blurred these constructed borders was thus perceived as a dangerous threat to the Cold War political and social order.

Given these circumstances, change occurred only slowly. The most powerful force for a shift in the image of the working mother—but not in attitudes towards all-day education—in West Germany was the economy.

From the late 1950s on, booming industry was confronted with a growing labor shortage. Until the building of the Berlin Wall in 1961 sealed the border with the GDR, the FRG had been able to rely on a steady influx of qualified workers from the East. With this labor source no longer available, West German industries began to import more foreign labor and promote part-time employment of married women and mothers. In fact, in the boom period of the West German economy, it was only possible to limit married women to part-time work because of the extensive recruitment of "guest workers." West Germany imported more foreign labor than any other Western European country in the active recruitment period between 1955 and 1973.[44] In 1968, 1.9 million "foreigners" lived in the FRG; 1 million of them were employed.[45] Their number increased to 4 million in 1973, with 2.6 million of them holding jobs. The largest groups were migrants from Turkey, Yugoslavia, and Italy. Although in 1973 the West German government decreed a "ban of recruitment," the increase continued until the early 1990s. One reason was that more and more family members followed.[46]

Parallel to the recruitment of "guest workers," part-time employment of mothers rose. The attitudes towards mothers' employment gradually changed as it became increasingly accepted by society and politicians. An early indicator of this change in public discourse is the government's report *Woman in Employment, Family, and Society* that was presented to the parliament in September 1966. Painting a much more complex picture of maternal employment, it no longer claimed that it had only negative effects on child development.[47] By the mid-1960s, social scientists also began to support part-time paid work for mothers.[48] As a result, it became increasingly acceptable for women to earn at least a "supplementary income" from part-time work, which was now recommended as the best possible solution to reconciling motherhood and employment. By 1971, 19 percent of all employed women in West Germany were working part-time, up from only 7 percent a decade earlier.[49] The gradual introduction of part-time employment was accompanied by a rise in the overall proportion of women in the workforce (see Table 13.3).[50] Married women with children accounted for the largest share of this increase, although the greatest rise had already occurred in the 1950s. Between 1950 and 1961, their employment rate rose from 23 to 32 percent, and in 1982 it reached 39 percent.[51] Despite the increase in the number of employed mothers, the expansion of childcare and all-day schools stagnated in West Germany until the early 1970s (see Tables 13.1 and 13.2). The dominant family model continued to prevail, but in a new form: the "male-breadwinner/female-homemaker-and-supplementary-income-earner" family. Married women and mothers now had to fulfill a "dual role."[52]

TABLE 13.3: Development of women's employment in West Germany, 1950–1989[53]

Year [a]	Women in the workforce	The proportion of employed women in the working age female population (15–65 years)	The proportion of employed women of the total female population
1950	7,267,000		30%
1954	8,050,000		32%
1960	9,747,000	47%	33%
1964	9,785,000	50%	32%
1968	9,412,000	50%	30%
1972	9,760,000	48%	31%
1980	9,829,000	50%	37%
1989	10,794,000	56%	39%

Note:
(a) Until 1958 without West Berlin.

Reform and Stagnation: The 1960s through 1980s

It was not until the mid-1960s and the beginning of a new period of reform that West Germany, like many other countries in Western Europe, experienced an increasingly intense debate over educational reform. This debate was sparked by the broad public perception of a "crisis of the educational system."[54] In the interest of economic development, the main goals of both major parties—the CDU/CSU and the SPD—were to make more "efficient use" of "educational reserves" and to promote a "maximization" of learning. This economic approach to education was accompanied by social and political demands for "increased equal opportunities." Education was now defined as a "right of each citizen."[55] This debate focused primarily on equal educational chances for children from lower social backgrounds and girls. The education of the increasing number of children from migrant families was not yet on the agenda.[56] In 1965, the KMK established the Education Council (Bildungsrat) as a national body charged with developing new proposals for a fundamental reform of the education system. Over the course of the next few years, the Council published detailed reform programs. Most important for the time policy were two recommendations: In 1968, the Council proposed a rapid expansion of the number of kindergartens (*Kindergärten*) and preschools (*Vorschulen*), which it classified as "educational institutions" that should be open to all children. One year later, it called for the "experimental" introduction of comprehensive schools, which were generally to be organized on an all-day basis.[57] The reform plans of the Education Council were actively supported by the grand coalition of CDU/CSU and SPD, which had replaced the long-standing conservative Christian-liberal government in 1966, as well as the social-liberal coalition formed by the SPD and the FDP that came to power in 1969. However, in the federative system of West Germany, the *Länder* were ultimately responsible for the realization of these plans.

The Council's recommendations for kindergarten and preschool education were enacted by most federal states with remarkable speed. Beginning in 1970, most states passed laws that defined kindergarten and preschool as the "lowest level of the school system."[58] They greatly expanded the number of kindergarten and preschool places from 952,900 in 1965 to 1,478,000 in 1975, enough for 66 percent of all three- to six-year-old children. Still, only 20 percent of all facilities were open all day and their places were reserved mainly for so-called social problem cases. Thus, despite all educational reforms in this period, the old division between full-time childcare as "social welfare" and half-day childcare as an "educational program" that supplements the upbringing of children in the family remained firmly in place.[59] In the mid-1970s, the expansion of the number of childcare places came to a halt. The further increase of the overall extent of coverage, which in 1989 reached 79 percent of all three- to six-year-old children, was primarily the result of the decreasing birth rate. (See Table 13.1.) Citing their high cost, policymakers rejected a further increase of the number of places and were not willing to finance more all-day facilities. With unemployment on the rise, they did not want to support anything that might facilitate the full-time work of mothers.[60]

The number of all-day schools also rose following the recommendations of the Education Council. The majority of all-day schools that existed in West Germany prior to unification had been founded by the late 1970s. By 1977, their number had increased to 311 and would grow to 672 in 1988 (see Table 13.2). Of these schools, 246, or 44 percent, were private (compared to 9 percent of all schools in the FRG). The relatively high percentage of private all-day schools had a long tradition and indicates that they needed to respond more swiftly to parental demand because they depended on the tuition parents had to pay. In 1988, only forty-four all-day schools were primary schools. The federal states with the highest number of all-day schools were Bavaria (192), North Rhine-Westphalia (117), and Baden-Wurttemberg (116). Only in social-democratic-governed NRW, however, were they for the most part public; in the other two states, which were governed by the CDU/CSU, the majority of these schools were private. Moreover, in NRW more than 50 percent were comprehensive schools, which were rare in Bavaria and Baden-Wurttemberg. On average, until the 1990s only 5 percent of all West German schools were open all day, and only 5 percent of these were primary schools.[61]

Two major factors prevented the further expansion of the number of all-day schools in the 1970s and 1980s: First, heated ideological conflicts over questions of education began after the grand coalition split up. One subject of these debates was the comprehensive school, which was denounced by the CDU/CSU as an institution that sought to "equalize" children from different social backgrounds. In this conflict, the conservatives deliberately equated the comprehensive school with the all-day school (despite the fact that until the late 1980s, only one-third of all-day schools were comprehensive schools). As a result, the all-day school once again came under fire.[62] Second, since the beginning of the economic recession in the 1980s, opponents cited the higher costs of all-day schools to argue against their expansion.[63]

Even during the reform era of the 1960s and 1970s, there was surprisingly little protest against the still-dominant time policy of half-day childcare and schooling. To be sure, criticisms of the gendered division of labor in the family, society and politics, the related "patriarchal" family model, and the "authoritarian" family education had emerged in West Germany within the context of the student movement and the new women's movement. This critique, however, was rarely associated with demands for more state funded all-day childcare and schooling. Two factors were at work here. First, the majority of the young and educated women in both movements simply had no children, so that childcare and school education were not important issues for many of them.[64] Second, both movements shared a critical attitude towards the state and preferred greater autonomy from its institutions. Not surprisingly, those parents who were involved in the students' and women's movements chose instead to found private childcare and after-school institutions, which they could run themselves. The aim of this *Kinderladen* (child storage) movement was an "antiauthoritarian" education. The self-organized *Kinderläden* were often only open part-time and demanded a very active involvement of the parents, who not only had to provide services like shopping, cooking, and cleaning but often also had to take care of the children. These tasks were difficult to combine with a full-time job.[65]

As a result of this development, at the end of the 1980s, the time policy of the FRG childcare and school system was unique in Western Europe. No other country, with the exception of Austria (and the German parts of Switzerland), clung so tightly to the half-day system. Already at this point, however, many working parents perceived this time structure as a problem. Since the late 1960s, the demand for all-day schools and out-of-school care for primary school children exceeded by far the number of places.[66] A representative survey of the women's magazine *BRIGITTE* in 1992 revealed that 87 percent of all mothers with under-thirteen-year-old school children wanted out-of-school care in the afternoon and 45 percent demanded compulsory all-day schools.[67]

Solidification and Change: Reunited Germany

At first glance, unification appears not to have had a substantial impact on the time policy of childcare and schooling in West Germany. This was not, however, the case for the six newly incorporated federal states from the former East Germany. Western politicians demanded that the new states quickly adapt to the structures and laws, policies and practices of the West.[68] The extended system of all-day childcare and after-school care and the comprehensive school system of the former GDR were thus quickly dismantled, not only because of their association with "collective socialist education" and Marxist indoctrination, but also because the new states had difficulty continuing to finance them to the former extent. The percentage of children in all-day childcare and after-school programs, however, remained much higher than in the West. In 2006, the Organisation for Economic Co-operation and Development (OECD) reported that the federal states in the West provided childcare places for only 3 percent of all children under three and 90 percent of all three- to six-year-olds, 24 percent of which were full-time places. The new states in the East, in contrast, provided childcare places for 37 percent of all children under three and almost all three- to six-year-olds, of which 98 percent were full-time places. Likewise, after-school programs were offered in the West for only 6 percent of all primary school children aged six to ten, compared to 68 percent in the East. The overall figures for out-of-school provision in the FRG were in the same year 14 percent and for children in all-day schools, 13 percent.[69] All-day schools are also much more common in the East. In 2004, the federal states with the highest percentage of children between six and ten in all-day schools were Saxony (58 percent) and Thuringia (52 percent), and the capital, Berlin (22 percent).[70]

In retrospect, the consequences of unification for the time policy of childcare and schooling were, paradoxically, far more problematic in West Germany, whose politicians were so heavily involved in the attempt to reform the East along Western lines that they ignored the necessity of reforms at home. Thus, at a time when other Western European countries began or even finished important structural reforms that bridged the gap between economic and social changes and policies and practices by providing more all-day childcare and schools, the traditional half-day structure was being reinforced in West Germany by the attempt to implement it in the East.

The consequences of this outdated policy can be clearly observed today. Combining work and family remains much more difficult in the FRG than in most other countries of the European Union. One of the clearest indicators is the marked disparity between the employment rate of single women and mothers. In contrast to the situation twenty years ago, the FRG now ranks among those EU countries with a relatively high rate of female employment. In 2006, the OECD reported that 66 percent of all women aged fifteen to sixty-four in the FRG were employed, a higher rate than the EU average. At the same time, however, only 38 percent of all mothers with children under the age of twelve and 43 percent with children under the age of six worked outside the home.[71] Moreover, in no other EU country do so many women leave the labor force when they become mothers and then not go back to work before their children reach the age of three (50 percent). And with the exception of Ireland, nowhere else in the EU do so many women with two or more children leave the labor force entirely.[72] Part-time work remains the most common form to combine family and work in the FRG. As a result, more mothers are employed part-time than in most other EU countries, and the proportion of part-time working women among all employed women is unusually high—37 percent in 2006 compared to 21 percent in Sweden and 24 percent in France.[73] However, the constraints on mothers seeking employment are far more developed in West Germany, where the rate of part-time working mothers stood at 76 percent in 2005. In East Germany this proportion was significantly lower at 43 percent. (See Table 13.4.)[74]

TABLE 13.4: The percentage of working mothers (full- and part-time) according to their children's ages in 2005[75]

Age of the youngest child under 15 [a]	West Germany (without Berlin)			East Germany (including Berlin)		
	Percentage of working mothers [b]	Full-time [c]	Part-time [c]	Percentage of working mothers [b]	Full-time [c]	Part-time [c]
Together	56%	24%	76%	61%	57%	43%
Under 3	31%	32%	68%	41%	55%	45%
3–5 years	54%	21%	79%	64%	54%	46%
6–9 years	64%	20%	80%	69%	57%	44%
10–14 years	71%	26%	74%	72%	60%	40%

Notes:
(a) All children under 15 who live in the household.
(b) Percentage of actively working mothers (without women on maternity leave) of all working women between, 14 and 65.
(c) Percentage of all full-time/part-time working mothers of all working mothers.

In addition to the much better provision of all-day childcare and after-school programs in the East, these differences also mirror the still widely varying attitudes towards mothers' employment and public childcare in both parts of Germany. In the West, the model of the "male-breadwinner/ female-homemaker-and-supplementary earner" family continues to prevail. Thus, the overwhelming majority of mothers in the Western states of the FRG share the predominant view that small children belong with their mothers, who at best should only work part-time. The enduring influence of GDR socialization seems to be an important reason for a very different attitude in the East. The communist state officially had supported full-time work for mothers, and in the final years of the GDR, more than 88 percent of women with children had worked full-time. All recent surveys show that East German women continue to regard full-time employment for mothers as "normal." In an official survey taken in 2003, only 37 percent of all East German women who work part-time stated that they did so because of "personal or familial reasons," as compared to 85 percent of women in the West. On the contrary, 47 percent of the East German women who worked part-time actually wanted to work full-time, but had not yet found a full-time job. In West Germany this was only the case for 4 percent of all part-time working women.[76] Collective childcare from an early age also continues to enjoy far greater acceptance in East Germany than it does in the West.[77] In a 2005 survey, only 25 percent of eastern women stated that all-day childcare is "harmful" to child development as compared to 40 percent of their counterparts in the West.[78]

Attitudes are, however, changing. The percentage of West German women who believe that small children cannot develop well if their mother works has fallen from 78 percent in 1982 to 68 percent today, a significant decrease, even if it is still high when compared to the 39 percent of women in the East who feel the same way. More importantly, 65 percent of all West German mothers surveyed stated that they would work longer hours if their children had places in an all-day childcare or school. Likewise, more and more women no longer believe in the myth of the "good mother" who sacrifices her career for her children. The model of the male-breadwinner/female-homemaker family is slowly but steadily eroding. In a representative survey in 2000, only 42 percent of all West Germans and 31 percent of all East Germans stated that this is the best possible family form. In the under-thirty age group, the percentage was even smaller—29 percent in the West and 21 percent in the East.[79]

Arguably one, if not the most serious, consequence of this situation, is the decline of Germany's birth rate. At 1.3 children per woman, Germany has one of the lowest fertility rates in the EU.[80] In particular, educated younger women seem to be on a "birth strike": 65 percent of women with a university education aged thirty-three to thirty-six have no children, compared to 36 percent of all women in the same age group.[81] According to a recent census, 65 percent of female university graduates stated that they want to have children, but hesitate to do so because of the difficulties of reconciling a career with a family. In addition to the general lack of all-day childcare and schools and the inflexible schedules of existing facilities, they fear the judgment of public opinion. Career women with children are often still perceived as "neglectful mothers."[82]

This situation has sparked an intense political debate and helped to change attitudes towards all-day education. The media and politicians alike have linked the dramatic social consequences of the decreasing birth rate to the future of the labor market, the welfare state, and the education system. The demand for a "population-oriented family policy," which includes all-day childcare and schools, has thus received increasing support in recent years.[83]

Another important factor that generated support for all-day education was the "PISA shock." After the publication of the results of the 2000 study by the Program for International Student Assessment (PISA), it was no longer possible to deny the shortcomings of the German education system. Out of the thirty-two industrialized countries in the study, Germany scored far below the OECD average. When compared to other countries, it scored especially poorly in the performance of children from lower social and migrant backgrounds. This was perceived as a major failure of the German education system and a serious social and economic problem.[84] One-third of all German students reach a general qualification for university entrance (*Abitur*), and only 9 percent leave school without any degree. For students from a migrant family, these percentages are 16 percent and 17 percent.[85] The result is that young men and women with a migrant background often have fewer chances on the labor market and in the end are more often unemployed.[86] This is an increasingly serious problem for the German economy, because the percentage of children with a migrant background is constantly rising. The major reason is that the birth rate of women with a migrant background is on average higher than that of native-born German women. As a result, 33 percent of all children under five, compared to 20 percent of the German population as a whole, had a "migrant background" in 2006.[87]

In the ensuing public debate after the PISA shock, two main causes were singled out as responsible for the poor showing: the tripartite school system and its half-day structure. According to many analysts, both have had a particularly deleterious effect on the academic performance of children from disadvantaged social and minority ethnic backgrounds.[88] Among the solutions proposed to remedy this structural deficiency was a quantitative and qualitative expansion of all-day childcare and schooling. To pursue this goal, in 2002 the government, at the time controlled by the SPD and Green Party, initiated the program *The Future of Education and Care,* which earmarked €4 billion for the expansion of all-day schools between 2003 and 2007.[89]

This program, which the CDU/CSU-SPD coalition government that took power in 2005 also supported, at first glance appears to be a major step in the right direction. Its implementation, however, has been highly disappointing, despite all public pronouncements. The *Twelfth Children's and Youth Report* of the Federal Ministry for Family Affairs, Senior Citizens, Women and Youth, published in September 2005, as well as the recent KMK statistics from 2008 (which report development until 2006) have shown that thus far, this program and all other initiatives by the federal government have changed little. The number of primary schools with "all-day offerings" rose from 1,757, 10 percent of the total, in 2002 to 4,878, 29 percent, in 2006. However, the proportion of students in schools with "all-day offerings" only increased from 4 percent in 2002 to 13 percent in 2006. Furthermore, this increase was more a result of new definitions than of new schools.[90] The program spoke of *all-day offerings* rather than *all-day schools,* and promised money to schools that remain open for seven hours at least three days a week and serve a hot meal on those days. Their afternoon programs can be voluntary and offered by any private provider, but must bear a "conceptual relationship" to the half-day school in the morning, which can otherwise continue as usual. In addition, parents have to pay for the lunch and often for the afternoon care too. This new type of so-called all-day school, known as "open schools," merely adds a very inadequate afternoon care program to the traditional half-day school, a far cry from what advocates of all-day education had hoped for. The same half-hearted attitude prevails in the program to extend all-day childcare for two- to six-year-olds.[91] In short, thus far, new policy has done very little to help parents who work all day, nor has it improved—as it was supposed to—the education of children from disadvantaged social and migrant backgrounds. The declared objective of the federal government and the KMK in 2008 was that "all-day schools [will be] the norm in Germany" in 2020. However, if these are "open schools" with voluntary "all-day offerings," the new policy will not have solved the discussed problems.[92]

Conclusion

The preceding historical analysis confirms the strong path dependency of the half-day time policy in West Germany, which was cemented by a combination of multiple political, economic, social, and cultural factors. First, the legal and institutional foundations established in the nineteenth and early twentieth century created an especially high degree of path dependence that produced the half-day time policy of the public system of childcare and schools. In particular, the institutional structures for childcare and schooling established at the beginning of the Weimar Republic proved their staying power not just in postwar West Germany, but continued to manifest themselves in a reunified Germany after 1990. The experience of the Third Reich intensified the recourse to traditional structures of the childcare and school system after 1945. As a result, a strong prejudice against collective education prevailed within the political class and society in general, and the approaches and projects of reformist pedagogy were largely forgotten.

Second, economic and financial factors played an important role in creating and then perpetuating the half-day system. The introduction of the half-day schedule for lower schools was in large part a result of the financial difficulties of the states to finance the traditional form of all-day schooling with a long lunch break for all children in compulsory school age. The expansion of all-day childcare in turn depended in large measure on the needs of the labor market. World War II, when female labor was in high demand, was especially important in this regard. During the reform period of the 1960s and 1970s, an economic approach to education dominated. Politicians wanted to make more "efficient use" of "educational reserves" and promoted a "maximization" of learning. This policy enforced the growth of half-day childcare and all-day schools. In the 1980s, the limits of their expansion were determined above all by the financial capacity of the state. The supposedly prohibitive cost now became the single most important argument leveled against a further expansion of half- and all-day childcare and all-day schools.

Third, the culturally constructed concepts of the gender order and education that emphasized the family as the primary site of childrearing and rejected any form of collective education played an integral part in shaping the time structure of childcare and schooling. For decades, these remarkably durable cultural concepts acted as a brake on the expansion of all-day education. This is particularly true for the male-breadwinner/ female-homemaker family model, which had exerted a powerful influence on German educational and social policy since the nineteenth century. To this day, the majority of West Germans still do not question this family model in its current form, which accepts part-time work for mothers. Moreover, until recently, fathers occupied only a very marginal role in this debate. And while a new and more assertive women's movement has since the late 1960s challenged the hegemony of this family model, for a variety of reasons the time policy of childcare and schooling never stood very high on its agenda.

Finally, the political context of the Cold War and its aftermath also served to reinforce the half-day system for childcare and schooling. Above all, West Germany's confrontation with the GDR—which, by valorizing the working mother and relying on collective childcare, promoted the ideal of the double-earner family—strengthened the influence of the male-breadwinner/female-homemaker family model in the FRG and related ideas about the importance of the family for the upbringing of children. The postwar gender order in the West, which was rooted in this family model, and the half-day childcare and school system were key Cold War markers of the fundamental difference between the FRG and the GDR. The West German half-day policy can thus only be explained in relation to developments in the GDR, because here, as in other fields of politics, the two German states engaged in a complex relationship of "distancing and interconnection."[93]

The reunification of the two German states has reinforced the structures of the half-day time policy of childcare and schooling—at least in the West. Whether or not the recently declared policy shift of the federal government will indeed result in a paradigmatic change of practical childcare and school policies remains to be seen.

Notes

I would like to thank Myra Marx Feree, Brandon Hunziker, Konrad H. Jarausch, Sonja Michel, Bob Moeller, and Ann Taylor Allen for their helpful comments on earlier versions of the paper.

1. Bundesministerium für Familie, Senioren Frauen und Jugend (BMFSFJ), *Seventh Family Report: Families between Flexibility and Dependency—Perspectives for a Life Cycle–related Family Policy: Statement by the Federal Government and Summary* (Bonn, 2006), 2. See also the German original: BMFSFJ, *Siebter Familienbericht. Familie zwischen Flexibilität und Verlässlichkeit. Perspektiven für eine lebenslaufbezogene Familienpolitik. Bericht der Sachverständigenkommission* (Bonn, 2006), XXVIIf.
2. BMFSFJ, *Seventh Family Report*, 2.
3. BMFSFJ, *Siebter Familienbericht*, 229–32.
4. See Karen Hagemann and Karin Gottschall, "Die Halbtagsschule in Deutschland—ein Sonderfall in Europa?" *Aus Politik und Zeitgeschichte*, B 41 (2002): 12–22; Karen Hagemann, "Between Ideology and Economy: The 'Time Politics' of Child Care and Public Education in the Two Germanys," *Social Politics* 13, no. 1 (2006): 217–260; Karen Hagemann, "Die Ganztagsschule als Politikum: Die westdeutsche Entwicklung in gesellschafts- und geschlechtergeschichtlicher Perspektive," *Zeitschrift für Pädagogik* (Beiheft) 54 (2009): 209–29.

5. See Institut für Demoskopie Allensbach, *Monitor Familienleben 2010. Einstellungen und Lebensverhältnisse von Familien. Ergebnisse einer Repräsentativbefragung* (Allensbach, 2010), 8.

6. Paul Pierson, "Increasing Returns, Path Dependency, and the Study of Politics," *American Political Science Review* 94, no. 2 (2000): 251–67. For more on this concept see the introductions in this volume by Karen Hagemann, Cristina Allemann-Ghionda and Konrad H. Jarausch.

7. For more, see Hagemann, "Between Ideology," 229ff.; Ann Taylor Allen, *Feminism and Motherhood in Germany, 1800–1914* (New Brunswick, NJ, 1991).

8. See Jürgen Reyer et al., *Materialienband zur Hortgeschichte* (Cologne, 1989).

9. On the development of the Prussian and German school system, see Karl-Ernst Jeismann and Peter Lundgreen, eds., *Handbuch der deutschen Bildungsgeschichte*, vol. 3, *1800–1870. Von der Neuordnung Deutschlands bis zur Gründung des Deutschen Reiches* (Munich, 1987); Christa Berg, ed., *Handbuch der deutschen Bildungsgeschichte*, vol. 4, *1870–1918. Von der Reichsgründung bis zum Ende des Ersten Weltkrieges* (Munich, 1991).

10. See Hagemann, "Die Ganztagsschule"; Harald Ludwig, *Entstehung und Entwicklung der modernen Ganztagsschule in Deutschland*, 2 vols. (Cologne, 1993), 1: 32–39; Joachim Lohmann, *Das Problem der Ganztagsschule. Eine historisch-vergleichende und systematische Untersuchung* (Ratingen, 1965), 13–24.

11. See Ibid., 37–47.

12. See Ludwig, *Entstehung*, 1: 255–324.

13. See, for example, Hans-Peter de Lorent and Volker Ullrich, eds., *Der Traum von der freien Schule. Schule und Schulpolitik in Hamburg während der Weimarer Republik* (Hamburg, 1988); Inge Hansen-Schaberg, *Koedukation und Reformpädagogik. Untersuchung zur Unterrichts- und Erziehungsrealität in Berliner Versuchsschulen der Weimarer Republik* (Berlin, 1999).

14. See Hilmar Hoffmann, *Sozialdemokratische und kommunistische Kindergartenpolitik und -pädagogik in Deutschland* (Bochum, 1994).

15. Hagemann, "Between Ideology," 229ff.

16. Ibid.

17. See Ludwig, *Entstehung*, 1: 315–25.

18. Günter Erning et al., eds., *Geschichte des Kindergartens*, 2 vols. (Freiburg/Br., 1987), 1: 70ff.

19. Ibid., 2: 37.

20. See Ludwig, *Entstehung*, 1: 326–53.

21. On the background see Christoph Führ and Carl-Ludwig Furck, eds., *Handbuch der deutschen Bildungsgeschichte*, vol. 6, pt. 1, *1945 bis zur Gegenwart. Bundesrepublik Deutschland* (Munich, 1998); Karl Neumann, "Geschichte der öffentlichen Kleinkindererziehung von 1945 bis in die Gegenwart," in Erning et al., *Geschichte*, 1: 83–116.

22. See Hans-Werner Fuchs and Klaus-Peter Pöschl, *Reform oder Restauration? Eine vergleichende Analyse der schulpolitischen Konzepte und Maßnahmen der Besatzungsmächte 1945–1949* (Munich, 1986).

23. See the chapter on the GDR by Monika Mattes in this volume.

24. Ludwig, *Entstehung*, 2: 354–63.

25. Hagemann, "Between Ideology," 229ff.; Christoph Führ, "Zur deutschen Bildungsgeschichte seit 1945," in Führ and Furck, *Handbuch*, vol. 6, pt. 1, 1–21, 10–11.

26. See Karl Dienst, "Die Rolle der evangelischen und der katholischen Kirche in der Bildungspolitik zwischen 1945 und 1990," in Führ and Furck, *Handbuch*, vol. 6, pt. 1, 110–27, 110ff.; Robert G. Moeller, *Protecting Motherhood: Women and the Family in the Politics of Postwar West Germany* (Berkeley, CA, 1993), esp. 38–75; Lukas Rollikemper, *Familie im Wiederaufbau. Katholizismus und bürgerliches Familienideal in der Bundesrepublik Deutschland, 1945–1965* (Paderborn, 2000).

27. See Ludwig, *Entstehung*, 2: 463.

28. Ibid., 498–511 and 516–23.

29. Ibid., 497ff., 514f., and 523; *Tagesheimschule* 6 (1966): 56f and 77; *Die Ganztagsschule* 17, no. 3/4 (1977): 76–79; *Die Ganztagsschule* 27, no. 3 (1987): 90–93.

30. Neumann, "Geschichte," 2: 37ff and 70ff.

31. For example, Herman Nohl, "Pädagogische Aufgaben der Gegenwart," *Die Sammlung* 2 (1947): 694–701.

32. Lina Mayer-Kulenkampf, "Gedanken zur Schule heute," *Die Schule* (Aug. 1947), reprint in Joachim Lohmann, ed., *Die Ganztagsschule* (Bad Heilbrunn, 1967), 31–36.

33. See Ludwig, *Entstehung*, 2: 463–68.

34. Ibid., 475–86; Hagemann, "Die Ganztagsschule."

35. Ibid.; Ludwig, *Entstehung*, 2: 486–97.

36. Hagemann, "Die Ganztagsschule." See also, Ingrid Sommerkorn, "Die erwerbstätige Mutter in der Bundesrepublik: Einstellungen und Problemveränderungen," in *Wandel und Kontinuitäten der Familie in der Bundesrepublik Deutschland*, ed. Rosemarie Nave-Herz (Stuttgart, 1980), 114–44.

37. Cited in Mechthild Koppel, "Für das Recht der Frauen auf Arbeit. Ein Kampf gegen Windmühlenflügel in den Jahren 1945–1960," in *"Da haben wir uns alle schrecklich geirrt ..." Die Geschichte der gewerkschaftlichen Frauenarbeit im Deutschen Gewerkschaftsbund von 1945 bis 1960*, ed. DGB (Pfaffenweiler, 1993), 38. See also Sigrid Ingeborg Bachler, "Frauenleben und Frauenideal in der Frauenpolitik des DGB der Fünfziger Jahre," in *"Da haben wir uns alle schrecklich geirrt ..."*, 133–77, esp. 158ff.

38. DGB, Bundesvorstand, Hauptabteilung "Frauen," *Geschäftsbericht 1962–64* (Düsseldorf, n.d.), 16.

39. See Karin Gottschall, "Erwerbstätigkeit und Elternschaft als Gegenstand soziologischer Forschung," *Zeitschrift für Frauenforschung* 3 (1999): 19–33; Wiebke Kolbe, "Kindeswohl und Mütterwerbstätigkeit: Expertenwissen in der schwedischen und bundesdeutschen Kinderbetreuungspolitik der 1960er und 1970er Jahre," *Traverse* 2, no. 2 (2001): 12–135.

40. Hagemann, "Ganztagsschule"; BMFSFJ, *Siebter Familienbericht*, 69–70. For the historical background, see Merith Niehus, *Familie, Frau und Gesellschaft. Studien zur Strukturgeschichte der familie in Westdeutschland, 1945–1960*, (Göttingen, 2001), esp. 214–96.

41. Christine Feldmann-Neubert, *Frauenleitbild im Wandel 1948–1988: Von der Familienorientierung zur Doppelrolle* (Weinheim, 1991); Astrid Vornmoor, "Genderkonstruktionen in Leitbildern (west-)deutscher Familienpolitik von der Nachkriegszeit bis in die Gegenwart," *Femina Politica* 13, no. 1 (2003): 17–26.

42. For example, F. Pöggeler (Verein katholischer Lehrerinnen), "Tagesheimschule und Ganztagsschule," *Der katholische Erzieher* (1957): 19.

43. Gunilla-Friederike Budde, "'Tüchtige Traktoristinnen' und 'schicke Stenotypistinnen': Frauenbilder in den deutschen Nachkriegsgesellschaften—Tendenzen der 'Sowjetisierung' und der 'Amerikanisierung'?" in *Amerikanisierung und Sowjetisierung in Deutschland 1945–1970*, ed. Konrad Jarausch and Hannes Siegrist (Frankfurt/M., 1997), 243–73; Uta C. Schmidt, "Das Problem heißt: Schlüsselkind. Die Schlüsselkinderzählung als geschlechterpolitische Inszenierung im Kalten Krieg," in *Massenmedien im Kalten Krieg*, ed. Thomas Lindenberger (Cologne, 2006), 171–202.

44. See Rita Chin, *The Guest Worker Question in Postwar Germany* (Cambridge, UK, 2007); Monika Mattes, *"Gastarbeiterinnen" in der Bundesrepublik. Anwerbepolitik, Migration und Geschlecht* (Frankfurt/M., 2005); Christine von Oertzen, *Teilzeitarbeit und die Lust am Zuverdienen. Geschlechterpolitik und gesellschaftlicher Wandel in Westdeutschland 1948–1969* (Göttingen, 1999); Christine von Oertzen, *The Pleasure of a Surplus Income: Part-Time Work, Gender Politics and Social Change in West Germany, 1955–1969* (Oxford, 2007).

45. The official statistic of the FRG defines "foreigners" as people without German citizenship. The number of "people with a migrant background," which includes migrants of the first, second, and third generation with and without citizenship, is much higher. See Veysel Özcan and Stefan Grimbacher, "Focus Migration Deutschland," *Länderprofil Europäische Union*, ed. Hamburg Institute of International Economics (HWWI), no. 1 (May 2007): 1–9.

46. Ibid., 2; European Parliament, *The Teaching of Immigrants in the European Union.* Retrieved 1 January 2010: http://www.europarl.europa.eu/workingpapers/educ/pdf/100_en.pdf, 12–14; see also Ulrich Herbert, *A History of Foreign Labor in Germany, 1880–1990: Seasonal Workers, Forced Laborers, Guest Workers* (Ann Arbor, MI, 1990).

47. Bundesministerium für Frauen und Familie, *Bericht der Bundesregierung über die Situation der Frauen in Beruf, Familie und Gesellschaft, 1966* (Bonn, 1966), 6. See also Bundesministerium für Familie und Jugend, *Bericht der Bundesregierung über die Lage der Familien in der Bundesrepublik Deutschland* (Bonn, 1968). On the development of the German federal government's family policy in the 1960s and 1970s, see Ute Behning, "Zum Wandel des Bildes 'der Familie' und der enthaltenen Konstruktionen von 'Geschlecht' in den Familienberichten 1968 bis 1993," *Zeitschrift für Frauenforschung* 14, no. 3 (1996): 146–56.

48. Gottschall, "Erwerbstätigkeit."

49. Marianne Assenmacher, *Frauenerwerbstätigkeit in der Bundesrepublik Deutschland. Eine demographisch-ökonomische Analyse* (Frankfurt/M., 1988), Table 9.

50. Angelika Willms, "Grundzüge der Entwicklung der Frauenarbeit zwischen 1880–1980," in *Strukturwandel der Frauenarbeit 1880–1980*, ed. Walter Müller et al. (Frankfurt/M., 1985), 141. See also Friederike Maier, "Zwischen Arbeitsmarkt und Familie—Frauenarbeit in den alten Bundesländern," in *Frauen in Deutschland 1945–1992*, ed. Gisela Helwig and Hildegard Maria Nickel (Bonn, 1993), 257–80.

51. Maier, "Zwischen Arbeitsmarkt," 259–60.

52. Alva Myrdal and Viola Klein, *Women's Two Roles: Home and Work* (London, 1956).

53. Maier, "Zwischen Arbeitsmarkt," 257f.

54. Georg Picht, *Die deutsche Bildungskatastrophe. Analyse und Dokumentation* (Olten, 1964).

55. Ralf Dahrendorf, *Bildung als Bürgerrecht—Plädoyer für eine aktive Bildungspolitik* (Hamburg, 1965).

56. One of the first German publications that discussed this issue was Herbert R. Koch, *Gastarbeiterkinder in deutschen Schulen* (Königswinter/Rhein, 1970).

57. Deutscher Bildungsrat, ed., *Empfehlungen der Bildungskommission: Einrichtung von Schulversuchen mit Gesamtschulen* (Stuttgart, 1969); Deutscher Bildungsrat, "Empfehlungen der Bildungskommission: Einrichtung von Schulversuchen mit Ganztagsschulen," in *Sicherung der öffentlichen Ausgaben für Schulen und Hochschulen bis 1975* (Bonn, 1968). See also Kulturministerkonferenz (KMK), "Vereinbarung zur Durchführung der Empfehlung der Bildungskommission des Deutschen Bildungsrates vom 23./24. Februar 1968 zur Einrichtung von Schulversuchen mit Ganztagsschulen. Beschluß vom 3. Juli 1969," *Bundesanzeiger* 21, no. 137 (1969): 7; and Ludwig, *Entstehung*, 2: 534–66.

58. Neumann, "Geschichte," 83–116.

59. Ibid.; Erning, *Geschichte*, 2: 37.

60. Hagemann, "Die Ganztagsschule."

61. Ibid.

62. Ludwig, *Entstehung*, 2: 567–83.

63. Ibid. 549ff., 567f.; Carl-Ludwig Furck, "Allgemeinbildende Schulen. Entwicklungstendenzen und Rahmenbedingen," in Führ and Furck, *Handbuch*, vol. 6, pt. 1, 251ff.

64. See Ute Frevert, "Umbruch der Geschlechterverhältnisse? Die 60er Jahre als geschlecht-erpolitischer Experimentierraum," in *Dynamische Zeiten: Die 60er Jahre in beiden deutschen Gesellschaften,* ed. Axel Schildt et al. (Hamburg, 2000), 642–60; Kristina Schulz, *Der lange Atem der Provokation: Die Frauenbewegung in der Bundesrepublik und in Frankreich 1968–1976* (Frankfurt/M., 2002).

65. Gerda Tornieporth, "Familie, Kindheit, Jugend," in Führ and Furck, *Handbuch,* vol. 6, pt. 1 175ff.; Dagmar Herzog, *Sex after Fascism: Memory and Morality in Twentieth-Century Germany* (Princeton, NJ, 2005), 171–72.

66. See Heinz Günter Holtappels, "Ganztagserziehung," in *Ganztagserziehung in der Schule: Modelle, Forschungsbefunde und Perspektiven,* ed. Heinz Günter Holtappels (Opladen, 1995), 35ff; Tino Bargel, "Bestands- und Bedarfsanalysen zu Ganztagsschulen und Ganztagsangeboten," in *Ganztagserziehung in der Schule,* 67–85; Tino Bargel and Manfred Kuthe, *Ganztagsschule. Untersuchungen zu Angebot und Nachfrage, Versorgung und Bedarf* (Bad Honnef, 1991), 137ff.

67. Julia Ohde, *Kinderbetreuung in Deutschland. Eine repräsentative gesamtdeutsche Studie über die Situation von Müttern mit Kindern unter 13 Jahren im Auftrag der Zeitschrift BRIGITTE,* (Hamburg, 1992), 38f and 54.

68. Rosemarie Nave-Herz, "Die institutionelle Klein-Kindbetreuung in den neuen und den alten Bundesländern—ein altes, doch weiterhin hochaktuellen Problem für die Eltern," *Zeitschrift für Frauenforschung* 8 (1990): 45–59.

69. OECD, *Starting Strong II: Early Childhood Education and Care* (Paris, 2006), 334; KMK, *Bericht über die allgemeinbildenden Schulen in Ganztagsform in den Ländern der Bundesrepublik Deutschland, 2002 und 2006* (Bonn, 2008), 10.

70. Miriam Beblo et al., "Gantagsschulen und Erwerbsbeteiligung von Müttern—eine Mikrosimulation für Deutschland," discussion paper, German Institute for Economic Research (Berlin, Dec. 2005), 5.

71. OECD, *Starting Strong II,* 309, 320, 325, 333, and 408.

72. Ute Klammer, "Vom 'Ernährermodell' zum 'Erwerbstätigenmodell.' Zum gesellschaftlichen und sozialpolitischen Umgang mit Fürsorgearbeit in Europa," in *Sozialstaat in Europa. Geschichte, Entwicklung, Perspektiven,* ed. Katrin Kaus and Thomas Geisen (Wiesbaden, 2002), 272–84; Ute Gerhard et al., eds., *Working Mothers in Europe: A Comparison of Policies and Practices* (Cheltenham, 2005).

73. OECD, *Starting Strong II,* 333.

74. See Karin Esch and Sybille Stöbe-Blossey, "Kinderbetreuung: Ganztags für alle? Differenzierte Arbeitszeiten erfordern flexible Angebote," *IAT Report* 9 (2002): 4; Felix Büchel and C. Katharina Spiess, *Form der Kinderbetreuung und Arbeitsmarktverhalten von Müttern in West- und Ostdeutschland* (Stuttgart, 2002).

75. Statistisches Bundesamt, *Leben und Arbeiten in Deutschland—Sonderheft 2: Vereinbarkeit von Familie und Beruf. Ergebnisse des Mikrozensus 2005* (Wiesbaden, 2006), 10.

76. Statisches Bundesamt, "Mikrozensus 2003: Müttererwerbstätigkeit steigt," news release, no. 191, 28 April 2004.

77. Nave-Herz, "Die institutionelle Klein-Kindbetreuung"; Hildegard Maria Nickel, "Frauenarbeit in den neuen Bundesländern: Rück- und Ausblick," *Berliner Journal für Soziologie* 1 (1992): 39–48.

78. BMFSFJ, *Monitor Familienforschung. Mütter und Beruf: Realitäten und Perspektiven,* no. 4. (Bonn, 2005): 7–8.

79. Ibid.; BMFSFJ, *Siebter Familienbericht,* 72; BMFSFJ, *Frauen,* 248–49.

80. Population Reference Bureau, *Fertility Rates for Low Birth-Rate Countries, 1995 to most recent Year.* Retrieved 1 July 2008: http://www.prb.org/pdf07/TFRTable.pdf.

81. See Julia Bornsteiner et al., "Generation kinderlos," *Der Spiegel*, no. 37 (12 Sept. 2005): 62–72, 36, and 66; see also BMFSFJ, *Siebter Familienbericht*, 176–78.

82. Susanne Gaschke, "Kinder, Küche, Karriere? Nicht bei uns," *DIE ZEIT*, no. 33, 11 August 2005; BMFSFJ, *Seventh Familiy Report*, 11.

83. BMFSFJ, *Wachstumseffekte einer bevölkerungsorientierten Familienpolitik*, ed. with the Bundesverband der Deutschen Industrie and the Institut der Deutschen Wirtschaft Cologne (Bonn, 2006).

84. See Cornelia Kristen, "Ethnische Unterschiede im deutschen Schulsystem," *Aus Politik und Zeitgeschichte*, B 21-22 (2003): 26-32; Ludger Wößmann, "Familiärer Hintergrund, Schulsystem und Schülerleistungen im internationalen Vergleich," *Aus Politik und Zeitgeschichte*, B 21-22 (2003): 33-38.

85. Bundesministerium für Forschung und Bildung, *Förderung von Jugendlichen mit schlechteren Startchancen*. Retrieved 1 January 2010: http://www.bmbf.de/de/9036.php.

86. For more, see Bundesministerium für Forschung und Bildung, *Berufsbildungsbericht 2008* (Bonn, 2008); Beauftragte für Migration, Flüchtlinge und Integration, ed., *Daten – Fakten – Trends: Bildung und Ausbildung* (Berlin, 2004).

87. Özcan, "Focus Migration Deutschland," 3; The group of people "with a migrant background" include in the official statistic everyone who migrated after 1949 in the FRG, as well as all children of migrants ("citizens" as well as "foreigners") who were born in the FRG. See Statistisches Bundesamt Deutschland, *Bevölkerung und Erwerbstätigkeit. Bevölkerung mit Migrationshintergrund—Ergebnisse des Mikrozensus 2005* (Bonn, 2007).

88. See OECD, Program for International Student Assessment (PISA), *Schülerleistungen im internationalen Vergleich. Im Auftrag der Kultusminister der Länder und in Zusammenarbeit mit dem Bundesministerium für Bildung und Forschung* (Bonn, 2001); Jürgen Baumert et al., eds, *Herkunftsbedingte Disparitäten im Bildungswesen: Differenzielle Bildungsprozesse und Probleme der Verteilungsgerechtigkeit: Vertiefende Analysen im Rahmen von PISA 2000* (Wiesbaden, 2006).

89. See BMFSFJ, *Ganztagsschule—eine Chance für Familien* (Berlin, 2006).

90. Sekretariat der KMK, *Allgemeinbildende Schulen in Ganztagsform in den Ländern in der Bundesrepublik Deutschland—Statistik 2002 bis 2006* (Bonn, 2008), 8 and 11.

91. Ibid., 4; see also BMFSFJ, *Zwölfter Kinder- und Jugendbericht. Bericht über die Lebenssituation junger Menschen und Leistungen der Kinder- und Jugendhilfe in Deutschland* (Berlin, 2005), 484–505; Deutsches Jugendinstitut e.V., *Abteilung Kinderbetreuung, Zahlenspiegel 2007. Kindertagesbetreuung im Spiegel der Statistik* (Dortmund, 2008), 55.

92. Barbara Gillmann, "Bund setzt Förderung fort: Die Ganztagsschule soll 2020 der Normalfall sein," *Handelsblatt*, 14 September 2008. Retrieved 14 February 2009: http://www.handelsblatt.com/politik/deutschland/die-ganztagsschule-soll-2020-der-normalfall-sein.

93. Christoph Kleßmann, "Abgrenzung und Verflechtung: Aspekte der geteilten und zusammengehörenden Nachkriegsgeschichte," *Aus Politik und Zeitgeschichte* 29/30 (1995): 30–41.

Chapter 14

FROM PART-TIME TO ALL DAY?

Time Policies in the Swiss Childcare, Preschool,
and Primary School System since 1945

Claudia Crotti

The public education system of the Swiss Confederation has undergone relatively few changes since it was institutionalized throughout the country during the first half of the nineteenth century. The Swiss political system is characterized above all by two closely linked principles: federalism and subsidiarity. Under the federal structure of the Swiss republic, the confederation possesses competency only where it is specifically empowered under the federal constitution. Prior to the passage of the new constitution in 2006, which enabled the creation of a more centralized and coordinated education policy, Switzerland's twenty-six cantons were responsible for compulsory education.[1] These cantons are politically autonomous, not merely administrative subdivisions of a centralized state. According to the principle of subsidiarity, a higher political authority should take on administrative responsibilities only if those authorities below it are unable to do so. The consequence of these basic political principles is a childcare and education policy that lacks coherences and raises questions about the efficient use of resources and an equal treatment of citizens.[2]

The differences between cantons are increased by the diverse cultural traditions of the German- (64 percent), French- (20 percent), and Italian- (7 percent) speaking parts of the country (the rest of the population speaks other native languages); a religious divide (41 percent of the Swiss citizens are Roman Catholic and 40 percent Protestant); as well as economic and social disparities between urban and rural regions. Switzerland stands among the most affluent countries in the Organisation for Economic Co-operation and Development, with a per capita GDP roughly 20 percent above the OECD average. There are considerable variations of income from

Notes for this chapter begin on page 317.

canton to canton, however, with the Canton Zurich (German) being one of the richest and the Canton Ticino (Italian) one of the poorest. Together with the Canton Vaud (French), these cantons constitute about 30 percent of the entire Swiss population. Zurich is also the largest canton in Switzerland in terms of both population size and density. All three cantons, moreover, have very high percentages of foreigners, as their nearness to national borders and their strong economies make them accessible and attractive to foreign workers. As a result, these cantons exhibit a high degree of ethnic and linguistic diversity, which poses special challenges for their childcare and education system.[3]

Despite the many political and cultural differences that separate them, the education systems in all Swiss cantons are based on a similar tripartite model consisting of preschool, primary school (in some cantons grades 1–4, in others grades 1–6), and secondary school levels (grades 5–9 or 7–9). Secondary education is organized according to achievement levels in different types of schools. Only the "more gifted students" move on to the *Gymnasiale Maturitätsschule* (a special form of high school), which, upon successful graduation (the *Matura*), qualifies them to study at a university. The five-day school week, moreover, is the norm across the country. Preschools and primary schools in the German-speaking regions are usually organized as "part-day schools," which are only open in the morning. In addition, preschool children attend one afternoon and first and second graders in primary school one or two afternoons each week. From the third grade on, students usually go to school every morning and up to three afternoons each week. However, they are rarely provided with lunch at school, which they usually take at home during a long lunch break. This makes it difficult for parents, in particular mothers, to combine family and work. In the French- and Italian-speaking parts of the country a divided school day with a long lunch break, during which students also usually eat at home, is the norm. They follow the model of the traditional divided all-day school.[4] Preschool children, however, generally attend for only a half-day period of three to four hours per day.[5] In most cantons, every child has the right to attend a preschool for one or two years before attending primary school. According to the OECD, childcare beyond the half-day preschool remains "underdeveloped" in comparison to most other European countries.[6] In 2004, the OECD reported that on average, 29 percent of children under the age of three in Switzerland attend some kind of formal childcare, usually a crèche. For children aged three to six, that number is somewhat higher at 39 percent (7 percent of three-year-olds, 31 percent of four-year-olds and 84 percent of five-year-olds).[7]

Despite these basic similarities, the twenty-six cantons differ in numerous and highly consequential ways. Although all cantons have established preschool institutions that are attended by a majority of Swiss children, only six cantons actually require children's attendance.[8] In addition, cantons set different age levels for entry into preschool. Primary school starts in most cantons at the age of six. In addition, the range of childcare options for young children still varies considerably, not only between the three main language regions (because of their different institutional and cultural traditions), but also between more urban areas and rural regions. According to a 1999 survey, in German-speaking Switzerland only 27 percent of all children under fifteen attended childcare, while in the French- and Italian-speaking parts some 35 percent did.[9] Particularly prominent are the differences in respect to all-day care: in the German- and French-speaking parts of the country, only 2 and 7 percent of all children under fifteen were enrolled in all-day childcare, respectively. In contrast, 33 percent of children in the Italian-speaking part were.[10]

The fact that the public education system in Switzerland provides school education and childcare only for a limited part of the day has proved to be a major problem for parents, and particularly mothers, seeking to reconcile family and paid work. The part-day system of most kindergartens, preschools, and primary schools, which the German-speaking part of Switzerland shares with Austria and Germany, requires that families look after children before school, at lunchtime, and after school. As a result of this time policy, most parents who seek all-day care are forced to combine several types of childcare, a situation that becomes even more difficult if they have more than one child requiring care.

The Swiss childcare and education system is—as is the country's entire family policy—based on the traditional model of the male-breadwinner family, a model that has been rendered increasingly obsolete by a variety of social changes. As is the case elsewhere in Europe, the general trend in Switzerland is that fewer women marry and their marriages are more likely to end in divorce.[11] Increasing numbers of married women seek paid employment outside of the home. In 1970, men were the sole breadwinners for 68 percent of two-parent families with children; in 2000, in almost 52 percent of the families both parents were engaged in paid work. Compared to the EU average of 70 percent, the Swiss employment rate of women aged twenty-five to sixty-four was high in 2000 at 78 percent. However, in the EU, 70 percent of all mothers with children under sixteen were employed, compared to only 60 percent in Switzerland. Moreover, the rate of female part-time work is, at 45 percent, the second highest in the OECD. For mothers with dependent children, this rate soars to almost 75 percent in Switzerland.[12] One consequence of the difficulties of combining family and paid work is Switzerland's very low birth rate of 1.4, one of the lowest rates in Europe. Similarly to West Germany, women in

Switzerland who want to pursue a professional career do not want to become mothers.[13]

These social changes have had a major influence on the public discourse on educational policy in Switzerland, which culminated in a soon-to-be-implemented reform that aims to effect a fundamental change to the Swiss education system. Among other things, this reform establishes a uniform age for children to enter school and standardizes the duration of the same school grades and their aims. In the future, upon reaching the age of four, all children will attend compulsory preschool for two years. At the same time, teaching hours will, whenever possible, be regular and fixed. Finally, the cantons will be responsible for providing supervision and childcare during the time spent outside of the classroom, for example, supervised lunch meals and after-school homework assistance.[14]

This shift in priorities in the organization of public education, which I explore in this chapter, reflects the social changes that have occurred since 1945. In order to reconstruct these changes, I first focus on the development in three areas—the economy, gender equality, and the family—that form the historical background. In a second step, I demonstrate how these changes have shaped discussions on time policies for childcare and schooling in the three main linguistic regions of Switzerland and explain the differences between them.

From "Housewife-and-Mother" to "Part-Time-Employed-Mother"

The ideal of the male-breadwinner family, according to which men were gainfully employed and women worked as housewives and mothers at home, prevailed for most of the twentieth century in Switzerland. But as was the case elsewhere in Europe, women from lower social strata always had to earn a living through paid work. In 1910, 47 percent of all women aged fifteen to sixty-four were employed. Many more worked in the agricultural sector, but their labor as "family assistants" was not counted in official statistics. In contrast to most other European countries, the female employment rate decreased in the following decades to 45 percent in 1920 and 35 percent in 1935. Those women who could afford to do so increasingly gave up their gainful employment outside the home upon getting married. Politically and socially influential voices, with the two major churches and conservative political parties and pressure groups leading the way, declared that married women's gainful employment was not only detrimental to family life and children's welfare, but politically and economically undesirable as well.[15]

This widespread sentiment concerning the employment of women only began to erode in the 1960s, when increasing numbers of wives without children and mothers with older children began working outside of the home. The female employment rate increased from 43 percent in 1971 to 58 percent in 2000. And yet still, female work for many years stayed within the widely accepted "three-phase model" for women's lives. This model legitimized women's employment before marriage, then denied it to them on the birth of their first child, before finally granting them the privilege to work outside the home again once their children had left home and they had fulfilled their family duties.[16]

Most of the expansion of female employment occurred in the service sector. While in the 1960s almost half of the Swiss workforce was still employed in the industrial sector, today nearly three-quarters (73 percent) are employed in the service sector. The expansion of this sector would have been unimaginable had female employment not increased dramatically during the last third of the century.[17] During this period, the ratio of working women in Switzerland rose dramatically: in the 1960s, one-third of all employees were women, while today they constitute half of the workforce.[18]

Most working women, however, work only part-time. The prevailing part-day time structure of the preschool and primary education system and the "underdeveloped" infrastructure of childcare have made it extremely difficult for women with children to balance family obligations and paid work. Moreover, women's attitude towards their working life outside the home helps to defuse potential conflicts over clashing family and job interests. And yet at the same time, it can also lead to job insecurity, less generous social security benefits, and much more limited prospects for further advancement. Mothers who work part-time continue to be constrained by the burden of combining work and family. Although no longer practical, the traditional family ideal in which the two sexes were assigned specific roles in the public and private spheres continues to shape patterns of women's employment, above all in regard to mothers who work part-time. As was the case in Austria and West Germany, the traditional model of the male-breadwinner family in Switzerland was simply replaced by a "modernized" variation of the same ideal: "the male-breadwinner/female homemaker and part-time-earner" family.[19]

According to a 2004 survey conducted by the Swiss Federal Bureau of Statistics, "Slightly more than one-quarter of all women with children under the age of fifteen would like to change their professional life and reduce the amount of time they spend taking care of their children so that they can either resume gainful employment or increase the number of hours that they work. For 44 percent of these mothers, the lack of suitable childcare services is the primary problem."[20] Helping women balance their working and private lives is thus a key issue for Swiss society.[21] In 2004, the OECD issued a report recommending that Switzerland should reform its childcare and education system by implementing childcare for small children and replacing the half-day time schedule for pre- and primary school and the full day interrupted by an extended lunchtime with continuous, all-day childcare, preschool, and primary schooling. Moreover, the report proposed that the Swiss state should invest in an extended "out-of school service," which, wherever possible, needs be integrated with schools in order to better "align children's schedules with parents work hours." The OECD judged that Switzerland, as one of the richest countries in the world, should be able to afford this reform.[22]

Towards Greater Gender Equality

As Switzerland modernized economically and socially in the decades following World War II, gender equality became enshrined in law. Still, it was not until 1971 that Swiss women were given the right to vote and be elected at the national level, making Switzerland the last Western country to grant women equal political rights. The two main reasons for this delay were the Swiss tradition of direct democracy (initiatives and referendums), which gives disproportionate influence to specific interest groups and can impede new policy initiatives and reforms, and widespread antifeminist sentiment in the male population.[23]

Until the 1960s, the consensus among the leading political parties was that the terms "Swiss" and "citizen" in the federal constitution's article pertaining to universal suffrage, which represented "a fundamental principle of the federal public law," applied solely to male Swiss citizens.[24] The same antifeminist attitude prevailed among the male voting population, which rejected the legislative proposal for equal women's suffrage in 1959. When in 1968 the federal government planned, although with reservations, to sign the European Convention on Human Rights, feminists protested. Switzerland, they argued, had not yet introduced women's suffrage, and thus stood in open breach of the regulations of the Human Rights Convention. Faced with this deadlock, the government finally chose to grant women equal active and passive suffrage. On 7 February 1971, 66 percent of the male voters voted in favor and 35 percent against the introduction of women's franchise; eight cantons (of twenty-six) rejected the female vote altogether.[25] This decision on the national level was followed by the cantons, which gradually introduced women's political participation at the cantonal and communal levels. It was not until the early 1990s, however, that equal political rights for women were fully implemented throughout the country.

Women's entry into the arena of politics prompted a fundamental dispute about the position of women in society. The legal inequality of the sexes with regard to employment, family, upbringing, and education became an increasingly important topic of public discussion. As a result, the following article on gender equality was adopted in the federal constitution in 1983: "Men and women have equal rights. The law ensures their legal and actual equality, especially with regard to the family, education, and to employment. Men and women are entitled to the same salary for equal work."[26] Finally, in April 1997, Switzerland ratified the UN Convention on the Elimination of All Forms of Discrimination Against Women, again one of the last countries to do so.

From Charitable to Family-Friendly Policies

While the "protection of the family" remained the guiding principle of welfare policy well into the 1970s, the growing participation of women in political life in the following decades gradually brought a change in direction. The compatibility of family work and gainful employment occupied an increasingly prominent place in the formulation of family policies. In 1982, a federal task force issued a report on Swiss family policies that recommended the expansion of facilities to support families and the reform of school organization. One of the specific reforms proposed by the task force dealt with all-day schools: "Gainfully employed mothers have a need for all-day schools. Other groups also demand such schools as an alternative to the current school system, not least of all as a way of advancing equal opportunities."[27] Although the report met with approval and there was increasing acceptance of the fact that the compatibility of working in the family and gainful employment outside of the home was a key issue that needed to be addressed, the government made little effort to implement its recommendations.

In the 1990s, however, the situation began to change. By then it had become clear that more and more women and men were refraining from having children. The number of children in Switzerland had dropped steadily since the 1960s. The birth rate declined from 2.3 in 1960 to 1.5 in 1990.[28] When asked why they were not having children, the majority of men and women cited the difficulty "women have in combining motherhood and gainful employment."[29] In his speech presenting the Swiss family report of 2004, Pascal Couchepin, a member of the Federal Council, emphasized that the realization of the desire to have children is inextricably linked to the difficulties of reconciling professional and family life. Helping families do this should, he thus concluded, become a priority for policymakers. The cornerstones of any sustainable family policies must include the standardization of time schedules for preschool and primary school, early school entry, and an increase in the number of crèches. He also noted that "the number of all-day schools offered at the cantonal level needs to be increased as well."[30]

As a result of the family report from 2004, the question of all-day childcare and schools quickly climbed to the top of the political agenda and became a focus of public discussion. In March 2000, Jacqueline Fehr, a member of the National Council, submitted a parliamentary initiative that requested initial state funding for the expansion of daycare facilities and all-day schools. The following year, the National Council took the initiative into consideration and appropriated 200 million Swiss Francs for the first four years. This financial contribution focused on three kinds of facilities: nurseries, day-care families (*Tagesfamilien*), and "out-of-school care" facilities. This third type applied specifically to school-aged children. "Out-of-school care is offered outside of compulsory school hours, i.e., in the morning before school starts, during lunch, and in the afternoon after school."[31] Such out-of-school childcare is thus to be expanded throughout Switzerland in the coming years. And yet still, there is no coherent plan for how this expansion is to be implemented. Instead, in keeping with the federalist tradition in Swiss education policies, cantons have simply expanded their already existing facilities for out-of-school care, i.e., these facilities have developed differently in the French, Italian, and German parts of the country.

All-Day Schools and Out-of-School Childcare Facilities in Switzerland Today

All-Day Schools in the German-Speaking Part of Switzerland

During the previous decades, the preferred form of "out-of-school" care in the German-speaking part of Switzerland became the all-day school (*Tagesschule*). While only 14 of these schools existed in all of Switzerland in 2000, by 2007 their number had risen to 83, with places for 4,660 students. This number is still very low when compared to the existing three thousand Swiss school communities (*Schulgemeinden*), only 3 percent of which have an all-day school. The vast majority of all-day schools are located in only three of the twenty German-speaking cantons:[32] Bern (33 schools for 1,306 students), Zurich (20 schools for 1,001 students), and Basel (city) (11 schools for 317 students) in 2007.[33] Most all-day schools are located in urban regions, where the percentage of working mothers, married or single, is usually much higher.[34]

The currently existing all-day schools, which are usually open from 7:00 A.M. until 6:00 P.M., are part of the public school system. They provide school education *and* care throughout the day. They offer supervision before the start of the school day, morning lessons, and a lunch at noon. In addition, they provide courses in the afternoon, help with homework, and organize recreational activities after school. Teaching and care occur in the same location, with pedagogic personnel and teachers working under one management as part of a single team. Teaching in all-day schools is based on the cantonal curricula, which can differ from canton to canton. The size of all-day schools, however, varies greatly, with the smallest among them teaching and supervising as few as 12 children and the largest up to 150.[35] Another factor contributing to the wide variety of all-day schools is the difference in respect to the grade levels they encompass. Of the 83 existing all-day schools, 22 include pre- and primary school, 38 are primary schools only, while a further 19 institutions accommodate all levels including the secondary school (6 starting in preschool and 13 in primary school).[36] Thus, up until now, all-day schools have catered primarily to the educational and care needs of children between the ages of five and twelve.

Despite the great diversity among them, all-day schools can be grouped into two main types—*compulsory* and *voluntary*. In compulsory all-day schools, children are required to participate in extracurricular activities on a regular basis, as they are considered an integral part of the overarching pedagogical philosophy. While offering out-of-school activities, voluntary open all-day schools, in contrast, do not require children to participate in them. Moreover, like the compulsory all-day schools, voluntary schools offer teaching, supervised lunches, help with homework, and recreational activities. The pupils can, however, choose for each semester of the school year which recreational activities they wish to attend and for how many days each week.[37] Of the sixty-four all-day schools that exist in the German- and French-speaking parts of Switzerland, fifty are voluntary and fourteen compulsory. Voluntary all-day schools have proven to be more easily adaptable to parents' needs and wishes than compulsory all-day schools, especially since only a minority of parents desires comprehensive care facilities during the whole week.[38] According to a survey conducted by the city of Bern, a mere one-third of parents use more than three child-care units per week.[39]

All-day schools are funded by three groups of people or institutions: public funds furnished by local communities and cantons, parents, and private sponsors. Parents' contributions are calculated according to two models: a fixed fee or a flexible amount based on their income. In the first instance, all parents pay the same amount for their children to attend all-day school. Siblings, moreover, are usually admitted at a reduced rate. In the second model, parents' contribution is deducted as a portion of their taxable income. Sixty-four all-day schools prefer the second model, while only twelve all-day schools require the same fixed monthly fee from all parents, which ranges from 300 to 720 Swiss francs.[40]

The institutionalization of all-day schools in Switzerland has occurred relatively recently, and only after having been demanded in the 1970s and 1980s by women's organizations, left-wing parties, and alternative groups.[41] At first, parliamentary initiatives concerning the introduction of all-day schools in the cantons of Basel, Bern, and Zurich were rejected by cantonal administrations. When in 1972 one of the first political initiatives was submitted in the city of Basel, the local government dismissed the request, arguing, "The advocates are not primarily concerned with easing individual hardship and the hardships of particular groups of the population, but instead have launched the idea of all-day schools as part of a social agenda regarding gender relations."[42] The majority of politicians were neither in favor of the concept of gender equality nor aware of the problems of reconciling paid work and family. However, because of the changes in the economy, gender equality, and family life, they were unable to push the issue of all-day schools off the table completely. Therefore, the cantonal authorities responded by allowing local communities to introduce all-day schools on a trial basis, as "laboratory schools." In doing so, the state effectively passed the initiative off to local groups and dedicated teachers, who then pushed the idea of all-day schools further through their work as volunteers. Indeed, they formed the nucleus out of which the cantonal all-day school associations would be established. One of the first was the All-Day School Association for the Canton Zurich, which was founded in 1974.[43]

Permission to found the first all-day school was granted to local communities by Zurich's Cantonal Council of Education in 1974. Six years later, school authorities in the city Zurich founded the first two all-day schools in a working-class neighborhood, where the majority of the mothers worked outside the home and had to leave their children alone and unsupervised.[44] The hope of the local authorities was that the all-day schools would create a more favorable environment that would enhance the quality of education and equal opportunity while at the same time improving the socialization of children and preventing delinquency.[45] Basel and Bern followed the example of Zurich for similar reasons, albeit slowly and with a good deal of hesitation. By the end of the 1980s, a total of five all-day schools had been established in Switzerland.

In addition to the pedagogical and social reasons for the founding of all-day schools, geographical and economical arguments also played a role. The first all-day school in the French-speaking part of Switzerland opened in Vissoie (Valais) in 1991. Because the villages in the Val d'Anniviers lie relatively far apart from one another, the walk to school can take up to forty minutes. School officials thus decided to establish the central school as an all-day school for the whole valley. As the number of pupils declined, smaller communities in the German-speaking part also began to see all-day school facilities and services as a way to keep their local schools open and thus remain attractive for families with children.[46]

It was not until the 1990s that the all-day school issue received further impetus for expansion. While women's organizations, left-wing parties, and alternative groups had been the main advocates of all-day schools in the 1970s and 1980s, more mainstream groups now began to embrace the idea.[47] The major middle-class parties, including the Liberal Democratic Party and the Christian Democratic Party, as well as important economic interest groups called for the creation of new all-day schools as a way of meeting the new challenges posed by the economy, gender equality, family policy, and demographic changes. The recommendations of the Swiss Conference of Cantonal Education Ministers in 1992 lent further and particularly crucial support for this proposal. Cantons that in the 1970s had shied away from regulating the issue of all-day schools by law now put it squarely on their political agenda. As a result, since the end of the 1990s, the number of all-day schools has increased significantly. While only twenty-two all-day schools were founded in the 1990s, another sixty-seven all-day schools have been opened since 2000.[48] Despite this rapid increase in the number of all-day schools, it is still too early to speak of an actual trend in their direction.

Out-of-School Childcare in the French-Speaking Part of Switzerland

In the French-speaking part of Switzerland, which encompasses four cantons in which French is the only official language and three where both French and German are spoken, all-day schools in the form of the conjunct *Tagesschule* are almost completely unknown. Only in the Canton of Vissoie do we find a similar institution (*écoles à horaire continu*).[49] Instead, in this region, schools follow the traditional French model of time policy: they are divided all-day schools with lessons in the morning and the afternoon, interrupted by a long lunch break. Thus they needed another form of out-of-school childcare. In August 1999, the Canton Vaud started a regionwide system of "all-day childcare centers for school children," the so-called *accueils pour enfants en milieu scolaire* (APEMS). The major aim of these centers is to provide out-of-school supervision for seven- to ten-year-old children in the first four grades of primary school, which is necessary because of the specific time structure of schools in the French-speaking part.

Since their introduction, the number of children enrolled in APEMS has increased by about 15 percent each year. But most of the centers were founded in Lausanne, where in 2005 about one-third (1,300) of all children in compulsory education (4,700) attended one.[50] Only parents who are gainfully employed or who are pursuing higher education or job training can take advantage of this childcare option. Most centers are open "between 7:00 A.M. and 8:30 A.M., during lunchtime, and from 4:30 P.M to 6:00 P.M," and offer numerous opportunities for learning and playing. Children can also receive help with their homework. Although these centers are closed during the long school holidays in the summer, they continue to offer recreational activities. A lead staff member with pedagogical training and untrained "monitors" supervise the children. If the school buildings can accommodate them, the centers are located in the primary schools themselves. In many school districts of the city of Lausanne, however, they are situated in apartments. Each semester parents must renew their enrollment, and fees depend on the family income. The local communities cover 67 percent of the costs.[51]

The situation in the other communities of the Canton Vaud is very different. Although most of them offer childcare facilities for children in compulsory education, with a great deal of variation in regard to both their enrollment capacity and the facilities, they fell short a staggering six thousand-plus places in out-of-school childcare facilities in 2004 alone.[52] The financial burden on the parents for out-of-school childcare thus differs considerably in the communities, with many having to rely on very expensive private childcare services.[53] To address this situation, the new 2003 constitution of the canton declared that the canton and its constituent communities, in cooperation with private partners, should seek to create both preschool and out-of-school care facilities for children (Art. 63, Par. 2). A law that went into effect in January 2007 details these intentions and regulates the preschool and out-of-school care facilities for children up to the age of twelve. Its primary goal is to ensure a sufficient number of places in childcare facilities and the quality of the childcare services they offer, and make childcare fees more affordable for parents. To accomplish this goal, the law also created a foundation tasked with coordinating daycare facilities for children. Although this expansion of out-of-school care facilities is based on already existing structures, it seeks to expand preschool nurseries, out-of-school childcare facilities, and care within day families.[54]

Like the Canton Vaud, the Canton Geneva has declared that out-of-school childcare facilities are the responsibility of the canton. Since 1994, it has thus been working to expand childcare facilities in thirty-nine of its forty local communities.[55] An Intercommunal Group for Extracurricular Services has been placed in charge of all childcare facilities throughout the canton. Here too, three time units of childcare—in the morning, noontime, and afternoon—are available and complement the all-day time structure of the schools. While only three out of forty-five local communities provide childcare before the start of school in the morning, thirty-eight do offer childcare during the noon break and another thirty-one after school. Only three communities in the entire canton provide childcare for the entire day.[56]

On the whole, with the exception of Geneva and Lausanne, childcare facilities inside and outside of schools are not well developed in the French-speaking part of Switzerland. Smaller towns and rural communities spend considerably less for childcare than the two cities. At the present time, there are also no plans to introduce conjunct all-day schools similar to those in the German-speaking part of the country. Rather, new legislation from the Canton Vaud suggests that it will expand its own model of out-of-school childcare in the future, which, unlike the *Tagesschulen* in the German-speaking part of the country, does not have a common pedagogical philosophy and a single management and will not combine teaching and childcare in a shared space.[57]

All-Day and Out-of-School Childcare in the Italian-Speaking Part of Switzerland

For several decades now, the Canton Ticino, the center of the Italian-speaking part of Switzerland with two cantons, has been pursuing comprehensive family-friendly policies, including the expansion of childcare.[58] Here too, out-of-school childcare has historically followed a different path, one that was geared to the Italian childcare and education system. In this system, the focus of early childhood education has and continues to be preschools (*scuola dell'infanzia*), which in 2004 were attended by 58 percent of three-year-old children, 95 percent of four-year-olds, and 100 percent of five-year-olds in the entire Canton Ticino.[59]

The first *scuola dell'infanzia* was established in Lugarno in 1844 as a way of dealing with the consequences of neglected children as more and more working-class women entered factory employment. Following the model of the Italian School Law from 1923—the so-called Gentile Reform—the Canton Ticino increasingly understood the education of young children as a task of both the state and society.[60] Preschools were perceived as an important part of the public education system. As was the case in Italy, after World War II a reform pedagogical approach influenced by the ideas of Maria Montessori became increasingly common.[61]

Following Montessori pedagogic philosophy, three- to five-year-old children are educated together in mixed-age groups, which are allowed a maximum of twenty-five children. In these groups, children learn, play, and work together. Teachers and staff aim to foster children's cognitive development and motor and communication skills. They cooperate closely with parents to improve children's social skills in preparation for primary school. In close consultation with parents, they also determine how long children attend preschool. During the first few months in preschool, most three-year-old children come only in the mornings or in the afternoons, but are required to attend lessons for at least four half-days per week. The length of attendance is then steadily increased so that, by the age of four, children usually attend for the whole day.[62]

The new School Law of the Canton Ticino from 1996 defined the *scuola dell'infanzia* not only, as the former law had, as part of the education system, but also stipulated that the communities need to provide preschool and all-day childcare for children aged three to six, usually from 8:30 A.M. until 4 P.M., with a supervised common lunch. Today, 78 percent of preschools in the Ticino are equipped accordingly.[63] During summer vacation, which lasts from mid-June to the beginning of September, preschools are, like all other schools, closed. The costs of the *scuola dell'infanzia* are covered by the local communities, which in some instances are subsidized by the canton. In addition, parents pay on average a monthly fee of 60 Swiss Francs for the school meals.[64]

After-school programs are sometimes available, but mostly concentrated in the urban municipalities. However, the new School Law from 1996 encouraged the development of "school centers" (*istituti scolastici*), which encompass preschools and primary schools, especially in localities with high numbers of students. Until then, separate laws had existed for each school level. This new legislation regulates both pre- and primary schools, which both follow like in the French areas the tradition of the divided all-day school. The intention of the law was not to create a new school model for all children between the ages of three and ten, but instead was prompted by the desire to improve the quality of education in different school districts by linking them together more closely. Thus preschool, which is not compulsory in the Canton Ticino, emerged in the new law as a more integral part of the state's educational system.[65]

Although it does not provide childcare for the entire day, the Canton Ticino does possess a fairly well developed childcare system for children between the ages of three and five in preschools that parents can take advantage of. Similar childcare opportunities are also available to some extent for older children in the primary school system, as are supervised lunches and after-school supervision. Nonetheless, there remains a clear difference between pre- and primary school in Ticino. While preschools are required by law to provide lunch for children, primary schools are not. Local communities are only required to provide lunch if children live too far from school. Thus, it comes as little surprise that only one-third of all primary schools provide supervised lunch for their students. In contrast, nearly two-thirds of all secondary schools, which are administered and financed by the canton, have their own cafeterias, although this is largely due to the fact that they are centrally located and serve several communities.[66] Thus, the situation in the Canton Ticino also creates serious problems for parents who are trying to balance family and paid work.[67]

Conclusion

Changes in the economy, gender equality, and the family as well as the impact of globalization have together contributed to the emergence of new social needs that have had an enormous effect on the childcare and education system in Switzerland. In order to meet these needs, politicians have been forced to pay more attention to these policy fields. The country's educational landscape, which has long since been shaped by a federalist political system, has reacted to these challenges by implementing a new policy that aims for greater coordination and standardization among the cantons. The goal, however, is not just a greater level of standardization of the vastly different education systems in its twenty-six cantons and thus more equal chances for children from different social and ethnic backgrounds, but also their expansion so that they can meet new social and economic needs. Recent attempts at reform include increasing the duration of compulsory school education, implementing new quality standards, and expanding conjunct all-day schooling (at least in the German-speaking part) so that parents can more effectively combine the responsibilities of work and family.

Above all, these reforms, guided by new concepts of social and gender equality, have made it easier for women to pursue better job opportunities. And with more and more women entering the work force, tax revenues have increased. Moreover, an array of new family supplements have been implemented to help single parents and lower-income families avoid falling into poverty, thus reducing the national poverty rate overall. Finally, the human capital represented by mothers can contribute more effectively to the labor market and, by extension, the economy in general.[68] There exists today a widespread consensus in Switzerland that policies designed to support families, although driven by the narrower interests of specific groups, are a crucial part of the solution to numerous social problems. As new federal funding suggests, there are plans to expand nurseries and increase the availability of childcare in day families.

Policies, institutions, and cultural traditions with deep historical roots have shaped the responses of the cantonal education systems to the new demands for greater access to all-day childcare and education. While in the German-speaking part of Switzerland, the conjunct all-day school model is increasingly being implemented and may one day become the norm, a similar trend cannot be observed in either the French- or Italian-speaking parts of the country, where the traditional divided all-day school is still dominant, and the idea of a modern conjunct all-day school like the *Tagesschule* has yet to gain more widespread influence in educational discourse. Whereas associations that lobbied for modern conjunct all-day schools had been founded in the 1970s in the German-speaking part of the country, it was not until 2004 and 2006 that similar organizations were established in the French- and Italian-speaking parts, respectively.

According to the official definition of all-day schools in Switzerland, the various forms of out-of-school childcare in both the French- and Italian-speaking parts of Switzerland cannot be correctly called modified versions of the modern conjunct all-day school. Above all, childcare and teaching are perceived as separate spheres that are not unified by a common pedagogical philosophy. Instead, childcare services and the school system have and continue to develop independently of each other. As a result, in many cantons, childcare and school education are even the responsibilities of different administrative departments. "The varying arrangements of services offered are no longer up-to-date, which makes both overall conception and planning more difficult."[69]

In light of the state's increased financial commitment to providing out-of-school childcare, the conjunct all-day schools in the German-speaking part of Switzerland will in all likelihood undergo further expansion, especially in the suburbs. However, modern conjunct all-day schools are unlikely to become the dominant model of education for the entire country, as the long-term issue of cost, despite the state's initial funding, has not been resolved and the benefits of such schools have only been seen in Zurich, Berne, Vaud, and Aargau. Moreover, the firmly entrenched tradition of federalism places clear limits on any unified, nationwide educational policy. Especially the cantons in the French- and Italian-speaking parts of Switzerland are likely to pursue their individual paths regarding the question of childcare services, with many choosing to maintain diverse models of all-day education and childcare over a single unified all-day school model, the *Tagesschule*. Nevertheless, this form of education will be also in the future an important model for school reform. But, as the Swiss Association of All-Day Schools declared in 2007, "If children, parents, the economy, and society as a whole should benefit from a school with a comprehensive range of services provided by professionals, day schools must be free of charge for parents. This is our vision for 2012: In five years there will be day schools in Switzerland for everybody, and they will be free of charge."[70] It remains to be seen whether this goal becomes a reality.

Notes

I would like to thank Marianne Junger and Brandon Hunziker for their translation of the text and Karen Hagemann for her careful editing.

1. See Daniel Bochsler et al., eds., *Die Schweizer Kantone unter der Lupe. Behörden, Personal, Finanzen* (Bern, 2005).
2. OECD, *Babies and Bosses. Reconciling Work and Family Life*, vol. 3, *New Zealand, Portugal and Switzerland* (Paris, 2004), 49.
3. Ibid., 18 and 35.
4. For more, see Franzisca Regi and Hans Furer, *Schulsysteme der Schweiz. Eine tabellarische Übersicht des Bildungswesens in der Schweiz* (Basel, 1996); Schweizerische Konferenz der Kantonalen Erziehungsdirektoren, Studiengruppe Bildung und Erziehung der vier- bis achtjährigen Kinder im schweizerischen Bildungswesen, *Bildung und Erziehung der vier- bis achtjährigen Kinder in der Schweiz. Die Basisstufe als Ort für die Bildung und Erziehung der vier- bis achtjährigen Kinder in der Schweiz* (Bern, 1997); Der schweizerische Bildungsserver, *Das schweizerische Bildungssystem*. Retrieved 8 September 2008: http://www.educa.ch/dyn/73136.asp.
5. OECD, *Babies and Bosses*, 3: 95.
6. OECD, "Give Swiss Working Mothers More Support to Avoid Labour Shortages and Foster Economic Growth," 24 October 2004. Retrieved 8 September 2008: http://www.oecd.org/document/57/0,2340,en_2649_34487_33844665_1_1_1_1,00.html.
7. OECD, *Babies and Bosses*, 3: 97.
8. *Statistisches Jahrbuch der Schweiz* (Zurich, 2007), 343.
9. Council of Europe, *Conference of European Ministers, Familiy Affairs, XXVI Session, National Reports: Social Cohesion and Quality of Life, Switzerland* (Stockholm, 1999).
10. OECD, *Babies and Bosses*, 3: 97f.
11. The rate of first female marriages decreased from 0.66 to 0.58 between 1980 and 2001, while during the same period the divorce rate increased form 31 to 44 per hundred marriages. OECD, *Babies and Bosses*, 3: 41.
12. Ibid., 77 and 81; OECD, *Babies and Bosses — Reconciling Work and Family Life: A Synthesis of Findings for OECD Countires* (Paris, 2007), 44–47.
13. OECD, *Babies and Bosses — Reconciling*, 16. See for West Germany the chapter by Karen Hagemann in this volume.
14. Schweizerische Konferenz der kantonalen Erziehungsdirektoren, ed., "Harmonisierung der obligatorischen Schule Schweiz (HarmoS). Kurz-Information." Retrieved 25 January 2007: http://www.edudoc.ch/static/web/aktuell/medienmitt/harmos_kurzinfo_d.pdf.
15. See Anne-Lise Head-König, "Frauenwerbsarbeit," in *Historisches Lexikon der Schweiz* (Bern, 1998–2008). Retrieved 8 September 2008: http://hls-dhs-dss.ch/textes/d/D13908.php; Regina Wecker and Brigitte Schnegg, eds., *Frauen. Zur Geschichte weiblicher Arbeits- und Lebensbedingungen in der Schweiz* (Basel, 1984).

16. See Alva Myrdal and Viola Klein, *Women's Two Roles: Home and Work* (London, 1956).

17. *Statistisches Jahrbuch der Schweiz*, 81.

18. A person is considered as gainfully employed part-time if she or he works for less than 90 percent of the working hours. See Bundesamt für Statistik, *Teilzeitarbeit in der Schweiz*. Retrieved 25 January 2007: http://www.bfs.admin.ch/bfs/portal/de/index/themen/03/22/publ.html?publicationID=2328.

19. Francois Höpflinger, "Familie und Beruf heute—ausgewählte statistische Informationen," in *Zeit für Familien. Beiträge zur Vereinbarkeit von Familien- und Erwerbsalltag aus familienpolitischer Sicht*, ed. Eidgenössische Koordinationskommission für Familienfragen (Bern, 2004), 35–51.

20. Bundesamt für Statistik, *Wichtigste Ergebnisse der Schweizerischen Kräfteerhebung* (Neuchâtel, 2005), 8.

21. OECD, "Give Swiss Working Mothers More Support."

22. Ibid.

23. See Claudia Weilenmann and Eva Sutter, *Frauen, Macht, Geschichte: Frauen- und gleichstellungspolitische Ereignisse in der Schweiz 1848–1998* (Bern, 1998/99).On the history of the movement for women's suffrage in Switzerland, see Sibylle Hardmeier, *Frühe Frauenstimmrechts-Bewegung in der Schweiz (1890–1930): Argumente, Strategien, Netzwerk und Gegenbewegung* (Zurich, 1997).

24. Schweizerischer Verband für Frauenstimmrecht, *Frauenstimmrecht in der Schweiz* (Zurich, 1950), 7.

25. Lotti Ruckstuhl and Lydia Benz-Burger, *Frauen sprengen Fesseln: Hindernislauf zum Frauenstimmrecht in der Schweiz* (Bonstetten, 1986), 151.

26. Bundesverfassung der Schweizerischen Eidgenossenschaft vom 18. April 1999, art. 8. Retrieved 8 August 2006: http://www.admin.ch/ch/d/sr/1/101.de.pdf.

27. Arbeitsgruppe Familienpolitik, *Familienpolitik in der Schweiz* (Bern, 1982), 53.

28. Globalis, *Switzerland: Total Fertility Rate*, 1855–2005. Retrieved 8 September 2008: http://globalis.gvu.unu.edu/indicator_detail.cfm?IndicatorID=138&Country=CH.

29. Alexis Gabadinho, *Mikrozensus Familie in der Schweiz 1994/95* (Bern, 1998), 33.

30. Eidgenössisches Departement des Innern, *Familienbericht 2004. Strukturelle Anforderungen an eine bedürfnisgerechte Familienpolitik* (Bern, 2004), 6. Retrieved 8 September 2008: http://www.bsv.admin.ch/themen/zulagen/00058/01380/index.html?lang=de.

31. Bericht der Kommission für soziale Sicherheit und Gesundheit des Nationalrates. *Parlamentarische Initiative Anstossfinanzierung für familienergänzende Betreuungsplätze*, 22.2.2002. Retrieved 8 September 2008: http://www.admin.ch/ch/d/ff/2002/4219.pdf.

32. In 16 of 17 cantons German is the offical language; in 3 German and French are offical languages.

33. Verein Tagesschulen Schweiz, *Tagesschulen Schweiz—Übersicht* (Zurich, 2007), 1–4.

34. Susan Wirz, "Sollen Tagesschulen in der Schweiz eingeführt werden?" (MA thesis, University of Basel, 1998), 15.

35. Christian Aeberli and Hans-Martin Binder, *Das Einmaleins der Tagesschule* (Bern, 2005).

36. Verein Tagesschulen Schweiz, *Tagesschulen Schweiz*, 1–4.

37. Aeberli and Binder, *Das Einmaleins*, 117.

38. Markus Mauchle, "Die öffentliche Tagesschule in der Schweiz," *Schulverwaltung*, no. 1 (2003): 45.

39. Renate Stohler Berger, "Tagesschule—eine Schulform der Zukunft?" (MA thesis, University of Bern, 2000).

40. Hans-Martin Binder et al., *Handbuch für die Planung und Realisierung öffentlicher Tagesschulen* (Zurich, 2000), 73–75.

41. Max Mangold and Andreas Messerli, "Die Ganzstagsschule in der Schweiz," in *Die Ganztagsschule,* ed. Volker Ladenthin and Jürgen Rekus (Weinheim, 2005), 108.
42. Quoted after Wirz, "Sollen Tagesschulen," 4.
43. Mangold and Messerli, "Die Ganzstagsschule in der Schweiz," 108.
44. Wirz, "Sollen Tagesschulen," 4.
45. Aeberli and Binder, *Das Einmaleins,* 38.
46. Binder, *Handbuch,* 6–10.
47. Mangold and Messerli, "Die Ganzstagsschule," 108f.
48. Ibid.; Verein Tagesschulen Schweiz, *Tagesschulen Schweiz.*
49. Gabriela Chaves, *Etude sur l'accueil extrascolaire en Suisse Romande menée pour la Verein Tagesschulen Schweiz.* Retrieved 25 January 2007: http://www.tagesschulen.ch/Download .html.
50. Ibid.
51. Aeberli and Binder, *Das Einmaleins,* 44.
52. Chaves, *Etude,* 31–35.
53. Philipp Lavenchy and Gabriela Chaves, "Vorentwurf für ein Gesetz des Kantons Waadt über familienergänzende Betreuungsstrukturen für Kinder im Alter von null bis zwölf Jahren," in *Educare: betreuen—erziehen—bilden,* ed. Schweizerische Konferenz der kantonalen Erziehungsdirektoren (Bern, 2005), 73–78.
54. Philippe Lavanchy, "La Loi sur l'accueil du jour des enfants est en marche." Retrieved 13 December 2006: http://www.avenirsocial.ch.
55. Chaves, *Etude,* 17.
56. Ibid.
57. Verein Tagesschulen Schweiz, ed., *Qualitätsmerkmale von Tagesschulen.* Retrieved 8 September 2008: http://www.tagesschulen.ch/PDF/Qualitaetsmerkmale.pdf.
58. Ticino is the only canton in which Italian is the only offical language. In the Canton Grisson, Italian and German are spoken.
59. OECD, *Babies and Bosses,* 3: 97.
60. On the Italian development and the Gentile Reform, see the chapter by Cristina Allemann-Ghionda in this volume.
61. Mangold and Messerli, "Die Ganzstagsschule," 108f.
62. Aeberli and Binder, *Das Einmaleins,* 40.
63. Legge sulla scuola dell'infanzia e sulla scuola elementare del 7 febbraio 1996, della Repubblica e Cantone Ticino. Retrieved January 2007: http://www.ti.ch/CAN/argomenti/ leislaz/rleggi/rl/dati_rl/f/f/05_04.htm.
64. Aeberli and Binder, *Das Einmaleins,* 40.
65. Dipartimento dell'istruzione e della cultura: Divisione della schola—Ufficio dell'educazione prescolastica, ed., *La Scuola dell'infanzia nel Cantone Ticino.* Retrieved 8 September 2008: http://www.scuoladecs.ti.ch/ordini_scuola/asilo_riforme.htm.
66. Aeberli and Binder, *Das Einmaleins,* 41.
67. OECD, *Babies and Bosses,* 3: 96; Cesiro Guidotti and Barbara Rigoni, *La scuola ticinese in cifre 2005.* Retrieved 14 January 2007: http://www.ti.ch/decs/ds/usr/download/ Ticifre2005.pdf.
68. Beat Uebelhart and Barbara Krattiger, *Anstossfinanzierung des Bundes für familienergänzende Kinderbetreuung. Quo vadis?* Retrieved 14 January 2007: http://www.edk.ch/xd/ 2005/35.pdf, 26.
69. Ibid., 36.
70. Verein Tagesschulen Schweiz, *Tagesschulen für alle und zwar gratis.* Retrieved 7 October 2007: http://www.tagesschulen.ch/PDF/Vision2012_d.pdf.

Section C

All-Day Childcare and Part-Time Pre- and Primary School Systems in Eastern Europe

Chapter 15

BEYOND IDEOLOGY

The Time Policy of Russian School Education since 1945

Anatoli Rakhkochkine

Since the Russian Revolution of 1917, time policy in Soviet school educa-tion has been driven not only by the desire to increase the effectiveness of education and issues of children's health but also by ideology, economic considerations, demographic changes, and family policy. This basic path did not change after World War II. Although ravaged by the war, the Soviet Union emerged victorious from the conflict and became an acknowledged superpower and the primary model for other communist states during the Cold War. Since the dissolution of the Soviet Union in 1991, almost all former Soviet republics, including the Russian Federation, have disman-tled their centrally planned economies and adopted neoliberal, market-oriented policies. After a period of turmoil during the economic transition in the 1990s, rising oil prices, increased foreign investment, higher domes-tic consumption, and greater political stability have bolstered economic growth in Russia since the turn of the century.

This development also influenced changes in the time policy of the Russian childcare and education system, which will be the focus of this study. Together with the above-mentioned economic, political, social, and cultural factors, it produced a wide-ranging mix of all-day provisions, in-cluding boarding schools, extended-day programs, all-day schools, all-day and all-year educational provision, and extracurricular activities. In the 1950s and 1960s, the expansion of all-day education in the Soviet Union was motivated above all by both economic and ideological motives. As was the case in other communist countries, the Soviet state faced a labor shortage that compelled it to bring more married women, in particular mothers, into the workforce. To do this, the government needed to expand

---

Notes for this chapter begin on page 340.

all-day childcare and education. Because of a dramatically declining birth rate, in the 1970s and 1980s the extension of all-day education became an important part of a broader pronatalist family policy that sought to increase the fertility rate. After the dissolution of the Soviet Union and the transition to a neoliberal economy, diminishing financial resources forced the Russian state to rapidly dismantle the public system of all-day education of the communist regime. Today, educational experts and state officials advocate a return to all-day schooling for two main reasons. On the one hand, they now see all-day schools and after-school programs as a way to provide additional time for learning and thus reduce stress on students. By extending the school day, they hope to create a healthier learning environment for school children. On the other hand, the growing need to care for homeless and neglected children has motivated Russian politicians to expand all-day education.[1] One indicator for the latter is the high percentage of children of primary school age (seven to nine years old) who are not attending school, which according to a UNESCO report stood at 11 percent in 2001–2002, compared to an average of 2 percent in the industrialized countries of the West.[2]

As was the case under Soviet rule, Russian school education today is provided predominantly by the state and regulated by the Federal Ministry of Education. Regional and local authorities govern the school system within the framework of federal laws.[3] Compulsory education, which was introduced in the communist period, starts at the age of seven and lasted first six and later ten years. It was and remains free. In September 2007 it was extended to eleven years. Today children are accepted to the first grade at the age of six or seven, depending on their individual development. The eleven-year school term is split into primary (grades 1–4), middle (grades 5–9), and senior (grades 10–11) classes. The absolute majority of children attend full program schools providing an eleven-year education. Schools limited to primary or middle grades are located predominantly in rural areas. Everywhere, the school capacity is so insufficient that students often cannot be taught on the normal morning to afternoon schedule. Local authorities have to resort to "double shift schools" in which two groups of students in a morning and evening shift share the same facility. Of the 59,260 schools in Russia, in 2007–2008, more than 13,100 were taught in "double shifts" and 75 even in "triple shifts," compared to 19,201 and 235, respectively, in 2001–2002.[4] In these schools, as in many others, a half- or part-time school schedule is common.[5]

Kindergartens and preschools are defined, as they were under Soviet rule, as an integral part of the education system and are funded by regional and local municipalities. When in 2004 the government attempted to charge parents the full cost of kindergarten, widespread public opposition forced the proposal to be withdrawn. Today, local authorities can legally charge parents up to 20 percent of the cost of kindergarten and pre-school. The majority of children between the ages of three and six are still enrolled first in a kindergarten and later in a preschool. However, due to the economic crisis that followed the transition to a market economy in the 1990s, public childcare provision was dramatically scaled back. Between 1990 and 2000, the number of these childcare institutions declined from 87,900 to 53,000, and the number of children in those facilities dropped by more than 50 percent from 9,009,000 to 4,263,0000. In addition, the costs and eligibility requirements for the remaining childcare centers increased, while at the same time the quality of the provided care declined. This decrease was much higher than the decline of the birth rate.[6] The booming Russian economy over the past several years enabled more communities to reopen childcare facilities while giving parents the means to pay for them. The enrollment in kindergarten and preschool programs increased again, from 67 percent in 1999 to 84 percent in 2005. As in the past, most of these institutions are located in urban regions. According to the 2002 census, 78 percent of all children aged five living in urban areas were enrolled in a kindergarten compared to only 47 percent in rural areas.[7]

The decrease of all-day childcare and school education in postcommunist Russia created severe problems for working parents, in particular working mothers. The employment of women (aged sixteen to fifty-four) declined between 1992 and 1998 from 78 to 64 percent. Since the turn of the century, when the economic situation improved and the number of childcare facilities increased, the female employment rate began rising again, reaching 69 percent.[8] In particular, working mothers were forced to leave the workforce because they no longer had access to all-day childcare and schooling. Unlike many Western European societies, the Russian economy does not offer many part-time jobs. The percentage of full-time employed women is therefore very high. It increased from 73 percent in 1994 to 80 percent in 2001.[9] Today, 94 percent of all employed women are engaged in full-time work, much more than in most other European countries. Indeed, most working women in Russia cannot afford to work part-time. Therefore, despite the economic boom of the past decade, the financial situation of many families has deteriorated. The Soviet family model of the "two-income family/female-homemaker" family is still the norm. Sixty-three percent of all marriages are dual-earner couples, compared to only 24 percent of marriages in which the husband is the sole breadwinner, 9 percent in which only the wife is employed, and 4 percent in which both spouses are unemployed. Only with two incomes a family can survive.[10] The difficult situation of working women and mothers in Russian society during the past two decades is also reflected in the development of the fertility rate, which fell from 2.23 in 1990 to 1.14 in 2005, one of the lowest in the world.[11]

Because of the complex relationship between the political, economic, and social changes in post-1945 Russia, I focus in this chapter on ideological and pedagogical discourses, economic conditions, as well as social and family policies that shaped the time policy of school education in Russia. First, I briefly define my understanding of "school time" and discuss the consequences of this understanding for an analysis of time policies of education. From there, I examine the evolution of the discourse on all-day education in Russia since 1945 and reflect on the implications of the changing time policies for school organization as well as for individuals.

"School Time"—Some Conceptual Reflections

Recently, educationalist Cristina Allemann-Ghionda has argued that the all-day school has become the norm for education systems in the industrialized world.[12] For Russia, however, this statement must be qualified, because all-day schools such as those that exist in Britain, France, or Sweden are not common there.[13] However, the time policy of the Russian school system was and is not based solely on the model of the half-day school model either. In fact, the interplay of economic, social, demographic, and cultural factors produced a wide range of forms of daily and weekly time structures, which include boarding schools, various kinds of all-day schools, and special schools that integrate formal and informal education, as well as the combination of half-day schools with after-school care and extra-curricular activities.

Time policies for childcare and school education have become an increasingly important subject of comparative research. Compared with other factors that determine the quality of education such as economic conditions, the education of teachers and childcare workers, or the excellence of teaching, the organization of time is a relatively formal component. Nevertheless, it has emerged as one of the central dimensions of comparative studies, because the time structure of a childcare and school system has far-reaching consequences beyond the education process. But what is actually meant by "school time"? This is often unclear. It is important to realize that "school time" includes more than just the time spent in the classroom. I therefore use in the following the concept proposed by the comparative research project *Time for Schooling* (*Zeit für Schule*) organized by the German Institute for International Pedagogical Research, which has resulted in a new approach to the analysis of school time that takes into account the various physical and psychological factors that influence educational outcomes. They differentiate between *teaching time*, the *time spent in school*, and *school-related time*.[14] This concept emphasizes that school time constitutes a substantial portion of children's lives and structures their daily routine, and thus needs to be balanced with their leisure time and physical activities.

In addition, more recent research has highlighted the substantial financial, economic, and social consequences of the time structure of a school system, because it constitutes an important part of a broader social, family, and gender policy. Political decisions concerning the daily and weekly school schedule reflect not only national concepts on the supposedly "right" balance between the responsibilities of the state and families for children. They also reflect prevailing views on women's roles in society and the gendered division of labor in the family. They have a lasting influence on the possibilities of mothers to engage in paid work outside the home.[15]

The Time Policy of School Education in Early Post-1945 Russia

After World War II, the major aim of Soviet education policy was the enforcement of a seven-year compulsory education for all children. It was not until 1958 that eight years of compulsory education were introduced. With towns and the economy in ruins, providing education proved extremely difficult, as the basic material conditions, including classrooms, teachers, and schoolbooks, were all in severely short supply. In addition, many children, especially in rural areas, had to work to support their families. In order to enroll all children in school, teaching in "double shifts" became common: half of the students had lessons in the morning, the other half in the afternoon. Under these challenging conditions, all-day school education was simply not possible. The common practice was a half-day school in combination with various extracurricular activities, most of which were organized by the communist children's and youth organizations. These social and political activities were so extensive that the Communist Party (CPSU) regularly criticized the "overburdening" of school children and in 1948 even decreed that all activities outside of school had to be subordinated to school curricula.[16] The practice of half-day "shift-schools" stood in sharp contrast to the discussion about a reformed communist pedagogy, which had begun in the 1920s. The vision of Soviet school reformers was the "socialist education" of the "new man." One of their major aims was an eight-year comprehensive all-day school, which would combine school education, vocational training, social and cultural activities, and leisure time and offer students regularly scheduled meals during the whole year.[17]

The primary objective of family policy after World War II was to restore the nation's population and provide care for orphans and homeless children. The Soviet Union suffered the highest number of casualties during the war. The estimates range from 21 to 40 million (25 million of them civilians) dead, or as much as one-fifth of the prewar population.[18] In addition, the war had orphaned or rendered homeless millions of children. "Children's homes," residential institutions for orphans and homeless children, thus assumed an important place in the state's welfare policy of the postwar era. These institutions had existed prior to 1945. They were first established to deal with the effects of the 1917 Revolution, the subsequent civil war, and the famine in the Ukraine during the early 1930s, not to mention the restrictive policy towards illegitimate children. But the effects of World War II were much greater than these previous crises. By 1950, 6,395,900 children were being cared for and educated in 5,643 of these children's homes, twice as many as existed a decade earlier.[19] Until the early 1950s, there were three types of boarding institutions: schools for orphans and homeless children, schools for handicapped children, and boarding schools in rural areas, which allowed children in sparsely populated regions to get a primary education or to continue with their secondary education. All three fulfilled important social functions in the Russian postwar society.

The Time Policy of Soviet Schools in the Post-Stalinist Era

The year 1956 proved crucial in the evolution of time policy in the Soviet education system, particularly in regard to all-day schooling. On 15 September of that year, the government issued a decree establishing a new kind of boarding school that was to become an integral component of a grand but unrealistic plan to restore the belief in communist ideas after the mass repressions and personality cult of the Stalin era. The decree was in part the result of a public debate concerning the improvement of the shortcomings of parental education, which was perceived as too "traditional" and "conservative." In this debate, which began shortly after Stalin's death, the Communist Party demanded that schools play a more central role in young people's development. In response, educational reformers and experts proposed boarding schools and claimed that they would not only "collectivize" the education of children and youth but also make their education more systematic and efficient. They would improve young people's character by ensuring continuity in moral and ideological education.

In addition, they declared that boarding schools would "relieve" mothers from family and housework and thus advance their social and economic position in society. Finally, they argued that boarding schools would help poor families, who in many regions were still suffering from a shortage of housing a decade after the war. Boarding schools, it was thought, would help reduce some of the pressure on these families.[20]

As a result of this debate, the CPSU advocated establishing boarding schools as the prototype "for the school of the future" since the mid-1950s. The party leadership declared that these schools should initially focus on underprivileged children. Over time, however, they should be expanded to encompass all children, regardless of social background.[21] While schools and parents were to continue working together and provide each other mutual support in the raising of children, boarding schools were supposed to reduce the negative influences that families and other less-regulated environments could have on children. To counter strong cultural, religious, or nationalistic influences, they would endeavor to inculcate proper communist values in Soviet children. In extreme cases of child neglect, boarding schools would assume a compensatory or surrogate role, effectively acting as a substitute for the family.[22]

Boarding schools were also viewed by the CPSU as a way of reviving the tradition of collectivism in education that was being threatened by the increasing number of one-child families. Indeed, already in the early 1960s, about half of all Russian families had only one child. This trend led in the second half of the 1950s to the growing fear of an increase of "spoiled and self-centered" children.[23] The trend toward a one-child family was enhanced by a change of the policy towards illegitimate children. To increase the population after World War II, family policy under Stalin had provided single mothers with an allowance, which effectively relieved the unmarried father of his financial responsibility. As a result, the number of single mothers rose rapidly. By 1956, their children were either in primary school or just entering secondary school. Since these women were needed to work in agriculture and industry but found it increasingly difficult to combine work and childcare, the demand for residential care grew.[24]

In a 1956 decree, the communist government planned for all Soviet children to be educated in boarding schools by 1980.[25] Soon after its publication, the Soviet state began establishing boarding schools. The process, however, was poorly organized. The major problem was the lack of appropriate buildings. In most cases, the administration either used common school buildings, which often proved ill-suited to serve the special requirements of the new boarding schools, or reorganized "children's homes" into boarding schools. The staff was selected and prepared in seminars and summer schools. However, despite the efforts of regional and local educational authorities and the enthusiasm of the directors of these new institutions, the ambitious initial targets could not be reached. By 1 September 1960, 540,000 students were enrolled in boarding schools, a far cry from the target of 2,500,000 that had been set for 1965.[26]

In 1961, the social scientist Effie Ambler described in an article in the journal *American Slavic and East European Review* the usual practice of Soviet boarding schools at the time:

> The ideal boarding school contains, in a potentially almost self-sufficient children's village, about 550 students from nursery age to eleventh grade; except for brief vacations at home the child will live in this same school from age four to seventeen or eighteen. Emphasis is placed on the unity and continuity of the student body, which is supposedly slowly welded into a family-like, multi-age collective of the type found most effective by Soviet pedagogical theorist A. S. Makarenko, whose ideas are currently in high favor. Classes are small; twenty-five is the largest group considered practical. In addition to a large teaching staff, there are special tutors, who have had higher education in guidance and who live at the school and work with the pupils in their production training and practice.[27]

However, as the author emphasized, this was only the ideal practice. In reality, the initial shortcomings continued and led officials to rethink the program of boarding schools altogether in 1963. The lack of infrastructure, financial resources, and trained staff prevented boarding schools from being opened in sufficient numbers. In addition, the existing boarding schools did not often function as hoped. The weaknesses of this educational program thus became increasingly obvious. Numerous teachers reported problems with "difficult," i.e., academically poor and undisciplined students. Their attempts "to improve their character," they noted, often failed. In addition, education experts and psychologists increasingly emphasized the harmful effects of residential care and the importance of families in the raising of children. Such criticism led officials to urge an improvement in the relationship between schools and families and to abandon the vision of boarding schools as the future for all students.[28]

Although the experiment, on the whole, failed to meet its lofty goals, boarding schools remained important institutions that served a crucial welfare function in the Soviet and Russian education systems. As the social scientist John Dunstan concluded in an article on "Soviet Boarding Education," published in 1980:

> The (boarding) schools' achievement was that they provided a second chance for at least some of their thousands of underprivileged pupils—indeed, it should be stressed that they continue to offer enhanced opportunities to chil-

dren in certain remote rural areas—and they gave thousands of women, particularly unmarried mothers the possibility of improving their socio-economic position.[29]

In the early 1960s, the focus of Soviet education policy shifted from boarding schools to "extended-day schools" (*shkola prodlennogo dnya*), which were from the start envisioned for all children. A decree of 15 February 1960 established an extended-day school program and described the general goals of this new type of schooling.[30] Further regulations followed in 1962. Initially, extended-day schools were presented as a step in the long-term program of the boarding schools. The declared goals of the new program were remarkably similar to those laid out for boarding schools. The Ministry of Education aimed for

- the enhancement of communist ideological education;
- a reduction in the number of school periods in which children and adolescents were unsupervised;
- support for parents in regard to the provision of all-round education for their children, as many parents were not deemed qualified to accomplish this task on their own;
- the improvement of educational achievement through close supervision of homework, which also could not be guaranteed in many families;
- the promotion of equality of men and women by offering relief for employed women, who still shouldered the dual responsibilities of taking care of the household and children;
- relieving parents of their supervision duties so that they would have more time to focus on their own ideological and political development.[31]

This new form of all-day education promised several advantages over the existing half-day school system, especially since it allowed more flexibility. The extended school day could be organized in different ways, which included extended-day schools, extended-day grades, and extended-day groups. The choice depended on local demand for extended-day provision and on the availability of staff and suitable facilities. If the number of students attending extended-day groups exceeded 80 to 85 percent of all students in grades one through eight, the school would be designated as an extended-day school and, as such, become entitled to additional financial support and staff.[32] The Soviet educationalist Eduard G. Kostyashkin emphasized two major advantages of the new program: First, extended-day services could be established at all general half-day schools without the need for new rooms or extensive reorganization. Second, the costs per student of extended-day schools were five to six times lower than they were in boarding schools. Thus, extended-day schools accommodated the political and financial realities in the Soviet Union much better than boarding schools.[33]

The number of students enrolled in extended-day schools increased rapidly between the early 1960s and the mid-1980s (see Table 15.1). In 1985, nearly 37 percent of all students in primary and middle classes (grade 1-9) attended extended-day schools. These schools were popular because they offered a free all-day education.

TABLE 15.1: Students in extended-day schools (compulsory grades 1–8) in Russia, 1960–1985[34]

Year	Total Number of Students	Percentage of Total
1960	160,000	n/a
1970	2,471,000	12%
1975	3,489,000	n/a
1980	4,912,000	33%
1985	5,941,000	37%[(a)]

Note:
(a) 32 percent in urban areas, 49 percent in rural areas.

To persuade parents to send their children to these new extended-day schools, officials tried to improve their pedagogic organization and efficiency based on scientific research, which they had begun commissioning 1960s. This research, as well as actual experience with successful activities and methods, formed the basis of regulations and compulsory programs in extended-day schools. Research-based decision making became an important element of the centrally planned time policy of school education in the Soviet Union. As illustrated by an article titled "The Resolution of Teaching, Upbringing, and Health Problems in Prolonged-Day Schools" that was published in the journal *Sovetskaya pedagogika* in 1980, the question of children's physiological and mental health was one of the areas where research played an important role in the discourse on and practice of all-day school education. The research of medical scientists and educationalists directly informed daily practice. Among other things, they recommended that extended-day schools try to mix different activities in the daily schedule of children from different age groups in a way that corresponded to their daily physiological rhythm. The authors reported:

> Students in the elementary grades attend prolonged-day schools ten or eleven hours a day—almost all the waking hours for these youngsters, who are between 7 and 10 years of age. Therefore, it is very important to organize properly all types of their activity and recreation, physical education, and nutrition. Under natural experimental conditions ... , medical researchers and peda-

gogues have amassed sufficient data to define certain physiological and hygienic requirements for the organization of the prolonged-day routine. Above all, it is essential that this routine take into account the age of the children and the human body's periodic physiological functions. In the course of their development, children of a given age are prepared for different mental and physical workloads. ... Given the long period of time that pupils spend in school, learning, labor, and creative activity can be distributed from 8:00 A.M. to 6:00 or 7:00 P.M., with due regard to the periodicity of the body's physiological functions and its efficiency. The efficiency of healthy children reaches a peak in the morning hours (from 8:00 to 11:00 A.M.). By 2:00 P.M., there is a marked decline in efficiency, especially in its qualitative indicators. A second, smaller rise in efficiency is observed between 4:00 and 5:00 P.M., then efficiency drops sharply. Consequently, it is important to schedule the most difficult school subjects before lunch. It is also better to transfer independent study activity by pupils to the morning hours, when the functioning of higher nervous activity and mental efficiency are at their peak. During the periods of relatively high efficiency, pupils should spend relatively less time on homework than they do on independent work in the second half of the day, after 3:00 or 4:00 o'clock. ... Therefore, in the prolonged-day school there is hygienic justification for conducting activities in the fine arts, music, nature studies, reading, rhythmics in the second half of the day on specific days of the week.[35]

Usually, the morning in extended-day schools was reserved for teaching, while the afternoon was used for supervised homework and extracurricular activities. Here, students were to pursue their individual interests and participate in social, political, and sport activities. While there were experimental attempts to achieve a more balanced distribution of learning and leisure activities throughout the day, they did not become the norm. This research-based time policy allowed the Soviet state to provide a similar temporal organization of extended-day schools and extracurricular activities all over the country. Its centrally planned character, however, was also responsible for the increasing formalism of the time structure, which did not offer much room for individual initiative at the everyday level.

As before, more than anything else, it was difficult material conditions that hampered the development of the pedagogically ambitious extended-day school program. The main obstacle for a general introduction of all-day schools was the lack of school buildings. Many Russian school administrations were forced to use existing school buildings in a "double shift system." In some cases, schools were even forced to introduce a "three-shift system." The number of schools running on a shift system was considerable, as was the number of students who attended them. In the school year 1970–1971, more than 38 percent of all Russian schools representing 29 percent of the students operated with two or three shifts. These numbers declined somewhat over the course of the 1970s so that by

1980–1981 "only" 22 percent of schools had two or three shifts. Due to a rise in the number of students, the number of such schools began to grow again, reaching 35 percent by 1995–1996 with 25 percent of all students.[36]

One side effect of this situation was the boost in the number of after-school programs in facilities outside of school, for example sport clubs and "pioneer palaces," youth centers administered by the communist children's and youth organizations. Indeed, the all-day provision that exists in Russia today continues to rely on the integration of formal and informal education.[37] In addition to serving educational purposes, the expansion of extended-day schools was also a key component of the state's pronatalist family policy, which took on increasing importance since the birth rate started falling significantly in the 1960s. Between 1960 and 1980, it fell from 2.82 to 1.94.[38] The CPSU viewed the increasing participation of Soviet women in the labor market as one important reason for this trend. Compared with most other Eastern and Western industrialized countries, female work force participation in the Soviet Union was very high. In 1989, women made up the majority of the workforce (51 percent) and comprised 44 percent of the industrial labor force. Since 1970, the average proportion of full-time employed women aged sixteen to fifty-four was a constant 90 percent.[39] The Communist Party considered women's employment not only as necessary for the economic modernization of the Soviet Union. In keeping with the tradition of the socialist emancipation theory, it also promoted female employment as the precondition for the political, economic, and social equality of men and women.[40]

The decreasing birth rate, however, forced Soviet leaders to reevaluate existing social and family policy. In the Khrushchev era (1953–1964), its focus was on the relative liberalization of private life and the improvement of housing conditions and living standards. While the CPSU continued this social policy under Leonid Brezhnev (1964–1982), it also attempted to develop a more pronatalist family policy. In his opening address to the 26th Congress of the Communist Party in 1981, Brezhnev therefore emphasized the difficulties that mothers faced in combining their dual roles as workers and mothers. To help them cope with this burden, he promised new state measures including up to one year of partially paid leave for childcare, an increase in children allowances (especially following the birth of a second and third child), a shorter workday for mothers with infants, an increase of the number of day nurseries, kindergartens, and preschools and an improvement of their quality, more schools with extended-day groups, and additional consumer services.[41]

The Soviet state, however, found it very difficult to fully realize these promises. Since the extended-day programs were often in short supply, a relatively large number of school-aged children were not involved in any kind of extended-day education. As an alternative, in the 1970s the CPSU began advocating "self-education" and education by the communist children's and youth organizations as the best possible way for young people to spend their leisure time after school.[42] To realize this, the state established a number of programs and facilities that would enable children to use their leisure time in a way that would promote "socialist socialization" as well as prevent "child neglect." Among other things, the government recommended that regional and local authorities introduce optional courses in schools, social clubs, pioneers' palaces, music schools, and sports schools, all of which were designed to meet students' extracurricular interests. Between 1970 and 1980, enrollment in these extracurricular activities increased significantly. The number of students enrolled in sports schools rose from 1,323,000 to 2,525,000; the number of young participants in the programs of the Palaces of Culture increased from 1,601,000 to 3,149,000, and in the programs of the Academies of Art, Music, and Choreography from 762,000 to 1,416,000. In addition, the government expanded the funding of summer camps. As a result, the number of camps and the level of participation in them grew rapidly, from 8,806,000 children in 1970 to 12,085,000 in 1980.[43] And yet despite these impressive numbers, the press and various studies regularly reported on the lack of such facilities, especially in rural areas, as well on the problems caused by unstructured leisure time.

The Transition from a Communist to Neoliberal Education Policy

By 1985, the political, economic, and social problems that had long plagued the Soviet Union could no longer be ignored. To address them, Mikhail Gorbachev, who assumed the leadership of the CPSU in March 1985, declared a new policy of glasnost and perestroika. Among other things, Gorbachev's reforms included a reduction of state control over schools; efforts to combat formalism, including in education; and a further liberalization of private life. In respect to family policy, Gorbachev advocated what amounted to a paradigmatic change. He wanted to see women return "to their purely feminine mission" and criticized communist societies for their failure to leave women sufficient time to "perform everyday tasks in housework, child rearing and simple coziness in the heart of the family."[44] Indeed, he considered it a historic error that the communist state had assumed the responsibility, if only in part, for the raising of children.

This was a dramatic shift from the earlier education and family policy, undermining the ideological foundations of the former system of all-day education.[45] Parents' new freedom to decide whether to send their children to the ideologically aligned, pedagogically inflexible, formalized extended-day schools or other public educational institutions for children quickly sent such institutions into a steep decline. From 1985 to 1991, the percentage of students in extended-day schools fell by nearly half, from 37 percent to 19 percent.[46] One result of this individual protest again the collective Soviet education, however, was that children and young people increasingly lacked afternoon supervision. In several cities, such as Moscow and Kasan, gangs of teenagers began to terrorize citizens, while conflicts among them often exploded into violent confrontations. To meet this new challenge, schools were required to keep their doors open through the evening hours. But many teenagers showed little interest in spending their free time in schools, no matter what activities they offered. Their attitude was the result of the overregulation of students' time in the previous decades.[47]

After 1991, the financial crisis of the Russian state accelerated the deterioration of the system of extended-day education and informal extracurricular education of the former Soviet Union. The proportion of students in extended-day schools fell from 19 percent in 1991 to 15 percent in 1997.[48] Many pioneer palaces and smaller youth clubs as well as other activities and programs were also shut down or reorganized into a new system of extracurricular education. In addition, state and municipal institutions that had provided informal extracurricular education began to face competition from churches and other private educational organizations after the transition. But following a period of consolidation, new and more flexible forms of all-day provision began to emerge that, in keeping with the Soviet tradition, integrated formal and informal education. Moreover, schools began cooperating with institutions of informal education or founded such departments on their own initiative. Most of the successful private schools have been running as all-day schools, providing education and supervision from 8:00 A.M. until 7:00 P.M. and in some cases even later.[49]

Shortly after Vladimir Putin became president of Russia in 2000, the government presented its National Doctrine of Education and the Program of Modernization of Education to 2010, which outlined the state's educational policy for the next decade. Above all, the new doctrine sought to protect young people's health and eliminate the "overburdening" and stress that they faced in school. In order to achieve these goals and at the same time raise educational standards, the former policies that had been inherited from the Soviet era desperately needed to be reformed. The new policy led to a considerable revision and reduction of school curricula, but it was not enough to meet the ambitious goal of eliminating the overburdening of students. Instead, that goal was expected to be accomplished by increasing the duration of school education from ten to twelve years, which has been implemented gradually since 2000.[50]

However, both teachers and parents harshly criticized the Ministry of Education's plans to introduce a new entry-level grade (*nulevoy klass*) for six-year-olds, which forced this proposal to be withdrawn. Moreover, it was argued that greater flexibility could be achieved if regional authorities or schools themselves determined the school year calendar and the duration of the school week (five or six days). The new policy also highlighted the importance of the system of extracurricular education, especially in terms of its benefits for improving young people's character and offering greater opportunities for recreation.[51]

As was the case in the early postwar period, the raising of children has once again assumed new importance in Russia. Both schools and institutions of extracurricular education are required by the government to provide "character and moral education" by offering more after-school programs. Such programs should provide much-needed supervision for children, who should be kept off the streets. This is especially important given that there were an estimated one hundred thousand homeless and one million neglected Russian children in 2003.[52] In order to fight and prevent homelessness and child neglect, the new policy seeks to expand again after-school programs and extended-day programs that are accessible to underprivileged children.[53]

Another new development is the revival of all-day schools. Since the turn of the century, the idea of all-day schools has found new proponents in Russia, especially in Moscow, where 218 of all 1,522 schools (14 percent) moved to an all-day schedule in 2003. Still, in developing this new all-day policy, the Moscow Department of Education has drawn directly on the concept of the all-day school that first emerged in the 1960s under communist rule. Like their predecessors, the new all-day schools are open from 7:45 A.M. until 7:00 P.M, and no less than 80 percent of the students must attend the all-day program. They are guided by a clear concept for organizing the second part of the school day by integrating formal (compulsory) and extracurricular education. Overall, they have proved quite successful.[54]

There are several reasons for the reintroduction of all-day schools. Above all, female labor force participation is growing once again, and, due to the nuclear structure of most families, grandparents or other relatives who could look after the children in the afternoon are seldom present. Increasingly well-educated and career-oriented women, particularly in large cities, seek secure supervision and education for their children until the late afternoon. In addition, the current government recommends all-day schooling as a means of preventing homelessness and child neglect, an argument that also has its roots in the Soviet period. These changes in time policy were made possible by the economic boom, which increased the state's financial resources and allowed for greater expenditure on education as well as a new pronatalist policy. In the early 1990s, the birth rate, which had increased from 1.94 to 2.13 between 1980 and 1990, began to decline again.[55] The reduced number of school-aged children made more space available, which can be used for afternoon programs. For the same reason, the number of schools that are forced to teach in double shifts is also decreasing, although 22 percent of all Russian schools still have to teach in shifts.[56]

Despite the obvious increase in the demand for all-day education, educational experts, school directors, and teachers fear that the reintroduction of all-day schools "from above" is nothing more than a fashionable political trend that will ultimately lead to a reintroduction of central state control and formalism in education.[57] They are concerned that the discredited reputation of Soviet-era extended-day schools, which were "boring and formalized," might undermine the idea of a new democratic all-day school that is designed to meet the "real needs and interests" of children and adolescents.[58] In addition, they criticize the reduction of school autonomy and point out that the overly detailed regulation of time in education hinders the development of sustainable all-day schools. They also reject the rule that teaching time during the school week be subject to strict physiological requirements, even if those requirements are based on current research. And they perceive the Ministry of Education's requirement that a break of forty-five minutes between compulsory and optional classes as an example of an encroaching "overregulation." In particular, they question regulations that stipulate when certain subjects are to be taught during the school day.[59] Finally, teachers and administrators worry that the system of extracurricular education, which has begun to recover after the upheavals of the 1990s, might be destabilized or even destroyed altogether.[60]

Many parents and students share similar reservations. According to a survey carried out in Tambov in 2005, only 22 percent of the parents interviewed wanted their children to attend all-day school.[61] The older the child is, the less likely it is for parents to see the need for an institutionalized all-day education. Moreover, there exists an enormous disparity between rural and urban areas. In rural parts of the Tambov region, for example, only 15 percent of parents would send their children to an all-day school, whereas in the city of Tambov itself, 94 percent would do so. And while 48 percent of teachers are convinced that all-day school is needed, only 25 percent would actually like to work in such a school.[62] As in other countries with a half-day system like Germany, these teachers are attempting to protect their professional interests.

However, the major reason for criticism is that many schools find it impossible to meet all of the new requirements of the educational authorities. In Moscow, reaching compulsory enrollment of at least 80 percent of students in the all-day program, especially if children are also expected to use the facilities of extracurricular and informal education in cooperation with the school, has proved to be the most difficult goal of all. As a result, school directors and educationalists have begun to advocate delegating local school governments and individual schools with the authority to develop their own concepts for all-day education that would take into consideration the needs and interests of students, parents, and teachers as well as their particular financial resources, educational traditions, existing forms of cooperation with the community, and the local institutions of informal education.[63] These contradictions and problems are a result not only of current strategies in Russian school education, but also the longer-lasting influence of the tradition of communist educational policy.

Conclusion

A mix of economic necessities, pronatalism, and the vision of a "socialist education" shaped the time policy of Russian school education after World War II. The result was a complex system of all-day provision in childcare that coexisted with a combination of "shift schooling" in half-day schools and additional extracurricular activities. Although the goals of Soviet time policy were informed primarily by communist ideology, economic needs, and pronatalism, they were also based on solid educational research that sought to transform political goals and communist visions into pedagogical programs. Factors such as a poor infrastructure and a lack of qualified teaching and educational staff determined the practical outcomes of these policies. Thus, the communist theory of all-day care and education reflects only one aspect of time policy under Soviet rule. It was up to local education authorities and teachers, however, to realize this policy at the everyday level.

By applying Wolfgang Mitter's concept of school time analysis to Russia, it becomes clear that the *teaching time* has changed only slightly since the Soviet era. While minor shifts occurred in official school schedules for various subjects, on the whole, the long tradition of physiological arguments for a specified day routine and temporal organization of the curricula has perpetuated a largely static allocation of time for learning. In terms of *time spent in school*, the effects of time policy can also be observed in the attempts to structure the extended day by detailed regulations that determined times for breaks, meals, and recreation. In regard to *school-related time*, the attempts to utilize students' leisure time for school-related purposes must also be considered. The most far-reaching changes stemmed from a long process leading to the expansion of compulsory education to ten years by 1981 and then twelve years after 2000.

Qualitatively, time policy in Soviet and Russian education can be characterized by a high degree of political, ideological, social, and financial control over individuals and schools by the state. Above all, time policy was used to socialize students into a collectivist culture. Prescriptive time policy also produced a considerable bureaucratization of school organization, which to some degree still hinders the development of local and more flexible concepts of all-day education. However, in comparison to Western countries, between 1945 and 1990 the time policy of the Soviet education system proved to be a relatively successful component of a broader paternalist communist welfare state and family policy. It achieved considerable success in fighting the homelessness and child neglect after World War II, in reconciling family and work for women, and in providing after-school supervision as well as sports and arts education to all children that were mostly free of charge.

The new neoliberal Russia has still yet to reach the level of full-day educational provision that existed before the transition, but it also needs to avoid the mistakes of the past. Time policy in Russian education must find answers to massive demographic problems and the need for women to fulfill the dual role of mothers and workers. In addition, it must address the problems associated with the reorganization of residential institutions for orphans and homeless children as well as the lack of participation of underprivileged children in extracurricular education beyond the compulsory minimum in the morning hours. Finally, it needs to meet the challenge of raising educational standards of all students after the abysmal results of the worldwide tests of fifteen-year-old school children's scholastic performance conducted by the international Program for International Student Assessment (PISA).

Notes

1. For an overview of the development of the Soviet Education system, see Oskar Anweiler, "Sowjetunion," in *Bildungssysteme in Europa*, ed. Oskar Anweiler et al. (Weinheim, 1976), 143–58; Oskar Anweiler, *Geschichte der Schule und Pädagogik in Russland* (Heidelberg, 1964); Ben Eklof and E. D. Dneprov, *Democracy in the Russian School: The Reform*

Movement in Education Since 1984 (Boulder, CO, 1993); Ben Eklof et al., eds., *Educational Reform in Post-Soviet Russia: Legacies and Prospects* (London, 2005); Gerlind Schmidt, "Russian Federation," in *The Education Systems of Europe*, ed. Wolfgang Hörner et al. (Dordrecht, 2007), 646–68.

2. UNESCO Institute of Statistics, *Children out of School; Measuring Exclusion from Primary Education* (Montreal, 2005), 17, 25, and 70.

3. UNESCO, *Education For All By 2015: Will We Make it?* (Oxford, 2007), 284.

4. Russian Ministry of Education, *Statistics: Number of Schools by Type and Year* (Moscow, 2008). Retrieved 16 October 2008: http://www.ed.gov.ru/uprav/stat/1849/.

5. UNESCO Institute of Statistics, *Education Counts: Benchmarking Process in 19 WEI Countries: World Economic Indicators—2007* (Montreal, 2007), 140.

6. Tatyana Teplova, "Welfare State Transformation, Childcare and Women's Work in Russia," *Social Politics* 14, no. 3 (2007): 292.

7. "Data Tables of 2002 Census: Shares of Children aged 3–9 Attending School and Preschool Institutions." Retrieved 15 October 2008: http://en.wikipedia.org/wiki/Education _in_Russia#cite_note-ME1–14; UNESCO, *Education For All*, 39, 268f.

8. Akvile Moticjunaite and Zhanna Kravchenko, "Family Policy, Employment and Gender-role Attitudes: A Comparative Analysis of Russia and Sweden," *Journal of European Social Policy* 18, no. 1 (2008): 40.

9. Teplova, "Welfare State," 304.

10. Ariane Pailhe and Oxana Sinyavaskaya (Independent Institute for Social Policy [INED]), "Labor Force Participation of Men and Women and Gender Relations in the Framework of Women-Friendly Policies in France and Russia," paper presented at the international conference, "How Generations and Gender Shape Demographic Change," Geneva, 14–16 May 2008, 11.

11. Globalis, *Russia: Total Fertility Rate, 1955–2005*. Retrieved 16 October 2008: http://globalis .gvu.unu.edu/indicator_detail.cfm?Country=RU&IndicatorID=138.

12. Cristina Allemann-Ghionda, "Between Pedagogy and Ideology: Some Transnational Topoi in the Discussion about Half-Day and All-day Schooling," paper presented at the Interdisciplinary Workshop "Welfare State Regimes, Public Education and Child Care: Theoretical Concepts for a Comparison of East and West Potsdam," Potsdam, 31 March–1 April 2006, 2.

13. See the chapters by Cristina Allemann-Ghionda, Lisbeth Lundahl, and Sally Tomlinson in this volume.

14. Wolfgang Mitter, "Einführung des Projektleiters," in *Zeit für Schule. Polen, Sowjetunion*, ed. Heliodor Muszynski and Leonid Novikov (Cologne, 1990), vii–xii. For more, see the introduction by Karen Hagemann, Konrad H. Jarausch, and Cristina Allemann-Ghionda in this volume.

15. Cf. Karen Hagemann, "Between Ideology and Economy: The 'Time Politics' of Child Care and Public Education in the Two Germanys," *Social Politics* 13, no. 1 (2006): 217–60.

16. Mikhai.M. Deineko, *40 let narodnogo obrazovaniya v SSSR* (Moscow, 1957).

17. Anatoli Rakhkochkine, "Schulische und 'ergänzende' Bildung in Russland," in *Ganztägige Bildungssysteme. Innovation durch Vergleich*, ed. Hans-Uwe Otto and Thomas Coelen (Münster, 2005), 106.

18. Milton Leitenberg, "Deaths in Wars and Conflicts in the 20th Century," Cornell University: Peace Studies Program. Occasional Papers, no. 29, 3rd ed. (Ithaca, NY, 2006), 11.

19. Deineko, *40 let narodnogo*, 206.

20. John Dunstan, "Soviet Boarding Education: Its Rise and Progress," in *Home, School and Leisure in the Soviet Union*, ed. Jenny Brine et al. (London, 1980), 117ff.

21. Ibid.
22. Ibid., 119.
23. Ibid. Between 1955 and 1970, the fertility rate declined from 2.85 to 2.02; see Globalis, *Russia: Total Fertility Rate.*
24. Dunstan, "Soviet Boarding Education," 119.
25. Bernice Q. Madison, *Social Welfare in the Soviet Union* (Stanford, CA, 1968), 69.
26. Dunstan, "Soviet Boarding Education," 122.
27. Effie Ambler, "The Soviet Boarding School," *American Slavic and East European Review* 20, no. 2 (1961): 251.
28. Dunstan, "Soviet Boarding Education," 125ff.
29. Ibid., 135.
30. Eduard G. Kostyashkin, *Shkola prodlennogo dnja* (Moscow, 1965), 27.
31. See Oskar Anweiler et al., eds., *Die sowjetische Bildungspolitik von 1958 bis 1973. Dokumente und Texte* (Berlin, 1976), 151; Kostyashkin, *Shkola prodlennogo dnja,* 4ff.; Josef Scheipl, "Ganztägiges Schulwesen im internationalen Vergleich," *Erziehung und Unterricht* 140, no. 6 (1990): 327.
32. Kostyashkin, *Shkola prodlennogo dnja,* 4.
33. Ibid., 53f.
34. Goskomstat Rossii, *Rossiyskiy statisticheskiy ezhegodnik* (Moscow, 1997), 192.
35. Antonina G. Khripkova et al., "The Resolution of Teaching, Upbringing, and Health Problems in Prolonged-Day Schools," *Soviet Education* 22, no. 4 (1980): 28.
36. The birth rate increased after a long period of decline between 1980 and 1990 from 1.94 to 2.14. Globalis, *Russia: Total Fertility Rate.* See also Goskomstat Rossii, *Rossiyskiy statisticheskiy ezhegodnik,* 237.
37. Rakhkochkin, "Schulische und 'ergänzende' Bildung," 110ff.
38. Globalis, *Russia: Total Fertility Rate.*
39. Elain Bowers, "Women in Employment in Russia" (Ph.D. diss., University of Warwick, 1993), 21ff.
40. Barbara Alpern Engel, *Women in Russia, 1700–2000* (Cambridge, UK, 2004), chap. 12 and 13.
41. Leonid Brezhnev and Nikolay Tikhonov, "On Pronatalist Policies in the Soviet Union," *Population and Development Review* 7, no. 2 (1981): 373.
42. See Lyubov' K. Petrova, "Osnovnye vorposy organizatsii svobondogo vremeni shkolnikov," in *Svobonoe vremya shkol'nikov,* ed. Lyubov' K. Petrova (Moscow, 1969), 8–32.
43. Judith Harwin, *Children of the Russian State: 1917–95* (Avebury, 1996), 39.
44. Cited in ibid., 69.
45. Ibid., 70.
46. Goskomstat Rossii, *Rossiyskiy statisticheskiy ezhegodnik,* 192.
47. Leonid Novikov, "Zeit für Schule: Sowjetunion," in Muszynski and Novikov, *Zeit für Schule,* 94f.
48. Goskomstat Rossii, *Rossiyskiy statisticheskiy ezhegodnik,* 192.
49. Konstantin Sumnitel'nyy, "Polnokrovnaya zhizn' polnogo dnja: vozmozhno li eto v nyneshney shkole?" *Narodnoe obrazovanie* 59, no. 8 (2005): 148–55.
50. Ministerstvo obrazovaniya Rossiiskoi Federatsii, "Prikaz N 393 ot 11.02.2002 O Konceptsii modernizatsii rossiyskogo obrazovaniya na period do 2010 goda." Retrieved 4 January 2007: http://www.edu.ru/db/mo/Data/d_02/393.html. However, the plans to introduce a twelve-year general course of education seem to have been abandoned; cf. Schmidt, "Federation," 55.
51. Ministerstvo obrazovaniya Rossiiskoi Federatsii, "Prikaz N 393."

52. Valentina S. Demina, "O likvidatsii detskoy beznadzornosti i besprizornosti v Rossiyskoy Federatsii kak sotsialnogo yavleniya," in *Problemy detskoy beznadzornosti i besprizornosti v Rossiyskoy Federatsii: sotsial'no-politicheskie posledstviya i sovremennye tekhnologicheskie resheniya*, ed. Analiticheskiy vestnik Soveta Federatsii FS RF, no. 207 (2003), 8–13.

53. Demina, "O likvidatsii detskoy."

54. Tatyana N. Dement'eva, "Analititcheskiy obzor materialov eksperimenta 'Shkola polnogo dnya v g, Moskve," *Zavuch* 3, no. 3 (2003): 74ff.

55. Globalis, *Russia: Total Fertility Rate*.

56. Russian Ministry of Education, *Statistics*.

57. Cf. Tatyana. Dement'eva, "V shkole polnogo dnya: organizatsiya uchebno-vospitatel'nogo protsessa v shk. N 1148, 1958, 1976 Moskvy," *Narodnoe obrazovanie* 60, no. 5 (2006): 99–105; Sumnitel'nyy, "Polnokrovnaya zhizn'"; Anatoly Vitkovskiy, "Zadachi na 'polnyy den,'" *Pervoye Sentyabrya*, no. 68 (2005). Retrieved 4 January 2007: http://ps.1september.ru/article.php?ID=200506807; Anton Zverev, "Pedagogika polnogo dnya: prostranstvo svobodnogo tvorchestva uchitelya i shkol'nikov," *Narodnoe obrazovanie* 60, no. 4 (2006): 227–32.

58. Cf. Vitkovskiy, "Zadachi na 'polnyy den.'"

59. Glavnyy gosudarstvennyy sanitarnyy vrach RF, *Postanovleniye ot 28 noyabrya 2002 g. no. 44 g. "O vvedenii v deistviye sanitarno-epidemiologicheskikh pravil i normativov SanPiN 2.4.2.1178–02"* (Moscow, 2002).

60. Sumnitel'nyy, "Polnokrovnaya zhizn'."

61. Redaktsia PS, "Kto khochet prodlit' shkol'noe vremya?" *Pervoye Sentyabrya*, no. 68 (2005). Retrieved 4 January 2007: http://ps.1september.ru/article.php?ID=200506806.

62. Ibid.

63. Sumnitel'nyy, "Polnokrovnaya zhizn'."

Chapter 16

ECONOMY AND POLITICS
The Time Policy of the East German Childcare
and Primary School System

Monika Mattes

With its high rate of female employment and its elaborate infrastructure of state-run childcare, East Germany differed greatly from its Western counterpart. In 1989, more than 91 percent of working-age women (including students and apprentices) were gainfully employed. Moreover, 95 percent of all three- to six-year-old children attended preschool, and 81 percent of primary school children went to an after-school childcare center.[1] Until reunification in 1990, all-day education and childcare was thus the norm in the German Democratic Republic (GDR). Even today, all-day childcare and mother's employment remain widely accepted in the six eastern *Länder* (federal states) of the unified Federal Republic of Germany, which belonged to the former GDR. Such acceptance stands in stark contrast to the West, where more ambivalent attitudes towards all-day childcare and mother's employment persist.[2]

In this chapter, I address the question of how and through which arguments all-day education and childcare for school-aged children were established in the former GDR.[3] As Karen Hagemann demonstrates in this volume, East and West Germany shared a common tradition that defined education as the obligation of the state and childrearing as the responsibility of parents. This tradition was deeply rooted in the bourgeois model of the breadwinner-and-housewife family. All-day childcare institutions were thus accepted only as welfare measures for children of working mothers.[4] To what extent, then, did East Germany depart from this traditional German understanding of women's work and childcare? As the following will show, the GDR developed a unique response to the question of how best to divide the responsibilities of education and childcare between family and state. In this new, socialist model, the family would exercise considerably less influence on the raising of children than had traditionally been the case. We can thus characterize the GDR as a state socialist welfare regime in which the state assumed the primary responsibility for providing childcare and educating children.[5] As a result, the GDR broke institutionally from the former tripartite division of school as well as the organization of childcare along class lines. To this day, children in the West are separated after the primary school into different tracks of the school system. Only the highest level, the *Gymnasium,* allows students to advance to a university. Under the new GDR system, preschools and after-school childcare programs were integrated into a single educational administration.[6] The employment of women, moreover, assumed enormous significance in both economic and ideological terms. Nevertheless, old ideas about "appropriate gender roles" continued to shape the division of work between men and women so that women remained primarily responsible for domestic responsibilities, above all the provision of childcare.

In the context of the Cold War, the GDR presented itself as an alternative model to West Germany, proclaiming itself "the better German state." In the West, on the other hand, the GDR was viewed as a state that forced women into the labor market and collectivized education in the name of communism.[7] Both German states thus defined themselves in reference to each other, and their competitive relationship shaped the development of different time policies in their respective education systems.[8]

Why, then, did all-day education of school children in East Germany become increasingly important in the late 1950s? And how did it become institutionalized? To answer these questions, I examine the interplay of several different factors, including the political and ideological intentions of the state as well as the social and economic needs of East German society. First, I briefly describe the development between 1945 and 1958, and then I explore the specific political and social circumstances that produced in the 1950s and early 1960s a critical juncture that led to the introduction of the all-day education system in East Germany, while also discussing the debates and politics concerning the so-called "day school" (*Tagesschule*) in this period. And finally, I integrate the analysis of this critical period of reform into the broader historical and societal context of the 1960s and 1970s.

Childcare, Education, and "Socialist Construction"

In contrast to West Germany, in East Germany there was a deep institutional break in the education system. After the experience of war and National Socialism, in April 1946 the Communists and Social Democrats who united in the Socialist Unity Party of Germany (Sozialistische Einheitspartei Deutschlands, SED) had common education policy objectives: the denazification of schools, both in terms of personnel and on an intellectual level, the separation of school and church, and the provision of equal opportunities for education. In May 1946, a new School Law was decreed. This school reform was a turning point in the history of German education. It represented not only a decisive break with National Socialism but also with the social order that existed before 1933. With the introduction of the eight-year comprehensive school (*Einheitsschule*) for all children, the traditional tripartite division of German schools was abandoned. Compulsory schooling started with the age of six.[9] For the first time, all childcare facilities and after-school care centers were declared to be educational institutions and, as such, integrated into the state-financed and -controlled national education system. Already by 1946, 80 percent of the childcare institutions in the GDR had come under the jurisdiction of municipalities, while only 13 and 7 percent remained run by the church or were attached to workplaces, respectively.[10]

The school reform became increasingly drawn into the process of German division that occurred in the context of growing East-West confrontation. From 1949 on, the SED, the governing party of the state, suppressed the influence of former Social Democrats on school policy.[11] Though the constitution of the young GDR, which was founded in October 1949, defined childrearing as the "natural right of parents and their foremost duty to society,"[12] child education, in contrast to West Germany with its plural structure of charity organizations, was established as a state function. The traditionally strong influence of the churches on childcare and education was marginalized. The family, traditionally charged with the education of children, was considered complicit in the Nazi project and was thus politically disqualified from participating in the education of children in the new socialist state.[13] In 1952, after-school care facilities (*Horte*), which had in the GDR previously been mostly part of the daycare centers of the municipalities (*Kindertagesstätten*) or the kindergartens at the workplace (*Betriebskindergärten*), were placed under the control of the schools. In the 1950s, however, the network of state-run childcare remained loosely coordinated. The great majority of school children were not enrolled in a childcare or after-school care program. In 1955, around 35 percent of all three- to six-year-old children had a place in a childcare facility, and only 5 percent of six- to fourteen-year-old school children. (See Table 16.1.)

In addition to traditional forms of childcare and after-school care, new forms were increasingly offered during the 1950s by mass political organizations like the German Democratic Women's Association (Demokratischer Frauenbund, DFB), National Front (Nationale Front), as well as

TABLE 16.1: Childcare for three- to six-year-old children in the GDR, 1955–1989[14]

Year	Number of childcare facilities	Number of places	Degree of coverage [a] (percent of all children in the age group)
1955	8,527	350,332	35%
1960	11,508	458,678	46%
1970	13,105	654,658	65%
1980	12,233	664,478	92%
1989	13,452	747,140	95%

Note:
(a) Until 1985, the places refer to children 3–5 years old plus 75 percent of the children from six to seven years. From 1986 on, it includes children from three to five as well as 58 percent of the children from six to seven years.

Young Pioneers (Junge Pioniere) and Free German Youth (Freie Deutsche Jugend, FDJ). They organized and improvised rooms for doing homework (*Hausaufgabenzimmer*) and school clubs. The great majority of children with working parents, however, spent their afternoons in the 1950s either with their grandparents or on their own.

The Pressure to Reform: Women's Work, Childcare, and Education Policy

The period between 1958 and 1960 witnessed a critical juncture that proved crucial for the implementation of all-day childcare and education. Never before had both been discussed so intensely as they were during these years. But why did they suddenly climb to the top of both the pedagogical and political agenda? The answer to this question is to be found in a specific historical constellation of developments in the labor market, education policy, and political and ideological concepts that together produced a new debate on childcare and education. This debate, moreover, quickly led to the implementation of a new educational policy.

The Labor Market

By the late 1950s, the GDR faced a growing shortage of workers that threatened its seven-year plan to overtake West Germany economically. At the time, thousands of people, especially men and younger citizens, were leaving the country through the still-open border to the West. To meet the demands of the labor market, the state made an unprecedented appeal to women to enter the workforce. The female proportion of the working population, however, had been stagnant since 1955. After the war, it was primarily unmarried women, war widows, and single mothers who entered the labor market. But in order to accomplish its ambitious economic plans, it now became necessary for the state to mobilize married women and mothers for the workforce.[15] Drawing heavily on the socialist rhetoric of female emancipation, in 1958 the SED thus launched an elaborate ideological campaign. Above all, it appealed to unemployed women to realize their inherent right to work, which was, not surprisingly, also framed as the duty to work. In concert with the party's efforts, the DFB, a mass women's organization with broad membership, initiated a campaign of "housewife brigades" to "help" women emancipate themselves and broaden their domestic horizons by taking jobs in industry.[16] The old bourgeois concept of the mother and "unproductive housewife," moreover, drew sharp criticism from several quarters. The new cultural ideal of the "good mother" was the working mother, who, by participating in the building of socialism, exercised a healthy influence on her children. As an article in the magazine *Woman of Today* (*Frau von Heute*) from 1957 claimed:

> More and more women recognize that in addition [to the economic benefits of work] having a job contributes enormously to the development of their personality. To an ever greater degree, women are completely fulfilled by their jobs. For them, working in socialism is liberating and educating. By engaging in such social work, a woman will become a better role model for her child.[17]

The lack of childcare institutions, however, proved to be one of the main obstacles to mothers' employment in the GDR. As the SED pointed out in 1958, mothers' employment was stagnating because there were hardly any after-school childcare centers, especially for school-aged children. (See Table 16.2.) Only 8 percent of six- to eleven-year-old children were enrolled in an after-school care center. In contrast, at least 45 percent of all children between the ages of three and six attended kindergarten and preschool. The SED was thus concerned that many mothers were leaving their jobs after their children entered school.[18]

Education Policy

Beginning in the late 1950s, the SED began to develop an ambitious new education policy.[20] To accelerate education reform, in 1958 the Politburo set up a school commission that included party members, officials from the Ministry of Education, and education experts. According to the School Law of 1959, the old comprehensive school with eight grades was to be replaced by a general polytechnical high school (*Polytechnische Ober-schule*) that would last ten years. However, this goal would not be realized

TABLE 16.2: Childcare for school children[a] and day schools in the GDR, 1955–1989[19]

Year	Number of after-school childcare centers (*Schulhorte*) until 1965	Number of children in all-day care and education (*Kindertagesstätten,* and after 1965 also *Schulhorte*)	Degree of coverage (percent of all children in the age group)	Number of day schools (*Tageschulen*)
1955	2,310	98,444	5% [b]	—
1958	3,126	133,515	7% [a]	9
1960	5,022	266,946	13% [b]	56
1962	5,737	361,981	16% [b]	—
1965		424,347 [c]	—	133
1970		595,268	47% [c]	
1980		627,401	75% [c]	
1989		760,740	88% [c]	

Notes:
(a) Since 1965, polytechnical high schools (*Polytechnische Oberschulen*) and schools for handicapped children (*Sonderschulen*).
(b) The places refer to children 6–14 years old.
(c) The places refer to children 6–10 years old.
(d) This number refers to children only at the polytechnical high school.

throughout the country until the late 1970s.[21] In addition, this new school law established a closer connection between school and after-school care. Indeed, after-school childcare and all-day school education played a crucial role in these educational debates, which involved education experts, SED members, and officials in the education administration. Studies revealed that many students, especially those with working-class or peasant backgrounds, had difficulty meeting the standards of the curriculum and completing their homework. In some regions of the GDR, in particular the agricultural areas at the periphery of the state, the percentage of students who needed to repeat a grade was very high.[22] For many government officials, SED members, and education experts, all-day school education appeared to offer an effective way to improve student performance, particularly in the new ten-year high schools. Education experts from the Central German Pedagogical Institute thus began developing concepts and time schedules according to which an entire school day could be organized. Their primary goal was to promote student success in the ten-year high school.[23]

Political-Ideological Concepts of Education

In addition to the specific new education policies developed and implemented in the late 1950s, the SED and the government also envisioned a much broader education policy that would be an integral component of the project of "building socialism." Indeed, as part of their attempt to mobilize society for this grand objective, they strengthened the rhetoric of education and morality. In the field of education, Soviet pedagogy had become the leading model. The Soviet program to create the "New Socialist Man (*Mensch*)" inspired educational discourses in the GDR that were guided by the idea of "socialist communal education." The emerging debates on the expansion of state-run childcare illustrate the pedagogical optimism, which was characterized by the belief in the omnipotence of education, of these years. The visions of an extensive system of institutionalized childcare were based on a rote input-output model of education that would supposedly optimize the shaping of the human character.[24]

From the perspective of the SED, the success of this ambitious educational project was contingent upon reducing the influence of competing educational agencies such as the family and churches. The fact that the broad majority of school children were spending the afternoon in the streets or with their supposedly "unprogressive" families was interpreted as an obstacle not only for mothers' employment but also for the socialist state and its educational agenda. Grandparents, in particular, were criticized as

> relicts, in their consciousness and lifestyle, of capitalist society that have a deleterious influence on the adolescent generation. It is a fact that these petit-bourgeois ideas and attitudes emerged more clearly in the family than at the workplace. State-run, all-day childcare eliminates these uncontrollable and often negative influences and replaces them with a planned and systematic education.[25]

Despite the deep mistrust of the family as a deficient educational agency, Party and government officials advocated a closer connection between the school and family. According to the Sixth Pedagogical Congress held in 1961, school and family needed to develop a "simultaneous heartbeat."[26] After-school childcare centers, moreover, were supposed to "help" the family educate their children in a more socialist way.[27] But for all of the educational efforts undertaken by the party and government, by 1960 schools continued to suffer from large classes that, due to shortages of teachers and space, often had to be taught in shifts.

The "Day School": Actors and Arguments

The discourse and political efforts surrounding the all-day school developed during two brief periods that together constitute a critical juncture in the formulation of a new path in education and childcare policy in the GDR. First, the years 1958 and 1959 represent a kind of incubation period that witnessed the establishment of several experimental all-day schools and a growing debate on all-day education. Second, in 1960 the political campaign to introduce the all-day school culminated throughout the country.

During this first period, eleven "day schools" (*Tagesschulen*) were established on a trial basis. Already in 1957, the SED had instructed the Central German Pedagogical Institute to conduct an experiment with all-day schools. Beginning in 1958, these "laboratory schools" were supposed to develop all-day education as a permanent institution, particularly for children from working-class or peasant backgrounds.[28] This decision was influenced by two major factors. On the one hand, the Soviet Union introduced after 1956 first boarding schools and later "extended-day schools" and "groups of the extended-day" (*Gruppen des verlängerten Tages*) as part of a new education policy that sought to "connect school to life." These schools were to be open the entire day and offer a curriculum that included cognitive learning, sports, and other social activities. The communist government of the SU hoped that this collective approach to education would have a beneficial impact on the development of a "socialist personality" of children.[29] On the other hand, East Germany closely observed developments in all-day education in West Germany, where the first all-day schools were founded in the second half of the 1950s.[30] Indeed, there appears to have been some contact and interaction between Eastern and Western educational experts. Representatives of the East German Ministry of Education attended, for example, conferences organized by the West German supporters of all-day schools like the GGT, the Gemeinnützige Gesellschaft Tagesheimschule.[31]

Pedagogical journals and the archives of the East German Ministry of Education show that beginning in 1958, the discourse on all-day education in the GDR became increasingly shaped by the following related arguments. Within the context of polytechnic education, all-day education was discussed as a way of establishing a closer connection between the workplace and schools so as to prepare students for their future profession.[32] In addition to citing the Soviet idea of "collective education," proponents of all-day education emphasized the needs of the children of working mothers and the desire for "our working mothers" to be "relieved" from their "double burden."[33] In this context, childcare was clearly defined as a "maternal" rather than a "parental" responsibility. Other concepts that defined this discourse were "class" and "social equality." At the time, day schools and after-school care centers were intended primarily for working-class and peasant children. On the one hand, this restriction was due to a lack of space and learning materials; on the other, it was formed by the ideological idea that workers' and peasants' children required greater support and attention, and an intensified ideological education. Only such an education, the SED and the Ministry of Education argued, would enable working-class children to realize their historical mission as the new "leading class."[34] In this regard, its proponents viewed the day school also as an instrument to compensate for these children's lack of social and cultural capital.[35] A place in a conventional after-school childcare center or a day school was thus reevaluated as a "privilege." This interpretation was compatible with the widely accepted social-pedagogic rationale that all-day childcare was a sociopolitical measure designed to help realize the broader political goal of supporting working-class families.

Contrary to the official discourse in the GDR, the realization of day schools in East and all-day schools in West Germany exhibited important similarities. In both German states, these schools were at first established primarily in industrial regions with high rates of female employment. Moreover, in both states, working-class children represented the majority of their students. In the GDR, however, a higher proportion of them, despite political rhetoric to the contrary, were classified as "difficult."[36] But whereas in West Germany, the so-called latchkey child dominated the discussion on mothers' employment, that image was entirely incompatible with the policy of the communist state.[37] It was therefore avoided in East German discourse on the subject. Because of the striking similarities in respect to the social background of the students enrolled in the first all-day schools in East and West Germany, pedagogues in the GDR were compelled to emphasize clearly the principal difference between the two German states. In the words of Horst Drewelow, an educationalist from the University of Rostock:

> The all-day school of the GDR is not an institution in terms of capitalist welfare institutions and is not at all an institution for underperforming and neglected children. … The point is that with the day school, the children of workers' and peasants' families receive an education which enables them 'to continue the great work of their fathers,' that is, to direct the socialist state, [and] its economy, and culture.[38]

The second phase of the day school, which began in early 1960, was marked by the political and ideological campaign for the implementation of all-day education for the entire country. Already in November 1959, the Central Committee of the SED had written to its party organizations in the schools that they needed to prepare for the transition to "full all-day education."[39] In order to accelerate the "socialist reorganization" of the school system, the party decided to transform all East German high schools into all-day schools by 1966. Moreover, the discourse on all-day education no longer focused solely on workers' and peasants' children. Instead, all children were now to be integrated into this "school of the communist future."[40] The school commission, which was staffed by the SED with pedagogical researchers and school administrators, defined all-day education as a "higher level of our socialist school" and as a more effective way "to reach our educational goals."[41] These new schools should be created by merging existing schools and after-school childcare centers. Not surprisingly, the new education policy had a hidden agenda. Day schools were designed as an intermediate step. In keeping with the Soviet model, boarding schools, the final step in the transformation of the educational system, were to be introduced starting in the 1980s.[42]

In January 1960, the SED leader, Walter Ulbricht, initiated a political campaign to implement this new policy to create all-day schools. There was, however, no public mention of the future plan to introduce boarding schools. The education administration, together with the party organizations and the principals, had to decide whether schools were politically and practically "ripe" enough for the new all-day time structure. The most important criterion was the degree of cooperation between teachers and the so-called educators (*Erzieher*, i.e., the childcare personnel in after-school programs), their political attitudes, and the available rooms in schools. Initially, the campaign for day schools seemed to have developed its own self-sustaining dynamic. In several districts, school councils and party secretaries pushed for day schools without taking into account the financial limits of the plan. In the countryside, moreover, the introduction of all-day education overlapped with the collectivization of agriculture. Here too, female labor was increasingly needed. An extension of all-day education was seen as one precondition for a rise in female employment.[43] In this historical context, day schools had an impressive start: 56 were established in 1960. By 1965, their number increased to 133. (See Table 16.2.)

But how did the political intentions of the communist state and party filter down to the level of institutional actors? Moreover, how did non-institutional actors, above all parents and other social and professional groups, react to this new policy? As it was, Ulbricht's campaign met with massive resistance from a variety of quarters. Along with the Protestant and Catholic Churches, many parents, physicians, and teachers strongly opposed the state's plan. Defending their traditional prerogatives concerning their children, parents argued that all-day education would destroy the family and overstrain children. This reflects the strong Germanic tradition of a division between the responsibility of the parents for the education (*Erziehung*) of their children in the family and the state's obligations for their school education (*Bildung*). They also complained that the day school would imprison their children for the entire day like an unfree "herd."[44] Indeed, it quickly became clear that many workers' and peasants' families did not share the educational goals of the state. Instead, they were more interested in seeing their children begin work as soon as possible to ease their financial burden. Others rejected the idea of all-day education because it would mean that their children would have less time to complete their chores at home. For their part, Christian families and the churches argued that children would no longer have time for religious instruction in the afternoon.[45] In addition, childcare personnel worried that the plans to unify schooling and after-school programs in one institution and mix them during the day might lead to the abolition of their profession altogether in the near future. Finally, many schoolteachers resisted all-day education as well. They maintained that their primary duty was knowledge-based teaching and thus refused to undertake the onerous task of nonacademic afternoon teaching. Such concerns were particularly prominent among the growing numbers of female primary school teachers who feared extended working time because of their own family obligations.[46] In fact, such concerns contributed to the exodus of teachers to the West before the border was closed with the building of the Berlin Wall in August 1961. Indeed, the SED itself conceded that one of the primary reasons for the migration to the West by members of this profession was the unpopular campaign for the day school.[47]

But in the end, it was not this deep mistrust of an omnipotent state felt by parents and other social groups that prevented the realization of day schools throughout the country. Instead, the policy failed due to the lack of funds for the construction of new buildings and purchase of materials that were deemed necessary for all-day education to succeed. Moreover, the Ministry of Education apparently failed to discuss its plans with the State Planning Commission. As a result, the needs of all-day education were never incorporated into central planning figures. In the summer of 1960, the SED therefore decided that the transition to the all-day school could only be carried out gradually and without the additional resources it had initially foreseen as necessary.[48] Although financial reasons were primarily responsible for preventing the implementation of day schools, social and cultural factors also played a role. The fact that in the following years, the SED and the government stressed the voluntary character of after-school childcare suggests that they realized—and accommodated themselves to the fact—that a broad part of the society did not share their ideas for greater state influence over the raising and education of children.[49]

While several new day schools were founded in the early 1960s, the day school as a means of transforming education was increasingly marginalized on the political agenda. Instead, it became largely an object of academic interest. In 1962, the German Pedagogical Central Institute founded a "day school" research group that was charged with studying the transition from half-day to all-day education in laboratory schools.[50] In the mid-1960s, a study undertaken by the Ministry of Education revealed that in practice, there was no major difference in the academic performance of children who attended all-day schools and those who attended schools with integrated after-school childcare centers (*Schulhorte*).[51]

All-Day Education in the Later GDR

Following the construction of the Berlin Wall in August 1961, the East German economy and society slowly began to stabilize. Women's employment and education both became highly politicized and were offered as proof of East Germany's modernity and progressiveness, especially in comparison to West Germany. The rate of female employment increased steadily from 66 percent in 1970 to 78 percent in 1989. (See Table 16.3.) The extension of all-day childcare centers and after-school programs became crucial for increasing economic productivity, because there remained an urgent need for female labor. With opening hours from 6:00 A.M. to 6:00 P.M. or later in the evening, they allowed women to pursue both a professional career and a family. Moreover, all-day care and education also promised to prepare children better for life and work in the high-tech communist society envisioned by the state.

TABLE 16.3: Women's employment in the GDR, 1955–1989[52]

Year	Women of working age (15–65 years)	Women in the workforce	Female employment rate [(a)]
1955	6,182,000	3,244,000	53%
1970	5,011,000	3,312,000	66%
1980	5,257,000	3,848,000	73%
1989	5,074,000	3,962,000	78%

Notes:
(a) Percent of working women in the working age of 15–65 years (not including apprentices and students).

Rather than establishing more day schools, however, after-school childcare was expanded. In 1960, only about 13 percent of children of primary school age attended an after-school program.[53] In 1970 that number had climbed to 47 percent and by 1980, it reached 75 percent (see Table 16.2).[54] The growing percentage of children in after-school care was largely the result of a real extension of the places, but also reflected the demographic development. In the mid-1960s, the East German birth rate had begun to decline, a trend that accelerated rapidly in the following decade.

Acceptance of after-school care in the GDR population grew slowly but steadily. In the 1960s, many parents still seem to have believed that it would be better to take care of children at home after school. In 1960, the German Pedagogical Central Institute reported that parents appeared to threaten their children with after-school care to get them to behave. They thus concluded that they needed "to educate the whole population to refrain from making threats such as 'if you don't obey, you have to go to the after-school care center.'"[55] To counter these "traditional" attitudes, the state attempted to make all-day education more attractive for children and their parents. If the state could win over children by offering appealing afternoon activities, parents might also come to sympathize with the goals of the communist state.

The utilitarian economic and political purposes of all-day education could also not be ignored. The 1960s were the height of the East-West competition on the field of educational reform, as many European countries realized that a better education for the broad population would produce the much-needed "economic reserve." For the GDR, the "exhaustion of the educational reserve" (Ausschöpfung der Bildungsreserve) and the mobilization of the education system for a "scientific technical revolution" became important goals. The grand vision of a communist society based on science and technical know-how informed the socialist discourses on schooling and education in the 1960s. Schools were supposed to "educate personalities who could manage and direct the process of the scientific technical revolution." Because the curricula of the half-day school were already too packed, time for additional instruction had to be found outside of the conventional classroom.[56] The state thus needed to further children's interests and abilities, which themselves had to be geared more towards the kinds of qualifications the future economy would require. According to the "Socialist Education Law" of 1965, the general goal of education was to create "broadly educated and harmoniously developed socialist personalities" that possess a positive attitude towards work and social usefulness.[57]

With the passage of this education law, the GDR's leadership believed it was finally on the way to becoming a modern "educated nation" and defined all-day care and education as an "integral part" of schooling.[58] However, the cooperation between schools and their integrated after-school centers remained a problem. In most cases, they were essentially two separate, coexisting institutions in one building. Principals and teachers often showed little interest in after-school childcare. They neither took the childcare personnel nor their work in the afternoon-care centers seriously, and therefore refused to invite them to teachers meetings.[59] One reason for this reservation was their poor training. Until the 1960s, the majority of the childcare personnel had only attended a few introductory courses or even no professional training at all.[60]

The quality of after-school education was also impaired by the lack of attractive recreational facilities as well as competition from the different actors involved in extracurricular activities. Since the mid-1960s, an increasingly dense network began to emerge that linked afternoon childcare with the offerings of the working groups and sports clubs of the school, and the activities of the Young Pioneers and Free German Youth, the socialist children and youth organizations.[61] For many principals, the coordination of these many different activities proved quite difficult. In May 1966, Minister of Education Margot Honecker issued a sharp criticism of this situation. She complained that a "collective" that included teachers and "educators" still did not exist at most schools and both groups were not willing to give the children's interests, represented by the Young Pioneers, serious consideration. She therefore concluded that "at the majority" of "schools the quality of education could not be considered satisfactory."[62] In the following years, many after-school care centers were beset by problems resulting from this competition as well as the deficiency of qualified educators. It was not until the late 1970s that the government finally merged the training for the staff of afternoon childcare centers and primary school teachers. For the childcare personnel, this was an important step toward the professionalization of their occupation. In spite of all efforts to improve after-school programs, there was little doubt that the academic curriculum had taken precedence over afternoon childcare activities. As a result, the Soviet concept of school education in which the teacher played a central and leading role remained firmly entrenched throughout the forty-year existence of the GDR.[63]

Despite its early deficits, all-day care and education continued to expand and became more and more accepted as a cultural norm in East Germany. Parallel to this development, women's employment grew steadily throughout the 1960s and 1970s. The concept of the "working woman and mother" gained increasing acceptance in the population. Already by 1976, 79 percent of working-age women were gainfully employed (see Table 16.3).[64] In addition to the general expansion of education, which offered broader social strata than ever before access to higher education, women also benefited from training and advancement programs designed specifically for them. But despite these changes, the labor market remained strongly divided along gender lines. The introduction of the five-day workweek in 1967, which extended the workday by forty-five minutes, made it more difficult for mothers to combine paid work and family. The result was an increasing demand for part-time work. In contrast to other communist countries like the Soviet Union, the Czech Republic, and Hungary, the GDR accepted part-time work as an imperative, and all attempts to reduce it failed.[65] As a result, already by 1970 more than 33 percent of all women worked part-time.[66]

Family policy in the GDR worked to institutionalize the "two-breadwinner family" as a way of stabilizing "socialist society." The Family Law of 1965 was based on the premise that the state and families shared a common interest. This law redefined the importance of the family not only for raising children but also for reproducing society in general. Indeed, the main purpose of marriage was to bear and raise children for the socialist state; gender equality came second. Thus, the practice in the GDR was the "two-breadwinner/female-homemaker" family. Shortly after the Family Law came into force, the growing divorce rate and the declining birth rate made it increasingly apparent that women were overburdened by the dual workload inside and outside the home. Beginning in the early 1970s, the state, under the new leadership of Erich Honecker, responded with extensive family policy measures that sought to help women combine motherhood and employment. Pregnancy and childbirth leave were expanded, and an optional one-year maternity leave was introduced. Men, however, were ineligible for parental leave. This policy not only valorized women's role as mothers, but it also perpetuated the putative responsibility of women for family matters.[67]

Conclusion

Throughout its forty-year existence, the main argument to expand state-run childcare in the German Democratic Republic was that it would facilitate the integration of women into the labor market, which from the very beginning was recognized as absolutely necessary. At first, married, widowed, and single women provided the main female labor reserve. Only later in the 1950s were mothers increasingly needed to sustain the workforce. This forced the regime to extend all-day childcare for toddlers and kindergarten and increase the number of places in afternoon-programs.

The traditional half-day structure of the school system, however, persisted until the fall of the wall. The first new School Law only abolished the traditional Germanic path of the tripartite school system and introduced comprehensive schooling. The SED also tried to reform the time structure of the school system, but with little success. Beginning in the mid-1950s, the education policy of the GDR focused increasingly on social equality and the shaping of the "socialist personality." Following the model of the

Soviet Union, the communist government accelerated the development of day schools. Despite resistance from the population as well as educational professionals, its implementation was possible because the GDR was a highly centralized authoritarian state that sought to regulate aspects of social and political life through extensive planning. In this paternalist "welfare dictatorship," the SED thoroughly controlled all political decision-making processes by eliminating the kinds of competing political forces and ideas that had prevented the development of all-day education in West Germany. In the end, not primarily political and cultural causes, but the financial constraints of the GDR in the 1960s stopped the extension of the number of day schools. Instead the SED systematically expanded state-subsidized all-day care and education in daycare centers and after-school care programs.

During the 1970s and 1980s, this expanded network of all-day care and education represented a crucial component of the paternalistic East German welfare policy. Despite the image of the "modernity" of East German society propagated by the SED, the break with the traditional German path in family and schooling was less decisive than the politics and rhetoric of state socialism implied. The continuity of traditional gender relations in the family and at the workplace is well known. In the school system, Soviet pedagogical concepts existed alongside of a traditional professional culture of teachers, and the persistence of the half-day structure, together with resistance against all-day schools for very similar reasons by the same groups as in the FRG, suggest a complex mix of continuity and change in the GDR school system.

West German observers long overlooked the fact that the traditional half-day school survived in the GDR, even if it was supplemented with an extensive all-day childcare program with crèches, daycare centers, and after-school care programs. This state-run all-day care and education in the GDR served both as a way to integrate mothers into the workforce and as an instrument of political power used to stabilize family and society. In the long-run, however, it proved extremely costly and contributed to the growing economic difficulties that produced the crisis of the East German state in the late 1980s.

Notes

The research for this paper was funded by a grant of the Volkswagen Foundation for a research project entitled "Between Ideology and Economy: All-Day School in East and West Germany in Comparison (1945–1980)," which is directed by Karen Hagemann (University of

North Carolina, Chapel Hill). I would like to thank her for her extensive support and critical comments.

 1. Gunnar Winkler, ed., *Frauenreport 90* (Berlin, 1990), 143f.
 2. For more see the chapter by Karen Hagemann in this volume; Karen Hagemann, "Between Ideology and Economy: The 'Time Politics' of Childcare and Public Education in the Two Germanys," *Social Politics* 13, no. 2 (2006): 221f.; Ute Gerhard, "Mütter zwischen Individualisierung und Institution: Kulturelle Leitbilder in der Wohlfahrtspolitik," in *Erwerbstätige Mütter: Ein europäischer Vergleich*, ed. Ute Gerhard et al. (Munich, 2003), 80ff.
 3. Until recently, relatively little research has been done on this topic. Most studies focus on education and generally neglect the cultural and gender dimension. Karen Hagemann has suggested that new research on the time politics of the German case of childcare and education should strive to integrate the cultural and gender dimension. Karen Hagemann and Karin Gottschall, "Die Halbtagsschule in Deutschland—ein Sonderfall in Europa?" *Aus Politik und Zeitgeschichte*, B 41 (2002): 12–22; Hagemann, "Between Ideology." See for research that does not include the gender dimension, Birgit Gebhardt, "Die Tagesschule der DDR: Betrachtungen zum sozialistischen Konzept der Ganztagserziehung," *Zeitschrift für Pädagogik* 39, no. 6 (1993): 991–1006; Gert Geißler, "Ganztagsschule in der DDR: Großer Sprung, kleine Schritte und allmähliche Erschöpfung," in *Ganztagsangebote in der Schule. Internationale Erfahrungen und empirische Forschungen*, ed. Falk Radisch (Bonn, 2005), 81–100; Monika Müller-Rieger, ed. *"Wenn Mutti früh zur Arbeit geht …" Zur Geschichte des Kindergartens in der DDR* (Dresden, 1997).
 4. See the chapter by Hagemann in this volume; Hagemann, "Between Ideology."
 5. Toni Makkai, "Social Policy and Gender in Eastern Europe," in *Gendering Welfare States*, ed. Diane Sainsbury (Cambridge, UK, 1994), 189.
 6. Julius Hoffmann, "Jugendämter im Wandel: Zur staatlichen Kinder- und Jugendpolitik in der SBZ/DDR," in *Jahrbuch für zeitgeschichtliche Jugendforschung 1994/95* (Berlin, 1995), 40–57; Hilmar Hoffmann, "Zwischen Kontinuität und Diskontinuität: Zur Geschichte der Kindergartenpädagogik in der DDR," in Müller-Rieger, *Wenn Mutti*, 19–39.
 7. Hagemann, "Between Ideology"; Thomas Lindenberger, ed., *Massenmedien im Kalten Krieg: Akteure, Bilder, Resonanzen* (Cologne, 2006).
 8. Hagemann, "Between Ideology"; Robert Moeller, *Protecting Motherhood: Women and the Family in the Politics of Postwar West Germany* (Berkeley, CA, 1996).
 9. For more on this tradition, see the chapter by Hagemann in this volume. For the early GDR see, Gert Geißler, "School Reform between the Dictatorships? Pedagogics and Politics during the Early Years in the Soviet Occupation Zone of Germany," in *Education for the New Europe*, ed. Dietrich Benner and Dieter Lenzen (Oxford, 1996), 69–92.
10. See Christoph Führ and Carl-Ludwig Furck, eds., *Handbuch der deutschen Bildungsgeschichte*, vol. 6, *1945 bis zur Gegenwart*, pt. 2, *Deutsche Demokratische Republik und neue Bundesländer* (Munich, 1998); Dieter Höltershinken et al., *Kindergarten und Kindergärtnerin in der DDR*, 2 vol. (Neuwied, 1997); Hilmar Hoffmann, *Sozialdemokratische und kommunistische Kindergartenpolitik und -pädagogik in Deutschland* (Bochum, 1994).
11. Geißler, "School Reform."
12. Hagemann, "Between Ideology."
13. Leonore Ansorg, *Kinder im Klassenkampf. Die Geschichte der Pionierorganisation von 1948 bis Ende der fünfziger Jahre* (Berlin, 1997), 15f.; Heinz-Elmar Tenorth, "Die Bildungsgeschichte der DDR—Teil der deutschen Bildungsgeschichte?" in *Bildungsgeschichte einer Diktatur. Bildung und Erziehung in der SBZ und DDR im historisch-gesellschaftlichen Kontext*, ed. Heinz-Elmar Tenorth (Weinheim, 1997), 83f.
14. Winkler, *Frauenreport '90*, 143.

15. Heike Trappe, *Emanzipation oder Zwang? Frauen in der DDR zwischen Beruf, Familie und Sozialpolitik* (Berlin, 1995); Gunilla-Friederike Budde, ed., *Frauen arbeiten: Weibliche Erwerbstätigkeit in Ost- und Westdeutschland* (Göttingen, 1997); Hildegard Maria Nickel, "'Mitgestalterinnen des Sozialismus': Frauenarbeit in der DDR," in *Frauen in Deutschland 1945–1992*, ed. Gisela Helwig and Hildegard Maria Nickel (Bonn, 1993), 233–56.

16. Gesine Obertreis, *Familienpolitik in der DDR 1945–1980* (Opladen, 1986), 140ff.; Monika Mattes, "'Vom Ich zum Wir': Hausfrauenbrigaden in der DDR, 1958–61," *1999: Zeitschrift für Sozialgeschichte des 20. und 21. Jahrhunderts* 11, no. 2 (1996): 36–61.

17. "Unsere große Aussprache: Wir und unsere Kinder," *Frau von heute* 12, no. 42 (1957): 10 and 17; *Frau von heute* 12, no. 45 (1957): 31; *Frau von heute* 12, no. 47 (1957): 17; *Frau von heute* 12, no. 49 (1957): 14; Horst Drewelow, *Die Schule der Zukunft: Die Tagesheimschule in der Deutschen Demokratischen Republik und ihre Bedeutung für die Entwicklung der Ganztagserziehung* (Berlin, 1962).

18. "Protokoll von der Sitzung der Arbeitsgruppe für die Erarbeitung des Mittelschulprogramms am 1.11.1958," Stiftung Archiv der Parteien und Massenorganisationen im Bundesarchiv (hereafter SAMPO-Barch), DR 2/4624.

19. *Statistisches Jahrbuch der DDR 1963* (Berlin 1964), 405; *Statistisches Jahrbuch der DDR 1968* (Berlin 1969), 455; Winkler, *Frauenreport '90*, 144.

20. Führ and Furck, *Handbuch*, vol. 4; Tenorth, "Die Bildungsgeschichte."

21. Gert Geißler, *Zur Zeitgeschichte von Bildungs- und Schulpolitik in Deutschland* (Berlin, 2006), 48f.

22. "Schreiben von Neugebauer an Senf, vom 5.2.1960," Bibliothek für Bildungsgeschichtliche Forschung, Bestand Deutsches Pädagogisches Zentralinstitut (hereafter BBF, DPZI), 2538; Horst Drewelow, "Praktiker und Wissenschaftler lösen gemeinsam Probleme der Tagesheimschule in der DDR," *Pädagogik* 15, no. 2 (1960): 178–81.

23. "Schreiben von Neugebauer an Senf vom 5.2.1960."

24. Dorothee Wierling, "Die Jugend als innerer Feind: Konflikt in der Erziehungsdiktatur der sechziger Jahre," in *Sozialgeschichte der DDR*, ed. Hartmut Kaelble et al. (Stuttgart, 1994), 417.

25. Drewelow, *Schule der Zukunft*, 11.

26. *Elternhaus und Schule—es muß ein Herzschlag sein. Erfahrungsaustausch über die Zusammenarbeit zwischen Lehrern und Eltern: Materialien und Beispiele* (Berlin, 1961).

27. "Alle Eltern gewinnen: Zur Arbeit der neu gewählten Elternräte," *Pädagogik* 15, no. 3 (1960): 263–68.

28. Werner Lindner, "Auszüge aus Materialien und Dokumenten der Partei und Regierung zu Fragen der Ganztagserziehung," BBF, DPZI, 2322

29. "Die Internatsschulen in der Sowjetunion," *Pädagogik* 13, no. 6 (1958): 464–68; Flora Lompscher, "Erfahrungen und Probleme der Ganztagserziehung in der Sowjetunion," *Pädagogik* 15, no. 6 (1960): 546–61; "Über die Organisierung von Ganztagsschulen: Mitteilung über eine gemeinsame Verordnung des ZK der KPdSU und des Ministerrats der DDR, veröffentlicht am 15.3.1960," in *Die sowjetische Bildungspolitik seit 1917. Dokumente und Texte*, ed. Oskar Anweiler (Heidelberg, 1961), 402f. See also the chapter by Anatoli Rakhkochkine in this volume.

30. Harald Ludwig, *Entstehung und Entwicklung der modernen Ganztagsschule in Deutschland*, 2 vol. (Cologne, 1993), 2: 498ff.

31. "Protokoll der Arbeitstagung der Gemeinnützigen Gesellschaft Tagesheimschule vom 2.4.1959 in der Tagesheimschule Frankfurt/M., Am Bornheimer Hang," SAPMO-BArch, DR 2/23560. For more on the GGT see the chapter by Hagemann in this volume.

32. Sektor Polytechnische Bildung und Oberschulen, "Arbeitsplan für die Zeit vom 1.1.-30.6.1960," SAPMO-BArch, SED, DY 30//IV 2/9.05/9.

33. Helga Schünemann, "Mutti ist jetzt ganz beruhigt," *Frau von heute* 13, no. 5 (1959): 12f.; DPZI, ed., *Aus der Arbeit in den Schulhorten: Gedanken und Erfahrungen* (n.p., 1960), 5; "Erfahrungen der Ganztagserziehung im Hort gründlich auswerten!" *Pädagogik* 15, no. 2 (1960): 160f.; Walter Günther et al., *Rahmenplan für die Bildung und Erziehung im Schulhort: Empfehlungen für die Arbeit der Horterzieher* (Berlin, 1972), 11.

34. "Gesichtspunkte für die Arbeit in den Ganztagsschulen vom 6. Mai 1958," BBF, DPZI, 2322.

35. DPZI, ed., *Aus der Arbeit*, 53 and 67.

36. Falk Goetze, "Bericht über die wissenschaftliche Arbeitskonferenz über Probleme der Tagesheimschule in der DDR vom 14.10–16.10.1959 an der Universität Rostock," BBF, 2046a; A. Döbler, "Bericht über die Konferenz der Pionierleiter der Tagesheimschulen am 13.2.1960 in der Zentralleitung," BBF, 2538; Helmut Dombrowski, "Die Tagesschule kann sich nur schrittweise entwickeln," *Ganztägige Bildung und Erziehung* 2, no. 2 (1964): 6–10.

37. Uta C. Schmidt, "Das Problem heißt: Schlüsselkind. Die Schlüsselkinderzählung als geschlechterpolitische Inszenierung im Kalten Krieg," in Lindenberger, *Massenmedien im Kalten Krieg*, 171–202.

38. Drewelow, *Schule der Zukunft*, 49.

39. Lindner, "Auszüge aus Materialien," 2322.

40. Gebhardt, "Die Tagesschule der DDR."

41. "Schlußbemerkungen der Genossen Neugebauer und Prof. Hager auf der Sitzung der Schulkommission über Fragen der ganztägigen Bildung und Erziehung am 23.3.1960," BBF, 2538.

42. "Beschluß über die Einführung der ganztägigen Bildung und Erziehung in der DDR," SAPMO-BArch, DR 2/5390.

43. "Die Schule im schönen sozialistischen Dorf—eine begeisternde Aufgabe," *Pädagogik* 15, no. 5 (1960): 482–89; Heinz Lindner and Hans Rettke, "Die Schule im vollgenossenschaftlichen Dorf," *Pädagogik* 15, no. 5 (1960): 406–14.

44. Ministerium für Volksbildung Abt. Hauptinspektion, "Schreiben vom 23.12.1959," SAPMO-BArch, Nationale Front, DY 6/3939; "Schreiben des Direktors der Oberschule Etzdorf an Ministerium für Volksbildung vom 15.9.1960," BArch, DR 2/7293.

45. "Information an die Genossen Kurz Hager und Werner Neugebauer über die Verbreitung der Elternbeiratswahlen," SAPMO-BArch, DY 30/IV 2/9.05/141; "Argumentation zu Verleumdungen des Schulgesetzes und der Schulordnung durch einige reaktionäre Kirchenkreise," SAPMO-BArch, DY 6/3939; "Maßnahmen kirchlicher Kreise gegen das Schulgesetz," SAPMO-BArch, DY 30/IV 2/9.05/9.

46. "Einschätzung über den Stand der Volksdiskussion (Min. Volksbildung)," 12 December 1959, SAPMO-BArch, DY 6/3939.

47. Gebhardt, "Die Tagesschule der DDR," 1002.

48. "Notiz über die Zusammenarbeit der verantwortlichen Genossen des Ministeriums für Volksbildung mit den Genossen der Abt. Volksbildung der Staatlichen Plankommission vom 21.7.1960," SAPMO-Barch, DR 2/5390; Gebhardt, "Die Tagesschule der DDR," 1002.

49. "Schreiben von Werner Lindner (DPZI) an Lorenz, Staatssekretär im Min. für Volksbildung vom 31.5.1963," SAPMO-BArch, Ministerium für Volksbildung, DR 2/23562.

50. Werner Goetze, "Beratung der Forschungsgemeinschaft Tagesschule," *Pädagogik* 18, no. 2 (1963): 218f.; "Beschluß des Präsidiums des Ministerrates über den schrittweisen Aufbau der Tagesschulen in Berlin-Köpenick und Leipzig-Südwest," SAPMO-BArch, DR 2/23561.

51. "Einschätzung des Entwicklungsstandes der Tagesschulen," SAPMO-BArch, DR 2/23569.
52. Winkler, *Frauenreport '90*, 63.
53. *Statistisches Jahrbuch 1960/61 der Deutschen Demokratischen Republik* (Berlin,1961).
54. Winkler, *Frauenreport '90*, 144.
55. DPZI, ed., *Aus der Arbeit*, 33. See also Paul Janke, "Vom Mehrstufenunterricht zur Ganztagserziehung: Erfahrungen aus dem Kreis Sondershausen," *Pädagogik* 15, no. 6 (1960): 562f.
56. "Der Klub ist kein Privileg der Tagesschule," *Ganztägige Bildung und Erziehung* 2, no. 7 (1964): 11f.
57. Kanzlei des Staatsrates der DDR, ed., *Unser Bildungssystem—ein wichtiger Schritt auf dem Wege zur gebildeten Nation: Materialien der 12. Sitzung der Volkskammer der DDR und das Gesetz über das einheitliche sozialistische Bildungssystem* (n.p., 1965).
58. Ibid., 100f.
59. Eckard Milde and Hannelore Wasser, "Wir beseitigen das Nebeneinander von Schule und Hort," *Ganztägige Bildung und Erziehung* 2, no. 1 (1964): 15–16; Clara Bolz, "Alte Vorstellungen vom Hort hemmten unsere Arbeit," *Ganztägige Bildung und Erziehung* 2, no. 3 (1964): 18–20; Roland Rudolf, "Pädagogen dritter Klasse?" *Ganztägige Bildung und Erziehung* 2, no. 8 (1964): 16–19.
60. After 1978, the plan of studies for primary school teachers included an internship in an after-school childcare center, which would prepare them to work in such a facility. See Dietmar Waterkamp, *Handbuch zum Bildungswesen der DDR* (Berlin, 1990), 384f.
61. For the early period of the GDR, see Ansorg, *Kinder im Klassenkampf.*
62. Margot Honecker, "Nächste Schritte bei der Verwirklichung des Gesetzes über das einheitliche sozialistische Bildungssystem: Referat des Ministers für Volksbildung, Margot Honecker, auf der zentralen Arbeitsberatung der Bezirks- und Kreisschulräte zur Vorbereitung des Schul- und Lehrjahres 1966/67 am 12. und 13. Mai 1966 in Berlin," *Deutsche Lehrerzeitung* 13, no. 21 (1966): 32f.
63. Heinz-Elmar Tenorth, *Geschichte der Erziehung: Einführung in die Grundzüge ihrer neuzeitlichen Entwicklung* (Weinheim, 2003), 285.
64. *Statistisches Jahrbuch 1976/77 der Deutschen Demokratischen Republik* (Berlin, 1977), 37.
65. See the chapters by Hana Hašková and Dorottya Szikra in this volume.
66. Obertreis, *Familienpolitik*, 306.
67. Ute Gerhard, "Die staatlich institutionalisierte Lösung der Frauenfrage: Zur Geschichte der Geschlechterverhältnisse in der DDR," in Kaelble, *Sozialgeschichte*, 391f.; Obertreis, *Familienpolitik*, 292ff.

Chapter 17

TRADITION MATTERS

Childcare, Preschool, and Primary Education in Modern Hungary

Dorottya Szikra

Hungary has long been a leader among European countries in the development of publicly supported family policies. This has been true both in the case of direct payments to families and state provision of social services such as early childhood care. Despite the implementation of neoliberal economic policies since the political transition of 1989, most of the family policy measures and basic childcare arrangements that were established during the communist era have been kept in place. The real value of those payments, however, has fallen steadily throughout the 1990s.[1] Nevertheless, the level of cash transfers and the extent of childcare arrangements in Hungary are today relatively generous compared with most of the other countries of the former Soviet bloc. Thus the Organisation for Economic Co-operation and Development (OECD) reported in 2004 that 85 percent of the three- to four-year-old children, 91 percent of the four- to five-year-olds, and 97 percent of the five- to six-year-olds in Hungary attend kindergarten or preschools (*óvoda*). The percentage of children under three in childcare centers and crèches (*bölcsőde*), on the other hand, was lower than the EU average at 9 percent, but still higher than in other countries such as the Czech Republic (1 percent) or Germany (3 percent). Moreover, both types of childcare offer all-day services of up to ten hours for fifty weeks per year. The final year of kindergarten for five- to six-year-olds is compulsory. Primary school starts at age six, and because it is a half-day school, over 40 percent of all students between the ages of six and twelve attend after-school programs.[2]

At first glance, it is surprising that the generous maternity and parental leave policy and the high percentage of three- to six-year-olds in childcare has not produced a higher rate of female employment, which at 54 percent is slightly below the EU average of 56 percent. Rather, the level of mothers' participation in the labor market is strikingly low. According to a 2004 OECD study of twenty states, the percentage of employed mothers with children under three in Hungary was at 31 percent the second lowest, after the Czech Republic's rate of 14 percent. The employment rate of mothers with children under six is at 30 percent nearly the same. Hungary's fertility rate of 1.3 is also far below the EU average.[3] How can we explain this situation?

According to the OECD report, one major reason for this is that Hungary, with its high levels of unregistered work and various work disincentives, has one of Europe's lowest rates of formal employment. This situation results from the very sparse employment opportunities for people with limited education in the formal labor market.[4] For women, an additional factor is the insufficient opportunity to work part-time. Ninety-five percent of all employed women had to work full-time in 2004, compared to an average of 32 percent in the EU. The rigidity of the working schedules and the amount of working hours make it extremely difficult to balance family and work, even with older children, yet another reason why Hungary posts the lowest rate of employed mothers with children under sixteen in Europe.[5]

Above all, the Hungarian family policy and its childcare and preschool system face two major challenges that are the root cause of this situation. The first challenge is the low rate of childcare provision for small children and the unbalanced regional distribution of crèches and kindergartens throughout the country, which has resulted in a very unequal access. As in the past, the agrarian poor in rural regions at the periphery of the country and ethnic minorities in particular have been effectively excluded from high-quality social and educational services. The most disadvantaged and poorest minority group in the country are the Roma, who represent about 6 percent of the population. The percentage of Roma has increased rapidly since World War II. Today every fifth or sixth newborn in Hungary is Roma, and the country has the largest proportion of Roma in the world.[6]

This inequality is related to a second major problem, namely, Hungary's high rate of female economic inactivity, particularly among women from lower social strata. Because poor mothers and women from minority groups have limited access to childcare and after-school programs, they have much greater difficulty returning to the labor market after childbirth. The extremely long period of maternal and parental leave provided by the Hungarian state along with insufficient provision of childcare for small children has also served to raise the rate of women who do not return to the labor market. Insured (employed) women are entitled to a maternity leave of twenty-four weeks, which is remunerated at 70 percent of the employee's average salary with no upper limit. Afterwards they may still receive 70 percent but with a limit set at the minimum wage until the child's second birthday. In addition, Hungary provides a universal, flat-rate parental leave allowance until the third birthday of all children, which employed and unemployed mothers can receive.[7] As a result, women in Hungary take much longer leaves from work when they have children compared with their counterparts in most other European countries. This is a result not only of the difficult labor market, but also because family policy focuses on providing options for lengthy parental leaves backed by cash benefits. Long absence from the labor market, however, often has a deleterious effect on women's career prospects. Indeed, women encounter greater difficulties returning to their former jobs or the workforce in general, which increases their risk of long-term unemployment. The OECD has thus recommended that the Hungarian family policy should "focus more on helping parents combine work and family roles" by allowing for more flexibility in respect to working hours and improving and expanding the choices for childcare service for small children.[8]

The aim of this chapter is to show how and why Hungary's family and childcare policies embraced a form of "optional familialism" that offers a wide range of social transfers and services for families with children.[9] I describe the shortcomings of this system and its time policy and reveal how it remains shaped by persistent traditions that offer different welfare arrangements for certain social and ethnic groups. I begin by briefly sketching my theoretical approach to the analysis of welfare-state systems in East-Central Europe. From there, I will examine the history and present state of childcare policies in Hungary by analyzing the development of crèches, kindergartens, and after-school programs.

Welfare, Gender, and Family Policy in East-Central Europe

With the collapse of communism in Eastern Europe in 1989 and the introduction of neoliberal capitalism in all East-Central European countries (the Czech Republic, Hungary, Poland, and Slovakia), the once sharp East-West divide that characterized the Cold War receded quickly. Indeed, all of these countries joined the European Union in 2004.[10] Although feminist scholars have produced an ever-growing body of research on welfare and gender in Eastern Europe, they continue to struggle with the question of whether and how these countries can, in fact, be analyzed with the help of already existing conceptual frameworks.[11] The historian Sonya Michel, for example, has recently argued that the "greatest challenge" to existing conceptual frameworks for welfare state research "comes from the former Eastern bloc cases."[12] But despite these difficulties, it remains fruitful to test well-developed theories of feminist scholarship against communist and postcommunist welfare practices.

Citizenship Theory and Welfare State Typology

Sociologist Thomas H. Marshall's pioneering history of the development of citizenship rights and obligations identifies three major forms of citizenship rights: civil and economic rights, political rights, and social rights.[13] These rights have been elaborated and expanded over time, with each building upon and reinforcing the other. While Marshall's typology has proven very influential, feminists have criticized its usefulness, because for much of history, "women were denied the formal status and rights of citizens."[14] Moreover, women as mothers were sometimes accorded social rights earlier and in different forms than men before they received civil and political rights.[15]

Even before they became part of the Soviet bloc, economic and political rights in the countries of East-Central Europe had been granted on a much more limited basis and much later than in most Western European countries. Hungary provides a useful example. As a result of its defeat in World War I, the Austro-Hungarian monarchy collapsed and Hungary became for the first time in its history an independent state. Under the new authoritarian regime led by the regent Miklós Horthy, only 26 percent of the Hungarian population possessed the right to vote, while the majority of the population, especially agricultural workers, lacked almost all political rights.[16] Even during the brief period of democracy between 1945 and 1949, Hungarians did not enjoy real political freedom. In the first elections in 1945, the Communist Party of Hungary received only 17 percent of the vote. Nevertheless, under Soviet pressure, a coalition government under the direction of the Communists was formed. They gradually gained political control and were able to take power with the new constitution in August 1949. A new era of totalitarian dictatorship began.[17] When viewed through the lens of Marshall's typology, this meant that political rights, which had never been very developed to begin with, were completely revoked after the communist takeover.

The rigidity of Hungary's Stalinist system, the lack of political rights, and the persistent economic problems and social disparities—despite the communist rhetoric of wealth and class equality—led to the anti-Stalinist rebellion of 1956. This uprising and its bloody suppression had enormous consequences for the subsequent development of the Hungarian welfare state. A political "compromise" was established between the regime and the people according to which they, in return for accepting the Communist Party's monopoly on power, would receive new welfare services, not least of all in the area of childcare. In addition, the state promised to provide more consumer goods and a higher standard of living. Thus, in the case of communist Hungary (and other communist states), Marshall's theory of citizenship was effectively turned on its head: the state provided extensive social rights while at the same time stripping its citizens of their ability to exercise many civil and almost all meaningful political rights.[18]

This unique development makes it difficult to place communist and postcommunist countries into mainstream welfare regime typologies.[19] Social scientist Bob Deacon, for example, has described communist welfare regimes as "bureaucratic state collectivist systems of welfare." At the same time, he has pointed to the difficulties of comparing these systems with those of capitalist democracies and "placing" them into Gøsta Esping-Andersen's classic typology of "conservative-corporatist," "liberal," and "social democratic" welfare states.[20] This typology has been widely criticized for not being able to grasp the real variations that exist among capitalist welfare states, let alone communist welfare states. The same is true for the postcommunist welfare systems. The vastly different pre- and postwar experiences of the East-Central European countries had a lasting influence on the development of their welfare state policies. Indeed, the constantly changing features of the welfare regime in Hungary have led historian Bela Tomka to label it as "institutionalized volatility." Others have described the current system of Hungarian family policies as a "mixed welfare regime,"[21] or argue that the Hungarian welfare state has emerged from the period of transition in the 1990s as a "corporatist-liberal" welfare regime in which corporatist state provisions for the well-off effectively serve to maintain the dual class structure of society.[22]

Maternalism and Familialism

Among the most important gendered concepts that seek to go beyond traditional analysis of welfare development are *maternalism* and *familialism*. Both concepts were developed in the 1990s to overcome the former dichotomy between the "male-breadwinner" and "dual-earner" models in gendered regimes. According to the concept of maternalism, women played a central role in the process of welfare state formation in two ways.

On the one hand, historians have used the term maternalism to describe a political strategy that was developed in the late nineteenth century by certain segments of the middle-class women's movement to achieve equal political participation of women on the basis of their "natural" difference. These women claimed female expertise and responsibility for all issues related to welfare, childcare, and education, and indeed made an enduring contribution to the development of the modern welfare state.[23] The women's movement in East-Central Europe, especially after World War I when the independent process of state formation began there, also promoted a maternalist strategy. In interwar Hungary, where the influence of the Roman Catholic Church was strong, mostly Catholic middle-class women became active outside of the home by doing charity work. One field of their philanthropic activities was childcare.[24] The legacy of the maternalist approach to women's politics lived on after 1945. Although the constitution of 1949 defined women as "equal" to men, in the political realm, their main area of responsibility became "social issues" and education.[25]

On the other hand, sociologists have used the term maternalism to describe the development of pronatalist programs for women that are designed above all to raise fertility rates. Sociologist Lynne Haney, for example, has argued that the welfare state in Hungary that existed between 1968 and 1985 could be described as maternalist because the needs of its female clients were effectively "maternalized."[26] Both usages of the concept of maternalism offer a useful tool for analyzing childcare policies before, during, and after the communist era.

The concept of familialism proved to be even more useful for understanding the nature of welfare policies before and after the fall of communism. Familialism can be seen as an "extended" concept of maternalism that emphasizes how "states attempted to mobilize families and deploy familial images for a variety of political ends."[27] More than just a set of welfare measures, familialism is also an ideological tool employed by states to strengthen the image of the ideal family and achieve their aims by shaping the discourse on the family. Many studies, especially those that have incorporated the feminist critique of traditional research on the welfare state and family policy, have successfully employed the concept of defamilialization.[28] Among other things, these studies have shown how different care arrangements assign responsibility for care within the overall mix of welfare policies. Policies can be more or less familialistic depending on the extent to which they assign responsibility for care to the family. Conversely, they can be considered as defamilializing when care becomes socialized. Moreover, when responsibility for care is located within the family, different kinds of dependencies are created. In this case, family members who require care (children, elderly, disabled) depend on mostly female care providers—mothers and grandmothers, daughters and sisters. At the same time, those family members who provide care within the family—again usually women—depend on the breadwinners—in most cases men. The policies that are geared towards the defamilialization of care thus relax these two kinds of dependencies. Above all, by facilitating access to public care services, they enable women, who in most cases are the primary care providers, to join the workforce.[29]

As Lynne Haney and fellow sociologist Sigrid Leitner have shown, familialism can assume a variety of forms depending on how much and what kind of support the state provides to families.[30] Leitner differentiates between four types of policy mixes based on the degree of familialistic and defamilializing elements they contain: The first type is "implicit familialism," where the state does not provide any significant support for families in meeting their care responsibilities. The second is "explicit familialism," under which states pay for care, for example, by making possible longer parenthood-related leaves from work. In the third type, "optional familialism," both elements—the opportunity to use publicly provided care services and/or to receive generous payments for home-based care—are mixed. Finally, the fourth type, "defamilialization," is a policy mix in which the element of cash payments for family-delivered care is weaker; instead, the state invests more money in institutionalized care. The last policy type encourages families to use publicly provided care services rather than forcing (female) caregivers to stay at home with the family member who requires care. As a result, the responsibility for care is shifted away from the family.[31]

When all of these diverse provisions are viewed together, it becomes clear that Hungary's welfare system is characterized by a kind of optional familialism that embodies elements of social democratic, conservative, and liberal traditions.[32] However, because the system creates different "welfare tracks" for mothers with different social and ethnical backgrounds, the optional familialism is limited.

From Worker's Welfare to Optional Familialism

The history of social insurance and direct payments to families in Hungary reveals a two-track welfare development with a tradition that reaches back to the Austro-Hungarian Empire. From the late nineteenth century on, industrial workers, especially those employed in factories, were the primary focus of welfare policy. In addition, civil servants benefited from state support, with the royal government introducing generous family allowances for them in 1912. Agricultural workers, on the other hand, who constituted the majority of the labor force until the middle of the 1940s, were effectively excluded from all major state welfare provisions. The state supported these workers only with residual, personal, and discretionary welfare services, combined with strict social discipline and control. This two-track welfare policy did not change when Hungary became independent after

World War I, and was effectively pursued by the communist government of the newly founded People's Republic of Hungary after 1949 as well. This indicates the high degree of path dependency in Hungarian welfare policy.[33] The postwar regime was controlled by the Hungarian Working Peoples Party (Magyar Dolgozók Pártja, MDP), which was formed by the merging of the Communist Party and Social Democratic Party in 1947. The MDP focused its efforts to reconstruct the devastated economy on heavy industry, which claimed more than 90 percent of total industrial investment in the "planned socialist economy." In contrast, the consumer industry, where most women worked, and farming had long since garnered less attention from the communist state. As a result, the workers in these branches and their families received fewer social services. It was only with the universalization of cash welfare arrangements in 1975 that agricultural workers were finally accorded the same welfare benefits as industrial workers and state employees.[34] Nevertheless, the earlier pattern of discriminating against the most vulnerable groups persists. Today, the poorest segments of the population, especially those living in remote rural areas of the country, encounter similar structural inequity once faced by agricultural workers. In particular, the Roma experience racial and ethnic discrimination. This is most glaring in the provision of childcare services and preschools.[35]

Crèches: Childcare for Children under Three

Hungary's first crèches were opened in the 1850s in Budapest for the children of working-class mothers who had to earn a living. They were usually open all day. As industrialization accelerated in the larger cities towards the end of the century, it became increasingly common for factories to organize welfare services for their employees, including childcare. As was the case in Czechoslovakia, these early crèches placed a strong emphasis on social hygiene and healthcare, thus initiating a tradition that lasted throughout the communist era and continues on today. Female agricultural workers, however, did not have access to crèches for their children before World War II, and even under communism, crèches remained primarily an urban phenomenon. Women who worked in agriculture were expected to rely on their family members for childcare (mainly grandmothers and older daughters who had to look after their younger siblings) or take along their children to work.[36]

World War II devastated Hungary's economy, reducing its overall production by 60 percent. The new postwar government thus embarked on an ambitious program of reconstruction, which led to a rapid reindustrialization and a growing labor shortage. The constitution of 1949 proclaimed the right and the obligation of equal work for women and men. Women were increasingly required to fuel the labor market of the booming socialist economy, which by 1955 had seen industrial employment rise by nearly 50 percent. Most of these new workers were women. In 1941, less than 20 percent of all working-age women were employed outside the home. But by 1955, their percentage increased to 50 percent, rising still further to 63 percent by 1965.[37]

To attract women into the workforce, the MDP initiated an extensive propaganda campaign. Beginning in the early 1950s, it promoted the "double-earner" family model, although without questioning the gender division of labor in the family and society.[38] As in other states of the Soviet bloc, the communists legitimized this family model with the traditional rhetoric of the prewar socialist women's movement, which had equated female work with women's independence and emancipation. In addition, the propaganda emphasized the importance of women's collective work for both society and the individual family. With their earnings, the communists argued, women could increase the family income and "ultimately contribute to the building of socialism."[39]

The dramatic rise of female employment in industry was due not least of all to an increase in the rate of working mothers. To enable more mothers to work in industry, in 1953 the communist regime issued an order to increase the number of crèches and kindergartens. Despite this measure, however, the daily lives of Hungarian families witnessed little improvement during the 1950s. Living standards and life expectancy remained quite low, while fertility rates, after witnessing a brief spike following the passage of strict abortion legislation in 1953, continued to sink from 2.7 in 1955 to 2.2 in 1960, and 2.0 in 1970, which was, after Czechoslovakia (1.9), at the time the lowest in Europe.[40]

More than anything else, the "demographic crisis" signaled by the rapidly declining birth rate pushed the communist regime to introduce a radical maternalist family policy in the mid-1960s. Family allowances targeting factory workers and civil servants had already been introduced in the 1930s as a way to encourage them to have larger families. In 1948, the new government controlled by the MDP extended eligibility to all industrial workers; in 1959, allowances were expanded to agricultural workers with three children. By 1975, both agricultural and industrial workers had equal access to family allowances. However, allowances still remained contingent upon full-time employment, which excluded many of the poorest families in which mothers stayed at home with children. Paradoxically, family allowances became universally available for all families only after the systemic change in 1990. In addition, maternity leave provisions during the communist era were available only to women who were employed for at least 270 days prior to childbirth. They were provided with twelve weeks of leave at 50 percent of their previous salary.[41] In 1967, a three-year, flat-rate maternity leave with a generous payment was introduced for all mothers who worked full-time.[42] The major aim of the long-term maternity leave was to raise the birth rate.[43]

In formulating this new policy, the state carefully considered the expert opinions of child psychologists, who, like their counterparts in other East and West European countries, argued that it was in a child's best interest to stay at home with its mother during the first three years of its life.[44] Also influencing the new policy was the fact that crèches were simply more expensive than cash transfers to mothers.[45] Finally, maternalizing care offered a way to cope with the declining need for female labor as the economy began to stagnate. Indeed, the three-year-long period of mother-provided childcare helped to mask a growing "labor surplus," which had become an inconvenient fact for the communist regime. As a result of this policy, the employment rate of Hungarian women increased only slightly until the end of the 1980s, from 64 percent in 1970 to 71 percent in 1980 to 74 percent in 1989.[46]

In the context of the maternalist policy change in the 1960s, the interests of women were increasingly defined by the demographic needs of the state, which focused mainly on their role as mothers. As sociologist Maria Adamik has pointed out, the discourse on childcare completely excluded—and thus effectively marginalized—women's sexual and reproductive rights.[47] The policy change also affected public childcare policy for small children under the age of three. Between the early 1970s and the late 1980s, the percentage of children in this age group in a crèche increased, especially when compared to the growth of kindergarten enrollment, only modestly, from 9 to almost 14 percent. During the transition to a market economy in the 1990s, it decreased again to the level of the late 1960s. (See Table 17.1.)

TABLE 17.1: Crèches and kindergartens in Hungary, 1938–2000[48]

Year	Number of crèches	Percent of children of the age cohort in crèches	Number of kindergartens	Percent of all 2–6-year-old children in a kindergarten
1938			1,100	26%
1955			2,503	28%
1960			2,865	34%
1970	1,044	9.0%	3,457	51%
1980	1,305	13.6%	4,690	78%
1990	1,003	13.7%	4,718	87%
1995	628	9.0%	4,720	91%
2000	532	8.7%	4,643	92%

The 1960s discourse that defined the mother as the best possible caretaker for small children continues to shape childcare arrangements in Hungary today. While public opinion is slowly changing, it remained rather conservative throughout the last decade. In 2002, for example, 66 percent of the population still believed that a small child is likely to suffer if its mother worked.[49] This mentality was reinforced by the rhetoric of the postcommunist governments, all of which advocated, although to different degrees, for female caring roles. The 1990 election was won by the center-right Hungarian Democratic Forum (HDF), which supported a gradual transition towards capitalism and presided over the first years of the difficult transition to a liberal market economy. Already in 1991, the HDF government removed most state subsidies for the economy, which led to a severe recession. As one strategy to combat the climbing unemployment rate, it tried to reduce female employment. The rhetoric of the HDF and other conservative parties therefore emphasized "female choice." They proclaimed that women "finally" could stay home with their children and thus fulfill their "true motherly obligations," which had supposedly been "suppressed" during the communist regime.[50] Not surprisingly, they reduced the support for crèches, which led to the closure of many since 1990. (See Table 17.1.) In light of this discourse, sociologists Anna Kwak and Gillian Pascall have discerned a "new maternalism" or "re-traditionalization" of childcare in the family policies. Likewise, fellow sociologist Éva Fodor has argued that the state viewed the restoration of traditional roles of mothers as "the way to the West."[51]

This policy did not undergo much change with the following governments. In 1994 the social democratic Hungarian Socialist Party (HSP) won an absolute majority in parliament. While voters hoped that HSP would halt the declining living standard, they were soon disappointed by its policies. Between 1998 and 2002, a conservative coalition led by the Hungarian Civic Union (FIDEZ) formed the government, which pursued a new family policy for the "working middle class." One of its most important provisions has been the introduction of a family tax allowance, which became the primary instrument for providing cash transfers in the current family policy.[52] Since 2002, the HSP has been the strongest party in the parliament and the head of a coalition government. In 2006, it introduced an important change in family policies, which, for the first time in Hungary, concentrated on the issue of child poverty. Within this program, the amount of the universally available family allowance was raised while tax allowances were restricted to families with three or more children. However, the HSP did not introduce major changes in childcare policy for children under three.

Today, it is above all financial barriers that stand in the way of opening new crèches. Although the HSP government subsidizes them, by providing a set sum per child, its contribution only amounts to about one-third of the total costs. The remainder must be furnished by the municipalities, which own and operate the vast majority of crèches, and parents themselves. Due to the lack of financial resources, many local governments find it difficult to justify opening new crèches. In principle, crèches are available for all families in Hungary, but the reality is that the number of places is much lower than the demand for them. Moreover, although the current law explicitly states that priority should be given to "underprivileged children," crèches often determine admission on the basis of other, more exclusionary criteria. In general, they accept children whose parents work while refusing children whose parents are unemployed but still need childcare if they are to return to work. There are also signs that they discriminate against children from poor and especially Roma families. Indeed, it is often said that women in poor families "choose" to have more children and stay at home since they see little chance for entering or returning to the labor market at all.[53] The recent government program to reduce child poverty in Hungary emphasizes the implementation of already existing legislation. Above all, it seeks to establish greater oversight of crèches to ensure whether or not they are following guidelines established by the law. In addition, it encourages the opening of new crèches with flexible hours, especially in small villages and impoverished areas.[54]

Kindergarten: Childcare and Preschool Education for Three- to Six-Year-Old Children

The first kindergartens in Hungary—and indeed all of East-Central Europe—were opened in the 1820s with the goal of promoting Hungarian national values. In 1836, middle- and upper-class national liberals formed an association for establishing kindergartens. Most of them were part-time services with an educational agenda. It was not until 1879, however, that the first state-funded kindergarten was established, which provided all-day childcare for the children of "needy" working-class families, in particular employed mothers.[55]

In 1891 a new Act on Kindergartens was passed, the same year that saw the introduction of the first compulsory social insurance act. The two major aims of the kindergarten act were to provide childcare for the children of working-class families that needed the income of both parents, and to promote the cultural homogenization of Hungarian society and teach small children the Hungarian language. As in the Czech territories

of the Austro-Hungarian Empire, kindergartens here also served nationalist aims. The act stipulated that the administrative responsibility for kindergartens was to be shared by the Ministry of Education and the Ministry
of the Interior, and thus all kindergartens were generally defined as educational institutions. The act however, differentiated between three types
of kindergartens, each with a different curriculum: first, all-day childcare
centers providing care and nutrition mostly for the children of employed
working-class mothers; second, kindergartens offering mainly middle-
class children a preschool education in the morning and the afternoon,
sending children home for a long lunch break; and third, summer childcare centers providing these services during the agricultural labor season
for peasant children. The act called for local authorities to establish and
finance kindergartens not only in the industrial centers but also in regions
dominated by ethnic minorities. The principle of subsidiarity, which allowed the state to take independent action only if no nonprofit provider
was available for the task, and obligated the government to finance their
activity, was anchored in the law. The municipalities should support the
churches, civil or religious associations, charity foundations, or private
persons that continued to be the main providers of childcare.[56]

After World War I, Hungary gained its national independence but lost
two-thirds of its territory, thus making it an ethnically much more homogeneous country. As a result, one of the state's main motives for establishing new kindergartens, an early nationalist education, disappeared. They
were now mainly perceived as a welfare provision for children from needy
working-class families and became a responsibility of the Ministry of Welfare. As a result, the number of state-funded kindergartens decreased. This
trend was enhanced by the difficult economic situation following the loss
of some of the main industrial regions in South Slovakia and Transylvania,
which led to a financial crisis that left little public funding for kindergartens. Those that survived were mostly located in and around the capital
Budapest, where heavy and light industries were concentrated.[57]

Instead, new forms of childcare, organized by the Catholic Church,
religious women's organizations, or female middle-class philanthropic
associations, gained increasing influence in the interwar period. As a result, the percentage of children in childcare slowly increased after the first
postwar decline. By 1938, 26 percent of all three- to six-year-old Hungarian
children were already attending kindergartens. Their agenda, however,
had shifted during this period yet again, and now included the improvement of the health and social hygiene of children. This aim was part of
an increasingly pronatalist and racist family policy of the Horthy regime,
which sought the "protection of the Hungarian people and families." An
important component of this shift in policy, which came into force in 1938,

the same year when Hungary became an ally of the Axis powers, was the introduction of a family allowance for factory workers as well as a major social program for poor agrarian families in 1940.[58]

Until 1945, the Catholic Church had a far-reaching influence on both state-funded childcare and the education system in general.[59] To limit the influence of the church and its organizations, in 1948 the new government, led by the MDP, nationalized all kindergartens and schools and prohibited church-sponsored welfare. The responsibility for kindergartens switched again, this time back from the Ministry of Welfare to the Ministry of Education, thereby bringing them into the larger system of universal education. This change, however, was not accompanied by an increase in the percentage of children in kindergarten, because in the immediate postwar years, the communist regime concentrated all financial resources in the reconstruction of heavy industry. It also had little impact on the prevailing understanding of kindergartens as an institution, which in the early postwar period continued to be seen primarily as providing care, not education. Most kindergartens were still open only in the morning and afternoon, sending children home during lunchtime. In contrast to factories and agricultural cooperatives, which increasingly opened their own kindergartens, local authorities were not able to provide all children with a warm meal. They lacked the financial resources in the first postwar decade.

In 1953, the government introduced a new Kindergarten Law that created a "unified" system of kindergarten and preschool education. Above all, the law aimed to provide childcare services for employed mothers, because of the growing demand for female labor. It granted access to services only to double-earner families or single mothers who could not provide care "in other ways." If their children were older than two-and-a-half years, they had a chance of enrolling them in a kindergarten.[60] For the next two decades, and especially after the suppression of the 1956 revolution, kindergartens played an important role in educating children in good "communist behavior." It was not until the mid-1970s, when the physical and psychological needs of children as well as the preparation for primary schools became the focus of kindergarten care and education that this policy began to change.[61]

In the 1950s, the percentage of children in kindergartens slowly increased, reaching 34 percent by the end of the decade. During the second half of the 1960s, however, a time that also saw the introduction of new cash transfers for mothers, the growth in the number of kindergartens accelerated so that by 1980 nearly 78 percent of all two- to six-year-old children were enrolled. (See Table 17.1.)

The collapse of communism did not lead to a drop in the percentage of children in kindergarten. Instead, the ensuing decade witnessed a slow but steady increase from 87 percent in 1990 to 92 percent in 2000. Kindergartens were now perceived in the public discourse as "early childhood education" and, more than that, an important part of the system of universal education. At the same time, however, the disparity in access to kindergartens grew. The reasons were similar to those that have diminished access to crèches. The state only covers about half of the total costs of running a kindergarten, while local governments and parents substitute the rest according to their own financial situation. As a result, the majority of poor children do not start kindergarten before the obligatory age of five. This, in turn, contributes to the greater number of poor children who later encounter more problems in primary school.[62]

The National Core Curriculum from 2000, introduced by the Ministry of Education, defines the guidelines for education and the administrative control of education. It is, however, decentralized, thereby allowing local governments to administer kindergartens, preschool, primary, and secondary education. Kindergartens are in general open ten to twelve hours per day, mostly from 7:00 A.M. to 5:00 or 6:00 P.M. Like crèches, most kindergartens are still run by municipalities, with a minority of 10 percent being operated by independent private organizations or churches. Most of these private kindergartens are available only to a minority of well-off families.

"Afternoon Programs" for Primary School Children

"All-day schools" are not common in Hungary, which shares the half-day school tradition of other countries that were once part of the Austro-Hungarian or German Empires. The 2000 National Core Curriculum stipulates the maximum number of lessons at each educational stage, with the number of daily hours increasing with the age of the child: children in the first to third school year (ages six to nine) attend class for a maximum of four hours per day, while those in the fourth to sixth school year (ages nine to twelve) spend four to five hours (the weekly average must not exceed 4.5 hours per day) in the classroom.[63] Education provided by primary schools is complemented by "daytime homes" (*napköziotthon*), extracurricular afternoon programs in schools. Students take the usual classes in the morning and then participate in less-structured recreational activities such as sports in the afternoon. These afternoon-programs in primary schools can differ from school to school and, depending upon available resources, the number of trained staff and the level of fees paid by parents.

As their name suggests, *napköziotthon* were introduced to offer children a "home" while their mothers were at work. The first programs were organized at the end of the 1890s by factories in Budapest. In 1902, the municipal government ordered that all school districts should create daytime homes for needy school children.[64] By 1912, 14 percent of all primary school children in Budapest were attending an afternoon program. The stated goal of the government was "to provide education and healthcare for primary school children who cannot be taken care of by their parents because they work in the factory or elsewhere until late in the evening." It was feared that unsupervised children might come to harm.[65]

After World War I, the need for such services increased, because more mothers worked outside the home. But now, as in the other sectors of childcare, the government lacked sufficient financial resources. Therefore, in the early 1930s, civil associations, welfare organizations, and churches began to offer "work afternoons" and "story-time afternoons" for working-class children.[66] After 1938, the aim of education policy became more overtly nationalist. Afternoon programs were now required to focus above all on the "moral, religious, and patriotic education" of children. However, it was not the nationalist policy, but, as elsewhere in Europe, the increasing demand for female labor in war industries that led to a major expansion of afternoon programs for children in the early 1940s. In 1941, the Hungarian army joined the invasion of Yugoslavia and the Soviet Union by the Axis powers. Women had to replace the soldiers in industry. By 1943, approximately ten thousand children attended these services in 106 schools and 272 daytime homes in Budapest alone.[67]

Following World War II, the percentage of Hungarian children in an afternoon program was very low and increased only slightly. The enormous economic problems plaguing the country at the time did not allow an extension of such a program. In 1949, only 2 percent of all primary school children attended an afternoon program, in 1956, 4 percent, and in 1960, 8 percent. The stated aim of the Ministry of Education was to provide children of working parents a "friendly, warm home" so that they "would be at ease about them while working." The idea of a "socialist education" was only secondary.[68] It was not until the mid-1960s, with the introduction of the pronatalist family policy, that the communist regime expanded the number of afternoon programs to include more children. By the end of the 1960s, 17 percent of students attended afternoon programs, which became increasingly available in rural areas as well. For a child to be eligible for afternoon education, however, both parents had to work and no private care arrangement was available. The number of places continued to expand through the late communist era so that by the 1980s, some 35 percent of school children were attending "daytime homes."[69]

During the 1990s, this percentage continued to increase, but only slightly, and today the rate has stabilized at about 40 percent. Two major issues in the current public debate about after-school programs are their accessibility and quality. These programs are mainly accessible for younger school children and children from better-off families, as the costs for the meals are prohibitively expensive for many parents who, unless they have three or more children or their income falls below the poverty line, must pay for meals in the daycare centers. Municipalities provide only poor parents with a certificate for free meals, free books, and some other benefits. However, when their children reach the fifth grade, they must assume half the cost of school meals. Recent surveys have shown that poor parents find it difficult to afford this cost, and thus their children often go to afternoon programs without warm meals or just go straight home after school.[70] Therefore, only two-thirds of the children receive a meal in school.[71] The quality of the afternoon programs, which vary from school to school, is in many cases also insufficient. Education experts criticize that most schools simply provide supervision, and very few have designed a pedagogical program for their afternoon services. Most afternoon programs simply offer students a place to do their homework or participate in some kind of arts and crafts activity.[72] Therefore, it is mostly younger students who attend afternoon programs. By the time they reach the age of ten or twelve, their parents usually let them go home after school.[73]

A third problem with afternoon programs is the widespread segregation of and discrimination against poor children and Roma in the preschool and primary school system. In 2005, about one-fifth of the population under twenty was counted as poor. Roma, who constitute 6 percent of the population and make up half of the bottom poorest 10 percent, are overrepresented.[74] In the 1999–2000 school year, afternoon programs were available in 85 percent of all schools, but their distribution was regionally and socially very uneven.[75] They were less available in poorer rural areas with a high percentage of Roma. In Budapest, for example, the percentage of children who attended afternoon services was much higher (42 percent) than in rural Borsod-Abauj-Zemplén county, which has the highest proportion of Roma in Hungary (27 percent).[76] These differences reflect the social and ethnic segregation of the primary school system in Hungary, which increased after 1989 when the new government granted parents more freedom to choose their children's school.[77] Despite repeated attempts by later governments to change the pattern of unequal distribution of care and education, local actors, including kindergarten nurses, teachers, and parents, have been successful in protecting the interests of better-off parents and children.

Conclusion

When compared to other European countries, the family and childcare policy in Hungary can be viewed as an example of optional familialism, because families can choose how they want to balance family and work. Long maternity leave payments allow mothers to stay home for up to three years following the birth of their child. Those who do wish to work, however, often have trouble finding a place in a crèche. Services for kindergarten and primary school children are, in contrast, relatively extensive.[78] Still, the social exclusion of poor and Roma children from these services continues to be widespread. This situation has contributed to the persistence of a low rate of female employment, especially among the less-educated, poorer portion of the population. Moreover, family policies have failed to raise Hungary's extremely low birth rate, which for years has been among the lowest in Europe.

Kindergarten and primary schools could serve as important agents of social integration. In Hungary, as has been repeatedly shown by the reports of the Program for International Student Assessment, they actually reinforce and reproduce social differences. Among the OECD countries, Hungary ranks as second to last in Europe, behind only Germany, in terms of the performance of students from disadvantaged social and ethnical backgrounds.[79] This poor result is due above all to the segregation of and discrimination against poor and Roma children that begins at the crèche and kindergarten level and continues on for the rest of their school education.[80] If steps are not taken to reduce this discrimination, Hungary soon threatens to become a "dual society" in which a growing proportion of the population is socially and economically marginalized. There is thus an urgent need for more flexible and accessible childcare services for both poor and well-off families than currently exists today.

Notes

1. For a discussion of cash transfers for families with children, see Dorottya Szikra, "Family and Child Support in a Post-communist Society: Origins of the Mixed Hungarian Welfare Capitalism," in *Fighting Poverty and Reforming Social Security: What Can Post-Soviet States Learn from the New Democracies of Central Europe?* ed. Michael Cain et al. (Washington, DC, 2007), 29–45.
2. OECD, *Starting Strong II: Early Childhood Education and Care* (Paris, 2006), 32ff.
3. Ibid.; UNICEF, *At a Glance: Hungary.* Retrieved 28 October 2008: http://www.unicef.org/infobycountry/hungary_statistics.html.
4. Károly Fazekas, "A magyar foglalkoztatási helyzet jelene és jövője," in *Munkaerőpiaci Tükör* (Budapest, 2007), 128–29.
5. Ibid.
6. Gábor Kertesi and Gábor Kézdi, *Roma Children of the Transformational Recession: Widening Ethnic Schooling Gap and Roma Poverty in Post-Communist Hungary*, Working Papers on the Labour Market BWP 2005/8, Corvinus University of Budapest (Budapest, 2005).

7. "1998. évi LXXXIV. törvény a családok támogatásáról. 20. §." Retrieved 28 October 2008: http://www.1000ev.hu/index.php?a=3&param=9662.

8. OECD, "Improving Reconciliation between Work and Family," in *Economic Survey of Hungary 2007* (Paris, 2007), chap. 4. Retrieved 28 October 2008: http://www.oecd.org/document/29/0,3343,en_2649_34569_38616413_1_1_1_1,00.html.

9. Sigrid Leitner, "Varieties of Familialism: The Caring Function of the Family in Comparative Perspective," *European Societies* 5, no. 4 (2003): 353–75.

10. Angelika von Wahl, "The EU and Enlargement: Conceptualizing Beyond 'East' and 'West,'" in *Gender Issues and Women's Movements in the Expanding European Union,* ed. Silke Roth (London, 2008), 19–36.

11. See Steven Saxonberg, "Polish Women in the Mid-1990s: Christian Democrats in a Country without a Christian Democratic Party," *Czech Sociological Review* 7, no. 2 (2000): 233–53; Éva Fodor et al., "Family Policies and Gender in Hungary, Poland and Romania," *Communist and Post-Communism Studies* 35, no. 4 (2002): 475–90; Gillian Pascall and Jane Lewis, "Emerging Gender Regimes and Policies for Gender Equality in a Wider Europe," *Journal of European Social Policy* 33, no. 3 (2004): 373–94; Sabine Hering and Berteke Waaldijk, *Guardians of the Poor—Custodians of the Public: The History of Eastern European Welfare* (Opladen, 2005); Gillian Pascall and Anna Kwak, *Gender Regimes in Transition in Central and Eastern Europe* (Bristol, 2005); Lynne Haney, *Inventing the Needy: Gender and the Politics of Welfare in Hungary* (Berkeley, CA, 2005).

12. Sonya Michel, "Introduction: Perspectives on Child Care, East and West," *Social Politics* 13, no. 2 (2006): 146.

13. Thomas H. Marshall, *Citizenship and Social Class* (Cambridge, UK, 1950; repr. London, 1992), 8–48.

14. Barbara Hobson and Ruth Lister, "Citizenship," in *Contested Concepts in Gender and Social Politics,* ed. Barbara Hobson et al., (Cheltenham, 2002), 25.

15. Ibid.

16. Ignác Romsics, *Magyarország története a XX. Században* (Budapest, 2004), 145.

17. Ignác Romsics, *Hungary in the 20th Century* (Budapest, 1999), 512.

18. Zsuzsa Ferge, "Freedom and Security," *International Review of Comparative Public Policy* 7 (1996): 19.

19. Gøsta Esping-Andersen, *The Three Worlds of Welfare Capitalism* (London, 1990), 26–29.

20. Bob Deacon, *The New Eastern Europe: Social Policy Past, Present and Future* (London, 1992), 167–69. For more on Esping-Andersen's model, see the introduction to this volume by Karen Hagemann, Konrad H. Jarausch, and Cristina Allemann-Ghionda.

21. Szikra, "Family and Child"; Bela Tomka, "The Politics of Institutionalized Volatility: Lessons from East Central European Welfare Reforms," in Cain et al., *Fighting Poverty,* 67–87.

22. Julia Szalai, "Poverty and the Traps of Postcommunist Welfare Reforms in Hungary: The New Challenges of EU-accession," *Revija za Socijalnu Politiku* 13, no. 3 (2005): 309–33.

23. Seth Koven and Sonya Michel, eds., *Mothers of a New World: Maternalist Politics and the Origins of Welfare States* (New York, 1993).

24. Susan Zimmermann, *Die bessere Hälfte? Frauenbewegungen und Frauenbestrebungen im Ungarn der Habsburgermonarchie 1848 bis 1918* (Vienna, 1999); Andrea Petö, "Hungarian Women in Politics, 1945–51," in *Power and the People: A Social History of Central European Politics, 1945–56,* ed. Eleonore Breuning et al. (Manchester, 2005), 266–81; Andrea Petö, *Hungarian Women in Politics, 1945–1951* (New York, 2003); Eva Bicskei, "'Our Greatest Treasure, the Child': The Politics of Child Care in Hungary, 1945–1956," *Social Politics* 13, no. 2 (2006): 158ff.

25. Petö, "Hungarian Women."

26. Haney, *Inventing the Needy*, 165–80.

27. Lynne Haney and Lisa Pollard, "In a Familial Way: Theorizing State and Familial Relations," in *Families of a New World: Gender, Politics, and State Development in a Global Context*, ed. Lynne Haney and Lisa Pollard (New York, 2003), 1–14.

28. For example, see Jane Lewis, "Gender and the Development of Welfare State Regimes," *Journal of European Social Policy* 2, no. 3 (1992): 159–73; Gøsta Esping-Andersen, *Social Foundations of Postindustrial Economies* (Oxford, 1999).

29. Leitner, "Varieties of Familialism."

30. Ibid.; Lynne Haney, "Welfare Reform with a Familial Face," in Haney and Pollard, *Families*, 159–78.

31. Haney, "Welfare Reform."

32. Szikra, "Family and Child."

33. On the concept of path dependency, see the introductions of this volume.

34. "1975. évi II. törvény a társadalombiztosításról." Retrieved 28 October 2008: http://www.1000ev.hu/index.php?a=3&param=8505.

35. Kertesi and Kézdi, *Roma Children*.

36. Ferenc Gergely, *A magyar gyermekvédelem története, 1867–1991* (Budapest, 1997), 167.

37. Lynne Haney, "Familial Welfare: Building the Hungarian Welfare Society, 1848–1968," *Social Politics* 7, no. 2 (2000): 105.

38. See Andrea Pető, "Women's Associations in Hungary: Mobilisation and Demobilisation, 1945–1951," in *When the War was Over: Women, War and Peace in Europe, 1940–1956*, ed. Claire Duchens and Irene Bandhauer Schöffmann (London, 2000), 132–46.

39. Haney, "Familial Welfare," 106.

40. Globalis, *UN Common Database on Fertility Rates.* Retrieved 28 October 2008: http://globalis.gvu.unu.edu.

41. Haney, "Familial Welfare," 109.

42. Szikra, "Family and Child," 35.

43. Ezster Varsa, "Class, Ethnicity and Gender—Structures of Differentiation in State Socialist Employment and Welfare Politics, 1960–1980: The Issue of Women's Employment and the Introduction of the First Maternity Leave Regulation in Hungary," in *Need and Care—Glimpses into the Beginnings of Eastern Europe's Professional Welfare*, ed. Kurt Schilde and Dagmar Schulte (Opladen 2005), 197–221.

44. See the chapters by Karen Hagemann, Hanna Hašková, and Tora Korsvold in this volume.

45. See Szikra, "Family and Child."

46. Catherine Saget, "The Determinants of Female Labor Supply in Hungary," *Economics of Transition* 7, no. 4 (1999): 577.

47. Mária Adamik, "A 'gyes-diskurzus'" (PhD diss., Corvinus University Budapest, 2001).

48. OECD Directorate for Education, *Early Childhood Education and Care Policy: Country Note for Hungary* (Paris, 2004), 13 and 17.

49. Zentralarchiv für Empirische Sozialforschung, *International Social Survey Program (ISSP) 2002: Family and Changing Gender Roles III* (Cologne, 2004).

50. Ibid.

51. Pascall and Kwak, *Gender Regimes*, 13–18; Éva Fodor, "A Different Type of Gender Gap: How Women and Men Experience Poverty," *East European Politics and Societies* 20, no. 1 (2002): 18.

52. Ágnes Darvas and Mózer Péter, "Kit támogassunk?" *Esély* 15, no. 6 (2004): 32–55.

53. Judit Durst, "Fertility and Childbearing Practices among Poor Gypsy Women in Hungary: The Intersections of Class, Race and Gender," *Communist and Post-Communist Studies* 35 (2002): 457–74.

54. Ágnes Darvas and Katalin Tausz, *Tackling Child Poverty and Promoting the Social Inclusion of Children. A Study of National Policies, Hungary* (Brussels, 2007) 47ff.
55. Bicskei, "Our Greatest Treasure," 155f.
56. Ibid.
57. Ibid., 155ff.
58. Ibid., 158.
59. Ibid., 158ff.
60. Ibid., 165
61. Országos Egészségnevelési Intézet, *Az óvodások egészséges életmódra nevelése*. I. TIT Természettudományi Stúdió (Budapest, 1981).
62. European Commission against Racism and Intolerance, *Third Report on Hungary*, European Commission (Strasbourg, 2004), 25–30; OECD, *Early Childhood: Country Note for Hungary*, 342–50.
63. International Review of Curriculum and Assessment Frameworks Internet Archive, "INCA Summary Profile—Education in Hungary." Retrieved 28 October 2008 from: http://www.inca.org.uk/hungary-system-mainstream.html.
64. Sándor Füle, *Az iskolai napközi otthoni nevelőmunka fejlődése és perspektívái* (Budapest, 1966), 123.
65. Quoted by Füle, *Az iskolai napközi*, 311.
66. Ibid., 320.
67. Ibid., 316.
68. Ibid., 321.
69. Ibid.; Központi Statisztikai Hivatal (KSH), *Statisztikai Tájékoztató, Alapfokú oktatás, 1999/2000* (Budapest, 2001), 30–34.
70. Sándor Füle, "Az iskolai napközi otthoni nevelőmunka fejlesztése," *Új Pedagógiai Szemle* 9, no. 5 (2005): 43–62.
71. KSH, *Magyar Statisztikai Évköny* (Budapest, 2004), 22.
72. Füle, *Az iskolai napközi*, 55.
73. KSH, *Statisztikai Tájékoztató, 1999/2000*, 30–34.
74. Darvas and Tausz, *Tackling Child*, 47ff.
75. KSH, *Statisztikai Tájékoztató, 1999/2000*, 30–34; KSH, *Statisztikai Tájékoztató. Óvodák 1999/2000* (Budapest, 2001), 12.
76. KSH, *Statisztikai Tájékoztató,1999/2000*, 30–34.
77. For the issue of segregation in Hungarian schools, see Gábor Havas and Ilona Liskó, *Szegregáció a roma tanulók általános iskolai oktatásában. Kutatási zárótanulmány*, (unpublished manuscript, Budapest, 2004); Gábor Kertesi, *A társadalom peremén. Romák a munkaerőpiacon és az iskolában* (Budapest, 2005).
78. Dorota Szelewa and Michal P. Polakowski, "Who Cares? Changing Patterns of Childcare in Central and Eastern Europe," *Journal of European Social Policy* 8, no. 2 (2008): 21–23.
79. OECD, *PISA 2006, Science Competencies for Tomorrow's World*, vol. 2 (Paris, 2006), table 4.4a, table 4.7c. Retrieved 28 October 2008: http://www.pisa.oecd.org.
80. Éva Fodor, *Women at Work: The Status of Women in the Labor Markets of the Czech Republic, Hungary and Poland*, United Nations Research Institute for Social Development (UNRISD) Occasional Paper (Geneva, February 2005).

Chapter 18

Female Employment, Population Policy, and Childcare

Early Childhood Education in Post-1945 Czech Society

Hana Hašková

In the aftermath of the revolutionary political changes of 1989, the over-all number of childcare facilities and preschools in the newly founded Czech Republic[1] declined rapidly. Most notably, day crèches (*Denní jesle*) for children under the age of three effectively disappeared. Since 1990, their number shrank from 1,040 to a mere 54. In 2006, the Organisation for Economic Co-operation and Development reported that center-based, municipal day crèches provided care for less than 0.5 percent of all children under three; almost all children in this age group are now cared for by their families or through informal care arrangements. In its report, the OECD sharply criticized the Czech Republic, which before 1989 had one of the highest percentages of small children in formal childcare, for abandoning its exemplary childcare policy. It now ranks among the countries with the lowest percentage of children in out-of-home care. The decrease in the percentage of three- to six-year-old children in public all-day kindergartens (*Mateřská škola*), the dominant form of childcare service for this age group, however, occurred slowly. In 2006, the percentage of three-, four-, and five-year-olds in childcare remained at 76, 93, and 94 percent, respectively, quite high when compared with other European countries. Parents' fees are capped at 50 percent of costs for the first two years of the *Mateřská škola*. In general, the fee amounts to only about 3 percent of the median family income. The third year is free. Compulsory school starts at six years and is usually—following the Germanic tradition—a half-day school. But in 2006, 36 percent of children between the ages of six and twelve years were enrolled in an after-school program (*Školní družina*).[2]

The decline in the number of childcare facilities and preschools, in particular for small children, has also been observed in other East-Central European countries during the 1990s. The scholarly consensus is that this decline is the result of several related factors, including the decentralization of social policies and services; budgetary difficulties faced by state, local governments, and municipalities; the restructuring of the labor market that has forced the closure of employer-based childcare facilities and preschools; the commercialization of childcare and preschool education and the resulting increases in costs; and a decline in fertility rates.[3]

The rate of decline of early childhood education services since 1989, however, has varied widely among these countries, which is in part a reflection of the fact that formerly communist countries already had considerably different percentages of children under six in childcare. And yet still, the decrease of childcare for small children in other countries was not as distinctive as in the Czech Republic. In Hungary, for example, between 1989 and 2002 the proportion of children under three in childcare fell from 12 to 10 percent (and from 11 to 10 percent in crèches for children under three), a very modest drop. In Poland, where the percentages were already quite low during the communist period, the decline was more pronounced, from 9 to 5 percent (9 to 4 percent in crèches). In contrast, between 1989 and 2000, East Germany, where the percentage of children in such facilities was the highest in Eastern Europe during the communist period, saw its rate plummet from 80 to 35 percent. Although its overall percentage was lower than East Germany's, the Czech Republic experienced a similar decline, with its rate falling from more than 20 to 10 percent (and a striking 18 to less than 1 percent in crèches) between 1987 and 2002. Not surprisingly, this reduction was matched by the Slovak Republic, which until 1992 was joined with the Czech Republic as Czechoslovakia. Its number of children under three in such facilities dropped from 18 to 6 percent overall (15 to less than 1 percent in crèches).[4]

The family policies pursued by communist and postcommunist governments in East-Central Europe exhibit important continuities. Sociologists Steven Saxonberg and Tomáš Sirovátka have argued that the main differences among the postcommunist countries of East-Central Europe today reflect differences that already existed during the communist era.[5] Their research suggests that these differences may have originated even before the communist takeover in the immediate prewar years. The importance of studying past political decisions and institutions for understanding current policymaking has been well established. Indeed, once a government embarks on a certain course of social policy, it is easier for political actors to continue along basically the same "path" than to initiate an entirely new policy. This does not, however, mean that social policies do not undergo change. While policymakers do tend to follow the same basic "path" that they or their predecessors have established, the outcomes of the policy change over time, thereby altering, if often only gradually, the direction of the "path" itself.[6]

However, given the scarcity of scholarly research on the origins and evolution of early childhood education policy in the countries of East-Central Europe, our understanding of their individual policies and practices as well as the differences among them remains limited, and numerous questions are yet to be answered.[7] Why, for example, did—in contrast to, say, East Germany—the proportion of children under the age of three in formal (i.e., institutionalized) childcare never exceed 25 percent in communist Czechoslovakia, even if this percentage was relatively high for Europe at the time? Why did the postcommunist Czech Republic experience such a dramatic drop in the number of crèches while at the same time seeing the proportion of four- to five-year-old children in kindergartens increase? And, above all, how have "critical junctures," namely, the points at which multiple alternatives were available before a certain tradition was started, that existed both during and before the communist regime contributed to the origins and evolution of the "paths" of childcare and preschool education policy in this region?

In this chapter I seek to answer these questions through a close analysis of the evolution of early childhood education and its time policy in the territory that forms the current Czech Republic (Bohemia and Moravia). My analysis focuses on the availability, time structure, and use of childcare and education for children under the age of six. Above all, I seek to uncover some of the key "critical junctures" in the history of early childhood education policy. By doing so, we can achieve a better understanding of the current and possible future course of this policy field in the Czech Republic. In the following, I first describe briefly the development of early childhood education before World War II. From there, I examine more closely the two important periods in communist Czechoslovakia, the immediate postwar years and the 1950s, and the 1960s and 1970s, before concluding with a discussion of the current situation.

The Development of Early Childhood Education before World War II

As was the case nearly everywhere in Europe, the beginnings of formal childcare and preschool education in Bohemia and Moravia, which until 1918 were part of the Austro-Hungarian Empire, date back to the first half of the nineteenth century. The first crèches and kindergartens were established along with other childcare facilities that varied according to their providers, goals and rules, the age of the children they admitted, and their opening hours.[8] In 1872, a ministerial decree differentiated between three major types of childcare institutions: crèches for children up to the age of three that would be governed by healthcare regulations; children's asylums for children aged three and older; and preschools, above all kindergartens for children aged four and older. The first two institutions were usually open all day and supervised working-class children whose mothers had to earn a living. Kindergartens and preschools were—as elsewhere in Central Europe—usually half-day institutions dedicated to early education. Most of the children who attended them came from middle-class families. In the late nineteenth century, the majority of kindergartens in Bohemia and Moravia were German, even though the Czech nationalist movement pushed for a rapid increase in the number of Czech kindergartens in order to prepare children for Czech schools.[9]

In the First Czechoslovak Republic (ČSR) (1918–1939),[10] early childhood education became an important and widely discussed topic. During this period, approximately 20 percent of children between the ages of three and five attended a kindergarten. In the early 1920s, the government—a coalition of the republican Agrarian Party, the Social Democratic Party, the liberal National Socialist Party, and the Catholic People's Party—drafted a Kindergarten Law, which aimed for a reorganization of the entire system of preschool education. The draft stated that both public and private early childhood education for children aged three and up would be approved, supervised, and funded by the state. They were to be governed by guidelines established by the Ministry of Education, the Ministry of Social Care, and the Ministry of Healthcare and Sports.[11] This draft was widely criticized for two reasons: first, the division of responsibilities caused conflicts between the ministries that would be involved in implementation; second, the very well-organized and vocal professional organization of kindergarten teachers demanded that kindergartens be "nationalized" and become the responsibility of the Ministry of Education. By doing so, they would cease to be perceived simply as caring facilities, but would instead become recognized and respected as an established component of the Czech education system. Critics thus sought the removal of the guidelines set by the Ministry of Social Care.[12] Such criticism, which focused on the question of whether early childhood education is "education" or "care" and which institutions therefore are responsible for it, prevented the completion of this reform bill. As a result, both privately and publicly funded facilities continued to be governed by legislation that had originated under the Austro-Hungarian Empire.

Female Work and Childcare in the
Early Post-1945 Czech Republic

Before World War II, Czechoslovakia stood among the most developed, industrialized, and urbanized countries in Central Europe. War and occupation by Nazi Germany, however, did serious damage to the Czech economy. As a result, after 1945 the Third Czechoslovak Republic (1945–1948) had to focus above all on economic reconstruction. Following liberation, a broad coalition of political parties and associations formed the National Front of Czechs and Slovaks for the rebuilding of the devastated country that would be guided by the far-reaching socialist Košice Governmental Program. From the beginning, the Communist Party of Czechoslovakia (Komunistická strana Československa, KSČ) dominated the new coalition government. It decreed that employment was to be mandatory, because all available human resources were needed for reconstruction. This decree, however, did not specifically mention women, whose participation in the labor market had increased dramatically during the war as they had entered war industries in large numbers.[13]

The question of whether women should, like men, be compelled to enter into gainful employment was a highly contested issue in the National Women's Front. This umbrella organization of the women's movement brought together female members from the main political parties as well as representatives of the Czechoslovakian Women's Council.[14] The female leaders of the KSČ were especially interested in recruiting women to work in industry, as they believed that female employment was a precondition for women's independence and emancipation. Their social democratic counterparts, however, advised waiting until social conditions had improved sufficiently before calling for the mass participation of women in the labor market. They believed that their families urgently needed them in their everyday struggle for survival. The double burden of paid work and housework, especially under difficult postwar conditions, would be too much for them to bear. Women from the liberal National Socialist Party, on the other hand, favored women's professional employment in specific "female segments" of the labor market such as education, healthcare, and social services. They were also keen to see women in more leading positions. Conversely, the more conservative women from the Catholic People's Party feared that female employment would lead to a population decrease and also have a detrimental effect on family life and children. They thus promoted the idea of a "family wage" for the male breadwinner.[15]

The majority in the Czechoslovakian Women's Council and the National Women's Front, however, agreed that women should have the same right to gainful employment as men. They called for the state to help women achieve this right, not least of all through the provision of services designed to facilitate housework and childcare.[16] Among other things, they wanted the state to "establish or expand school canteens, factory canteens, crèches, children's shelters, cheap laundries, repair shops, and everything that can ease women's work."[17] After all, the Košice Program had promised to help working women with childcare and housework and ensure the provision of necessary social services from the time of pregnancy all the way through after-school programs and extracurricular activities for older children.[18]

But the realization of these aims would take many years. When Czechoslovakia became a communist state in 1948, the economic and social situation was still so acute that all resources were needed to rehabilitate industry. The government tried to solve these problems with a centrally planned economy, which was based largely on extractive and manufacturing industries. Relatively little was invested in the consumer sector. The so-called women's question was, rhetorically at least, on the agenda of the communist leaders, but in practice was not made a high priority. For them, the idea of "women's emancipation" meant that *women* had to change, not men. They never questioned the conventional division of labor and power in the family. Like men, women should also become earners in addition to doing the house and family work they had always done. As was the case elsewhere in Eastern Europe, the KSČ advocated the double-earner family. In practice, however, until 1989 it pursued policies that effectively demanded that women bear a double burden.[19]

Throughout the postwar period, Czechoslovakia suffered from a chronic labor shortage. To overcome this shortage, it sought to integrate as many women as possible into the labor market. Between 1948 and 1955, the rate of employed women rose from 38 to 43 percent of the total workforce. Previously, unemployed housewives represented the primary reserve for the labor market. By the mid-1950s, however, this reserve had been exhausted, forcing the state to recruit mothers, which proved a more difficult task. The female employment rate thus more or less stagnated until the mid-1960s. By 1965, it remained below 45 percent.[20] Moreover, because most companies rejected part-time work as "uneconomic," most employed women worked full-time. The desire for a decent standard of living motivated married women and mothers to shoulder the double burden work.

As women's economic activity outside of the home increased, so too did the need for the construction of preschools and childcare facilities. But while the communist state expanded childcare steadily, progress remained slow. Between 1950 and 1960, the number of children under three in crèches increased from 3 to 8 percent, and the percentage of kindergarten children aged three to five grew from 26 to 37 percent. (See Table 18.1.)

TABLE 18.1: Children (zero to five years old) in crèches and kindergartens in Czech society, 1948–2005[21]

Year	Places in crèches	Children in kinder-gartens	Children in half-day kinder-gartens	Percentage			
				of 0–2-year-olds in crèches	of 3–5-year-olds in kindergarten	of 3-year-olds	of 4-year-olds
1948	5,300	148,817	128,363 [(b)]	0.1%			
1950	16,321	187,427	125,077	3.0%			
1955	26,718	169,156	36,435	5.4%	28.9%		
1960	30,711	201,988	24,633	7.8%	37.4%		
1965	44,917	221,914	11,545	10.1%	50.0%		
1970	53,272	258,567	9,666	12.7%	56.0%		
1975	57,634	316,991	7,657	10.3%	59.7%		
1980	69,829	463,565	4,544	13.9%	70.7%		
1985	72,773	432,067	1,449	17.9%	80.5%		
1990	39,829	352, 139	–	17.9%	81.1%		
1995	7,574	333,433	–			55.7%	81.3%
2000	1,867	279,838	–			71.4%	93.0%
2005	1,708 [(a)]	280,487	–			75.0% [(a)]	90.4% [(a)]

Notes:
(a) Places in 2004.
(b) Places in 1949.

The growth was especially prominent in kindergartens with all-day services (about ten hours per day). By the end of the 1950s, 88 percent of children in kindergartens attended all-day facilities that were also required to provide boarding and two-hour sleeping breaks.[22] The increase in the percentage of children in public all-day nurseries and kindergartens owed much to new laws. The 1948 Act on Unified Education and the act on its implementation in kindergartens from the same year nationalized all kindergartens and set standards for their work. With these two acts, they became fixed components of the unified schooling system, even if they were not compulsory. Henceforth, the establishment of all kindergartens required the approval of the National School Office. This controlling authority demanded that kindergartens provide free, standardized training, preschool education, and preparation for basic school. The only cost borne by parents was a government-regulated fee for boarding. In addition, two acts from the Ministry of Healthcare from 1951 and 1952 defined crèches as preventive healthcare facilities in which children would receive care from pediatric nurses and weekly check-ups from pediatricians. These two acts replaced a law from 1947 that authorized the Ministry of Social Care to implement a new organization of care for youth, including the organization of crèches.[23]

The number of childcare facilities and preschools thus began to grow, but their numbers remained insufficient and they were not evenly distributed throughout the country. Most of these facilities were public and concentrated in urban industrialized centers. Support, however, also came from companies and agrarian cooperatives, which wanted to ensure that their female employees went back to work after childbirth. Company trade organizations and cooperative trade unions played an especially important role in establishing and administering company or cooperative childcare facilities and preschools. As a result, by 1950, 27 percent of crèches were being run by companies and cooperatives, a figure that remained steady until the late 1980s. In time, they began to establish kindergartens as well. In the late 1960s, such company-run facilities constituted only 8 percent of all kindergartens, but that number would grow to 28 percent by the end of the 1980s. These forms of crèches and kindergartens were promoted as an especially convenient solution for working mothers because they could drop their children off on the way to work.[24]

From the beginning, public discourse on early childhood education focused on crèches for young children. Kindergartens were widely accepted as the first stage of children's education that would prepare them for primary school. During the 1950s, however, crèches were primarily discussed as an issue of labor and women's policy. In 1956, the State Statistical Office conducted a large survey on parenthood, the results of which shed light on the closely linked discourses of the economic costs of crèches and women's emancipation:

> It is known that the costs of a single place in a crèche are high and sometimes exceed the contribution of the mother of a child in such a facility. Nevertheless, we will continue to build crèches because they achieve an important political goal: they allow each employed mother to have gainful employment, and thus help her maintain economic independence, liberate her socially and economically from her dependence on the husband; therefore, it is not essential that her contribution to society always be greater than the costs of her child's enrollment in a social facility.[25]

The 1956 survey revealed that only about one-third of gainfully employed women who were pregnant or had a child aged one or under had placed (or would place) their child in a crèche if one existed close to where they lived. According to the authors of the survey, the unpopularity of crèches resulted from the fact that they were frequently closed due to the outbreak of contagious illnesses, which prevented mothers from going to work. Nevertheless, approximately two-thirds of employed women who became mothers returned to the labor market. And of these "returning" mothers, about half went back to work immediately after maternity leave, entrusting their children to the care primarily of their grandmothers, but also to other relatives or neighbors.[26]

Despite all of its efforts, in the eyes of employed women, the help offered by the communist state was not nearly enough. The regime was unable to keep its promise of increasing the number of quality childcare facilities and collective housework services or improving housing conditions. Indeed, the housing situation was a constant source of complaints, as the majority of Czech families lived in crowded apartments. So too was the poor provision of consumer goods of all types. The rationalization and mechanization of housework, commerce, and services came nowhere close to the standards of most Western European countries at the time.[27] One option available to married women attempting to manage their workload and improve their living standard was to use birth control, which became widely available in the 1950s. The fertility rate thus dropped quite dramatically, from 2.8 children per woman in 1950 to 2.1 at the end of the 1950s. This decline was accelerated after 1957 when the regime, following the lead of the Soviet Union in 1955, legalized abortion.[28]

Concerned by these trends, the communist regime made increasing women's participation in the workforce while at the same time increasing the fertility rate major policy goals. Therefore, already the 1956 survey by the State Statistical Office included the question whether these two political goals were contradictory. The results led the authors of the study to conclude that it was not women's participation in the labor market that had caused the birth rate to drop. Instead, the real issue was the condition of working women, which needed to be improved. They therefore recommended the establishment of more childcare facilities and preschools as well as a gradual reduction in the number of hours that mothers worked. Only the first recommendation found public support. The second proposal was quashed due to resistance from employers, who argued that employing workers with shorter and longer working hours in the same workplace would lower productivity.[29]

"The Women's Issue" and "The Children's Issue" in the 1950s and 1960s

Because of the urgent need for more female labor, in the second half of the 1950s, the government began an ambitious program aimed at increasing the number of childcare facilities and preschools. In addition, the School Act of 1960 called for "joint facilities of crèches and kindergartens" to be established in order to make it easier for children to advance from crèches to kindergartens. Although crèches remained administered by the Ministry of Healthcare, they were now also classified as preschools. Legislation on "joint facilities," however, proved to be particularly complex, not least of all because of the legal requirement to provide different arrangements for children of crèche and kindergarten age. Thus, the number of joint facilities remained quite small throughout the communist era.[30]

The program continued in the 1960s, but only the number of kindergartens increased. Their total rose from 6,633 in 1960–1961 (with 285,863 children) to 8,624 in 1973–1974 (with 414,433 children). The number of crèches stagnated (1,617 in 1960–1961 and 1,622 in 1973–1974) while the total of enrolled children increased modestly, from 65,276 to 67,657.[31] (See Table 18.1.) Despite the lack of crèches, women with small children increasingly worked outside of the home. The female employment rate rose from 45 percent in 1965 to 48 percent in 1973.[32] On average, employed mothers who first gave birth in the 1960s spent less time at home caring for their children before going back to work than mothers in any other decade of the communist period.[33] However, by the end of the 1960s, because of a change in the family policy, this trend slowly began to subside.

After 1945, the coalition government had introduced family allowances and tax deductions. This policy was motivated by social, not demographic, concerns. These family allowances were increased during the 1950s. Still, the fertility rate continued to fall, a trend that the regime saw as a "threat" for the future of Czech society.[34] An intense debate over the causes of this decline began at the Twelfth Congress of the KSČ in 1962. As a result, the supposed contradiction between women's productive roles in the economy and reproductive roles in society gained new currency. Pressured by this discussion, a State Population Committee was set up in the same year, which together with other institutions in the 1960s conducted a number of studies on the links between women's participation in the workforce, working women's fertility rate, and their children's development. Contemporary research by pediatricians and child psychologists drew attention to the possible psychological deprivation and socialization deficiencies of children who grew up in public facilities, especially "children's homes" and "week nurseries," where children of employed mothers stayed overnight during the workweek.

Criticism had already begun to appear by the late 1950s, but in the 1960s, the debate on the optimal age of children to enter a collective childcare facility intensified. Some psychologists and social scientists argued that the optimal age for children to begin attending a collective care facility was one year, while others advocated three years.[35] In addition, an economic argument was now used against crèches: the high morbidity among children who attended crèches was seen as one of these facilities' long-term problems, because it caused mothers' absence from work. This argument contributed to an equally powerful discourse on the supposed ineffectiveness of employing mothers with small children.[36] When in the late 1960s the fertility rate fell below the population-replacement level, the focus of the public discourse and social policy increasingly drifted away from "the women's (emancipation and labor market participation) issue" to "the children's issue."[37]

Population Policies, the Baby Boom, and Family Consumerism in the 1970s

The widespread fears sparked by the decline in Czechoslovakia's fertility rate resulted in a series of measures, already begun in the 1960s, designed to increase population. Among others, they included a stricter policy on abortion. New guidelines for the "interruption committees," which decided whether a woman could have an abortion, were introduced. Moreover, paid maternity leave was extended from 18 to 22 weeks and later to 26 weeks for married and 35 weeks for unmarried mothers, while the allowance for the leave was also increased.[38]

After the Soviets crushed the movement for greater democratization in Czechoslovakia in the spring of 1968, the communist state attempted to soothe people's disappointments by offering more consumer goods to families. This policy corresponded to the reaction of the population. With their hopes for political reform dashed, many citizens withdrew from public life and focused more on their private lives. The family became the one space that remained somewhat beyond the control of the state. This more consumer-friendly policy was made possible by the period of relative prosperity and abundance in the 1970s.[39]

The communist regime also introduced further measures designed to combat the falling birth rate, such as a housing distribution that prioritized married couples with children, interest-free loans for young married couples who had children in quick order after marriage, saving plans for young people, increased family allowances, tax breaks for children, free school supplies, grants for housing and travel, and other kinds of family-friendly subsidies. In general, social policy was increasingly geared towards raising women's employment by granting longer and longer full-time leaves—"extended maternity leave"—that would also guarantee job security for mothers caring for small children. The law on maternity allowances from 1970 provided a maternity leave and a monthly allowance for all employed women until the child reached the age of one. In 1971, this allowance was also applied to housewives and its duration extended to two years. A decade later, it was increased to three years.[40] At the same time, the construction of new childcare centers, preschools, and after-school facilities also continued. (See Table 18.1.) Following the introduction of these measures, the fertility rate did indeed begin to rise rapidly, if not necessarily as a direct result of them. More important than state policy was the fact that towards the end of the 1960s, the large cohort of people who had been born immediately after World War II reached childbearing age. In 1974, the birth rate reached 2.5, its highest point during the communist era. In the following years, however, it resumed its slow but steady decline.[41]

As a result of these and other policies, which codified the double-earner family model but did not question the gender division of labor, the difference between the continuous professional careers of men and the interrupted careers of women was effectively institutionalized. Indeed, policymakers made no effort to use gender-neutral terms in this legislation.[42] As was true for other Eastern European countries, the late 1960s and early 1970s were another "critical juncture" period for family and childcare policy during the communist regime. The new "policy path" blazed during this period sought to achieve full-time work for all women. To do so, it increased their entitlement to paid, extended maternity leave. Family-friendly work arrangements, however, such as part-time work or flexible working hours, remained, like in Hungary, very limited. Instead, mothers usually returned to the labor market after an extended maternity leave to work full-time with fixed working hours set by their employers. In practice, the major question was not what combinations of employment and public and family childcare parents should choose, but rather how long a mother should stay at home full-time with her child before going back to work full-time and relying on an all-day childcare or preschool facility.[43] While institutional public childcare outside the home and women's participation in the labor market were supported by the state, gender segregation and inequalities persisted in the labor market, and the gender division of work and responsibilities in the family was reproduced.

Restructuring Childcare in the Postcommunist Czech Republic

In addition to new political, economic, and social regimes, the revolutionary changes that occurred in East-Central Europe at the end of the 1980s brought a new discourse about gender roles. During the communist era, the discourse and practices regarding gender roles, women's participation in the labor market, and early childhood education were shaped by a mixture of conservative and progressive attitudes. After 1989, however, one can discern a marked increase in a more conservative rhetoric on gender. As the new capitalist Czech Republic began to encounter its first problems with unemployment, many politicians began to allude to the abolition of the "mandatory work rule," even if it in fact never applied to mothers with young children. They propagated the neoliberal concept of "freedom of choice," which was understood as the supposedly "voluntary" and "natural" return of women to the household and family responsibilities.[44]

The conservatism of the early 1990s was not just evident at the rhetorical level but was also reflected in childcare policies. For example, the mid-1990s debate over the question of whether the eligibility for the maternity allowance should be extended until a child's fourth birthday was settled when the government ended up taking the established path of extending the full-time, at-home period of care. Due to opposition from employers, however, the period of time during which a parent on parental leave was entitled to return to their original employer and a job matching their original work contract was not extended from three to four years.[45]

At the same time, the number of childcare facilities dropped sharply.[46] Indeed, the crèche system for children under the age of three basically collapsed altogether, and today only 54 crèches with a total of 1,671 places for children remain in the Czech Republic. One reason for this precipitous decline was that company and cooperative childcare facilities vanished completely, due to the massive restructuring and often closing of companies that accompanied the postcommunist marketization of the economy. Another reason was the decline in the birth rate, from 1.8 children per woman in the late 1980s to 1.3 children in the mid-1990s, although this alone cannot explain the massive decrease in the number of crèches. More important was the combined impact of a public discourse that did not value crèches and a legal framework and administrative system that did not protect them.[47]

One major reason for the contrasting development of crèches and kindergartens was the different legal tradition and administrative responsibility for both: the Ministry of Education was responsible for kindergartens and the Ministry of Health for crèches. This institutionalized separation of responsibilities and rules for providers of care for children up to the age of three (pediatric nurses) and children from the age of three and up (teachers) has been well established since the late 1940s and early 1950s. So, too, has been the inclusion of kindergartens into the unified school system. The inclusion of crèches among facilities for preschool education that occurred in 1960, however, has always been complicated by the continued dominance of rules set down by the Ministry of Health. To remedy this situation, in 1991 it was decided that crèches were no longer to be included among preschools, a policy change that accelerated the decline in the number of crèches in the 1990s. As a result, less than 1 percent of children under the age of three attend crèches today. The ones that remain in operation are mainly private and demand high enrollment fees, in some cases as much as a third of the average worker's salary. Conversely, only 2 percent of kindergartens are private or run by the church. Most kindergartens are operated by the municipal governments, which set the fees for children's enrollment according to guidelines issued by the Ministry of Education.[48]

As the number of crèches fell, it became increasingly difficult to obtain formal daycare for very young children. It is clear that trouble finding a place in a childcare facility has contributed to the high percentage of mothers who do not return when their maternity leave ended. Forty percent of these women cited the inability to find a crèche or kindergarten place as the main reason for their long-term absence from the labor market.[49] Historically, inflexibility in work schedules has contributed to the increase in length of time Czech mothers remain out of the labor market. Even today, only 9 percent of employed women hold a part-time job.[50] The constraints of working full-time make it very difficult to combine work and family—even with childcare. As an alternative, the ability of parents to look after their children full-time was, at least in theory, being encouraged through the extension of the eligibility period for the parental allowance to a full four years. This measure was part of a broader set of social policy measures intended to preserve social peace and thus the viability of the neoliberal market reforms of the 1990s that had produced so much economic hardship and anxiety.[51] These policies, along with a host of other social and economic factors, led to an increase in the amount of time mothers spent at home providing full-time care for their children and thus outside the labor market.[52]

The policy of long parental leaves with an even longer flat-rate parental allowance for mothers on full-time and uninterrupted leave did not endanger female participation in the centrally planned economy of the communist regime. But after 1989, this same policy has put them at much higher risk of unemployment. A comparative international survey of workforces published by the European Commission in 2006 showed that among EU countries, parenthood in the Czech Republic has the greatest negative impact on female employment.[53] Czech employers claimed the highest percentage of mothers that do not come back to work for them after parental leave.[54]

As we have seen, the decline in the number of places in kindergartens was not nearly as great as that of crèches. Due to the dramatic drop in fertility in the 1990s, the percentage of children between the ages of three and five enrolled in kindergartens did not begin to decline until 2004. This decrease may be explained by the fact that the birth rate started to rise again while the reduction in the capacity of kindergartens continues. One result of the large drop in the number of crèches was that more parents with two-year-old children tried to place them in kindergartens.[55] The vast majority of kindergartens maintain the tradition of the all-day schedule, running, on average, for ten hours each day. Most children spend every working day, seven hours a day, in kindergarten, but nearly 25 percent stay for more than eight hours. Seventy percent of kindergartens open at 7:00 a.m., but only 8 percent remain open after 5:00 p.m. More than half of all parents who use kindergarten services also use them during summer vacation, when they are usually open for five of the eight weeks of summer vacation.[56]

Only after the turn of the millennium has it become indisputably clear that women's long-term unemployment experienced a steady rise, especially among women in the age group most likely to be caring for small children. During the accession process into the European Union, the Czech Republic was criticized for its neglect of an active and effective employment policy. In response, the Czech government began drafting National Action Plans for Employment. Work offices began offering programs that targeted women with small children as a way of helping them return to the labor market. However, they focused on unemployed mothers, not those mothers receiving the parental allowance in the fourth year after the birth of their child.[57]

Towards the end of 1990s and the beginning of the new millennium, the Czech government implemented several legislative changes that aimed to increase the flexibility of parental leave and the parental allowance as a way to help mothers return to work. These changes came largely from the Ministry of Labor and Social Affairs, the main coordinator of policies promoting equal opportunity in the economy and society. In the first half of 1990s, in order to be eligible for the parental allowance, a parent had to provide full-time care and was not allowed to have unlimited income from gainful employment (the limit for income was so low that it prevented the parent from any paid work). Moreover, the parent was not permitted to use formal childcare facilities and preschools. These gradual legislative changes were introduced by the government in the last decade, especially at the beginning of the new millennium. They allow a parent receiving the parental allowance to have an unlimited income from their employment and to use collective childcare facilities and preschools (for five days a month if the child is under three and for four hours a day if the child is three or four years old). Thus, a parent receiving the parental allowance can choose between full-time care and combining a paid job and care. Before these changes in the law, a parent receiving the parental allowance only had the option of full-time care without any help and without any gainful work activity. If a parent worked and/or used a childcare facility, s(he) lost the entitlement to the parental allowance. Moreover, the parental allowance was increased at the beginning of 2007, making it easier for some parents to afford private childcare. But while these legislative changes have in theory made using parental leave and parental allowance more flexible, in practice the requisite conditions for them to succeed do not yet exist.[58] Above all, the Czech Republic lacks a family-friendly labor market policy, and the number of childcare facilities and preschools continues to decline.

This development is still not viewed as a major problem by the conservative government. Policy changes after 1989 resulted in a general decentralization of services that were once provided by the state. At the same time, municipalities obtained greater rights to determine their budgetary priorities. But due to the large decline in fertility in the 1990s, it was difficult for many of them to maintain kindergartens. The lack of incentives designed to encourage municipalities to maintain their existing kindergartens, along with the fact that there are few mothers among the ranks of municipal representatives, makes it unlikely that the decline in the number of kindergartens will abate anytime soon.

Conclusion

In this chapter, I have argued that there were four critical junctures that institutionalized a specific path of childcare and preschool education in the Czech Republic. On the one hand, these critical junctures and the resulting policy path established the norm that mothers stay at home with their child for the first three years with the help of a state-funded allowance. After 1989, this policy was reinforced due to the dramatic drop in the number of crèches. On the other hand, this policy path has led to one of the highest percentages of four- to five-year-old children in public childcare in Europe, because it was defined as preschool education provided by teachers and understood as a part of the universal schooling system.

The first critical juncture on this path occurred in 1872, when the government of the Austro-Hungarian Empire institutionalized the division between "care" facilities (crèches and children's asylums) and preschool "education" facilities (kindergartens). The care in all-day crèches was defined for "younger" children from families suffering from a "lack of adequate care" and the preschool "education" in half-day kindergartens for "older" children from better-off social backgrounds.

The second critical juncture happened in 1948, when the new communist regime passed the Act on Unified Education that institutionalized all-day kindergartens as the only officially sanctioned facilities for preparing children over the age of three for primary school education according to the standardized guidelines of the Ministry of Education. Because of this integration of kindergartens into the schooling system, their construction far outpaced the construction of any other kind of childcare facility. Today they are still widely accepted.

The third critical juncture occurred in 1952, when nonfamily care for children under three was institutionalized as part of a government-sponsored preventive healthcare scheme under which care was provided by pediatric nurses and pediatricians in order to ensure strict hygienic conditions. Not only because of its tradition, but also because it was mostly "endangered" children from poor families who attended crèches in the first decades of the communist regime, the debate on crèches has been framed by health-related social terms ever since.

The fourth critical juncture came in the 1960s and early 1970s, when the "additional maternity leave" and the maternity allowance became the main tools of the communist regime for a population policy that sought to halt and then reverse the dramatic decline of the fertility rate, which was indeed closely followed by, if not necessarily responsible for, an increase of the number of births. This trend, however, did not last very long. Since then, the path of continuing to extend paid leave, if only for mothers, was followed consistently, first as a way to tackle "the fertility problem" and then, after 1989, as a means of dealing with "the unemployment problem."

Although the percentage of children in both crèches and kindergartens in Czechoslovakia increased steadily until the 1980s, medical, psychological, and economic discourses critical of crèches intensified since the second half of the 1960s. These discourses opposed collective facilities as the primary providers of childcare and preschool education. In addition, they questioned the notion that they would emancipate women by enabling them to achieve economic independence and freedom from the very time-consuming and unpaid tasks of housekeeping and childcare. A very similar argument was used after 1989 during the restructuring of the Czech welfare state and childcare system, when in a neoliberal vein, "free choice" for women became the slogan of politicians who wanted to cut expenditures for publicly funded crèches.

As this chapter has shown, childhood education has been highly path dependent in the Czech Republic. Above all, its four critical junctures led to the institutionalization of a specific division of rules and concepts regarding "adequate" early childhood education. The result has been a system unlike any other in Europe. Recently, the aims of the European Union in respect to gender equality, women's and mother's employment, and early childhood education, which are most clearly defined in the targets set at the Lisbon and Barcelona conferences in 2000 and 2002, respectively, have begun to influence Czech policymaking. Moreover, some nongovernmental women's organizations established after 1989 have started to employ the EU discourse in their lobbying efforts.[59] However, the already-established path of childcare and preschool education policy places clear limits on the development of new policies.

Notes

The chapter is based on research that was carried out as part of the grant project "Gendered Citizenship in Multicultural Europe: The Impact of Contemporary Women's Movement (FEMCIT)," Sixth Framework Program, European Union, no. 028746–2.

1. The First Czechoslovak Republic was established after World War I in 1918. In 1948, when the communists assumed power, they first kept the name Czechoslovak Republic, but changed it in 1960 to the Czechoslovak Socialist Republic (CSSR). In 1989, the communist regime came to an end. In 1993, Czechoslovakia split into the Czech Republic and Slovak Republic.

2. OECD, *Starting Strong II: Early Childhood Edcucation and Care* (Paris, 2006), 304.

3. See Steven Saxonberg and Tomáš Sirovátka, "Failing Family Policy in Post-Communist Central Europe," *Journal of Comparative Policy Analysis* 8, no. 2 (2006): 185–202; Jacqueline Heinen and Monika Wator, "Childcare in Poland before, during, and after the Transition: Still a Women's Business," *Social Politics* 13, no. 2 (2006): 189–216.

4. Saxonberg and Sirovátka, "Failing Family Policy," 190; Michal Bulíř, Zařízení *předškolní péče a výchovy v ČSR: retrospektiva let 1881–1988 a 1921–1988*, Czech Statistical Office (Prague, 1990), appendix, table 6, n.p.; Christina Klenner, "Gender Equality and Work in Germany," *Willamette Journal of the Liberal Arts* 15 (2005): 21; Silke Bothfeld et al., *WSI—FrauenDatenReport 2005* (Berlin, 2005), CD-ROM, Kapitel 6—Soziale Sicherung, table 6.A.3., n.p.

5. Saxonberg and Sirovátka, "Failing Family Policy," 190; see also Heinen and Wator, "Childcare in Poland."

6. See Richard Rose, "Inheritance Before Choice in Public Policy," *Journal of Theoretical Politics* 2, no. 3 (1990): 263–91; James Mahoney, "Path Dependence in Historical Sociology," *Theory and Society* 29, no. 4 (2000): 507–48. See also the introductions to this volume.

7. See as one example Karen Hagemann and Sonya Michel, eds., "Perspectives on Child Care and Education in Eastern and Western Europe," special issue, *Social Politics: International Studies in Gender, State, and Society* 13, no. 2 (Summer 2006).

8. For more, see Ann Taylor Allen, *Feminism and Motherhood in Western Europe, 1890–1970: The Maternal Dilemma* (New York, 2005).

9. Věra Mišurcová, *Dějiny teorie a praxe výchovy dětí předškolního věku v 19. a 20. století*, (Prague, 1980).

10. In addition to Bohemia and Moravia, the first Czech Republic incorporated parts of Silesia, Slovakia, and sub-Carpathian Ruthenia.

11. Mišurcová, *Dějiny teorie*, 213–18.

12. Ibid.

13. Eva Uhrová, "Národní fronta žen." Retrieved 15 January 2007: http://www.feminismus .cz/fulltext.shtml?x=720276.

14. The Czechoslovak Women's Council (dissolved after the communist takeover in February 1948) was a nongovernmental women's umbrella organization that contained representatives from the Central Trade Union Council, the Central Cooperative Council, and political parties. The National Women's Front copied the structure of the National Front of Czechs and Slovaks.

15. Eva Uhrová, "Národní fronta žen."

16. Ibid.

17. *Československá žena*, no. 42 (1946): 3; Eva Uhrová, "Rada československých žen." Both retrieved 15 January 2008: http://www.feminismus.cz/fulltext.shtml?x=473896.

18. Similarly in Hungary: Éva Bicskei, "Our Greatest Treasure, the Child: The Politics of Childcare in Hungary, 1945–1956," *Social Politics* 13, no. 2 (2006): 151–88.

19. Saxonberg and Sirovátka, "Failing Family Policy," 185.

20. Alena Heitlinger, "Pro-natalist Population Policies in Czechoslovakia," *Population Studies* 30, no. 1 (1978): 124.

21. Database of Czech Statistical Office in Bulíř, *Zařízení předškolní*; Database of Office for Information in Education in Věra Kuchařová and Kamila Svobodová, *Síť zařízení denní péče o děti předškolního věku v ČR*, Research Institute of Labor and Social Affairs (Prague, 2006); Database of Office for Information and Statistics in Health in Kuchařová and Svobodová, *Síť zařízení*; Database of Czech Statistical Office. Retrieved 1 October 2007: http://www.czso.cz; Database of Czech Republic Population Information. Retrieved 1 October, 2007: http://popin.natur.cuni.cz/html2/index.php.

22. See the data in Bulíř, *Zařízení předškolní*.

23. See the Act on Unified Education No. 95/1948 Coll., the Government Act No. 195/1948 Coll. on implementation of the Act on Unified Education in kindergartens, the Act of the Ministry of Healthcare on unified preventive and medical care No. 130/1951 Coll., the Act of the Ministry of Healthcare on organizing of preventive and medical care No. 24/1952 Coll., and the governmental Act No. 202/1947 Coll. on organization of care for the youth.

24. See the data in Bulíř, *Zařízení předškolní.*

25. Vladimír Srb and Milan Kučera, *Výzkum o rodičovství 1956*, State Statistical Office (Prague, 1959), 115. A total of 11,126 Czech and Slovak women 15–39 years old were surveyed. Fifty-five percent of them were economically active.

26. Ibid., 115–20.

27. Heitlinger, "Pro-natalist Population," 125.

28. Ibid., 129

29. Ibid., 135f.

30. Miloš Klíma, *Pečovatelská služba jako forma péče o děti jeslového věku a důsledky vyplývající z jejích zavadení* (Brno 1969), 11; Bulíř, *Zařízení předškolní*, appendix, table 11.

31. Heitlinger, "Pro-natalist Population," 134.

32. Ibid., 124.

33. Data from a representative survey of 1,330 Czech and Slovak women: the Institute of Sociology, Academy of Sciences of the Czech Republic, "Women in Social Structure — Czechoslovakia 1991" (Prague, 1991).

34. Irina Kolorosova, "Czechoslovakia: One Culture in Two States," in *Population, Family and Welfare: A Comparative Survey of European Attitudes* (Oxford, 1995), 102–21.

35. See, for example, Martin Marušiak, *Rodina a manželství* (Svobodné slovo, 1964); Josef Langmeier and Zdeněk Matějček, *Psychická deprivace v dětství* (Prague, 1963); Jiřina Máchová, *Spor o rodinu* (Prague, 1970).

36. See M. Jančíková, *Dlohodobý vývoj jeslí,* Czech Statistical Office (Prague, 1979), 11.
37. Alena Wagnerová, "Ženy socialisticky osvobozené," *Literární noviny,* no. 5 (2007): 8.
38. Milada Bartošová, *Populační politika v ČSSR 1945–1975,* Czechoslovak Research Institute of Labor and Social Affairs (Prague, 1978), 38–48.
39. Ladislav Rabušic, *Kde ty všechny děti jsou? Porodnost v sociologické perspektivě* (Prague, 2001).
40. Heitlinger, "Pro-natalist Population," 131.
41. "Women's Fertility Rates in Czechoslovakia during 1970–1979," *Demosta* 14, no. 2 (1981): 44–49.
42. In fact, it was not until 1990 that the "maternity allowance" was renamed "parental allowance." It would take another ten years, in 2000, to change "extended maternity leave" to "parental leave." Only single fathers, and then not until the 1980s, received something close to the same rights as mothers in regard to childcare.
43. See Gerlinda Smauss, "K čemu českým ženám feminismus," *Literární noviny,* no. 5 (2007): 9.
44. Irena Hradecká, "Výrobní dělníci, industriální vztahy a sociální politika: základní orientace a postoje," *Sociologický časopis* 31, no. 4 (1995): 485–99; Sharon L. Wolchik, "Women and the Politics of Transition in the Czech and Slovak Republics," in *Women in the Politics of Postcommunist Eastern Europe,* ed. Marylin Rueschemeyer (Armonk, NY, 1995), 3–27.
45. Věra Kuchařová et al., *Zaměstnání a péče o malé děti z perspektivy rodičů a zaměstnavatelů,* Research Institute of Labor and Social Affairs (Prague, 2006).
46. Saxonberg and Sirovátka, "Failing Family Policy," 190.
47. Kuchařová and Svobodová, *Síť zařízení.*
48. Ibid.
49. Kuchařová et al., *Zaměstnání a péče.*
50. Claire Wallace, "Work Flexibility in Eight European Countries," *Czech Sociological Review* 39, no. 6 (2003): 773–93.
51. Tomáš Sirovátka, "Family Policy in the Czech Republic after 1989: From Gendered and Enforced De-Familialism to Gendered and Implicit Familialism," in *Society, Reproduction and Contemporary Challenges,* ed. Petr Mareš (Brno, 2004), 97–117.
52. The Institute of Sociology, Academy of Sciences of the Czech Republic, Survey: "Parents 2005" (Prague, 2005).
53. European Commission, *Indicators for Monitoring the Employment Guidelines 2006 Compendium* (Brussels, 2006), 47.
54. European Foundation for the Improvement of Living and Working Conditions, *Working Time and Work-Life Balance in European Companies* (Luxembourg, 2006), 37f.
55. Kuchařová and Svobodová, *Síť zařízení.*
56. Ibid.
57. Kuchařová et al., *Zaměstnání a péče.*
58. Institutional incentives to bring men into care have also been neglected in Czech society. Even today, there is no "paternity leave" or "daddy days," and only 1 percent of all parental leave takers are men.
59. Other women's nongovernmental organizations argue for "active motherhood" (a term already being used in Czechoslovakia before 1989) and for a clearer differentiation between women's and men's roles. These groups have lobbied against the Barcelona and Lisbon targets.

SELECTED BIBLIOGRAPHY

The following selection includes some of the most important publications on the subject. It is organized in six sections:

1. Theories and Methodologies
2. Families and Family Policies
3. Demographic Trends and Population Policies
4. Gender, Work, and Welfare
5. (Primary) School Education
6. Childcare and Early Childhood Education

1. Theories and Methodologies

"AHR Forum: Revisiting 'Gender: A Useful Category of Historical Analysis.'" *American Historical Review* 113, no. 5 (2008): 1344–430.

"Gender and Change: Agency, Chronology and Periodization." Special issue, *Gender & History* 20, no. 3 (2008): 453–678.

Allemann-Ghionda, Cristina. *Einführung in die vergleichende Erziehungswissenschaft.* Weinheim, 2004.

Cohen, Deborah, and Maura O'Connor, eds. *Comparison and History: Europe in Cross-National Perspective.* New York, 2004.

Haupt, Heinz-Gerhard, and Jürgen Kocka, eds. *Geschichte und Vergleich.* Frankfurt/M., 1996.

Kaelble, Hartmut. *Der historische Vergleich. Eine Einführung zum 19. und 20. Jahrhundert.* Frankfurt/M., 1999.

Kaelble, Hartmut, and Jürgen Schriewer, eds. *Diskurse und Entwicklungspfade. Der Gesellschaftsvergleich in den Geschichts- und Sozialwissenschaften.* Frankfurt/M., 1999.

Lister, Ruth. *Citizenship: Feminist Perspectives.* London, 1997.

Marshall, Thomas Humphrey. *Citizenship and Social Class, and Other Essays.* Cambridge, UK, 1950. Reprint. London, 1992.

O'Connor, Julia S. "Gender, Class and Citizenship in the Comparative Analysis of Welfare State Regimes: Theoretical and Methodological Issues." *British Journal of Sociology* 44, no. 3 (1993): 501–18.

Orloff, Ann Shola. "Gender and the Social Rights of Citizenship: The Comparative Analysis of Gender Relations and Welfare States." *American Sociological Review* 58, no. 3 (1993): 303–28.

———. "Gender in the Welfare State." *Annual Review of Sociology* 22, no. 1 (1996): 51–78.

Pierson, Paul. *Politics in Time: History, Institutions, and Social Analysis.* Princeton, NJ, 2004.

———. "Increasing Returns, Path Dependence, and the Study of Politics." *American Political Science Review* 94, no. 2 (2000): 251–67.

Scott, Joan Wallach. *Gender and the Politics of History.* New York, 1988.

Thelen, Kathleen. "Historical Institutionalism in Comparative Politics." *Annual Reviews in Political Science* 2 (1999): 369–404.

———. "How Institutions Evolve: Insights from Comparative-Historical Analysis." In *Comparative Historical Analysis in the Social Sciences,* edited by James Mahoney and Dietrich Rueschemeyer, 208–40. New York, 2002.

2. Families and Family Policies

Childers, Kristen Stromberg. *Fathers, Families, and the State in France, 1914–1945.* Ithaca, NY, 2003.

Crompton, Rosemary et al., eds. *Women, Men, Work and Family in Europe.* Basingstoke , 2007.

Creighton, Colin. "The Rise and Decline of the 'Male Breadwinner Family' in Britain." *Cambridge Journal of Economics* 23, no. 5 (1999): 519–41.

Daly, Mary. "The Functioning Family: Catholicism and Social Policy in Germany and Ireland." *Comparative Social Research* 18 (1999): 105–33.

Ehrmann, Sandra. *Familenpolitik in Frankreich und Deutschland im Vergleich.* Frankfurt/M., 1999.

Fagnani, Jeanne F. "Family Policy in France." In *International Encyclopedia of Social Policy,* edited by Tony Fitzpatrick et al., 3: 501–6. Oxford, 2006.

———. "Family Policies in France and Germany: Sisters or Distant Cousins?" *Community, Work and Family* 10, no. 1 (2007): 39–56.

Fagnani, Jeanne F., and Marie Thérèse Letablier. "Caring Rights and Responsibilities of Families in the French Welfare State." In *Care Arrangements and Social Integration in European Societies,* edited by Birgit Pfau-Effinger and Barbara Geissler, 153–72. Berlin, 2005.

Ferree, Myra Marx. "The Rise and Fall of 'Mommy Politics': Feminism and Unification in (East) Germany." *Feminist Studies* 19, no. 1 (1993): 89–115.

Fodor, Éva et al. "Family Policies and Gender in Hungary, Poland and Romania." *Communist and Post-Communism Studies* 35, no. 4 (2002): 475–90.

Gauthier, Anne H. "Family Policies in Industrialized Countries: Is There Convergence?" *Population* 57, no. 3 (2002): 447–74.

————. *The State and the Family: A Comparative Analysis of Family Policies in Industrialized Countries*. Oxford, 1996.

Gerhard, Ute. *Debating Women's Equality: Toward a Feminist Theory of Law from a European Perspective*. New Brunswick, NJ, 2001.

Hantrais, Linda, and Marie Thérèse Letablier. *Families and Family Policies in Europe*. London, 1996.

Horska, Pavla. "Historical Models of Central European Families: Czechs and Slovaks." *Journal of Family History* 19, no. 2 (1994): 99–106.

Kaufmann, Franz-Xaver. "Politics and Policies towards the Family in Europe: A Framework and an Inquiry into their Differences and Convergences." In *Family Life and Family Policies in Europe*, vol. 2, *Problems and Issues in Comparative Perspective*, edited by Franz-Xaver Kaufmann et al., 419–77. Oxford, 2002.

Kaufmann, Franz-Xaver et al., ed. *Family Life and Family Policies in Europe*, 2 vols. Oxford, 1998 and 2002.

Leitner, Sigrid. "Varieties of Familialism: The Caring Function of the Family in Comparative Perspective." *European Societies* 5, no. 4 (2003): 353–75.

Moeller, Robert G. *Protecting Motherhood: Women and the Family in the Politics of Postwar Germany*. Berkeley, CA, 1993.

Motiejunaite, Akvile, and Zhanna Kravchenko. "Family Policy, Employment and Gender-role Attitudes: A Comparative Analysis of Russia and Sweden." *Journal of European Social Policy* 18, no. 1 (2008): 38–49.

Obertreis, Gesine. *Familienpolitik in der DDR 1945–1980*. Opladen, 1986.

Petö, Andrea, and Béla Rásky, eds. *Construction—Reconstruction: Women, Family and Politics in Central Europe. 1945–1998*. Budapest, 1999.

Rölli-Alkemper, Lukas. *Familie im Wiederaufbau. Katholizismus und bürgerliches Familienideal in der Bundesrepublik Deutschland, 1945–1965*. Paderborn, 2000.

Saxonberg, Steven, and Tomáš Sirovátka. "Failing Family Policy in Postcommunist Central Europe." *Journal of Comparative Policy Analysis* 8, no. 2 (2006): 185–202.

Szikra, Dorottya, and Dorota Szelewa. "Passen die mittel- und osteuropäische Länder in das 'westliche' Bild? Das Beispiel der Familienpolitik in Ungarn und Polen." In *Wohlfahrtsstaaten und Geschlechterungleichheit in Mittel- und Osteuropa. Kontinuität und postsozialistische Transformation in den EU-Mitgliedstaaten*, edited by Christina Klenner and Simone Leiber, 88–123. Wiesbaden, 2008.

Williams, Fiona. *Rethinking Families*. London, 2004.

3. Demographic Trends and Population Policies

Ahn, Namkee, and Pedro Mira. "A Note on the Changing Relationship between Fertility and Female Employment Rates in Developed Countries." *Journal of Population Economics* 15, no. 4 (2002): 667–82.

Bernhardt, Eva M. "Fertility and Employment." *European Sociological Review* 9, no. 1 (1993): 25–42.

Bertram, Hans. "Nachhaltige Familienpolitik und demografische Entwicklung. Zeit, Geld und Infrastruktur als Elemente einer demografiebewussten Familienpolitik." *Zeitschrift für Pädagogik* 55, no. 1 (2009): 37–55.

Brewster Karin L., and Ronald R. Rindfuss. "Fertility and Women's Employment in Industrialized Nations." *Annual Review of Sociology* 26 (2000): 271–96.

Caldwell, John C., and Thomas Schindlmayr. "Explanations of the Fertility Crisis in Modern Societies: A Search for Commonalities." *Population Studies* 57, no. 3 (2003): 241–63.

Di Prete, Thomas A. et al. "Do Cross-national Differences in the Costs of Children Generate Cross-national Differences in Fertility Rates?" *Population Research and Policy Review* 22, no. 4 (2003): 439–77.

Goldstein, Joshua et al. "The Emergence of Sub-replacement Family Size Ideals in Europe." *Population Research and Policy Review* 22, no. 5/6 (2003): 479–96.

Hobson, Barbara, and Livia Sz. Oláh. "Birthstrikes? Agency and Capabilities in the Reconciliation of Employment and Family." *Marriage and Family Review* 39, no. 3/4 (2006): 197–227.

Kreyenfeld, Michaela. "Fertility Decisions in the FRG and GDR: An Analysis with Data from the German Fertility and Family Survey." *Demographic Research, Special Collection* 3, art. 11 (2004): 275–318.

McDonald, Peter. "Gender Equity, Social Institutions and the Future of Fertility." *Journal of Population Research* 17, no. 1 (2000): 1–16.

———. "Low Fertility and the State: The Efficacy of Policy." *Population and Development Review* 32, no. 3 (2006): 485–510.

Presser, Harriet B. "Comment: A Gender Perspective for Understanding Low Fertility in Post-Transitional Societies." *Population and Development Review* 27, supplement "Global Fertility Transition" (2001): 177–83.

Rindfuss, Ronald R. et al. "The Changing Institutional Context of Low Fertility." *Population Research and Policy Review* 22, no. 5/6 (2003): 411–38.

Rindfuss, Ronald R., and Karin L. Brewster. "Childrearing and Fertility." *Population and Development Review* 22, supplement, "Fertility in the United States: New Patterns, New Theories" (1996): 258–89.

Sardon, Jean-Paul. "Recent Demographic Trends in the Developed Countries." *Population* 59, no. 2 (2004): 263–314.

4. Gender, Work, and Welfare

Anttonen, Anneli, and Jorma Sipilä, "European Social Care Services: Is It Possible to Identify Models?" *Journal of European Social Policy* 6, no. 2 (1996): 87–100.

Bergqvist, Christina et al., eds. *Equal Democracies? Gender and Politics in the Nordic Countries.* Oslo, 1999.

Bock, Gisela, and Susan James, eds. *Beyond Equalities and Difference: Citizenship, Feminist Politics and Female Subjectivity.* London, 1992.

Bock, Gisela, and Pat Thane, eds. *Maternity and Gender Politics: Women and the Rise of the European Welfare States, 1880s-1950s.* London, 1991.

Boje, Thomas P., and Arnlaug Leira, eds. *Gender, Welfare State and the Market: Towards a New Division of Labor.* London, 2000.

Breen, Richard, and Lynn Prince Cook. "The Persistence of the Gendered Division of Domestic Labor." *European Sociological Review* 21, no. 1 (2005): 43–57.

Brush, Lisa D. "Love, Toil, and Trouble: Motherhood and Feminist Politics." *Signs* 21, no. 2 (1996): 429–54.

Bussemaker, Jet. *Citizenship and Welfare State Reform in Europe.* London, 1999.

Daly, Mary E. *The Gender Division of Welfare: The Impact of the British and German Welfare States.* Cambridge, UK, 2000.

Daly, Mary E., and Katherine Rake. *Gender and the Welfare State: Care, Work and Welfare in Europe and the USA.* Cambridge, UK, 2003.

Deacon, Bob. *The New Eastern Europe: Social Policy Past, Present and Future.* London, 1992.

Del Boca, Daniela, and Cecile Wetzels, eds. *Social Policies, Labor Markets and Motherhood: A Comparative Analysis of European Countries.* Cambridge, UK, 2007.

Ellingsæter, Anne Lise, and Arnlaug Leira, eds. *Politicizing Parenthood: Gender in Scandinavian Welfare States.* Bristol, 2005.

Esping-Andersen, Gøsta. *Social Foundations of Postindustrial Economics.* Oxford, 1999.

———. *Three Worlds of Welfare Capitalism.* Princeton, 1990.

———, ed. *Welfare States in Transition: National Adaptations in Global Economies.* London, 1996.

Esping-Andersen, Gøsta, et al., eds. *Why We Need a New Welfare State.* Oxford, 2002.

Evers, Adalbert et al., eds. *The Changing Face of Welfare.* Aldershot, 1987.

Fagnani, Jeanne, and Marie Thérèse Letablier. "Work and Family Life Balance: The Impact of the 35 Hour Laws in France." *Work, Employment and Society* 18, no. 3 (2004): 551–72.

Ferge, Zsuzsa, and Jon Eivind Kolberg, eds. *Social Policy in a Changing Europe.* Boulder, CO, 1992.

Fraser, Nancy. "After the Family Wage: Gender Equity and the Welfare State." *Political Theory* 22, no. 4 (1994): 591–618.

Fultz, Elaine et al., eds. *The Gender Dimensions of Social Security Reform in Central and Eastern Europe: Case Studies of the Czech Republic, Hungary and Poland.* Budapest, 2003.

Gatens, Moira, and Alison Mackinnon, eds. *Gender and Institutions: Welfare, Work, and Citizenship.* Cambridge, UK, 1998.

Gerhard, Ute et al., eds. *Working and Mothering in Europe: A Comparison of Policies and Practices.* Cheltenham, 2005.

González, María José et al., eds. *Gender Inequalities in Southern Europe: Women, Work, and Welfare in the 1990s.* London, 2000.

Gordon, Linda, ed. *Women, the State and Welfare.* Madison, WI, 1990.

Gornick, Janet C., and Marcia K. Meyers. *Families That Work: Policies for Reconciling Parenthood and Employment.* New York, 2003.

———. "Welfare Regimes in Relation to Paid Work and Care." In *Changing Life Patterns in Western Industrial Societies,* edited by Janet Zollinger Giele and Elke Holst, 45–67. Amsterdam, 2001.

Gornick, Janet C. et al. "Supporting the Employment of Mothers: Policy Variations Across Fourteen Welfare States." *Journal of European Social Policy* 7, no. 1 (1997): 45–70.

Gottfried, Heidi, and Jacqueline O'Reilly. "Reregulating Breadwinner Models in Socially Conservative Welfare Systems: Comparing Germany and Japan." *Social Politics* 9, no. 1 (2002): 29–59.

Haney, Lynne. "'But We are Still Mothers': Gender and the Construction of Need in Post-Socialist Hungary." *Social Politics* 4, no. 2 (1997): 208–24.

———. "Familial Welfare: Building the Hungarian Welfare Society, 1948–1968." *Social Politics* 7, no. 1 (2000): 101–22.

———. *Inventing the Needy: Gender and the Politics of Welfare in Hungary.* Berkeley, CA, 2002.

Hantrais, Linda, ed. *Gendered Policies in Europe: Reconciling Employment and Family Life.* London, 2000.

Hašková, Hana et al., eds. *Women and Social Citizenship in Czech Society: Continuity and Change.* Prague, 2009.

Heinen, Jacqueline. "Clashes and Ordeals of Women's Citizenship in Central and Eastern Europe." In *Women and Citizenship in Central and East Europe*, edited by Jasmina Lukic et al., 81–100. Aldershot, 2006.

———. "East European Transition, Labor Markets and Gender in the Light of Three Cases: Poland, Hungary and Bulgaria." *Polish Population Review* 15 (1999): 106–27.

Heinen, Jacqueline, and Heini Martiskainene de Koenigswarter. "Framing Citizenship in France and Finland in the 1990s: Restructuring Motherhood, Work, and Care." *Social Politics* 8, no. 2 (2001): 170–81.

Heinen, Jacqueline, and Stéphane Portet. "Social and Political Citizenship in Eastern Europe: The Polish Case." In *Gender Justice, Development and Rights*, edited by Maxine Molyneux and Shahra Razavi, 141–69. Oxford, 2002.

Heinen, Jacqueline, and Monika Wator. "Child Care in Poland before, during, and after the Transition: Still a Women's Business." *Social Politics* 13, no. 2 (2006): 189–216.

Hobson, Barbara, ed. *Gender and Citizenship in Transition.* New York, 2000.

Hobson, Barbara, and Marika Lindholm. "Collective Identities, Women's Power Resources, and the Making of Welfare States." *Theory and Society* 26, no. 4 (1997): 475–508.

Hobson, Barbara, et al., eds. *Contested Concepts in Gender and Social Politics.* Cheltenham, 2002.

Hong, Young-Sun. *Welfare, Modernity, and the Weimar State.* Princeton, NJ, 1998.

Huber, Evelyne, and John D. Stephens. "Partisan Governance, Women's Employment, and the Social Democratic Service State." *American Sociological Review* 65 (2000): 323–42.

Jaumotte, Florence. "Labor Force Participation of Women: Empirical Evidence on the Role of Policy and Other Determinants in OECD Countries." *OECD Economic Studies*, no. 37 (June 2004): 53–112.

Klenner, Christina, and Simone Leiber, eds. *Wohlfahrtsstaaten und Geschlechterungleichheit in Mittel- und Osteuropa. Kontinuität und postsozialistische Transformation in den EU-Mitgliedstaaten.* Wiesbaden, 2008.

Kolbe, Wiebke. *Elternschaft im Wohlfahrtsstaat. Schweden und die Bundesrepublik im Vergleich 1945–2000.* Frankfurt/M., 2002.

Kulawik, Teresa. *Wohlfahrtsstaat und Mutterschaft. Schweden und Deutschland 1870–1912.* Frankfurt/M., 1999.

Leira, Arnlaug. *Welfare States and Working Mothers: The Scandinavian Experience.* Cambridge, UK, 2002.

Lewis, Gail. *'Race,' Gender, Social Welfare: Encounters in a Postcolonial Society.* Cambridge, UK, 2000.

———, ed. *Forming Nation, Framing Welfare.* London, 1998.

Lewis, Gail et al., eds. *Rethinking Social Policy.* London, 2000.

Lewis, Jane. "The Decline of the Male Breadwinner Model: Implications for Work and Care." *Social Politics* 8, no. 1 (2001): 152–169.

———. "Gender, The Family and Women's Agency in the Building of the 'Welfare State': The British Case." *Social History* 19, no. 1 (1994): 37–55.

———. *The Politics of Motherhood: Child and Maternal Welfare in England, 1900–1939.* London, 1980.

———. "Women's Agency: Maternalism and Welfare," *Gender & History* 6, no. 1 (1994): 117–23.

———, ed. *Women and Social Policies in Europe: Work, Family and the State.* Aldershot, 1993.

———, ed. *Women's Welfare, Women's Rights.* London, 1983.

Lewis, Jane et al., eds. *Gender, Social Care and Welfare State Restructuring in Europe.* Aldershot, 1998.

Lewis, Jane, and Gertrude Åström. "Equality, Difference, and State Welfare: Labor Market and Family Policies in Sweden." *Feminist Studies* 18, no. 1 (1992): 59–87.

Lewis, Jane, and Susanna Giullari. "The Adult Worker Model Family, Gender Equality and Care: The Search for New Policy Principles and the Possibilities and Problems of a Capabilities Approach." *Economy and Society* 34, no. 1 (2005): 76–104.

Mahood, Linda. *Policing Gender, Class and Family: Britain, 1850–1940.* Edmonton, AB, 1996.

Michel, Sonya, and Seth Koven, eds. *Mothers of a New World: Maternalist Politics and the Origins of Welfare State.* London, 1993.

Moeller, Robert G. "Reconstructing the Family in Reconstruction Germany: Women and Social Policy in the Federal Republic, 1949–1955." *Feminist Studies,* no. 1 (1989): 137–69.

———. "The State of Women's Welfare in European Welfare States." *Social History* 19, no. 1 (1994): 384–92.

Morgan, Kimberly J. "The Politics of Mothers' Employment: France in Comparative Perspective." *World Politics* 55, no. 2 (2003): 259–89.

———. *Working Mothers and the Welfare State: Religion and the Politics of Work-Family Policies in Western Europe and the United States.* Stanford, CA, 2006.

Noble, Virginia Anne. *Gender and the Practice of Welfare Provision in Britain, 1946–1966.* Chapel Hill, NC, 2001.

O'Connor, Julia S. et al., eds. *States, Markets, Families: Gender, Liberalism and Social Policy in Australia, Canada, Great Britain and the United States.* Cambridge, UK, 1999.

Pascall, Gillian, and Anna Kwak. *Gender Regimes in Transition in Central and Eastern Europe*. Bristol, 2005.

Pascall, Gillian, and Jane Lewis. "Emerging Gender Regimes and Policies for Gender Equality in a Wider Europe." *Journal of Social Policy* 33, no. 3 (2004): 373–94.

Pascall, Gillian, and Nick Manning. "Gender and Social Policy: Comparing Welfare States in Central and Eastern Europe and the Former Soviet Union." *Journal of European Social Policy* 10, no. 3 (2000): 240–66.

Pedersen, Susan. *Family, Dependence, and the Origins of the Welfare State, Britain and France 1914–1945*. New York, 1993.

Perrons, Diane et al., eds. *Gender Divisions and Working Time in the New Economy*. Northampton, 2006.

Plantenga, Janneke, and Chantal Remery. *Reconciliation of Work and Private Life: A Comparative Review of Thirty European Countries*. Luxembourg, 2005.

Randall, Vicky, and Georgia Waylen, eds. *Gender Politics and the State*. London, 1998.

Sachsse, Christoph. *Mütterlichkeit als Beruf. Sozialarbeit, Sozialreform und Frauenbewegung 1871–1929*. Frankfurt/M., 1986.

Sainsbury, Diane. "Gender and the Making of Welfare States: Norway and Sweden." *Social Politics* 8, no. 1 (2001): 113–43.

———. *Gender and Welfare State Regimes*. Oxford, 1999.

———. *Gender, Equality and Welfare States*. Cambridge, UK, 1996.

———, ed. *Gendering Welfare States*. London, 1994.

Schram, Sanford F. et al., eds. *Race and the Politics of Welfare Reform*. Ann Arbor, MI, 2003.

Schröder, Iris. *Arbeiten für eine bessere Welt. Frauenbewegung und Sozialreform, 1890–1914*. Frankfurt/M., 2001.

Skocpol, Theda, and Gretchen Ritter. "Gender and the Origins of Modern Social Policies in Britain and the United States." *Studies in American Political Development* 5, no. (1991): 36–93.

Szalai, Julia. "Poverty and the Traps of Postcommunist Welfare Reforms in Hungary: The New Challenges of EU-accession." *Revija za Socijalnu Politiku* 13, no. 3 (2005): 309–33.

Szikra, Dorottya. "Family and Child Support in a Post-communist Society: Origins of the Mixed Hungarian Welfare Capitalism." In *Fighting Poverty and Reforming Social Security: What Can Post-Soviet States Learn from the New Democracies of Central Europe?* edited by Michael Cain et al., 29–45. Washington, DC, 2007.

Torstendahl, Rolf, ed. *Social Policy and Gender System in the Two German States and Sweden 1945–1989*. Uppsala, 1999.

Verdery, Katherine. "From Parent-State to Family Patriarchs: Gender and Nation in Contemporary Eastern Europe." *East European Politics and Societies* 8, no. 2 (1994): 225–55.

Williams, Fiona. *Social Policy: A Critical Introduction. Issues of Race, Gender and Class*. Cambridge, UK, 1989.

Williams, Fiona et al., eds. *Welfare Research: A Critical Review*. Berkeley, CA, 1999.

Wolchik, Sharon L. "The Status of Women in a Socialist Order: Czechoslovakia, 1948–1978." *Slavic Review* 38, no. 3 (1978): 123–42.

———. "Women and the Politics of Gender in Communist and Post-Communist Central and Eastern Europe." In *Eastern Europe: Politics, Culture and Society since 1939*, edited by Sabina R. Ramet, 285–304. Bloomington, IN, 1998.

5. (Primary) School Education

Allemann-Ghionda, Cristina. "Ganztagschule im europäischen Vergleich: Zeitpolitiken modernisieren—durch Vergleich Standards setzen?" *Zeitschrift für Pädagogik*, supplement no. 54 (2009): 190–208.

———. "Ganztagssysteme in Europa—Zeitstrukturierung im internationalen Vergleich." In *Grundbegriffe der Ganztagsbildung: Das Handbuch*, edited by Hans-Uwe Otto and Thomas Coelen, 674–83. Wiesbaden, 2008.

Arnesen, Anne-Lise, and Lisbeth Lundahl. "Still Social and Democratic? Inclusive Education Policies in the Nordic Welfare States." *Scandinavian Journal of Educational Research* 50, no. 3 (2006): 285–300.

Baumert, Jürgen et al., eds. *Herkunftsbedingte Disparitäten im Bildungswesen: Differenzielle Bildungsprozesse und Probleme der Verteilungsgerechtigkeit: Vertiefende Analysen im Rahmen von PISA 2000*. Wiesbaden, 2006.

Bonfiglioli, Sandra. "Le politiche di riorganizzazione dei tempi della città: sviluppo della qualità della vita e del territorio." In *Cosa vogliono le donne. Cosa fanno le donne per conciliare lavoro e famiglia*, 54–59. Milan, 2001.

Bourdieu, Pierre. *Reproduction in Education, Society, and Culture*. London, 1990 (in French, 1970).

Bourdieu, Pierre, and Jean-Claude Passeron. *Die Illusion der Chancengleichheit. Untersuchungen zur Soziologie des Bildungswesens in Frankreich*. Stuttgart, 1971.

Brehony, Kevin J. "Primary Schooling under New Labor: The Irresolvable Contradiction of Excellence and Enjoyment." *Oxford Review of Education*, 312, no. 1 (2005): 29–46.

———. "Representations of Socialist Educational Experiments in the 1920s and 1930s." In *Passion, Fusion, Tension. New Education and Educational Sciences: End 19th-Middle 20th Century*, edited by Rita Hofstetter and Bernard Schneuwly, 271–304. Bern, 2006.

Brine, Jenny et al., eds. *Home, School and Leisure in the Soviet Union*. London, 1980.

Commission of European Communities. *Education of Migrant Workers' Children in the European Community*. Luxembourg, 1975.

Compère, Marie-Madeleine. *L'histoire de l'education en Europe. Essai comparatif sur la façon dont elle s'écrit*. Paris, 1995.

———, ed. *Histoire du temps scolaire en Europe*. Paris, 1997.

Döbrich, Peter et al. *Zeit für Schule*, 6 vol. Cologne, 1990–1991.

Eklof, Ben et al., eds. *Educational Reform in Post-Soviet Russia: Legacies and Prospects*. London, 2005.

Eklof, Ben, and E. D. Dneprov. *Democracy in the Russian School: The Reform Movement in Education Since 1984*. Boulder, CO, 1993.

European Commission, *Key Data on Education in Europe 2005*. Brussels, 2005.

European Parliament. *The Teaching of Immigrants in the European Union*. Luxembourg, 1997.

EURYDICE, *Organization of School Time in Europe: Primary and General Secondary Education, 2007–08 School Year*. Brussels, 2009.

Gebhardt, Birgit. "Die Tagesschule der DDR: Betrachtungen zum sozialistischen Konzept der Ganztagserziehung." *Zeitschrift für Pädagogik* 39, no. 6 (1993): 991–1006.

Geißler, Gert. "Ganztagsschule in der DDR: Großer Sprung, kleine Schritte und allmähliche Erschöpfung." In *Ganztagsangebote in der Schule. Internationale Erfahrungen und empirische Forschungen*, edited by Falk Radisch, 81–100. Bonn, 2005.

Grew, Raymond, and Patrick J. Harrigan, eds. *School, State and Society: The Growth of Elementary Schooling in Nineteenth-Century France*. Ann Arbor, MI, 1991.

Hagemann, Karen. "Die Ganztagsschule als Politikum: Die westdeutsche Entwicklung in gesellschafts- und geschlechtergeschichtlicher Perspektive." *Zeitschrift für Pädagogik*, supplement no. 54 (2009): 209–29.

Hagemann, Karen, and Karin Gottschall. "Die Halbtagsschule in Deutschland — ein Sonderfall in Europa?" *Aus Politik und Zeitgeschichte* B 41 (2002): 12–22.

Holtappels, Günter, ed. *Ganztagserziehung in der Schule. Modelle, Forschungsbefunde und Perspektiven*. Opladen, 1995.

Hörner, Wolfgang. "Das französische Ganztagsmodell." *Aus Politik und Zeitgeschichte* B 23 (2008): 15–21.

Hörner, Wolfgang et al., eds. *The Education Systems of Europe*. Dordrecht, 2007.

Ladenthin, Volker, and Jürgen Rekus, eds. *Die Ganztagsschule. Alltag, Reform, Geschichte, Theorie*. Weinheim, 2005.

Lindblad, Sverker et al. "Educating for the New Sweden?" *Scandinavian Journal of Educational Research* 46, no. 3 (2002): 283–303.

Ludwig, Harald. *Entstehung und Entwicklung der modernen Ganztagsschule in Deutschland*, 2 vols. Cologne, 1993.

Lundahl, Lisbeth. "A Matter of Self-Governance and Control: The Reconstruction of Swedish Education Policy 1980–2003." *European Education* 37, no. 1 (2005): 10–25.

Mattes, Monika. "Ganztagserziehung in der DDR. 'Tagesschule' und Hort in den Politiken und Diskursen der 1950er bis 1970er Jahre." *Zeitschrift für Pädagogik*, supplement no. 54 (2009): 230–46.

Organisation for Economic Co-operation and Development (OECD). *Education at a Glance*. Paris, 2007.

———. *PISA: Measuring Student Knowledge and Skills: The PISA 2000 Assessment of Reading, Mathematical and Scientific Literacy*. Paris, 2000.

———. *Where Immigrant Students Succeed: A Comparative Review of Performance and Engagement in PISA 2003*. Paris, 2006.

Otto, Hans-Uwe, and Thomas Coelen, eds. *Ganztägige Bildungssysteme. Innovation durch Vergleich*. Münster, 2005.

———, eds. *Grundbegriffe der Ganztagsbildung: Das Handbuch*. Wiesbaden, 2008.

Prost, Antoine. *Education, société et politiques. Une histoire de l'enseignement en France, de 1945 à nos jours.* Paris, 1992.

Stecher, Ludwig et al., eds. *Ganztägige Bildung und Betreuung. Zeitschrift für Pädagogik* supplement no. 54. Weinheim, 2009.

Tomlinson, Sally. *Education in a Post-Welfare Society.* Berkshire, 2005.

———. *Race and Education in Britain: Policy and Politics.* Berkshire, 2008.

6. Childcare and Early Childhood Education

Allen, Ann Taylor. *Feminism and Motherhood in Germany, 1800–1914.* New Brunswick, NJ, 1991.

———. *Feminism and Motherhood in Western Europe, 1890–1970: The Maternal Dilemma.* Basingstoke, 2005.

Bicskei, Eva. "'Our Greatest Treasure, the Child': The Politics of Child Care in Hungary, 1945–1956." *Social Politics* 13, no. 2 (2006): 151–88.

Brehony, Kevin J. "Transforming Theories of Childhood and Early Childhood Education: Child Study and the Empirical Assault on Froebelian Rationalism." *Paedagogica Historica* 45, no. 4/5 (2009): 585–604.

Choi, Soo-Hyang. "Early Childhood Care? Development? Education?" *UNESCO Policy Brief on Early Childhood* 1 (March 2002).

Del Boca, Daniela. "The Effect of Child Care and Part-Time Opportunities on Participation and Fertility Decisions in Italy." *Journal of Population Economics* 15, no. 3 (2002): 549–73.

Depaepe, Marc, and Ferre Laevers. "Preschool Education in Belgium." In *International Handbook of Early Childhood Education,* edited by Gary A. Woodwill et al., 93–103. New York, 1992.

Fix, Birgit. "Church-State Relations and the Development of Child Care in Austria, Belgium, Germany, and the Netherlands." In *Families and Family Policies in Europe: Comparative Perspectives,* edited by Astrid Pfennig and Thomas Bahle, 305–21. Frankfurt/M., 2000.

Haddad, Lenira. *An Integrated Approach to Early Childhood Education and Care. UNESCO Early Childhood and Family Policy Series,* no. 3. Paris, 2002.

Hagemann, Karen. "Between Ideology and Economy: The 'Time Politics' of Child Care and Public Education in the Two Germanys." *Social Politics* 13, no. 1 (2006): 217–60.

Hašková, Hana. "Factors Contributing to the Decline in Childcare Services for Children Under the Age of Three in the Czech Republic." In *Manka Goes to Work: Public Childcare in the Visegrad Countries 1989–2009,* edited by Agota Scharle, 4–20. Budapest, 2010.

Höltershinken, Dieter et al., *Kindergarten und Kindergärtnerin in der DDR,* 2 vols. Neuwied, 1997.

Kocourková, Jirina. "Leave Arrangements and Childcare Services in Central Europe: Policies and Practices before and after the Transition." *Community, Work & Family* 5, no. 3 (2002): 301–18.

Křížková, Alena, and Hana Hašková. "Gender (In)Equalities in Employment and Care in the Czech Republic during the EU accession and EU Membership." In *Gender Equality in the Enlarged European Union,* edited by Verena Kaselitz and Petra Ziegler, 45–60. Frankfurt/M., 2008.

Lamb, Michael E. et al., eds. *Child Care in Context: Cross-Cultural Perspectives.* Hillsdale, NJ, 1992.

Luc, Jean-Noël. *L'invention du jeune entfant au XIXe siècle. De la salle d'asile à l'école maternelle.* Paris, 1998.

———, ed. "L'école maternelle en Europe XIXe–XXe siècles." *Numéro spécial de la revue Histoire de l'Èducation. Service d'Histoire de l'Éducation,* INRP (1999).

Mahon, Rianne. "Child Care in Canada and Sweden: Policy and Politics." *Social Politics* 4, no. 3 (1997): 382–418.

Mahon, Rianne, and Sonya Michel, eds. *Gender and Welfare State: Restructuring through the Lens of Child Care.* London, 2002.

Michel, Sonya. *Children's Interests/Mothers' Rights: The Shaping of America's Child Care Policy.* New Haven, CT, 1999.

Morgan, Kimberly J. "Forging the Frontiers between State, Church, and Family: Religious Cleavages and the Origins of Early Childhood Care and Education Policies in France, Sweden, and Germany." *Politics and Society* 30, no. 1 (2002): 113–48.

———. "'The 'Production' of Child Care: How Labor Markets Shape Social Policy and Vice Versa." *Social Politics* 12, no. 2 (2005): 243–63.

Morgan, Kimberly J., and Kathrin Zippel. "Paid to Care: The Origins and Effect of Care Leave Policies in Western Europe." *Social Politics* 10, no. 1 (2003): 49–85.

Moss, Peter. *Childcare and Equality of Opportunity: Consolidated Report to the European Commission.* Final Version. Brussels, 1988.

Müller-Rieger, Monika, ed. *"Wenn Mutti früh zur Arbeit geht ..." Zur Geschichte des Kindergartens in der DDR.* Dresden, 1997.

Naumann, Ingela K. "Child Care and Feminism in West Germany and Sweden in the 1960s and 1970s." *Journal of European Social Policy* 15, no. 1 (2005): 47–63.

Nyberg, Anita. "How Are Swedish Women Faring? Child Care as a Gauge." *Social Politics* 8, no. 2 (2001): 206–9.

OECD. *Babies and Bosses: Reconciling Work and Family Life,* vol. 1–5. Paris, 2002–2007.

———. *Starting Strong I: Early Childhood Education and Care.* Paris, 2001.

———. *Starting Strong II: Early Childhood Education and Care.* Paris, 2006.

Penn, Helen. "Childcare Market Management: How the United Kingdom Government Has Reshaped Its Role in Developing Early Childhood Education and Care." *Contemporary Issues in Early Childhood* 8, no. 3 (2007): 192–207.

Plaisance, Eric. *L'école maternelle en France depuis la fin de la Seconde Guerre mondiale.* Paris, 1984.

Plantenga, Janneke, and Melissa Siegel, eds. *Child Care in a Changing World.* Groningen, 2004.

Presser, Harriet B. "Can We Make Time for Children? The Economy, Work Schedules and Child Care." *Demography* 26, no. 4 (1989): 523–43.

Randall, Vicky. "Childcare Policy in the European States: Limits to Convergence." *Journal of European Public Policy* 7, no. 3 (2000): 246–368.

———. *The Politics of Child Daycare in Britain.* Oxford, 2000.

Rostgård, Tine, and Torben Fridberg. *Caring for Children and Older People: A Comparison of European Policies and Practices.* Copenhagen, 1998.

Teplova, Tatyana. "Welfare State Transformation, Childcare and Women's Work in Russia." *Social Politics* 14, no. 3 (2007): 284–322.

Valiente, Celia. "Central State Child Care Policies in Postauthoritarian Spain: Implications for Gender and Carework Arrangements." *Gender & Society* 17, no. 2 (2003): 287–92.

Whitbread, Nanette. *The Evolution of the Nursery-Infant School: A History of Infant and Nursery Education in Britain, 1800–1970.* London, 1972.

Wincott, Daniel. "Paradoxes of New Labor Social Policy: Towards Universal Child Care in Europe's 'Most Liberal' Welfare Regime." *Social Politics* 12, no. 2 (2006): 286–312.

Wollons, Roberta Lyn, ed. *Kindergartens and Cultures: The Global Diffusion of an Idea.* New Haven, CT, 2000.

NOTES ON CONTRIBUTORS

CRISTINA ALLEMANN-GHIONDA is Professor of Comparative Education at the Institute of Comparative Education and Social Sciences of the University of Cologne. Her main research fields are international and intercultural comparative studies on issues referring to educational policies and theories, and intercultural communication and competence in selected professional settings. She is coeditor of the German educational journal Zeitschrift für Pädagogik. Her recent publications include: *Bildung für alle, Diversität und Inklusion: Internationale Perspektiven* (Paderborn, 2013); "Ganztagsschule im europäischen Vergleich. Zeitpolitiken modernisieren – durch Vergleich Standards setzen?," *Zeitschrift für Pädagogik* 55, Supplement 54 (2009): 190-208; "Ganztagssysteme in Europa – Zeitstrukturen (vor-)schulischer Bildung in Europa" in Grundbegriffe der Ganztagsbildung: Das Handbuch, ed. Hans-Uwe Otto and Thomas Coelen (Wiesbaden, 2008), 674–83; with Deloitte Consulting, *Intercultural Education in Schools: A Comparative Study* (Brussels, 2008); and *Einführung in die Vergleichende Erziehungswissenschaft* (Weinheim, 2004).

KEVIN J. BREHONY is Froebel Professor of Early Childhood Studies and Director of the Early Childhood Research Centre, in the School of Education at the University of Roehampton. He is also President of the International Froebel Society. His main research fields are: education policy, school governance, the history of education, child-centered education, social theory, ideologies, discourse, historiography, and historical sociology. His recent publications include: "Transforming Theories of Childhood and Early Childhood Education: Child Study and the Empirical Assault on Fröbelian Rationalism," *Paedagogica Historica* 45:4 (2009): 585–604; "Fröbel's Religious Beliefs: The Transition from Alternative to Oppositional and its Bearing on the Diffusion of the Kindergarten post 1848," in *Fröbelpadagogik im Kontext der Moderne. Bildung Erziehung und soziales Handeln,* ed. Karl

Neumann et al. (Jena, 2010), 73–92; "Stat och förskola i England och Wales, 1900–1918," in *Förskolans aktörer: Stat, kår och individ iförskolans historia,* ed. Johannes Westberg (Uppsala, 2011), 23–48; and "Play, Work and Education: Situating a Fröbelian Debate," Bordon 65:1 (2013): 55–73.

CLAUDIA CROTTI is Professor at School for Teacher Education, Institute for Primary Education, University of Applied Sciences, Northwestern Switzerland. Her main research fields are: gender and education, teacher education, and the history of education systems. Her recent publications include: "'Mehr Männer in die Klassenzimmer!' Lehrtätigkeit – als Frage des 'richtigen' Geschlechts – eine zeitlose Debatte?" in *Die Zeit der Pädagogik. Zeitperspektiven im erziehungswissenschaftlichen Diskurs,* ed. Marie-Theres Schönbächler et al. (Bern, 2009), 197–210; ed. with Fritz Osterwalder, *Das Jahrhundert der Schulreformen. Internationale und nationale Perspektiven, 1900–1950* (Bern, 2008); "Bildungspolitische Steuerungsversuche zwischen 1875 und 1931. Die pädagogischen Rekrutenprüfungen," in *Bildungsraum Schweiz. Historische Entwicklungen und aktuelle Herausforderungen,* ed. Lucien Criblez (Bern, 2008), 131–54; *Lehrerinnen - frühe Professionalisierung. Professionsgeschichte der Volksschullehrerinnen in der Schweiz im 19. Jahrhundert* (Bern, 2005); ed. with Jürgen Oelkers, *Ein langer Weg. Die Ausbildung der bernischen Lehrkräfte von 1798–2002* (Bern, 2002); "Higher Education for Women in Switzerland during the 19th Century or A History of Inequality," in *Gender Perspectives on Vocational Education. Historical, Cultural and Policy Aspects,* ed. Philipp Gonon et al. (Bern, 2001), 95–113.

JEANNE FAGNANI is Emeritus Senior Research Fellow at CNRS (National Center for Scientific Research), University of Paris 1-Sorbonne and Associate Researcher at the Institut de Recherches Economiques et Sociales. She is co-editor of the *Revue Française des Affaires Sociales* (Ministry of Social Affairs). Her main research fields are: comparisons between national family policies in Europe, interactions between family policies, female employment, fertility, and labor markets. Her recent publications include: "Childcare Policies in France: The Influence of Organizational Changes in the Workplace," in *From Child Welfare to Child Well-being: An International Perspective on Knowledge in the Service of Making Policy,* ed. Sheila Kamerman et al. (Dordrecht, 2009), 385–402; "Recent Reforms in Childcare and Family Policies in France and Germany: What Was at Stake?" *Children and Youth Services Review* 34:3 (2012): 509–16; and "Work-Family Life Balance: Future Trends and Challenges," in *The Future of Families to 2030,* ed. OECD (Paris, 2012), 119–88.

UTE GERHARD is Professor Emerita of Sociology and Director of the interdisciplinary Cornelia Goethe Centre for Women's and Gender Studies at the University of Frankfurt am Main. Her main research fields are: women's rights, social policy in European comparison, the history of women, women's movements, and feminist theory. Her recent publications include: ed. with Trudie Knijn and Anja Weckwert, *Working Mothers in Europe. A Comparison of Policies and Practices* (Cheltenham, 2004); "The Women's Movement in Germany in an International Context," in *Women's Emancipation Movements in the 19th Century. A European Perspective,* ed. Sylvia Paletschek and Bianka Pietrow-Ennker (Stanford, CA, 2004), 102–22; "Engendered Citizenship: A Model for European Citizenship? Considerations against the German Background," in *The Politics of Inclusion and Empowerment: Gender, Class and Citizenship,* ed. John Andersen and Birte Siim (New York, 2004), 100–15; *Debating Women's Equality: Toward a Feminist Theory of Law from a European Perspective* (New Brunswick, NJ, 2001).

KAREN HAGEMANN is James G. Kenan Distinguished Professor of History at the University of North Carolina at Chapel Hill. Her main research fields are Modern German and European history, especially the history of education, welfare states, labor culture, and women's movements, as well as the history of the nation, the military, and war. Her recent publications on the subject of gender, citizenship, education, and welfare include: ed. with Konrad H. Jarausch, *Halbtags oder Ganztags?: Zeitpolitiken von Kindergarten und Schule nach 1945 im europäischen Vergleich* (Weinheim, 2014); ed. with Stefan Dudink and Anna Clark, *Representing Masculinity: Citizenship in Modern Western Culture* (New York, 2008/2012); ed. with Sonya Michel and Gunilla Budde, *Civil Society and Gender Justice: Historical and Comparative Perspectives* (Oxford, 2008/2011); ed. with Sonya Michel, "Childcare in Transition: Eastern and Western Europe in Comparison," special issue, *Social Politics* 13:1 (2006), which includes her article "Between Ideology and Economy: The 'Time Politics' of Childcare and Public Education in the Two Germanys," 217–60; written with Karin Gottschall, "Die Halbtagsschule in Deutschland—ein Sonderfall in Europa?" *Politik und Zeitgeschichte* B 41 (2002): 12–22.

HANA HAŠKOVÁ is Senior Research Fellow at the Institute of Sociology, Department of Gender and Sociology of the Academy of Sciences of the Czech Republic and Lecturer of Gender and Family Studies at the Charles University in Prague. Her main research fields are: gender and family policies, fertility, motherhood and childlessness, and combining quantitative and qualitative research methods. Her recent publications include: with Steven Saxonberg and Jiří Mudrák, *The Development of Czech Childcare Policies* (Prague, 2012); with Christina Klenner, "Why Did Distinct Types of Dual Earner Models in Czech, Slovak and East German Societies Develop and Persist?" *Zeitschrift für Familienforschung / Journal of Family Research* 22:3 (2010): 266–88; *Fenomén bezdětnosti* [Phenomenon of Childlessness] (Prague, 2009); ed. with Zuzana Uhde, *Women and Social Citizenship in Czech Society: Continuity and Change* (Prague, 2009); "Structural and Value Influences on the Entry into Parenthood in the Czech Republic," in *Demográfia* 52:5 (2009): 66-84.

JACQUELINE HEINEN is Professor Emerita of Sociology at the University of Versailles-Saint-Quentin-en-Yvelines, former director of *Cahiers du Genre* (Centre National de la Recherche Scientifique), and former president of the Conseil national des universités of France. Her main research fields are gender and social policies in Western and Eastern Europe. Her recent publications include: ed. with Isabelle Clair Rétrospectives, *Cahiers du genre* 54 (2013); "Le droit de choisir, hier et aujourd'hui," in *Imaginer la citoyenneté*, ed. David Paternotte und Nora Nagels (Louvain-la-Neuve, 2013), 59-77; ed. with Shahra Razavi *Religion et politique: Les femmes prises au piège, special issue Cahiers du Genre* (2012); written with Stéphane Portet, "Reproductive Rights in Poland: When Politicians Fear the Wrath of the Church," *Third World Quarterly* 31, no. 6 (2010): 1007–21; written with Ruth Lister et al., *Gendering Citizenship in Western Europe: New Challenges for Citizenship Research in a Cross-national Context* (Bristol, 2007); "Clashes and Ordeals of Women's Citizenship in Central and Eastern Europe," in *Women and Citizenship in Central and East Europe*, ed. Jasmina Lukic et al. (Ashgate, 2006), 81–100.

KONRAD H. JARAUSCH is Lurcy Professor of European Civilization at the University of North Carolina at Chapel Hill, and Senior Fellow of the Center for Research on Contemporary History in Potsdam. His main research fields are: German history before and during the First World War, the social history of German students or professions, the course of German unification in 1989–1990, and the problem of interpreting German history in general. His most recent publications include: with Matthias Middell and Annette Vogt, *Sozialistisches Experiment und Erneuerung in der Demokratie – Die Humboldt Universität zu Berlin 1945-2010* (Berlin, 2013); "Contemporary History as Transatlantic Project: The German Problem, 1960-2010," *Historical Social Research,* supplement 24 (2012); *Reluctant Accomplice: A Wehrmacht Soldier's Letters from the Eastern Front* (Princeton, 2011); *Gebrochene Wissenschaftskulturen: Universität und Politik im 20. Jahrhundert* (Göttingen, 2010); ed., *Das Ende der Zuversicht? Die Siebziger Jahre als Geschichte* (Göttingen, 2008); ed. with Klaus J. Arnold, *"Das stille Sterben." Feldpostbriefe von Konrad Jarausch aus Polen und Russland, 1939–1942* (Paderborn, 2008); ed. with Thomas Lindenberger, *Conflicted Memories: Europeanizing*

Contemporary Histories (New York, 2007); and *After Hitler: Recivilizing Germans, 1945-1995* (Oxford, 2006).

TORA KORSVOLD is Professor of Early Childhood Education at the Queen Maud University College in Trondheim, Norway. Her main research fields are: the history of welfare states, childcare systems in a historical and comparative perspective, and how childhood has changed with time and space. She is coeditor of the journal *Nordic Research in Early Childhood Education*. Her recent publications include: *Barn og barndom i velferdsstatens smaabarnspolitikk. En sammenlignende studie av Norge, Sverige og Tyskland 1945–2000* (Oslo, 2008); "Der Wohlfahrtsstaat, der Kindergarten und die Behinderten," in *"Dabeisein ist nicht alles." Inklusion und Zusammenleben in Kindergarten,* ed. Borgunn Ytterhus and Max Kreuzer (Munich, 2007), 92–110; and "Kinder und Familienpolitik. Vereinbarkeit von Familie und Beruf in Skandinavien. Das Beispiel Norwegens am Ende des 20. Jahrhunderts," *Norröna* (2002), no. 31: 23–32 and no. 32: 65–71.

LISBETH LUNDAHL is Professor at the Department of Applied Educational Research of the University of Umeå. Her main research interests are: education policy, youth policy, and young people's school-to-work transitions. She is one of the team leaders of a new Nordic Centre of Excellence, Justice for Education. Her recent publications include: with Maria Olson, "Democracy Lessons in Market-oriented Schools: The Case of Swedish Upper Secondary Education," *Education, Citizenship and Social Justice* 8:2 (2013); "Educational Theory in an Era of Knowledge Capitalism," *Studies in Philosophy and Education,* 31:3 (2012): 215–26; "Leaving School for What?: Notes on School-to-work Transitions and School Dropout in Norway and Sweden." in *Education for Social Justice, Equity and Diversity,* ed Torill Strand and Merethe Roos (Zurich, 2012), 85-108; ed. with Elisabet Öhrn and Dennis Beach, "Young People's Influence and Democratic Education: Ethnographic Studies in Upper Secondary Schools" (London, 2011).

MONIKA MATTES isResearch Fellow at the Center for Research on Contemporary History, Potsdam, in a research project funded by the Volkswagen Foundation and the Federal Ministry of Education and Research and directed by Karen Hagemann and Konrad Jarausch with the title "Between Ideology and Economy: The All-Day School as a Political Issue: East and West Germany in Comparison (1945–1949)." Her main research fields are: migration history, women and labor market in the two Germanys, and the history of childcare and education. Her recent publications include: *"Gastarbeiterinnen" in der Bundesrepublik. Anwerbepolitik, Migration und Geschlecht* (Frankfurt/M., 2005); "Les travailleuses immigrées, la politique de genre et le marché de travail ouest-allemand 1955–1973," *Sextant. Revue du Groupe interdisciplinaire d'Etudes sur les Femmes* 21–22 (2004): 161–84; "Hindernisse und Strategien der staatlichen Anwerbung von 'Gastarbeiterinnen' in der Bundesrepublik 1955–1973," *Archiv für Sozialgeschichte* 42 (2002): 105–21; written with Esra Erdem, "Gendered Policies – Gendered Patterns: Female Labour Migration from Turkey to Germany from the 1960s to the 1990s," in *European Encounters: Migrants, Migration and European Societies since 1945,* ed. Rainer Ohliger et al. (Aldershot, 2003), 167–85.

KIMBERLY J. MORGAN is Associate Professor of Political Science and International Affairs at George Washington University. Her main field of research is on the politics of the welfare state, with a particular interest in childcare, parental leave, health care, and public finance. Her recent publications include: with Andrea Louise Campbell, *The Delegated Welfare State: Medicare, Markets, and the Governance of Social Policy* (Oxford, 2011); *Working Mothers and the Welfare State: Religion and the Politics of Work-Family Policy in Western Europe and the United States* (Berkeley, CA, 2006); written with Andrea Louise Campbell, "Federalism and the Politics of Old-Age Care in Germany and the United States," *Comparative Political Studies* 38 (2005); 887–914; "The Production of Childcare: How Labor Markets Shape Social Policy and Vice Versa," *Social Politics* 12, no. 2 (2005): 243–63; "The Politics of Mothers' Employment: France in Comparative Perspective," *World Politics* 55, no. 2 (2003): 259–89; written with Kathrin Zippel, "Paid to Care: The Origins and Effects of Care Leave Policies in Western Europe," *Social Politics* 10, no. 1 (2003): 45–85.

KRISTEN D. NAWROTZKI is Senior Research Fellow at the Early Childhood Research Centre of the School of Education at Roehampton University and Lecturer at the University of Education in Heidelberg, Germany. Her main research fields are: the comparative historical analysis of early childhood advocacy, policy, and provision, especially in the United States and United Kingdom; and perceptions and performances of motherhood and childhood. Her recent publications include: ed. with Jack Dougherty, *Writing History in the Digital Age* (Ann Arbor, MI, 2013); "Parent–School Relations in England and the USA: Partnership, Problematized," in *Mapping Families: Practices and Concepts of Children, Parents, and Professionals,* ed. Sabine Andresen and Martina Richter (Heidelberg, 2012), 69–83; and "'Greatly changed for the better': Free Kindergartens as transatlantic 'Reformance,'" *History of Education Quarterly* 49, no. 2 (2009): 182–95. She also edited the special issue of the *History of Education Quarterly* 49:2 (2009): *New Perspectives on Preschooling: The Nation and the Transnational in Early Childhood Education.*

LIVIA SZ. OLÁH is Associate Professor for Demography at the Department of Sociology at the University of Stockholm. Her main research fields include: family demography in comparative perspective (partnership formation, fertility, family dissolution, the impact of public policies on demographic behavior, with special emphasis on Scandinavia and Central-Eastern Europe), and gender issues including societal level and familial gender relations in industrialized countries. Her recent publications include: ed. with Ewa Fratczak *Childbearing, Women's Employment and Work-Life Balance Policies in Contemporary Europe* (Basingstoke, 2013); with Frances Goldscheider and Allan Puur, "Reconciling Studies of Men's Gender Attitudes and Fertility: Response to Westoff and Higgins," *Demographic Research* 22, article 8 (2010): 189–98; with Barbara Hobson, "Birthstrikes? Agency and Capabilities in the Reconciliation of Employment and Family," *Marriage and Family Review* 39, no. 3/4 (2006): 197–227.

ANATOLI RAKHKOCHKINE is Professor of International and Intercultural Comparative Education at the University of Leipzig. His main research fields are: international and comparative education, transmigration, internationalization in education, systems of education, and educational policies in Eastern Europe. His recent publications include: "On the Dichotomy of Teacher-centred Instruction and Self-regulated Learning in Russian Didactics," *Zeitschrift für Erziehungswissenschaft* 15 (2012): 555–71; "Didactics in Russia: National Traditions and International Influences," in *Beyond Fragmentation: Didactics, Learning and Teaching*, ed. Brian Hudson and Meinert A. Meyer (Opladen, 2011), 338–52; "Education of Children of Circular Migrants in the EU – A Case of Exclusion?," *Panorama: Intercultural Journal of Interdisciplinary Ethical and Religious Studies for Responsible Research* 21 (2009): 101–10; "Schulische und 'ergänzende' Bildung in Russland," in *Ganztägige Bildungssysteme. Innovation durch Vergleich*, ed. Hans-Uwe Otto and Thomas Coelen (Münster, 2005), 105–19.

DOROTTYA SZIKRA is Associate Professor at Eötvös Loránd University, Budapest, Faculty of Social Work. Her main research fields are: history of social policy and social work, the development family policies, and comparative social policy. Her recent publications include: "'Welfare Co-operatives' and Social Policy Between the Two World Wars in Hungary," in *Co-operatives and the Social Question: The Co-operative Movement in Northern and Eastern Europe, 1880–1950*, ed. Mary Hilson et al. (Cardiff, 2012), 153–67; with Dorota Szelewa, "Do Central and Eastern European Countries fit the 'Western' Picture? The Example of Family Policies in Hungary and Poland," in *Welfare States and Gender Inequality in Central and Eastern Europe. Continuity and Post-socialist Transformation in the EU Member States,* ed. Christina Klenner and Simone Leiber (Brussels, 2010), 81–117; "Eastern European Faces of Familialism: Hungarian and Polish Family Policies From a Historical Perspective," in *Selektive Emanzipation: Analyse zur Gleichstellungs- und Familienpolitik*, ed. Diana Auth et al. (Opladen, 2010), 239–54; with Béla Tomka, "Social Policy in East Central Europe. Major Trends in the 21st Century," in *Post-Communist Welfare Pathways: Theorizing Social Policy Transformations in Central and Eastern Europe*, ed. Alfio and Pieter Vanhuysse (Basingstoke, 2009).

SALLY TOMLINSON is Professor emerita of Education Policy at Goldsmiths College, University of London and a Research Fellow in the Department of Education, University of Oxford. She has researched and published in the areas of education policy, race, ethnicity and education, and special education. Her recent publications include: ed. with Tehmina Basit, *Social Inclusion and Higher Education* (Bristol and Chicago, 2012); *A Sociology of Special Education* (Abingdon: 2012); "Eltern und Bildungpolitische Dynamik in Grossbritannien," in *Migration und Schiulischer Wandel: Elternbeteiligung*, ed. Sara Furstenau and Mechthild Gomolla (Wiesbaden, 2009), 161–80; *Race and Education in Britain: Policy and Politics* (Maidenhead 2008); *Education in a Post-Welfare Society* (Maidenhead, 2005); "Race, Ethnicity and Education under New Labor," *Oxford Review of Education* 31, no. 1 (2005): 153–71; written with Martin Thrupp, "Education Policy, Social Justice and 'Complex Hope,'" *British Educational Research Journal* 31, no. 5 (2005): 549–56.

CELIA VALIENTE is Associate Professor in the Department of Economic History and Institutions at Universidad Carlos III de Madrid. Her main research interests are gender-equality policies and the women's movement in Spain from a comparative perspective. Her most recent publications are: "Are Gender Equality Institutions the Policy Allies of the Feminist Movement? A Contingent 'Yes' in the Spanish Central State," *South European Society & Politics* 12: 3 (2007): 315–34; "Developing Countries and New Democracies Matter: An Overview of Research on State Feminism Worldwide," *Politics & Gender* 3:4 (2007): 530–41; with Monica Threlfall and Christine Cousins, *Gendering Spanish Democracy* (London, 2005); *El feminismo de Estado en España: El Instituto de la Mujer (1983–2003)* (Valencia, 2006); "Central State Child Care Policies in Postauthoritarian Spain: Implications for Gender and Carework Arrangements," *Gender & Society* 17, no. 2 (2003): 287–92; "State Feminism and Gender Equality Policies: The Case of Spain (1983–95)," in *Sex Equality Policy in Western Europe*, ed. Frances Gardiner (London, 1997), 127–41; "The Power of Persuasion: The Instituto de la Mujer in Spain," in *Comparative State Feminism*, ed. Dorothy McBride Stetson and Amy G. Mazur (London, 1995), 221–36.

INDEX